METROPOLITAN AMERICA IN
CONTEMPORARY PERSPECTIVE

METROPOLITAN AMERICA

in contemporary perspective

Edited by

AMOS H. HAWLEY
University of North Carolina

and

VINCENT P. ROCK
National Research Council

Prepared for the Social Science Panel on the Significance
of Community in the Metropolitan Environment of the
Advisory Committee to the Department of Housing
and Urban Development

National Academy of Sciences

Sage Publications

Halsted Press Division
JOHN WILEY & SONS
New York–London–Sydney–Toronto

Distributed by Halsted Press, a Division of
John Wiley & Sons, Inc., New York

Printed in the United States of America

Library of Congress Cataloging in Publication Data

Metropolitan America in contemporary perspective.

   Papers prepared for the Social Science Panel on the Significance of Community in the Metropolitan Environment of the National Research Council.
   1. Metropolitan areas—United States. I. National Research Council. Social Science Panel on the Significance of Community in the Metropolitan Environment. II. Hawley, Amos Henry. III. Rock, Vincent P.
HT334.U5M38   301.36'4'0973   '75-8613
ISBN 0-470-36305-3

FIRST PRINTING

CONTENTS

Part III. GOVERNANCE OF METROPOLITAN COMMUNITIES

PREFACE

As the nation has become more urban, it has also become increasingly metropolitan in form. The metropolitan community is now the predominant urban unit. For decades, metropolitan settlements have been growing faster than the general population. Today, two out of three Americans live within metropolitan areas narrowly defined, and more than nine out of ten Americans live within commuting distances.

Metropolitan settlements, as they have grown, have also increased in complexity. The larger metropolitan communities include old central cities and suburbs, newer suburbs and satellite towns, and a widening zone of formerly rural areas now undergoing urbanization. The parts of a metropolitan settlement are increasingly interdependent. They are served by common social and economic institutions.

Individuals circulate throughout the metropolitan region on a daily basis for purposes of work, shopping, and recreation. Mobility, derived from rising incomes, lower residential densities, and reliance on the automobile, has changed the relative importance of the local neighborhood or vicinage in the lives of most urban dwellers.

The Department of Housing and Urban Development (HUD), in view of these developments, sought assistance in obtaining a broader understanding of the changing character of urban organization and urban life. The Assistant Secretary for Research and Technology of HUD indicated a particular need for scientific and technical advice to assist HUD in relating housing policy to urban growth patterns and objectives.

As a response to these interests, the Advisory Committee to the Department of Housing and Urban Development of the National Academy of Sciences–National Academy of Engineering requested that the Assembly of Behavioral Sciences initiate a "study of the significance of community in the metropolitan environment."

To provide the assistance requested, the Assembly of Behavioral Sciences of the National Research Council established a Panel on the Significance of Community in the Metropolitan Environment. The members of the panel were: Amos H.

EDITOR'S NOTE: The project which is the subject of this report was approved by the Governing Board of the National Research Council, acting in behalf of the National Academy of Sciences. Such approval reflects the Board's judgment that the project is of national importance and appropriate with respect to both the purposes and resources of the National Research Council.

The members of the committee selected to undertake this project and prepare this report were chosen for recognized scholarly competence and with due consideration for the balance of disciplines appropriate to the project. Responsibility for the detailed aspects of this report rests with that committee.

Each report issuing from a study committee of the National Research Council is reviewed by an independent group of qualified individuals according to procedures established and monitored by the Report Review Committee of the National Academy of Sciences. Distribution of the report is approved, by the President of the Academy, upon satisfactory completion of the review process.

This is a report of work prepared under Contract H-1077 between the National Academy of Sciences and the U.S. Department of Housing and Urban Development.

Hawley, Kenan Professor of Sociology, University of North Carolina, Chapel Hill, Chairman; Brian J.L. Berry, Irving B. Harris Professor of Urban Geography and Director of Training Programs in Urban Studies, University of Chicago; Angus Campbell, Director, Institute for Social Research, University of Michigan; John M. DeGrove, Director, Joint Center for Environmental and Urban Problems, Florida Atlantic and Florida International Universities; and Melvin M. Webber, Director, Institute for Urban and Regional Development, University of California, Berkeley.

The panel undertook the task of setting forth in the clearest way possible the present knowledge of urban organization and life. Specifically, it sought to examine the basic characteristics of the metropolitan settlements and the adaptation of urban neighborhoods and political units to their increasing scale and complexity. The findings of the Social Science Panel are set forth in the report, *Toward an Understanding of Metropolitan America* (Washington, D.C.: National Academy of Sciences, 1974). The report also provides a basis for conclusions and recommendations by the NAS-NAE Advisory Committee to the Department of Housing and Urban Development (ACHUD).

At the outset of its deliberations, the Social Science Panel agreed on the necessity for an overview of the empirical knowledge and research bearing on the process of metropolitanization. To this end, it commissioned the several papers brought together in the present volume.

These papers, which, in the main, seek to review the state of the knowledge, played a critically important role in the deliberations of the panel. Although the papers were primarily intended to make a substantive contribution, their preparation and utilization illustrates a way in which the scientific advisory process may be made to work with some effectiveness.

The papers were drawn from the work in several different disciplines. They provided a body of knowledge essential to the panel in developing a common perspective. The panel recognized, of course, that because urbanization as a major field of inquiry is still under development, and because of time constraints, there are gaps in the empirical material.

As the papers were received, they were read by the panel and discussed with the authors. The papers served to extend and correct the information available to members of the panel. In the discussions with the authors, the issues to be addressed by the panel were sharpened and elaborated. Conversely, in a number of instances the authors revised their papers to take account of the questions raised by the panel. The panel, of course, relied heavily on the state-of-knowledge papers in preparing its final report and findings. In addition, as the papers were reviewed, they were made available to key officials in the Department of Housing and Urban Development.

The papers are being made available here in full, both because of their intrinsic scientific interest and because of the background they provide for issues that will continue to concern policy makers and the public for years to come.

Amos H. Hawley
Chairman, Social Science Panel

FOREWORD

by

Morris Janowitz and Gerald D. Suttles

In the three decades since World War II, the decay and deterioration of our central cities have been pressing realities. The range of strategies available to restore our central cities—from urban renewal in the 1950s to the War on Poverty in the 1960s—have been widely assessed as modest and limited in their objectives and coherence. Some of these efforts may have had discernible and positive effects, and some of them may have resulted in much effective social learning. But the desired, fundamental reconstruction of the central cities has not been achieved.

The abrupt emergence of the "new economics" in the first half of the 1970s has exhausted further public confidence in piecemeal efforts at problem-solving in the post-automobile city. The "new economics" has brought chronic inflation accompanied by high levels of unemployment, the escalation of energy costs, and the near bankruptcy of local governments. We need innovative approaches to organize our knowledge in order to frame a new and more unified set of social policies for our central cities.

It is a grave error only to extrapolate ongoing trends in social analysis or social policy. It is doubtful whether collective judgments on contemporary America can be based on available data from the recent past. Fortunately, there has been an expansion of research and scholarly writing about growth and change in metropolitan areas. The importance of this body of research is that it seeks to present a systematic overview of metropolitan America and thereby helps to avoid any mechanical extrapolations in the analysis of social change.

This volume is an effort to organize and present varied elements of the contributions of contemporary social research on metropolitan America in a meaningful format. As such, it represents an enormous intellectual and critical effort. Of course, the expansion of work in a field of social research scarcely guarantees its intellectual vitality or its relevance for policy. However, under the sponsorship of the National Academy of Sciences, an interdisciplinary group of scholars was assembled. They did not try to develop or create a single or even a series of models or paradigms of the metropolitan community. They have conformed rather to the prescription of Robert K. Merton, who speaks of codifying the findings of social research. Each author begins with an essential theoretical orientation and seeks to assemble a pertinent body of research to explicate his initial formulations. The result is a contribution which is both analytic and substantive. This volume thus presents a unified strategy for reporting the state of knowledge about a variety of themes that are at the core of the interdisciplinary study of metropolitan affairs.

The contributors are fully aware of the pressing problems of public policy and of the need for developing new solutions and new strategies. But their work is first designed to assess existing knowledge and to assemble substantive findings in a comprehensive fashion. Nevertheless, from their efforts come a perspective and intellectual orientation that have profound implications for public policy. Both the substantive content of this volume and the new perspectives in urban public policy stress more holistic concepts of metropolitan affairs and seek to fashion urban strategies that are more comprehensive in scope and intent. The implication is hardly a renunciation of partial and incremental strategies of change and development, since these are inherent dimensions of a multilayered political system. However, the intellectual approach is to seek an overview in analysis and in public policy that explores the interrelations of institutions and programs in order to avoid limited and even contradictory policies. Metropolitanization emerges here as a central concept. Both research findings and the scope of public policy require a structure comprehensive enough to encompass the complexities that operate in the contemporary American metropolis.

The morphology of the "urban problem" has been repeatedly described both in scholarly documents and in the mass media. In fact, the amount of material is so great that the evidence of counter-trends and innovative solutions is often overlooked. But there can be no doubt that metropolitan centers have proliferated beyond the point where political and administrative boundaries can be effective. The segregation of socioeconomic and racial groups has become massive. Despite the chronic shortage of housing, significant stocks of decent dwelling units in the central cities have been permitted to deteriorate and have ultimately been abandoned. While educational institutions have increased the cognitive skills in the population at large, the quality of schooling in the central cities has fallen off. The capacity of educational institutions to perform the socialization tasks assigned to them has been strained. The separation of residence and employment has deprived an important segment of the population of reasonable access to work opportunities. The disorder of metropolitan life has become epitomized by dissatisfaction with private transportation and by the spread of alarm about "crime in the streets."

The state-of-knowledge papers contained here have special relevance in that they help to clarify the sources of the uncoordinated and contradictory efforts to deal with the decay of the center of the metropolis. For example, municipalities have sought to subsidize mass public transportation while simultaneously supporting the expansion of downtown parking structures. Urban clearance projects in the central city have been accompanied by generous federal subsidies for building single-family houses in the suburbs. Efforts to increase municipal tax revenue have been counterbalanced by federal interstate highway programs that have removed large residential areas from municipal tax rolls. Given the continued deconcentration, the investment of the private sector in the central business district has generally failed to have a direct positive impact or create the multiplier effect so often expected.

The underlying issue is more than the documentation of these grave problems. It is the analysis, as pursued in these papers, of the weakness of institutional mechanisms in integrating, balancing, and adjudicating competing public and private municipal enterprises. In the end, the efforts at metropolitan redevelopment have been exhausted by diffusion and overspending, both public and private. In the private sector, the key misallocation has been the resource commitment to the capital plant for producing automobiles and to the purchase of automobiles (and, to a lesser extent, relative overinvestment in single-family houses). In the public sector, the main misallocation, along with the massive investment in the highway system, has been to the less-effective portions of the welfare system, those so beset with bureaucratic rigidities, limited moral legitimacy, and mechanistic criteria that they have served to segregate their "beneficiaries" from the larger society.

Immediately after World War II, most scholars turned their attention away from the realities of urban environment in order to create highly generalized and abstract systems of analysis. Neighborhoods and communities were viewed as residues and parochial elements that would decline with the growth of a cosmopolitan outlook. It was believed that localism would decline as opportunities for solving contemporary problems by more effective administrative and bureaucratic coordination were presented. The distinction between local and cosmopolitan appears, in retrospect, however, to be little more than intellectual snobbery when one takes into consideration the realities of the search for a grass-roots basis for political power. The publication of this book indicates the emergence of a more comprehensive, more creative, and more responsible approach to urban studies.

The concept of metropolitanization has raised fundamental intellectual issues. It raises the questions of what variables can be changed at what points. One can choose increased costs of energy, limits in the efficiency of automotive transportation, organizational character of educational institutions, distribution of housing, fragmentation of municipal agencies, changing life styles, or experiments in community participation. Each variable, in its own right or in combination with others, highlights elements of actual and potential transition and modification, however limited. As the authors explore these issues, recent trends in the organization of the metropolis and the points of possible public intervention are indicated.

Metropolitanization addresses itself to the problem of the appropriate interface between the levels of government and the population that governmental institutions are required to serve. Given the outmoded boundaries and fragmentation of governmental units, it is understandable that the central cities have become the foci of vast transportation networks and industrial concentrations, with disarticulated areas of residence for upper- and lower-income groups. The suburbs are very fragmented entities without appropriate cultural and civic institutions, whose governmental agencies are unable to supply the required large-scale services for their residential concentrations. Under these circumstances, especially when they are faced with the impact of the "new economics," the central cities understandably press the federal government to assume the economic burden of welfare and education. However, there is little confidence that the intervention of the federal government will create administrative institutions that will cope effectively with the management of local functions. While federal economic aid to meet the costs of local government and welfare is essential, metropolitanization implies the development of administrative and political institutions appropriate for a greater degree of self-regulation.

Likewise, in the suburbs, the notion of metropolitanization is directed to comparable patterns of civic responsibility and administrative effectiveness. The problems of the suburbs, however, are complicated by their opposition to the intervention of the federal government on the ideological and political ground that it serves as an instrument of racial and socioeconomic integration.

We are dealing, then, with more than fragmented and outmoded boundaries and structures. We are dealing with perspectives of civil servants and elected officials that are not congruent with those of their clientele. Each specialized group—police, educators, social welfare workers, or traditional social planners—is eager to present itself as composed of skilled professionals. But it is reluctant to assume the broad responsibilities which metropolitanization requires. The citizenry and its elected officials emerge as the active agents.

Metropolitanization manifests itself in a concern with formal restructuring of the boundaries and organization of government to conform more to the realities of contemporary population aggregates. But metropolitan government is more than a tidying up of boundaries and is therefore a long-term aspiration. Even the three most metropolitanized local governments in the United States have not achieved striking advantages and benefits, nor have they stimulated other centers. Naturally, the opposition to metropolitan government is immense; and, in reality, it does produce only incremental progress.

These state-of-knowledge papers emphasize that, in the absence of metropolitanization, the cost of racial and socioeconomic segregation is high for the entire metropolitan community. The papers also point up the extensive economic and social costs imposed by low-density population—costs certain to rise with the shortage of cheap energy. They highlight the fact that the central city, with all its cultural and leisure-time resources, is still unable, because of poor schooling and widespread crime, to remain competitive in attracting residents. They demonstrate how ill-balanced are current attempts to make the positive benefits of urban life accessible.

The idea of metropolitanization requires institution-building at the national level. It is not merely a matter of a new balance between the central city and the suburbs. At the national level, the emergence of interest in a federal land-use bill signals the potentialities of a more comprehensive approach to "urban problems" for the first time. National initiative could supply a broad context in which metropolitan growth and transformation would develop in the next half-century. The very belief in a national crisis has at least the potential for mobilizing national decision-making.

If the contemporary scene is truly transitional, and if the definition of a "crisis" leads to new political initiative, there is every reason to believe that urban policies will continue to be defined in terms of economic and physical categories, for such is the language of an advanced industrial society. In effect, the issues are being posed as needs for new forms of transportation and for an increased supply of housing. But in the context of the new research literature, as reflected in this volume, and because of increased, vocal political demands about the "quality of life," human dimensions the sense of personal identity and group cohesion—are certain to figure more centrally than in past government attempts to intervene.

Even our economic and physical approach to metropolitanization has come to mirror more concern with "social definitions." Both imaginative speculation about urban development and careful institutional planning have begun to focus on the centrality of the schools and the educational system. If schooling is seen as a lifelong process which is related to public welfare, then the school supplies a physical and cultural focal point for effective metropolitanization. Effective schools are essential parts of any countertrends that will keep and attract middle-income families to the central city and thus arrest long-term trends toward deterioration.

There is every reason to believe that schools and schooling supply an appropriate point of entrance for a new metropolitanization. The idea of the school as the focal point of the community of limited liability makes much sense. The community of limited liability is designed to hold its residents as long as it supplies effective services—physical and human. The services of the schools are elemental, since they are widely regarded as symptomatic of the quality of local community life. Not only do the schools represent our most immediate sense of community well-being, they stand for the main elements of a meaningful social and moral order.

INTRODUCTION

From a variety of perspectives, the papers in this volume seek to bring relevant behavioral and social science knowledge to bear on the question: What is the scope and nature of the urban unit in America today? In addressing that question, they contribute to our understanding of urban processes and urban life. They help to correct traditional perceptions of city, small-town, and rural life that are no longer an accurate reflection of reality in the present stage of the society. They provide a foundation for a series of findings with respect to twentieth-century urbanization in America. They suggest approaches to policy formulation that may increase the congruence between urban problems and the policy instruments selected to deal with them. Finally, they provide a good many ideas for an experimental and research agenda to improve our understanding of the processes of urban change.

The papers were prepared at the request of a Social Science Panel of the Assembly of Behavioral and Social Sciences of the National Research Council. The panel was responding to a question posed by the Department of Housing and Urban Development. HUD, which had its historical roots in housing finance, was attempting to acquire a broader urban orientation. The experience of HUD in seeking to carry out its programs suggested that urban life had become increasingly metropolitan in scale. Federal programs outside the jurisdiction of HUD, such as those conducted by the Department of Transportation, appeared to play a critical role in the urbanization process. At about the same time, many program proposals continued to assume a need to strengthen the role of micro-communities, or neighborhoods, in larger urban settlements. As a result of these interests, the Social Science Panel was requested to review the state of knowledge concerning the significance of community in the metropolitan environment.

IDENTIFICATION OF KEY ISSUE AREAS

At the outset, as a framework for responding to the interests of HUD, the Social Science Panel identified a number of key issue areas.

First is the set of issues that stems from the changing scale of urban life. The tendency for social units to increase in scale is widespread and underlies many concrete questions. Thus, the panel asked: What are the implications of the increasing scale of society? What are its causes and consequences? What is the relevance of scale for understanding such notions as "the metropolitan community"?

Second are the issues that surround mobility as a key variable in urban life and the panel asked: What are the implications of mobility for physical and social density and for the utilization of the physical environment? How is the character of urban settlements shaped by various mobility patterns, including differential socioeconomic movements? What are the implications of mobility for urban neighborhoods and fragmented political units of government? To what extent have changes in urban organization been a response to improvements in transportation and communication? What can be established with respect to the increasing range of circulation in the daily movements of metropolitican residents? Finally, what is the relation of increased mobility to the density of urban settlements?

Third are questions that derive from the internal differentiation taking place in urban environments. To what extent is differentiation found, not only in geographic subareas, but in the differentiation in roles, statuses, and political structures? What are the implications of differentiation for racial segregation and for socioeconomic stratification? What are the implications of an increasingly complex urban environment for the way in which individuals relate to one another? How does this complexity affect the attributes of communities from which people derive satisfaction?

Fourth are issues connected with the changing social characteristics of residential areas. What are the conditions necessary for a viable neighborhood? How do mobility and differentiation affect the possibilities of local areas being social units of any operative kind? Is there a wide range of activities that take place within typical local neighborhoods, or is their function now largely limited to social control? How widespread is the perception of residential areas as communities of limited liability? Is the homogeneity of residential areas in terms of class, race, and stage-in-life-cycle increasing or decreasing?

Fifth, recognizing that all human activities have a time-space location, what are the significant spatial dimensions of national life? As organizations increase in size and interdependence, as wealth accumulates and incomes rise, as knowledge and information channels multiply, as the non-space orientation of roles and institutions spreads, in what respects is it useful to focus on metropolitan areas and their surrounding territories? When urbanization is viewed as a process of acculturation, rather than simply as a physical task of city-building, what are the significant regional dimensions?

Sixth, a series of issues relates to how effectively government is responding to the increasing scale of urban life. What changes are taking place as a result of local initiative, state intervention, or federal action? Is it possible to identify additional ways in which the federal government could exercise leverage to achieve more effective government at the metropolitan level? What can the federal government do to facilitate intergovernmental cooperation or changes in the structure of metropolitan government? What are the alternatives to increased state and federal involvement in the government of urban settlements?

What are the implications for urban life of an increasing array of private institutions, national in scale, that perform public functions? Finally, as urban life increases in scale, what are the requirements for local differentiation and decentralization?

REVIEW OF RELEVANT KNOWLEDGE

Having identified a number of key issues, the Social Science Panel met with the authors of the papers in this volume to discuss the availability of behavioral and social science knowledge that might be brought to bear on the questions posed. The authors were asked to undertake a state-of-the-knowledge review of the literature. However, in certain cases it was understood that the review would emphasize certain recently available special studies, and in one case provision was made for what was in effect a policy analysis of key issues in a particular area. In all cases, the policy views and research suggestions of the authors were sought.

The papers, as they finally emerged, fall into three broad groups. The first group deals broadly with the metropolitan context. "The Urban Centrifugal Drift," by Basil G. Zimmer of Brown University, examines the demographic characteristics of the urbanization of the United States during the present century, as well as the growth and development of metropolitan centers historically. Data bearing on various aspects of the increasing scale of urban life are considered. The paper points up the fact that functional interdependent communities have grown beyond the boundaries of any single municipality. "Beyond the Suburbs: The Changing Rural Scene," by Rex R. Campbell of the University of Missouri, focuses on the implications of the increasing scale of urban life for individuals and communities outside the boundaries of metropolitan areas. It deals not only with rural areas that are feeling the effects of loss of population, but also with many others on the periphery of metropolitan centers which are experiencing rapid growth. While recognizing the effect of urbanization on rural value systems and behavior patterns, the primary focus is on demographic changes in rural areas. "Urban Concentration and Deconcentration," by Matthew Edel, Queens College, and John R. Harris and Jerome Rothenberg of the Massachusetts Institute of Technology, examines the spatial spread of urban systems from the perspective of economic causation. The paper considers two sets of related questions. One set centers on the factors affecting the total number and size of metropolitan agglomerations, and the other on the degree to which individual agglomerations are compact or dispersed in their internal arrangements. The economic arguments that have been developed to explain the current metropolitan patterns in the United States are considered. "Accessibility for Residents in the Metropolitan Environment," by Donald L. Foley, University of California at Berkeley, explores a number of facets of the concept of accessibility. Special attention is devoted to a study of motor-vehicle availability in the San Francisco Bay area, as revealed in a study by the Survey Research Center, University of California at Berkeley. The survey results warrant attention because of the fresh conceptual and classificatory system used and because the metropolitan area surveyed may be fairly typical of much of the United States.

The second group of papers focuses on the quality of urban life in a metropolitan environment. They approach this topic from a number of different points of view. "The Metropolitan Experience," by Claude S. Fischer of the University of California at Berkeley, is a systematic review of the literature concerned with the effects of population agglomeration on behavior and attitudes. Dr. Fischer reviews three data sources: ethnographic studies, community studies, and national and international attitude surveys. Urban agglomerations, he indicates, provide opportunities for many sorts of varied experiences. Moreover, the variety of experience tends to generate social change. Thus, it is possible to conclude, as one authority did, that the metropolitan experience is profoundly civilizing. "Community Design: The Search for Participation in a Metropolitan Society," by Gerald D. Suttles of the State University of New York at Stony Brook, considers such current issues as community control and decentralization. The paper begins with an examination of the literature on the traditional view of communities and the decline of community. It moves then to a historical review of community development in the United States, tracing the tradition of physical design and the movement toward urban and social planning. Moving beyond the review of literature, Dr. Suttles then makes his own innovative proposal for community design. "Toward an Understanding of Community Satisfaction," by Robert W. Marans and Willard Rodgers of the Institute for Social Research, University of Michigan, deals with one particular aspect of the quality of American life—people's level of satisfaction with their residential communities. While primarily concerned with research under way at the Survey Research Center of the Institute for Social Research at the University of Michigan, it takes account of the work of others who have investigated people's responses to residential environment.

The third group of papers is concerned with the problems of governance associated with the increasing scale of urban life. They seek to answer three main questions. First, in what respects does the present system fail to meet the needs of an increasingly metropolitan society? Second, to what extent do specific initiatives or programs undertaken at the various levels of government give promise of providing more effective government for metropolitan communities? Third, what are the approaches that warrant consideration in seeking to achieve a closer correspondence between social and economic institutions on the one hand and governmental institutions on the other? "Governance in a Metropolitan Society," by Alan K. Campbell and Judith Dollenmayer of Syracuse University, is a comprehensive review of the shortcomings of urban government and of the devices that have been used to improve its effectiveness. An assessment of the substantially greater efforts that will be required in the future to reduce the social inequities and fiscal disparities presently embedded in the system is also provided. "Fiscal and Productive Efficiency in Urban

Government Systems," by Lyle C. Fitch of the Institute of Public Administration, looks at the organization of urban government primarily from the viewpoints of economics and public administration, somewhat tempered by viewpoints usually associated with political science and sociology. Fitch assumes that the three main values of urban government are: efficiency in the delivery of public goods, equality of income distribution, and the preservation of domestic tranquility. The paper provides a cogent policy analysis of alternative approaches to the design of urban government, in order that it may achieve these purposes more effectively. "The Patchwork Approach: Adaptive Responses to Increasing Urbanization," by Joseph F. Zimmerman of the University of New York at Albany, examines in systematic fashion the actions short of general reorganization being undertaken by governments in metropolitan areas to cope with areawide problems. These include initiatives such as regional planning, the establishment of councils of governments, intergovernmental service agreements, upward transfer of functional responsibility, creation of special district governments, tax sharing, and direct state government action. Significant court decisions bearing on the effectiveness of urban government are also briefly considered.

As a group, the state-of-the-knowledge papers mirror the uneven development of research on urban processes and urban life. Urban studies have only recently emerged as a major field of inquiry. This is reflected in the literature review found in the papers. A good deal of the literature is concerned with the how, rather than the why, of urban change. Empirical examination of urban life and theories to explain urban processes have sometimes tended to develop independently. The invention of objective and of subjective measures of quality of life has, up until recently, proceeded along separate paths. Government reorganization has often moved ahead without attention to the underlying characteristics of the social and economic institutions. In regard to urban studies, sociology, economics, political science, and social psychology have tended to follow the interests of the disciplines rather than those of the policy makers. Both in the preparation of the review papers and in the subsequent discussions with the authors, the Social Science Panel sought broader understanding of urban processes and an appreciation of a wider range of policy alternatives.

METROPOLITAN COMMUNITIES—THE PREDOMINANT URBAN UNIT

The review of the literature points to the metropolitan community as the predominant urban unit. In the nineteenth century, the urban population concentrated in cities that grew up at the junctures of ports and railroads. Cities were centers of commerce and industry with rather well-defined boundaries. The country came up to the edge of the city. As municipal corporations, cities encompassed most of the activity that gave them vitality.

In the twentieth century, a number of factors, particularly improvements in short-haul transportation, tended to erase the dividing line between city and country. As the cities grew, they also dispersed, and multiple centers of commerce and industry rose within single metropolitan areas. The density of urban settlements tended to decline. The primacy of the old city tended to become less significant. Manufacturing, retailing, wholesaling, and households located in growing numbers beyond municipal boundaries, even as occasionally extended by annexation. Social and economic institutions that served the people of the primary city also served many more beyond its boundaries. Services for the entire metropolitan population came to originate in one or another suburban center. Whether for work, residence, shopping, or leisure, the urban population moved about with little regard for the boundaries of the city. In short, the primary city, to the degree that it persists, functions as a part of a larger, multicentered, interactive, metropolitan complex. This complex includes old and new suburbs, satellite towns, and a widening fringe of formerly rural areas characterized by rapid growth.

As the city has lost its singular identity, the distinctive features of rural America have also eroded. Improved transportation and communications have fostered the spread of urban values throughout most of the nonmetropolitan population. Indeed, most of the population classified as rural lives within commuting distance of jobs and other opportunities provided by the metropolis. In short, while significant differences in the density of settlement remain, the values and activities of city and country have tended to converge.

Neighborhood life has also been affected by the changing scale of institutions and the increasing mobility of individuals. The intensity of relationships found at the level of the neighborhood has tended to decline. While the neighborhood retains some utility as an area of social control, interactions are increasingly translocal and metropolitan in scale. Urban neighborhoods, however, may provide the arena for intermittent communities organized for particular purposes at particular times in the family life-cycle of inhabitants. Neighboring, in any case, tends to be rather limited. In short, the traditional view of the small town as a community of shared sentiment, if indeed it was ever widely prevalent even in rural America, is inappropriate as a model for urban neighborhoods. Mobility rather than proximity is the primary factor influencing the pattern and meaning of human interaction at the metropolitan scale.

PROBLEMS OF METROPOLITAN COMMUNITIES

Although metropolitanization has been going on for a long time, the pace accelerated after World War II. Rapid change has accentuated old problems and created new ones. Many of these problems are common to a significant number of metropolitan communities.

As cities have declined as centers of manufacturing, retailing, and personal services, residential abandonment has increased. Meanwhile, the costs of suburban sprawl have tended to outrun the benefits. Ill-equipped rural areas on the periphery have found difficulty in coping with unplanned growth. Delivery of services has remained markedly unequal as between various population groups. Segregation has tended to increase as blacks and other minorities concentrated in the central cities and whites moved out. To a significant degree, a mismatch has developed between the location of jobs and the residential location of people with the skills to fill them. While mobility is essential for access to the opportunities in a metropolitan area, there are constraints on movement associated with race, income, age, or physical condition. Residential movement within a metropolitan area is selective in terms of socioeconomic status, resulting in stratification of population groups not only between the central city and the suburbs, but also among the various suburbs as well.

The increasing scale of the urban system, the fragmentation of local government, and the stratification of population groups result in serious disparities between taxable capacity and social needs. While the unequal distribution of income and services is not new, nor is discrimination, the territorial scale of metropolitan settlements accentuates these problems, and brings new ones in its wake. Frequently, there is an uneven distribution of costs and benefits between governments within the metropolitan complex. For example, part of the costs of suburbanization are reflected in the cost of operating central-city governments. Improvements that will facilitate orderly processes of government and permit an equitable allocation of costs and benefits throughout the metropolitan community are far from self-evident. The extent to which such governmental processes can and should be unique to each metropolitan community and the degree to which they must originate at the state or national level is a complex question. On the one hand, metropolitan settlements are part of the national network and tend to manifest common problems. On the other hand, the political-economic-cultural ecology of each metropolitan community is in some respects unique. The communities vary in centrality and unity, in culture and competence. All are affected by the actions of an array of national institutions, but they are often affected differentially.

In sum, behavioral and social-science research is relatively conclusive with regard to the emergence of metropolitan settlements and their common problems. However, the evidence with respect to the future evolution of urban society is much more uncertain. The following findings drawn from the report of the Social Science Panel of the Assembly of Behavioral and Social Sciences of the National Academy of Sciences, *Toward an Understanding of Metropolitan America,* provide a terse, evaluated summary of the present state of knowledge:

(1) Thus far in the twentieth century, metropolitan communities have increased in scale and become more multicentered.

(2) Since the rapid growth of metropolitan areas in the United States has been accompanied by an even more rapid centrifugal movement of population within metropolitan areas, there has been a general decline of urban densities.

(3) The dispersion of population within metropolitan areas has been almost exclusively white, resulting in an increasing segregation of blacks in central cities. However, late in the 1960 decade, there were indications that the outward movement of minorities was accelerating somewhat. There then began a trend toward blacks, especially middle-class ones, moving from the central cities to the suburbs.

(4) As metropolitan areas develop, there is a tendency for the jobs best suited for the labor force of the suburbs to remain concentrated in the central cities, particularly the downtown, central business district, while the jobs best suited to the type of labor force locked into the central city move to the suburbs.

(5) Historically in the process of metropolitanization, there has been suburban selectivity of the higher socioeconomic groups. As multicentered metropolitan communities evolve, however, selectivity *among* suburbs appears likely to be of increasing significance; different suburbs will draw disproportionately from different socioeconomic classes. Construction of multiple-dwelling units in the suburbs has increased sharply. Hence, a corresponding broadening in the stages of the family life cycle represented in the suburbs may be expected, including young adults and older couples as well as families with children.

(6) The proliferation of government units and the development of urban services in suburban territory have contributed to acceleration of population scatter, as have certain federal programs.

(7) The fragmentation of government in metropolitan communities in the context of the positive tendency toward increasing scale in urban areas, results in disadvantages for the community as a whole. The centrifugal movement of population, as it has become increasingly intergovernmental, has aggravated fiscal and social inequities in the metropolitan areas at large.

(8) It appears that residents who remain in the central city subsidize the suburban residents' use of public services.

(9) With rising income, more education, and greater knowledge about the metropolitan environs, most metropolitan residents are able to benefit from the array of opportunities open to them, over and beyond the actual destinations to which they customarily travel. The aged, the physically handicapped, and the poor, however, suffer a deprivation of access, since these are the predominant groups lacking use of autos, which are now necessary for metropolitan mobility, particularly in low-density suburban districts.

(10) The centrifugal movement of urban populations and the diffusion of urban characteristics are not confined to metropolitan areas; they have extended into the adjacent rural territory to produce there the country's highest growth rates. Ninety-five percent of the nation's population lives within the labor shed of metropolitan central cities. This may be delineated by the time-distance (distance that can be traveled in a specific time) required to commute to major places of employment.

(11) The overall conclusions about urban sprawl seem to be the following: The benefits of this process are distributed regressively with respect to income and wealth. While obvious benefits have been derived from lowered residential densities in the past (at least compared with nineteenth-century levels), the current marginal social net benefits may be negative. Sprawl appears to have outrun the ability of government to meet requirements of urban settlements. Moreover, given the present structure of government, distortions in the distribution of costs and benefits are not readily correctable. There is reason to require more equitable sharing of costs, not only between the suburbs and the central city, but increasingly among suburbs also. There is also an argument for ending or modifying subsidies that have favored single-family, auto-owning, low-density suburbanization.

(12) Metropolitan experience is manifold. It offers a great range of opportunity and substitutes trans-local for neighborhood associations and interests.

(13) At present, the best evidence is that the urban experience, as indicated by size of place, does not affect individual behavior in any substantial way. It does not seem to change the ways in which people relate to each other, or to whom they relate.

(14) When factors such as class and ethnicity are taken into account, it is not clear that cities per se breed violence. Indeed, cross-culturally and historically, rural areas have predominated in violent lawlessness.

(15) There is very little support for the prediction that city life impairs mental functioning in ways that can be related to psychiatric disorders.

(16) City-suburban differences in life-style are almost entirely socioeconomic differences. The remaining differences are probably caused by self-selection.

(17) People's perceptions of their residential environments vary in both scale and attribute content. This may help to account for the fact that, while there is a tendency for higher levels of satisfaction to be associated with a higher degree of residential site-planning, no clear patterns of attributes liked or disliked are associated with different site plans. Moreover, studies of quality-of-life indicate that satisfaction with community is partially based on assessments of particular extra-site attributes such as public schools, police-community relations, and local taxes.

(18) Multivariate analysis shows that the links between objective and subjective measures of environmental attributes are substantial.

(19) People have difficulty making a clear distinction between their micro- and macro-neighborhoods. The characteristics of one are often confused with those of the other.

(20) Rising household incomes, lower residential densities, and a preponderant reliance on the automobile have contributed to a lowering of the importance of the more traditional neighborhood, or micro-community, pattern. In the metropolitan context, the local vicinage or micro-community has become relatively less significant as a locus of interaction

and a force in personality formation. Except perhaps in poor residential areas, it survives principally as a means of control over the immediate physical and/or service environment, and in that respect tends to operate as a unit only when it is threatened.

(21) A central problem in the development of micro-communities as control devices is the absence of any authoritative way in which residents can appeal to a single set of boundaries.

(22) While residents of micro-communities often share similar life-styles, residential mobility is often high, and social participation in community affairs is usually limited. There is instead a tendency to rely on professionals and formal organizations for the discharge of community responsibilities. The micro-community is a community of limited liability, that is, one in which people invest their efforts and resources for achievable gains with the expectation that they can pull out on short notice.

(23) Federally and municipally guided attempts at decentralization and sub-community participation have frequently floundered because adversarial relationships between community groups and public agencies have developed.

(24) At the national level, there is a need for: (a) a broader, more empirically based understanding of urbanization processes; (b) support for innovation and experimentation in the urban development process; (c) a sensitive information collection and analysis network to monitor the outcomes of public and private initiative; and (d) feedback of findings and forecasts to provide a more reliable basis for public and private decisions.

(25) The present system of local government fails to answer the needs of a clearly metropolitan society. Fragmented and overlapping government in metropolitan areas (a) aggravates the mismatch between resources and social needs, (b) makes the solution of metropolitan social problems more difficult, and (c) inhibits efficient administration of services.

(26) Although no coordinated national policy has responded to the by-products of metropolitanization, all levels of government have undertaken certain specific programs of action. If the federal response has been inadequate or misconceived, the same generalization can be made with much greater force concerning the states.

(27) Of the external forces influencing the governmental system of metropolitan areas since 1962, none has had a greater impact than the federal courts. Unfortunately, from the central-cities' viewpoint, the judicial requirement of fair representation in state legislatures came after the cities had already lost to the suburbs their prominent position in state populations. The cities no longer had the votes to redress the balance between resources and social needs. The chief beneficiaries of reapportionment were suburban jurisdictions, and suburbs will gain even more as population continues to move outward. The courts, however, in issues recently and currently before them, have the potential to reduce some of the inequities caused by fragmentation.

(28) Historical experience indicates that voter approval of metropolitan reorganization outside the South has been virtually impossible to obtain. In lieu of reorganization, a large number of special districts have been created to meet the service needs of metropolitan communities.

(29) While the county scale seldom includes the total interactive and interdependent area of a metropolitan community, enlarging the responsibilities of the counties may improve local government for smaller metropolitan areas. Counties may also serve as effective subunits in a larger metropolitan regional system.

(30) Councils of governments have been put forward as one solution to the metropolitan governmental problem. Although the councils of government are easily organized, flexible, and adaptable governmental units, none of the large number created in the 1960s has solved a major metropolitan problem. There is no evidence that they are beginning to take on a metropolitan governance function.

(31) A large number of intergovernmental service arrangements has been created. Sixty-three percent of the 2,375 municipalities responding to a mailed questionnaire have entered into formal and informal agreements with other units for the supply of services.

(32) It can be stated with reasonable confidence that major problems with which local governments cannot cope will have to be confronted by state or federal governments, unless new area-wide mechanisms are developed.

IMPLICATIONS FOR POLICY

While the papers in this volume were intended primarily as reviews of the state of the knowledge of urban processes and urban life, a number of important inferences with respect to policy may be drawn from them.

First, the papers suggest the need for a national urban social policy. Many of the forces that shape urban life are national in scope. National public decisions with respect to transportation, communications, energy, and housing have important consequences for the quality of urban life. Major private-investment decisions tend to have a similar impact. The urban settlements in which most Americans live and work share common demographic attributes and experience similar problems. Moreover, there is evidence of a growing interdependence among all urban settlements. As wealth and knowledge have accumulated, large-scale national and international institutions have developed. As the service sector of the economy has grown relative to industrial production, new activities are less tied to particular locations. In effect, as the papers by Zimmer, by Edel, Harris, and Rothenberg, and by others suggest, a national network of urban settlements has grown up, tied together by a growing array of national institutions. Each urban settlement is multicentered and in turn is part of a larger national or even international multicentered urban network of communities performing different roles. The relationships among the parts are not so much territorial as functional and transactional; a complex web of interdependencies has developed. Since the network is still changing in scale and intensity of transactions, the lack of a national urban policy is in fact a policy of random intervention.

Second, the papers indicate that the social unit for national programs ought to be the metropolitan communities and the territories they serve. The increasing scale of urban settlements presents both problems and opportunities. Viewed from the national level, the congruence between problems and opportunities is greatest at the scale of the metropolitan community, which contains a wide range of facilities and diverse interest groups. People circulate about the entire metropolitan area on a daily basis. Fischer documents the main characteristics of this metropolitan experience. Marans and Rodgers analyze the subjective attributes of community satisfaction that derive from this experience. While the search for improved design of neighborhoods has been pursued since the turn of the century, the achievements have been absorbed frequently by the metropolitan scale of life which the designs failed to take into account, Suttles finds. Decentralization of functions may be useful at a certain metropolitan scale, but rarely so to the neighborhood as traditionally conceived.

Third, the papers suggest the main substantive elements with which policy must deal. These include: (1) the distributional impact of major decisions, (2) income distribution and metropolitan stratification, (3) transportation and communications essential to ensure equal access to opportunities, and, finally, (4) effective metropolitan government.

If, as was indicated in a number of papers (e.g., Edel, Harris, and Rothenberg; Campbell and Dollenmayer; Fitch; and Foley), national decisions (both public and private) have distributional impacts on population and enterprise, a first task of policy is to develop processes for understanding what the impacts of such decisions may be and procedures for taking them into account. In the case of some federal programs that are intended to have distributional impacts, the analysis of actual effects is inadequate. More commonly, major decisions are taken for which these impacts are unanticipated and often unintended. Moreover, the long-term distributional impact of major technological developments, such as the energy crisis or the communications revolution, require far more systematic procedures for analysis and action than presently exist. These developments may constrain the spread of urban settlements or facilitate the evolution of more effective settlement patterns. National urban policy ought to provide a decision process in which these distributional impacts are taken into account.

As Fischer indicates, the major differences between central cities and suburbs, as well as among suburbs, are socioeconomic. If so, urban policy must direct a good deal of attention to present income-distribution patterns and to whether the their modification would contribute to overall improvement in the quality of life in metropolitan settlements. This in turn, of course, requires a much more systematic understanding of the capital, labor, and housing markets within each of the major metropolitan communities.

As urban settlements increase in scale, their effectiveness in meeting human needs depends to an increasing degree on systems for the circulation of men, ideas, and materiel. As Foley demonstrates, urban-settlement patterns tend to assume the availability of the automobile. Access to urban opportunities depends in large measure on the availability of automobile transport. Yet, for something like a quarter of the population, such transport is not available. Even mass-transportation systems emphasize bringing people into the city to work, rather than taking people from the cities to jobs in the suburbs. The result is considerable inequity in access to the opportunities provided by the metropolitan region as a whole.

Improved communications may be a partial substitute for mobility, but little is known yet about how expected improvements may affect either the settlement pattern as a whole or the differential access of various groups.

Housing, of course, is one of the basic needs of an urban population. Freedom of choice in housing, however, is not effective for large portions of the population for two quite different reasons: (1) A subtle web of segregationist attitudes and practices tends to limit the access of minorities to suburban housing which their incomes would otherwise allow them to rent or purchase. (2) There are large groups for which the locations of employment and suitable housing are not economically interrelated. The most numerous of these groups are the lower-skilled, lower-income people who find employment in the suburbs, but who must continue to reside in the central cities. Dealing with the problem of housing on a metropolitan scale could increase choice and reduce commuting.

Finally, there is the question of effective government for metropolitan communities. As both the Campbell and Dollenmayer and Fitch papers point out, fundamental questions of the equity and effectiveness of the governments of metropolitan communities from the perspective of the nation have seldom been addressed. The federal system of government ought no longer to be viewed as a set of separate entities. The federal, state, and local levels retain appropriate responsibilities, but effectiveness is achieved only when the various levels find means to move in common directions. The federal government must explicitly affirm the goal of effective government at the metropolitan scale. Sound policy operationally requires evaluating revenue-sharing and federal grants-in-aid in terms of their potential impact on the development of effective government for metropolitan communities, as well as in terms of other substantive purposes.

In sum, the papers tend to support the view that a national urban policy is needed since many of the forces that affect the quality of urban life are national. Yet, the focuses of policy should be metropolitan because the daily experiences of most people are on that scale. The substantive questions have to do with distributional impact, income distribution, access to opportunities, and effective government for metropolitan communities. Expanded experimentation and research are essential to provide a sounder basis for future policies.

PART I
METROPOLITAN CONTEXT

Part I provides the demographic context of metropolitanization. What movements of firms and households have been and are taking place among and within metropolitan areas relative to race and income, and what are the implications of the new residential patterns for equity?

The first two papers draw heavily on census data to sketch the major population migrations with which metropolitanization is concerned: the movement from the central city to the suburbs, and the movement from rural to urban areas. Zimmer comprehensively documents the outward movement from the cities that has occurred in recent decades in terms of people, employment, and services. He notes that this outward movement has greatly increased the scale of local community life. It has resulted in a new type of urban settlement, geographically much more extensive than the city: the metropolitan community. The widespread settlement pattern has resulted in a decrease of population density in both the central cities and the outlying areas.

Campbell details the rural-to-urban movement and notes the increasing urbanization of life that is occurring even in nonmetropolitan areas. He feels that the traditional rural-urban dichotomy obscures many important changes taking place around metropolitan areas and suggests a new ecological classification that would take these changes into account.

While Zimmer and Campbell describe what has been happening in the buildup of metropolitan areas, and within them the drift to the suburbs, Edel, Harris, and Rothenberg attempt to explain why and to evaluate these phenomena. In regard to the increasing urbanization, or concentration in cities, they suggest that optimal city size should be viewed in new terms—i.e., that the net benefits associated with various urban scales should be determined. They attempt to demonstrate with a preliminary model that this net can be captured through aggregate land values. Furthermore, they hypothesize that different sizes of cities may be most efficient for different functions.

In regard to increasing deconcentration of the cities into the suburbs, they present an implicit model indicating the several kinds of factors that enter into the location decisions of households and businesses within a metropolitan area. They also consider how markets coordinate the decisions into a location pattern that is usually reflected in a rough balance between horizontal and vertical expansion. They observe that the historical form of settlement of the American city and its recent evolution conform to this model.

In their evaluation of concentration into metropolitan areas and deconcentration within metropolitan areas, Edel, Harris, and Rothenberg argue that a circumstantial case can be made, on grounds of overall allocative efficiency, that both these processes have progressed too far. Overconcentration into metropolitan areas raises social overhead costs, which are distributed unequally among various groups of the population. The benefits of the spread to suburbia are distributed regressively with respect to wealth.

Foley's contribution to the metropolitan context is more specialized. He discusses the changes in population density and land-value structure in terms of access to metropolitan opportunities, particularly automobile access, since it has become the common presumption that residents will have and rely on cars. Drawing on data from the Bay Area Survey on automobile availability conducted by the Survey Research Center at Berkeley, Foley finds that certain population categories (e.g., women, blacks, and the elderly) are seriously deprived. Since there is an increasing recognition that "community" is a sharing of access to opportunities, there are certain negative implications in this situation for community-building.

CHAPTER 1

THE URBAN CENTRIFUGAL DRIFT

Basil G. Zimmer

Brown University

METROPOLITAN GROWTH

DURING THE PRESENT CENTURY, the United States has changed from a predominantly agricultural to an urban society. By the turn of the century, the nation had been settled and the urban network largely established (Hawley, 1971: 83). The shift in population distribution since that time has been toward the city. For example, during the short span of only thirty years, 1880-1910, the number of people living in places of 250,000 and over increased from less than 4.5 million to more than 15.4 million. The number of urban places (2,500 and over) increased from 939 to 2,266 (U.S. Bureau of the Census, 1971a: 464-467). In the years to follow, the urban population continued to increase more rapidly than the total population, and by 1920, for the first time in history, a majority of the population lived in urban areas. The United States had become an urban society.

The same pattern of growth continued at a rapid pace throughout the century, except for a slowdown during the depression years of the 1930 decade. At each successive census period, an even larger proportion of the population was living in cities. For example, in 1940 the number of urban places had increased to nearly 3,500, and by 1970 to 7,062.[1] In 1970, three out of every four people lived in an urban setting. The changing distribution of population, however, was not only in the direction of urban places. Population was concentrating particularly in large urban centers—first, in the industrial Northeast, and then throughout the country. As the centripetal movement continued, the urban population expanded in size.

This increase was largely at the expense of the rural area—the rural farm areas in particular. As a consequence, in the early stages of the redistribution of population, the farm population lost its natural increase to the cities. The total out-migration during the half century 1910-1960 was equal to the total farm population at the beginning of the period—i.e., the net movement from farm areas was approximately 32 million, which was the size of the farm population in 1910 (Landis and Hatt, 1954: 403-410; Bowles, 1961).[2] And still the movement continues. In the last decade, another third of the population migrated to urban areas at the beginning of the decade. With the persistent movement out of farm areas in excess of natural increase, the farm population declined in absolute size. By 1971, the farm population had been reduced to less than 10 million, and less than 5 percent of the total population (U.S. Bureau of the Census, 1972a).[3]

In the early stages of urban development, with limited local transportation available, the population necessarily settled in rather compact units. As one author (Hawley, 1971: 88-89) has noted, "the city of this period (nineteenth century) was a pedestrian city; it was confined, therefore, to a radius of not more, and usually less, than three miles . . . houses were closely built on lots of 20 to 30 foot frontages. . . . Space could not be squandered on yards and open spaces about each house." In a study of the population of Chicago in 1898, it was reported that half of the 1,690,000 inhabitants lived within a radial distance of 3.2 miles of the center of the city (Cressey, 1938: 59). As short-distance transportation and communication improved, and cities continued to increase in size, rapid growth took place on the periphery. A reversed pattern of population movement as well as communal organization was set in motion. The compact urban center of the nineteenth century rapidly gave way to a much more widespread type of community organization. The city gave way to the metropolitan community.[4]

The concept of *community* that will be used throughout the following discussion is the one defined by Hawley (1956: 246, 257-258, 1971: 10-11):

> The community includes the area the population of which, however widely distributed, regularly turns to a common center for the satisfaction of all or a major part of its needs. . . . Thus, from a spatial standpoint, the community may be defined as comprising that area the resident population of which is interrelated and integrated with reference to its daily requirements, whether contacts be direct or indirect. From a functional standpoint the urban (metropolitan) community is a mechanism for relating a local population to a larger universe of activity. On the one hand, through its organization it produces products, services, or information for export to other communities. On the other hand, its organization is adapted to receiving and distributing imports, as well as locally produced goods and services, among its members. The two-way flows of interaction are decisive factors in determining the content of communal life.[5]

The purpose of this paper is to examine some of the trends that have been under way in the community settlement pattern in the United States, particularly during the present century, and to examine some of the consequences of these trends. The radius of daily interaction and the opportunities for increased contacts within the local community setting have grown as the barriers to communication and short-distance travel have decreased. The process of local expansion has been under way throughout the present century, involving a reconstitution of the old, compact, urban community on a new territorial basis and a different pattern of functional as well as spatial alignments (Hawley, 1971: 145).[6] The same author (1971: 148) continues:

> Local expansion created a new kind of urban center at the core of the enlarged and more highly integrated urban region. Instead of the dense, compact, settlement unit laid down in the preceding century, there emerged a new, much more diffuse type of communal unit. Not only was the territorial scope of the sixty-minute radius increased to approximately 25 miles, the frequency and intensity of interactions within that expanded area were multiplied several-fold by the motor vehicle, the telephone, and other changes that facilitated communications. . . . Within the enlarged radius of daily communications, villages and open-country settlements that had lived more or less aloof from the large center nearby were in a short space of time incorporated into an urban community.

The following discussion will focus on the increased scale of local community life. It should be noted, however, that increased scale refers to something quite different from the distances that people must travel in order to satisfy many of their daily needs. While there may be a close relationship between changes in scale and changes in daily travel patterns, the two refer to quite different dimensions of community life (see Foley, this volume). For our purposes, increased scale is reflected in changes in the overall spatial patterning of the population. This is measured in terms of change in the territorial scope of daily activities.

These changes are reflected in the rate of growth and the changing distribution of population within metropolitan areas during the present century, as shown in Table 1.1. Throughout the seventy-year period, metropolitan-area growth exceeded the growth rate of the total population. But even more important, while metropolitan areas exceeded the nonmetropolitan areas by twofold at the beginning of the century, this increased to nearly fourfold by 1950 and remained at that ratio again in 1960. By 1970, however, while metropolitan areas continued to increase, nonmetropolitan areas actually declined in size.

Table 1.1: Percentage of Change in Population in the United States in Metropolitan Areas and in Nonmetropolitan Areas, 1900-70

Selected Periods	Total Population	No. of Metro Areas	Metro Population	Central Cities	Outside Central Cities	Non-Metro Areas
1900-10[a]	21.0	44	34.6	33.6	38.2	16.4
1910-20[a]	14.9	58	26.9	25.2	32.0	9.6
1920-30[a]	16.1	97	28.3	22.3	44.0	7.9
1930-40[a]	7.2	140	8.1	5.1	15.1	6.5
1940-50[b]	14.5	168	22.0	13.9	35.9	6.1
1950-60[c]	18.5	212	26.3	10.7	48.6	7.1
1960-70[d]	13.3	243	16.6	6.5	26.7	−4.0

a. Thompson, 1943.
b. Hawley, 1956, p. 2.
c. U.S. Bureau of the Census, 1961, p. xxvi.
d. U.S. Bureau of the Census, 1971a, p. 143.

Within metropolitan areas, there has been a centrifugal drift of population since the turn of the century. For every census period, the population in the areas outside of the central cities increased more rapidly than the population in the central cities. At the beginning of the century, the gap was small, but in more recent years the city-suburban differentials have increased markedly.[7]

In the 1950-60 period, the U.S. census reported a population increase of approximately 28 million. Of this increase, 23.6 million were added to the 212 metropolitan areas, which accounted for 84.3 percent of the total increase. Of even more significance is the differential growth pattern within metropolitan areas. Of the 23.6 million increase in such areas, 18 million were added in the areas outside the central city. This represents a doubling of the population in the suburbs during a single decade. According to the census, during the 1950-60 period, the growth rate outside exceeded the central-city growth rate fivefold, and was seven times the rate of growth outside metropolitan areas.

In the 1960-70 decade, the outside areas increased at a rate more than four times that of the central cities, while nonmetropolitan population actually declined in size. But these data understate what is happening in metropolitan areas, since most of the increase in population in central cities was caused by the annexation of suburban territory. Of the 5.6 million increase in central-city population during this period, 4.9 million, or 86.3 percent, was due to annexation. Thus, of the 23.6 million increase in metropolitan areas, not 18 million but, in effect, 22.9 million were added outside the boundaries of the central city at the beginning of the period.

The same pattern continued in metropolitan areas during the next decade. Of the 3.9 million increase in central cities, more than 3.8 million, or 98.7 percent, were added through annexation. Actually, the centrifugal drift is even more substantial than the data in Table 1.1 indicate. The increases outside of the boundary of the central cities at the beginning of the period for both decades is shown in Table 1.2. Clearly, growth in the suburban areas would have been much higher if the suburbs had not lost population to the central cities through annexation.

The centrifugal drift of population during the present century has substantially changed the distribution of population within metropolitan areas. The

Table 1.2: Rate of Population Growth in Metropolitan Areas by Type of Place, With and Without Annexation, 1950-60 and 1960-70

Area	1960-70[a]		1950-60[b]	
	With Annexation	Without Annexation	With Annexation	Without Annexation
Total U.S.	13.3	13.3	18.5	18.5
Metropolitan areas	16.6	16.6	26.3	26.3
Central cities	6.5	0.1	10.8	1.5
Outside area	26.7	33.1	48.5	61.6
Number of areas	243	243	212	212

a. U.S. Bureau of the Census, 1971a, p. 193.
b. U.S. Bureau of the Census, 1961, p. xxvi.

consistent trend has been a decline in the proportion of the population living in central cities. Since 1940, in particular, the proportion of the metropolitan population living in the rings has increased markedly. In 1910, three-fourths of the metropolitan population lived in central cities, but this had decreased to only 45 percent by 1970.[8] Thus, by 1970, a distinct majority of the metropolitan residents lived in the rings. By that time, the metropolitan population had become a largely suburban population. Central cities had already lost their dominant position in terms of population. As will be noted later, this increasing scale of local community life had repercussions that affected the whole metropolitan community.

The changing distribution of population has been more significant than the number of people involved, since only selected segments of the population have taken part in the widespread pattern of settlement. This becomes evident when the characteristics of the population that were a part of this centrifugal drift are examined. But before pursuing that problem, the metropolitan population will be considered according to changing definitions and criteria; data on this are presented in Table 1.3.

Although the actual size of the metropolitan area population varies by the definition used, by 1950, under any of the definitions, a majority of the people in the United States lived in metropolitan areas. It was not until after 1960, however, that a majority of the metropolitan population lived outside of the

Table 1.3: Metropolitan Area Population, 1950-70

| Population | No. of Metro-politan Areas | Size of Population (in millions) | | | Percent Metro-politan in CC | Percent U.S. Popu-lation Metro-politan |
		Metro-politan Areas	CC	Out-side CC		
1950[a]	168	83.9	49.1	34.9	58.5	55.5
1950[b] (Adj. for 1960 areas)	212	89.3	52.4	36.9	58.7	59.0
1950[c] (Adj. for 1970 areas)	243	94.6	53.7	40.9	56.8	62.5
1960[b]	212	112.9	58.0	54.9	51.4	63.0
1960[c] (Adj. for 1970 areas)	243	119.6	60.0	59.6	50.1	66.7
1970[c]	243	139.4	63.8	75.6	45.8	68.6
1970[d] (Adj. for 1960 areas)	212	130.9	—	—	—	64.4

a. 1950 Census of Population, 1951, p. 68.
b. U.S. Bureau of the Census, 1961, p. xxvi.
c. U.S. Bureau of the Census, 1971a, p. 180.
d. U.S. Bureau of the Census, 1971a, p. 191.

central cities. The number of metropolitan areas, using constant criteria, increased from 168 in 1950 to 243 in 1970—an increase of 44 percent. At the same time, the population in metropolitan areas, as defined at the time of the census, increased from 83.9 million to 139.4 million—a 66 percent increase. Thus, metropolitan population increased much more rapidly than metropolitan areas. This is due to the continued concentration in the larger metropolitan areas.

If one adjusts for the new areas added and then looks at the changes in population in the 243 metropolitan areas reported in the 1970 census, one finds that the population increased from 94.6 million to 139.4 million, or nearly 50 percent, during the period. Thus, whether one holds the number of areas constant or not, the metropolitan population is the most rapidly growing segment of the total population, and the rings of metropolitan areas are increasing more rapidly than the central cities. The centrifugal drift is apparent, regardless of what adjustments are made in classifying metropolitan areas. The absolute size of the metropolitan population increase is not due either to definitional change or to the inclusion of new areas since, even when the 1950 metropolitan areas are adjusted to 1970 areas, the increase accounts for more than 85 percent of the total population growth. While the metropolitan population increased by 68 percent, the ring areas increased by 85 percent, compared with a 19 percent increase in the central cities (based on 1970 metropolitan areas). The evidence is clear that the population is becoming increasingly concentrated in metropolitan areas and, at the same time and at an even more rapid rate, the population is becoming more widely distributed within the metropolitan community, with a substantial majority living in suburban areas.[9]

It should be noted that the increased scale of local community life, as reflected in the urban centrifugal drift within metropolitan areas, focuses only on the changes that are taking place within the local community setting. The increase of scale of the metropolitan community should be clearly differentiated from the related concept, "metropolitanization of society." The latter refers to "a comprehensive reorganization of the entire structure of the society leaving no sector or sphere untouched. 'Town' and 'country' are merged under a single set of institutions and a common set of processes" (Hawley, 1971: 219).[10] These processes, while related, are outside the scope of the present discussion, which focuses only on the growth, development, and territorial expansion of the population at the local community level.

EXPANSION OF THE URBAN UNIT

The growth of metropolitan organization, which has greatly expanded the scope of daily life, has resulted from "the conquest of distance" as a barrier to community size. The reduction of the limiting effects of distance has made possible an extension of the radius of community. In the compact city of the nineteenth century, the radial scope of local organization rarely exceeded ten miles. By contrast, the metropolitan community, even as early as 1950, embraced in a single organization the population within a radial distance of thirty-five miles or more from the central city (Hawley, 1956: 3). Comparable data for a more recent period are not at hand, but the scale of community life as reflected in the growth of urbanized areas, which are much more limited in scope than the metropolitan community, has increased markedly during the past twenty years as the highway system has expanded, thus further reducing "time-distance" cost at the local level.

How the improved road system has effectively reduced distance is illustrated by the data shown in Figure 1.1 for the state of Rhode Island. In the short period of only ten years, the distance that could be traveled with no increase in time has expanded substantially. While the increase is evident in all time zones away from the central city, the amount of change increases as one moves further away from the city. If we focus our attention on a line drawn from the city center in a southwesterly direction to the border of the state, it permits a rough measure of changes in time-distance zones. For the 1955-65 period in the zone closest to the city, the ten-minute zone had increased by about two miles. The twenty-minute zone had doubled from seven to fourteen miles, and the forty-minute zone had increased from eighteen to more than twenty-five miles. It is now possible to travel approximately fifteen miles further in fifty minutes than in the earlier period. With the expanded highway system, the distance (forty miles) that previously had required seventy minutes can now be traveled in fifty minutes.

This is the type of change that has occurred in metropolitan areas throughout the country. This type of decrease in travel time has been one of the major factors that has made the expansion of the urban unit possible. The extent of expansion of the urban unit is partially evident from the growth of urbanized areas over the past twenty years.

While the urban centrifugal drift extends beyond the boundaries of the metropolitan community, a large proportion of the population is concentrated in the urbanized area.[11] This is the population that is densely settled beyond the corporate limits of the city. The present discussion examines the changes that have taken place in these areas over the twenty-year period from 1950 to 1970. While there are difficulties in comparison from one census to the next, the area boundaries are generally determined on the basis of constant criteria. As new areas meet the criteria, they are included. According to the census, the number of urbanized areas increased from 157 in 1950 to 250 by 1970. Table 1.4 shows two ways of measuring the changes in urban areas over a twenty-year period. In order to measure change in population and land area, the number of urbanized areas was held constant throughout the period (see Table 1.4, top). Overall change during this period, according to constant criteria, has been observed by including the new urban areas as they developed (see Table 1.4, bottom).

For the 155 urbanized areas identified in the 1950 census, several significant trends are evident.[12] A marked centrifugal drift of population is observed. While central cities increased from 48 to 56 million (32 percent), the outlying

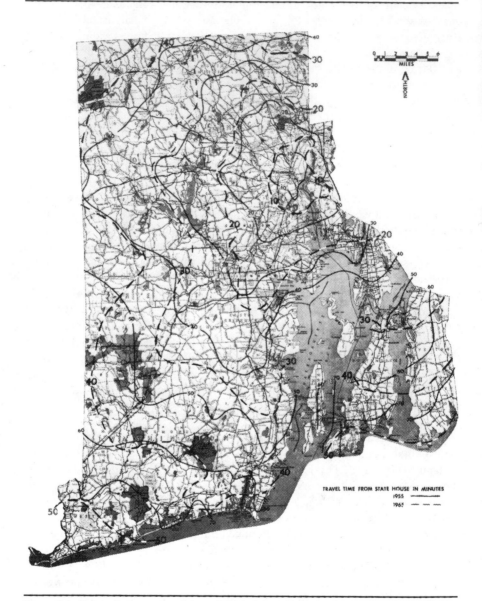

Figure 1.1: Past and present travel times (Rhode Island Statewide Planning Program, Rhode Island Development Council Research Division, 1969).

Table 1.4: Changes in Population, Land Area, and Density in Urbanized Areas, by Type of Area and Proportion in Central Cities, 1950-70

Year	Urbanized Area	Central City	Outside Central City	% in Central City
	Constant (1950) Number of Urbanized Areas			
Population				
1950[a]	69,288,234	48,377,240	20,910,994	69.8
1960[b]	89,983,910	53,477,361	36,506,549	59.4
1970[b]	107,827,098	56,352,118	51,474,980	52.3
Land Area (sq mi)				
1950	12,805	6,214	6,591	48.5
1960	23,111	9,169	13,941	39.7
1970	30,465	11,368	19,098	37.3
Density (per sq mi)				
1950	5,411	7,785	3,173	
1960	3,894	5,832	2,619	
1970	3,539	4,957	2,695	
	Constant Criteria			
Population				
1950	69,288,234	48,377,240	20,910,994	69.8
1960	95,848,487	57,975,132	37,873,355	60.5
1970	118,446,566	63,921,684	54,524,882	54.0
Land Area (sq mi)				
1950	12,805	6,214	6,591	48.5
1960	25,546	10,838	14,707	42.4
1970	35,081	14,297	20,786	40.8
Density (sq mi)				
1950	5,411	7,785	3,173	
1960	3,752	5,349	2,575	
1970	3,376	4,471	2,623	

a. U.S. Bureau of the Census, 1961.
b. U.S. Bureau of the Census, 1971a.

areas increased from 21 to nearly 52 million (160 percent). Consequently, the proportion of urbanized population in the central cities declined from nearly 70 percent to only 52 percent during the twenty-year period. The data also show that the urbanized territory in these 155 areas increased substantially from 12.8 thousand square miles in 1950 to more than thirty thousand square miles in 1970. Most of the expansion took place outside of the central city. Thus, while nearly half of the urbanized territory was in central cities in 1950, it had declined to only 37 percent by 1970, for the same areas. Land areas expanded more rapidly than population, causing a decrease in density of settlement not only in the expanded urbanized area but also in the central cities.[13]

In the lower portion of Table 1.4, areas are not held constant, but conform to a constant definition. The general pattern of change already observed persists;

only the scale of expansion has increased. Urbanized population and urbanized land have increased sharply, and urban density in all segments of the urbanized areas has declined. The proportion of change over the twenty-year period is shown in Table 1.5.

Table 1.5: Percent Change in Population, Land Area, and Density in Urbanized Areas by Type of Area, 1950-70

Years	Urbanized Area	Central City	Outside Central City	Urbanized Area	Central City	Outside Central City
	Constant (1950) Number of Urbanized Areas			Constant Criteria		
Population						
1950-60	1.30	1.11	1.75	1.38	1.20	1.81
1960-70	1.20	1.05	1.41	1.24	1.10	1.44
1950-70	1.56	1.17	2.46	1.71	1.32	2.61
Land Area						
1950-60	1.81	1.48	2.12	2.00	1.74	2.23
1960-70	1.32	1.24	1.37	1.37	1.32	1.41
1950-70	2.38	1.83	2.90	2.74	2.30	3.15
Density						
1950-60	0.72	0.75	0.83	0.69	0.69	0.81
1960-70	0.91	0.85	1.03	0.90	0.84	1.02
1950-70	0.65	0.64	0.85	0.62	0.57	0.83

NOTE: Calculated from Table 1.4.

Table 1.6: Size of Urbanized Population, Land Area, Density, and Percent of Population in Central City by Size of Urbanized Areas, 1950 and 1970

Population Class of Area[a]	No. of Area	Size of Population (000)		Land Area		Density (per sq mi)		% of Population in CC	
		1950[d]	1970[e]	1950	1970	1950	1970	1950	1970
(3,000,000 or more	3	21,214	31,273	2,832	5,274	7,490	5,929	67.0	51.6
1,000,000– 3,000,000	9	16,640	23,382	2,450	5,476	6,791	4,270	60.6	37.6
500,000– 1,000,000	13	8,851	15,085	1,961	5,357	4,515	2,816	74.0	53.6
250,000– 500,000	24	8,780	15,049	1,920	5,259	4,445	2,862	75.7	57.0
100,000– 250,000	69[b]	10,765	18,767	2,781	7,240	3,870	2,492	76.8	61.4
Under 100,000	37[c]	3,019	4,270	801	1,859	3,771	2,298	85.8	75.5

a. Size classes are based on 1950 census; the number of areas has been held constant.
b. Schenectady has been subtracted; it was incorporated into another area in 1960.
c. Niagara Falls has been subtracted; became part of the Buffalo urbanized area in 1960.
d. U.S. Bureau of the Census, 1961.
e. U.S. Bureau of the Census, 1971a.

As the centrifugal drift is examined in more detail, it is found that, while it has occurred in all metropolitan areas combined, there are substantial differences in the amount of drift by size of urbanized area, as shown in Table 1.6. During this period, the widespread pattern of settlement was particularly marked in the one- to three-million population-size class. In this group, land increased by nearly 125 percent, while population grew by only 40 percent. Thus, density declined by more than one third, and the proportion of urbanized population in the central city decreased from 60 percent to around 38 percent. A similar pattern of change also was found in the other size classes. In the smaller areas, a majority of the population continued to live in the central city even though the proportion had declined substantially during the period. In all areas, regardless of size, land area expanded more rapidly than population, causing a decrease in population density. A high proportion of population in the central city does not necessarily mean that the population is not more widespread in distribution than at an earlier period, since land areas in cities increased by 80 percent during the period. In the smaller urbanized areas (under 500,000), the central cities doubled their land area over the twenty-year period.

The increased scale of local community life is partially evident in the expanded radial distance from the center to the outer boundary of the urbanized areas, as shown in Table 1.7. (Radial distances to the borders of metropolitan, as opposed to urbanized, areas would show a much larger scale of community organization.) The radial distance to the border of the urbanized area increases consistently with the size of the urbanized area. These data understate the distances involved, since it assumes equal development in all directions from the center, whereas actual development tends to be uneven and tends to extend along radial highways. Thus, the scope of activities would be much more extensive than these data indicate. Except for the smallest areas, the radial distance over the twenty-year period increased inversely by size of area. The largest areas increased their radial distance by approximately one-third, while the next three size classes (as of 1950) increased radial distance by nearly two-thirds.

Density of settlement has declined in all size classes of urbanized areas, and in central cities as well as in the outside areas. As is evident from the data

Table 1.7: Average Radial Distance of Urbanized Area and Percent Change by Size of Area, 1950-70

Size of Area[a]	Distance in Miles			Percent Increase 1950-1970
	1950	1960	1970	
3,000,000 or more	17.34	21.16	23.66	36.5
1,000,000 to 3,000,000	9.31	12.49	13.92	49.5
500,000 to 1,000,000	6.93	10.00	11.45	65.2
250,000 to 500,000	5.12	7.03	8.35	63.0
100,000 to 250,000	3.58	4.89	5.78	61.5
Under 100,000	2.62	3.57	4.00	52.7

NOTE: Calculated from Table 1.6.
a. Based on 1950 population of urbanized areas.

123999

Table 1.8: Density of Central City and Urbanized Area Outside Central City by Size of Place, 1950-70[a]

Size of Place[b]	Central City		Ratio	Outside Central City		Ratio
	1950[c]	1970[d]	1950-70	1950[c]	1970[d]	1950-70
3,000,000 or more	14,079	12,881	.915	3,838	3,764	.981
1,000,000 to 3,000,000	13,580	11,603	.854	3,817	3,091	.810
500,000 to 1,000,000	6,066	3,937	.649	2,612	2,118	.811
250,000 to 500,000	5,905	3,613	.612	2,512	2,243	.893
100,000 to 250,000	4,969	3,107	.625	2,233	2,052	.919
Under 100,000	4,407	2,646	.600	2,019	1,634	.809

a. Per square mile.
b. Area held constant based on 1950 data.
c. U.S. Bureau of the Census, 1961.
d. U.S. Bureau of the Census, 1971a.

presented in Table 1.8, density in the central cities decreased more in the smaller than in the largest urbanized areas. The decrease was less than 10 percent in the largest areas, as compared with 35 percent or more in areas below 1,000,000. Areas outside central cities experienced a much lower rate of decline in density, ranging from only 2 percent in the largest to 20 percent in the smaller areas. The decline in density of settlement must be viewed with caution, since much of the change is due to an expansion of area on the fringes of built-up areas. Cities have annexed territory on their fringes, which were less densely settled than the population living within the earlier boundaries. This would have the effect of decreasing overall density, even though the overall pattern of settlement in the original city may have remained largely unchanged.

By definition, the density in the outside areas could change only within certain limits, since in order to be incorporated into the urbanized area, a minimum density of settlement is necessary. Thus, regardless of the amount of expansion of urbanized areas outside of the city, density will not change substantially. In short, the area of dense settlement continues to increase in size as residents move to the fringes of the already built-up areas. Consequently, the scope of daily life has increased in scale. But as noted elsewhere, not all segments of the population participate equally in this widespread pattern of settlement. We turn now to a discussion of the selective aspects of the centrifugal drift.

CHANGES IN POPULATION COMPOSITION

The composition of the population involved in the changing distribution within metropolitan areas is a very significant dimension of the suburban movement. Not only are the central cities growing at a less rapid rate, or in many cases even declining in size, but there is a selectivity in the changes that are taking place within segments of the metropolitan area. The differences that evolve are likely to have significant implications for a number of communitywidc functions. Thus, attention will be focused on the type of people taking part in this widespread settlement pattern and the type of people left behind in the central city.

Most of the literature in this area is based either on single case studies or is limited to the larger metropolitan areas, but, in general, the findings quite consistently show that there is a marked selectivity in the movement to the suburbs. In an analysis of four large metropolitan areas in 1960, Schnore (1964) reported that it was the lower educational groups that were left behind in thc central city in the redistribution of population within metropolitan areas.[14] Looking at the proportion of each educational group that resided in the central city, he found that it decreased consistently as the level of education increased. The range of difference was substantial. In three of the four areas, the college-educated group had the lowest index of concentration in the central city. In all areas (Los Angeles excepted), the (central-city) index of concentration in the central city was highest at the lower levels of education.[15] Part of the city-suburban difference was probably due to age composition.

In an attempt to observe change longitudinally, Schnore (1964) has also examined the index of concentration in the suburbs by level of education for several decennial census periods for a single metropolitan area (Detroit). According to his data, in 1940 Detroit had a very slight over-representation of the lowest levels of education and of those who had attended high school. However, in the next census period, a period of rapid suburban growth following World War II, it became evident that it was the population in the lower educational categories who were being left behind in the city. Disproportionate over-representation in the city was found for those who had not attended high school. And during the next census period, 1950-60, there was an even larger disproportionate concentration of the lower educational group in the central city.

Clearly, either the higher educational groups were moving to the suburbs or migrants to the metropolitan area displayed great selectivity in location; it is likely that both movement patterns were occurring. At any rate, the city was left with a high disproportionate number of those with low educational attainment. When Detroit was compared with a number of other large cities for thc same time period, it was found to be quite consistent with a general pattern.

However, if one examines all metropolitan areas in more detail, it becomes evident that the Detroit pattern is more representative of the metropolitan areas where the central cities are larger and older and have not extended their boundaries in recent years. In the smaller, newer, central cities, and in areas where the central city is expanding through annexation, the central city-suburban differences are less marked. To pursue this issue further, let us examine the findings reported by others.

Duncan and Duncan (1955), for example, in a study of Chicago based on 1950 census data, showed that centralization of residence was inversely related to socioeconomic status. It can be said that this generalization, based on a single community that is both large and old, may not apply to other metropolitan areas. However, we find some support for this observation in an analysis of the central city and rings of all 168 SMAs in 1950. Schnore and Varley (1955: 413) concluded that "the larger the central city the more likely it is that the socioeconomic status of ring residents will be higher than that of city residents." Studies of the types of people moving into such areas also indicate that the same selectivity takes place as occurs within an area (Kirschenbaum, 1972). The lower status migrants to metropolitan areas are moving into the central city, while the higher status migrants disproportionately move directly to the suburbs.

In a study of Providence, Rhode Island, Mayer and Goldstein (1964) found that, during the 1940 decade, the central city experienced a heavy out-migration made up disproportionately of persons in the higher socioeconomic categories, but the movement also included a number of persons in manual occupations. They also observed that movement from the suburbs to the central city was predominantly by the lower socioeconomic groups.

In a more recent analysis of the twelve largest SMSAs, Taeuber and Taeuber (1964) reported that the net effect of migration flows was to diminish the educational and occupational levels of the population in the central cities and to increase these levels in the suburbs. They felt that the lowering of educational and occupational levels of central-city populations should be attributed almost entirely to the heavy out-migration of high-status whites rather than to any significant in-migration of low-status whites or Negroes.

As a consequence of these movement patterns, the socioeconomic gap between cities and suburban areas is increasing. As Schnore (1964) has noted in the case of Detroit, the central cities are left with a disproportionate number of the disadvantaged. Schnore hypothesized that, while Detroit was quite representative of a class of cities, the same pattern of redistribution would not find support if a number of other variables were taken into account. However, at this stage he shifted his analysis to the more limited urbanized area, so his findings are not an adequate test of what is happening in metropolitan areas.

Nonetheless, we find at least for income that the central-city/suburban differences are much less marked in the smaller areas than in the larger metropolitan areas. It is in the smaller areas that only a limited amount of suburbanization has taken place. In metropolitan areas of less than 250,000, half or more of the residents still live in the central city. It is in the areas of from one to three million that the suburbanization movement has reduced the central-city population to only slightly more than one-third of that of the metropolitan area. For the most part, these are the older metropolitan areas of the North and Northeast, and it is in these areas that the higher socioeconomoc groups have moved disproportionately to the metropolitan ring.

Table 1.9 illustrates that this selectivity in the suburban movement is most evident in the larger metropolitan areas. For the population residing in the largest metropolitan areas (1,000,000 and over), individual incomes were nearly 20 percent higher in the suburban areas than in the central city. The difference in favor of the suburbs declines to only 10 percent in the smaller areas, how-

Table 1.9: Mean Per Capita Income in Metropolitan Areas by Size, Place of Residence, Race, 1970

Size and Place of Residence	Total[a]	White Males	Negro Males
1,000,000 or more	6,475	9,150	5,854
Central city	5,868	8,258	5,773
Outside central city	6,939	9,660	6,177
OCC/CC ratio	1.183	1.170	1.070
Under 1,000,000	5,690	8,061	4,674
Central city	5,398	7,848	4,769
Outside central city	5,963	8,224	4,427
OCC/CC ratio	1.109	1.048	.928

NOTE: Data from U.S. Bureau of the Census, 1971d, pp. 89-92.
a. Includes all persons 14 years of age and over as of March 1971.

ever.[16] But these differences are found only for whites. For Negro males, there is a slight selectivity in the large area suburbs, but in the smaller ones, suburban Negroes appear to have a slight disadvantage.

In a study of six metropolitan areas in three different size classes, it was reported that central-city and suburban areas tended to disproportionately attract residents who are closely similar to the residents already living in each subarea of the metropolitan community (Hawley and Zimmer, 1970). The movement to the suburban zones drew off the better educated from among the central-city residents, whereas those moving from the suburbs to the central city tended to be the least educated. A similar type of selectivity was found for income groups. In the redistribution of population, the central cities gained low-income earners from the suburbs and lost the higher-income earners to the suburbs. The authors noted further that the suburbanward movers had incomes considerably above the residents already living in the suburbs. It is evident that this type of movement is to the disadvantage of the central city. Not only are the cities left with the lower-income groups, but they are placed at a further disadvantage by attracting lower-income earners from both their own metropolitan areas and from outside.

In further analyzing these data, the authors found that the suburbanward movement drew off the top income level in each education class. When suburban residents who had moved from the central city were compared with central-city residents who had lived only in the city, the income differentials were marked. On the other hand, the more general pattern, with some exceptions, was that movers from suburbs to central cities were drawn from the lower-income levels of the suburban population. However, such movers tended to have higher incomes than those who had lived only in the central city.

The authors also showed that the effects of residence change with reference to occupation were similar to those reported for education. At every occupational level but one (the "professional, managerial and official" in the largest areas), suburbanward movers had higher incomes than did central-city household heads who had lived only in the city. And in the reverse movement (i.e., suburban to central city), the movers were for the most part low-income earners when compared with other suburbanites in similar occupations.

The net effect has been to increase the average level of income in the suburban areas. The selectivity of the suburban movement in the areas covered in this study has meant that the central cities have lost many citizens who are successful by one or more of several criteria, and are left with those who have not been successful.[17]

Schnore (1964) has shown that a number of factors are related to whether or not there are high-status groups in the suburbs (at least for urbanized areas, which include only the city and the densely settled area around the city). He has shown that it is only in the large, older areas with non-expanding central cities that the suburban population consistently exceeds the city in socio-economic status (using education as an index). Conversely, in the smaller (under 250,000) urbanized areas, in the newer areas (those that reached 50,000 in 1910 or later) and in areas where the central city has annexed territory, either the higher educational classes are over-represented, or both the highest and lowest educational classes are over-represented in the city.

While these data suggest that we may have overgeneralized the selectivity of the suburbanward movement, the findings must be viewed with caution since the Schnore analysis is limited territorially. It includes only a small part of the metropolitan area population living outside of the central city—i.e., that part of the population that lives contiguous to the city in the older suburban areas.[18] Since the higher-status groups tend to live furthest from the city, it may be that a more complete analysis would show quite different results. But regardless of the generalizability of his findings, Schnore nonetheless makes the point that the differences found between cities and suburbs in all metropolitan areas combined may not represent the differences that exist in any given metropolitan area. He has identified a number of factors that should be taken into account as we attempt to understand the processes at work in the redistribution of population within the metropolitan community.

In a special tabulation of the 1960 census (U.S. Bureau of the Census, 1967: x), socioeconomic status categories were constructed by combining occupational and educational attainment scores of the chief income recipient of a family with current family income. In Table 1.10, we have summarized the distribution of scores by color within selected residential categories. Even admitting the limitations of the data, the distribution of scores is informative.[19] Status scores differ markedly by place of residence. Within each residential status category, there are substantial differences in the scores for whites and Negroes. While 60 percent of the whites in the central city and more than 70 percent in other urban areas outside the central cities have scores about 50, fewer than one-fourth of the Negroes are found with such scores. Also of interest here is that the status scores of Negroes are the same whether they live in the central city or in the urban areas outside the city. In other words, the suburban areas have not attracted the higher-status Negroes as they have the higher-status whites.

Table 1.10: Percent Distribution of Socioeconomic Status Scores by Place of Residence and Color, 1960

Socioeconomic Status Scores	Metropolitan					
	Central Cities		Other Urban		Rural	
	Whites	Negroes	Whites	Negroes	Whites	Negroes
80 or more	15.5	2.7	22.7	2.7	12.1	1.1
50-79	46.8	21.0	50.2	19.3	41.7	8.3
20-49	31.6	55.2	23.6	53.7	36.9	42.8
Under 20	6.1	21.0	3.5	24.0	9.3	47.7

NOTE: Data from U.S. Bureau of the Census, 1967.

In most studies of metropolitan areas, the ring or suburban area usually refers to all of the metropolitan area outside of the central city. That this has the effect of veiling the real central city-suburban differences is suggested by the last two columns of Table 1.10. Actually, the socioeconomic status of the population living in the rural portion of metropolitan areas is even lower than the status of the central-city population. The difference is particularly marked for Negroes. Since 25 percent of the whites and approximately 40 percent of the Negroes in the rings of the metropolitan areas lived in these lower-status residential categories, they can substantially affect the overall status of the metropolitan rings by bringing down their average score. In short, the lower status of central-city residents would be even more marked if the rural segment of the ring were not counted as part of the suburban population. The urban parts of the suburbs are even more selective of the higher socioeconomic status groups than the usual city-ring classification of metropolitan areas indicates.

Quite apart from, but not independent of, the socioeconomic factors in the redistribution of population within metropolitan areas is the racial dimension. The widespread pattern of settlement has been almost exclusively white, thus sharpening racial segregation. During the 1960-70 decade, the central cities underwent a major racial change. This was most extreme in the Northeast, where the white population declined by 9.3 percent, while the Negro population increased by 35.5 percent (Morrison, 1971). This same general pattern prevailed in all regions except the West. Even in the West, however, the Negro population increased by 52 percent, compared with an increase of less than 3 percent for the whites. In 1970, for all metropolitan areas of one million or more, nearly 80 percent of the Negroes lived in central cities, as compared with 36 percent of the whites. In metropolitan areas below one million, about two-fifths of the whites and nearly three-fourths of the Negroes lived in central cities.

It is likely that the Negro concentration in central cities will increase in the future. According to unpublished estimates prepared in 1971 by the U.S. Census Bureau for the Commission on Population Growth and the American Future, nonwhites will make up between 37 and 42 percent of the central-city population by the year 2000, as compared to only 22.5 percent in 1970. Central cities have become increasingly segregated. In 1970, there were sixteen cities where blacks outnumbered whites. In Washington, D.C., an extreme example, seven out of ten residents were black (U.S. Bureau of the Census, 1971b). Clearly, the racial selectivity in the suburban movement is much more evident and even more important than the differentials by socioeconomic status.

The literature on suburban selectivity is not clear, since no research has covered all metropolitan areas at any given time. Most research has been limited either to single metropolitan areas or to the older, larger, metropolitan areas. Size, age, rate of growth, region of the country, annexation history by size of area, and a number of other comparable and important variables have not been consistently taken into account. While Hawley and Zimmer (1970) made an effort to examine the selectivity by size of metropolitan area, their sample was such that it excluded the very large metropolitan areas that have attracted most research attention. Thus, while their findings are suggestive, the study excluded the areas that have provided the empirical evidence for most of the generalizations on central city-suburban differences which have become a part of the popular literature.

There is a need for further research on this topic, particularly historical research. Obviously, at some point in time the suburban populations become quite different from city populations, but at what point this occurs is not at all clear from the evidence at hand. It is not enough to demonstrate that in the older, larger areas there is such selectivity; what we need to know is at what point in the growth and development of the metropolitan community this type of differential becomes sociologically significant. We also need to know at what point and under what circumstances different segments of the population participate in the widespread settlement pattern.

DEVELOPMENT OF A METROPOLITAN AREA

Before returning to a further discussion of metropolitan areas in general, we will focus attention on the pattern of development of a single metropolitan area—Flint, Michigan—to illustrate specifically the type of changes that have taken place in the "urban centrifugal drift" in recent years. While no claim is made that this metropolitan or urbanized area is representative of any class of metropolitan area, the data at hand illustrate rather dramatically the general pattern of change that has taken place as the scale of local community life has expanded (Zimmer, 1958).

In the more advanced state of development of the metropolitan area, as shown in a comparison of Figures 1.2 and 1.3, the densely settled population has burst over the boundary lines of the central city. As a result, in all directions, but particularly along major highway routes, there is a continuously settled population beyond the corporate limits of the city. A star-shaped pattern developed early and is still clearly evident for the urbanized area in 1970. It is also evident that up to 1920 there were frequent enlargements of the city area.

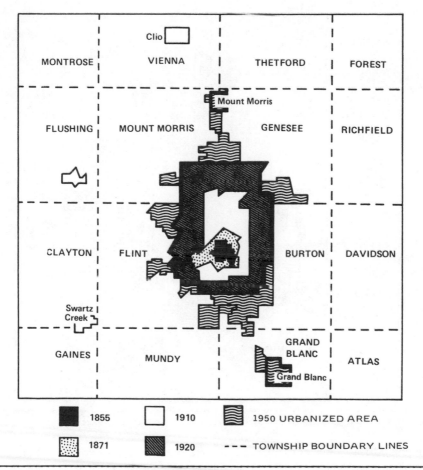

Figure 1.2: Growth of city of Flint, 1855-1920; Flint urbanized area, 1950 (Zimmer, 1950).

The central city was incorporated in 1885, and in the years to follow, as the population increased in size and as more land was developed, the political limits of the city were extended outward in order to continue to encompass the densely settled areas in a single municipality for the provision of services. In some instances, the enlargement of the city may have lagged behind the development of urban areas, but, regardless of the sequence, there was an adjustment of the boundaries as the urban population grew. The largest annexation occurred in 1920, which was the last time that any sizable boundary changes were made.[20] For the next twenty years, most of the growth of the metropolitan area took place in the central city. By the late 1940s and early 1950s, the city had largely developed its available vacant land, and, as the population of the metropolitan area continued to expand, residential (as well as nonresidential) concentrations developed beyond the city limits.

At the beginning of the century, the central city had a population of only 13,000, but it experienced a rapid population growth during the decades to

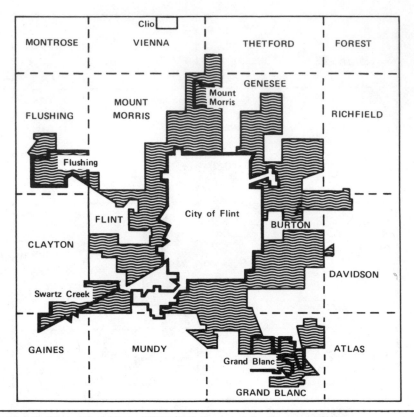

Figure 1.3: Flint urbanized area, 1970 (U.S. Bureau of the Census, 1972c).

follow. At least some of the increase at the center was at the expense of the outlying areas, which experienced population losses. This was a period of rapid centripetal growth.[21] The concentration of the population in the central city continued until 1930, when three out of every four people in the metropolitan area lived in the central city. It was not until after 1930 that the centrifugal drift got under way. The following reasons have been given by Hawley and Zimmer (1961: 150) for the change in pattern of settlement:

> Just as Flint's growth was based on the rise of the automobile industry, the automobile in turn revolutionized the pattern of local life in and around Flint. Whereas at the turn of the century Flint, as a prosperous small city, existed more or less independently of its hinterland, the motor vehicle converted it into the functional center of an expanding metropolitan community. That effect was not immediate, however. Adapted at first primarily to intra-city use, the automobile had to await the development and surfacing of rural roads before its potentialities as an agent for change could be realized.

Once the road improvements in the metropolitan area began, after 1910, there was a continuous development of hard-surfaced roads which has resulted

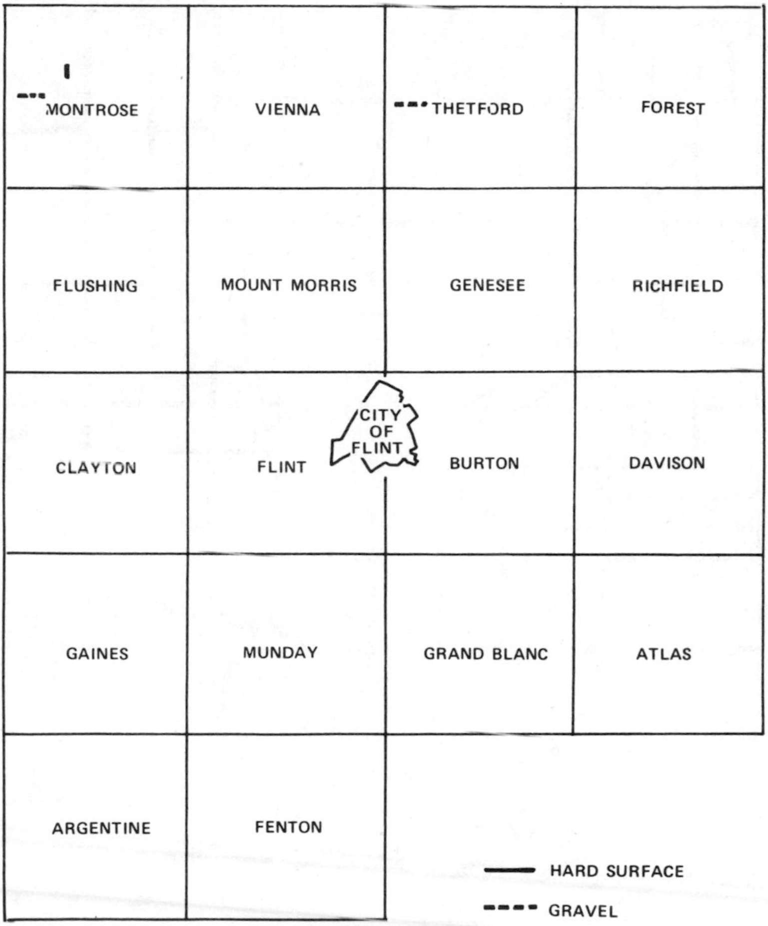

MONTROSE	VIENNA	THETFORD	FOREST
FLUSHING	MOUNT MORRIS	GENESEE	RICHFIELD
CLAYTON	FLINT	CITY OF FLINT BURTON	DAVISON
GAINES	MUNDAY	GRAND BLANC	ATLAS
ARGENTINE	FENTON	— HARD SURFACE ▬▬▬ GRAVEL	

Figure 1.4: Improved roads in Genesee County, 1909 (Zimmer, 1958).

in an efficient highway transportation system. Even as late as 1909, nearly all of the roads in metropolitan areas outside of the central city were unimproved, thus making transportation, particularly at certain times of the year, difficult (see Figure 1.4). However, by 1920 nearly all segments of the county had been interconnected by a system of improved roads, surfaced at least with gravel (see Figure 1.5). A hard-surfaced road ran the full length of the county up through the center from the south to the northern limits of the county. Two other hard surfaced roads extended to the southeast of Flint and directly east through to the county boundary. The basic improved road system showed signs of becoming developed throughout the county by this date. During the next eighteen years, nearly all of the section line roads and main roads leading in all directions out of the central city were hard-surfaced (see Figure 1.6). The free flow of traffic throughout the county was no longer limited by the seasonal ravages of the weather. From 1938 to 1956, the major changes involved convert-

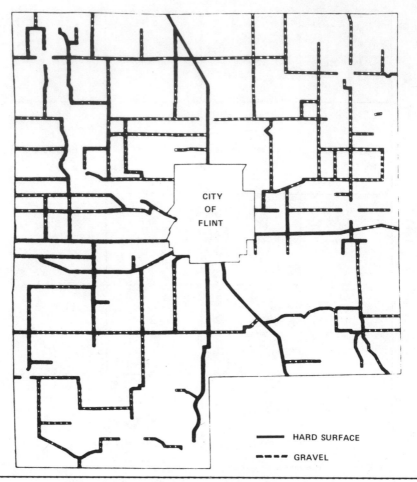

Figure 1.5: Improved roads in Genesee County, 1920 (Zimmer, 1958).

ing gravel surfaces of many of the heavily traveled roads to hard surfaces (see Figure 1.7). This has had the effect of increasing the traffic capacity of these roads as well as the ease of movement (Zimmer, 1958).

The continuous need for an improved system of highways in the area can be found in the increase in the number of automobiles registered. From 1930 to 1955, motor-vehicle registrations increased continuously from slightly more than 57,000 to more than 151,000.[22] Passenger cars and commercial vehicles increased by 167 percent and 134 percent, respectively. The increase in motor-vehicle registrations was much more rapid than the increase in population. From 1930 to 1940, the population of the metropolitan area increased 7.7 percent, whereas passenger-vehicle registration increased 17 percent. During the next decade, although the population increased by less than 20 percent, passenger vehicles increased nearly 60 percent. Throughout the period from 1930-55, the rate of increase in passenger vehicles in the county was triple the rate of growth in population.

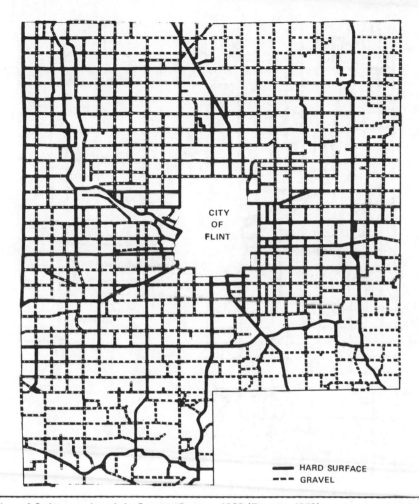

Figure 1.6: Improved roads in Genesee County, 1938 (Zimmer, 1958).

Let us further examine how the improved road system and the increase in the number of automobiles affected the pattern of settlement within the metropolitan area. The increased scale of local community life is reflected in the changing distribution of population within the metropolitan area, as shown in Figure 1.8. It becomes evident that the outlying areas that were abandoned in the centripetal movement to the central city in the early part of the century began to attract residents. This occurred first in the areas immediately adjacent to the city, and in more recent years the rate of growth has been highest in the outer ring of the metropolitan area. While the centrifugal drift had started as early as the 1910-20 decade, in that the contiguous townships showed increases of 145 and 106 percent, in the two decades ending in 1930, the largest increases in numbers were still added to the central city. Little growth had occurred in the outer ring of the metropolitan area. But between 1930 and 1950 the town-

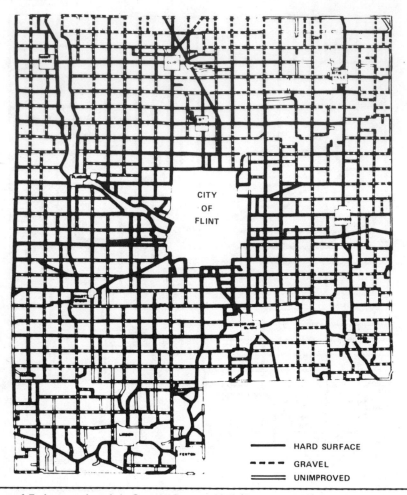

HARD SURFACE
GRAVEL
UNIMPROVED

Figure 1.7: Improved roads in Genesee County, 1958 (Zimmer, 1958).

ships contiguous to the central city experienced the largest absolute growth in numbers.

Thus, while the central city contained three-fourths of the metropolitan population in 1930, by 1950 this had declined to three-fifths. The population of contiguous townships during this same period increased from 11 percent to 21 percent of the metropolitan total. This area is a zone that is approximately five to ten miles from the center of the city. The outer ring remained largely unchanged (Zimmer, 1958). However, since 1950, the centrifugal drift continued to spread further from the central city. During the 1950 and 1960 decades, the largest rates of increase as well as the largest size of increase were beyond ten miles from the center in the outer ring of the metropolitan area. The development of a road system and the increase in automobile ownership had made the more widespread settlement pattern possible. Thus, in the past decade the central city actually experienced a decline in population, while the

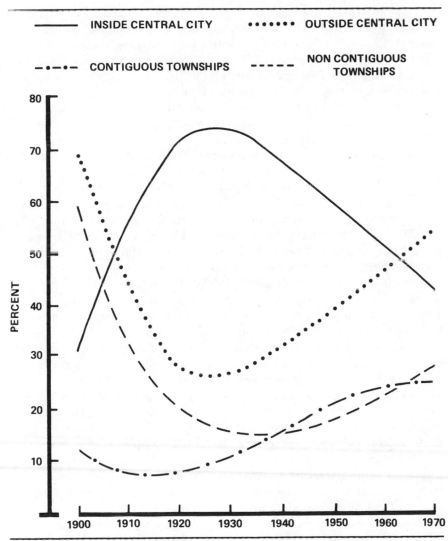

Figure 1.8: Changing distribution of population within the Flint metropolitan area, 1900-70
(Zimmer, 1958; updated by U.S. Bureau of the Census, 1961, 1971a).

outer ring showed the largest increases. By 1970 the population of the central city had declined to 43.5 percent of the metropolitan total.[23]

Another way of viewing the centrifugal drift is to examine changes in population in the central city by mile zones out from the center. In 1909, the population of the city of Flint was 25,034.[24] Of this number, all but 31 persons, 0.1 percent, lived within two miles of the center of the city, and nearly 85 percent lived within the first mile zone. By 1950 the population had increased to 163,143. Only 18 percent lived within one mile, whereas 45 percent lived more than two miles distant from the center. The relative importance of the first zone decreased markedly, declining from 85 percent to less than 20 percent during that period. After 1940 the first mile zone experienced an absolute decline in numbers. Thus, before the centrifugal drift beyond the corporate limits of the central city, there was a period of "filling up" the city. As the population spread out into the ring areas, the central core was the first area to experience a population decline, starting in the 1920 decade (Zimmer, 1958).

The expansion of the population beyond the corporate limits of the central city is evident, in part, in the changing size and shape of the urbanized areas for the period from 1950 to 1970, as shown in Figures 1.2 and 1.3. The expansion of the urbanized area occurred disproportionately along major thoroughfares leading out from the central city. The lack of congruence between the pattern of settlement and municipal boundary lines is partially evident from the development of the urbanized area. During the twenty-year period for which data are available, the urbanized population increased by 67 percent—from 197,000 to 330,000. The central-city population increased by only 18 percent, while the outlying areas increased by 296 percent. As a result of differentials in growth rates, the proportion of the urbanized population living outside of the city increased from 17.5 percent in 1950 to 41.4 percent by 1970.

In terms of land area, the urbanized population occupied 44.8 square miles in 1950, with only one-third of this being outside of the central city. The urbanized land area had more than doubled by 1970, to 96.4 square miles. By this time, two-thirds of the area was beyond the city boundary. During the past twenty years, the city area increased by only 11.9 percent, while the urbanized area outside of the city increased by more than 300 percent. With the rate of expansion of the urbanized area exceeding the growth in population, there has been a general decrease in density of settlement during the period. Thus, starting with a compact population of 13,103 occupying a land area of only six square miles at the turn of the century, the urbanized population has increased to 330,000 and the size of the area of dense settlement has expanded to encompass nearly 100 square miles. As roads were improved to withstand the ravages of changing seasons and as the private automobile became more available, the population moved outward.

In more recent years, the areas of rapid increase are beyond the 1970 urbanized area. The areas of most rapid growth were only five to ten miles from the center until 1950, but since that time the most rapid increases have been in the outer ring of the metropolitan area, which is from 10 to 25 miles from the center of the central city.[25]

A study of one of the outlying villages (Linden) in the metropolitan area illustrates the impact of efficient highway transportation on the enlargement of local community life (Pratt, 1957). Linden is less than twenty miles from the central city, but at the turn of the century it required a full day to travel to Flint by railroad, since contact was not direct. Freight shipments from Flint seldom consumed less than two days. But with the coming of improved roads, the village was brought within less than one hour's travel of Flint. As a result, the village underwent a profound reorientation. It declined as a trade center, and the workers in the village became absorbed into the Flint labor force. Whereas it was impossible to live in the village and work in Flint in 1900, by 1930, 14 percent of those gainfully employed worked in Flint, and twenty years later the proportion had increased to 46 percent. Linden became drawn into, and was made a part of, an enlarged community with the metropolitan area central city as its service and administrative center. It had become a suburban area (Hawley and Zimmer, 1961: 150-151).

When the Flint metropolitan population growth trends were compared with other comparable areas for the same time period, it was found that the Flint experience was but an extreme manifestation of what had been a general tendency. Central cities at first grew rapidly and then more and more slowly. Rates of growth in the outside areas, relative to those of the central cities, have increased rapidly from decade to decade (Hawley and Zimmer, 1961: 152). While this discussion has focused only on population changes, other significant changes, largely in response to the same forces, were also happening at the same time. For example, after an initial high growth rate in the central city, industry gradually experienced a redistribution similar to that which we have observed for population, and the central business district declined in importance in recent years as the major retail center. In short, the centrifugal drift affected all aspects of community life.

EXPANSION OF TELEPHONE SERVICE

One index of the expanding scale of local community life is to be observed in the expansion of the telephone network and the territorial changes in the area within which telephone communication is possible without paying a toll charge. This is the area in which there are no obstacles to communications—everyone in the area is as accessible as one's telephone.

That such areas of "free" communication have expanded rapidly in the last 40 years is demonstrated by the data for a single metropolitan area—Providence, Rhode Island—as shown in Figure 1.9. In 1935, non-toll calls to the center were limited to the City of Providence and parts of the contiguous towns. At that time, non-toll calls were limited to an area of less than ten miles from the center of the central city. The area of local service covered an area roughly twelve miles by twenty miles, or 240 square miles. This area remained unchanged for the next fifteen years. In 1950, the area of local service expanded greatly, up to at least 25 miles from the center. The area had expanded to approximately 800 square miles, which was more than a threefold increase. Thus, for a zone approximately twenty to twenty-five miles from the center, there were increased communication possibilities without additional costs. Ten years later, in 1960, the area was expanded again to include areas slightly more than thirty miles from the central city, which added more than 200 square miles to the local service area. Since that time, the area of equal access has remained unchanged.[26]

As the area of free access in communications increased, the number of persons who could be contacted increased markedly. These data are shown in

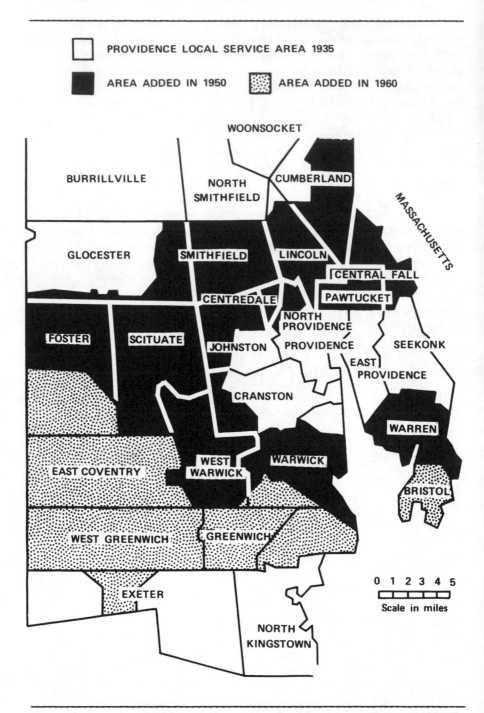

Figure 1.9: Expansion of toll-free telephone service, Providence metropolitan area, 1935-70 (data from the New England Telephone and Telegraph Co., Providence, R.I.).

Table 1.11: Number of Telephones in Each Exchange and Number of Telephones in Local Service Area, 1951-70

Telephone Exchange	Number of Telephones			Number of Telephones Within Contact[a]		
	1951	1960	1970	1951	1960	1970
Bristol	3,453	5,149	8,633	8,998	178,671	244,847
Centredale	3,846	7,284	14,502	167,331	224,279	310,973
Coventry	763	1,467	2,590	763	186,362	267,911
Greenwich	3,025	6,142	14,430	13,808	198,402	304,437
Warwick (Hillsgrove)	3,738	15,569	29,936	139,927	151,858	289,150
Pawtucket	35,995	50,214	69,575	165,960	221,653	338,350
Providence	126,119	164,155	221,709	183,659	273,945	405,062
Scituate	1,371	2,626	5,187	138,381	186,037	273,755
West Warwick	7,045	11,972	23,075	141,298	202,031	297,847
Warren	5,545	9,367	14,505	135,117	178,671	244,847

NOTE: Data from New England Telephone and Telegraph Co., Providence, R.I.
a. Non-toll.

Table 1.11, for the years 1951 to 1970. Ten separate exchanges had become part of the central city exchange by 1970. While there was a substantial increase in the number of telephones in each area, the significant change was the very marked increase in the number of phones that could be contacted toll-free from any one area. The most rapid increase in the number of telephones that could be contacted occurred in the central area. Thus, in Providence, the number of phones that could be contacted toll-free increased from only 73,000 in 1940 to over 400,000 by 1970, due in part to the increase in number of phones in the area, but more particularly to the expansion of the area of free access.

While central-area residential and commercial phones have access to all of the phones in the enlarged area, and all areas have access to the central area, the outlying areas do not have access to the total area. Bristol, for example, which had an increase of 236,000 phones in its non-toll area from 1951 to 1971, still has only about 60 percent of the number of contacts available to and from the central area. This, of course, clearly demonstrates the dominant position of the central city in the metropolitan area.

Clearly, the opportunities for telephone contacts over an expanded area, out from the center, have increased substantially during recent years. This is but another dimension of the increased scale of local community life. Prior to 1950, the areas of non-toll calls were limited largely to the compact city, but twenty years later the area has expanded to include almost all of the metropolitan area. The area of free access had spread from a radius of less than ten miles to thirty miles or more.

CHANGES IN JOB OPPORTUNITIES

Even prior to the beginning of World War II, the exodus of manufacturing industry from our central cities, based largely on highway accessibility, assumed

major proportions. For example, between 1939 and 1947, the number of production workers in manufacturing industries rose by about 50 percent in the ring
areas and by less than 25 percent in the central cities (Grebler, 1956).

In a recent analysis of metropolitan areas of more than one million, it was
found, for the period 1947-1958, that fourteen of the twenty-two core areas
actually lost manufacturing employment (Kenyon, 1967: 106-109). When all
metropolitan areas included in the study were combined, the overall loss in
manufacturing employment in the core areas was 6.8 percent, as compared with
a 40 percent increase in the metropolitan peripheries.

While employment figures clearly demonstrate that there is a changing distribution of manufacturing within metropolitan areas, even larger differences are
found if one focuses on "value added by manufacture." The reason for this
difference is that it is the industries that are undergoing rapid modernization
that tend to locate in the outside areas, and increased modernization results in
greater output per worker. Value added increased by 150 percent in the ring
areas, as compared with little more than 100 percent in the central cities in
the 1939 through 1947 period (Grebler, 1956). More recently, the per-capita
investment in 1958 in plant and equipment was twice as high in the peripheries
as in the core areas.

In an analysis of the thirty-nine largest metropolitan areas (with New York
City excluded), Niedercorn and Kain (1963) also showed a very rapid suburbanization of employment for the 1948-58 period. Their data further support the
marked suburbanization of manufacturing which has already been noted, but
they also showed that other types of employment were suburbanizing at an even
more rapid rate. Both wholesaling and retailing increased in the suburbs more
than seven times the rate of increase in the city. This is double the city-suburban
ratio observed for manufacturing. While services also increased more rapidly in
the suburbs, the rate of increase, relative to the growth in the central city, was
less than that for any other type of employment.

Quite a different picture emerged, however, when the authors corrected for
annexation. Instead of manufacturing increasing approximately 3 percent per
year in the central cities, it actually declined and the rate of increase in the ring
was 15 percent, rather than 10 percent. The rates of increase for wholesaling,
retailing, and service employment in the ring were also substantially higher. In
the case of wholesaling and retailing, the increase reported for the city was due
almost entirely to annexation, as was nearly half of the central-city increase in
service employment during the ten-year period.[27] But even including
boundary changes, the rate of increase in employment of all types was much
higher in the suburbs than in the central cities. Thus, employment opportunities
during this period were becoming more widespread throughout the metropolitan
area.[28]

Suburban growth has been largely a result of spillover from the central city,
as both residents and employers have sought space for expansion. Industrial
and population growth have occurred in response to the changes that have
already taken place in the outside areas. In short, changes in population and in
employment feed on one another, and each contributes to the attractiveness of

the area for the other. This complementary relationship is not as readily available for all segments of the population, however. For example, in New York, manufacturing industries have been moving to the suburbs, but housing and transportation have not been adequate in such areas to allow low-income and minority workers to move in close proximity to the expanding job opportunities (Hamovitch and Levinson, 1969: 459 ff.).

Dorothy Newman (1967: 7) has noted that, while there is high unemployment, particularly among minority groups living in central cities, many jobs in the metropolitan area are vacant. One of the main reasons why jobs and workers are not matched is that new jobs in the suburbs are not "available" to unemployed city workers who lack access to them.[29] The new jobs are too distant from their place of residence and too difficult to reach.[30] On the other hand, the types of jobs remaining in the city tend to demand qualifications that are not met by low-income workers.

One of the major problems associated with this widespread distribution of jobs is that it has been more difficult for the poor and minorities to obtain employment. They are likely to occupy the older residential areas in or near the center of the city abandoned by previous generations of workers who had lived and worked in the same area. These areas are now far removed from the expanding job opportunities in the suburbs. Not only are suburban jobs (if available) inaccessible because of distance and lack of transportation, but the traditional channels of labor market information about job openings have become less effective (Weber, 1964: 73). Ordinarily, marginal workers (i.e., those least knowledgeable about job opportunities and most in need of work) tend to rely largely on friends or neighbors for information concerning "who is hiring" or to make direct application for jobs at the plant gate. However, these opportunities are denied them when jobs are widely dispersed throughout the metropolitan area, and are largely unknown to their usual informants in the older core residential areas.

Thus, not only are the poor and minorities lacking in information about job openings in suburban areas, but they are also likely not even to know where to go or how to get to plants that might want workers.[31] The problem is complicated further by the higher skill requirements of the new expanded industrial plants in the suburbs. More than likely, due to mechanization, the openings for the unskilled and poorly trained are very limited. Consequently, the poor and minority-group members are left in the central city with contracting opportunities, while jobs that they would have held at one point in time are either moving away from their place of residence or are being eliminated in the modernized plants being built in the suburban zone. One of the consequences is a high disproportionate number of unemployed in the areas that are effectively isolated from the mainstream of American life (Weber, 1964: 74).

The large number of potential industrial workers in the core of the central city have no means of access to these distant locations in the periphery. Thus, even if those living in the abandoned portions of the central city succeed in finding employment in the suburbs, they face a major problem connected with the daily journey to work. The consequences of this pattern of reverse commuting were indicated by a Chicago study that reported that Negro workers, on the average, traveled twice as far to work as their white counterparts (National Committee Against Discrimination in Housing, 1968).[32] It has also been reported that central-city residents using public transportation spend both more time and more money to reach suburban jobs than those commuting to the city (Meyer, Kain, and Wohl, 1965).

If Negroes attempt to reduce their travel time, however, by moving closer to their work in the suburbs, it becomes evident that there is a general lack of low-income housing available in the suburbs and a more specific lack because of discrimination. In a very real sense, the wide-spread pattern of distribution of jobs has worked to the disadvantage of those who are least able to compete in the labor market. The lack of adequate housing and free access to housing in the right location probably accounts for as much unemployment as the lack of jobs in the metropolitan area. As new industry is attracted to an area, or as those already in the area expand, the added jobs contribute little if anything to the opportunities available for the minority groups in the city, since such jobs are scattered throughout the metropolitan area. In effect, such jobs do not exist for the slum dweller who does not have access to an efficient transportation system.

Minority group members and other urban poor are largely denied access to the private automobile, which is the mode of travel that was used as early as 1960 by nine out of every ten male workers who lived in the city and commuted to the suburbs in the daily journey to work. Most Negro families living in central cities do not own an automobile. In Chicago, for example, four out of five Negroes do not have cars.

One of the major problems posed by the suburbanization of manufacturing is that of transportation. Since such locations tend to be widespread in distribution, there is no single concentration that would permit efficient use of public transportation.[33] In actual fact, both jobs and residences of workers tend to be diffused throughout the metropolitan area, making automobile travel the only mode available, since the journey to work generates a large number of different travel paths. That this is so is evident from the predominant mode of travel in the largest metropolitan areas, as reported by the 1960 census.

In an analysis of these data, it was found that workers in the core cities of the twenty-two largest metropolitan areas were four times as likely (37.3 percent vs. 10.5 percent) to use public transportation as mode of travel to work as those who lived in the outside areas. On the other hand, nearly eight out of ten in the outside areas traveled to and from work by car, as compared with less than half the central-city workers (Kenyon, 1967). When all metropolitan areas combined are examined, we continue to find the same pattern, but the size of the central city-ring difference is less marked. Apparently, in the smaller metropolitan areas the proportion of central city workers driving to work increases, while there is a slight decline in the suburban areas.

The automobile as a mode of travel to work varies by distance to work as well as by sex. In the following discussion distance is operationalized in terms

Table 1.12: Percent of Workers Traveling to Work by Automobile, by Place of Residence and Place of Work, by Sex, 1960

	Place of Work	
Place of Residence	Central City	Outside CC
Males		
Central city	62.8	88.3
Outside central city	83.8	77.2
Females		
Central city	39.0	71.5
Outside central city	70.7	65.0

NOTE: Data from U.S. Bureau of the Census, 1964, Table 216.

of whether or not a worker crosses the city boundary line in moving from residence to work. It is assumed here that, if a person lives and works in a different zone, he travels a greater distance to work than if he lives and works in the same city or ring zone. According to the data presented in Table 1.12, males are much more likely to travel to work by automobile than female workers. The highest use rate (88.3 percent) is found among males who live in the city but work in the outside area. The next highest rate is found among suburban males who work in the central city. The lowest use rate (39.0 percent) is for females who live and work within the central city. However, the rate nearly doubles if they work outside the city.

In an analysis of central city-suburban employment for eight cities (which are also counties) in different size classes and in various regions of the country, the rapid increase in jobs in the suburbs that occurred from 1959-65 was found to have continued in all but one of the areas during the period 1965-67. In commenting on these data before a congressional committee, Garn (1971: 98) noted that, even with these changes, the ratio of jobs to labor force is still much higher in the central cities than in the suburbs and that the job/population ratio increased during the 1959-67 period in the central cities studied. Thus, there is still sufficient centralization of jobs in the central cities to which suburban workers must commute.

This is not, however, inconsistent with our observations elsewhere that the suburbanization of jobs creates a shortage of job opportunities for the minority groups and other poor who continue to live in the city. The job/labor force ratio is misleading in this context, since it does not take into account the type of jobs available in the city and the qualifications of the work force residing in the city. Thus, while the ratio of jobs to labor force is favorable in the city, the types of jobs available are not types that can be performed by those low in education and lacking in occupational skills, and in many instances these jobs may not be available to minority group members. Equally important to note is that the low ratio of jobs to work force in the suburbs does not mean that suburban residents are in a highly competitive job market, for the types of jobs that are increasing most rapidly in the suburbs are not the types that would be held by the kind of people who have moved to the suburbs.

Consequently, within the metropolitan community a residential-employment pattern is developing that will further increase the distance between home and work. Jobs best suited for the type of labor force that is "locked" in the city are moving to the suburbs, while the labor force best suited for the types of jobs that are disproportionately concentrated in the city is moving to the suburban areas. Limited support for this is found in an analysis of recent job trends in eleven large cities, shown in Table 1.13. While total employment increased, there were marked differences in the rate of change of different industry groups. Manufacturing, wholesale, and retail employment declined over the period, with manufacturing showing the largest decrease. In 1950, 28 percent of the jobs were in manufacturing, but this had declined to around 22 percent in 1967. On the other hand, employment in selected services and in government, transportation, finance, and utilities increased markedly. The largest increase was in the services. During the 1950-67 period, the eleven cities lost almost 600,000 jobs in manufacturing and trade, but at the same time gained more than a million government, business, and personal-service activity jobs.

While the data at hand are limited, the author concludes that "a qualitative upgrading of the economy of the cities has been taking place" (Ganz, 1971: 125). This is based on the 5.3 percent increase in employment over the period 1963-67, and the fact that the loss of manufacturing jobs has been more than offset by a rise in government, business, and personal-service jobs. While it is risky to project a long-term trend on such a short experience period, this position does find support from other sources. Vernon (1957: 25), for example, reported that, while manufacturing jobs in New York City declined by 42,000 between 1947 and 1955, jobs in finance, insurance, and real estate as well as jobs in corporate offices increased by 28,000. Hawley (1971: 169) has observed that "while producing activities were moving in one direction (suburban) administrative and related functions have moved in an opposite direction."

Hawley (1971: 166) has noted that the centrifugal movement of industry has been long-range, starting as early as the mid-nineteenth century. After 1899, industrial locations were scattering from the central cities to the suburbs with increasing frequency, interrupted only by depression and war-time materials

Table 1.13: Changes in Employment by Type and in Distribution of Employment by Type in 11 Large Cities, 1950-67

Type of Employment	Ratio of Jobs 1967/1950	Percent Distribution	
		1950	1967
Total	1.060	100.0	100.0
Manufacturing	.838	27.7	21.6
Wholesale trade	.920	8.4	7.3
Retail trade	.876	16.1	13.3
Selected services	1.431	7.5	10.1
Government, et al.[a]	1.254	40.3	47.6

NOTE: Data from Ganz, 1971, p. 126.
a. Includes construction, transportation, utilities, finance, and other.

shortages. Wage jobs in manufacturing located in central cities declined from 63 percent of the metropolitan total, in 1940, to 51 percent in 1960.

Hawley (1971: 167) has suggested that the changes in space requirements of manufacturing have been instrumental in this decentralization:

> The outward movement has attracted the large plants primarily, particularly those requiring specially designed buildings. A continuous, assembly-line mode of production is more satisfactory if laid on a single horizontal level. Hence the single-story building has replaced the multi-storied building. But the single-story building uses much more ground space and involves much greater cost for land. The assembling of land in sufficient quantity for a large sprawling building in a densely occupied area has proved to be too costly and time consuming to be worth the effort. Furthermore, space for parking workers' automobiles, in amounts rivaling that occupied by buildings, has become mandatory. These enlarged space requirements can be easily and rather inexpensively obtained in the suburban belt.

In the modern context, the most efficient physical plant layout is a single-story structure often spread out over a relatively large area. Thus, a suburban location becomes attractive because, as noted, land is much cheaper than in the central cities. Also, land is more readily available.

A RAND report (Niedercorn and Hearle, 1963) showed that the supply of vacant land has fallen sharply in central cities in recent years, and that few large vacant parcels now remain. For example, the fraction of land in Washington, D.C., that was vacant dropped from 22 percent in 1928 to 4 percent in 1955. In Detroit, 22 percent of the land was vacant in 1943, but only 8 percent in 1954. Land in the newer and larger city of Los Angeles was 64 percent vacant in 1940, but had declined to 31 percent vacant by 1960.

In regard to the cost of land, the (U.S.) President's Committee on Urban Housing (1968: 141) noted that:

> Within any given metropolitan area, the cost of land tends to rise as one moves toward the center of the city. Land costs in downtown areas, even in slum areas, are extremely high compared to suburban land. . . . However, the steepness with which land prices drop off as one travels away from the city center is less pronounced than it used to be. In other words, the curve which plots land prices against distance from the central city, is flattening out.

Nonetheless, the large uses both for production and space for parking find the suburban areas attractive sites.

Hawley (1971: 168) elaborated on two other factors that have been important in the centrifugal drift of industry within metropolitan areas: significant improvement in transportation and communication facilities, and the presence of urban services in outlying areas. The motor vehicle and the extensive network of paved roads have made it possible for a plant to draw its working force from a radius of 25 miles or more. Also, the increased reliance on the motor truck for short-haul freight transfers has made a peripheral location far more convenient than a central location. In effect, metropolitan streets and roads have become extensions of assembly lines. The more recent extension of urban services to small towns and unincorporated territory has also been important in the deconcentration of industry.

One other factor is important in the movement of places of employment to the suburbs, but to date it has not received much research attention. While it is generally recognized that the suburbanization of population and jobs tend to be closely related, the evidence at hand showing a direct link between the two is, at best, limited. There is, however, some evidence that suggests that the movement of business owners to the suburbs may precede the movement of the place of business away from the central city (Zimmer, 1964). These findings must be viewed with caution, however, since the study is not based on a representative sample of business owners, but rather is limited to the type of business that was displaced during a five-year period because of either urban renewal or highway construction programs.[34] Nonetheless, the observations are such that they would appear to merit attention.

It is of interest to note first that the differences in personal characteristics of the business owners by place of residence within the metropolitan area followed the same general pattern frequently observed for central city-suburban populations. Also, the proportion of owners that lived in the suburbs increased consistently by size of business measured by number of employees. A large majority (71 percent) of the owners of the larger business establishments lived in the suburbs.

When these businesses relocated following displacement, the place of residence of the owner became a significant variable in the selection of a new location in the suburbs. For a distinct majority of those moving to the suburbs, the move decreased the distance between place of business and place of residence. Relocation in the city had this effect in only one-fifth of the moves. These data, while limited in scope, suggest that the suburbanization of population may well portend changes in the metropolitan area that are far more significant than the changing distribution of residences. It may be that central-city businessmen first change their residences to the suburbs and later move their businesses out of the city also.[35]

In general, the proportion of units moving to the suburbs varied directly by size of business. The median-sized business that relocated in the city employed 3.8 workers at the time of displacement, while those moving to the suburbs averaged 7.2 workers. This, of course, means that the suburbanization of "jobs" far exceeded the suburbanization of establishments.

In a further analysis of these data, it was found that suburban residents were five times as likely as central-city residents to move their business to the suburbs. Less than 5 percent of those living in the city selected a site in the suburbs, but, of those living in the latter area, 27 percent moved outside of the central city. It was also noted that, of the businesses that relocated in the city, only 47 percent of the owners lived in the suburbs, but, of those that moved out of the city, 87 percent lived in the outside area. It is of interest that those who moved to the suburbs were much more likely to move into a newly constructed building specifically designed for their use and with ample parking facilities. Also, those moving to the suburbs occupied larger buildings; the median size of structure in the city was 2,500 square feet as compared to 4,500 in the suburbs. Land area differences between the central city and suburbs were even more marked.

The conclusions reached in the Zimmer (1964: 332-333) study may well serve as an appropriate summary of the changes observed in respect to the more widespread pattern of jobs in metropolitan areas:

> It may be that we have observed the early stages of a new rationale for an even more widespread settlement pattern in urban centres than has developed to date. Owners of businesses apparently now have a greater amount of free-dom and wider range of choice in the selection of a site. . . . The problem of space in the traditional sense seems to have lost much of its meaning in the local community setting. Because of the higher incomes and higher levels of living in general, workers and customers alike appear to be willing and able to overcome the costs of distance. Thus, in the modern context . . . nearly any location is readily accessible. Employers seem to be no longer dependent on workers living in close proximity. Also businesses can more effectively attract customers from greater distances. Consequently business owners in relocation have been able to select sites largely in relation to their own place of residence. . . . Many businesses seem no longer to be as dependent upon a specific location. This suggests that the time-cost variable may have lost much of its original significance as a limiting factor influencing either residential locations, places of employment, or the sites for many commercial establish-ments.

More recently, Hawley (1972: 519) has observed that the reduction of density associated with the centrifugal movement of urban population has important implications for the metropolitan area:

> It marks a general subsiding of the importance of proximity. Whereas it was once necessary that closely related activities be located within hailing dis-tances of one another, that is no longer the case. The distances that can separate interdependent units at no loss of access continue to increase. The other side of the coin is that units are no longer under any compulsion to accept what is close at hand, whether that be services from nearby insti-tutions or associations with neighbors. One can choose his services and his personal associations from a progressively widening area.[36]

CENTRAL BUSINESS DISTRICT

The central business district (CBD) has experienced marked changes with the expansion of local community life. Once the center of all major activities in the city and even the hinterland, the central business district has continued to decline in importance, particularly as a retail center, as mass public transporta-tion has been replaced by the private automobile as the principal mode of travel. Once the hub of the local transportation system and the point of maximum accessibility in the community, it has lost this advantage as the community has expanded in size, with a road system not oriented to the center. In a distinct break with the past, deliberate efforts have been made in recent years to move traffic away from the center. These changes have weakened the dominance of the CBD as a shopping center.

By the end of the 1930s, CBDs were already experiencing serious competition from outlying shopping centers (Isard and Whitney, 1949). The latter were at that time contributing to the decline of the center in shopping-goods sales, and were moving ahead in selected sales such as automobiles, furniture, and hardware. From 1940 until 1960, approximately 2,500 shopping centers were constructed, and in more recent years, not only the number but the size of such centers have increased. With the automobile widely available, particularly for that segment of the population which had moved away from the city, it is not surprising that an increased proportion of shopping would be done in accessible outlying areas with ample parking space. While the decline of the CBD has been well documented, it is still of interest to examine the changes that have taken place in recent years.[37]

The following analysis is limited to metropolitan areas of 250,000 and over for which data on CBDs are available for both 1954 and 1967. The 1950 population was used to establish size classes. We are looking for the changes that have taken place in retail sales in metropolitan areas of a given size class during this period, with attention focused on selected types of activity. No attempt has been made to correct for changes in definition. (For example, in 1954 leased departments were separately classified as stores whereas starting in 1958 figures for leased departments are incorporated with the main store. While this does not affect changes in sales, it does affect the number of establishments, but certainly not to an extent that would change any of the observed patterns.) That marked changes are taking place in the distribution of retail establishments and sales in metropolitan areas is evident from the data presented in Table 1.14.

During the 1954-67 period, there was a substantial decline in the number of retail establishments in the central city. (The changes observed will actually understate the deconcentration of retail activity to the area outside the central city since no correction has been made for annexations, which have been sizable in some areas and size classes. While such corrections would increase the magnitude of the change, it would not affect the pattern of change.) The decline increases inversely by size of metropolitan area. Thus, it would appear that it is in the smaller metropolitan areas that the CBD has been most affected by the new widespread settlement pattern. However, we must view these changes with caution since they represent only what is happening at a given point in time. Clearly during the period under study the smaller areas were more affected than the larger areas, but one reason for this is that the larger areas had, during an earlier period, already experienced declines in the CBD. This is reflected in the proportion of metropolitan area sales in the CBD in 1948 by size of area, which was only 17 percent in the largest metropolitan areas but 40 percent in the 250,000 to 500,000 size class (Casparis, 1967: 213). For the same time period

Table 1.14: Percent Change in Establishments and Sales in Selected Areas of Metropolitan Areas by Type of Sales and Size of Metropolitan Area, 1954-67

Size of Area	CBD		City		Outside City		SMSA	
	Est.	Sales	Est.	Sales	Est.	Sales	Est.	Sales
Total Sales								
Total	−32.4	2.6	18.7	44.0	37.7	167.2	3.3	89.7
3,000,000 +	−26.0	12.1	−26.3	34.3	29.9	132.2	−7.4	70.4
1,000,000 to								
3,000,000	−26.9	8.3	−23.7	26.8	30.3	175.0	3.6	97.6
500,000 to								
1,000,000	−38.2	−3.7	−8.4	58.4	51.3	209.0	14.1	104.0
250,000 to								
500,000	−37.6	−6.7	−8.6	61.4	48.0	193.1	13.4	104.2
General Merchandise								
Total	−22.1	5.5	−21.0	76.4	40.0	470.6	2.0	165.6
3,000,000 +	−16.7	12.9	−32.5	68.1	16.2	395.0	−16.9	158.2
1,000,000 to								
3,000,000	−11.7	8.2	−25.0	29.1	36.9	467.0	9.6	153.5
500,000 to								
1,000,000	−28.3	−1.5	−8.0	95.3	47.8	707.8	17.0	177.2
250,000 to								
500,000	−26.1	2.0	−2.8	118.6	41.4	486.6	17.1	181.0
Apparel								
Total	−39.8	−7.6	−24.5	18.5	23.1	133.6	−8.5	49.1
3,000,000 +	−32.2	−1.4	−23.7	14.5	7.3	105.6	−14.7	37.5
1,000,000 to								
3,000,000	−34.8	4.5	−34.0	12.8	25.8	148.2	−6.3	64.8
500,000 to								
1,000,000	−46.6	−15.3	−19.8	30.6	35.0	138.5	−1.2	55.3
250,000 to								
500,000	−45.2	−17.8	−23.0	21.4	45.6	192.0	−0.8	56.8
Furniture								
Total	−39.8	−10.6	−18.7	19.3	38.6	165.9	3.5	65.2
3,000,000 +	−45.1	−11.1	−25.2	−5.7	12.9	146.5	−11.2	43.0
1,000,000 to								
3,000,000	−32.8	−3.4	−27.5	11.6	44.3	169.1	8.7	77.3
500,000 to								
1,000,000	−42.0	−8.8	−8.3	48.5	72.3	183.1	19.9	84.0
250,000 to								
500,000	−36.7	16.6	−9.3	45.9	51.7	198.8	12.3	81.4

NOTE: Data from U.S. Bureau of the Census, 1958, 1970.

it was found that CBDs in the largest metropolitan areas experienced a decline in sales, while sales in the smaller metropolitan areas increased (Dessel, 1957).

At any rate, the number of establishments in CBDs during the 1950-67 period declined slightly more than one-fourth in the largest areas and nearly two-fifths in the smaller metropolitan areas. While sales remained largely unchanged, the smaller areas experienced a decline. For each type of sales included, the same general pattern is observed, but it is the numbers of "apparel" and "furniture" establishments that have shown the largest changes. Here, too, the declines have been most marked in the smaller metropolitan areas.

Not only the CBDs, but also the central cities, have been affected by the widespread settlement pattern. The pattern of change in the central cities, however, is the opposite of that observed for CBDs. The rate of decrease of establishments varies directly by size of metropolitan area, ranging from a low of only 8 percent to a high of 26 percent. In all size classes, sales increased, but the increases were much larger in the small than in the larger metropolitan areas. Again, the same general pattern is observed for each type of sales, but general merchandise showed the least loss in number of establishments and the largest increase in sales. These data suggest that, once a metropolitan population reaches a certain size, the CBD is affected first, but later the central city also decreases in importance as a retail center. After a certain amount of decline, the rate of decrease becomes smaller. Conversely, after a certain amount of growth has taken place in the suburbs, the rate of increase there becomes less, even though there is a continued suburbanization of activities. Again, the data in Table 1.14 show that the rate of increase in the suburban area for both establishments and sales varies inversely by size of area.

The differential rates of change for selected areas within the metropolitan area have resulted in a marked change in the distribution of retail establishments and sales in the metropolitan area. In all size classes, there has been a decline in

Table 1.15: Percent of Metropolitan Area Establishments and Sales in Central Business District, 1954-67

Year of Business Census	Total Establishments	Sales	General Merchandise Establishments	Sales	Apparel Establishments	Sales	Furniture Establishments	Sales
1954	14.5	27.4	13.7	68.7	33.9	56.0	17.5	32.6
1967	12.0	19.5	13.5	50.3	27.1	43.7	12.9	24.4
Difference	−2.5	−7.9	−0.2	−18.4	−6.8	−12.3	−4.6	−8.2
3,000,000 and Over								
1954	10.2	20.8	7.5	56.7	21.4	41.6	11.7	21.2
1967	10.2	17.3	9.3	38.1	19.0	35.8	8.6	20.0
Difference	——	−3.5	+1.8	−18.6	−2.4	−15.8	−3.1	−1.2
1,000,000 to 3,000,000								
1954	14.8	30.2	13.4	72.1	34.3	60.3	16.9	36.3
1967	14.2	25.8	15.8	60.5	33.8	55.8	15.7	31.4
Difference	−0.6	−4.4	+2.4	−11.6	−0.5	−4.5	−1.2	−4.9
500,000 to 1,000,000								
1954	17.4	31.4	17.7	72.4	48.0	70.7	21.5	39.6
1967	11.8	19.1	13.8	36.6	32.0	45.8	13.6	24.3
Difference	−5.6	−12.3	−3.9	−35.8	−16.0	−24.9	−7.9	−15.3
250,000 to 500,000								
1954	20.3	33.2	24.8	79.7	56.3	74.5	25.4	44.9
1967	13.9	19.2	18.8	37.2	40.1	50.5	17.7	25.7
Difference	−6.4	−14.0	−6.0	−42.5	−16.2	−24.0	−7.7	−19.2

NOTE: Calculated from Table 1.14.

the proportion of establishments and sales in the CBD during recent years. In each size class, the proportion of sales declined more than the proportion of establishments (see Table 1.15). It is worthy of note that the CBD held the dominant position in 1954 in general merchandise sales, even though only a small proportion of the establishments were in the center. By 1967, the proportion of sales of this type had dropped markedly in all size classes, except in the 1,000,000 to 3,000,000 size class, in which the CBD still accounted for 60 percent of metropolitan sales. In the smaller metropolitan areas, in particular, the drop in general merchandise sales was substantial. Apparel and furniture establishments and sales declined in all metropolitan-area size classes, and the declines were more marked in the small than in the large areas. These data indicate that while there has been more change in the CBD in recent years in the smaller metropolitan areas, the CBDs in such areas continue to play a more dominant retail role in their metropolitan areas than they do in the larger metropolitan areas. It is equally clear in all size classes, however, that the widespread settlement pattern within the metropolitan community has shifted much, if not most, of the retail activity away from the CBD.

While the CBDs have generally declined as retail outlets, the rate of growth in the rings of metropolitan areas has been such that an increased proportion of the establishments and sales has been concentrated in the areas outside the central cities. In 1954, as shown in Table 1.16, approximately two-fifths of the retail activity in metropolitan areas was outside the central city, but by 1967 more than half of the establishments and sales were in the ring of metropolitan areas. The centrifugal drift of retail activity was particularly marked in the 1,000,000 to 3,000,000 size class, but the outward movement occurred in all size classes.

More recent changes are shown in Table 1.17 by type of area. During the 1963-67 period in the 25 largest metropolitan areas, sales increased four times as much (43.0 percent) in major retail centers as in the CBDs (10.5 percent). These data also show that the major retail outlets increased much more rapidly than did sales in the metropolitan areas. When all metropolitan areas were combined, the actual volume of sales in the major retail centers exceeded the CBDs by 200 percent in 1967. While the CBDs reported 9.5 percent of all

Table 1.16: Proportion of Retail Establishments and Sales in Ring of Metropolitan Area by Size of Metropolitan Area, 1954-67

	1954		1967	
Size of Metropolitan Area	Establish-ments	Sales	Establish-ments	Sales
Total	39.0	37.0	52.0	52.2
3,000,000 +	33.7	37.0	47.2	50.3
1,000,000 to 3,000,000	50.5	47.8	63.5	66.5
500,000 to 1,000,000	37.7	30.3	50.0	45.9
250,000 to 500,000	38.9	32.5	50.8	46.6

NOTE: Calculated from Table 1.14.

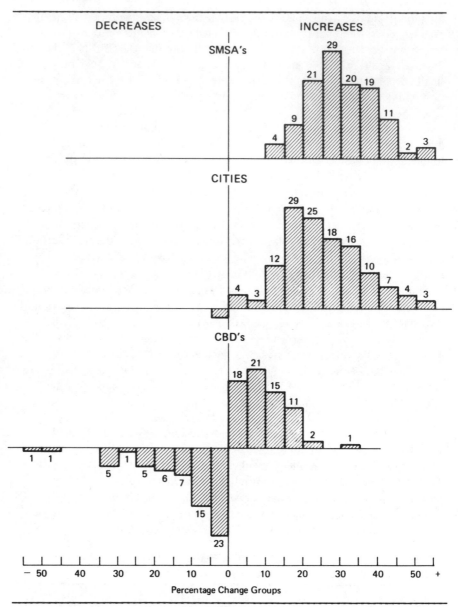

Figure 1.10: Major retail centers summary—retail sales: 1963-67 number of SMSAs, cities, and CBDs by percentage change groups (U.S. Bureau of the Census, 1970). Includes only those areas with a CBD.

metropolitan-area sales, the major retail outlets accounted for 19.1 percent during the same period. Thus, in 1967 a substantial proportion of metropolitan area sales were outside the central city.

What has happened to the distribution of the retail function is dramatically shown in Figure 1.10. In all metropolitan areas, sales increased during the

Table 1.17: Percentage Change in Sales for 25 Largest SMSAs by Type of Area, 1963-67

Type of Area	Percentage Change
Central business district	10.5
Central cities	25.1
Standard metropolitan areas	27.1
Major retail centers[a]	43.0

NOTE: Data from U.S. Bureau of the Census, 1970, pp. 1-3.
a. Those concentrations of retail stores located within the SMSA but outside the CBD, having at least $5 million in retail sales and at least 10 retail establishments, one of which is classified as a department store.

period, and in a large majority of the areas, sales increased between 20 and 40 percent. Sales in the central cities also increased, but considerably less than in the metropolitan area. The most significant change, however, occurred in CBDs. Nearly half actually lost sales during the period, and only three increased by more than 20 percent. Since these figures have not allowed for inflation, the absolute level of sales in the CBD is even less than these data show. Clearly, the CBD is declining in importance as a retail outlet. The evidence is so consistent and convincing that further elaboration is not needed, yet it might be of interest to specifically examine the impact of the widespread distribution on use of the CBD.

In a recent random sample survey in the Providence metropolitan area, it was found that the widespread pattern of settlement had a profound effect on the use of the CBD for shopping (Hilferty, 1972). As in other metropolitan areas, the core of the central city as a market center is diminishing in importance, while outlying shopping centers and other retail outlets are absorbing an increased proportion of the sales volume in the metropolitan area. Part of the decline in Providence is due to the decrease in central-city population. From a peak population of 253,504 in 1940, the city had declined to 179,213 in 1970. Thus, during the last 30 years, the city experienced a 29 percent loss of population. At the same time, the metropolitan ring was increasing in size. As a result, by 1970 the central city contained only 19.7 percent of the metropolitan population and 18.9 percent of the total state population.[38]

It is readily apparent from the data shown in Table 1.18 that the CBD in the central city is not the major retail outlet for the metropolitan area. Shopping centers are almost as frequently reported as the place where residents do most of their shopping, but it is the discount stores that are most frequently used. About as many report that they do most of their shopping in satellite central business districts and strip commercial developments as shop in the major central business district. While there has been a marked deconcentration of retail outlets most frequently used by the residents of the area, it is noted that two-fifths of the sample report that at some time during the past year they did shop in the CBD. But an even larger proportion had at one time or another shopped at one of the discount stores in the area. It should be noted, since this is one of the crucial reasons why the CBD has lost out as the major retail outlet, that the private

Table 1.18: Location of Most Frequent Shopping Places and Total Places Shopped During Past Year: Providence, Rhode Island, 1968

Area	Place Shopped Most	Places Where Shopped Past Year
Number	1,127	1,127
CBD — Providence	24.1	60.3
Shopping centers	20.1	62.3
Discount houses	30.9	72.5
Other[a]	24.7	55.0
Percent	100.0	

NOTE: Data from Hilferty, 1972.
a. Includes CBDs of suburban towns and strip commercial developments and stores not otherwise classified.

Table 1.19: Percentage of Population Using Central Business District by Zone of Residence: Providence, Rhode Island, 1968

Selected Indices of Use of CBD	Zone of Residence[a]				
	CC	1	2	3	4
% reporting most shopping done in CBD	47.3	24.1	19.1	9.2	7.7
% shopping in CBD during year	76.4	66.3	55.9	49.0	34.3
% reporting trips to CBD					
Monthly or more	54.8	33.5	27.1	19.6	11.2
Few times per year	28.3	41.1	38.3	36.6	34.3
Rarely or never	15.1	24.4	34.6	42.5	54.6

NOTE: Data from Hilferty, 1972.
a. Zones are determined by contiguous cities and towns, i.e., Zone 1 is a ring composed of the complete jurisdictions of all cities and towns bordering on Providence City; Zone 2 is a ring composed of the complete jurisdictions of the cities and towns touching on Zone 1, and so forth.

automobile is the mode of travel used in shopping by 80 percent of the respondents in the sample. Fewer than 10 percent travel by bus, and only two-thirds as many walk.

As shown in Table 1.19, distance is a crucial variable influencing use of the CBD of the central city. While only one-fifth of the respondents in the sample reported that their families did most of their shopping in the CBD, the proportion ranges from almost half of those living in the city to less than one-tenth of those living beyond the second zone in the suburbs. The same pattern by distance from the city is found in terms of whether people ever shop in the CBD. Even when we focus on a broader use of the CBD and include frequency of trips for any purpose, we continue to find that the proportion drops sharply beyond the city limits and continues to decline by distance from the center.

The evidence clearly shows that, as the population becomes more widely scattered throughout the metropolitan area, the CBD declines in importance, not

Table 1.20: Percentage of Population Using Downtown During Past Year by
Socioeconomic Status: Providence, Rhode Island, 1968

Socioeconomic Status	Total Number[a]	% Used Downtown
Total	1,127	60.5
Income		
Under $3,500	230	57.4
$3,500 - $5,499	170	53.5
$5,500 - $7,499	241	56.0
$7,500 - $12,249	313	69.6
$12,250 and over	151	73.5
Occupation		
Unskilled	108	54.7
Operatives	182	55.5
Craftsmen	223	56.1
Clerical-sales	107	75.7
Manager-officials	115	71.3
Professionals	135	74.1
Education		
8th Grade or less	291	50.5
Some high school	335	58.2
High school graduate	338	64.2
College	156	75.6

NOTE: Data from Hilferty, 1972.
a. Nonresponses excluded.

only for retailing but for any use.[39] Distance from the center does not affect
all segments of the population equally, however, since there are selective factors
that influence the use of the CBD. As Table 1.20 indicates, use varies directly by
socioeconomic status, and the size of the difference is substantial whether status
is measured in terms of income, occupational status, or level of education. These
findings are consistent with numerous traffic surveys, which show that members
of the upper occupational and income groups visit CBDs most frequently, especially for shopping and the transaction of business. Individuals with lower socioeconomic status are more often confined to the immediate neighborhood.[40]

Looking at this in more detail, in Table 1.21 we find that, within each
distance zone, use of the CBD increases substantially by socioeconomic status.
Least use is made by the lowest status groups in the more distant zones, and
most use is made of the central zone by highest status persons living in the inner
ring. But the significant point here is the variation of ratios by zone within
status levels. The decrease by distance is markedly larger in the lower status
levels. That is, use of the CBD declines from the inner to the outer zone by
about 40 percent at the lower status levels, as compared with only 20 percent
at the higher levels.[41]

As a retail center, the CBD has become less important, but this does not mean
that other functions of the center have been affected equally. On the contrary,
the center continues to perform crucial functions for the metropolitan area. For
example, it shows considerable vitality as a location for central office functions,

Table 1.21: Percentage of Population Using Downtown by Ring Population, and Distance from Central City, and Socioeconomic Status: Providence, Rhode Island, 1968

Socioeconomic Status	Inner Ring[a]	Outer Ring[b]	OR/IR Ratio
Income			
Under $3,500	45.3	27.0	.596
$3,500 - $5,499	51.1	31.4	.614
$5,500 - $7,499	55.6	37.3	.671
$7,500 - $12,249	76.0	51.0	.671
$12,250 and over	81.4	52.3	.643
Occupation			
Unskilled	54.4	33.3	.612
Operatives	55.1	33.3	.604
Craftsmen	63.6	37.3	.586
Clerical-sales	75.0	58.8	.784
Manager-officials	82.6	47.1	.570
Professionals	78.8	63.6	.807
Education			
8th Grade or less	51.0	27.2	.533
Some high school	60.7	40.5	.667
High school graduate	66.7	46.5	.697
College	84.5	67.5	.799

NOTE: Data from Hilferty, 1972.
a. Zones 1 and 2 combined.
b. Zones 3 and 4 combined.

and there are some indications that it may grow even more important in that respect. According to the Committee for Economic Development (1960: 18), business and governmental services, which require face-to-face contact or depend upon female labor, continue to show a strong preference for office space in the core of large metropolitan areas. The committee further indicates that central locations have also retained their hold on manufacturers of unstandardized products and those dependent upon a diversified mix of skills and materials. In addition, Hawley (1971: 172) suggests that, as long as the CBD continues to be a major employment center, it also will continue to be an important shopping center.

SCHOOLS

In the early 1950s, when the suburbanization movement reached major proportions in many metropolitan areas following World War II, a substantial burden was placed on suburban school systems. As the population continued to grow at increasingly rapid rates and as young families with children became more and more concentrated in the suburbs, there were expanding needs for added school facilities and programs. These educational demands were made in many cases on essentially new residential communities, which often lacked an industrial or commercial tax base to help carry the tax burden for new schools. In some suburban communities, particularly those in former rural areas, not only was the tax base lacking, but there was strong and persistent opposition from the older residents who, with no children in school, resented the changes that were taking place in their areas. The "original" local population were not educationally oriented and were not anxious to take on an added tax burden to finance elaborate school buildings (Dobriner, 1963). Yet, with the rapid growth in school-age population, the need for schools increased.

In the mass-produced suburbs, such problems were particularly acute. Levittown was one such case. For example, shortly after the end of the war, in 1947-48, there were 40 students in daily attendance at the one local school. By 1960, the number of school buildings had increased from 1 to 15, the number of teachers from 2 to 678, and the tax rate had jumped from $0.73 to $6.45. Since the community had no industry and little business property, its main tax resource was the homeowner (Dobriner, 1963, p. 113). However, only in rare instances is it possible to support an adequate school system through local resources where the tax base is limited to residential property. [42]

During this period, the taxable resources and the per capita expenditure for education were substantially higher in the central-city areas. In one metropolitan area in the late fifties, for example, the taxable wealth behind each membership in the city was more than double the resources of the suburban areas ($16,658 vs. $7,008). But equally important were the wide disparities in resources among the suburban school systems in this area. The range in per capita taxable wealth in the suburbs was from $42,379 to only $4,408, nearly a tenfold difference. One suburban school district assessed only 8.35 mills and realized more than $350 per membership, whereas a neighboring district assessed 18.35 mills and obtained only $81. Although the state's contribution decreased the differential between the districts, the gap still remained large. In one district, the total per capita expenditures for school operations was $475, while it was only $258 in the other districts (Zimmer and Hawley, 1968: 22). Funds for buildings showed an even larger differential.

This type of differential was found in many metropolitan areas. For example, in St. Louis County, Bollens (1961: 44) reported that in 1956-57, one school district spent $308 per pupil in average daily attendance, another had a comparable expenditure of $337, and still another spent $615 per pupil. [43] Similar differentials were observed in New Jersey in a New York suburb. In 1959-60, Garden City had approximately $48,000 of full-value taxable property for each of its pupils, while Levittown had only $11,000. Consequently, Garden City raised more than $700 per pupil from property taxation, and Levittown raised slightly less than $225 (Dobriner, 1963: 126). In Los Angeles County, the amount per average daily attendance among elementary school districts in 1965-66 ranged from a high of $133,300 in one district to a low of $1,800 in another, predominantly Negro, district (Advisory Commission on Intergovernmental Relations, 1967: 340). Such were the disparities in the period of rapid growth of suburban areas that took place in the first two decades following the war.

This suburban movement was made up disproportionately of the population in the higher socioeconomic status categories who were "child-oriented." Indeed, one study (Seeley, Sims, and Loosley, 1964) concluded that the major institutional focus in suburban areas was on child-rearing. Thus, most of the interest suburban residents showed in community affairs centered around the schools. Critical problems resulted from a rapid increase in the number of school children, a new emphasis on the quality of education provided, and the lack of local resources. Since the suburban areas lacked an industrial or commercial tax base, the expanded school facilities had to be financed almost exclusively by the private homeowner (Dobriner, 1963: 113). While the suburbs grew rapidly, local resources lagged behind population growth.

A 1957 study (Advisory Commission on Intergovernmental Relations, 1967) of the thirty-seven largest metropolitan areas found that central-city schools had a distinct advantage over suburban schools, at least in terms of the funds expended for each pupil in school. City school expenditures exceeded the suburban areas by nine dollars ($312 vs. $303) per pupil. However, this differential was short-lived. Suburban resources which could be put toward education increased substantially, while in central cities, noneducational needs increased as overall resources declined. As a result of this combination of forces, by 1959 the cities were spending $64 less on each child in school than were the suburbs. Two years later, the gap had doubled to $124 in favor of the suburbs. While this was a period of rapid increase in school expenditures, the rate was more marked in the suburbs than in the central cities. From 1957 to 1964, cities increased their per-pupil expenditures from $312 to $449, while the suburban areas increased theirs from $303 to $573.

This initial city advantage was lost for several reasons. While city school systems benefited temporarily from the exodus of middle- and upper-middle-income families, since these were the ones that placed a high value on quality schools, fewer demands were then made on the cities to develop quality programs. While resources remained high, capital improvements in building were largely neglected. This neglect was to have serious implications in the next decade as cities were left with "high cost" citizens at the very time their resources were contracting relative to the suburbs and their schools were becoming obsolescent through aging.

This was particularly important in the older and larger central cities. For example, in a 1965 analysis of fifteen selected large cities, it was reported that 40 percent of the elementary schools were over forty-five years old. In two of the cities, Boston and Cleveland, more than 60 percent of the schools were this old. Only one-fourth of the junior and senior high schools were this old, but the proportion ranged above 40 percent in six of the fifteen cities (U.S. House of Representatives, 1966: 357). At the same time, cities were faced with growing enrollments, largely because of the rapid increase in the young black population with children and because of the decline in parochial schools.

With a need for school expansion as well as replacement of facilities, with a contracting tax base, and with heavy demands for noneducational expenditures, the cities lost their original advantage over the suburbs. By this time, the suburbs had built up an inventory of school facilities and had expanded their nonresidential resources. As a consequence, the city-suburban gap worked to the disadvantage of the central city. The disparities had been reversed over a period of less than two decades. This change was clearly a response to the increasing scale of local community life and the selective processes under way in terms of who could and could not participate in this new widespread settlement pattern. Schools, more than any other single community institution, were profoundly affected by this new and enlarged pattern of settlement.

This more widespread settlement pattern, as already noted, had a marked impact on the composition of the central-city population. The poor, the less well educated, the disadvantaged blacks, and other minority group members have been left behind in the city, and they make up an increasing proportion of the school population. This has important implications for the city schools, since such a population places heavy demands on the resources of the community, which in turn decreases the proportion of funds available for the schools. It has been suggested that the municipal over-burden of cities is supported at the expense of the education function (Campbell and Meranto, 1971). At the same time, there has been a substantial shift of taxable resources away from the central city. In recent years, there has been a movement of industrial and commercial property to the suburbs. The pattern for manufacturing, employment, and retail sales reflects the fact that economic activities are an integral part of this more widespread settlement pattern (Newman, 1967). This movement has had a significant impact on the tax base of the city. As industry continues to move to the suburbs, central cities barely hold their own, or in some cases experience actual declines in taxable property (The Research Council of the Great Cities Program for School Improvement, 1964). Campbell and Meranto (1971: 343) have noted that: "It is now clear that the suburbanization of the country, by draining the higher-income families and much economic activity from the central cities, produced greater problems for education in central cities than it did for the suburbs."

Enrollment changes for the 36 largest metropolitan areas from 1960 to 1970 indicate that the school burden continued to increase in both central city and suburban areas (see Table 1.22). The relative burden, however, is to the disadvantage of the central city, particularly at the elementary level. This has been caused by the sharp decline in non-public-school enrollment (largely parochial), which has led to disproportionate increases in the number of children in public schools as overall population (and resources) has declined. Nearly two-fifths of the increase in public schools in the central cities has been due to the decline in non-public-school enrollment. No doubt much of the remaining increase is due to the rapid increase in the Negro population in these areas, which is made up disproportionately of young families with children in school. At the high school level, public school enrollments increased by four times the rate of non-public schools. While non-public high schools accounted for slightly more than 20 percent of total enrollments in 1960, they accounted for only 6 percent of the

Table 1.22: Percent Change and Percent Distribution of School Enrollments in Central-City and Suburban Areas by Type of School in 36 Largest Metropolitan Areas,[a] 1960-70

Areas	Elementary			High School		
	Total	Public	Non-Public	Total	Public	Non-Public
Percent Change 1960-70						
SMSA	25.1	34.5	−9.2	64.2	70.6	32.8
Central cities	7.9	16.6	−19.2	35.7	42.4	11.2
Suburbs	37.8	47.1	0.0	86.3	90.5	59.1
Percent Distribution						
Central cities						
1960	100.0	75.7	24.3	100.0	78.7	21.3
1970	100.0	81.8	18.2	100.0	82.6	17.4
Suburbs						
1960	100.0	80.3	19.7	100.0	86.5	13.5
1970	100.0	85.7	14.3	100.0	88.4	11.6

NOTE: Data from U.S. Bureau of the Census, 1964, 1972b; compiled by P. Jackson, Department of Sociology, Brown University.
a. New York metropolitan area has been excluded.

increase in enrollments during the decade. Thus, almost all of the increase during the period added to the burden of the central-city public schools.

While the rate of enrollment increases was substantially higher in the suburban areas, the relative burden was probably less marked since these areas were also increasing in taxable resources. But here, too, it is evident that all of the increase in enrollments at the elementary level was in the public schools. In 1960, out of a total of five million elementary enrollments, nearly one-fifth were in non-public schools, but of the increase of almost two million during the decade, only 445 were added to the non-public schools. At the high school level, also, public schools absorbed a major portion of the increase. Thus, in both segments of the metropolitan area, the non-public schools are declining in importance. This is shown in the bottom panel of Table 1.22. In all areas, the proportion of enrollments in public schools has increased during the decade.

Recent data indicate that suburban schools have a distinct advantage over central city schools in terms of funds available, in part because of the changing distribution of industrial and commercial property, but mostly because of the higher noneducational expenditures in the city. For the 36 largest metropolitan areas, central-city noneducational expenditures were $232 per capita in 1964-65, compared to only $132 in suburban areas (Advisory Commission on Intergovernmental Relations, 1967: 72). This differential takes on added significance when it is noted that the outside areas are made up disproportionately of high-income residents. This means that the per capita tax burden in relation to income is much higher in the city than in the suburbs.

Even though the total tax burden is substantially higher in the city, the per-pupil expenditure for education is lower. While the disparity in favor of the suburbs is of recent origin, the gap is increasing. As already noted, a slight central-city advantage in 1957 changed to substantial suburban advantage by 1964-65 (Campbell and Sachs, 1967: 120; Sachs and Ranney, 1966: 64). By way of emphasis, it is noted that the gap for noneducational expenditures also grew, but in the opposite direction. By 1968, central cities devoted 63.4 percent of their expenditures to non-education purposes, while the suburban areas devoted only 44.4 percent. In terms of taxes, central cities raised $144 per capita in noneducational taxes, whereas, in the suburbs, the per capita local tax was only $76 (Advisory Commission on Intergovernmental Relations, 1970: 7).

The favored position of the suburbs may be short-lived, however. While it is more than likely that suburban school systems will continue to expand more rapidly than the central cities in the decades ahead, the composition of the school population will change as the flight from the central city continues. To data, the suburban areas have been successful in skimming off the top of each status group in the city, but in the future the movement out of the city is likely to be made up of whites with working-class or lower-middle-class backgrounds. And the higher status groups now living in the suburbs or those who are upwardly mobile are likely to move further out or at least become concentrated in selected high status residential areas. [44]

With the changing distribution of manufacturing and industrial firms to the more spacious suburbs, it is to be expected that blue-collar workers in search of manufacturing jobs will leave the city in order to be closer to place of work. Thus, the population characteristics of the suburbs will change in the coming years. As the suburban population continues to grow, there will be increased demands for a range of community services, which will require the suburbs to devote larger proportions of their resources to noneducational services. This will necessarily decrease the relative funding of the school system (Meranto, 1970: 57). These added costs may more than absorb the gains brought by the changing distribution of economic activities. Wood (1958: 135) has noted that suburban governments are potentially the most expensive of all local governments in the next twenty-five years. Even though the central cities face financial crisis because of obsolescence, the proportion of tax-exempt property, and suburban-imposed costs, the suburbs' problems are just beginning. Building new communities is likely to be at least as expensive as restoring old areas.

This point, rarely reported in the literature, has also been briefly discussed by Professor Brazer (1964: 135):

> Strong pressures have developed which have resulted in the growth in suburban communities of conditions once confined to low-income central city residential sections. In some of these, fiscal problems that exist are even more intense than those experienced by the central city because the suburban community which houses the low-income worker is frequently not the location of the industrial plant employing him. Lower-income families no longer necessarily occupy with increasing density the older residential sections of the central city. They are found concentrated as well in development tracts in suburban communities where the tax base represented by their houses is far too low to permit the financing of an acceptable level of public services.

It is more than likely, also, that federal grant programs in the future will encourage low-income housing and other programs in the suburbs, so that suburbanized manufacturing jobs will become more accessible to the poor and minorities.[45] Such developments will not only place an added burden on the schools, but will also increase the need for suburban areas to devote a larger proportion of their resources to noneducational needs. Even though the resources of the suburbs are likely to continue to increase, the demand for services will increase disproportionately as the population increases in size, as well as changes in composition. It is already evident that the larger metropolitan suburban areas provide a wide range of services. Obsolescence, particularly in the older suburban areas, will add to their burdens, as will the increases in the aged, the poor, and minority groups.

The more distant suburban areas, however, will continue to have marked advantages over the central cities and the close-in suburban areas for many years to come. Such areas will continue to devote a high, disproportionate share of their resources to education. Thus, the gap in educational resources will not only be between the central cities and the suburbs, but the gap will be marked between inner and outer suburban areas. This pattern is likely to develop as population and economic activities continue to push out and expand on the fringes of previous settlements.

The major threat to the suburban advantage, however, is the possibility that the federal government will force a reorganization of school districts in metropolitan areas in order to equalize resources and to make racial integration more feasible. Racial integration would probably be less complex if it involved only a single district rather than the multiple districts currently found in metropolitan areas. Most of these districts are either predominantly white and middle class, or predominately black and lower class.

Since each district tends to be an independent taxing unit with its own governing board, it becomes increasingly difficult to work out programs that cross district lines. While the probabilities of bringing about reorganization through popular vote are at best slight, such a change may very well come through legislation from outside the separate districts (Hawley and Zimmer, 1970: chs. 6 and 7). Such a reorganization would make the current central city-suburban differentials lose their meaning. Taxable wealth, affluence and/or poverty, would be shared throughout the community regardless of their concentration in specific locations within the metropolitan area. The artificial boundary that now divides the community would no longer serve as a barrier for community-wide attention to area-wide problems.

HOUSING

It has previously been suggested that the favored position of the suburban areas may be only temporary because of the changes likely to occur in the near future. That such changes are under way is evident from the type of residential

Table 1.23: Housing Units Added in Metropolitan Areas by Type of Unit, 1960-70

Type of Unit	Metropolitan Area		Central City		Outside Central City	
	Number	%	Number	%	Number	%
1 Unit	3,082,228	40.2	468,761	22.0	2,613,467	47.3
2 Units +	4,154,255	54.3	1,584,067	74.3	2,570,188	46.5
Mobile homes	418,777	5.5	79,612	3.7	339,165	6.1
Total	7,655,260	100.0	2,132,440	100.0	5,522,820	100.0

NOTE: Data from U.S. Bureau of the Census, 1971c.

building that has taken place in recent years. The suburbs traditionally have been characterized largely as areas of owner-occupied single-family homes. While it is difficult to project a long-term trend on the basis of only ten years of experience, the available data nonetheless suggest that changes are in process. The following discussion will focus on residential structures added within metropolitan areas during the last decade.

While ownership continued to be much higher in the suburbs than in the city, in the 1970 census the proportion of owner-occupied units in metropolitan areas decreased from 72.4 to 70.3 percent. The size of this decline is not large, but its direction takes on added significance when viewed in terms of the type of structure added during the last decennial period, as shown in Table 1.23. Less than half of the residential structures added to the housing inventory in the suburbs were single-family units. Actually, the number of multiple-unit structures nearly equalled the number of single-unit structures. Of the total multiple-unit structures added in metropolitan areas, more than three out of five were added in the suburban areas. Mobile housing units accounted for 5 percent of the added inventory, but four-fifths of the units were in the suburban areas. The change in type of structure is becoming significant. In 1960, only 22 percent of multiple units in metropolitan areas were in the suburbs, but by 1970 this had increased to 33 percent.

The rate of change by type of structure during the 1960-70 period is shown in Table 1.24. It is evident that growth in housing was much more rapid in the suburbs than in the central city, but the differential was more marked for multiple units than any other type. In short, in recent years there has been a marked increase in the number of multiple-unit structures being built in the suburbs. This in turn will affect the ownership rate, and in the long run will substantially change the composition of the suburban population. This pattern is likely to accelerate in the future as the demand for low-income housing increases and government support programs encourage low-cost housing programs near the industrial development in the suburbs.[46] In the meantime, however, as of 1970, owner-occupied housing values in the suburbs averaged $20,800, as compared with only $16,500 in the central city. And rentals were 75 percent higher in the suburban areas. While the gap between city and suburb is substantial, if short-term trends continue, the gap may become less marked.

Table 1.24: Percentage Change in Housing Units in Metropolitan Areas by Type of Structure, 1960-70

Selected Areas	Units in Structure		
	1 Unit	2 Units or More	Mobile Home
Metropolitan areas	11.8	34.6	97.4
Central city	4.3	17.0	83.1
Outside central city	17.2	96.1	101.5
OCC/CC ratio	4.0	5.7	1.2

NOTE: Data from U.S. Bureau of the Census, 1971.

IMPACT ON CENTRAL CITY

The most obvious result of the changing distribution of population is that suburban residents do not share in the high costs of city services necessitated by the increasing concentration of nonwhites, the elderly, the unemployed, and other low-income persons. It has been shown that per capita governmental costs in central cities in metropolitan areas (exclusive of education) are much higher than in suburban areas. Apart from these differentials as such, a particularly significant question is the extent to which this new widespread pattern of settlement causes central-city municipal costs to be higher. This type of problem arises when people live in one community and work in another, when people live and pay taxes—particularly property taxes—in one municipality but consume public services in other areas besides their own (Brazer, 1964: 141).

Several studies have shown that the proportion of the metropolitan population that lives outside the central city is closely related to per capita expenditures in the city. These studies show that the central cities must provide services not only for their own residents but also for nonresidents during the time they spend in the city. There is abundant literature showing that the "community" population is larger than the number of people living within incorporated boundaries (e.g., McKenzie, 1933: Ch. 13). The added burden placed on the city by nonresidents living in close proximity to the city has been interpreted as the "suburban-exploitation-of-the-metropolis" hypothesis. Support for this is found in an analysis of tax rates in the San Francisco-Oakland area (Margolis, 1957: 232).

In a more extensive study of 76 cities of 100,000 or more population and their metropolitan areas (based on 1940 census data), Hawley (1951) found that per capita costs of government (computed on the population residing within the city) are more closely related to population living outside the city ($r = .554$) than with the population living in the city ($r = .398$). The difference was even more pronounced if expenditures were limited to operating costs only. The relationships were such that, where the author assumed linearity, every increase of one person in the central-city population increased the cost of government there by $1.30, whereas an increase of one person in the outside area added $2.77 to central-city costs.

Kasarda (1972) examined the same type of problem for 168 metropolitan areas, using 1960 and 1970 data, and reported essentially the same results. That is, size of the suburban population was more important than size or composition of the central-city population in determining central-city expenditures for public services. The impact of the suburban population on city expenditures was still evident, even when controls for central-city size, age, per capita income, and percentage of population nonwhite were introduced.

When the author specifically focused on the impact of suburban communities on cost of central-city services, he found that the number of suburbanites who commute to work in the central city had a direct impact on total per capita central-city operating expenditures. A more detailed examination of the public sector showed that the suburban population in general, and the commuting population in particular, exerted strong effects on central-city police, fire, highway, sanitation, recreation, and general administrative functions. Thus, it becomes abundantly clear that the daily use of central-city facilities by suburban residents substantially increases the cost of municipal services in the central city.

Still another factor that places a burden on central cities is the growth of tax-exempt property in such areas. For example, in Boston, more than 60 percent of the land in the city is occupied by governmental, religious, cultural, educational, and other institutions, which are exempt from the local property tax that finances more than half of the city's budget. This fact, combined with higher (than suburban) costs for a wide range of public services and a population made up disproportionately of minority groups and other low-income families, adds substantially to the financial burden of central-city residents.[47] As a result, city taxpayers pay more in local taxes than their suburban neighbors, even though there is a marked income difference in favor of the suburbs. In all metropolitan areas combined, as noted above, central-city residents pay 7.6 percent of their incomes in local taxes, while suburban residents pay 5.6 percent (Advisory Commission on Intergovernmental Relations, 1967: 72). And in some metropolitan areas, the central city-suburban disparity is even greater. For example, in Newark, the ratio is nearly two-to-one—13 percent to 6 percent (Danielson, 1971).

The changing distribution of population from central cities to suburban areas, along with obsolescence of property in the city, increases in tax rates, and declines in municipal services, has contributed to an increase in the abandonment of both residential and nonresidential structures in the older sections of the city. Abandonment of property adds further to the problems of the city. Once this process is under way it tends to spread rapidly. It has been noted that the abandoned building is not merely a symbol of the decline and dysfunction of the central core, but an active factor itself in the abandonment process (Sternlieb, 1972: 13).

That this is a problem of major dimensions is evident from the limited data available. The National Urban League Center for Community Change (1971: 1) has noted: "The [National Survey of Housing Abandonment] has produced extensive evidence that entire neighborhoods housing hundreds of thousands of central city dwellers are in advanced stages of being abandoned by their owners. The phenomenon affects many but not all Eastern and Midwestern cities." Data are available for only a few areas on citywide levels of abandonment, but these data indicate that the problem is becoming increasingly important. In New York City, it is estimated that approximately 2 percent of the existing housing stock has been abandoned. The National Urban League Center for Community Change (1971: 15) indicates that these figures understate the problem, since disinvestment—one stage of abandonment—is occurring in at least 7 percent of the housing inventory. This will probably lead to final abandonment unless something drastic intervenes. The problem is even more acute in St. Louis, where abandonment has affected 16 percent of the structures in selected neighborhoods. This is not unrelated to the fact that the central-city population actually declined by one-fifth during the last decade. In some neighborhoods, the abandonment rate runs as high as 20 percent.

The abandonment of property in the city is a result of the changes that have taken place in the growth pattern of cities in recent years. In the early stages of city growth, in the nineteenth-century pedestrian city, such property would have been held for speculation with the expectation that, as the city increased in size, there would be a land-use change that would enhance the value of the property (Burgess, 1923). Disinvestment and the withholding of services to an occupied building by the landlord, which are considered crucial ingredients of the abandonment process, are not of recent origin. On the contrary, these activities have characterized slum areas for years in most American cities. However, abandonment was not the end product of advanced stages of deterioration, since there were alternative uses for the property as other land uses in the city core expanded.

Abandonment has occurred in recent years not only because of obsolescence, since this is not new, but also because of the lack of alternative uses. The types of nonresidential functions that historically have displaced obsolescent residential structures have moved to outlying parts of metropolitan areas. It is the lack of alternative demands for property, reflected in abandonment, which adds further to the financial burden of cities.[48] This further reduces an already declining tax base, and there is little promise that conditions will improve in the future, unless there is a change in public policy. Such property is abandoned, since it is no longer profitable for private ownership. Perhaps some form of urban land bank that would permit community ownership of property to be held for future development would help to resolve some of the problems in this area.

INCREASE IN LOCAL GOVERNMENTS

One of the concomitants of the widespread settlement pattern has been the proliferation of autonomous governmental units at the local level. In the outlying portions of metropolitan areas in particular, frequent attempts have been made to replicate city governments by incorporating the population living in close proximity. And where replication has not taken place, alternative measures have been common, such as the establishment of single-function districts to provide selected urban services. Thus, from 1957 to 1967, the number of non-school-district governments in metropolitan areas increased from about 10,500 to about 15,700—an increase of slightly less than 50 percent in a single decade.[49] Most of these governmental units are small. Two-thirds of the municipalities in metropolitan areas have a population of less than 5,000 and one-third of the total have fewer than 1,000 residents. Of the 3,225 townships in metropolitan areas, over two out of three have a population of less than 5,000 (National Commission on Urban Problems, 1969: 7).

During this period, there was a substantial decline in the number of school districts (see Table 1.25). The average number of school districts per metropolitan area declined one-third, from 35.3 to 22.1 during the ten-year period. While data are not available to provide evidence on this, it is quite likely that most of this decrease occurred in the outer fringes of metropolitan areas, where the small rural school districts have been consolidated into larger districts. The decline in number of school districts may be misleading in terms of what is happening in metropolitan areas, since little or no change may have occurred in the more urbanized portions of metropolitan areas, where most of the major educational problems are found.

Partial evidence for this is found in the change in the number of school systems by size of enrollment, as shown in Table 1.26. It is evident that the largest declines occurred in the smaller districts, particularly in districts that enrolled fewer than 50 pupils and in nonoperating districts. Substantial decreases also occurred in districts that enrolled fewer than 300 pupils, but such districts are also more likely to be in the outer fringes of the metropolitan areas. What this means is that the sharp drop in the number of school districts cannot be accepted as evidence that the metropolitan school problems are being resolved through reorganization of school districts. It is probable that central cities and the close-in suburban areas have not experienced any substantial change in the organization of school systems, since resistance to reorganization on a metropolitan area scale has not changed in recent years (Zimmer and Hawley, 1968; Bollens, 1961; Greer, 1963).

Table 1.25: Number of Local Governments in Metropolitan Areas, 1957-67

Local Government	1957[a]	1962[a]	1967[b]	% Change 1957-67
Metropolitan areas	17,984	18,442	20,703	15.1
Total number of school districts	7,486	6,004	5,018	−33.0
Other governments	10,498	12,438	15,685	49.4
Municipal	3,844	4,144	4,977	29.5
Special districts	3,736	5,411	7,049	88.7
Other	2,918	2,883	3,659	25.4

a. U.S. Bureau of the Census, 1963, p. 2.
b. U.S. Bureau of the Census, 1969, p. 1.

Table 1.26: Number of School Systems in Metropolitan Areas, by Size of Enrollment, 1962 and 1967

Size of Enrollment	1962[a]	1967[b]	% Change
1,200 or more	2,556	3,112	22.0
300 to 1,199	1,410	1,218	−14.0
150 to 299	481	333	−31.0
50 to 149	585	358	−39.0
15 to 49	540	201	−63.0
1 to 14	120	57	−52.0
Nonoperating	912	250	−73.0

a. U.S. Bureau of the Census, 1963, p. 21.   b. U.S. Bureau of the Census, 1969, p. 19.

Table 1.27: Average Number of Local Governments in Metropolitan Areas for Selected Years

Local Government	1957[a]	1962[a]	1967[b]
Number of metropolitan areas	212	212	227
Total	84.8	87.0	91.2
Non-school districts	49.5	58.7	69.1
Municipalities	18.4	19.5	21.9
Special districts	17.6	25.5	31.3

a. U.S. Bureau of the Census, 1963.   b. U.S. Bureau of the Census, 1969.

Even with the substantial decline in school districts, there was an overall increase of more than 2,800 governmental units in metropolitan areas from 1957-67. This was due to the sharp increase in the number of municipalities and special districts. There was an increase of 4,400 such units from 1957-67. Three-fourths of the increase was due to the growth of special districts, which nearly doubled during the decade, from 3,736 to 7,049. While the average number of governments per metropolitan area increased during the ten-year period, the increase in total number of governmental units is much less than the rate of increase of nonschool districts, because of the sharp decrease in number of school districts (see Table 1.27).[50] While there was a decrease of approximately 2,500 school districts, there was an increase of more than 3,300 special districts during the period.

Thus, as the population continues to spread out from the center in a more widespread settlement pattern, it is being administered by increasingly fragmented units.[51] Not only have municipal governments been replicated in the outlying areas within commuting distance of metropolitan centers, but there also has been a substantial growth in ad hoc service districts in attempts to meet the urban service needs of small areas independently of the center. This had led to governmental chaos within an otherwise integrated unit. The pattern of metropolitan growth has divided among many governmental units what are actually indivisible problems (Gulick, 1962: 24). The present fragmentation of governmental units reinforces the socioeconomic differences within metropolitan areas, which results in vast inequities in the costs and benefits of government services to residents of different communities (Danielson, 1971).

SUMMARY

The early part of the present century was characterized by a pattern of centripetal movements, which resulted in a rapid period of urbanization. By 1920
a majority of the population lived in urban areas. The centripetal movement
continued not only to urban areas but more particularly to the larger urban
centers. A reverse pattern of movement was set in motion as the urban population in large centers began to expand beyond city boundary lines. This was a
period of increasing scale of local community life. A new type of communal
organization developed as the radius of daily activities increased in scope.
Villages and open countryside that had once been independent of the large
urban centers became engulfed in an enlarged community. The large city gave
way to the metropolitan community. The territorial scope of this metropolitan
community is more extensive than the city, but the function it serves is not
different. It has replaced the city as both the producing and consuming unit.
These changes are reflected in the growth and changing distribution of population and community activities at the local level.

In recent years, the most rapid increase in population has taken place in
metropolitan areas. While the population has become more concentrated in a
limited number of large centers, there has also been a centrifugal drift within
these centers, increasing the proportion of metropolitan population that lives
outside of central cities.[51] By 1970, nearly seven out of every ten people in
the United States lived in metropolitan areas and of this number, three out of
four lived in the suburbs. While a majority of those in the suburbs live in the
densely settled urbanized area beyond the corporate limits of the city, the
scope of daily life extends to a radius of thirty-five miles or more. And it is
the outer areas that are experiencing the most rapid growth.

Along with the centrifugal drift of population, there are a number of marked
changes under way within the metropolitan community that reflect this increased scale of daily life. The widespread settlement pattern has resulted in a
decrease in population density. Land area devoted to urban use has increased
much more rapidly than population. Not only has density declined in the
expanding urbanized areas, but in the central cities as well. The increased scale
of local community life is partially evident from the expanded radial distance
from the center to the outer boundary of the urbanized area.

Not all segments of the population have participated equally in the more
widespread settlement pattern. While evidence on this is limited, the data available generally agree that the suburban movement is made up disproportionately
of persons in the higher socioeconomic status groups, regardless of how social
status is measured. The net city-suburban movement within metropolitan areas
is such that it tends to lower the socioeconomic status of the city population.
The central cities are left with minority groups, the poor, the elderly, and other
disadvantaged groups low in education and occupational skills.

The widespread settlement pattern has been almost exclusively white. As a
consequence, racial segregation has sharpened. In the nineteenth-century

pedestrian city, segregation had been marked, but it was along neighborhood lines. With the development of the metropolitan community, however, blacks and other disadvantaged groups have become segregated along political lines. During the past decade, central cities underwent major racial changes as the black population, in particular, increased rapidly, while the white population decreased in number. And it is likely that the black concentration in central cities will continue to increase in the future.

In recent years, there has also been a marked centrifugal drift of jobs to the suburbs, causing employment opportunities to become more widespread throughout the metropolitan area. This has worked to the disadvantage of the blacks and other urban poor who do not have access to such places of employment, because of lack of transportation. Thus, the widespread pattern of distribution of jobs has worked to the disadvantage of those who are least able to compete in the labor market. The lack of low-income suburban housing and the denial of access to existing suburban housing near suburban jobs contributes to the high unemployment of blacks in metropolitan areas. In general, a residential-job opportunity pattern is developing that will further increase the distance between home and work and will increase unemployment in central cities. Jobs best suited for the type of labor force that is locked into the city are moving to the suburbs, while the labor force best suited for the type of jobs concentrated in the city is moving to the suburban areas.

The increased scale of local community life has had a marked impact on the central business district, reducing the taxable resources of the central city. Once the hub of local community life and the point of maximum accessibility, the CBD has continued to decline in importance, particularly in the retail area, but also in wholesaling, manufacturing, and selected services. Retail sales in the CBD, as a proportion of metropolitan sales, have been on a continuous decline as the centrifugal drift of the population has increased. Clearly, major suburban shopping centers have increased in importance as retail outlets. While the CBD has become less important as a retail center, it has retained other crucial functions for the metropolitan area, however. It continues to show considerable vitality as a location for central offices and for business and governmental services.

The urban centrifugal drift has had a marked impact on schools in the metropolitan areas. The early stages of suburbanization created a school crisis in the suburbs because there was a rapid growth in school population, while taxable resources were largely limited to residential property. More recently, however, the crisis has shifted to the central cities. This is caused, in part, by a declining tax base as commercial and industrial establishments move to suburban locations, and also by the changing city population composition. The present population has demands for noneducational expenditures, which further reduces the local resources available for schools. Problems of racial minorities add further to the school crisis in central cities. The favored position of the suburban areas may be short-lived, however. Public policy may force low-income housing into the suburbs, so that the urban poor and minorities will have access to housing where jobs are available. Also, as the suburban population becomes more heterogenous, noneducational expenditures are likely to increase, thus reducing the resources available for the schools.

There is a limited amount of data available which suggests that the type of housing is changing in suburban areas. In recent years, there has been a sharp decrease in the proportion of new construction in single-family units. In suburban areas during the past decade, less than half of the housing units added to the inventory were single-family structures. Multiple units in the suburbs nearly doubled during this period. If this trend continues, it will have a marked impact on the home-ownership rate and on the characteristics of the population living in suburban areas. Central city-suburban differentials will become less marked, particularly for the close-in suburban areas.

The changing distribution of population has placed heavy demands on the city, since it is necessary to provide services not only for their own residents, but for nonresidents as well when they come to the city. Available evidence indicates that per capita expenditures in the city increase directly as the proportion of metropolitan population outside of the city increases. The number of suburbanites who commute to work in the central city has a direct impact on the total per capita operating expenditures for central city services. In short, the daily use of central city facilities and services by suburban residents increases the cost of municipal services in the central city.

As the local community has expanded beyond the corporate limits of the central city into the suburban areas, there has been a proliferation of local governmental units. Frequent efforts have been made to replicate city governments in the outlying areas, and, where replication has not taken place, alternative measures have been taken in attempts to provide urban services independently of the central city. There has been a rapid growth of ad hoc special-service districts in metropolitan areas. Thus, as the population continues to spread out from the center, the metropolitan area becomes increasingly fragmented as an administrative unit. This adds to the total cost of government within the metropolitan area and precludes administrative units that can cope with metropolitan area problems. This fragmentation of local governmental units also effectively segregates socioeconomic and racial groups by political boundaries. Neighborhood segregation has given way to political segregation. Service needs and available resources vary markedly among the fragmented units. While many observers have recognized the need for some form of metropolitan-wide government for the enlarged community, efforts to bring about such change have met with very limited success (see Campbell and Dollenmayer, this volume).

Nonetheless, the overriding issue in this more widespread pattern of settlement is the need for an administrative structure large enough in scope to handle area-wide problems and to encompass all segments of the population. It is evident that the growth and development of the metropolitan community has been superimposed on an already existing political and educational administrative structure that was created for an earlier period, when the compact city of the nineteenth century was surrounded largely by rural areas. The social and economic structure of the local community has undergone significant changes, but there have not been corresponding changes in organizational structures to accommodate these new and different functional patterns. While the enlarged community is closely integrated into the daily economic and social activities of life, it is segmented into parts for the provision of community services. The need for reorganization of government in metropolitan areas is so apparent that it needs no elaboration.

NOTES

1. Includes 627 places under 2,500 that were defined as *urban* for the first time in the 1970 census. There were 6,435 urban places with a population of 2,500 and over (U.S. Bureau of the Census, 1971a: 46-47).

2. In the past 200 years, the proportion of the labor force engaged in agriculture has decreased from nearly 90 percent to less than 10 percent. Thus, there has been a complete reversal in the agriculture/nonagriculture ratio.

3. It is of interest to note that the mechanization of agriculture requires large farms and big investments. As a result, the total number of farms in the U.S. declined from 6.1 million in 1940 to 3.7 million in 1959. Older farmers are not migrating to urban areas, however; when they die or retire, their manpower is not replaced. Instead, their farms tend to be absorbed by other farms.

4. Metropolitan areas are operational concepts for the metropolitan community worked out by the U.S. Bureau of the Budget and used by the Census Bureau and other government agencies in reporting data. For a definition of metropolitan areas, see Bureau of the Budget, 1967.

5. It should be noted that there are a large number of other concepts of the community reported in the literature. See, for example, Hillery (1955).

6. See also McKenzie (1933: 81).

7. In the comparisons throughout the period, the same areas are used at both the beginning and the end of the decade to avoid the inclusion of new territory. However, during each decade, the number of metropolitan areas increased, caused either by natural growth or changes in definition. For a discussion of change in definition, see Gist and Fava (1964: 39-48).

8. If there had been no annexations during the decade, the proportion in central cities would have declined to 43 percent.

9. Within metropolitan areas, many central cities have lost population. Of the 292 municipalities designated as central cities, 130 lost population between 1960 and 1970. The aggregate population loss of these cities was 2.3 million (Lowry, 1971: 3-4).

10. For an extensive recent discussion of the metropolitanization of society, see Hawley, (1971: 219-240). For related literature, see Hathaway, Beegle, and Bryant (1968); Vance and Sutker (1954: ch. 6); Bogue (1949); Duncan, Scott, Lieberman, Duncan, and Winsborough (1960); Fuguitt (1963: 246-261).

11. The urbanized-area concept was first introduced in the 1950 census to provide a better separation of urban and rural population in the vicinity of the larger cities. An urbanized area contains at least one city of 50,000 inhabitants or more and includes the surrounding closely settled population. For a detailed description, see U.S. Bureau of the Census (1971a: xii-xiii).

12. The urbanized population accounted for only 85 percent of the metropolitan population in 1950 once the portion of the population that moved farthest from the city is excluded. Hence, it also excludes the areas with the highest rate of increase in metropolitan areas in recent years.

13. It has been observed that the trend toward a decline in density in metropolitan cores is consistent with the long-term trend in the growth of the urban areas of industrial societies generally (Hawley, 1972: 519 ff.).

14. The areas included the New York Standard Consolidated Area (several contiguous SMSAs), the Chicago SCA, the Philadelphia SMSA, and the Los Angeles SMSA.

15. We have referred to Schnore's index of suburbanization as an index of concentration, since his index is confusing to interpret. For a description of the calculation of the index, see Hoover and Vernon (1959: 303).

16. The average individual income of metropolitan residents in 1970 was nearly 10 percent higher than the national average ($6,140 vs. $5,590), and was more than 30 percent higher than the income of nonmetropolitan residents ($6,140 vs. $4,618).

17. For a general review of the literature on suburban selectivity, see Pinkerton (1969).

18. This pattern was observed by Warner (1969) as early as 1900. While he confirms the observation that the lower classes were left behind in the central city as the middle and upper classes moved to the outer ring, he notes that, within this ring, the band closest to the city contained the lower middle class, the next closest contained the upper middle class, and the wealthy were found farthest out. More recent support was found by Dobriner (1963), who compared the same area at two points in time. He reported that the first occupants of the suburbs were white-collar workers, but later they moved on to higher-status suburban areas and were replaced by blue-collar workers.

19. These scores have been criticized in the literature because the component variables in the index are not independent but are different aspects of the same thing, and because the variables are neither additive nor of equal weight. While these criticisms have merit, the scores nevertheless provide a crude index of status differences between races and among places of residence.

20. In the mid-1960s, a large industrial area contiguous to the city and the adjacent area occupied by the municipal airport were annexed.

21. The same centripetal pattern is reported by Hawley (1956: 49, 1971: 159) for metropolitan areas in general.

22. For the twenty-five-year period there were three exceptions. In 1933 the number of vehicles registered dropped significantly because of the Depression. Another decrease occurred in the mid-1940s as a result of the war, when automobile production was drastically curtailed, and a slight decrease also occurred in 1952 because of the temporary steel shortage which seriously curtailed production and employment in the area.

23. In this analysis the boundary lines of the metropolitan area have been held constant according to the 1950 definition, even though the area was expanded in 1970 to include an adjacent county.

24. The difference between this figure and the 1910 population of 38,550 reported by the census is due to annexation.

25. In recent years, population and growth have moved outward, spilling over the boundaries of central cities and invading even the outer zone, which had earlier been the scene of population decline (Hawley, 1972: 519 ff.).

26. It is of interest to note that in 1945, telephone contact between the city of Providence and the town of Warwick was limited, since a toll call was required. Twenty-five years later, Warwick had increased in size to the point where it became, by census definition, one of the three central cities by which the metropolitan area is identified. This observation dramatically illustrates the scope of increased activity within the local community.

27. These observations should be viewed with caution since the adjustments for employment data in relation to annexation were based on the authors' questionable assumption that the percentage of employment annexed in each category was the same as the percentage of annexed population (Niedercorn and Kain, 1963: 7).

28. A Bureau of Labor Statistics study showed that for the period 1960-65, at least 62 percent of the valuation permits for new industrial building were for construction in the suburbs (National Committee Against Discrimination in Housing, 1968: viii).

29. For an elaboration of this point, see Wetzel and Holland (1966); Orshansky (1966: 30).

30. The (U.S.) Commission on Population Growth and the American Future (1972: 219) has stated: "While the absence in the suburbs of an adequate supply of low- and moderate-income housing available to all races is certainly not the sole or even the primary cause of unemployment or underemployment in the central city, it is a contributing factor which needs to be remedied."

31. In discussing this issue, Berry (1971: 337) has stated: "The minority groups . . . have poured into the central cities in search of . . . opportunities . . . only . . . to find that the opportunities that they were seeking, as they moved into those areas in which they could gain a place of residence in the core of the city, were moving away from them out into the far periphery of these metropolitan areas. So that you have the decentralization within metropolitan areas creating the vacuum in the destination areas of the minority immigrants and in turn, the growing pool of minority immigrants, out of work, on the welfare rolls, increasingly visible, becoming another major reason why the emigration of the white population from the central cities out into the suburban areas and into the further peripheries has continued to increase in the past decade. We have trend and trend and countertrend here."

32. The National committee Against Discrimination in Housing (1968: 27-29) reports that "in fact residents of central city ghettos do not commute in significant number, despite suburban job growth . . . and that commuting is prohibitively expensive and too time-consuming to be a practical solution for ghetto residents to work in the suburbs."

33. Federally supported programs designed to provide bus service between ghetto residences and suburban jobs have not been very successful. See, for example, Herbers (1970).

34. Of the 292 business units in the study, 104 were displaced by urban renewal and 188 by highway programs (Zimmer, 1964: 36).

35. It may be that the same pattern holds for physicians, dentists, and other independent professionals.

36. See also Guest (1973).

37. For example, see Sternlieb (1963); Lynd (1960: 32-33); Casparis (1967); Tarver (1957); and Dessel (1957).

38. The metropolitan areas population is 910,781 compared to the state population of 946,725. The areas covered are not coterminous; however, the metropolitan area extends into Massachusetts and does not include some of the South Country area of the state.

39. In a multiple-regression analysis of data for 62 SMSAs, it was reported that population growth and decentralization were major explanatory variables for the decentralization of "shopping goods" sales (Taeuber, 1964).

40. Caplovitz (1963: 57) found that low-income families tended to shop mainly in their own neighborhoods because they are more familiar with the neighborhoods and because they can obtain credit there more easily.

41. Similar findings for an earlier period have been reported by Jonassen (1955).

42. This is the type of problem Wood (1961) has referred to as the "segregation of resources from needs."

43. See also Martin (1962).

44. In Levittown, for example, it was observed that as white-collar workers' incomes rose, they sought other suburban communities that were more compatible with their changing life-styles (Dobriner, 1963: 111).

45. In 1970, a White House advisory group recommended that all sorts of federal aid be withheld from local communities in order to break the suburban barrier around the central cities (Semple, 1970). However, plans developed by HUD to use water and sewer grants to promote low-cost housing were unsuccessful.

46. The (U.S.) Commission on Population Growth and the American Future (1972: 219) has noted: "Access to employment, particularly jobs offering opportunities for advancement, is often restricted not only by the inability of the poor to satisfy job require-

ments, but also the physical inaccessibility of many jobs. Blacks and the poor are, in part, locked out of jobs because they cannot get to the suburbs where opportunities open up. Reverse commuting can be expensive, time-consuming and difficult. Suburban housing, while closer to job opportunities, is often too expensive or simply unavailable because of racial discrimination."

47. For an elaboration of this point, see above discussion on schools.

48. Hawley (1972: 528) has noted: "The cycling of land from low to high intensity uses can no longer be expected. As a result the continuing centrifugal drift of urban population and urban institutions leaves a widening core of obsolescent, deteriorated and abandoned buildings where once stood the richest sources of municipal revenues."

49. Part of this increase was due to the addition of fifteen metropolitan areas during the period. While the 1951 figures are based on the 212 metropolitan areas reported in 1960, the latter figures are based on the number of metropolitan areas delineated at the time of the 1967 Census of Governments.

50. Part of this increase is caused by the addition of fifteen metropolitan areas during the period. When area is held constant (using 1967 metropolitan areas), the average number of nonschool governments in 1962 is 65.0.

51. The centrifugal drift is not of recent origin. In his study of London, Booth noted that there was a "centrifugal tendency" of the classes to move outward from the center of the city (Pfautz, 1967: 94). This is also what Burgess (1923: 85-89) discussed in his "Concentric Zonal Hypothesis."

REFERENCES

Advisory Commission on Intergovernmental Relations. *Fiscal balance in the American federal system.* Vol. 2. *Metropolitan fiscal disparities.* Washington, D.C.: U.S. Government Printing Office. 1967.

Advisory Commission on Intergovernmental Relations. *Metropolitan disparities: A second reading.* Information Bulletin No. 70-1. Washington, D.C.: ACIR, Jan. 1970.

Berry, B. Statement in Congressional Hearings. In U.S. House of Representatives, *Industrial location policy.* Hearings before the Ad Hoc Subcommittee on Urban Growth of the Committee on Banking and Currency, 91st Congress, 2nd Session. Part 3. Washington, D.C.: U.S. Government Printing Office, 1971. 327-339.

Bogue, D. J. *The structure of the metropolitan community: A study of dominance and subdominance.* Ann Arbor: University of Michigan Press, 1949.

Bollens, J. C. (Ed.) *Exploring the metropolitan community.* Berkeley: University of California Press, 1961.

Bowles, G. Net migration from the farm population. Paper presented at the 1961 Annual Meeting of the Population Association of America.

Brazer, H. Some fiscal implications of metropolitanism. In B. Chinitz (Ed.), *City and suburbs: The economics of metropolitan growth.* Englewood Cliffs: Prentice-Hall, 1964. 127-150.

Burgess, E. W. "The growth of the city: An introduction to a research project." Proceedings of the American Sociological Society, 1923, 18, 85-97.

Campbell, A. K., and Sacks, S. *Metropolitan America: Fiscal patterns and governmental systems.* New York: The Free Press, 1967.

Campbell, A. K., and Meranto, P. "The metropolitan education dilemma: Matching resources to needs." Urban Affairs Quarterly, Sept. 1966, 2, 42-63. Reprinted in B. T. Downes (Ed.), *Cities and suburbs: Selected readings in local politics and public policy.* Belmont, California: Wadsworth Publishing Co., 1971. 336-352.

Caplovitz, D. *The poor pay more: Consumer practices of low income families.* New York: The Free Press, 1963.

Carlos, S. "Religious participation and the urban-suburban continuum." American Journal of Sociology, March 1970, 75, 742-759.

Casparis, J. "Metropolitan retail structure and its relation to population." Land Economics, 1967, 43, 212-218.

Committee for Economic Development, Research and Policy Committee. *Guiding economic growth.* New York: CED, 1960.

Cressey, P. F. "Population succession in Chicago: 1898-1930" American Journal of Sociology, 1938, 44, 59-69.

Danielson, M. N. Differentiation, segregation, and political fragmentation in the American metropolis. Paper prepared for the U.S. Commission on Population Growth and the American Future, 1971.

Dessel, M. D. "Central Business districts and their metropolitan areas: A summary of geographic shifts in retail sales growth, 1948-1954." Area Trend Series, No. 1. Office of Area Development, U.S. Department of Commerce. Washington, D.C.: U.S. Government Printing Office, 1957.

Dobriner, W. M. *Class in suburbia.* Englewood Cliffs: Prentice-Hall, 1963.

Duncan, O. D., and Duncan, B. "Residential distribution and occupational stratification." American Journal of Sociology, March 1955, 60, 493-503.

Duncan, O. D., Scott, W. R. Lieberman, S., Duncan, B., and Winsborough, H. H. *Metropolis and region.* Baltimore: Johns Hopkins Press, 1960.

Fuguitt, G. V. "The city and the countryside." Rural Sociology, Sept. 1963, 28, 246-261.

Ganz, A. Our large cities: New directions and new approaches. In U.S. House of Representatives, *Industrial location policy.* Hearings before the ad hoc subcommittee on urban growth of the Committee on Banking and Currency, 91st Congress, 2nd Session, Part 3. Washington, D.C.: U.S. Government Printing Office, 1971. 221-227.

Garn, H. A. Statement in Congressional Hearings. In U.S. House of Representatives, *Industrial location policy.* Hearings before the ad hoc subcommittee on Urban Growth of the Committee on Banking and Currency, 91st Congress, 2nd Session. Part 3. Washington, D.C.: U.S. Government Printing Office, 1971. 95-99.

Gist, H. P., and Fava, S. F. *Urban society.* (5th ed.) New York: Thomas Y. Crowell Co., 1964.

Grebler, L. "Measuring the suburbanization of manufacture." Land Economics, Nov. 1956, 32, 380-381.

Greer, S. *Metropolitics: A study of political culture.* New York: John Wiley & Sons, 1963.

Guest, A. "Urban Growth and population densities." Demography, Feb. 1973, 10, 53-69.

Gulick, L. *The metropolitan problem and American ideas.* New York: Knopf, 1962.

Hamovitch, W., and Levenson, A. "Projecting suburban employment." Urban Affairs Quarterly, June 1969, 4, 459-476.

Hathaway, D. E., Beegle, J. A., and Bryant, W. K. *People of rural America.* 1960 Census Monograph Series. U.S. Department of Commerce. Washington D.C.: U.S. Government Printing Office. 1968.

Hatt, P. K. and Reiss, A. J. (Eds.) *Reader in urban sociology.* Glencoe: The Free Press, 1951.

Hawley, A. H. "An ecological study of urban service institutions." American Sociological Review, 1941, 6, 629-639.

Hawley, A. H. *Human ecology: A theory of community structure.* New York: Ronald Press, 1950.

Hawley, A. H. "Metropolitan population and municipal government expenditures in central cities." Journal of Social Issues, 1951, 7 (1-2), 100-108. Reprinted in P. K. Hatt and A. J. Reiss (Eds.), *Cities and Society: The revised reader in urban sociology.* Glencoe: The Free Press, 1959. 773-782.

Hawley, A. H. *The changing shape of metropolitan America: Deconcentration since 1920.* Glencoe: The Free Press, 1956.

Hawley, A. H. *Urban society: An ecological approach.* New York: Ronald Press, 1971.

Hawley, A. II. "Population density and the city." Demography, Nov. 1972, 9, 521-529.

Hawley, A. H., and Zimmer, B. G. Resistance to unification in a metropolitan community. In M. Janowitz (Ed.), *Community political systems.* Glencoe: The Free Press, 1961. 146-184.

Hawley, A. H., and Zimmer, B. G. *The metropolitan community: Its people and government.* Beverly Hills: Sage Publications, 1970.

Herbers, J. "Many post-riot bus projects to carry inner city poor to jobs are failing." The New York Times, May 29, 1970.

Hilferty, J. Use of the central business district by place of residence within the Providence Metropolitan Area. Unpublished senior honors thesis, Department of Sociology, Brown University, 1972.

Hillery, G. A. "Definitions of community: Areas of agreement." Rural Sociology, 1955, 20, 111-123.

Hoover, E. M., and Vernon, R. *Anatomy of a metropolis.* Cambridge: Harvard University Press, 1959.

Isard, W., and Whitney, V. "Metropolitan site selection." Social Forces, 1949, 27, 253-269.

Jonassen, C. T. *Downtown versus suburban shopping.* Columbus: Ohio State University, Bureau of Business Research, 1955.

Kaoarda, J. D. "The impact of suburban population growth on central city service functions." American Journal of Sociology, May 1972, 77, 1111-1124.

Kenyon, J. Manufacturing and sprawl. In J. Gottmann and R. A. Harper (eds.), *Metropolis on the move: Geographers look at urban sprawl.* New York: John Wiley & Sons, 1967. 102-121.

Kirschenbaum, A. "City-suburban destination choices among migrants to metropolitan areas." Demography, May 1972, 9, 321-335.

Landis, P. H., and Hatt, P. K. *Population problems: A cultural interpretation.* (2nd ed., prepared by P. K. Hatt). New York: American Book Co., 1954.

Lowry, I. S. *Housing assistance for low-income families: A fresh approach.* New York City: Rand Institute, 1971.

Lynch, K. *The image of the city.* Cambridge: Harvard University Press, 1960.

Margolis, J. "Municipal fiscal structure in a metropolitan region." Journal of Political Economy, June 1957, 65, 225-236.

Martin, R. C. *Government and the suburban school.* Syracuse: Syracuse University Press, 1962.

Mayer, K. B., and Goldstein, S. "Population decline and the social and demographic structure of an American city." American Sociological Review, Feb. 1964, 29, 48-54.

McKenzie, R. D. *The metropolitan community.* New York: McGraw-Hill, 1933.

Meranto, P. *School politics in the metropolis.* Columbus: Charles E. Merrill, 1970.

Meyer, J. R., Kain, J., and Wohl, M. *The urban transportation problem.* Cambridge: Harvard University Press, 1965.

Morrison, P. A. Population distribution policy: Issues and objectives. Paper prepared for the U.S. Commission on Population Growth and the American Future, 1971.

National Commission on Urban Problems. *Building the American city.* New York: Praeger, 1969.

National Committee Against Discrimination in Housing. *The impact of housing on job opportunities.* New York: NCDH, 1968.

National Urban League and Center for Community Change. *National survey of housing abandonment.* New York: NUL and CCC, 1971.

Newman, D. K. "The decentralization of jobs." Monthly Labor Review, May 1967, 90, 7-13.

Niedercorn, J. H., and Hearle, E.F.R. *Recent land-use trends in forty-eight large American cities.* MEM. RM-3664-FF. Santa Monica: RAND Corp., 1963.

Niedercorn, J. H., and Kain J. F. Suburbanization of employment and population, 1948-1975. RAND Corp., 1963. Paper presented at the meetings of the Highway Research Board, National Academy of Sciences, Washington D.C., Jan. 1963.

1950 Census of Population. The urban population of the United States. In P. K. Hatt and A. J. Reiss (Eds.), *Reader in urban sociology*. Glencoe: The Free Press, 1951. 57-69.

Orshansky, M. "The poor in city and suburb, 1964." Social Security Bulletin, Dec. 1966, 29, 22-37.

Pfautz, H. W. (Ed.) *Charles Booth on the city: Physical pattern and social structure.* Chicago: University of Chicago Press, 1967.

Pinkerton, J. R. "City-suburban residential patterns by social class: A review of the literature." Urban Affairs Quarterly, June 1969, 4, 499-519.

Pratt, S. A. "Metropolitan community developments and economic change." American Sociological Review, 1957, 22, 434-440.

Research Council of the Great Cities Program for School Improvement. *The Challenge of financing public schools in great cities.* Chicago: Research Council of the Great Cities Program for School Improvement, 1964.

Sacks, S., and Ranney, D. C. "Suburban education: A fiscal analysis." Urban Affairs Quarterly, Sept. 1966, 2, 103-119. Reprinted in M. Gittell (Ed.), *Educating an urban population*. Beverly Hills: Sage Publications, 1966, 60-76.

Schnore, L. F., and Varley, D. W. "Some concomitants of metropolitan size." American Sociological Review, Aug. 1955, 20, 408-414.

Seeley, J. R., Sims, R. A., and Loosley, E. W. *Crestwood Heights: A study of the culture of suburban life.* New York: John Wiley and Sons, 1964.

Semple, R. B., Jr. "Panel bids Nixon promote housing." The New York Times, July 23, 1970.

Sternlieb, G. "The future of retailing in the downtown core." Journal of the American Institute of Planners, 1963, 29, 102-112.

Sternlieb, G. "Abandonment: Urban housing phenomenon." Challenge (U.S. Department of Housing and Urban Development), May 1972, 3 (5), 12-14.

Taeuber, A. F. Population redistribution and retail changes in the central business district. In E. W. Burgess and D. J. Bogue (Eds.), *Contributions to urban sociology.* Chicago: University of Chicago Press, 1964. 163-177.

Taeuber, K., and Taeuber, A. F. "White migration and socioeconomic differences between cities and suburbs." American Sociological Review, October 1964, 29, 718-729.

Tarver, J. J. "Suburbanization of retail trade in the Standard Metropolitan Areas of the United States, 1948-54." American Sociological Review, Aug. 1957, 22, 427-433.

Thompson, W. S. *The growth of metropolitan districts in the United States: 1900-1940.* Washington, D.C.: U.S. Government Printing Office, 1947.

U.S. Bureau of the Budget, Office of Statistical Standards. *Standard metropolitan statistical areas.* Washington, D.C.: U.S. Government Printing Office, 1967.

U.S. Bureau of the Census. The urban population of the United States. In P. K. Hatt and A. J. Reiss, Jr. (Eds.), *Reader in urban sociology.* Glencoe: The Free Press, 1951. 57-69.

U.S. Bureau of the Census. U.S. Census of Business: 1958. *Central business districts.* Vol. 7. Washington, D.C.: U.S. Government Printing Office, 1958.

U.S. Bureau of the Census. U.S. Census of Population: 1960. *Number of inhabitants.* Final Report PC(1)-1A. U.S. Summary. Washington, D.C.: U.S. Government Printing Office, Nov. 1961.

U.S. Bureau of the Census. U.S. Census of Governments: 1962. Vol. 5: *Local governments in metropolitan areas.* Washington, D.C.: U.S. Government Printing Office, 1963.

U.S. Bureau of the Census. U.S. Census of Population: 1960. *Characteristics of the population.* Vol. 1, Part 1, PC(1)A-D. U.S. Summary. Washington, D.C.: U.S. Government Printing Office, 1964.

U.S. Bureau of the Census. U.S. Census of Population: 1960. *Socioeconomic status.* Subject Reports, PC(2)-5C. Washington, D.C.: U.S. Government Printing Office, 1967.

U.S. Bureau of the Census. U.S. Census of Governments: 1967. Vol. 5: *Local governments in metropolitan areas.* Washington, D.C.: U.S. Government Printing Office, Nov. 1969.

U.S. Bureau of the Census, U.S. Census of Business: 1967. *Major retail centers.* Vol. 6, Retail trade. BC67-MRC-1. Washington, D.C.: U.S. Government Printing Office, 1970.

U.S. Bureau of the Census. U.S. Census of Population: 1970. *Number of inhabitants.* Final Report PC(1)-A1. U.S. Summary. Washington, D.C.: U.S. Government Printing Office, 1971. (a)

U.S. Bureau of the Census. U.S. Census of Population: 1970. *Negro population in selected places and selected counties.* Supplemental Report, Series PC(S1)-2. Washington, D.C.: U.S. Government Printing Office, June 1971. (b)

U.S. Bureau of the Census. U.S. Census of Population and Housing: 1970. *General demographic trends for metropolitan areas, 1960-1970.* U.S. Summary, Final Report, PHC(2)-1. Washington, D.C.: U.S. Government Printing Office, Oct. 1971. (c)

U.S. bureau of the Census. *Income in 1970 of families and persons in the United States.* Series P-60, No. 80. Washington, D.C.: U.S. Government Printing Office, Oct. 1971. (d)

U.S. Bureau of the Census. *Farm population.* Current Population Reports. Series Census, ERS, P-27, No. 43. Washington, D.C.: U.S. Government Printing Office, May 1972. (a)

U.S. Bureau of the Census. U.S. Census of Population: 1970. *General social and economic characteristics.* PC(1)-C1. U.S. Summary. Washington, D.C.: U.S. Government Printing Office, June 1972. (b)

U.S. Bureau of the Census. U.S. Census of Population: 1970. Vol. 1, Part A, *Number of inhabitants.* No. 24 (Michigan). Washington, D.C.: U.S. Government Printing Office, 1972. (c)

U.S. Commission on Population Growth and the American Future. *Population and the American future.* New York: Signet, New American Library.

U.S. House of Representatives. *School construction.* Hearings before the General Sub-committee on Education of the Committee on Education and Labor, 89th Congress, 1st Session, July and August 1965. Washington, D.C.: U.S. Government Printing Office, 1966.

(U.S.) President's Committee on Urban Housing. *A decent home.* Washington, D.C.: U.S. Government Printing Office, 1968.

Vance, R. B., and Smith, S. Metropolitan dominance and integration. In R. B. Vance and H. J. Demerath (Eds.), *The Urban South.* Chapel Hill: University of North Carolina Press 1954. 114-134.

Vernon, R. "Production and distribution in the large metropolis." Annals of the American Academy of Political and Social Science, Nov. 1957, 314, 15-29.

Warner, S. B. *Streetcar suburbs: The process of growth in Boston, 1870-1900.* New York: Atheneum, 1969.

Weber, A. R. Labor Market perspectives of the new city. In B. Chinitz (Ed.), *City and suburbs: The economics of metropolitan growth.* Englewood Cliffs: Prentice-Hall, 1964. 66-81.

Wetzel, J. R., and Holland, S. S. "Poverty areas of our major cities." Monthly Labor Review, Oct. 1966, 89, 1105-1110.

Wood, R. C. *Suburbia: Its people and their politics.* Boston: Houghton, Mifflin Co., 1958.

Wood, R. A., and Almendinger, V. V. *1400 governments: The political economy of the New York metropolitan region.* Cambridge: Harvard University Press, 1961.

Zimmer, B. C. Flint area study. 1958.

Zimmer, B. G. *Rebuilding cities: The effects of displacement and relocation on small business.* Chicago: Quadrangle Books, 1964.

Zimmer, B. G., and Hawley, A. H. "Suburbanization and church participation." Social Forces, May 1959, 37, 348-354.

Zimmer, B. G., and Hawley, A. H. "Suburbanization and some of its consequences." Land Economics, Feb. 1961, 37, 588-593.

Zimmer, B. G., and Hawley, A. H. *Metropolitan area schools: Resistance to district organization.* Beverly Hills: Sage Publications, 1968.

CHAPTER 2

BEYOND THE SUBURBS:
THE CHANGING RURAL SCENE

Rex R. Campbell

University of Missouri

> *In these days of rapid transportation and easy communication, the country*
> *village and town are submerged by the streams of influence which pour in*
> *upon them from the distant cities [Gillette, 1922: 473].*

THE TERM "RURAL" still brings visions to many people, including leaders and
legislators, of nostalgic scenes—farms with grazing cattle, neat white farm houses
with red barns, and placid small villages with main streets and small stores. The
rural-urban dichotomy which is still used to classify the geographic areas of the
United States was developed at a time when such scenes were typical for most of
the population. At that time, rural areas were primarily agricultural, and cities
were smaller, much more compact, and less pervasive in their influence. Today,
however, while many social science researchers recognize that this dichotomy is
too simple to accurately describe the United States, they continue to use it.

Rural communities were once culturally distinct from urban ones and could
be defined as subcultural areas. The relative geographic isolation, when the only
transportation was walking, horseback, or perhaps trains, helped to preserve
differences in dress, behavior, and value systems. These differences were
reflected in distinctive individual demographic traits such as educational attainment, income, and occupation. Much of the early distinctiveness resulted from
the uniqueness of farming as a way of life, and the tendency of immigrants from
the agrarian areas of Europe to settle in rural areas of the United States with
others of their kind. Thus, there were German, Swedish, Italian, and Polish
farming communities.

Rural hamlets were relatively complete communities with close interpersonal
ties. The rural communities at one time provided most of the necessary social
and economic services for their residents, including churches, schools,
physicians, retail stores, and a psychological sense of belonging together.
Gradually many of these institutions which provided the social glue have been
integrated with larger units in other, larger communities. Today, rural villages

have only limited functions. The primary one is residential—they serve as a type of bedroom community similar to suburbs. So-called "rural" areas today range all the way from traditional to highly urbanized communities.

The greater availability of mass media, the automobile, and the high mobility rates of the American people have been strong influences in lessening the subcultural differences among regions and communities. Virtually the same programs are watched on television regardless of whether the child is residing in an Ozark rural village or a Manhattan apartment. The styles of houses being built are similar regardless of whether they are located in suburbs, small towns, or in open country. And as a result of the marketing practices of the large corporations of today, the clothes, the toothpaste, and the tomatoes are the same. Perhaps the ultimate question is: How much does a MacDonald's hamburger vary from Key West, Florida, to Seattle, Washington? From the metropolitan to the nonmetropolitan?

Increasingly, the social values of rural communities are coming into line with those held in other parts of the United States. A mass society is developing at a level including both the metropolitan and nonmetropolitan areas. The place of residence, whether rural or urban, of an individual or a family is less indicative today of patterns of behavior than a number of other characteristics such as socioeconomic class and ethnicity.

These statements should not be taken to suggest that ecological patterns of residence are no longer important. The suburbs around metropolitan areas are typified by certain socioeconomic class and race stratification, for example. But the rural-urban dichotomy or any other division based on the premise that residence in small villages or open country in some way results in distinctive resident characteristics is no longer valid.

Certainly differences within and between communities and areas still exist, and some small differences in behavior patterns between geographic regions exist today and will remain in the future. However, such geographic differences do not have the magnitude and consistency of earlier times. Major differences exist between the socioeconomic classes and the ethnic groups within communities regardless of whether they are rural or urban.

The theme of this article is what is becoming obvious to most Americans: We are living in an industrialized, urbanized society which extends its influence to the most remote rural hamlets (Bishop, 1967). Rural and urban as widely varying styles of life may still exist in other parts of the world. For the United States, however, they are for the most part superannuated terms which confuse our mental images of communities and may be analytically misleading. Yet they are still widely used in government agencies, colleges, and universities and by people in general.

I will examine first the utility of the rural-urban dichotomy—metropolitan-nonmetropolitan—which may serve as a "stopgap" measure.[1] Then I will describe some of the major changes in nonmetropolitan communities, both at the individual and community levels. Finally, I will suggest some research needs for the nonmetropolitan areas which will produce alternatives to the above dichotomies.

THE RURAL-URBAN DICHOTOMY

Wirth (1938), in one of the classic conceptions of the city, used size, density, and homogenity-heterogenity as primary dimensions of defining the city. The Bureau of the Census uses two of these—size and density—in their definition of rural and urban areas and undoubtedly assumes the third. This dichotomization is an oversimplification, but it has served in the past as a useful starting point in defining the differences between agricultural and urban-industrial areas. Its utility in today's society is questionable, however. Hathaway, Beegle, and Bryant (1968: 233) concluded:

> It has been known for some time that the use of the simple three-fold residence categories of urban, rural-nonfarm, and rural-farm without refinement leads to numerous absurdities. On the one hand, the urban population may encompass a metropolis such as Detroit or New York containing millions and a Podunk Center containing a scant 2,500 persons. On the other hand the rural population is a composite which includes persons residing on farms as well as persons in rural areas but classified as "nonfarm." A large fraction of these people are fully associated with the life of urban areas. In contemporary America, it is patently absurd to use the term "rural" to describe a large part of the population which is identified as rural by census definition.

In the United States, population increase has been the norm for the country as a whole and for a vast majority of the incorporated areas. As a rural village grew beyond a certain size (2,500 population) or an area beyond a specified density, it was automatically reclassified from rural to urban. This process has made rural a residual, constantly declining category, and not necessarily a functional category in which the people are distinctive in character from those living in cities.

Since areas with population growth are the norm, however, it is possible that the people in the rural areas which do not have enough population increase to be reclassified to urban would remain distinctive in some characteristics. Perhaps differences might be found when comparisons are made of the characteristics of rural and urban areas. Thus, the idea that rural may be a misleading concept has not been adopted by all scholars. For example, Schnore (1966: 143), in an examination of the rural-urban dichotomy, concluded on the basis of 1960 data that:

> rural-urban divergences in the United States are still substantial and well worth studying, despite the apparent fact that they are diminishing. Rural and urban types of community display patterned differences, while place of residence and place of origin are fundamental characteristics of individuals that permit the analyst to predict human behavior.

CENTRAL PLACE THEORY

Even though differences may continue to exist between rural and urban populations in total, such a comparison overlooks the possibility of very vital interrelationships between a metropolitan center and its "rural" hinterlands. The very character of rural communities and their role in the greater metropolitan areas has been changed significantly by the automobile and the highway systems. Thus, a better conceptual basis for delineating ecological units in the United States than rural-urban may be central place theory.

The following description of central place theory draws on Hawley (1971: 221-2). According to this theory, as formulated by Walter Christaller (1933) and modified by August Lösch (1954), the greater the number and variety of services provided from a center to a hinterland, the greater is the geometric centrality of its location. But to serve a large area at minimum transport costs, lower-order (i.e., more standardized and more frequently used) services are offered from successively smaller-size centers nested in groups of sixes. According to Lösch, it is only in the shape of hexagons that market areas can efficiently fill an area. Thus, urban centers form a numerical and functional hierarchy in a region. The smallest centers, providing the lowest-order functions, are most numerous; the next larger size class of centers, only one-sixth as numerous, offers all of the lowest-order functions and a selection of somewhat more specialized services; at the apex is the regional capital, from which are available all lower-order services and also the most specialized or highest-order services.

The relationship of surrounding territories which are not included in the urban centers is not specified exactly by central place theory. The idea of metropolitan dominance and subordination of the territory around the metropolis is one method of conceptualizing the influence of the urban centers. The theory of patterns of dominance holds that urban characteristics are distributed in rural areas to form gradients of decreasing incidence with increasing distance from the urban center. The hypothesized inverse relationship is due primarily to the decreasing influence at increasing distance from metropolitan centers of communications media, transportation facilities, and interactions between rural and urban people.[2]

Krugel (1971: 141-3), in reviewing the literature on metropolitan dominance in a study of the influence of metropolitan areas on human fertility, concludes that:

there is substantial evidence of metropolitan dominance at any given point in time, as indicated by gradient patterns in economic, demographic, and other variables. A second conclusion is that although much attention has been given to the metropolitan dominance of economic variables, relatively little attention has been given to social or cultural dominance, though this interest is sometimes implicit. A third and related conclusion is that few investigators have attempted to link the theory of metropolitan dominance to other areas of sociological interest, two examples of which are the spatial distribution and diffusion of norms and values and the cultural role of cities.

Krugel (1971: 141) found the following patterns in Kentucky:

(1) Metropolitan centers partially dominate and organize social norms, (2) theory of metropolitan dominance is insufficient as a general explanation of the spatial distribution of social norms, (3) the location of inner-metropolitan highways is not highly related to the distribution and change of norms, and (4) the concept of subdominance has limited usefulness when applied to cities of small population.

The gradient principle may be less in evidence now than at an earlier time, because the widespread utilization of mass media and rapid transportation has caused the urban influence to spread much more evenly. If the hypothesis concerning the development of a mass culture is correct, then the distance gradient is likely to disappear.

Hoover (1969) found that there is less differentiation in economic and social structure between broad regions in the country now than in the past and that there is increasing differentiation between large and small centers within the urban hierarchy. This suggests that a more profitable way of analyzing the social and economic ecological structure would be to use a hierarchy of urban centers including their surrounding hinterlands. While some comparative analyses have been made of urban centers, relatively little work has been done which includes the hinterlands of urban centers.

The number of ecological classifications currently available, besides the rural-urban dichtomy, is very limited. One very crude dichotomization which is available, and which takes into account size of place at a level which is more meaningful than the rural-urban division, is the metropolitan-nonmetropolitan classification. The rural-urban division is made at 2,500 population in incorporated places, and the metropolitan-nonmetropolitan division is made at 50,000. Hathaway, Beegle, and Bryant (1968) support the use of a metropolitan-nonmetropolitan division and suggest that while it is a basic proposition that urban-influenced changes in rural areas are related to the size of the urban center, urban influence on rural areas is also closely related to distance from large centers. They conclude (p. 235):

These (rural-urban) differences no longer appear to be related primarily to the occupation of farming. The large commercial farmer in a metropolitan county may have more in common with his urban business counterpart in a nearby metropolis than with either the subsistence farmer in the rural South or the banker in a remote village removed from a metropolitan area. Our results indicate that much of the economic and social variations in rural areas are a function of the proximity to metropolitan areas and that future census classifications should recognize this fact.

However, the metropolitan-nonmetropolitan categorization suffers from a number of serious faults. For example, hinterland counties adjacent to a metropolitan area are not included by the Bureau of the Census as a part of the Standard Metropolitan Statistical Area (SMSA) unless they meet certain requirements. While Hathaway et al., take distance from a metropolitan center into account, the Bureau of the Census does not. In addition, this simple dichotomy does not take into account the large amount of variation among different sized places.

Also, specialization of employment results in other distinctive qualities. Many of the smaller towns and cities have changed from primarily agricultural trade centers to manufacturing, recreational, or some other type of employment base. Thus, any type of categorization which is based upon size alone will miss these significant variations. Although these faults are recognized, the metropolitan-nonmetropolitan categorization will be used for some broad generalizations in this article because it is available now and it is better than the rural-urban alternative. However, research should be undertaken to conceptualize and refine an ecologically based delineation which is more sensitive to the reality of today's nonmetropolitan society.

POPULATION CHANGES

Rural-Urban: A Historical Analysis

Since the rural-urban dichotomy had considerable utility in the past, it is worthwhile to examine briefly some of the major dimensions of the rural-urban population change from a historical perspective. In 1900, only four out of every ten persons in the United States were urban residents. By 1920 the rural proportion had declined, and the country's population was one-half urban. But, at the same time, the rural population had continued to increase from 46 million to 52 million. The proportion of urban population continued to increase until in 1970 the country was almost three-fourths urban.

The population of rural areas has remained relatively stable since 1930— around 54 million persons. The United States has continued to grow in population, and the rural percentage has declined from 44 to 26 percent. As mentioned earlier, rural is a residual category. The amount of territory which is considered rural today is less than it was earlier. For example, the land area in the 290 largest cities increased from 7,610 square miles in 1950 to 15,588 in 1970, or an increase of 104.8 percent (International City Management Association, 1972: 85). Since the area has decreased and the population has remained relatively stable, this means that the actual density of population of the rural areas has increased (see Table 2.1).

The rural nonfarm increase has not been distributed equally in all areas, but has been concentrated around metropolitan areas and other cities. The majority of counties in the United States have lost substantial population from their peak numbers. The U.S. Commission on Population Growth and the American Future (1972: 31) notes:

> The territory involved in this rural exodus is immense; but, relative to the national population, the number of people leaving is small. The growth of the nation has been so great that even if all rural counties were repopulated to their historical maximum, they would absorb a population equivalent to no more than five years of national growth.

Table 2.1: Population of the United States by Urban and Rural Residence, 1900-70

Year	Total	Urban	Rural	% Urban
1900	76,212	30,215	45,997	39.6
1910	92,228	42,064	50,164	45.6
1920	106,022	54,253	51,768	51.2
1930	123,203	69,161	54,042	56.7
1940	132,165	74,705	57,459	56.5
New definition				
1950	151,326	96,847	54,230	64.0
1960	179,323	125,269	54,045	69.9
1970	203,212	149,325	53,887	73.5

NOTE: Under the current definition, the urban population is comprised of all persons living in urbanized areas and in places of 2,500 inhabitants or more outside of urbanized areas. In previous years, the urban population was comprised of all persons living in incorporated places of 2,500 inhabitants or more. In both definitions, the population not classified as urban constitutes the rural population. Data from U.S. Bureau of the Census, 1961, 1971.

In 1920 the farm population was about three-fifths of the rural population and 30 percent of the total United States population. Between 1940 and 1950, the farm population declined to less than one-half of the rural population, and today it is only one-fifth of the rural population and less than five percent of the total United States population.

From these data two generalizations can be made. The first is that the rural nonfarm population has had a major increase during this period. This has undoubtedly resulted from the increased off-farm employment available in the rural areas and from commuting to work from rural communities to urban places. Hawley (1971) points out that the decentralization of population started as early as 1920.

The second generalization is that a benchmark toward the urbanization of rural areas was established when rural nonfarm included more than 50 percent of the rural population. This occurred between 1940 and 1950 (see Table 2.2). From this time onward, if not before, the rural population was for the most part urbanized—i.e., no longer were the rural areas primarily agricultural. The residents were now employed in a diversity of occupations, and the homogenity of interests and other characteristics was disappearing.

There is further evidence of urbanization of rural areas—the migration of persons who are likely to bring urban value systems into rural areas. It was found in a recent study that urban-to-rural migrants made up 24 percent of the total rural white population, while rural-to-urban migrants have made up 20 percent of the white urban population. For the black population, the rural-to-urban migrants were a higher percentage than the urban-to-rural migrants (see Table 2.3).

In 1970, 27 percent of the population was rural, but five out of every six rural people were nonfarm residents (see Table 2.4). In 19 of the 50 states, over 90 percent of the rural population was nonfarm. No state had a majority of rural population in the rural farm category.

Table 2.2: Farm Population, 1920-70

Year	Farm Population (in thousands)	% of Total U.S. Population
1920	31,974	30.1
1925	31,190	27.0
1930	30,529	24.9
1935	32,161	25.3
1940	30,547	23.2
1945	24,420	17.5
1950	23,048	15.3
1955	19,078	11.6
1960	15,635	8.7
1965	12,363	6.4
1970	9,712	4.8

NOTE: Data from U.S. Department of Agriculture, May 1971, p. 4.

Table 2.3: U.S. Population by Residence, Race, and Migration Status, 1967

Population	% of Total[a]	
	White	Negro
Urban		
Rural to urban migrants[b]	20	21
Urban to urban migrants	39	33
Nonmigrants	41	46
Rural		
Urban to rural migrants	24	11
Rural to rural migrants	29	17
Nonmigrants	47	72

NOTE: Data from U.S. Department of Agriculture, May 1971.
a. Population 14 years old and over by 1967 residence and residence at age 16 or earlier.
b. Migrants are persons who have ever lived more than 50 miles from their 1967 address.

Nonmetropolitan Places

Over two-thirds of the United States population is located in Standard Metro-politan Statistical Areas which are defined on the basis of the population size of a central city (50,000 minimum) and by county boundaries. The majority of the population has been in this category since before 1950, increasing 4 to 6 percent per decade to the present time.

The 1970 metropolitan population was distributed remarkably evenly among the four Bureau of the Census geographic regions (see Table 2.5). Only the West had less than 25 percent. The South, which has increased its proportion of metropolitan population rapidly in recent years, still has the lowest proportion of intra-regional metropolitan population.

Interestingly, in a few states which have a large number of metropolitan areas, the percentage of nonmetropolitan population is lower than the percentage rural. Some "rural" population is included in what the census defines as metro-

Table 2.4: Rural and Rural Nonfarm Population, 1970

State	% of Total Nonmetropolitan[a]	% of Total Rural[b]	% of Rural Nonfarm[c]	State	% of Total Nonmetropolitan[a]	% of Total Rural[b]	% of Rural Nonfarm[c]
United States	31.4	26.5	84.6	Montana	75.6	46.6	74.5
Alabama	47.7	41.6	88.8	Nebraska	57.2	33.5	58.2
Alaska	100.0	51.6	99.3	Nevada	19.3	19.1	91.7
Arizona	25.5	20.4	93.6	New Hampshire	72.7	43.6	97.2
Arkansas	69.1	50.0	81.9	New Jersey	23.1	11.1	95.9
California	7.3	9.1	89.8	New Mexico	68.9	30.2	87.7
Colorado	28.3	21.5	81.8	New York	13.5	14.4	92.8
Connecticut	17.4	22.6	97.8	North Carolina	62.7	55.0	86.6
Delaware	29.6	27.8	92.6	North Dakota	88.1	55.7	55.8
Florida	31.4	19.5	94.5	Ohio	22.3	24.7	85.9
Georgia	50.3	39.7	90.6	Oklahoma	49.9	32.0	78.6
Hawaii	18.1	16.9	95.5	Oregon	38.8	32.9	85.2
Idaho	84.2	45.9	71.2	Pennsylvania	20.6	28.5	93.3
Illinois	19.9	17.0	77.3	Rhode Island	15.3	12.9	98.1
Indiana	38.1	35.1	79.4	South Carolina	60.7	52.4	91.8
Iowa	64.4	42.8	57.6	South Dakota	85.7	55.4	55.9
Kansas	57.7	33.9	68.8	Tennessee	51.1	41.2	80.4
Kentucky	60.0	47.7	75.1	Texas	26.5	20.3	83.0
Louisiana	45.2	33.9	90.8	Utah	22.4	19.6	87.2
Maine	78.4	49.2	95.3	Vermont	100.0	67.8	91.2
Maryland	15.7	23.4	93.2	Virginia	38.8	36.9	88.8
Massachusetts	15.3	15.4	97.9	Washington	34.0	27.4	88.0
Michigan	23.3	26.2	88.0	West Virginia	68.7	61.0	94.6
Minnesota	43.1	33.6	64.4	Wisconsin	42.4	34.1	72.5
Mississippi	82.3	55.5	82.9	Wyoming	100.0	39.5	76.2
Missouri	35.9	29.9	74.3	Washington, D.C.	—	—	—

a. U.S. Bureau of the Census, July 1972.

b. U.S. Bureau of the Census, 1971.

c. U.S. Bureau of the Census, August 1972.

Table 2.5: Metropolitan and Nonmetropolitan Population by Regions, 1970

	United States	North-East	South	North Central	West[a]
Number (000)					
Total	203,212	49,041	62,795	56,572	34,804
Metropolitan	139,419	39,188	35,199	37,658	27,373
Nonmetropolitan	63,793	9,852	27,596	18,913	7,431
Percent (within regions)					
Total	100.0	100.0	100.0	100.0	100.0
Metropolitan	68.6	79.9	56.1	66.4	78.6
Nonmetropolitan	31.4	20.1	43.9	33.6	21.4
Percent (between regions)					
Total	100.0	24.1	30.9	27.8	17.1
Metropolitan	100.0	28.1	25.2	26.9	19.6
Nonmetropolitan	100.0	15.4	43.3	29.6	11.6

NOTE: Data from U.S. Bureau of the Census, 1971.
a. Includes Hawaii and Alaska.

Table 2.6: Percent Population Change, 1960-70

Population Groups	Percent
United States total	13.3
Total metropolitan	16.6
Total nonmetropolitan	6.7
Nonmetropolitan nonfarm	19.3
Nonmetropolitan farm	−36.0

NOTE: Data from U.S. Department of Agriculture, May 1971, p. 21.

politan. Again this calls attention to one of the weaknesses of the metropolitan-nonmetropolitan dichotomy and to the need for a new ecological categorization.

The percentage change in the numbers of population between 1960 and 1970 indicates that the nonmetropolitan areas did not grow as rapidly as the metropolitan areas (see Table 2.6). The major difference in growth rates in nonmetropolitan areas was between nonfarm and farm. The nonmetropolitan nonfarm had a growth rate of 19.3 percent, while the farm population declined 36 percent.

The population distribution within various sizes of towns (incorporated places) is very unequal. In 1970, 61 percent of nonmetropolitan towns included 10 percent of the total nonmetropolitan town population, while 5 percent of the towns had almost one-half of this population (Fuguitt, 1971).

It is a popular belief that small towns and villages are dying unless they are near a metropolitan center. However, Fuguitt (1971: 460), in his study of small towns in America, concludes that there has been little change in the size of place distribution over the past two decades:

Approximately 90 percent of the places stayed in the same size class during each decade. The change that has occurred is one which on balance has favored growth and new incorporation over decline and disappearance.

Fuguitt reports that there has been an overall decline in the 1960-70 decade in the proportion of places over 2,500 population, which grew both in absolute numbers and in proportion to the smaller places which grew.

The larger nonmetropolitan places (10,000 and over) grew slightly more rapidly than did the smaller places. Twenty-two percent of the largest places increased over 20 percent in population during the decade, while 18 percent of the villages with less than 500 population had such an increase. At the other end of the change scale, 33 percent of this smallest sized category lost more than 10 percent of their population, and 10 percent of the largest category experienced such a loss (see Tables 2.7 and 2.8).

The popular mythology of small town demise is in part the result of the highly visibly functional changes. Many of the businesses have closed and the buildings have been abandoned. Many highways are routed through the business district, and thus to the casual visitor it appears that the town is dying. However, close inspection of the residential areas would reveal that most of the houses are occupied. Many of the occupants are retired farmers or businessmen, and the age structure of such small communities includes many older people.

In most nonmetropolitan areas the farm population has experienced a large loss. Where this has not been offset by increases in the rural nonfarm population, the total population served by the small businesses has been greatly reduced. Even where population has been replaced, the reduction in the number of farms has caused considerable dislocation in those businesses serving agriculture.

The decline of the economic functions of the small towns has resulted also from the improvements in transportation systems which permit people to travel longer distances to shop in large volume stores in larger towns (Ottoson, Birch, Henderson, and Anderson, 1966). Most small communities have a population too small to support supermarkets, discount stores, and other large volume merchandising outlets.

The supermarket and discount store originated in the metropolitan centers, but gradually such businesses have been established in modified form in the smaller metropolitan and larger nonmetropolitan centers. Even in the Plains States, which have low population densities, supermarkets and some types of discount stores are found in the county seat towns, and the large discount chains are now reaching into the smaller metropolitan centers. The resulting lower prices and larger selection of items produces competition which is very difficult for the "Mom and Pop" stores in the small villages to meet. As a result, small businesses have been forced out of small towns in the same manner as they were in the metropolitan centers at an earlier time. A few still remain in the villages for sales of convenience items. In the Midwest, most businesses in towns of less than 1,000 have been in severe economic straits for some time, and with the spread of chain discount centers into neighboring larger places, the future of these small businesses is very uncertain.

The loss of the tax base provided in the past by the small businesses has handicapped the towns in attempting to provide adequate roads, sewers, water systems, and other public services. These conditions, combined with the relative

Table 2.7: Number of Incorporated Places and Total Population by Size Class, Nonmetropolitan United States, 1950, 1960, 1970

Size Class	1950		1960		1970	
	Number	Population (in thousands)	Number	Population (in thousands)	Number	Population (in thousands)
Total	12,809	26,101	13,332	30,174	13,821	33,538
10,000 and over	555	10,560	673	13,714	748	16,215
2,500-9,999	1,718	8,300	1,874	9,152	2,019	9,882
1,000-2,499	2,483	3,888	2,561	4,017	2,649	4,173
500-999	2,728	1,930	2,600	1,861	2,646	1,893
Less than 500	5,325	1,423	5,624	1,433	5,759	1,415
Percentage Distributions						
Total	100	100	100	100	100	100
10,000 and over	4	40	5	46	5	48
2,500-9,999	13	32	14	30	15	29
1,000-2,499	20	15	19	13	19	13
500-999	21	7	20	6	19	6
Less than 500	42	6	42	5	42	4

NOTE: Table from Fuguitt, 1971, p. 452.

Table 2.8: Cross-classification of the Number of Incorporated Places by Size in Two Successive Censuses, Nonmetropolitan United States, 1950-60 and 1960-70

Size in Earlier Census	Size in Later Census					
	Less Than 500	500-999	1,000-2,499	2,500-9,999	10,000 and Over	Total
1960-1970						
New in 1970	344	73	43	23	6	489
Less than 500	5,220	393	9	1	1	5,624
500-999	192	2,050	347	11	--	2,600
1,000-2,499	3	129	2,200	229	--	2,561
2,500-9,999	--	1	50	1,735	88	1,874
10,000 and over	--	--	--	20	653	673
Total	5,759	2,646	2,649	2,019	748	13,821
1950-1960						
New in 1960	338	99	59	25	2	523
Less than 500	5,002	305	17	1	--	5,325
500-999	279	2,064	378	7	--	2,728
1,000-2,499	5	132	2,063	281	2	2,483
2,500-9,999	--	--	44	1,551	123	1,718
10,000 and over	--	--	--	9	546	555
Total	5,624	2,600	2,561	1,874	673	13,332

NOTE: Table from Fuguitt, 1971, p. 453.

isolation of many small towns from large metropolitan centers have made most small towns noncompetitive in attracting industry and population. This, in turn, has triggered unemployment and out-migration of the younger and better-educated people. Industrialization of small towns varies widely throughout the United States. Some small communities, however, especially in the South and the West, have attracted industry.

The consolidation of primary and secondary schools and other public services has also eliminated some of the main sources of employment of small communities. In some states there is a movement toward consolidation of governmental services on a regional basis, which will also reduce the economic functions of county seat towns.

All of these types of integration have greatly weakened the social bonds of most small communities so that today they are coming increasingly to resemble the suburbs, whose principal function is residential, with few social bonds.

Metropolitan Fringe Areas

The rate of centrifugal drift of people outward from the central cities into the "rural-urban" fringes of metropolitan areas has increased in the last decade. As the movement outward has occurred, the density of population has decreased in the growing fringes. This has resulted in part because, as the radius of a city increases, the geographic area included increases at a geometric rate, while the population increases only at an arithmetic rate. As an example, a city increasing in radius from ten to eleven miles would increase its area 66 square miles, while the same city at a later time which increased its radius from thirty to thirty-one miles would take in an additional 192 square miles. This "pancaking" of urban areas has resulted in spotty developments of housing, with large amounts of open country and low density population between the tract housing developments.

A large amount of farm land has been taken out of production for suburban development. The land area included in the 290 largest cities in the United States increased 7,978 square miles between 1950 and 1970, a 104.8 percent increase. Undoubtedly a much greater amount of land has been purchased from farmers and is being held for speculative purposes. This has driven the price of land and taxes up to the point where a large number of farm owners around cities have been forced to sell to developers and speculators. Land zoning does not exist around many metropolitan areas and, where it does, it is frequently controlled by real estate interests who change zoning to fit their desires (called "spot" zoning). Because much open country still remains in the large metropolitan fringe areas, the residents are a combination of metropolitan (those who commute to employment in the metropolitan area), nonmetropolitan-nonfarm (those employed and/or oriented to the local area), and farm populations.

The centrifugal drift has been facilitated by several factors. One of the most important has been the development of the interstate highway system. These major transportation routes have had major effects on fringe areas by opening

Table 2.9: Average Growth of All Places 10,000 and Over from 1950 to 1960 by Distance from Nearest SMSA and Accessibility to Interstate Highways

| Distance | High Access[a] | | Access[b] | | Low Access[c] | | No Access | | Distance Totals | |
	Percent of Growth	Number of Places	Percent of Growth	Number of Places	Percent of Growth	Number of Places	Percent of Growth	Number of Places	Percent of Growth	Number of Places
Within 50 miles of Nearest SMSA	27.6	585	16.7	399	15.5	41	14.6	24	22.7	1,049
50 to 100 miles	15.0	36	13.6	103	5.6	52	2.2	24	10.7	215
100 to 150 miles	15.4	15	15.1	114	10.0	98	6.7	111	10.9	338
150 miles and farther	14.7	3	17.2	55	4.2	22	7.1	64	10.7	144

NOTE: SMSA is determined by 1960 data. Source of table is unpublished data from Richard Sturgis, Urban Research Group Department, Oak Ridge National Laboratory, Oak Ridge, Tennessee.
a. Two or more interstate highways in county.
b. One interstate highway in county.
c. Interstate highway in adjacent county.

them to new settlement by the urbanite and by making easily accessible additional employment opportunities for the previously nonmetropolitan population.

The highways have fostered strip developments away from the metropolitan center with clusters at the major interchanges (see Table 2.9). At the end of the tentacles of development, the small, previously rural villages have experienced population increases as they have become suburban bedroom places. The open country population around the villages which had been losing population has ceased to decline or has had population increases. Some of these increases have resulted from the retention of young people; other increases consist of refugees from the city.

McNamara (1972), in a study of population migration between 1960 and 1970 in counties in the North Central Region, found that the metropolitan areas (SMSAs) had to be larger than one million population to have a major influence on the net migration in adjoining counties. While the region had a 1.7 percent out-migration, the counties adjoining cities of more than one million had a net in-migration. The counties adjoining cities of five million or larger had 9.7 percent in-migration, and for cities of one to two million there was in-migration of 4.4 percent. The adjoining counties for the small metropolitan areas of fifty to one hundred thousand had a 6.8 percent out-migration. These results suggest that the dominance of metropolitan areas for in-migration patterns is a function of metropolitan population size (see Table 2.10).

A major factor in centrifugal drift of population is the relocation of manufacturing and other major employers from the central cities to the fringes (Taysby, Davidson, and Clark, 1970). With the development of the interstate highway system and truck transportation, many of the manufacturers are less dependent on rail and water transportation. Racial and crime problems, high taxes, and the reluctance of some employees to work in the central cities have all contributed to an increased tendency for executives to relocate in the fringe areas or in smaller metropolitan centers. This relocation by major employers has compounded the centrifugal drift and has made places of employment much more accessible to previously rural areas. Another major factor influencing fringe area growth has been the economic affluence of the American middle class. A significant segment of the public is willing to spend a proportion of their

Table 2.10: Net Migration of North Central Region Counties Adjacent to Metropolitan Areas of Different Size Categories, 1960-70

Size Category	% Net Migration
Total	−1.7
5 million and over	9.7
2-5 million	3.0
1-2 million	4.4
500,000-1 million	−2.1
250,000-500,000	−2.8
100,000-250,000	−4.0
50,000-100,000	−6.8

NOTE: Data from McNamara, 1972.

affluence for automobile transportation to and from a metropolitan area, thus escaping from or avoiding the central cities.

The best way to delineate the "labor shed" of a city today is to consider the time-distance required to commute to the major places of employment, such as manufacturing, government, and retail services (Floyd and Robertson, 1972). Time-distance is the distance that can be traveled in a specific time. If the average commuter in a metropolitan area is willing to commute one-half hour time-distance, then the ring encompassing the labor shed is about one hour time-distance. One hour time-distance along a major freeway is at least forty or fifty miles from the place of employment. Such a distance, of course, encompasses a large amount of territory. In some parts of the United States where the metropolitan areas are relatively close together, almost all of the so-called rural territory is within one hour time-distance. Over one-third of the counties in the United States are either metropolitan counties or adjoining counties. Berry (1967), using the 1960 population distribution, found that 95 percent of the country's population lived within what he defined as the daily commuting field of metropolitan cities.

GROWTH COMMUNITIES

In nonmetropolitan areas, a number of specialized types of communities have developed recently. Four of these will be described here.

(1) Recreational Communities. Outdoor recreation has been growing rapidly in the United States, and the amount of money spent on recreation has increased very significantly. Segments of this industry are geographically limited, for example, water-based recreation which requires lakes, rivers, or oceans, and winter sports which require mountains. Many of the nonmetropolitan communities which have such facilities have had considerable population increases and economic development. The lake areas in the Ozark-Appalachian region have been growing, as have the winter sports areas in New England and the northern and central Rocky Mountains. While many of these communities have had significant population growth, the per capita income has not increased at the same pace because much recreational employment is seasonal and low-paid (Campbell and Hartman, 1972).

(2) Retirement Communities. Closely related to the recreational communities but not synonymous with them are communities catering to persons seeking places for retirement. Some of the earlier communities of this type were in the desert Southwest, but this phenomenon has now spread to many other parts of the United States. For two decades Florida has received large numbers of retirees, and in the last five years significant numbers of such communities have begun to develop in the Missouri and Arkansas Ozarks and, to a lesser extent, in the mountainous areas of southern Appalachia and the southern Rockies. The development of such communities involves a unique set of problems. Most of the retired people there are on fixed incomes and are often unable to meet the

threats of inflation. Their demands for medical services and other health care facilities are quite high. Such facilities, however, are not usually available in the original rural communities and must be provided. This, in turn, raises property taxes, which are a handicap to persons on fixed incomes.

(3) Educational Communities. Adolescents born in the post-World War II baby boom entered college in the 1960s. The result was a major expansion of higher educational institutions to meet the increased demand. Most state colleges, especially in the South and the Midwest, are located in small communities of less than metropolitan status. Since college students are counted by the Bureau of the Census as residents of the town or city in which they attend school, the increased enrollment in such institutions was reflected in a population increase in the college towns. The rate of increase in the college-age cohort will level off in the mid 1970s and begin to decline in the latter part of the decade. Thus, the rapid population and economic increases in these communities will not be sustained on the basis of college enrollments.

(4) Mining Communities. Throughout the United States, major mineral areas have opened and/or closed during the past several decades. The impact of a large mine either opening or closing is a major influence on the community in which it is located. Such was the case with the opening of copper mines in Montana and the closing of many coal mines in West Virginia. Other examples include the opening of major new lead mining areas in Missouri and uranium mines in various parts of the West. These communities must be considered as individual cases, and it is impossible to generalize except to say that mining has had a large impact on several communities.

Multi-Specialty Centers

Tarver (1972) reports, in a study of communities in the South during the decade of the 1960s, that multi-specialty centers consistently had higher rates of population growth than one-specialty towns. Of the ten types of one-specialty towns, three consistently had the highest rates of population growth: professional, public administration, and wholesale-retail centers (see Table 2.11). Three types experienced substantial reductions in the rate of population gains as compared to the previous decade—agricultural, manufacturing, and construction centers. The latter two are in contrast to the gains reported in a previous section for the total United States. Agricultural towns in the South suffered the greatest reduction in rates of gain.

MANUFACTURING IN NONMETROPOLITAN COMMUNITIES

Recent decades have witnessed a movement of many small labor-intensive industries into smaller communities. These currents have been especially strong in the South and parts of the Midwest. Large numbers of soft goods (primarily clothing), small electrical, furniture, and other industries which utilize compara-

Table 2.11: Population Changes of Southern Towns, 1960 to 1970, Classified by Major Types of Functions in 1960

Type of Industrial Function	Total	Number of Places With 1960 to 1970 Population Losses	Percentage Change in Population 1960 to 1970
One-specialty	352	106	13.9
1. Agriculture, forestry, and fisheries	23	10	2.5
2. Mining	32	21	−.4
3. Construction	30	8	11.5
4. Manufacturing	105	39	6.4
5. Transportation, communication, and other public utilities	29	5	13.8
6. Wholesale and retail trade	48	8	21.7
7. Finance, business and personal services and entertainment	17	3	17.1
8. Professional and related services	40	7	32.7
9. Public administration	21	2	21.6
10. Military	7	3	19.7
Diversified	106	61	8.9
Multiple-specialty	196	82	16.2
Unclassified in 1960[a]	35	18	4.6
Total	789	267	12.9

NOTE: Data from Tarver, 1972, p. 67.
a. Towns with fewer than 2,500 inhabitants in 1960.

tively large numbers of low-paid, low-skilled employees have moved into the Ozark-Appalachian area. These have hired large numbers of unemployed women and underemployed farmers. In the Midwest, the meat packing plants have moved from the metropolitan areas to small towns which are closer to the sources of supply.

The movement of industry into small communities has been very spotty. Parts of the Corn Belt and Great Plains have not received any large amounts of manufacturing or other types of off-farm employment. In such areas, especially those which are suited to large-scale agriculture, a considerable portion of the population remains redundant. Many of the farms are too small and under-capitalized to be competitive. The businesses in the small towns cannot compete with the discount house and supermarkets available in larger centers. Such areas are still experiencing large scale out-migration of the young people.

Small communities, because of their unique characteristics, cannot normally attract an automotive assembly plant. Wallace (in Ottoson et al., 1966) points out:

Rural communities have an advantage in attracting plants that (1) employ less than fifty workers, (2) do not require a highly skilled labor force, (3) are attracted to local raw materials, (4) do not require another local industry to service them, (5) have similar industries nearby, to contribute to a pool of trained workers, and (6) have managements that like a rural atmosphere.

Access to adequate rail and road transportation facilities are also essential.

FARMS AND FARM POPULATION

In 1971 the farm population of the United States was estimated to be 9,425,000 or 4.6 percent of the population—a decline of 0.2 percent in the year following the census, or a decrease in the size of farm population of almost 300,000 people (U.S. Bureau of the Census and U.S. Department of Agriculture, 1972).

The acreage in farms has remained relatively stable, however. It reached a peak in the mid 1950s and has declined almost 8 percent since then. The average size of farms continues to go up. The preliminary 1972 average size of farms is 394 acres—an increase of almost 80 acres in ten years. In 1925, the average was 143 acres.

The decline in the number of farms has been greatest for small commercial or family farms. In 1960 there were 1,277,000 farms which reported sales of from $2,500 to $10,000. In 1969 this number had declined to 675,000, a decline of almost one-half in ten years. In contrast, the farms of over $20,000 sales had increased from 340,000 to 568,000. Obviously some of the change in these two categories is a result of farms increasing the amount of sales and moving to a larger sales category. In the first category, those with less than $2,500 sales, the number of farms declined from 1,800,000 to 1,200,000, or 34 percent (see Table 2.12).

An obvious question which arises is how long the out-migration of the farm population will continue. This is unanswerable, but the rate must be reduced soon if any substantial number of farmers is to remain.

The migration rate for the farm population has been relatively constant since 1940 except for the 1945-1950 period. From 1940 to 1970, the rate of out-migration has varied from 5.2 to 5.8 percent per five-year period. The actual number of farm migrants has declined sharply. Between 1945 and 1950 the net out-migration from the farm population was 1,600,000, while the number was 582,000 from 1964 through 1969.

In some formerly agricultural areas, the growth in nonfarm employment has been enough to offset farm population losses or even to reduce these by making supplemental income available to small farmers. However, in parts of the Corn Belt and the Great Plains, many of the remaining commercial farms are not competitive in size, and little off-farm employment is available. Such areas, which frequently contain large proportions of older farmers, will continue to have out-migration and population losses.

Most farmers are no longer full-time farm operators. The Department of Agriculture estimated in 1971 that two out of every three farmers received over half of their total annual income from off-farm sources. In fact, the total off-farm income of farmers almost exceeded the net farm income (U.S. Department of Agriculture, 1971a).

Two types of integration, vertical and horizontal, can be used to describe most of the major changes in farming operations in the last decade. Vertical integration is the combination of two or more different levels of a process—for example, the combination of producers (farmers) and processors, such as meat packing plants. Vertical integration has been very common in the poultry, cattle feeding, vegetable, fruit, and portions of other agricultural industries. This has assumed two general types. In one the farm is absorbed into a large corporation with a large capital investment and highly specialized personnel. Examples of this type can be found in the fruit and vegetable industries, cattle feeding, and others. In the second type the farmer becomes a contractor of a large corporation and is little more than an employee. Examples are the broiler industry and some portions of the vegetable industry.

Horizontal integration is the combination of two or more units at the same level, such as the consolidation of two or more farms. This type has become common in all types of farming, especially in grain crops, cotton, and other field crops such as vegetables.

Horizontal integration has progressed to the point that by 1970 the largest 223,000 farms (those with sales over $40,000) comprised only 7.6 percent of the total farms but produced 52.5 percent of the total food and fiber output. It has been predicted that if this trend continues, 70 to 80 percent of the total farm production could be concentrated on about 100,000 farms in two or three decades (North Central Public Policy Education Committee, 1972).

These massive changes have been brought about by an explosive development of agricultural technology and an equally dramatic adoption of the technology (Hightower, 1972). The productivity per farmer has been increasing more rapidly than in manufacturing and most other sectors of the economy.

The term "farmer" covers a very broad spectrum, including everyone from the family on welfare with sales of two calves in the year prior to the Census of Agriculture, to the corporation with 50,000 calves on feed and a gross annual sales figure of several million dollars. These extremes have very little in common. As Hathaway et al. (1968: 233) conclude:

> On the basis of the existing definition, living on a farm brings relatively little homogeneity in either social or economic functions. As matters now stand, the major source of homogeneity within the farm population stems from the fact that residence is on a place defined by the census as a farm. These places vary immensely in both physical and economic attributes. Some are still little more than rural residences, while others are multi-million dollar investments in agricultural production facilities.

Table 2.12: Number of Farms by Value of Sales Classes, 1960-69

Year	$40,000 and over	$20,000 to $39,999	Farms with Sales $10,000 to $19,999	$5,000 to $9,999	$2,500 to $4,999	Less than $2,500	All Farms
Thousands of Farms							
1960	113	227	497	660	617	1,848	3,962
1961	123	239	494	625	576	1,764	3,821
1962	135	254	493	590	534	1,679	3,685
1963	144	267	491	558	496	1,605	3,561
1964	146	268	482	533	469	1,544	3,442
1965	160	287	487	502	430	1,474	3,340
1966	184	320	502	464	377	1,392	3,239
1967	182	317	491	447	361	1,348	3,146
1968	193	331	494	420	328	1,288	3,054
1969	211	357	505	389	286	1,223	2,971
Percentage Distribution							
1960	2.9	5.7	12.5	16.7	15.6	46.6	100.0
1961	3.2	6.3	12.9	16.4	15.1	46.1	100.0
1962	3.7	6.9	13.4	16.0	14.5	45.5	100.0
1963	4.0	7.5	13.8	15.7	13.9	45.1	100.0
1964	4.2	7.8	14.0	15.5	13.6	44.9	100.0
1965	4.8	8.6	14.6	15.0	12.9	44.1	100.0
1966	5.7	9.9	15.5	14.3	11.6	43.0	100.0
1967	5.8	10.1	15.6	14.2	11.5	42.8	100.0
1968	6.3	10.8	16.2	13.8	10.7	42.2	100.0
1969	7.1	12.0	17.0	13.1	9.6	41.2	100.0

NOTE: Data from U.S. Department of Agriculture, May 1971, p. 39.

DEMOGRAPHIC CHARACTERISTICS OF PEOPLE
IN NONMETROPOLITAN AREAS

The best comparison of characteristics of residents of various geographic areas would include such items as patterns of behavior and value systems as well as demographic characteristics such as age structure, level of education, and income. Unfortunately, comparisons of only demographic variables are generally available for any classification scheme, rural-urban or metropolitan-nonmetropolitan. The same statements can be made of comparisons at the community level. In recent years, rural sociologists and other students of rural or nonmetropolitan social and economic phenomena have made few systematic comparative studies, with comparative patterns of behavior especially neglected (Copp, 1972). Thus, in the following, a few demographic characteristics have been selected for comparison. If some of the major ecological variations in characteristics of the population in the United States are now based upon size of urban areas, then a metropolitan-nonmetropolitan comparison should reveal some of these differences.

Age. The average age for the United States population in 1970 was 28. The metropolitan average was very similar to this, while the places of 10,000 population or more outside metropolitan areas has a slightly younger average, 26.7. The rural areas were similar to the U.S. average—27.9. The small villages of 1,000 to 2,500 population were slightly higher—30.4 (U.S. Bureau of the Census, 1970). This similarity between most of the major categories is greater than it was in 1960 when there was a three-year variation between urban and rural. This adds additional support to the growing similarity between various categories.

Education. The residents of metropolitan areas remain better educated than do nonmetropolitan residents. Sixty-two percent of the metropolitan population over 25 years of age had completed twelve or more years of school. The comparable figure for nonmetropolitan areas was 50 percent, and only 42 percent for the farm sector. The difference between the two categories of areas was greater in the older age group (forty-five years and over) than in the younger group. In time the differences will be reduced and perhaps eliminated if this trend continues (see Tables 2.13 and 2.14). One possible reason for the nonmetropolitan areas' failure to attract and hold more educated people is that the annual income of nonmetropolitan males with more than four years of college was $1,600 less than that of metropolitan residents with same level of education. This was the largest income differential for any educational level.

Income. Nonmetropolitan per capita income remains substantially below metropolitan per capita personal income. However, during the past forty years the nonmetropolitan has been increasing more rapidly on a percentage basis than the metropolitan income. But the gap between the two groups in dollars has actually widened. In 1968 per capita personal income was $1,200 higher in the metropolitan counties than in the nonmetropolitan. The actual incomes were $3,811 and $2,614, respectively (see Table 2.15). When the income figures are examined by census region, it is found that the least gains have been made in the Southwest, which includes large Spanish-American and American-Indian

Table 2.13: Median Years of School Completed for Persons 25 to 29 Years Old, 1969 and 1960

Race and Year	Both Sexes	Male	Female
Metropolitan Areas			
1969			
All races	12.6	12.7	12.6
White	12.7	12.8	12.6
Negro	12.3	12.3	12.2
1960			
All races	12.4	12.4	12.3
White	12.4	12.5	12.4
Negro	11.4	11.3	11.4
Outside Metropolitan Areas			
1969			
All races	12.4	12.5	12.4
White	12.5	12.5	12.4
Negro	10.9	11.4	10.7
1960			
All races	12.2	12.1	12.2
White	12.1	12.2	12.3
Negro	9.0	8.3	9.5

NOTE: Data from U.S. Department of Agriculture, May 1971, p. 95.

Table 2.14: Educational Attainment of Persons 25 Years and Over by Race and Residence, March 1970

	Percent of Population			
	8 Years of School or Less		12 Years of School or More	
Age and Residence	White	Black	White	Black
Total	26.1	43.0	57.4	33.7
Metropolitan areas	22.1	36.0	61.5	38.8
Nonmetropolitan areas	33.2	60.9	50.0	20.6
Nonfarm	31.7	59.1	51.2	21.6
Farm	43.1	74.5	42.0	11.9
25 to 44 years	11.8	22.4	71.0	47.9
Metropolitan areas	9.4	18.0	74.7	52.2
Nonmetropolitan areas	16.5	36.3	65.9	34.2
Nonfarm	15.9	34.3	66.2	35.3
Farm	21.8	54.1	62.3	23.7
45 years and over	36.8	63.1	46.6	19.9
Metropolitan areas	32.1	55.7	51.2	24.2
Nonmetropolitan areas	44.9	78.9	38.7	10.5
Nonfarm	43.4	77.9	40.0	11.3
Farm	53.5	86.4	31.9	4.6

NOTE: Data from U.S. Department of Agriculture, May 1971, p. 93.

Table 2.15: Per Capita Personal Income by Metropolitan Status, United States, 1929-68

Year	Metropolitan Counties	Nonmetropolitan Counties
1929	$ 928	$ 402
1940	762	353
1950	1,745	1,088
1959	2,448	1,603
1962	2,658	1,791
1965	3,080	2,017
1966	3,296	2,281
1967	3,517	2,419
1968	3,811	2,614

NOTE: Data from U.S. Department of Agriculture, May 1971, p. 30.

populations. The most rapid gains have been in the Southeast, where the non-metropolitan and metropolitan incomes increased at the same rate, 7.6 percent.

The per capita personal income of the farming population was about $200 higher than it was for the total nonmetropolitan population. An increased proportion of the per capita income for the farm population has come from nonfarm sources. When income was examined as a function of the value of the farm products sold, it was found that only if the farms sold more than $10,000 of farm products did farm income become larger than nonfarm income. Interestingly, the total income was about the same, regardless of the amount of farm products sold, for farms selling less than $20,000. The $10,000 to $20,000 category has a total average income of $9,600, and the three lower income categories had incomes ranging from $7,000 to $8,000. The largest increase in total income was for farms with sales of more than $40,000 (see Table 2.16).

Poverty. In a metropolitan-nonmetropolitan comparison, the nonmetropolitan population has a 17 percent poverty rate, while the metropolitan population has a 9.5 percent rate. Within the metropolitan areas, 13 percent of the families in central cities were in poverty, the highest rate of any metropolitan subunit. The nonmetropolitan areas had higher proportions of population in poverty than the central cities, whose poverty situations have been well publicized.

According to the 1970 figures, almost one in five persons in farm families remains in poverty. This is a very marked decline from the 45 percent in 1959, but still remains much higher than the 11 percent for all families.

THE EX-RURAL IN THE UNITED STATES

In attempting to describe the "rural" population of today, we find it has become an urbanized but low density population which remains distinctive in many characteristics. Yet it is moving into the mainstream, the mass culture, of latter twentieth century America.

Table 2.16: Income Per Farm Operator Family by Major Source and by Value of Sales Classes, 1969

Value of Products Sold	Realized Net Farm Income[a]	Off-farm Income	Total Income Including Non-money Income from Farm Food and Housing	Percent Off-farm Income Is of Total Income
All farms	$ 5,437	$5,256	$10,693	49
$40,000 and over	27,503	5,464	32,967	17
$20,000 to $39,999	10,466	3,241	13,707	24
$10,000 to $19,999	6,481	3,141	9,622	33
$5,000 to $9,999	3,630	4,488	8,118	55
$2,500 to $4,999	2,122	4,895	7,017	70
Less than $2,500	1,082	7,011	8,093	87

NOTE: Data from U.S. Department of Agriculture, May 1971, p. 36.
a. Includes government payments.

Portions of the Corn Belt and the Great Plains probably remain as some of the most rural areas in the traditional sense. These areas have not experienced the influx of manufacturing or other types of employment and thus have high rates of out-migration.

The nonmetropolitan and the "rural" areas are heterogeneous both in variation between and within communities. A primarily agricultural community may have little similarity to a resort or mining community twenty miles distant. The welfare recipient has little in common with the airline pilot who lives down the road next to the large dairy farmer, and the latter two may be only nodding acquaintances. Thus, the trademark of rural communities, homogeneity, has largely disappeared.

NEEDED RESEARCH IN NONMETROPOLITAN AREAS

Many of the following suggestions have been made previously in the text or by other researchers.

(1) The whole relationship of nonmetropolitan to metropolitan areas needs to be reexamined for the purpose of establishing new methods of delineating functional ecological units larger than incorporated places. Rogers' (1971) matrix methods might be one point of departure. The conceptual framework of nodal regions has some potential.

(2) Community-wide or large scale studies of the type conducted by rural sociologists in the 1930s needs to be conducted in nonmetropolitan cities to determine the social and economic structure of such units. In recent years, rural sociologists and economists have virtually abandoned the community as a unit of analysis and concentrated on behavioral elements conducive to either statistical manipulation by use of computers, or survey methodology. This situation is the result in part of the funding available from governmental and other traditional sources of research funds.

(3) Time series analyses are needed, beyond those available from the Censuses of Population, Housing, Business, etc. However, even these census data have not been fully exploited. Fuguitt's (1971) study of small towns is a classic example and needs to be repeated for many other community attributes.

(4) A large number of comparative studies of the structure and function of communities in various parts of the U.S. should be made to verify the generalization made in this article concerning the development of a mass culture.

(5) Hathaway et al. (1968: 235-236) suggest the following refined categorization for analyzing the population:

We believe that metropolitan and nonmetropolitan categories now used by the Bureau of Budget should be retained as a fundamental part of a residence classification scheme. Within each of these categories there should be an urban and rural component, with the latter subdivided into village and open-country residence. Thus the proposed classification would appear as follows:

    1. Metropolitan county
      a. Urban
      b. Rural
        (1) Village
        (2) Open country
    2. Nonmetropolitan county
      a. Urban
      b. Rural
        (1) Village
        (2) Open country

(6) A combination of the above suggestions is needed to describe the non-metropolitan areas. First, the places and their hinterlands should be delineated using central place theory. Second, the places should be grouped into homogeneous classes according to some method, e.g., primary industry. The categories could then be examined and compared using the Hathaway et al. classification scheme.

(7) Finally, attention should be called to a workshop sponsored by the National Academy of Sciences (1971: 126-128) on the quality of rural living which resulted in a series of research priorities for rural areas. They include detailed recommendations in the general areas of health, nutrition, welfare, education, housing, employment, and income.

NOTES

1. It is doubtful whether "nonmetropolitan" will ever become as popular as "rural." The terms "rural" and "urban" are deeply ingrained in our vocabulary. The negative and the six syllables in "nonmetropolitan" will have an inhibiting influence on its use.

2. For literature on patterns of dominance and gradients in rural areas, see Bogue (1950: 5-6); Duncan (1956); Anderson and Collier (1956); Stoeckel and Beegle (1956: 346); and Berry (1967).

REFERENCES

Anderson, T. R., and Collier, J. "Metropolitan dominance and the rural hinterland," Rural Sociology, June 1956, 21, 152-157.

Berry, Brian J.L. Spatial Organization and levels of welfare: Degree of metropolitan labor market participation as a variable in economic development. Paper presented to the Economic Development Association Research Conference, Washington, D.C., October 9-13, 1967. Cited by N. Hansen, *Intermediate-size cities as growth centers.* New York: Praeger, 1967.

Bishop, C. E. "The organization of rural America: Implications for agricultural economics." Journal of Farm Economics, December 1967, 49, 999-1008.

Bogue, D. J. *The structure of the metropolitan community: A study of dominance and subdominance.* Ann Arbor: University of Michigan, School of Graduate Studies, 1950.

Campbell, R. R. and Hartman, J. A. "Influence of lakes on population change and characteristics: 1960-1970." Unpublished study submitted to Rural Sociology, August, 1972.

Christaller, Walter. *Die zentralen orte in Suddeutschland.* Jena: Gustave Fischer Verlag, 1933. Cited by A. H. Hawley, *Urban society: An ecological approach.* Ronald Press, 1971.

Copp, J. H. Rural sociology and rural development. Presidential address, annual meeting of the Rural Sociological Society, Baton Rouge, Louisiana, August 26, 1972.

Duncan, O. D. "Gradients of urban influence on the rural population." Midwest Sociologist, Winter 1956, 18, 27-30.

Floyd, F., and Robertson, T. D. "Some urban policy considerations of rural journey-to-work commuting." The Review of Regional Studies, Spring 1972, 1, 29-36.

Fuguitt, G. "The places left behind: Population trends and policies for rural America." Rural Sociology, December 1971, 36, 449-470.

Gillette, J. M. Rural Sociology. New York: Macmillan Co., 1922.

Hathaway, D. E., Beegle, J. A., and Bryant, W. K. People of rural America. 1960 Census Monograph Series. U.S. Department of Commerce. Washington, D.C.: U.S. Government Printing Office, 1968.

Hawley, A. H. Urban society: An ecological approach. New York: Ronald Press, 1971.

Hightower, J. Hard tomatoes, hard times: The failure of the land grant college complex. Washington, D.C.: Agribusiness Accountability Project, 1972.

Hoover, E. M. Some old and new issues in regional development. In E.A.G. Robinson (Ed.), Backward areas in advanced countries. New York: St. Martin's Press, 1969.

International City Management Association. Municipal yearbook, 1972. Vol. 39. Chicago: ICMA, 1972.

Krugel, D. L. "Metropolitan dominance and diffusion of human fertility patterns in Kentucky, 1935-1965." Rural Sociology, June 1971, 36, 141-156.

Losch, August. The economics of location. Trans. by W. H. Woglom. New Haven: Yale University Press, 1954, 105-134. Cited by A. H. Hawley, Urban Society: An ecological approach. New York: Ronald Press, 1971, p. 221.

McNamara, R. L. Population change and net migration in the North Central States, 1960-70. Report of the North Central Regional Project. Population Changes in the North Central States. NC-97. Missouri Agricultural Experiment Station, 1972, in press.

National Academy of Sciences, Agricultural Board, Division of Biology and Agriculture. The quality of rural living: Proceedings of a workshop. Washington, D.C.: NAS, 1971.

North Central Public Policy Education Committee. Who will control U.S. agriculture? Policies affecting the organizational structure of U.S. agriculture. Special Publication 27. Urbana-Champaign: University of Illinois, College of Agriculture Cooperative Extension Service, 1972.

Ottoson, H. W., Birch, E. M., Henderson, P. A., and Anderson, A. H. Land and people in the Northern Plain transition area. Lincoln: University of Nebraska Press, 1966.

Rogers, A. Matrix methods in urban and regional analysis. San Francisco: Holden-Day, 1971.

Schnore, L. F. "The rural-urban variable: An urbanite's perspective." Rural Sociology, June 1966, 31, 131-143.

Stoeckel, J., and Beegle, J. A. "The relationship between the rural farm age structure and the distance from metropolitan area." Rural Sociology, September 1966, 31, 346-354.

Tarver, J. D. "Patterns of population change among Southern non-metropolitan towns, 1950-1970." Rural Sociology, March 1972, 37, 53-72.

Taysby, F. A., Jr., Davidson, L. S., and Clark, D. D. "Flight to the fringes: An empirical study of office decentralization in Atlanta, Georgia." The Review of Regional Studies, Fall 1970, 1, 117-140.

U.S. Bureau of the Census. U.S. Census of Population: 1960. Number of inhabitants, PC(1)-1A U.S. Summary. Washington, D.C.: U.S. Government Printing Office, 1961.

U.S. Bureau of the Census. U.S. Census of Population: 1970. Number of inhabitants. Final Report PC(1)-A1 U.S. Summary. Washington, D.C.: U.S. Government Printing Office, December 1971.

U.S. Bureau of the Census. Statistical abstract of the United States: 1972 (93rd ed.). Washington, D.C.: U.S. Government Printing Office, July 1972.

U.S. Bureau of the Census. U.S. Census of Population: 1970. *Rural population by farm-nonfarm residence for counties in the U.S.: 1970.* Supplementary Report PC(S1)-27. Washington, D.C.: U.S. Government Printing Office, August 1972.

U.S. Bureau of the Census and U.S. Department of Agriculture. *Farm population of the U.S.: 1971.* Series P-27, No. 43. Washington, D.C.: U.S. Government Printing Office, May 1972.

U.S. Department of Agriculture, Economic Research Service, Economic Development Division. *The economic and social condition of rural America in 1970.* Committee Print, Part I. Prepared for the Committee on Government Operations, U.S. Senate, 92nd Congress, 1st Session, May 1971. (a)

U.S. Department of Agriculture, Economic Research Service. Farm income Situation, July 1971, 218. (b)

Wallace, L. T. Your community and industrialization. (mimeo EC-231) South Bend: Purdue University Extension Service. Cited by H. W. Ottoson, E. M. Birch, P. A. Henderson, and A. H. Anderson, *Land and people in the Northern Plain transition area.* Lincoln: University of Nebraska Press, 1966, p. 333.

Wirth, L. "Urbanism as a way of life." American Journal of Sociology, July 1938, 44, 8-14.

CHAPTER 3

URBAN CONCENTRATION AND DECONCENTRATION

Matthew Edel

Queens College

John R. Harris and Jerome Rothenberg

Massachusetts Institute of Technology

THEORIES AND POLICY ISSUES concerning urban concentration and deconcentration center on two distinct, but necessarily related, issues: the number and total size of metropolitan agglomerations, and the degree to which the individual agglomerations are compact or dispersed in their internal arrangements. In each case, a number of economic arguments have been presented concerning the reasons for current patterns in the United States, and concerning ideas of what an "optimal" arrangement might be. For example, new towns and migration affect the first form of concentration, intraurban transportation and central city-suburb fiscal disparities affect the second—and each affects the other. We include sections on both forms of concentration and deconcentration in our analysis.

URBAN AGGLOMERATION

America has been undergoing a steady process of urbanization for well over a century. According to the census, some 69 percent of the population in 1970 was resident in one of the 243 metropolitan areas having more than 50,000 persons. During the past decade, these metropolitan areas increased in population by some 14 percent, slightly in excess of total population growth in the country (U.S. Bureau of the Census, 1971; U.S. Commission on Population Growth, 1972). Undoubtedly, these data understate the full growth of metropolitanized population, since there is reason to believe that substantial growth has also occurred in the "fringe" areas lying immediately outside the officially-designated SMSA boundaries. However, this growth has been far from uniform—variation in growth by city size and region has been substantial.

Table 3.1: Population Growth of U.S. Metropolitan Areas, 1960-70

Metropolitan Area Population, 1970	Number of Areas, 1970	Population in 1970 Boundaries (millions)	Population 1960-70 (millions)	Increase (1970 boundaries) (Percent)
All areas	243	139	20	14
2,000,000 or more	12	52	6	12
1,000,000 to 2,000,000	21	28	6	27
500,000 to 1,000,000	32	22	3	18
250,000 to 500,000	60	20	3	16
Under 250,000	118	17	2	14

NOTE: Data from (U.S.) Commission on Population Growth and the American Future, 1972, p. 27.

Table 3.1 shows variation by city size, a pattern which is similar to growth patterns observed in the previous decade.[1]

The most rapid growth occurred in the South and West and, indeed, thirteen of the twenty-one cities in the one- to two-million class are in those regions, and all of the cities in this size class experiencing growth in excess of 27 percent are in the South and West. Similarly, the slowest growth has been in the North. Of the twelve cities over two million, only 4—Baltimore, Washington, Los Angeles, and San Francisco—are in the South or West. Significantly, these four centers had above-average growth rates as well. Particularly among the smaller cities, the average growth rates conceal wide variations in performance.[2] There seems to be some uniformity of differential patterns among regions. In the newer regions, especially the South and Southwest, particularly rapid growth is occurring in the major regional centers (e.g., Atlanta, Houston, and Phoenix), while in the older-settled regions, relatively smaller centers (e.g., Hartford) are experiencing the fastest growth within the region. In a multiple-regression framework, once region is controlled for, initial population does not explain growth.[3]

While it is interesting to document the patterns of growth and even to project them into the future, such exercises fail to ask why these patterns are emerging, what the consequences of the patterns are for the well-being of Americans, and to what extent the patterns are amenable to purposeful manipulation by government policy.

The fundamental question to ask is, why cities? It is true that measures of urbanization are highly correlated with measures of development in any historical or international cross-section study. This, however, merely indicates association—not causation. Do cities cause or merely follow economic growth? Furthermore, even if urbanization gives rise to—or is a necessary concomitant to—growth, is a pattern of increased concentration in super cities a requisite? Unfortunately, while passionate statements of opinion abound on all sides of these questions, there is a paucity of scientific evidence that can shed light on them.

The distinctive feature of urban complexes is the contiguity of a large variety of activities in space, and it is the possibilities for easy interaction among these diverse activities that give the raison d'être for urban development. Nevertheless, there are obvious costs associated with such concentrated growth: rising transport costs, congestion, high land prices, and rising costs of urban services are economic costs of increased urban scale; there are also social and political costs associated with alienation as local government becomes more remote. It is tempting to think that, up to some scale, the advantages of concentrated activities and eased communication, perhaps accompanied by some economies of scale in providing infrastructure and public services, outweigh the increased costs of scale, but that beyond that size, the costs outweigh further benefits of expansion. If so, can we not identify the optimal-sized city and direct public policy to see that cities are prevented from exceeding this size? This approach has led to the consideration of national urban growth strategies and new towns as a means for implementation (Rodwin, 1970; Moynihan, 1970).

Two main bodies of work have been addressed to this question of optimal urban scale. The first has concentrated on costs of infrastructure and urban services as they vary with city scale (e.g., Brazier, 1959; Hirsch, 1968), while the second has examined relationships between productivity and urban scale (e.g., Alonso and Mera, 1970; Mera, 1970). The evidence on costs has shown that per capita costs generally decline up to some population size ranging between 50,000 and 500,000, depending on the service, with little evidence that these costs start to rise again as population grows beyond these points. Problems abound in attempting to control expenditures for quality levels, and many studies have concentrated on the size of the political or administrative jurisdiction rather than on metropolitan population. Cogent arguments have been put forward that nonmeasured costs of congestion and pollution increase sharply with urban size and that, therefore, diseconomies of scale must exist beyond some finite city size. However, even if it were established that costs of urban infrastructure and services were minimized at some particular city size, it would not follow that this established an optimum size. It is possible that benefits of increasing scale would outweigh the concomitant rise in costs—or the contrary could also be true, that benefits were falling more rapidly than costs. Clearly, the optimum size is that at which *net* benefits are maximized.

What are the potential benefits arising from larger agglomerations of activity? From the standpoint of businesses, larger markets can be reached, more timely information can be obtained, there is access to a wide range of specialized suppliers, and it may be easier to recruit and retain a specialized work force in larger cities. It is clear that in industries marked by uncertain and fluctuating demands, there are advantages in being located in a city where specialized inputs can be obtained quickly (Vernon, 1960; Chinitz, 1961). For households, there are advantages of a larger range of potential employment opportunities, varied and specialized sources of consumer goods and services, and access to a number of cultural activities that are available only in the larger cities. Both firms and households benefit from better access to national transportation and communications facilities that center on large cities. These benefits, while real, are notoriously difficult to define and measure with precision. It is not unreasonable, however, to believe that most of these benefits should become manifest through improved productivity. Alonso (1971) and Mera (1970) have recently examined productivity (measured by per capita output or income) in relation to city scale in a number of countries, including the United States and Japan, and find that productivity so measured increases systematically with city size. There is no evidence that these productivity gains diminish at any existing scale. There are problems in interpreting these findings, since it is not clear to what extent some of the elements measured in the national accounts as output (e.g., transportation services) are in fact costs that should be subtracted from true productivity measures. Also, it does not follow that the larger is the city, the better from a net benefits standpoint, since both measured and unmeasured (e.g., congestion, pollution, social disorganization) costs may be rising even more rapidly than productivity over some range.

Furthermore, it is unlikely that the concept of "an optimal size of city" is meaningful. There may well be a range of optimal sizes for cities performing different functions and changes in transportation, communication and production technology and individual preferences may change these optimal configurations over time. Central place theory has emphasized that there is in fact a hierarchy of cities of differing size performing different functions, although the efficiency of such hierarchies has not been examined (Berry, 1964; Parr, 1970). Evans (1972) has demonstrated that if there are land, labor, and service costs which vary systematically with city size, industries having different input requirements will find it optimal to locate in different size cities. From this analysis, he derives the existence of a hierarchy of city sizes conforming to the rank-size rule. Research is now under way at the Urban Institute to identify the manner in which particular groups of economic activities cluster together in cities of different size (Bergsman, Greenston, and Healy, 1971a, 1971b).

While the evidence at hand is very scanty, it does seem clear that activities concentrated in the largest metropolitan areas are characterized by high dependence on timely information and specialized inputs or, increasingly, are suppliers of specialized inputs to larger markets. Thompson (1965) suggests a series of stages through which cities pass, the highest one being that of a service exporter. Indeed, just as central cities have been gaining in importance as centers for high-level business service activities serving metropolitan areas, so large metropolitan areas have been concentrating on these high-level services to be supplied throughout their hinterland. The continued growth of the largest cities may therefore be caused by technological, managerial, and administrative changes in the economy reinforced by changing patterns of demand.

In recent years, the most rapidly growing sectors of the U.S. economy have been in the services, particularly finance, insurance, data processing, health care, education, and local government. Within manufacturing sectors, it appears that management, control, and coordination are accounting for increasing proportions of costs and employment. And it is these service sectors, dependent as they are on enmeshing into an intricate web of complementary activities, that have been leading the growth of large urban centers. Within metropolitan areas, manufacturing has been leaving the center cities for the suburbs, only to be replaced by service activities (Ganz, 1972). There is some evidence that manufacturing activity is being drawn to smaller urban concentrations (at least relatively), while its place is taken in the largest centers by growing service complexes. Thus, the pattern of deconcentration within large cities may well repeat itself within the larger system of cities, perhaps to the detriment of the existing large centers.

Let us return again to the question of optimal-sized cities. The thread of argument to be followed is that different sizes of cities may be most efficient for different functions. It seems clear that high-level services clustering with corporate and government decision-making centers are most attracted to large metropolitan complexes and undoubtedly find such locations to be efficient. It is interesting to note that the fastest growing cities—Atlanta, Houston, Phoenix, and Denver—are emerging as major centers for corporate headquarters and specialized services serving the least-developed and fastest-growing regions of the country. These cities are emerging into roles already held by the largest centers in the established and slower-growing eastern and north-central regions, where now the fast-growing cities are the relatively smaller ones. These cities are attracting fabrication units and branches of established firms that have found costs and conditions in the largest cities unprofitable. But the essence of the regional "control and service center" is that it centralizes these functions into a single well-integrated complex serving a large area. Even if we found that in some sense per capita benefits were maximized in these large cities, it would not follow that all cities should be of the same size. Historically, the Midwest was too small for both Chicago and St. Louis to be regional centers, and Chicago won—who knows what the relative futures of Houston and Dallas will be!

It remains necessary, however, to identify some measures that will tell us about the net benefits of different urban scales, perhaps for groups of cities performing different functions. Concentrating only on costs or productivity is not sufficient. A case has been made by Harris and Wheeler (1971) that, given sufficient mobility of households and businesses among centers of different sizes, aggregate land values for metropolitan areas will capture the net benefits of agglomeration. That is, the land market capitalizes the net benefits of urban growth. Land-value measures, adjusted to reflect market prices, are available for almost all SMSAs in the United States for 1963; these were analyzed within a multiple regression framework to identify associated variables. The cities form three basic subsamples. One consists of cities that are based primarily on manufacturing; a second, which overlaps the first to some fair extent, contains cities with a high concentration of corporate headquarters and business services—the regional centers; the final group consists of the six largest cities that perform a large number of national and international control functions.

The regression analysis is consistent with the idea that there are increasing and then decreasing economies of agglomeration over a range of population up to about three million. Although one must be hesitant to draw conclusions from this study, given the relative crudeness of the data, it appears that manufacturing cities experience diminishing returns between 500,000 and 1,000,000 population. Beyond the million mark, total land values actually decline in cities without important regional headquarters functions. St. Louis and Pittsburgh are the most notable examples of cities that have grown larger than would be dictated by efficiency. In the second group of cities, those with a large number of corporate headquarters, there seems to be no sign of diminishing returns to scale until the population exceeds one million. Then the net gains diminish less rapidly than is the case with manufacturing-based cities, although beyond a million and a half there seem to be substantial diseconomies of growth. However, for the largest cities, with populations in excess of three million, land values and population rise proportionally, and there is no evidence of downturn in the net benefits as measured by land values. (Incidentally, New York lies close to the regression line calculated with New York excluded from the sample—that is, New York does not dominate the estimates simply because it is the outlying observation.) It seems reasonable to think of these largest cities as performing the high-level coordinating functions of "world cities." There is room only for a very few such specialized centers.

It is interesting to note that the partial relationship between population and land values is significantly nonlinear, which is the basis for the observation of increasing or decreasing returns to scale. We cannot be sure at this point, but it seems reasonable to argue that the assembling of a large labor pool, coupled with scale economies in the provision of some public services, explains the zone of net agglomeration economies, while diseconomies of scale in services and related congestion-pollution phenomena explain the zone of diseconomies of scale. Overriding economies of agglomeration centered around communications and control functions may explain the performance of the largest centers.

We also ran some simultaneous estimates to try to identify the lines of causation between location of manufacturing, administrative, and headquarters functions and population. Population seems to respond to manufacturing and administrative functions, but neither of these economic sectors appear independently drawn to population. Administrative headquarters are explained largely by the presence of Federal Reserve headquarters and headquarters of nonmanufacturing firms in banking, financial, and utilities sectors. Manufacturing activities are best explained by traditional location-theoretic factors, such as access to the transportation network.

There is clear evidence that money wages are positively correlated with city size after factors such as age, sex, race, and education are controlled (Fuchs, 1967; Wertheimer, 1971; Alonso, 1970). Furthermore, it is quite obvious that this variation exceeds differences in living costs, which are much less correlated with city size (Alonso, 1970; Wertheimer, 1971). It is most tempting to interpret these real-wage differentials as the necessary "bribes" that must be paid to attract and retain the urban labor forces. This is consistent with the well-known stories of the difficulty of living in congested, polluted, inadequately serviced, dangerous, and impersonal large cities. Although people might prefer more bucolic surroundings, they are compensated in order to put up with the frustrations of urban life. It is also interesting to note that a majority of respondents in a recent survey indicated their residential preference to be a small or rural community in proximity to a major metropolitan area (U.S. Commission on Population Growth and the American Future, 1972: ch. 4). If this is the case, we must ask why businesses continue to locate in these large cities, despite the higher labor and land costs which they face. We have already indicated that location decisions are a selective process and have identified the need for access to specialized pools of talent, information, and services as the key feature of those service activities that are locating in the largest cities. There is little systematic evidence available on profits related to city size, but what fragments exist do not suggest any systematic relationship. That is, the productivity gains associated with large cities are sufficient to compensate service activities for the higher urban costs which they face.

However, it would be a mistake to conclude that the present pattern is the "best possible in this best of all possible worlds." Indeed, the essence of urban economies is the systematic web of externalities generated as a result of spatial contiguity. We know that markets do not allocate efficiently when market signals received by individual decision units are distorted by the presence of externalities. In fact, a plausible case can be made that these externalities militate against small cities growing when it would be efficient for them to do so, while inefficient growth of very large cities is not discouraged. This is consistent with the empirical evidence of land-value/city-size relationships. We will return to the policy implications of this analysis in the final section.

INTRAMETROPOLITAN SPATIAL DISTRIBUTION

The previous section considered the determinants of city size and presented some evidence on the factors influencing the specific distribution of city sizes in the United States. This section turns to the second element of location, which has been referred to as "urban deconcentration": the dispersal of locations into areas surrounding the centers of cities. This deconcentration, or sprawl, as well as countervailing forces favoring concentration, can be studied as part of the analysis of general patterns of intrametropolitan location.

A considerable literature exists in urban economics (and in related work by urban economic geographers) explaining intrametropolitan location patterns. The analyses draw on the seminal model of land use around a central market first proposed by von Thunen (1966). Many variants of the von Thunen model have been elaborated, describing forces affecting the location of metropolitan activities around central business districts and other nodes of activities. The classic studies of metropolitan land values by Hurd (1903) and Hoyt (1933, 1939), and the work of the ecological school of sociologists, notably Park and Burgess (1925), drew upon its basic logic. In recent years, formal graphic and mathematical versions of the model emphasizing the role of transportation and accessibility have been elaborated by William Alonso (1960, 1965), Richard Muth (1961), Edwin Mills (1967), Lowdon Wingo, Jr. (1961), and Leon Moses and Harold Williamson, Jr. (1967). Ronald Grieson (1971) and Irving Hoch (1969) have added the role of building costs for different land use densities. These models, mathematical or otherwise, vary somewhat in the assumptions they make or the specific influences they take into account. But they share a common basic form, whose general logic we describe in this section.

The models of intrametropolitan spatial distribution we are discussing begin with the premise that the distribution of households and businesses within the metropolitan area is the result of the separate locational decisions made by these different decision makers. While their decisions are "separate," they are not independent of one another or of social constraints. The locational actions of these various actors affect both the relative attractiveness and the prices of different locations to the other actors. Furthermore, the decisions of actors are subject to incentives induced by taxes, regulations, and prejudices.

This section will try to indicate the several kinds of factors which enter into the locational decisions of households and businesses, and how they are affected by the competition of a multiplicity of actors for urban accommodation. A full, formal presentation, statistical estimation, or mathematical manipulation of a model will not be attempted here. We begin with a consideration of factors presumed to influence locational decisions of households and businesses respectively. From this, we pass to consideration of the manner in which markets coordinate these decisions into a location pattern. We also attempt to comprehend American patterns of urban concentration and deconcentration since 1950 in terms of the variables and relationships of the theoretical model implicitly presented here.

Household Location Choice

When a household chooses housing accommodations, it is choosing a bundle of attributes, which may be simplified to four types of components: (1) the housing unit itself, including its lot, (2) the neighborhood, (3) the location with respect to desirable destinations in the rest of the metropolitan area, and (4) the political jurisdiction:

(1) Housing unit—Many attributes are involved here, including size, number of rooms, architectural style and amenities, condition of structure, number of units in the structure, tenure class, and size, placement, etc., of the lot. These characteristics are relevant to the location decision because housing units are extremely durable, predominantly holding over from the past rather than being built afresh each period for each contemporary population. Thus, the characteristics and distribution of units built in previous periods determine to an important extent the alternatives facing a given population at a given time. This influence is strong, but it is not absolute, because existing units can be converted in various ways by their owners to adjust to changing market circumstances.

(2) Neighborhood—This comprises several types of factors: the social class and characteristics of the neighboring households and their housing units; the mix of land uses and their spatial distribution; physical characteristics of the

environment (topography, microclimate, etc.); the variety of private market goods available. Except for the "innate," immutable physical aspects of the neighborhood environment, most of the above refer to the consequences of the location decisions of other households and businesses. It is a particular example of the critically important principle of locational choice in urban areas; the evaluation of urban location is mainly a matter of co-locational economies and diseconomies, e.g., a site is prized or repellent to a given land user not for its intrinsic nature but because of its economic nearness or distance to other activities which are important positively or negatively to that user. Where activities whose relative location is unilaterally or reciprocally important are to be simultaneously located, atomistic market behavior may fail to achieve an appropriate reflection of these interdependencies. Where the interdependencies are reflected in existing, stable neighborhoods, i.e., where co-locators are already, and dependably, settled, atomistic choice can create the appropriate linkages. But in the latter case, under conditions of change, the interdependencies can lead to artificial rigidities of movement unless major portions of the neighborhood can relocate together in clusters.

(3) Location—The "economic distance" of a site with respect to other desirable destinations in the metropolitan area constitutes its "accessibility." Many models of intra-urban location treat accessibility in terms of a single destination—the "center" of the city. This is meant to reflect either an assumption that all desirable destinations are located in this "center," or that, where the locations of all activities are unsettled, location at the center minimizes the expected costs of transportation for any activity to its desirable, but as yet undetermined, destinations. Single-center models can be instructive, but they are potentially misleading, especially where business activities are subject to locational assignments as well as households, and where many of the important destinations have been determined and are not clustered in a single center. Recent American experience shows a considerable degree of multicenteredness in large metropolitan areas. There are many kinds of destination which comprise the household's trip-making behavior. Work trips are probably the most important in terms of total travel costs, but they are by no means the only kind. Moreover, with growing multiple jobs per household, work trips often involve more than one destination center. Other important trips involve school, recreation, shopping, and health care, and these typically involve less concentration of destination than work trips. Site location is significant to the household's choice of housing, not in terms of the sheer physical distances to their desirable destinations, but in terms of the economic costs of overcoming those distances the desired number of times. These costs reflect not only distance but also the travel modes available and their relative effectiveness for different trips. Thus, the placement and quality of different types of roads and public transit and the budget situation and mode preferences of households all affect the prospective travel costs of any trip set from alternative site locations.

(4) Political jurisdiction—Political jurisdiction is an explicit component variable in the choice of housing because the American metropolitan area com-

prises a number of local jurisdictions, and these jurisdictions differ appreciably in both the variety and level of public services provided and in the pattern and level of taxation. Since availability of public services and conditions of tax liability are imposed upon the household simply by its establishing legal residence, rather than subject to its voluntary choice thereafter, these jurisdictional differences are as much an integral part of different accommodations as are the other components discussed above. Jurisdictional differences are not innate. They stem from the political representation of the public service wants of the constituent populations of the several jurisdictions. Thus, they are likely to change either because given individuals change in what they would like the public sector to do or because the population composition of some of the jurisdictions change. Jurisdictional differences have as many dimensions as there are types of public services and tax liabilities. For analytic tractability, these may be simplified to four dimensions: variety of public services, quality level of public services, real property tax rate, and level of other types of tax. A further split of the second into education and all other public services may be warranted.

Each household can be treated as considering all of the available housing bundles in terms of these four attribute categories, and their relative prices, and selecting the one that represents the best price-attribute combination. For a given set of alternatives, their respective prices, and a set of prospective household settlers, these initial selections may not clear the market—i.e., some sites will receive more than one, some will receive no bids. But this disequilibrium is likely to induce changes in relative prices and a further approximation toward market clearing. Full clearing may not occur, because of a variety of informational and moving frictions.

For the question in hand, the pattern of urban concentration, the location process can be expressed in terms of choice of central city vs. suburb. Each household can be thought to consider whether moving to a suburb would bring more gains than costs relative to establishing in the central city.

In making these decisions, two sets of differences are likely to be very important: first, the set of alternative housing bundles is likely to elicit very different evaluations from any given household; second, a given housing bundle is likely to be quite differently evaluated by the set of different households. While some components of any pair of accommodations may elicit similar preferences, there will almost always be some that elicit different preferences. Tastes concerning structure characteristics, family age or size, the location of jobs, preferences about recreation or other private goods and public goods, will tend to establish important differences in relative judgments about alternatives among the population. These preferences are somewhat idiosyncratic to the individual household, but there exist a number of demographic variables that can help to explain systematic components of them. Some population variables are: level of household income, size of family, age of household head, location of principal work place, and racial or ethnic membership. They can be used to predict differences in choice with respect to each of the following aspects of the housing bundle: "quantity" of housing, "quality" of housing, rental vs. ownership tenure, single vs. multiple family occupancy of structure, lot size, density of land use in the neighborhood, public service-tax mix, "quality" of the sociophysical neighborhood environment, and relative and absolute accessibility of site location.

Selection of housing accommodation is a part of the overall budget allocation of the consumer goods, wherein the consumer is deemed to try to maximize his well-being. In making this allocation, patterns of relatedness between the housing package and other commodities are considered in the same manner as for other goods. Implications of this process for the degree of deconcentration in the metropolitan area will be discussed below.

Business Location

Much of what was said about household choice holds for the firm choosing among sites for business activity. Here, however, differences among structure characteristics are somewhat less important, as are lot characteristics other than size. To a greater extent than the household, the firm has significant relations with agents who must either travel or ship to the firm in question and with agents to whom the firm must either ship or travel. So co-locational interrelationships are of especially great importance. Some of these involve linkages that must be spatially intimate, and some involve spatial relations much looser. The former comprise the neighborhood "amenities"; the latter, the wider accessibility component. Unlike households, except for explicit linkages, firms are likely to be uninfluenced by indirect types of neighborhood interaction— i.e., the general environment of the neighborhood does not much affect firms.

The firm is assumed to select a site so as to maximize profits. There are four main issues involved: nearness to sources of input supply, nearness to customers for the firm's output, appropriateness of the cost and structure for efficient carrying out of the firm's business activity, and adequacy of public services and their associated tax liability.

Firms differ substantially with respect to sources of input supply. They range from those which are very heavily dependent on massive input flows from outside the metropolitan area to those which depend mostly on inputs from within the metropolitan area. With respect to customers, firms may cluster in three types: firms engaged mostly in export outside the metropolitan area; firms selling mostly within the metropolitan area, but without substantial clustering of customers in the area; and firms selling primarily to customers tightly clustered within the metropolitan area.

As remarked above, heterogeneity of structure is likely to be less important for firms than for households. The key variables seem to be size and horizontal vs. vertical layout. Similarly, the key land variable is lot size. Similarly, the public service variables are likely to be simpler and fewer than for households. Firms want streets and highways, water, sewerage, police protection, and enforcement of contract. Some of the most complex public services—i.e., education and welfare programs, have considerably less impact on businesses than on households.

From what has been said, it is clear that there are considerable sources of difference among firms in the evaluation of a given set of alternative sites and that these will generally differ appreciably from the evaluations of households. Nonetheless, there are likely to be clusters of likemindedness beyond that experienced with households. The influence of variations in specific determining variables on concentration and deconcentration will be traced below.

The Interactions of Land Users

The last two sections dealt with the nature of the two major kinds of land user (exclusive of government and nonprofit institutions like schools, hospitals, and churches). Their basic goals were noted, as well as the features of available location alternatives that related to goal achievement. Our description implicitly referred to typical individual members of each class of users. It is for each one of these that we can specify a given set of alternatives and their respective prices, and then, in terms of the implicit behavioral model, which underlies the discussion, predict—or explain—the choice that will be made.

In fact, the process to be explained is more complex than this. We are required to rationalize the behavior of the whole population of land users. What is added to the problem by this aggregative dimension is how the competing choices of different users, in their interplay with owners of accommodations, change the initial conditions facing each user. Two kinds of changes should be distinguished: the prices of given alternatives, and changes in the nature of the alternatives themselves. The first of these is essentially the conventional question of how the land market operates, albeit a market with notably special features dealt with below. The second is more novel. It is a reflection of the important role that spatial interdependencies among users play in location decisions. Two facets of this can be in turn distinguished—accessibility relationships and the responsiveness of public-sector variables to location decisions.

The accessibility of a site is the (inverse of the) economic cost of reaching desirable destinations from it. In traditional models, all relevant destinations within a metropolitan area were assumed to be located in a single cluster. This "single center" was thus not solely a description of business clustering, but a behavioral assumption about the overwhelming primacy of certain types of trips over others in defining the locational attractiveness of different sites. That the two aspects of the center are not equivalent can be seen by considering a hypothetical situation in which only one cluster of businesses exists in a given urban area and most businesses are located outside that cluster, but widely dispersed. In this situation, most work trips will not have the center as destination.

Both for descriptive relevance and analytic consistency, we do not assume either that there is only one business cluster, or that all trip destinations are at the center. Trip destinations are assumed to be wherever meaningful co-locational interdependencies exist. But these interdependencies are not innate; they depend on which activities are linked together, and where they decide to locate. Indeed, even this assumes too much, for the identity of linked activities (as for example, seller and customer) itself depends on relative location decisions (such as where a buyer selects the nearest seller from which to buy). So trip origins and destinations are simultaneously determined with location decisions.

In the context of the main question being considered here, this relativism means that the accessibility of a given site depends on where other activities are locating. At a time when most business firms are clustered near the center of the central city of the metropolitan area, a given suburban site may be quite inaccessible; but as more and more firms suburbanize, both job and specialized shopping destinations move closer to the given site: it becomes more accessible. Thus, over and above the changes in accessibility brought about by transportation improvements (such that given origin-destination trips incur lower real costs), accessibility changes when changing locations bring about new destination patterns for any given origin. In the model being implicitly developed here, such endogenous changes in accessibility will be significantly included. It is clear that it tends to augment a process of suburbanization that begins for whatever other reasons.

Accessibility to either a central business district or to preferred destinations in general is not, however, merely a function of location of a site and the other activities. The cost (in money and time) of transport between sites is more important than distance per se. Thus, the improvement of transport technologies in general, as by the invention of the automobile and truck (as well as, in earlier periods, by ferries, street railways, and other carriers), reduces the relative advantage of proximity. Such improvements can be expected to lead, fairly naturally, to a spreading out over wider areas of businesses and households when they occur. Similarly, the subsidization of cheaper or more rapid transportation on specific routes can give an advantage to some locations over others, which may be termed "artificial" by comparison with the situation that holds when all routes must pay their own costs. The relative roles of such "natural" and "artificial" factors in suburbanization are considered in the last section of this paper.

The public service-tax packages provided by different jurisdictions are endogenous in much the same way as accessibility. They depend on the relative locational choices—in this case, jurisdictional choices—of households and businesses. The relationships are, however, more complex. To see this, we must examine what determines the public service-tax packages of different jurisdictions.

We assume the public sector attempts to "represent" the interests of its population. This is perfectly definable only when all members of the population want the public sector to do the same thing. In the context of theory that predicts the average behavior of grouped individuals but not the idiosyncratic behavior of single individuals, this occurs only when the jurisdictional population is perfectly homogeneous. (Even here there is a possibility for ambiguity where a pure redistributional policy is involved: "Doing the same thing" does *not* mean that every household wants government to transfer to *it* the same net sum at the expense of everyone else. This is simply a general impasse. It means rather that all are agreed on some given pattern of net redistribution of assets among the population.)

Such perfect uniformity of population is significantly unrealistic. The inhabitants of any jurisdiction differ. As such, they are likely to disagree on exactly what they want local government to do. The public sector, in this more general case, attempts to compromise the differing interests of its constituents. No definitive theory of political compromise exists. An influential theory held by many economists requires the assumption that constituents' tastes for public action are constrained by a structural uniformity known as "single-peaked preferences." This essentially requires that, whatever the differences in preference, citizens agree on the differing degrees of "extremeness" possessed by different alternatives of public action and always prefer an alternative closer to their most preferred alternative than one more extreme from it. In effect, there is a single underlying dimension along which policy alternatives fall, and citizens always choose in terms of the relative distances of any two alternatives from their most preferred position on the dimension.

When this assumption holds, the compromise that will be adopted by majority rule can be unambiguously predicted. It will be the median preference position on the consensually agreed underlying policy dimension. Such a compromise will treat different constituents differently. There are two sources of difference: both the variety and level of public services and the distribution of tax liabilities are set as a uniform function of an agreed-upon tax base. Thus, the sources of inequality of treatment are the degree to which the compromise variety-level of public services diverges from that most preferred by the constituent and the divergence of his tax liability from the mean liability among all constituents.

The relative attractiveness of different jurisdictions can be seen from this characterization of public sector decision making. Three grounds for systematic preference can be noted. The first stems directly from the existence of inequality of treatment within jurisdictions. The treatment accorded any given individual depends on who are the other constituents. On the service side, the more dissimilar he is to the majority, the greater will be the discrepancy between the compromise service level (variety) and his own preferred level. On the tax side, the more his tax base exceeds the mean in the jurisdiction, the more he will be subsidizing other constituents in the financing of public services.

Thus, suppose a household head is faced with two alternative jurisdictions. In the first, the majority is very unlike him in policy tastes and much poorer in tax base, and in the second, they are very like him in policy tastes and either much richer or at least as rich. The household will thus be much better off in the second than in the first. If policy tastes are closely related to possession of tax base, the possibility of being heavily subsidized by tax differences is offset to some extent by a greater discrepancy between desired and actual public-service level.

What the above implies is that households will generally find it advantageous to reside in socially relatively homogeneous jurisdictions, rather than in those where they are significantly richer than the average or preponderant household. It will, on the other hand, pay some households to reside in jurisdictions where they are significantly poorer than the average or preponderant household. This latter incentive, however, is inconsistent with the advantage of those richer households. Consequently, the richer will have an incentive to exclude the poorer from locating among them (generally for reasons of neighborhood amenities as well as public fiscal advantages). Such exclusion can be accomplished explicitly through discriminatory land market transactions or indirectly through zoning and code regulations that make the jurisdiction less attractive—because more expensive—to the poor.

The second ground refers to the distribution of public services. Public services are not consumed equally by all constituents. Only families with school-age children use the schools, only certain families use mental hospitals, certain highways and parks, old-age facilities, and the whole apparatus of welfare aids. The presence of such special groups in large numbers may lead to unusually rich provision of these special services. But even where they have only minority voting power, these groups will generally share disproportionately in majority-voted programs and services. (In economic terms, many locally provided services are not "pure public goods," where the simple availability of the goods ensures equal consumption of them by all.)

Most models of urban location treat local public services as a single kind of homogeneous commodity. In these terms, the unequal distribution can be treated simply as a different quantity of the homogeneous "good" being consumed by different members of the population. At this level of abstraction, the most notable beneficiaries of unequal consumption are welfare clients, who have regular "amounts" of services available to them as well as the nontrivial extra services embodied in welfare aid. For simplicity, assume that this extra is a constant for any welfare client throughout the metropolitan area; then we may characterize the public-service distribution in any jurisdiction as an equal basic share for each nonwelfare family, and that same basic share plus the constant welfare extra for each welfare family.

Suppose two jurisdictions with the same overall populations have appreciably different numbers of welfare clients. Then the same total expenditure for public services in both will buy a considerably smaller basic share of services per family in the jurisdiction with the higher welfare load than in the one with the lower welfare load. Alternatively, the same basic public-service share per family will cost much more in the high-welfare-load jurisdiction than in the low-welfare-load jurisdiction.

Thus, *all* families—including welfare clients—have an incentive to reside in a low-welfare-load jurisdiction, since their expenditures there buy them more public services. Of course, the very universality of the incentive would tend to wipe out jurisdictional differences in this regard. But both "natural" and "artificial" circumstances operate to maintain significant differences and thus net fiscal advantages for those who can avail themselves of certain opportunities. High travel costs (a "natural" circumstance) and minimum lot zoning and various other forms of implicit and explicit exclusion ("artificial" circumstances) maintain these advantages. As a result, an impetus is given to wealthier families to locate in relatively homogeneous high-income suburbs some distance from job clusters and other main metropolitan trip destinations.

The first two grounds for fiscal advantage stem from the distributional effects of ordinary public-sector activities (i.e., from the fact that public output is not "sold" to each constituent at the marginal cost of providing it). The third ground, however, stems from a distortion in the allocation of resources that occurs because of interrelations across jurisdictional lines. Some public services cannot easily—or profitably—be restricted to the use of only jurisdictional residents. The streets, police and fire protection, garbage collection, etc., offered by one jurisdiction can be availed of by residents of other jurisdictions at zero or token cost, thereby increasing the cost of providing any given quality level of these services to its own residents. While some reciprocality of jurisdictional cross-use occurs, there is likely to be an important asymmetry in many metropolitan areas. Suburban residents are much more likely to make use of central-city public services than the reverse. The extent of the asymmetry depends on the degree to which desirable metropolitan trip destinations are located in the central city. Thus, it will differ among metropolitan areas. Since in each case genuine third-party interests are improperly represented in the resource-use decisions, efficient use of resources is frustrated by the public sector.

All three grounds of fiscal advantage favor suburban jurisdictions over the central-city jurisdiction, especially where relatively homogeneous high-income-level communities can be established there and remain protected by a variety of exclusionary factors. Like subsidization of transport on specific routes, this imparts an "artificial" boost to decentralization, over and above what might be called the "natural" stimulus from co-locational linkages of activities and relative attractiveness of different kinds of accommodation. It arises from the special nature of the local public sector, especially the absence of a single encompassing metropolitan level of government. It is discussed further below.

The relative attractiveness of different jurisdictions depends at any time on the particular collections of constituents that make them up, for differences among these determine the fiscal differentials. Thus, when events occur in the system that tend to change the respective population compositions of the different jurisdictions, their relative fiscal advantages will tend to change as well. This is the respect in which the public-sector components of accommodations are endogenous in the system instead of being fixed at will.

Along with jurisdictional effects and the effects of transport on accessibility, imperfections in the operation of land markets may affect the accommodations when individual site choices are aggregated. The multiplicity of user-seller interactions is mediated by the urban land market.

If the land market were perfect, lots of all sizes and characteristics would be available each market period, all traders would be fully informed about all market opportunities as well as their prices, all landowners and users would be active traders in each period, and the transactions engaged in by any group would have no effect on any other trader, except in influencing the availability and prices of different accommodations. Each lot would then be sold or rented to the highest bidder—i.e., the user with highest productivity (or utility) on that lot, and the price established would just equal the surplus of that productivity (utility) over what could be obtained on the next best lot. Similarly, for each user, the lot chosen would represent the best compromise between attractiveness of accommodation and price. As a result, the available land would be allocated among users in an efficient way: overall output would be maximized, each seller would be getting the highest price possible, and each buyer would be making the best deal available.

The real-world land market is not, however, perfect. It diverges in very important ways. First, urban land is not homogeneous. It is, for the most part, improved. The improvements are heterogeneous, highly durable, and expensive to remove. Second, transactions and resulting changes in occupancy (e.g., legal and moving costs) are very expensive. As a result, most users are active traders in the market only infrequently. Third, because of accommodation heterogeneity and the occasional availability of different accommodations, information requirements for active traders are great and costly, thereby aggravating the immobility of land owners and users. Lastly, the accommodation choices of groups of traders have important effects on other traders by changing the relative attractiveness of different accommodations as well as through availabilities and prices. These are the co-locational externalities discussed above which are so important in this market.

The upshot of these divergences is that there is no longer a presumption that land will be allocated efficiently. Frictions and the chance coincidences of being active traders will make some pairings of site and user less than optimal. Moreover, co-locational externalities will in some cases increase the frequency of required adaptations beyond what frictions will make worthwhile. In other cases, these externalities, especially in the form of neighborhood "character," will narrow relevant options to individual traders, sometimes to the point of significant rigidity. Owner transactors will not always obtain the highest price possible for their property; user transactors will not always obtain the best possible deal. Moreover, nonmovers will not in general be content with their present accommodations. Prices will not in general show the extent of surplus being enjoyed by users.

Lags of this sort can affect urban land use patterns in a number of ways. Situations may arise in which the land in some area is subject to high bids from one class of user, while buildings or neighborhood characteristics there may favor the occupancy of some other users. The problems that can arise in this case are discussed in Edel (1972) and Rothenberg (1967). Policies such as urban renewal that alter the composition of the building stock, or zoning and health codes that control its use, may speed or slow market adjustments in some cases. The cost of reconstruction or reassembly of land in old districts may be a factor leading to more rapid suburban deconcentration in some older cities. On the other hand, the immovability of some services, which might be located in diverse locations if built afresh, may impede deconcentration in other old cities with established central business districts. "History matters" in the current land market, but the extent to which it will cause either greater or lesser suburbanization may be a matter of institutional factors affecting the speed of land use conversions in existing areas. Inequality in treatment of new construction vs. reconstruction, for example, may be a biasing factor in the development of a city, parallel in its effects to jurisdictional pressures and transport subsidy.

Implications of the Model for Centralizing and Decentralizing Patterns

Our real-world context is that of growing metropolitan areas. Some sources of such growth have been touched on in the first part of this paper. If these growth forces do not affect any of the determinants of relative location, we would expect a balanced expansion both horizontally and vertically: the urban area would get larger, but some portions of the previously developed area would become more densely used. Because history matters, the CBD of the central city does have special status as an attractive force, despite the possibility of multi-centeredness. Development will breed a conflict in evolving urban form. The new population can establish itself either in the erstwhile undeveloped periphery of the urban area or can increase the density of the developed portions. The latter is usually more expensive than the former, involving conversion of existing structures or demolition and clearance of existing structures, plus new construction of higher-rise—and thereby typically more expensive—structures. But the option of horizontal expansion involves locations less accessible to existing desirable trip destinations, and this offsets the higher development cost of vertical expansion to some extent. As a city grows, there will be a balance of horizontal and vertical development, since otherwise the net attractiveness of the mode too heavily pushed will be considerably less than that of the mode neglected. Systematic choice in the latter, to take advantage of the differential, will bring them back into rough balance. Perhaps the *relative* distribution of densities would remain approximately unchanged, even as the overall density grew.

Prices of accommodations will reflect the attraction of accessibility and the high cost of dense land use. The price of land will tend to be least at the periphery of the urban area and will increase with higher accessibility as well as neighborhood quality. Thus, it will tend to increase irregularly toward the center, the irregularities reflecting richness of transportation facilities and neighborhood quality. The price of accommodations will reflect the underlying price of land as well as the reproducible—and convertible—quality of the existing structure. Its discrepancies from a smooth monotonic increase toward the center will be considerably more marked than the price of land alone.

The balance between horizontal and vertical expansion may be even more rough, however, because of a variety of factors. In what follows, we shall impose on the implicit model a number of essentially exogenous changes in some of the variables we have presented as influencing location. The changes are those that actually happened in the postwar period. Their impact on urban deconcentration will then be inferred from the properties of the model. We are thus to be interpreted as either making predictions from the model or as explaining historical occurrences in terms of the model. What follows is not simply historical narrative.

Economic growth brings two opposing influences to bear on mean family income. Most households already situated in the SMSA experience rising incomes over time. But the migration of population from rural to metropolitan areas consists disproportionately of poor people—many of them potential welfare clients. This increases the overall welfare load of the SMSA jurisdictions in which they choose to reside. This latter decision is essentially made for them by the combination of high clustering of unskilled jobs and nearly unique present availability of low-quality housing units and of additional existing units that are easy to convert to provide low-quality services.

Families with rising incomes are likely to want to purchase more land, more housing quality, and more accessibility. The first is cheaper in the suburbs, but the third implies a desire for closer location. On the basis of this alone, it is not possible to predict their location choices. Such choices depend on the relative preferences for land and accessibility, and the relative prices. In the postwar period in the United States, sociological factors probably raised the attractiveness of low-density living relative to dense urban interaction, especially to middle-class families with young children. In addition, the price of transport fell dramatically—i.e., the penalty for living in the suburbs declined. Thus, within this situational change, rising incomes induced heavy suburbanization beyond what would be predicted from growth alone. The mean density of the overall urban area actually fell.

The growing absolute presence of poor migrants in the SMSA augmented this trend through public-sector changes. It made the advantages of jurisdictional separation greater: a chance to upgrade neighborhood quality (including higher-level public services) that had slipped with migration flows, and the possibility of reaping fiscal advantages from increasing fiscal differentials. So suburbanization was fed by direct demand adjustments to own higher incomes and indirect adjustments to the effects of others' lower incomes on the fiscal advantages of changing jurisdictions.

Regarding transportation two extremely important forces operated to enhance its quality and lower the price in urban areas. First, the technological development of the automobile achieved significant improvements in personal transportation, perhaps even at lowered real cost (calculated in terms of constant quality). Second, the federal government heavily subsidized significant improvements and expansion of the urban highway system. This was especially notable in the growth of expressways for long-distance commuter traffic between outer suburbs and the inner city.

These events significantly lowered the economic penalty of long distances to the CBD. This was reinforced by another aspect of accessibility—the location of desirable trip destinations. The technological development of the truck as a cargo carrier and the interstate express-highway system made suburban sites for businesses near such highways more attractive than heretofore. A suburbanization of business followed. This further decreased the penalty on households for locating far from the center, since more job and shopping-trip destinations became suburban. Thus, for a variety of reasons the accessibility of suburban sites for residence increased markedly. The demand for more land could be achieved at low real costs.

Two factors concerning housing contributed further to the pattern of suburbanization. The middle-class demand for lower-density living was increased by a fall in the real price of single-family, owner-occupied units in the suburbs that resulted from the substantial federal subsidy to such dwellings through FHA and VA insured mortgages and from income-tax deductions for interest and real-estate taxes paid. No such subsidy went to multiple-unit structures or their renter occupants, and little went to units in central cities in any case, because of much lower availability of vacant land for FHA tract development. The asymmetry in subsidized-housing finance tilted incentives in the inner city toward converting existing units to low-quality occupancy, and thus contributed to the growing homogeneity of poor ghetto communities in the central city. This in turn aggravated the white, middle-class exodus to the suburbs by raising the potential gains from neighborhood improvement and the fiscal advantages of a separated jurisdiction.

Business suburbanization was abetted not only by the partially artificial subsidization of transportation but also by the more natural process of technical change. Horizontal layouts on large lots became more attractive for production efficiency in some industries than older vertical layouts. The resulting need for much larger lots and lower land-density operation made inner-city locations much less desirable relative to suburban locations than they had been. Not only were the former much more expensive, but lots of the requisite size were often simply unavailable, because of heavy development. Large enough lots were easily available and much cheaper in the suburbs. Moreover, such lots could be co-located to take better advantage of the newly attractive truck-expressway transportation than could inner-city locations. As noted above, business suburbanization is both an incident of suburbanization and an impetus to further suburbanization by households and other businesses for co-location reasons.

Some Empirical Evidence

The model we have been outlining, and which is presented more formally (in various aspects) in the works cited previously, predicts (at least retrospectively) the general form of settlement of the traditional American city and some of its recent evolution. That the city, in periods of high-cost transportation, should have evolved with a densely-settled core with high land values, and that density and land-value gradients should have grown flatter over recent decades, are observations consistent with the model. The general trend toward intraurban deconcentration has been amply documented by Basil Zimmer (this volume). Some statistical estimates by economists on the specific forms of the changes, particularly as they have affected land values, are worth mentioning.

The flattening over time of land-value gradients has been demonstrated for Chicago (Mills, 1969) and for the Boston Metropolitan Area (Edel and Sclar, 1971). Intercity comparisons covering recent periods indicate flatter density gradients, in general, for newer cities, and a trend toward the flattening of gradients (Muth, 1969). Recent suburbanization in older and newer cities has involved similar density patterns in newly urbanized sectors of metropolitan areas, even when net gradients are different because of differing sizes of old and new sectors (Kain and Quigley, 1969).

Several elements in the model have been shown to affect either land-use density or land values. Access to the central business district (Alonso, 1965), to additional centers of atrraction such as the Chicago waterfront for nineteenth-century businesses (Fales and Moses, 1971), to amenities such as parks (Wabe, 1971) and beaches (Kryzwicki, 1972), and to better-funded schools (Oates, 1969) have been shown to increase density or values. Negative factors have included pollution (Ridker and Henning, 1967) and higher taxes (Oates, 1969). The net effect of neighborhood segregation is more complex. Several studies have shown that the exclusion of blacks from some neighborhoods drives up land values in the ghetto to which they are confined (Laurenti, 1960). (One study finds that proximity to white neighborhoods may increase values, but whiteness here may index other amenities from which blacks have previously been excluded; see Bailey, 1966.)

These studies have given some support to the assumptions of the general land use model as to what kinds of influences may affect or repel users. However, they do not yet amount to a general modeling of land-allocation processes. The interrelations between different groups, either through rent competition for space or through negative or positive co-locational influences, are not explicitly shown in the mere fitting of gradients, nor is the simultaneous clearing of market for land in different parts of the metropolitan area. Attempts to build more complex models, showing the allocation of different properties to different users simultaneously, have been undertaken for several purposes. Some, designed to show the allocation of housing among different income groups, have over-simplified location and co-locational influences (Grigsby, 1962; Rothenberg, 1971). Others, designed to predict future use of transportation facilities, have not explicitly included pricing mechanisms, or have merely projected past trends into the future. (These studies are summarized in Lowry, 1968.) The modeling of more complex land-allocation processes is, however, being attempted in some new studies, now in their early phases, including a study of Detroit by the National Bureau of Economic Research (Ingram, Kain, and Ginn, 1972), and a study of Boston undertaken at MIT (Engle, Fisher, Harris, and Rothenberg, 1972).

Pending the improvement of modeling of specific cases (which will require both better data and better computational algorithms), much of what can be said about the relative weight of different factors in affecting urban land use and locational decisions is necessarily imprecise. Although the direction of influence of different factors can often be stated unambiguously, their quantitative contributions to change cannot always be known. The limits to knowledge implied become apparent when the magnitude of deconcentration is to be *evaluated*.

CONSEQUENCES OF CONCENTRATION AND DECONCENTRATION

We turn now to the problem of evaluating current trends in urban concentration and deconcentration. To the extent that population is concentrating more and more in large metropolitan areas, and dispersing to the suburbs within those metropolitan areas, questions may be posed about the desirability of those trends, either from the viewpoint of their effect on economic efficiency of the nation's productive apparatus or from the viewpoint of their effects on the distribution of benefits. In principle, there are often accepted—but not universally acceptable—methods of evaluating costs and benefits. In practice, however, the application of these is extremely difficult when dealing with large-scale or long-term trends, rather than single projects. One problem common to such analyses is the need to posit some alternative against which an existing degree of concentration is to be compared. When the simple "build/don't build" alternatives of standard project analysis do not apply, positing a "contrafactual alternative" requires considerable discretion. The problem has been discussed, although not resolved, in recent debates among economic historians. A second problem is one of whether or not prices and income distributions in the rest of the economy may be taken as givens for the purpose of a normative analysis.

The effect of these problems on the evaluation of urban concentration is potentially serious. One may argue, as above, that land values in part measure agglomeration economies. But such economies are system-dependent. Thus, for example, one may consider the probable change in land values in the area of Versailles after Louis XIV arranged that all nobles should move to the court and vie with each other in the display of loyal extravagance. Surely, for the nobles who were willing to join the competition, the benefits of nonexclusion from royal favor exceeded the costs. The net of these benefits from joining the agglomeration would, no doubt, have been reflected in land rents. By this land-value criterion, Versailles realized considerable agglomeration economies compared to the average feudal-castle complex. Nonetheless, history records that the drain of resources to the royal court was a factor in the undermining of the feudal economy of France, bankrupting the aristocracy and squeezing the peasants, with the result that two reigns later the entire system faced the deluge. Was agglomeration warranted? A believer in the divine right of kings could accept the land-value measure as indicating that the agglomeration was beneficial; we cannot.

Similar questions have been raised about the value of the large headquarters-city today. If corporate and public bureaucracies are accepted as a normal part of the workings of industrial society, then the only normative question about New York or Tokyo is whether they are a little too large for their headquarter roles; if the large institution is in a larger sense not necessary, then they may be costly aberrations like Versailles. On the one hand, William Alonso (1971) has argued the efficiency of the large city; on the other hand, Stephen Hymer (1972) has called the large metropolis a facet of the peculiar pattern of uneven development intrinsic to hierarchial capitalist systems, but having no intrinsic economic or ethical advantage. These different positions stem from different analyses and evaluations of the economy as a whole, not from observation of the big city per se. At a more microscopic level, the question of whether face-to-face contact or quick transfer of documents (as opposed to telecommunication alone) is necessary for higher-level decision making and contact in bureaucracies is an open one. It appears necessary for their operation; executives believe it necessary; and this has long been cited in agglomeration theory (Haig, 1926; Vernon, 1964). But is it really a technological necessity, or are executives trapped by custom against trying new technologies now available? Models of alternative communication systems would have to be developed and "costed-out" before a full answer could be given.

Similar considerations affect the evaluation of suburban deconcentration. Models of a "natural" market equilibrium of the city show a downward-sloping land-value gradient as one moves away from the center, but so do models of an equilibrium affected by negative externalities to residence at the core, or by vicious circles of fiscal balkanism. In either model, an improvement in transport technology will lead to a flattening of the gradient, but so will any unwarranted subsidization of transport. In most metropolitan areas, a downward sloping gradient is observed, and it has grown flatter in many cases over the past century. But these observations alone do not prove which of the alternative causes is at work or what proportion holds between the two. Similarly, models that consider the effect of transportation or of amenities on house values measure these, taking prevailing technologies, consumer awareness, and lack of alternatives as given.

For example, it may be asked whether the cost of pollution can be measured by the statistical association between pollution and property values. This association may measure the costs imposed on households by pollution, if the prices households bid for land rationally reflect the true cost and disutility of dirty air, and if the market selects the potential highest bidder efficiently. But it will be a poor measure if pollution varies little throughout the area, or if markets work poorly, or if households ignore the cost in their bids (Edel, 1971). Similarly, the effect of highway access on land values, or the effect of income increases on the demand for cars, are both measures by taking as given the existence of only sparse public-transit alternatives (Mohring, 1965; Kain, 1967a). Because of these uncertainties, the parameter values cannot be accepted as unambiguous evidence for the claim that the benefits of present urban form exceed their costs—that, in effect, the present situation reflects just what the population wants. Testing that claim requires consideration of the contrafactual alternative.

Lacking a single certain test to evaluate concentration and deconcentration, the economist is forced to fall back on more circumstantial evidence, which depends (like any such evidence) on the receptiveness of the interpreter for any credibility it may have. Taken in this perspective, however, circumstantial evidence is accepted within narrowly defined limits by the judiciary, and the economist cannot afford to reject it entirely. One can find a strongly suggestive circumstantial case, on grounds of overall allocative efficiency, for the existence of overconcentration of U.S. population in metropolitan areas larger than they need be, and for excessive deconcentration ("sprawl") through suburban development within these and other metropolitan areas. There is, in addition, some evidence of adverse distributional consequences: there is an unequal regressive incidence of the costs and benefits of these processes, which places particular burdens on specific groups and strata within the population. We now turn to brief "briefs" on the evidence.

Metropolitan Size Effects

The evidence on metropolitan size may be presented first. Leaving aside questions of the inevitability or dispensability of large organizations and their face-to-face communication at top levels, it does appear that agglomeration benefits are not uniform over the entire size range of American cities. The advantages of the four or five largest metropolitan areas may be unique, for it would appear that the smaller "regional headquarters" cities show declining returns above a certain size (still not precisely determined); the same is true, above a smaller size, for nonheadquarters industrial cities. Both the land-value approach (Harris and Wheeler, 1971; Edel, 1971) and the comparative-wages approach (Alonso and Fajans, 1970) show only a very weak size-value association in the middle-size ranges of metropolitan-area population. Thus, whatever the necessities of growth for New York in its competition with Tokyo, or the prospects of Houston or San Francisco in seeking to compete for those same functions, there are grounds for a size-limitation policy to slow down future growth of cities like Portland or Denver, which are out of that level of competition. From an efficiency viewpoint, there may be reason also to allow the population of Pittsburgh, St. Louis, and other manufacturing SMSAs to decline. On the other hand, evidence exists in favor of a new-towns policy that would stimulate growth in industrial areas of 250,000 or (where regions are not preempted) in commercial-bureaucratic centers of perhaps 750,000. For the largest cities, further study is warranted to discover which metropolitan functions could be removed or decreased in scale from present agglomerations and moved to new towns. The market appears to be presently deconcentrating the location of some manufacturing industries and retirement residences away from these cities. The prospects for other desirable deconcentration through public policy should be examined.

That there may have been agglomerative overconcentration from an efficiency viewpoint leads to consideration of the distribution of the costs of such concentration. Here the evidence is mixed.

The migration facet of urban concentration involves some of these costs. The plight of new migrants in cities has become better understood in recent years, especially as articulation of it gains in distinctness with political organization. This is often discounted as offset by the presumed greater gains from migration, since migration is voluntary. But this comparison is based on the prevailing rural and small-town conditions that induced departure. There is some presumption that the poverty and depression from which migrants have moved is the result of inappropriate public-policy commissions and omissions—e.g., the encouragement of farm consolidation and underinvestment in depressed-area urban centers (Kain and Persky, 1967). The resulting "artificial," or in any case avoidable, migration pattern may well be both inefficient and inequitable. Relative to an alternative policy of strengthening rural and small urban centers, the induced migrants are probably worse off in their present situation in the large cities.

Metropolitan concentration has had distributive consequences for nonmigrants as well. Urban growth raises some social overhead costs. The size of these diseconomies of scale, and the range of city sizes in which they occur, are debated. Adams (1965), in a comparative study of local government costs aggregated by counties, finds that density of population and proportion of area which is urbanized have a significant positive association with per capita expenditures in most categories. In all of these studies, however, there is no control for the quality and variety of public services rendered in an expenditure category. The apparent diseconomies of scale may actually be a reflection of higher quality, or even more likely, of the greater variety of services, which are only feasible at large scale. Where only specific public services that have easily quantifiable outputs have been studied, the literature on economies and diseconomies of scale uncovers neither measurable diseconomies nor economies for jurisdictional units above about a quarter of a million in population.

Other quasi- and non-governmental costs rise with urban size, most notably those of transportation. The level of congestion and air pollution and some other economic "bads" also tends to rise. Although Alonso and Fajans (1970) and Shaper (1970) argue, on the basis of Bureau of Labor Statistics data, that the cost of living does not rise in larger metropolitan areas as a direct function of size, their data groups too many cities together in size classes to be conclusive. It is also unclear whether the consumer price index counts all costs. Indeed, the coexistence of higher nominal wage levels in larger cities with more rapid migration to medium-sized cities suggests that the higher wage rates are compensating for higher hidden costs of living in the larger cities, and that real wage rates are actually higher in the smaller centers (Hoch, 1969).

Increasing costs with metropolitan growth may put a strain on the responsiveness of local governments. Ultimately, both increased public costs, reflected as taxes, and increased private costs such as commuting and health care, will be borne by businesses and individuals. The mobility of individuals in a job market means that some of the costs initially borne by households may be shifted to employers through demand for higher wages in high-cost areas (Strotz, 1966; Strotz and Wright, 1970). But capital is frequently more mobile than labor, so it is unlikely that most costs are shifted to employers. Within categories, too, mobility may vary. Employers with monopoly power may successfully pass on much of their tax, congestion, and wage costs to consumers and other businesses outside the specific metropolitan area. But not all agents have either high mobility or monopoly power. The less mobile the household or business, the greater will be the burden. Thus, the principal victims in a city when new individuals arrive are fixed-income individuals, less mobile workers, and immobile small businesses caught in the squeeze of rising taxes, transport costs, and delivered input or consumer-goods prices.

Effects of Suburbanization

In the case of suburbanization within metropolitan areas, it is possible to document a number of costs that are not internalized in decisions to suburbanize. Thus, a circumstantial case can be made that an inefficiently high level of deconcentration occurs; but this qualitative case does not indicate whether the optimum is considerably, or only slightly, less than the actual level.

One set of costs that are not borne fully by suburban land users and residents in many metropolitan areas are costs associated with commuter transportation. Both journeys to work (which account for approximately one-third of automobile trips) and a portion of all shopping, recreation, and business-to-business trips take place between suburbs and cities. They impose costs both on surrounding communities and on other road users. There are several reasons why automobile users do not bear all of the costs. In the first place, some of the costs of congestion-delay and auto-use are imposed on other cars, which are not compensated in the absence of adequate congestion tolls (Walters, 1961; Vickrey, 1963). Second, although costs of construction of the interstate highway system and some state highways are borne entirely through gasoline (auto-use) taxes, the collection of these taxes on a per-gallon basis rather than a true cost-per-car-mile basis involves some subsidization of the urban journey to work at the expense of intercity and other trips (Meyer, Kain, and Wohl, 1965). Third, not all road costs are borne by the gasoline tax. Often, only new road construction is subsidized from outside local jurisdictions. Road maintenance is often financed by local property taxes or other local levies. Costs of noise, air pollution, accidents, higher resident auto-insurance rates, costs of relocation, reduction of local-service scale economies through land-taking, and disruption of neighborhood communities may all be borne by the neighborhoods through which roads pass. Metropolitan-wide taxation helps to spread some of these costs to suburbanites, but even where there are formal metropolitan authorities (such as the Metropolitan District Commission parks district of Boston), the costs are still borne to a large measure by less-suburban communities.

The quantification of these costs is difficult. Air-pollution effects on land values have been measured, although the measurements suffer from the ambiguities mentioned above. The effect of automobile commuting on pollution itself can be measured partially with current computerized diffusion models of airsheds, while a study of lead content shows higher levels in the blood of those in the inner city of Los Angeles than of those in more suburban parts of the country. A study of land values in the San Diego metropolitan area shows lower land values within a quarter mile of freeways than at a half-mile distance, ceteris paribus (Kryzwicki, 1972). This has been replicated for Chicago (Burkhardt and Rothenberg, 1971). Finally, one of the authors is engaged in a study of Boston-area transport costs that shows higher costs of automobile insurance and local road maintenance, as well as a disproportionate bearing of metropolitan commission transport assessments, in the inner ring through which many commuters pass (Edel and Sclar, 1971). Further efforts in measurement are clearly called for, but it does appear that, in many cases, those remaining in the inner rings of a metropolitan area subsidize some of the costs of transit of those who are suburbanizing. This will, ceteris paribus, necessarily lead to a more dispersed pattern of settlement than would result if each commuter bore all of the costs he imposed, although the magnitude of this effect cannot be ascertained at present.

The fiscal balkanization of metropolitan areas creates a similar incentive to suburbanize in order to escape tax costs and differential public service levels, which would not be present given a wider uniform tax base. Evidence of differential tax rates, not accounted for by higher levels of service delivery in center cities, has been documented for a number of metropolitan areas. Artificial incentives given to higher-income persons to escape from poor-inhabited higher tax-rate jurisdictions decrease the ability of the local public sector to perform distributive functions, make for allocative inefficiency by generating inter-jurisdictional externalities that cannot adequately be adjusted for, and call for excessive provision of some public services, like transportation. Circumstances can be envisioned in which some jurisdictions are left with inefficiently small populations or inefficiently low population densities.

Public policy of another sort appears to create a third incentive to oversuburbanization. This is the availability of favorable credit-packages and tax treatment for owner-occupied housing. By reducing the relative cost of single-family house-and-lot packages in the suburbs, these policies have undoubtedly altered the composition of consumer demand toward a more decentralized urban form. These advantages have been harder to apply to older or multifamily dwellings because of the complexities of rehabilitation-loan policy and the condominium form of ownership. There has been little study, however, of the extent to which these laws have made a difference in location. The simultaneity of the availability of VA and other financing on a large scale with the expansion of automobile production after World War II makes such a test difficult.

The net effect of zoning is also difficult to determine. While maximum-density, minimum-lot-size zoning directly reduces densities in portions of the metropolitan area, it also raises the price of entry into these suburbs, and may thereby discourage net suburbanization, thus keeping core areas more crowded. Whatever the net overall impact on sprawl, though, the distributional effects are more important. Zoning gives a selective impetus to suburbanization by those who want to escape from residence near racial minority and poor groups, since it provides a device for successful exclusion of "undesirables." This leads to greater segregation of deprived minorities, and sometimes also to worsening real costs of housing for them, since they are restricted in market opportunities.

A final factor often presented as leading to urban sprawl is speculation—the holding of land out of development in the hope of eventual longer-term gains. Economists sometimes discount the possibility that speculation can have severe results on any market, because if the market does not later validate the predictions of speculators, they will lose money. But if real-estate speculations err, results may be irreversible. If housing is built farther from cities than it would be in the absence of speculation, there may be no economic way of moving the already-installed structures and residents when the speculator who has erred eventually sells at a loss. Lot-assembly problems on the urban fringe may also lead developers to select tracts at greater distances, where larger scale allows internalization of gains from infrastructure installation such as water supply, transit, or shopping-center development. While development nearer to the city core might yield greater total gains, there are fewer for the developers themselves. Although recent studies of suburban development patterns fail to uncover much evidence of speculative and assembly problems (e.g., Clawson, 1971), further study is probably warranted in view of widespread journalistic accounts of speculative problems, and because many economists have used inapplicable theory rather than detailed evidence to dispose of the problem.

All of the causes mentioned appear to have led to greater deconcentration of cities, and greater total social costs, than would prevail under a more optimally planned or coordinated pattern of metropolitan land use. The social costs involved include not only those of increased transport costs and inefficient public-service jurisdictional scale, but also several other social disadvantages stemming from a separation of different but linked land uses by distance. Among these are the lack of accessibility for elderly persons and those too young to drive, and the separation of the poor from services they could use. The separation of poor ghetto residents from suburban jobs (one example of this lack of access) has been the subject of several studies. The studies differ substantially, however, on the magnitude of the employment disability they are willing to ascribe to this spatial separation (Kain, 1968; Harrison, 1971).

Segregation of different class, ethnic, and racial groups also causes additional social problems but to what extent is also disputed. The Coleman report finding that classroom segregation lowered reading scores of minority students has been the subject of considerable debate. Recent studies indicate that segregationist attitudes of whites themselves are lessened by proximity to ghetto areas; however, borderline areas have been the scene of conflict. Within neighborhoods, greater dispersal of population and lack of diversity of ages among residents have been considered to inhibit community vitality. But so has overcrowding in the older slums. Gans (1962) has argued that community vitality is present in both urban and suburban neighborhoods.

Although a tendency toward excessive deconcentration is established, the exact degree of oversuburbanization is hard to measure. The gradual flattening out of land-value patterns with downward sloping gradients may be due to either natural market forces or to distortions. It is difficult to point to examples of genuine alternatives to the spread city pattern. Stockholm and the cities of the Netherlands are sometimes cited as partial models, as are Singapore and Hong Kong. The relevance of these examples for North America is disputed. One study (Schaeffer and Sclar, 1973) suggests that Edmonton, Alberta, may be worthy of study as an alternative city form. Although Edmonton grew to its population of one-half million mostly after World War II, its land use is more compact than most other North American cities, even those whose cores developed in the nineteenth century. Besides the lack of a definite contrafactual model for comparison, the possibility that suburbanization may possess hidden benefits also hampers measurement of social cost. In addition to a general appeal to moral virtues of uncrowded living, economists have proposed two such benefits.

First, it is sometimes argued that lower densities of settlement, fostered by suburbanization, reduce overall costs. Certainly beyond the point at which high-rise construction is required, density within a metropolitan neighborhood will raise costs. Some studies, however, find that, below a moderate level of density, costs begin rising again (Wheaton and Schussheim, 1955). John Kain (1967b), however, has argued that costs continue to fall with density. His reversal of the orthodox view depends, however, on quite special assumptions about sewage disposal (as well as an omission of radial transport costs). Kain assumes the low-density settlement can use septic tanks, while the more densely populated neighborhoods will use sewers. If all suburbs install sewer systems, their cost becomes a factor reinforcing other distribution costs that rise with decreasing density. Kain's argument thus appears unproven. What is more, if he is right on the matter of average costs, it would still not indicate that observed suburbanization falls short of what is cost-justified, because all of such benefits of low costs would be captured in lower land prices or taxes, and thus would attract additional urban migrants. Only noninternalized costs can be relevant in considering inappropriate degrees of suburban sprawl.

A second position sometimes presented to argue for the greater efficiency of dispersed suburbia is that, by homogenizing constituencies, it allows closer responsiveness of public service delivery to constituent desires. This argument, based on special theoretical considerations proposed by Tiebout (1956), rests on an implicit judgment that such responsiveness is worth the cost in virtual exclusion and seriously impaired exercise of the redistributional function of government. When it comes to cost-efficiency, the only evidence that smaller districts might have a significant effect in reducing costs is Adams' (1965) finding that more-fragmented counties spend less (per capita, ceteris paribus) than those with fewer jurisdictional subdivisions. However, an alternative explanation of these lower expenditures is that, because of insufficient scale or because many generated benefits might spill away across town lines, more fragmented districts provide fewer services. Any benefits of suburbanization brought about by greater public-service diversity must also be measured relevant to some alternative. If the alternative posed is one of a more compact area with sufficient community control of services, it is incorrect to attribute the benefits of diversity to the sprawl itself. Like the benefits of density, the benefits of diversity do not alter the qualitative conclusion that there is oversuburbanization. However, the two phenomena do further complicate its measurement.

Although neither the degree of excess deconcentration of cities nor the magnitude of the excess social cost involved has been measured, something can nonetheless be said about the distributional consequences. People who are able to move to suburbs are able to finance a higher level of public services at lower tax rates than those in the inner rings. People in neighborhoods which lose population suffer a loss of a sense of familiar social props, as friends move away or housing and facilities are removed to make room for transport corridors. This documented psychological loss is difficult to evaluate in money terms, but may be serious. Downs (1970) lists it as a cost omitted from compensation when public projects are built, and one which falls most heavily on the poor (although he argues that it may be considered a normal market risk which can be omitted from the calculation—a dictum with which we disagree). Increased segregation and decreased access are costs disproportionately borne by low-income, minority, and elderly individuals. The only possible offset of these costs, which fall on those who remain, might be accelerated filtering-down of old housing to the poor, as the total building stock expands. Vernon (1964) mentions this as an advantage of suburbanization, but only measures it compared with the alternative of no new construction rather than the alternative of building more at higher densities.

The distribution of land-value changes within metropolitan areas is another aspect of the distribution of net costs and benefits. At least some portion of these costs and benefits is apparently capitalized into site rents. To the extent that these values indeed capture all effects (which otherwise would appear as either producers' or consumers' surpluses), benefits and costs will be shared among landowners only. However, since mobility between sites is imperfect, the costs and benefits are incompletely capitalized; some limited evidence suggests only about 50 percent capitalization (Orr, 1968; Heinberg and Oates, 1970). The uncapitalized benefits and costs are distributed negatively among the entire urban population, while the capitalized portion is distributed regressively among the homeowning half of that population. The opening of new areas to suburban settlement lowers land values in older areas of the city. So do the co-locational influences of the aging of facilities within the same areas. Fiscal disparities and other distortions would appear to lower values further in the older neighborhoods occupied by poor renters and moderate- or low-income owners.

The overall conclusions about urban sprawl seem to be the following. The benefits of this process are distributed regressively with respect to income and wealth. While obvious benefits have been derived from lowered residential densities in the recent past (at least compared with nineteenth-century levels), the marginal benefits may already be negative. Sprawl appears to have gone "too far," even though we cannot now say by how much. There is thus a case for requiring suburbs to bear more of the costs they impose on inner-city areas. There is a case for reducing or ending artificial subsidies which now favor single-family, auto-using, low-density suburbanization. Possible reforms include meaningful levels of, and allocation formulas for, federal or state revenue-sharing;

metropolitan tax bases; more adequate compensation—for tenants as well as landlords—where land is taken for transport; diversion of highway trust funds toward forms of public transit; equal income-tax treatment for renters and homeowners and greater policy emphasis on rehabilitation of housing.

NOTES

1. Stanback and Knight (1970) break population-size groups differently and find the highest growth rate for cities in the 200,000-1,600,000 range, with cities of 50,000-200,000 growing at approximately 20 percent 1950-60. They also find negligible growth for nonmetropolitan counties, whereas the 1960-70 data suggest higher growth rates. Since total population increased by approximately 13.5 percent during the decade, and metropolitan population grew by 14 percent, nonmetropolitan population must have grown by about 12 percent.

2. Alonso and Medrich (1970) document the great disparities in growth within size classes and examine the duration of above-average growth in emerging centers.

3. We have experimented with a number of regression models for analyzing growth of SMSAs during the 1960s. This statement is based on preliminary results.

REFERENCES

Adams, R. F. "On the variation in the consumption of public services." Review of Economics and Statistics, November 1965, 47, 400-405.

Alonso, W. "A theory of the urban land market." Papers and Proceedings of the Regional Science Association, 1960, 6, 149-157.

Alonso, W. Location and land use. Cambridge: Harvard University Press, 1965.

Alonso, W. "The economics of urban size." Papers and Proceedings of the Regional Science Association, 1971, 26, 67-83.

Alonso, W., and Fajans, M. Cost of living and income by urban size. Working Paper No. 128. Berkeley: University of California, Institute of Urban and Regional Development, July 1970.

Alonso, W., and Medrich, E. Spontaneous growth centers in twentieth century American urbanization. Working Paper No. 113. Berkeley: University of California, Institute of Urban and Regional Development, January 1970.

Bailey, M. J. "Effects of race and other demographic factors on the value of single family homes." Land Economics, May 1966, 42, 215-220.

Baumol, W. J. "Macroeconomics of unbalanced growth: The anatomy of urban crisis." American Economic Review, June 1967, 57 (3), 415-426.

Bergsman, J., Greenston, P., and Healy, R. Explaining the economic structure of metropolitan areas. Working Paper No. 200-1. Washington, D.C.: The Urban Institute, December 1971(a).

Bergsman, J., Greenston, P., and Healy, R. The agglomeration process in urban growth. Working Paper No. 200-2. Washington, D.C.: The Urban Institute, December 1971(b).

Berry, B.J.L. "Cities as systems within systems of cities." Papers and Proceedings of the Regional Science Association, 1964, 13, 147-163.

Brazier, H. E. City expenditures in the U.S. Occasional Paper No. 66. Washington, D.C.: National Bureau of Economic Research, 1959.

Burkhardt, J. E., and Rothenberg, J. Changes in neighborhood social interaction. RMC Report UR-128. Washington, D.C.: U.S. Department of Transportation, Federal Highway Administration, 1971.

Chinitz, B. "Contrasts in agglomeration: New York and Pittsburgh." American Economic Review, Papers and Proceedings, May 1961, 51 (2), 279-289. Reprinted in M. Edel and J. Rothenberg (Eds.), Readings in urban economics. New York: Macmillan, 1972. Pp. 90-99.

Clawson, M. *Suburban land use conversion.* Baltimore: Johns Hopkins University Press for Resources for the Future, Inc., 1971.

Downs, A. Uncompensated nonconstruction costs which urban highways and urban renewal impose upon residential households. In J. Margolis (Ed.), *The analysis of public output.* New York. Columbia University Press, 1970. Pp. 69-106.

Edel, M. "Land values and the costs of urban congestion." Social Science Information, December 1971, 10 (6), 7-36.

Edel, M. Planning, market or warfare? Recent land use conflicts in American cities. In M. Edel and J. Rothenberg (Eds.), *Readings in urban economics.* New York: Macmillan, 1972. Pp. 134-150.

Edel, M., and Sclar, E. Differential taxation, land values and transportation. Paper presented to the Econometric Society, December 1971.

Engle, R., Fisher, F., Harris, J., and Rothenberg, J. "An econometric simulation model of intra-metropolitan housing location." American Economic Review, Papers and Proceedings, May 1972, 62, 87-97.

Evans, A. W. "The pure theory of city size in an industrial economy." Urban Studies, February 1972, 9, 49-77.

Fales, R. L., and Moses, L. N. Thunen, Weber and the spatial structure of the nineteenth century city. Evanston: Northwestern University, Department of Economics, 1971. (Mimeo.)

Fried, M. Grieving for a lost home. In J. Q. Wilson (Ed.), *Urban renewal: The record and the controversy.* Cambridge: MIT Press, 1967. Pp. 359-379.

Fuchs, V. L. *Differentials in hourly earnings by region and city size.* Occasional Paper No. 101, National Bureau of Economic Research. New York: Columbia University Press, 1967.

Gans, H. *The urban villagers.* New York: Free Press, 1962.

Gans, H. *The Levittowners.* New York: Knopf, 1967.

Ganz, A. *Our large cities: New light on their recent transformation; elements of a development strategy; a prototype program for Boston.* Cambridge: MIT, Laboratory for Environmental Studies, February 1972.

Grieson, R. E. The economics of property taxes and land values. Working Paper No. 72. Cambridge: MIT, Department of Economics, June 1971.

Grigsby, W. *Housing markets and public policy.* Philadelphia: University of Pennsylvania, Institute of Urban Studies, 1962.

Haig, R. "Toward an understanding of the metropolis." Parts 1 and 2. Quarterly Journal of Economics, 40, February 1926, 179-208; May 1926, 402-434.

Harris, J. R., and Wheeler, D. Agglomeration economies: Theory and measurement. Paper presented to the Urban Economics Conference, Keele, July 1971. (Mimeo.)

Harrison, B. Education, training and the urban ghetto. Unpublished doctoral dissertation, University of Pennsylvania, 1971.

Heinberg, J. H., and Oates, W. D. "The incidence of differential property taxes on Urbanization: Comment." National Tax Journal, March 1970, 23, 92-98.

Hirsch, W. The supply of public services. In H. S. Perloff and L. Wingo (Eds.), *Issues in urban economics.* Baltimore: Johns Hopkins University Press for Resources for the Future, Inc., 1969.

Hoch, I. The three dimensional city: Contained urban space. In H. S. Perloff (Ed.), *The quality of the urban environment,* Baltimore: Johns Hopkins University Press for Resources for the Future, Inc., 1969.

Hoyt, H. *One hundred years of land values in Chicago,* Chicago: University of Chicago Press, 1933.

Hoyt, H. *Structure and growth of residential neighborhoods.* Washington, D.C.: U.S. Government Printing Office, 1939.

Hurd, R. M. *Principles of city land values.* New York: The Record and Guide, 1903.

Hymer, S. The multinational corporation and the law of uneven development. In J. Bhagwati (Ed.), *Economics and world order.* New York: Macmillan, 1972.

Ingram, G., Kain, J. and Ginn, J. R. The Detroit prototype of the NBER urban simulation model. New York: National Bureau of Economic Research, February 1972. (Mimeo.)

Kain, J. F. "Postwar metropolitan development: Housing preferences and auto ownership." American Economic Association, Papers and Proceedings, May 1967(a), 57, 223-234.

Kain, J. F. *Metropolitan form and the costs of urban services.* Cambridge: Harvard University Preprint, 1967(b), (6).

Kain, J. F. "Housing segregation, Negro employment and metropolitan decentralization." Quarterly Journal of Economics, May 1968, 82(2), 175-197.

Kain, J. F., and Persky, J. J. The North's stake in Southern rural poverty. Discussion Paper No. 18. Cambridge: Harvard University, Program on Regional and Urban Economics, May 1967.

Kain, J. F., and Quigley, J. M. Measuring the quality and cost of housing services. Discussion Paper No. 54. Cambridge: Harvard University, Program on Regional and Urban Economics, July 1969.

Kryzwicki, J. Determinants of house values in San Diego. Unpublished S. B. essay, MIT, 1972.

Laurenti, L. *Property values and race.* Berkeley: University of California Press, 1960.

Levy, F. Revenue sharing, the Tiebout hypothesis and the urban crisis. Working Paper No. 10. Berkeley: University of California, Department of Economics, May 1971.

Lowry, I. S. Seven models of urban development: A structural comparison. In National Academy of Engineering, Highway Research Board, *Urban Development Models.* Special Report 97. Washington, D.C.: NAE, 1968. Pp. 121-146.

Margolis, J. "Municipal fiscal structure in a metropolitan region." Journal of Political Economy, June 1957, 65, 225-236.

Mera, K. On the concentration of urbanization and economic efficiency. Working Paper No. 74. Washington, D.C.: International Bank for Reconstruction and Development/ International Development Association, Economics Department, March 1970.

Meyer, J. F., Kain, J. F., and Wohl, M. *The urban transportation problem.* Cambridge: Harvard University Press, 1965.

Mills, E. S. "An aggregative model of resource allocation in a metropolitan area." American Economic Review, May 1967, 57, 197-210.

Mills, E. S. The value of urban land. In H. S. Perloff (Ed.), *The quality of the urban environment.* Baltimore: Johns Hopkins University Press for Resources for the Future, Inc., 1969. Pp. 231-255.

Mohring, H. Urban highway investments. In R. Dorfman (Ed.), *Measuring benefits of government investments.* Washington, D.C.: The Brookings Institution, 1965.

Moses, L., and Williamson, H. F., Jr. "The location of economic activity in cities." American Economic Review, Papers and Proceedings, May 1967, 57(2), 211-222.

Moynihan, D. P. *Toward a national urban policy.* New York: Basic Books, 1970.

Muth, R. "Economic change and rural-urban land conversions." Econometrica, January 1961, 29, 1-23.

Muth, R. *Cities and housing.* Chicago: University of Chicago Press, 1969.

Neutze, G. M. *Economic policy and the size of cities.* New York: Augustus M. Kelley, 1968.

Oates, W. E. "The effects of property taxes and local public spending on property values: An empirical study of tax capitalization and the Tiebout hypothesis." Journal of Political Economy, December 1969, 77(6), 957-971.

Orr, L. L. "The incidence of differential property taxes on urbanization." National Tax Journal, September 1968, 21, 253-262.

Park, R. E., and Burgess, E. W. (Eds.), *The city.* Chicago: University of Chicago Press, 1925.

Parr, J. B. "Models of city size in an urban system." Papers and Proceedings of the Regional Science Association, 1970, 25, 221-253.

Ridker, R. A., and Henning, J. A. "Determinants of residential property values with special reference to air pollution." Review of Economics and Statistics, May 1967, 49, 246-257.

Rodwin, L. Nations and cities: A comparison of strategies for urban growth. Boston: Houghton-Mifflin, 1970.

Rothenberg, J. Economic evaluation of urban renewal. Washington, D.C.: The Brookings Institution, 1967.

Rothenberg, J. Local decentralization and the theory of optimal government. In J. Margolis (Ed.), The analysis of public output. New York: Columbia University Press, 1970, Pp. 31-59.

Rothenberg, J. An econometric simulation model of the metropolitan housing market for public policy evaluation. Report to the National Urban Coalition. Washington, D.C.: NUC, 1971.

Schaeffer, K. N., and Sclar, E. Access. Harmondsworth (Middlesex, England): Penguin Press, 1973.

Shaper, D. "Comparable living costs and urban size: A statistical analysis." Journal of the American Institute of Planners, November 1970, 36(4), 417-421.

Sjaastad, L. "The costs and returns of human migration." Journal of Political Economy, October 1962, 70(5), Part 2 (supplement), 80-93.

Stanback, T. M., and Knight, R. V. The metropolitan economy. New York: Columbia University Press, 1970.

Strotz, R. H. The use of land rent charges to measure the welfare benefits of land improvement. Evanston: Northwestern University, Economics Department, 1966. (Mimeo.)

Strotz, R. H., and Wright, C. Spatial adaptation to urban air pollution. Prepared for Resources for the Future, Inc., Committee on Urban Economics. Evanston: Northwestern University, Economics Department, 1970. (Mimeo.)

Thompson, W. A preface to urban economics. Baltimore: Johns Hopkins University Press, 1965.

Tiebout, C. M. "A pure theory of local expenditures." Journal of Political Economy, October 1956, 64, 410-424.

U.S. Bureau of the Census. Census of Population and Housing: 1970. General demographic trends for metropolitan areas, 1960 to 1960. U.S. Summary, Final Report PHC(2)-1. Washington, D.C.: U.S. Government Printing Office, 1971.

U.S. Commission on Population Growth and the American Future. Population and the American Future. New York: New American Library (Signet), 1972.

Vernon, R. Metropolis 1985. Cambridge: Harvard University Press, 1960.

Vernon, R. The myth and reality of our urban problems. Cambridge: Harvard University Press, 1964.

Vickrey, W. S. "Pricing in urban and suburban transport." American Economic Review, Papers and Proceedings, May 1963, 53(2), 452-465.

Vincent, P. E. Fiscal impacts of commuters on core cities with varying revenue structures. Report MR-130. Los Angeles: University of California, Institute of Government and Public Affairs, 1969.

Von Thunen, J. H. The isolated state. (trans.) New York: Pergamon, 1966.

Wabe, J. S. A study of house prices as a means of establishing the value of journey time, the rate of time preferences, and the valuation of some aspects of the environment in the London metropolitan region. Economic Research Paper No. 11. Coventry: Warwick University, 1971.

Walters, A. A. "The theory and measurement of private and social costs of highway congestion." Econometrica, October 1961, 29, 676-699.

Wertheimer, R. F. Monetary rewards of migration within the U.S. Washington, D.C.: The Urban Institute, 1971.

Wheaton, W. C., and Schussheim, M. J. The cost of municipal services in residential areas. Washington, D.C.: U.S. Government Printing Office, 1955.

Wingo, L., Jr. Transportation and urban land. Baltimore: Johns Hopkins University Press Resources for the Future, Inc., 1961.

CHAPTER 4

ACCESSIBILITY FOR RESIDENTS IN THE
METROPOLITAN ENVIRONMENT

Donald L. Foley

University of California, Berkeley

METROPOLITAN AREAS have become the dominant community form in the
United States and in other countries with high levels of economic development,
primarily because they facilitate accessibility among the highly divergent and
specialized activities characterizing an industrial (now tending, we are told,
toward a post-industrial) society. The locational advantage is most apparent with
respect to business firms, professional offices, administrative headquarters,
medical centers, universities, and other nonresidential activities. Location in a
metropolitan area is also apparently a net advantage to people, for otherwise it
would be difficult to explain the persistent trend of people to migrate in force
to metropolitan areas. Whether metropolitan residents are actually better off for
having made that locational choice is less clear. Nevertheless, our population is
now preponderantly metropolitan.

As metropolitan areas proliferate, grow, and undergo significant change, it
becomes an intricate and difficult task to monitor and to interpret changes in
their structure. We may suggest two changes, not unrelated, which, in turn,
pose further questions as to how accessibility within metropolitan areas may be
changing.

First, we judge that metropolitan areas have been shifting toward a looser,
more dispersed, lower-density structure. The dominant center anchored by the
fixed radial transportation lines of an earlier period has given way to a plurality
of centers, often no longer compact or sharply delineated, largely held together
by the amazingly unfixed point-to-point capabilities of the auto or other motor
vehicle.

Second, we suspect that, for a great variety of reasons, metropolitan residents
are less likely to share patterns of work trips, facility use, and socializing than
may have been the case in the past. Greater choices are potentially open to individual residents than ever before. And the metropolitan environment attracts
and caters to persons with vastly different orientations toward living. Different

households—and even different members of the same household—may be characterized by distinctively different configurations of needs, interests, resources and physical capabilities. Thus, each metropolitan resident tends to have his own distinctive set of the channels and destinations that make up his "movement space" (to be discussed further, below) and his own subjective image of his working "community."

In addition, the very nature of accessibility in the metropolitan setting has certainly been undergoing significant changes in recent decades. This involves the distinct rise in dependence upon the auto, reliance upon the ubiquitous telephone, the pervasive impact of television, and, for many, the capabilities of air travel. It also involves unprecedented increases in income and the diffusion of expectations and consumption patterns which had previously been restricted to a much smaller number of residents—the elite. And it involves the rise of a new generation or two unfettered by the traditional encumbrances of earlier patterns and images of community. We are reaping the changes that mark a highly mobile, generally well-educated, and increasingly well-heeled people.

This, we hasten to note, is the larger, broad-brush view. It is certainly a facet of the American dilemma that our aspirations so far outrun our capacity to deliver with equity to all. In this paper we shall stress the deprivation and non-access suffered by selected categories of residents, in the midst of the larger trend toward affluence and access. Indeed, we shall particularly argue that the very widespread availability of the auto has both led us to think that most Americans are thereby well served and permitted our urban land use patterns and transportation systems to cater primarily to auto-users, to the specific and serious deprivation of those who lack access to the auto. While we touch upon various aspects of accessibility—and nonaccessibility—we look most pointedly at differential access to the auto.

VARIOUS FACETS OF THE CONCEPT, "ACCESSIBILITY"

We start by recognizing the idea of physical accessibility: the capability for getting directly into contact with persons or activities. This usually involves travel through space. Supplementary or alternative access may also be provided by other communication modes, particularly by telephone. The most ready and flexible short-distance travel mode is walking. Additionally, one may take "trips" (making use of a wheeled vehicle—or an air- or water-borne vehicle). Most metropolitan residents have essential physical access available to them, but a significant proportion, as we shall point out below, suffer physical disabilities that make walking or driving one's own vehicle difficult or impossible.

Differentials in available income are particularly significant. Income means purchasing power and hence power to choose. It bears on where one lives, what one can afford to do, what travel mode is at one's disposal, and how self-reliant one can be. It has been argued that the metropolis provides exceptional opportunities for the resident with higher income, but that it is likely merely to frustrate the resident who lacks the income to partake of the goodies latently available (Thompson, 1972).

Access also has subjective and social psychological aspects. Expectations on the part of the individual actor loom as overwhelmingly important. As Wildavsky (1968: 3) has suggested, a sure formula for revolt is to raise the level of expectations while failing to deliver the means for their fulfillment. Built into the social-psychological aspects of access are considerations of knowledge, self-confidence, capacity for initiative, and other requisites to the effective searching out and use of possible opportunities. The metropolitan arena has become an extremely complex setting within which a myriad of subsystems operate. Finding one's way through this maze may prove to be a forbidding challenge; we need to understand and to seek to alleviate the plight of the many metropolitan residents who are ill equipped to cope with this complexity (March, 1968).

Up to this point our discussion of access has assumed market-place circumstances by focusing on purchasing power and suggesting that metropolitan areas provide a very wide range of specialized goods and services. Another aspect of access relates to political participation and, generally, to one's capability to have access to political power or influence. A considerable research literature has reported on differential access to community power (Greer, 1972: ch. 9). Thus, we must consider accessibility not only as the bridging of physical distance, but also as the bridging of social and political distance.

In specific cases, accessibility may involve a mix of all of these aspects we have separately identified. It is, in fact, reasonable to presume that these different aspects tend to blur into each other and to be part of a larger syndrome. Thus, greater accessibility in any one sphere may well be associated with greater accessibility in other spheres. Greater income, for example, pervasively ramifies to an association with better health, with better chances for physical accessibility, with greater purchasing power, and with better opportunities for political influence. Conversely, lack of access in some spheres may reinforce the very lack of knowledge and lack of self-confidence that may make accessibility in other spheres less probable or more difficult.

THE INDIVIDUAL AND SUBJECTIVE ASPECTS
OF ACCESSIBILITY

It is undoubtedly a matter of cultural context whether, or to what degree, residents of a "community" share common interpretations and expectations as to a shared "turf." Even to ask the ordinary interview-type questions pose serious possibilities of contaminating replies by the interviewer's expectation that the respondent will be able to identify a "neighborhood" (Lee, 1968: 352-361). Our purpose here is not to provide any comprehensive review of research of this particular sort. At the risk of some selectivity or even personal bias, we merely stress that each urban resident inevitably has his own personal image of that portion of his urban environment of which he makes active working use. This reflects, to be sure, a land use pattern in the vicinity of the resident's home, and a broader pattern of transportation channels and activity centers more distant from his home. Only a selected number of stores, other facilities, friends, and possible points of contact are nearby. Others are more distant and require transportation or communication beyond the range of walking. Hence, physical-spatial constraints are imposed.

But each resident has a personalized interpretation of needs, a configuration of tastes, a sense of his financial resources, and his own physical condition (reflecting, in particular, his age) and role (reflecting sex, status within the household, whether employed outside the home, etc.). His conception of his own familiar turf interrelates with his habitual configuration of actual trips to various destinations—whether near his home or more distant.

We recognize the distinction between a resident's effective environment and his potential environment. The effective environment is "that version of the potential environment that is manifestly or latently adopted by users" (Gans, 1968: 6). Thus, the effective environment incorporates the user's subjective conception of his physical environment as this ties to the user's larger view of his world.

Hurst (1969: 75-76) has suggested a related concept, that of movement space:

> This is a perceived part of the environment within which movement occurs. . . . This concept of movement space is similar to Lewin's 'life space.' This is a universe of space and time in which the person conceives that he can or might move about, and is only a limited portion of the environment. . . .

> Movement space could be further refined. It might be possible to identify three types of movement space:

> 1. A *core,* which is the frequently travelled space with which the trip-maker is most familiar. This is the space within which regular journeys made, frequent visits to friends, and shopping trips.

> 2. A *median* area, the occasionally travelled space, within which journeys to visit relatives, and holidays would be made by many people.

> 3. An *extensive* movement space, which is the conceived, concept-learnt, or cosmological space. . . .

> The limits of the movement space, unique to a particular tripmaker, are set by his finite abilities to perceive, and by his learning experiences. Movement space will vary from the limited realm of the young child to the extensive realm of say an international movie-star. . . .

It would be misleading, however, to presume any tidy regularity of nested spaces. Even the core may reflect the traditional patterns of the individual in question and the urban topography (e.g., the particular configuration of land use and streets in the surrounding area). Characteristically, the resident may know and use certain routes or corridors, to the metropolitan center (if he goes there) or to specific other activity centers, without knowing or using many other sectors of the metropolitan area. The actual spatial pattern of his movement space may appear to be irregular—a distinctive set of destinations linked by a distinctive web of routes. We may speak of these routes as the resident's "Indian paths" through the city. We may expect that each urban resident has a unique configuration of Indian paths making up his effective environment or his movement space.

We may also cite Lee's findings (1968: 354) in the same vein, reflecting his 1954 study in Cambridge, England:

> It was found that people perceive, organize and react to their physical and social environment differently from their neighbours. Each person's constellation of experience and action is apparently unique, although there is some evidence of norm-formation. Repeated transaction with people and places in the urban environment leads, by a process of differentiation, to the separation of an organized socio-spatial whole. The processis is probably bi-directional—expanding outwards from the home and contracting inwards from the total city. We locate shops, cinemas, churches, parks and phone boxes; we learn the whereabouts of people who will cater to our specific needs—grocers, taxi-drivers, policemen and plumbers; and those who will give us the more general satisfactions of acquaintance and friendship. The roads and pathways which link them serve as a framework.

CHANGING METROPOLITAN STRUCTURE

We are undoubtedly trapped by very serious conceptual lags in our attempts to understand the functional-spatial organization of the contemporary large American metropolitan area. We persist in thinking of a traditional center serving both the main central city and the larger metropolitan area. We think of major transportation routes focusing on this center. And we think of suburbs as being adjuncts to the main central city. Even our data collecting efforts are, in part, caught by a certain inertia such that we continue to collect the types of data that reflect earlier circumstances.

We are, in fact, still influenced by the outpourings of the Chicago school of urban sociology that, during the 1920s and 1930s, produced an impressive and reinforcing set of empirical studies. We appear to lack an equally influential cutting edge that constantly brings us up to date on the incredibly powerful changes that have, if anything, basically altered the structure of metropolitan areas during the past few decades.

These changes appear to reflect in particular the interlocking impact of at least four major developments: (1) generally rising household incomes that have made it possible for households to have and use autos, and that have encouraged moves to lower-density suburban locations; (2) the very significant and pervasive rise in the availability of autos (the full import masked by the long period of time over which the change has been under way); (3) the great rise, both in absolute and relative terms, of the suburban portions of metropolitan areas at the inevitable expense of the central cities; and (4) the persistent drop in residential densities (and, more precisely, in the mix, within any given metropolitan area, between low-density and higher-density sectors, with the low-density suburban sectors becoming ever more dominant). Homeownership is also positively associated with lower density.

Over the past five or so decades the trend toward low-density dispersal and the increasingly heavy reliance on the private motor vehicle have had a cumulative and highly circular character, to the point where it becomes difficult and perhaps not very helpful to try to unravel the relative significance of the separate factors. As the suburbs have grown, new shopping centers and other service facilities have followed. A preponderance of employed persons residing in the suburbs of large metropolitan areas find employment in the suburbs. But to move around the suburbs means to have "wheels." The land use pattern makes it virtually imperative to have at least one car, and characteristically more than one auto, per household. In turn, the prevalence of autos has dictated the character of the shopping centers and the broader pattern of centers. The overall pattern has a looseness to it that is only understandable in terms of travel predominantly by auto. Given the auto, one merely extends in scale (as if stepped up by a giant pantograph) the freedom and flexibility of walking travel. Metropolitan residents "walk" in their cars.

The auto has already had profound impacts on both the overall land use pattern of the metropolis and on the individual lives of its residents. Further, the base for future development has vastly changed, and this foreshadows potential further changes that will cumulatively exert even greater long-range impact. While this is perhaps most evident in, say, Orange County, it is geographically pervasive; one could be dropped blindfolded by plane or helicopter into almost any suburban sector of a large American metropolitan area and be hard put to identify immediately precisely which metropolitan area he is observing.

While there are many threads to the overall trend, we single out the shifting residential densities as one broadly significant feature. We must recognize the difficulties in measuring densities. The main measure we employ, gross density, is exceedingly crude. And yet it permits a rough grasp of changes underway. Table 4.1 provides an initial overview for those urbanized areas of the U.S. with population of 100,000 or more. This shows that in the sixty years from 1920 to 1980 residential density on the average drops to 58 percent of the 1920 level. For that same sixty-year period, population in these urbanized areas increased 4.3 times while the land area included increased 7.2 times. This includes the additional urbanized areas, but reflects the average metropolitan environment for Americans.

Table 4.1: Gross Residential Densities, Population and Geographic Area in Large U.S. Urbanized Areas, 1920 to 2000

	1920	1940	1960	Projected 1980	Projected 2000
Persons (per square mile)	6,580	5,870	4,230	3,840	3,732
Population (in millions)	34.6	52.4	91.0	148.0	220.5
Square miles (in thousands)	5.3	8.9	21.6	38.4	60.6

NOTE: Includes only those urbanized areas with populations of 100,000 and over. In 1960 such areas represented about 95 percent of the population of all urbanized areas. Data adapted from Clawson, 1971, Table 39, p. 336 (in turn, from Pickard, 1967).

Table 4.2: Gross Residential Densities, Population, and Area in All U.S. Urbanized Areas, 1950-70

	1950	1960	1970
Population Per Square Mile			
Total urbanized areas	5,408	3,837	3,376
Inside central cities	7,786	5,502	4,463
Outside central cities	3,167	2,622	2,627
Total Population (000)			
Total urbanized areas	69,252	95,834	118,447
Inside central cities	48,377	57,966	63,922
Outside central cities	20,875	37,868	54,525
Percentage Distribution of Population			
Total urbanized areas	100.0	100.0	100.0
Inside central cities	69.9	60.5	54.0
Outside central cities	30.1	39.5	46.0
Land Area in Square Miles (000)			
Total urbanized areas	12.8	25.0	35.1
Inside central cities	6.2	10.5	14.3
Outside central cities	6.6	14.4	20.8

NOTE: Data from U.S. Bureau of the Census, 1961, 1971.

The drop in residential densities has affected both the central and the suburban portions of these urbanized areas. The trend for the most recent twenty years is shown in Table 4.2. We see that the drop in density was even more pronounced for the central cities than for the suburban portions, and that the densities of the central cities and the suburbs were more nearly equal in 1970 than they were in 1950. The suburban portions were, of course, growing more rapidly than the central cities. And whereas the central cities and the suburban portions were about equal in area in 1950, by 1970, the suburban portions had come to represent nearly 21,000 square miles, well over the 14,000 in central cities.

Table 4.3 shows more precisely the changing densities in four large urbanized areas, around New York, Chicago, Los Angeles, and San Francisco. The trends, when viewed in this detail, show some variations. Densities have generally been rising somewhat in the Los Angeles area, and Los Angeles as a central city is gradually moving a bit closer to the prevalent notion of higher densities for the central city than for the suburbs. Densities have generally fallen in the New York and Chicago urbanized areas and in the Bay Area.

These broad averages mask finer variations both within the central cities and within the suburbs. Table 4.4, for example, shows the variations in densities by geographic sector and the more refined alternative density measures that can be employed (in addition to gross density per square mile, the figure employed in Tables 4.1, 4.2, and 4.3). This table shows that quite beyond the simplifying dichotomy of inside and outside central cities used in Tables 4.2 and 4.3, there may well be much greater differences between the innermost part and the outer suburbs. We must bear in mind these very great differences and avoid undue

Table 4.3: Gross Residential Densities in the New York, Chicago, Los Angeles, and San Francisco Urbanized Areas, 1950-70

	1950	1960	1970
New York-Northeastern New Jersey			
Total urbanized area	9,810	7,512	6,683
Inside central cities	24,537	24,132	24,382
(New York City)	(25,046)	(25,966)	(26,343)
Outside central cities	4,066	3,541	3,580
Chicago-Northwestern Indiana			
Total urbanized area	6,954	6,238	5,257
Inside central cities	17,450	13,138	12,283
(Chicago)	(17,450)	(16,014)	(15,126)
Outside central cities	2,599	3,131	3,091
Los Angeles-Long Beach			
Total urbanized area	4,587	4,633	5,313
Inside central cities	4,370	5,475	6,135
(Los Angeles)	(4,370)	(5,547)	(7,364)
Outside central cities	4,821	4,134	4,818
San Francisco-Oakland			
Total urbanized area	7,038	4,213	4,387
Inside central cities	11,885	11,351	10,035
(San Francisco)	(17,385)	(16,307)	(15,764)
Outside central cities	4,545	2,734	3,252

NOTE: Data from U.S. Bureau of the Census, 1961, 1971.

generalization. Even so, we cannot avoid the important conclusion that very large numbers and proportions of persons are now living in relatively low-density portions of metropolitan environs.

Metropolitan development at low density brings certain inevitable correlaries. It brings vast increases in the land area within recognized urbanized areas. It brings an inability to provide effective public transportation—over half of our metropolitan residents report no available public transportation service (see Marans and Rodgers, this volume). It also brings to an end the traditional notion that local shops, schools, churches, and other community facilities will be within ready walking distance of homes. Densities have become so low that most residents are now beyond normal walking distance of these facilities, except for some elementary schools (Blumenfeld, 1967: chs. 10 and 16). These low-density residential areas have become autoland. Even in 1960 (and autos have become even more prevalent since that date), over 90 percent of the households in the most recently developed areas in metropolitan California had autos available to them. More specifically, 40-45 percent of the households had two or more autos available, 50-55 percent had one auto available, and only 3-5 percent had no auto available (Foley, Drake, Lyon, and Ynzenga, 1965: 202-203).

Autos have now become so prevalent, and have been in the ascendancy as a mode of personal transportation for so long in these lower-density portions of our metropolitan areas, that it has become the common presumption that residents will have and rely upon autos. This, in turn, has affected the very design of

Table 4.4: Residential Density Groups in the Baltimore-Washington Region for the Late 1950s

| Density Group | Neighborhood Density[a] (persons per acre) | | Net Residential Density[b] | | Gross Density[c] | |
	Range	Average	Persons Per Acre	Housing Units Per Acre	Persons Per Acre	Persons Per Mile
Inner city	50-120	100 (Balt.) 75 (Wash.)	120+	40+	20+	13,000+
Outer city	21-50	30	55-65	16-18	18	11,000
Inner suburban	12-21	15	20-25	6-7	8	5,000
Outer suburban	4-12	7	9-12	2-3	4	2,500
Rural	under 4	3	4-5	1-2	2	1,200

NOTE: Data adapted from Clawson, 1971; Table 36, p. 305 (in turn, from Baltimore Regional Planning Council and National Capital Regional Planning Council, 1960).
a. Persons on land devoted or to be devoted to residential use per acre of residential land, including residential streets and local neighborhood facilities.
b. Same, per acre of strictly residential land, exclusive of streets, neighborhood facilities, etc.
c. Residential population per acre of all land developed or to be developed.

these residential environments, including community facilities and their accessibility and, of course, the transportation channels as such. A perfect case in point is the large suburban shopping center locationally related to a comprehensive freeway system. It is virtually taken for granted that one gets to such a shopping center by auto.

We are not about to assert that low-density development and dependence upon the auto are in any simplistic way interlocked all by themselves. As Kain (1967: 233) has carefully stated: "It appears that income has been the most important factor underlying both higher post-war levels of automobile ownership and declines in residential density." He develops in greater detail the very real complexities of unravelling, out of a larger web, those factors that may be considered the most conclusively determinative. He also points to family size and to the pattern of labor force participation as affecting residential density. But when we talk about cities and about metropolitan areas in today's America, we are in fact dealing with a very different environmental setting than that which confronted the classic Chicago sociologists some fifty years ago.

ACCESS TO THE AUTO AS A PIVOTAL KEY TO THE BROADER QUESTION OF ACCESS

In very broad terms, then, we have been moving into metropolitan environments in which it has been assumed that the modal form of personal transportation is the auto. It has increasingly been assumed that, with the exception of certain high-density inner-city settings, most households would have an auto available. Further, and without our quite realizing the degree to which this has come about—since the evolution has been so gradual and we have been so immediately caught up in the process—we have in recent years been moving even beyond the point of the auto as *available to a household,* a logical earlier concept, to the point now where increasingly the auto is *personally available to each member* of the household. As we shall show below, this has now reached much more significant dimensions than many of us may have realized.

The thrust of our analysis from this point on will be to provide a summary of two trends over time and two types of differentials at any given time: (1) the availability of the auto to a household, and (2) the availability of an auto to a specific household member. These two are, in turn, interrelated. Quite obviously, as the number or proportion of households with one or more autos available rises, so, too, do the chances that individual members of that household have access to an auto. The further focus on individual members demonstrates certain persistent and significant differentials even within a given household. Thus, personal access to an auto reflects both the general level of auto availability to the household and each household member's own characteristics.

Concern about transportation, and a focus now on the availability of autos, inevitably raises difficult considerations about the ends at stake. Clearly, we do not want transportation only for transportation's sake. Fresh recognition that the primary goals are to improve urban livability and to provide access to opportunities has entered into recent analyses of the transportation problem. Webber (1971: 139) has effectively stated:

> A governmental strategy, aimed at improving human welfare by expanding individuals' accessibilities, must employ a spectrum of programmatic approaches in concert. Any modern strategy would be directed to improving educational opportunities, fostering positive mental and physical health, expanding the national and regional economies, improving the quality of the communications media, expanding the transportation networks and extending transport services to those presently excluded, raising family-income levels, expanding the range of housing choices, fostering diversity in the ranges of consumer goods offered for distribution, and more. Transport is clearly but one of many important inputs into such a strategy.

An exclusive focus on autos is of course incomplete. We ought to have a very full grasp of the effectiveness with which alternative modes of transport serve metropolitan residents. And, as we move toward an uncertain future, we should bear in mind that the auto, despite its fascinatingly relentless appeal, may well be superseded in coming decades by new versions of personal transport yet to be invented and translated to reality. But the auto has provided a personalized mode of transport so advantageous and so appealing to most present or would-be users that its acceptance and impact must be recognized.

There has been much written about the functional and social features underlying the auto's acceptance, and we shall not attempt to inventory these many features. We merely repeat that it permits residents to "walk" their metropolitan environs, but on the larger scale that more nearly matches the way in which metropolitan facilities and activity centers have come to be organized. It provides comfort and privacy; permits spontaneous starts, stops or changes in trip plan; encourages sociability or intimacy; serves to carry or to store many sizes of "things"; and lends itself to symbolic extension of self or home.

To have access to an auto is thus to provide potential "wheels" by which to do many things one needs to or desires to do. Transportation to work is overwhelmingly by auto. Other purposes are admirably served; formal traffic counts and our own personal experiences of living in cities attest to the increasing importance of weekend and evening travel.

In contrast, the urban resident lacking access to an auto is confronted with several forms of deprivation. First, he lacks the direct use of the auto. Second, he lacks choice of mode. Third, and increasingly serious, he lacks effective public transport. We have catered to those with autos and, in error, have come to act as though "everyone" had an auto. But various categories of persons comprising a sizeable minority in fact lack autos. And yet, increasingly, metropolitan residents find themselves in total environs (including the land use patterns and the available transportation channels) which are designed solely for auto users. The evolving land use changes reflecting auto predominance combine with the direct lack of auto and the absence of good public transportation to increase the relative deprivation of those who must continue to face life without autos in today's metropolitan environs.

This suggests that attacks on the problem include a fresh recognition of land use plans and controls, with an eye to lessening the need for transportation and, in particular, for reliance on the auto (Owen, 1972). We shall return to this implication at the end of the paper.

AUTO AVAILABILITY: A QUICK NATIONAL SUMMARY

We have not yet sought to break out the overall historical picture of auto availability for the United States on a household basis. The fifty-year trend based on the gross-autos-per-1,000-population basis customarily employed is shown in Table 4.5. This table is exceedingly crude: all of these autos were not necessarily in active use, and the population figure includes children and does

Table 4.5: U.S. Cars Per 1,000 Population, 1920-70, with Percentage Increases

Dates	Privately Owned Registered Cars Per 1,000 Population	Percentage Increase in Ratio Over Previous Ratio
1920	76.9	– –
1930	187.1	+143.3
1940	207.9	+11.1
1950	266.7	+28.3
1960	342.6	+28.5
1970	439.9	+28.4

NOTE: Data adapted from Automobile Manufacturers Association, 1972, p. 18, and U.S. Bureau of the Census, 1971.

Table 4.6: Percent of U.S. Households Owning Autos by Number of Autos and Auto/Household Ratio, 1960-70

Dates	Percent of Households Owning				Ratios of Autos to Households[a]
	No Auto	One Auto	Two Autos	Three Autos	
1960	25.0	58.6	16.4		0.91
1970	20.4	50.3	24.6	4.7	1.09

NOTE: Data adapted from U.S. Bureau of the Census, 1970, Table 1.
a. Calculated on the basis of a trichotomous classification—no auto, one auto, or two or more autos—with the latter class being treated only as though there were two autos. Thus, the ratio somewhat understates the precise number of autos in relation to households.

not take into account household size or composition. But it does suggest: a highly significant relative increase in the ratio of autos to people during the 1920s; some slowdown during the 1930s, reflecting mainly depression conditions; and quite remarkably, substantial increases of slightly over 28 percent in the ratio for each of the past three decades. It is particularly significant that the percentage increase in the ratio held up during the 1960s, despite the already very high base of auto availability by 1960, and despite the common presumption that we were nearing the saturation point. It seems further to support the degree to which the auto is becoming "indispensable," encouraged by a greatly augmented freeway and highway system and by the shifting land use pattern to which we have already alluded.

A look at the changing percentage of family ownership of autos from 1955 to 1969 also indicates increasing auto availability. In 1955, 71 percent of U.S. families owned autos. This number had increased to 77 percent in 1960, 79 percent in 1965, and 82 percent in 1969 (Automobile Manufacturers Association, 1972: 48). Another time-series measure, showing increased household ownership of autos, is shown in Table 4.6.

By either of these measures, it is quite clear that the 1960s saw our nation move much farther along the road toward the ubiquity of the auto. Over four-fifths of all households or families have an auto. And even with a conservative estimate for multi-auto households, we find that the average ratio of autos to households has risen from 0.91 to 1.09. We now have, on the average, more than on auto per household.

Table 4.7 summarizes the past decade's changes in this ratio of autos to households for separate regions of the United States and for selected large SMSAs. It can be seen that both the levels of auto ownership and the increases in auto ownership from 1960 to 1970 were generally high in all but the Boston, New York, and Pittsburgh SMSAs. The increases were notable in many of the SMSAs and in most of the regions of the United States. While in 1960 the Los Angeles-Long Beach SMSA in particular, and the Pacific and Mountain regions in general, led the rest of the nation by a considerable margin, by 1970 many other SMSAs and regions had reduced the gap.

Tables 4.8 and 4.9 show that both income of household and age of household head influence the ratio of auto ownership. In interpreting Table 4.8, we

Table 4.7: Changes in the Auto/Household Ratio in U.S. Geographic Regions and Selected Large SMSAs, 1960-70

	Auto/Household Ratio[a]				Auto/Household Ratio[a]		
Region	1960-1961	1969-1970	Change in Ratio	SMSAs	1960-1961	1969-1970	Change in Ratio
Total U.S.	0.93	1.09	+0.16				
New England	0.95	1.12	+0.17	Boston	0.84	0.85	+0.01
Middle Atlantic	0.81	0.94	+0.13	New York	0.72	0.77	+0.05
				Philadelphia	0.86	1.01	+0.15
				Pittsburgh	0.90	0.90	0
East N. Central	0.98	1.13	+0.15	Chicago	0.77	0.93	+0.16
				Detroit	1.05	1.21	+0.16
				Cleveland	1.06	1.14	+0.08
West N. Central	0.98	1.15	+0.17	St. Louis	0.85	1.03	+0.18
				Minneapolis-St. Paul	n.a.	1.28	n.a.
South Atlantic	0.86	1.04	+0.18	Washington	0.88	1.06	+0.18
East S. Central	0.83	1.08	+0.25				
West S. Central	0.95	1.11	+0.16				
Mountain	1.07	1.24	+0.17				
Pacific	1.07	1.19	+0.12	Los Angeles-Long Beach	1.13	1.21	+0.08
				San Francisco-Oakland	0.96	1.13	+0.17

NOTE: Data adapted from U.S. Bureau of the Census, 1970, Table 3.
a. Method of calculation understates precise number of autos in relation to households. See Table 4.6, Footnote a.

must bear in mind that an inflationary decade altered the relative purchasing power of the income classes shown. Two conclusions, however, stand out. The first is that the only gains, class by class, are for the two income classes over $10,000. The second, by inference, is that the bulk of the upward shift of .18 points in the overall ratios is due to redistribution of households into higher income groups—i.e., there were more households in the upper income groups and fewer in the lower income groups in 1970 than in 1960.

Table 4.9, breaking down the ratio by age of head of household, shows that by 1970 there were roughly three levels of auto availability. The highest was for households with heads aged thirty-five to fifty-four, the next highest for households with heads on either side in age (i.e., twenty-five to thirty-four and fifty-five to sixty-four, and the lowest, for households with heads under twenty-five or sixty-five and over. The table also shows that those age classes already associated with the highest levels of auto availability in 1960 had the greatest point gains, further reinforcing previous differentials.

Table 4.10 presents further auto/household ratio data for selected categories. We see that both the highest level of auto ownership and the greatest increase in

Table 4.8: U.S. Auto/Household Ratio by Income of Primary Family Individual, 1960-70[a]

Income	1960	1970	Change 1960-70
Total - All Incomes	0.91	1.09	+0.18
Under $3,000	0.48	0.47	−0.01
$3,000-4,999	0.90	0.83	−0.07
$5,000-7,499	1.11	1.09	−0.02
$7,500-9,999	1.27	1.26	−0.01
$10,000-14,999	1.38	1.44	+0.06
$15,000 and over	1.53	1.59	+0.06

NOTE: Data adapted from U.S. Bureau of the Census, 1970, Table 1.
a. See Table 4.6, Footnote a.

Table 4.9: U.S. Auto/Household Ratio by Age of Household Head, 1960-70[a]

Age of Household Head	1960	1970	Change 1960-70
Total — All Ages	0.91	1.09	+0.18
Under 25	0.85	0.87	+0.02
25-34	0.98	1.17	+0.19
35-44	1.06	1.30	+0.24
45-54	1.04	1.29	+0.25
55-64	0.89	1.04	+0.19
65 and over	0.57	0.64	+0.07

NOTE: Data adapted from U.S. Bureau of the Census, 1970, Table 1.
a. See Table 4.6, Footnote a.

Table 4.10: U.S. Auto/Household Ratio by Metropolitan-Nonmetropolitan Status and by Selected Other Categories, 1960-70[a]

Selected Characteristics	1960	1970	Change 1960-70
All households	0.91	1.09	+0.18
Metropolitan areas — total	0.83	1.08	+0.25
Central cities	0.72	0.88	+0.16
Outside central cities	1.03	1.26	+0.23
Nonmetropolitan areas — total	0.99	1.10	+0.11
Nonfarm	1.00	1.10	+0.10
Farm	0.93	1.14	+0.21
Owner occupied dwellings	1.04	1.25	+0.21
Renter occupied dwellings	0.70	0.81	+0.11
Black households	0.62	0.64	+0.02
White households	1.11	1.14	+0.02

NOTE: Data adapted from U.S. Bureau of the Census, 1970, Table 4.7.
a. See Table 4.6, Footnote a.

the ratios from 1960 to 1970 were to be found outside of the central cities in the metropolitan areas. This had the effect of pulling up the metropolitan-total ratios to the point where, by 1970, they were virtually the same as the ratios for nonmetropolitan areas. The final differences (which are marginal totals only, since they do not include any further cross tabulations) merely reinforce the type of difference we have between central cities and suburban areas, since both the owner category and the white category are so directly associated with suburban residence.

Table 4.11 shows the two-way impact of type of metropolitan setting and of income on auto/household ratios. The four metropolitan types give us an indirect sense of residential density, ranging from the highest density for the old, large central cities to the lowest for the suburban areas. Low-income households in the former had a ratio of only 0.15 autos per household; high-income households in the latter had on the average 1.60 autos per household. These are indeed very substantial differences. We may conclude that the differences between metropolitan settings account for more variation than differences in income. Even low-income households are shown to have autos in suburban areas.

Table 4.12, from the same survey and source, uses the identical breakdown by type of metropolitan setting and shows, for each setting, the distribution by mode of travel for regular trips (presumably excluding trips to work). In the old, large central cities, about half of the trips are taken by auto (always or sometimes), while for suburban areas this percentage rises to 90. Trips always taken by common carrier drop very low in the suburbs. These are not surprises, but hopefully these sample findings—for the broad, average basis they are intended to report—help us to understand the levels of auto ownership and use that characterize contemporary metropolitan situations.

Table 4.11: Metropolitan U.S. Auto/Household Ratio by Type of Metropolitan Environs and by Family Income, 1965

Family Income	Total U.S. Metro-politan	Old, Large Central Cities[a]	New, Large Central Cities[b]	Small Central Cities	Sub-urban Areas
(Sample Ns)	(1,474)	(117)	(111)	(474)	(772)
Total — all incomes	1.23 (308)	0.54	1.06	1.12	1.43
Under $4,000	0.64 (530)	0.15	0.58	0.55	1.04
$4,000-7,499	1.21 (636)	0.62	0.86	1.14	1.35
$7,500 and over	1.55	1.05	1.43	1.56	1.60

NOTE: Data adapted from Lansing and Hendricks, 1967, Table 5, p. 16.
a. The New York area is excluded.
b. The 11 largest SMSAs (excluding the New York area) were divided as follows: "old" central cities were Baltimore, Boston, Chicago, St. Louis, and Philadelphia; "new" central cities were Cleveland, Detroit, Los Angeles, Pittsburgh, San Francisco, and Washington, D.C.

Table 4.12: Metropolitan U.S. Percentage Distribution of Regular Trips by Type of Metropolitan Environs and Mode of Travel, 1965

Mode of Travel	Total U.S. Metro-politan[a]	Old, Large Central Cities[b]	New, Large Central Cities[b]	Small Central Cities	Sub-urban Areas
(Sample Ns)	(1,534)	(89)	(129)	(454)	(862)
Total trips — all modes	100	100	100	100	100
Walk or taxi	5	8	2	5	6
Always common carrier	8	37	15	7	4
Sometimes auto, some-times common carrier	7	20	18	10	3
Always auto	80	35	65	78	87

NOTE: Data adapted from Lansing and Hendricks, 1967, Appendix, Table 7.
a. The New York area is excluded.
b. See Table 4.11, Footnote b.

MOTOR VEHICLE AVAILABILITY: A MORE DETAILED LOOK AT THE SAN FRANCISCO BAY AREA

Bay Area Survey No. 1 was conducted during the summer of 1971 by the staff of the Survey Research Center, University of California, Berkeley. The major client for the survey was the BART Impact Study Group, Institute of Urban and Regional Development, University of California, Berkeley. The survey involved a rigorous random sample of household heads or their spouses in the five-county San Francisco-Oakland SMSA. Interviews were completed with 1,018 actual respondents, but final weighted results were adjusted so that the final results could be treated as a 1-in-a-1,000 sample of the Bay Area. Thus, a final 2,209 reported persons aged sixteen and over represented 2,209,000 household members sixteen and over in the five-county SMSA. We draw upon this survey in considerable detail because it provides data with a conceptual and classificatory system of fresh approaches to the phenomenon of personal access to autos. Despite the location in California, the Bay Area as a metropolitan area and San Francisco as the main central city are fairly typical for much of the United States (note Table 4.7), so that we may regard the findings for the Bay Area as deserving of considerable generalization.

In the analysis of survey findings, household "motor vehicle" was used as the basic unit rather than household "auto". Of the total of all motor vehicles, 88.6 percent were autos, 6.7 percent were pickup trucks, 2.8 percent were motorcycles, and 1.9 were other trucks for personal use. A first measure was the number of motor vehicles per household, shown in Table 4.13. It can be seen that only one out of every eight persons sixteen and over in the Bay Area lived in households lacking an auto, and four out of every eight lived in households with two or more autos.

A second, and more sophisticated, measure was the ratio of household motor vehicles to persons sixteen and over in that household, seen in Table 4.14. This shows that nearly half of the Bay Area households were, and over two-fifths of household members sixteen and over lived in, motor-vehicle saturated households (i.e., households in which there were at least as many personal motor vehicles as household members sixteen and over). About 35 percent of all households were, and 45 percent of household members sixteen and over lived in, unsaturated households, but households in which there was at least one auto. For persons sixteen and over this is, by a slight margin, the most frequent class.

A third, and more personalized, measure was to determine more exactly the type and level of direct personal access to an auto characterizing each household member sixteen and over, seen in Table 4.15. Thus, we see that over three-fifths of all household members sixteen and over are primary users, which is to say that they have either exclusive use of a household motor vehicle or have greater use of the motor vehicle than any other household member. This is, of course, a very high proportion to have such personalized access to a motor vehicle, and shows, for the Bay Area at least, how far we have moved toward direct personal access, in contrast to merely having an auto or a motor vehicle for the household.

As a further simplifying device, we added together two percentages: all of the percentage of primary use (63) and half of the combined secondary and shared users (6). Thus, for the total Bay Area this figure was 69 percent having direct access. Conversely, the remaining 31 percent of household members sixteen and over were grouped as lacking direct personal access to a household motor vehicle. We employ this simplifying dichotomy from this point on, and use the percentage *lacking direct personal access to a household motor vehicle* as our "thermometer" of nonaccess to motor vehicles. Overall, for the Bay Area, this 31 percent converts to an estimate of nearly 700,000 persons sixteen and over who lack direct personal access to a household motor vehicle. As might be expected, a large block of persons lacking access, numbering more than 250,000, is to be found in households having no motor vehicle. But an even larger number, estimated at about 375,000 and representing 55 percent of those persons lacking access, are from "unsaturated" households—where there is at least one motor vehicle, but not enough vehicles to match the number of adults.

The impact of household income on nonaccess to motor vehicles is very direct, as is shown in Table 4.16. The rates of nonaccess to motor vehicles, shown in the first column of the table, show a progressive drop from the high rate of 54 percent for members in households with income $20,000 and over. As one would expect, we have a disproportionately heavy clustering of household members lacking access in the two lower income classes. Those lacking access in these two lower income classes represent 65 percent of all lacking access, whereas only 45 percent of all household members are in these income classes.

There are also differentials between majority-white households and the various ethnic or racial minority households, as summarized for the entire Bay Area in Table 4.17. Overall, nearly two out of every four members sixteen and over of minority households lack access to a motor vehicle, while for majority-white households only about one out of every four members sixteen and lacks access. The more than a quarter-million minority household members sixteen and over lacking access to motor vehicles represent about three-eighths of all

Table 4.13: San Francisco-Oakland SMSA Distribution of Motor Vehicles Per Household, 1971

Type of Household	Households	Persons 16 Years of Age and Older
(Weighted-Sample Ns)	(1,087)	(2,209)
All Households	100	100
No motor vehicles	17	12
One motor vehicle	41	37
Two motor vehicles	31	34
Three motor vehicles	8	12
Four or more motor vehicles	3	5

Table 4.14: San Francisco-Oakland SMSA Ratio of Household Motor Vehicles to Persons Sixteen and Older by Type of Household, 1971

Type of Household	Ratio of Motor Vehicles to Persons 16 and Older	House-holds	Persons 16 Years of Age and Older
(Weighted-Sample Ns)		(1,087)	(2,209)
All Households		100	100
With no motor vehicle	0	17	12
Unsaturated with motor vehicles		35	45
	0.01 - 0.49	6	10
	.50	22	23
	0.51 - 0.99	7	13
Saturated with motor vehicles		49	43
	1.00	43	37
	1.01 or more	6	6

Table 4.15: San Francisco-Oakland SMSA Distribution of Type and Level of Access to Auto for Those Aged Sixteen and Older, 1971

Auto-access Status of Each Household Member	Persons 16 Years of Age and Older
(Weighted-Sample N)	(2,209)
All household members 16+	100
Subtotal-Member does not use motor vehicle	25
Member does not drive	22
Member drives, but is without household vehicle	3
Subtotal-Member has secondary or shared use of a motor vehicle	12
Member has secondary use of a motor vehicle	12
Member shares motor vehicle equally with another household member	1
Subtotal-Member is primary user of a motor vehicle	63

Table 4.16: San Francisco-Oakland SMSA Percent Household Members Sixteen and over Lacking Direct Personal Access to Motor Vehicles by Household Income, 1971[a]

Household Income	As Percent of All Household Members 16+ in That Income Class		Estimated Number
(Weighted-Sample Ns)	(2,209)		
All Households	31		689,000[b]
Under $5,000	54	(403)	217,000
$5,000-9,999	36	(521)	186,000
$10,000-14,999	23	(581)	136,000
$15,000-19,999	18	(280)	50,000
$20,000 and over	12	(260)	31,000

a. These figures are, at best, estimates, and carry possible sampling errors. These errors may be the largest for some of the internal cells of the table where the samples upon which they are based are the smallest. We report weighted-sample Ns; in general, the original Ns tend to be slightly smaller.
b. Households not reporting income numbered an estimated 69,999 and are not included. Therefore, the figures add to only 620,000.

household members sixteen and over lacking access to motor vehicles, whereas minority household members sixteen and over in total represent only a quarter of all household members sixteen and over. In Oriental households, nearly three out of four members sixteen and over lacked access, reflecting in part the heavy concentration of households in the high-density Chinatown area of San Francisco.

Table 4.18 shows the simultaneous impact of ethnic status and income as well as the differentials for geographic sector (San Francisco as the main central city, the main part of the East Bay, and the remaining more clearly suburban portions of the SMSA). In broad terms, it would appear that income is a more significant factor than ethnic status, but that the differentials between San Francisco and the other parts of the SMSA are also very marked and certainly persist even when we separately view particular "cells" in the ethnic-income cross classification. For San Franciscans sixteen and over with household incomes under $10,000, three out of every five lack personal access to a motor vehicle, and this rises to two out of every three for San Franciscans of minority ethnic status with household incomes under $10,000. At the opposite extreme, for household members sixteen and over with household incomes $10,000 or more in the more suburbanized portions of the SMSA, only 18 percent lacked direct personal access to a motor vehicle. This percentage did not appear to vary appreciably, whether majority-white or minority household.

Up to this point we have been examining the impact of *household* characteristics and have considered only the average situation for all household members sixteen and over in these categories of households. We now turn to differences within households, examining the impact of several characteristics that vary *person by person:* specifically, age, sex, and activity status (i.e., whether employed, in school, etc.).

Table 4.19 shows the very important breakdown by age and sex. This shows that women are strikingly deficient in their access to motor vehicles, with 43 per-

Table 4.17: San Francisco-Oakland SMSA Percent Household Members Sixteen and over Lacking Direct Personal Access to Motor Vehicles by Ethnic Status, 1971[a]

Ethnic Status	As Percent of All Household Members 16+ in That Ethnic Status		Estimated Number
(Weighted-Sample Ns)	(2,209)		
All Households	31		689,000
Majority-white households	26	(1,659)	435,000
All minority households[b]	47	(550)	256,000
Negro households	43	(252)	107,000
Spanish households	36	(142)	51,000
Oriental households	73	(97)	71,000
Other minority households	47	(59)	27,000

a. See Table 4.16, Footnote a.
b. The Bay Area Survey appears to have undersampled household members of Spanish surname, to have somewhat oversampled Negro households, and to have slightly oversampled Oriental households and other minority households. We may presume that the percentages in the first column are more reliable than the figures in the second column.

Table 4.18: San Francisco-Oakland SMSA Percent of Household Members Sixteen and over Lacking Direct Personal Access to Motor Vehicles by Geographic Sector, Ethnic Status, and Household Income, 1971[a]

Household Income	Total	Majority-White	Combined Minorities
Total — Five-County SMSA			
Total — all incomes	31	26	47
Less than $10,000	44	37	56
$10,000 and over	19	17	29
San Francisco			
Total — all incomes	50	43	59
Less than $10,000	60	53	66
$10,000 and over	28	25	36
Main Urbanized East Bay[b]			
Total — all incomes	26	32	38
Less than $10,000	37	32	45
$10,000 and over	17	14	27
Remainder of SMSA[c]			
Total — all incomes	23	22	32
Less than $10,000	29	27	
$10,000 and over	18	18	19[d,e]

a. See Table 4.16, Footnote a.
b. Generally western and central Contra Costa County and western Alameda County.
c. The remainder of Alameda and Contra Costa counties and all of Marin and San Mateo counties.
d. Base too small to percentagize (under 20 weighted cases).
e. Percentage based on N of only 20-49 weighted cases.

Table 4.19: San Francisco-Oakland SMSA Percent of Household Members Sixteen and over Lacking Direct Personal Access to Motor Vehicles by Age and Sex, 1971[a]

Sex	Total-All 16+	Age 16-24	Age 25-44	Age 45-64	Age 65 and Over
(Weighted-Sample Ns)	(2,209)	(530)	(764)	(671)	(244)
Total	31	38	22	27	58
Male (1,043)	19	25	12	16	36
Female (1,166)	43	49	31	38	71
Estimated Number Lacking Personal Access to Motor Vehicles					
Total	689,000	200,000	168,000	181,000	140,000
Male	194,000	61,000	49,000	51,000	34,000
Female	495,000	139,000	119,000	130,000	106,000

a. See Table 4.16, Footnote a.

cent of all women lacking access to motor vehicles in contrast to only 19 percent of men lacking access to vehicles. Nearly a half-million of the 689,000 persons sixteen and over lacking access are women. Both old (sixty-five and over) and young (sixteen to twenty-four) women have high nonaccess rates. The largest single block of household members sixteen and over, according to the breakdown employed in the lower part of the table, is women aged sixteen to twenty-four. Looking at the percentages of persons lacking access to motor vehicles, cell by cell, in the upper part of the table, we find great spread—from a high of 71 percent of women sixty-five and over lacking access, to a low of only 12 percent of men in the active age class, twenty-five to forty-four. The general pattern is an important one, showing the combined impact of both age and sex. While we do not carry the age-sex breakdown through many further tables in combination with other variables, the differences do in fact generally persist.

Table 4.20 combines the effects of age and sex with the additional effect of household income. The table shows a consistent pattern, with the impacts of income being very strong but being overlaid by the persistent impacts of age and sex. The highest percentage for any cell, not surprisingly, is 80 percent nonaccess for women aged sixty-five and over in households with incomes less than $5,000. We would expect that the lowest percentages would be for men in their active ages with high incomes. This is very nearly the case, for we find only 9 percent and 5 percent in the age twenty-five to forty-four and forty-five to sixty-four categories with household income $15,000 and over. Surprisingly, there is one female cell, for age twenty-five to forty-four, with income $15,000 and over, where the percentage drops to 5. This may, in part, reflect sampling error, but it appears to suggest that females in this active age group and in households with high income, may have percentages of nonaccess at approximately the same level as males.

In Table 4.21, we show the respective and combined impacts of ethnic status, household income and sex. We have not shown age in addition because that becomes unduly detailed and runs a bit beyond the capabilities of this particular

Table 4.20: San Francisco-Oakland SMSA Percent of Household Members Sixteen and over Lacking Direct Personal Access to Motor Vehicles by Age, Sex, and Household Income, 1971[a]

Household Income	Total-All 16+	Age 16-24	Age 25-44	Age 45-64	Age 65 and Over
Male					
(Weighted-Sample Ns)	(1,043)	(264)	(374)	(328)	(95)
All males	19	25	12	16	36
Less than $5,000	38	28	33[b]	50[b]	43[b]
$5,000-9,999	25	30	19	19	45
10,000-14,999	10	18	6	9	c
15,000 and over	9	19[b]	9	5	c
Female					
(Weighted-Sample Ns)	(1,166)	(284)	(390)	(343)	(149)
All females	43	48	31	38	71
Less than $5,000	66	58	62	62	80
$5,000-9,999	46	51	44	37	54[b]
10,000-14,999	36	46	24	36	c
15,000 and over	21	33	5	27	c

a. See Table 4.16, Footnote a.
b. Percentage based on N of only 20-49 weighted cases.
c. Base too small to percentagize (under 20 weighted cases).

Table 4.21: San Francisco-Oakland SMSA Percent of Household Members Sixteen and over Lacking Direct Personal Access to Motor Vehicles by Ethnic Status, Income, and Sex, 1971[a]

Household Income	Total	Majority White	Combined Minorities
Male			
Total — all incomes	19	15	31
Less than $10,000	30	25	39
$10,000 and over	13	8	18
Female			
Total — all incomes	43	36	61
Less than $10,000	55	46	71
$10,000 and over	29	27	40

NOTE: The cross tabulation for both sexes combined has already been shown as the upper part of Table 4.18.
a. See Table 4.16, Footnote a.

sample. One should understand that the age differentials would reflect the patterns already shown. Table 4.21 shows that sex has a strong and persistent impact, whatever cell or subcategory we examine. By far the highest percentage of those lacking access to a vehicle for any of the cells shown is 71, for women of minority status with household incomes under $10,000. The lowest percentage lacking access, as we might expect, is for majority-white males with incomes $10,000 and over—only 8 percent. Within each sex, both ethnic status and income have decided and persistent impact.

Table 4.22: Major Activity Status of Persons Sixteen and over Lacking Direct Personal Access to Motor Vehicle, San Francisco-Oakland SMSA, 1971

Major Activity Status	Percent of Persons 16+ Lacking Direct Access to Motor Vehicles	Estimated Number Lacking Direct Access to Motor Vehicles
(Weighted-Sample Ns)	(2,209)	
All persons 16+	31	689,000
Working	21 (1,255)	264,000
Attending school	43 (176)	76,000
Engaged in housework	43 (464)	199,000
Retired	52 (140)	72,000
Other status	45 (174)	78,000

Table 4.22 offers a breakdown by the major activity status of each household member sixteen and over, showing the number of persons in each status, the percentage lacking direct access to motor vehicles, and the number lacking access. The largest group (those employed) has the lowest percentage lacking access to motor vehicle, with only slightly over a quarter-million employed persons lacking access. Categories with high percentages of nonaccess were housewives (the largest group), those attending school, and those retired.

Table 4.23 shows that the much greater lack of motor vehicle access for household members who are not working carries persistently through, even when the further breakdowns by household income and by sex are introduced. One finding does emerge, however, and that is that working women are in a much more disadvantaged position with respect to motor vehicle access than are working men. In the three household income categories above $5,000, for example, the percentages of working women lacking personal access to motor vehicles very nearly equals the corresponding percentages for non-working men. It seems clear that the working male has by far the highest claim on personal use of a household motor vehicle. This may reflect either a situation of saturation where virtually all adult household members have direct access to a motor vehicle or a situation where the male has first claim to such vehicles as are owned, even though there are not enough vehicles to go around.

In Table 4.24 we present a further compound breakdown to show the respective and combined impacts of ethnic status, work or non-work status, and household income. This table, in addition to showing the impacts of all three of these factors on motor vehicle nonaccess, in particular shows the very high rate of nonaccess on the part of minority workers. While only about two out of ten majority-white workers with household income under $10,000 lack personal access to a motor vehicle, an average of five out of ten minority workers in this income class lack personal access.

In Table 4.25, the final reporting of Bay Area findings, we show the differences for the three main geographic sectors of the SMSA along with breakdowns by household income and by major activity status. In addition to the consistent differences between San Francisco and the other parts of the Bay Area, which we would fully expect, there is one particularly interesting feature of the middle

Table 4.23: San Francisco-Oakland SMSA Percent of Household Members Sixteen and over Lacking Direct Personal Access to Motor Vehicles by Activity Status, Income, and Sex, 1971[a]

Household Income	Total — All Statuses	Working	Other Than Working
Total			
Total — all incomes	31	21	42
Less than $5,000	54	46	58
$5,000-9,999	36	26	47
10,000-14,999	23	13	35
15,000 and over	15	12	20
Male			
Total — all incomes	19	12	32
Less than $5,000	38	30	43
$5,000-9,999	25	17	38
10,000-14,999	10	6	23
15,000 and over	9	7	18
Female			
Total — all incomes	43	35	45
Less than $5,000	66	61	68
$5,000-9,999	46	38	51
10,000-14,999	36	29	40
15,000 and over	21	21	21

a. See Table 4.16, Footnote a.

Table 4.24: San Francisco-Oakland SMSA Percent of Household Members Sixteen and over Lacking Direct Personal Access to Motor Vehicles by Ethnic Status, Income, and Major Activity Status, 1971[a]

Household Income	Total	Majority White	Combined Minorities
Working as Major Activity			
Total — all incomes	21	15	38
Less than $10,000	33	22	51
$10,000 and over	13	11	19
Other than Working as Major Activity			
Total — all incomes	42	36	56
Less than $10,000	52	48	62
$10,000 and over	29	26	43

NOTE: The cross tabulation for all activities combined has already been shown as the upper part of Table 4.18.
a. See Table 4.16, Footnote a.

("Working as a Major Activity") part of the table. The final column, for the remainder of the SMSA, represents a generally low-density suburban development in which there is the least available good public transportation. Note the extremely low percentage, 6.5, of workers with household incomes under $10,000 lacking personal access to a motor vehicle. It is possible, of course, that there is some sampling error involved, but, even so, it suggests that almost all workers in this area, regardless of income, need a personal motor vehicle. This is fully con-

Table 4.25: San Francisco-Oakland SMSA Percent of Household Members Sixteen and over Lacking Direct Personal Access to Motor Vehicles by Geographic Sector, Income, and Major Activity Status, 1971[a]

Household Income	Total Bay Area	San Francisco	Main East Bay[b]	Remainder of SMSA[b]
Total — All Major Activities				
Total — all incomes	31	50	26	23
Less than $10,000	44	60	37	29
$10,000 and over	19	28	17	18
Working as Major Activity				
Total — all incomes	21	40	14	11
Less than $10,000	33	54	23	7
$10,000 and over	13	22	9	11
Other than Working as Major Activity				
Total — all incomes	42	61	37	35
Less than $10,000	52	68	46	45
$10,000 and over	29	39	27	27

a. See Table 4.16, Footnote a.
b. For definition, see Table 4.18, Footnotes b and c.

sistent with the Lansing-Hendricks finding that we reported in Table 4.11. From this we can conclude that it might prove extremely difficult for a low- or moderate-income household moving to a suburban area lacking good public transportation to get along without a sufficient number of motor vehicles to at least match the number of workers in the household.

Let us summarize the findings from the Bay Area Survey data, so as to rise above the considerable detail just presented:

(1) Overall, Bay Area residents (i.e., household members sixteen years of age and over) have a very high level of direct personal access to motor vehicles, with nearly seven out of every ten enjoying such access. This quite obviously has permeated their living patterns and facilitated their out-of-the-home activities.

(2) Conversely, despite the fact that we have moved so overwhelmingly to a situation in which personal use of motor vehicles is so high, nearly three out of ten residents lack direct personal access to a motor vehicle. Some factors directly associated with this lack of access are household characteristics and include low-income, ethnic-minority status, and residence in the higher-density central city. This suggests that certain residential districts may be unusually dependent upon modes of transportation other than auto.

(3) Even within specific households it becomes very evident that highly significant differentials in access to a motor vehicle are common. Women, in particular, have much higher rates of nonaccess; household members in the sixteen to twenty-four and the sixty-five and over age groups have consistently higher rates; and household members who are not in a gainfully employed status have much higher rates. Such persons, we have found, are widely distributed, both in households without motor vehicles

and also, importantly, in households in which there are fewer vehicles than adults.

(4) The compound impacts of these various factors can be strongly reinforcing, with the result that it is not uncommon for certain subcategories of residents (specific cells in our detailed tables) to have very high rates of nonaccess to motor vehicles. In such cases, as many as six, seven, or even eight out of ten residents may lack direct personal access to motor vehicles.

(5) We need to know much more about how metropolitan residents lacking this access to motor vehicles actually cope. We should understand how much they go without trips they might take, were transportation not an impediment. We should learn how well such residents are served by walking and by public transport.

OTHER EVIDENCE REGARDING
OUT-OF-THE-HOME ACTIVITY PATTERNS

Certainly, powerful forces—rising household incomes, lower residential densities, and preponderant reliance on the auto—have contributed to a loosening of former more traditional neighborhood and community patterns. If urban residents increasingly use autos, we may fully expect that their orbits of travel, their freedom of movement, and their corresponding shifts in facilities relied upon will change. To bring direct evidence to bear on such hypothesized shifts proves, however, to be exceedingly difficult. We have few fully satisfactory comparative studies of shifts over time. The transportation studies tend to report only vehicular trips, and do not give us the full picture of the mix of walking and vehicular trips. This makes it difficult to understand the changing relative importance of walking trips. This, in turn, has a particularly pointed relevance if we want to understand how people who lack direct access to an auto get along.

A comparison for the Detroit area between 1953 and 1965 (restricted to vehicular trips) showed, as one might expect, a considerable increase in travel by auto (Bellomo, Dial, and Voorhees, 1970: 8-19). Using a 1953 base of 1.00, the number of trips in 1965 equalled 1.43. There was also a great drop in travel by public transit. With the same 1953 base, the number of trips in 1965 was 0.40. Shopping by auto showed the greatest increase (1965 trips = 1.99). Overall, auto trips did not show any great increase in distance; the average trip in 1953 was 5.1 miles, while in 1965 it was 5.5 miles. Nor was there much change in time; in 1953 the average trip took 12.7 minutes, while in 1965 it took 12.5 minutes. Transit trips, significantly, showed a marked increase in average time, up from 34.7 minutes in 1953 to 45.5 minutes in 1965, suggesting possible deterioration in headways and service as well as changes in the location of destinations.

According to Bellomo et al. (1970: 4), more complex changes were also under way in the Detroit area:

In 1953, the center-city resident had the lowest work trip length and the highest housing cost. . . . In the suburbs the trip lengths were higher but the housing costs were lower. In 1965 the pattern with respect to the transport costs completely reversed. People in the center city had higher trip lengths whereas those in the suburbs had lower trip lengths. These dynamic changes were brought about by factors such as the transportation system, the structure of the urban area, and socioeconomic conditions.

Work trips, particularly, increased in length and in time for low-income non-whites, with the most serious increases for those dependent upon public transportation.

Nor were increasing trip lengths restricted to large metropolitan areas like Detroit. Here are changes in average trips for two smaller urban areas:

Sioux City, Iowa	1955: 2.16 miles	1965: 2.39 miles
Reading, Pennsylvania	1958: 2.37 miles	1964: 2.67 miles

For both cases, as with Detroit, increases in mileage were brought about with little increase in time because of improved highway systems (Bellomo et al., 1970: 9). Hawley (1971: 191) has noted earlier increases in average work trip lengths, up to the 1950s, and surmises that since then they have probably further increased.

For work places have continued to scatter over metropolitan areas, a great amount of expressway mileage has been constructed, and multiple-car ownership has become more common. The centrifugal movement of blue-collar residences, however, have tended to shorten work-trip distances for that element of the population.

According to a national sample survey conducted in the summer of 1967 by Chiltern Research Services and National Analysts, respondents reported a great increase in auto use in the previous five years (see Table 4.26). The categories of persons showing the greatest relative increase in auto use included young persons, persons of intermediate education, blue-collar and intermediate white-collar levels, and males (McMilland and Assael, 1969: 44-54).

Still another sample survey was conducted in 1963, upon which Hawley and Zimmer (1970) based an extensive study. It was deliberately stratified to secure six types of community settings, breaking each of three size classes of metropolitan areas into central city and suburbs: (1) large metropolitan areas (about 1,000,000)—Buffalo, New York, and Milwaukee, Wisconsin; (2) medium metro-

Table 4.26: Percentages of Change in Auto and Public Transportation Use, 1962-67

	Auto	Public Transportation
Total	100%	100%
Decrease in use	9	11
No change in use	40	72
Increase in use	52	17
Net increase (difference in points, increase minus decrease)	+43	+6

Table 4.27: Percentage of Responses Identifying Selected Features as Attractive in Six Metropolitan Areas by Type of Metropolitan Setting, c. 1963

Attractive Features	Large SMSA		Medium SMSA		Small SMSA	
	Central Cities	Sub-urbs	Central Cities	Sub-urbs	Central Cities	Sub-urbs
Accessibility	52	46	57	37	52	25
Public transportation	22	11	28	10	14	2
Neighbors and property maintenance	24	33	26	37	30	34
Space, privacy, cleanliness	18	39	18	44	21	53

NOTE: Data from Hawley and Zimmer, 1970, Table 18, p. 48.

politan areas (about 450,000-500,000)—Rochester, New York, and Dayton, Ohio; (3) small metropolitan areas (about 150,000)—Saginaw, Michigan, and Rockford, Illinois. Several responses relevant to our present interests were obtained and analyzed. Responses concerning attractive features of a metropolitan setting are shown in Table 4.27. As Hawley and Zimmer (1970: 47) noted: "Central city households place a high value on accessibility. That advantage is also important to suburban residents in large metropolitan areas. But as size of area declines accessibility yields its primacy to the spaciousness, privacy and cleanliness of suburban neighborhoods.

Hawley and Zimmer also looked at the localization of several urban activities and constructed a scope-of-activity scale. Using eight dichotomized measures, they provided an additive scale score with each localized activity contributing a point to the score. The scale ranges from 1 (extreme localization) to 7 (extreme nonlocalization). Average scores are shown in Table 4.28, broken down by metropolitan setting, mobility, age of household head, education of household head, and income of household head. The table shows that household members tended to go farther for activities, and hence had higher mean scores (more nonlocalized) if they were in the suburbs, were in smaller metropolitan areas, had moved their residence, were young in age, had more education, and had higher incomes.

We cite one further empirical study. Haines, Simon, and Alexis (1972) examined the hypothesis that the poor in the inner city are restricted in their shopping habits. Four inner residential districts in Rochester, New York, were studied in the late 1960s. Food trading areas were found to be as large for these inner residents as for residents living farther out. Respondents usually also reported shopping at a second store representing an even larger area. Haines et al. (1972: 100) suggested that:

> One possible rationale is that people use their second major stores for rather specialized purposes such as to take advantage of sales or for the purchase of some particular categories of food which are felt to be better, say meat, at the second major store: that is, the difference may result from the second major store being more like a specialty goods store than a convenience goods store.

Table 4.28: Mean Scope-of-Activity Scale Score by Type of Metropolitan Setting and Selected Other Variables in Six Metropolitan Communities, c. 1963

Characteristics	Large		Medium		Small	
	Central Cities	Sub-urbs	Central Cities	Sub-urbs	Central Cities	Sub-urbs
Total	3.1	3.6	3.6	4.0	3.3	4.5
Lived only same zone	3.0	3.0	3.5	3.3	3.2	4.2
Moved from oppos. zone	3.7	4.0	3.9	4.2	3.7	4.6
Age of household head						
Under 30	3.2	3.9	4.1	4.0	4.0	4.5
30-44	3.3	3.7	3.6	4.0	3.4	4.6
45-64	3.3	3.6	3.8	4.2	3.3	4.5
65 and over	2.4	3.3	2.8	3.6	2.6	3.8
Education, household head						
Elementary school	2.9	3.5	3.3	4.0	3.2	4.3
High school	3.3	3.6	3.8	4.1	3.6	4.7
College	3.7	3.9	4.2	3.9	3.7	4.8
Income, household head						
Under $75 per week	2.7	3.3	3.0	3.8	2.9	4.0
$75-149 per week	3.5	3.8	4.0	4.0	3.6	4.6
150-299 per week	3.4	3.7	4.5	3.9	3.7	5.0
300 or more per week	—	4.1	3.7[a]	4.5	3.4[a]	4.9[a]

NOTE: 1.0, extreme localization; 7.0, extreme nonlocalization. Data from Hawley and Zimmer, 1970, Tables 4.24 and 4.25, pp. 60, 62-63.
a. Based on N of less than 25.

The study also showed that there are "fill-in" stores which do have smaller trading areas, but that these are not relied upon for the main purchases.

The following findings are suggested to summarize the studies reported in this section:

(1) There has indeed been a switch to increased reliance upon the auto, and a corresponding decrease in public transit use. This has increased trip distance, but more so in low-density settings (i.e., in smaller metropolitan areas and in suburban sectors).

(2) Because of the great improvements in the freeway-highway systems, greater distance can be covered without any necessary increase in time. Some studies, not reported here, also show that auto trips, in contrast to transit trips, increase the distance that can be covered within a given portal-to-portal time (Myers, 1970).

(3) As the auto supplants walking as a predominant mode, the range of distance that can be covered takes a quantum jump and the geographic area that comes within reach increases vastly. The auto also permits greater selectivity; a resident's movement space becomes less bound by contiguity as such and more nearly space-jumping in character.

(4) We might have added more, too, about the combined power of the telephone and auto. The telephone is available for exploratory inquiries or for confirming whether one will make a physical trip, and the auto is then available for the actual physical trip.

Table 4.29: U.S. Population by Chronic Condition, Mobility Limitations, and Age, 1965-67 Average

| Age Group | Total Population | With No Chronic Condition | With One Chronic Condition or More[a] | | With Some Limitation on Mobility | | | |
			Total	With No Limitation on Mobility	Total	Trouble Getting Around	Needs Help Getting Around[b]	Confined to the House[c]
Number of Persons (000)								
Total	191,537	96,684	94,853	88,541	6,312	3,114	1,766	1,432
Under 17	66,921	51,664	15,757	15,009	248	90	82	76
17-44	67,901	31,188	36,713	35,865	848	539	163	147
45-64	38,993	11,278	27,714	25,816	1,898	1,124	407	367
65 and over	17,723	2,553	15,169	11,852	3,318	1,361	1,114	843
As Percent of Age Group								
Total	100.0	50.5	49.5	46.2	3.3	1.6	0.9	0.7
Under 17	100.0	77.2	22.8	22.4	0.4	0.1	0.1	0.1
17-44	100.0	45.9	54.1	52.8	1.3	0.8	0.2	0.2
45-64	100.0	28.9	71.1	66.2	4.9	2.9	1.0	0.9
65 and over	100.0	14.4	85.6	66.9	18.7	7.7	6.3	4.8

NOTE: Data from U.S. Public Health Service, January 1971, adapted from Tables A, 1, 25.
a. Chronic conditions include some two dozen conditions ranging from asthma or hay fever to heart condition to physical impairments or disability.
b. Needs the help of another person or the use of some special aid such as a cane or a wheelchair.
c. May or may not be confined to bed.

PHYSICAL CONDITION, WALKING, BICYCLING

In a fundamental sense, walking provides a potentially effective means of physical mobility. But it presumes relatively good personal physical condition and land use arrangements such that the desired destinations are within ready walking range. Similarly, for those in very good physical condition, the bicycle offers a potentially important mode of transportation and has, of course, been enjoying a remarkable comeback in popularity. It has been reported that more bicycles than autos have been produced and sold during the past year or two.

Walking is important both as a mode complete in itself and as a supplementary mode, by which one gets to or from his auto or to or from public transportation. By and large, we simply lack systematic and reliable information on walking. As we have already indicated, the typical transportation study restricts "trips" to vehicular trips, dropping walking through the screen of concern. Obviously, the findings from such studies greatly distort the total out-of-home activity picture.

In this section, we look briefly at personal physical condition and at empirical evidence regarding walking (and, in passing, bicycling) trips.

Measures of physical disability and of mobility limitation are available nationally and for certain states or smaller geographic areas, although they vary from study to study. Since many measures are not very directly relevant to our concern for physical accessibility or mobility, we shall report only selected National Health Survey findings. As of the mid-1960s, it has been estimated that 6.3 million Americans (or 3.3 percent of the total population) have some limitation on mobility as well as one chronic condition or more. Table 4.29 shows the national breakdown by the type or seriousness of the mobility limitation cross-tabulated by age group. Not surprisingly, mobility limitations are most numerous for those sixty-five and over, being present in nearly one out of every five persons in this age group. For all age groups, 1.4 million persons are confined to their homes, 1.8 million need some help in getting around (either by another person or by the use of a special aid such as a wheelchair), and 3.1 million have some trouble getting around, but do not require help. The age group forty-five to sixty-four also contains a very sizable number of persons with mobility limitations, amounting to nearly 5 percent of the age group.

Table 4.30 includes only the 95 million Americans (all ages grouped together) with at least one chronic condition, ranging from disability or heart disease to more minor difficulties such as hay fever or asthma. For this large population block, the table provides a two-way classification: by mobility limitation and by activity limitation. As one would expect, there is an association between greater limitations on the activity one can carry on and the greater limitation on mobility. It is not clear from this table, however, whether overcoming mobility limitations would improve the chances for carrying on one's major activity or whether, in most instances, both types of limitation reflect personal physical condition.

Further evidence regarding the extent of personal disability is provided in Table 4.31. This shows that on the average each person in the United States

Table 4.30: U.S. Population with One Chronic Condition or More by Activity and Mobility Limitations, 1965-67 Average

Type of Activity Limitation	Total With One Chronic Condition or more[a]	With No Limitation on Mobility	With Some Limitation on Mobility			
			Total	Some Trouble Getting Around	Needs Help Getting Around	Confined to the House
Number of Persons (000)						
Total – all conditions	94,853	88,541	6,312	3,114	1,766	1,432
Not limited in activity	72,869	72,585	284	157	103	24
Total – Limited in activity	21,984	15,956	6,028	2,957	1,663	1,408
Limited, but not in major activity	5,637	4,785	852	633	161	58
Limited in major activity	12,269	9,517	2,752	1,661	699	392
Unable to carry on major activity	4,078	1,654	2,424	663	803	958
As Percent of Activity-Limitation Group						
Total – all conditions	100.0	93.4	6.6	3.3	1.9	1.3
Not limited in activity	100.0	99.6	0.4	0.2	0.1	– –
Total – Limited in activity	100.0	72.6	27.4	13.5	7.6	6.4
Limited, but not in major activity	100.0	84.9	15.1	11.2	2.9	1.0
Limited in major activity	100.0	77.6	22.4	13.5	5.7	3.2
Unable to carry on major activity	100.0	40.6	59.4	16.3	19.7	23.5

NOTE: Data adapted from U.S. Public Health Service, January 1971, Tables A, 1. The population figures inside the margins of the upper part of the table were estimated by applying the percentage figure in the lower part of the table.
a. For definitions, see Table 4.29, Footnotes a, b, and c.

Table 4.31: U.S. Distribution of Disability Days Per Person Per Year, by Type of Disability and Age Group, Mid-1960s

Age Group	Total Disability	Short-term Disability	Long-term Disability	
			Noninsti-tutional	Insti-tutional
Total — all ages	22.8	12.9	7.5	2.4
Under 15	11.3	10.3	0.6	0.5
15-44	14.8	11.5	2.1	1.2
45-64	29.1	16.6	9.9	2.7
65-74	57.4	20.8	30.3	6.3
75 and over	116.2	17.0	74.7	24.5

NOTE: Data from U.S. Public Health Service, July 1971, Table 3, pp. 8-9.

loses 22.8 days per year in disability. The table shows the variation by duration, by noninstitutional-institutional status, and by age group. Persons sixty-five to seventy-four spend one-sixth of their collective lives in a disabled status; persons seventy-five and over spend nearly one-third in such status.

As of 1969, an estimated 6.2 million persons in the civilian noninstitutional-ized population of the United States were reported to have one or more special orthopedic aids—aids for providing help in getting around. This represented 3.2 percent of the population; for males, 3.4 percent, and for females, 3.0 percent. A breakdown by type of special aid and by age group is provided in Table 4.32. The figures in the table are self-explanatory: 2.4 million persons require special shoes, 2.2 a cane or walking stick, 1.1 braces, and so on. Over 400,000 need wheel chairs and the same number need walkers.

In summary, it is clear that persons with serious limitations on mobility represent small proportions of the population, but that persons with some ill-health symptoms or low-energy levels are far more numerous. For older persons, even the numbers and proportions with mobility limitations are far more significant. These various statistics provide a powerful reminder that there are in fact very large numbers of persons with conditions that limit their abilities to walk or even to make fully effective use of normal modes of vehicular transportation.

We need systematically assembled data on walking: how many trips (e.g., as related to the number of vehicular trips), how far, for what purposes, and by whom. We need to study walking under different urban settings, with variations in density, land use, and other environmental differences. We need to find out the differentials in walking ability and in the willingness to walk as associated with such personal and household variables as age, sex, physical condition, income, and personal access to other transportation modes.

We will present a few extremely scattered findings, not necessarily current. In a study in a medium-density district in St. Louis, in 1948, it was estimated that over one-third of all trips from home to various facilities, including employment, were by walking (Foley, 1948: Tables 7 and 9). The purpose for which walking was most frequently employed were elementary school attendance (97 percent), food shopping (69 percent), church attendance (63 percent), and

Table 4.32: U.S. Population Using Special Orthopedic Aids by Type of Aid and Age Group, 1969

Age Group	Special Shoes	Cane or Walking Stick	Brace	Crutches	Wheel-chair	Walker	Artificial Leg or Foot	Artificial Arm or Hand	Artificial Other
Number of Persons Using Aids (000)									
All ages	2,377	2,156	1,102	443	409	404	126	46	140
Under 45	1,620	94	518	147	100	b	b	b	51
45-64	444	444	363	158	94	57	57	b	b
65 and over	313	1,618	221	137	215	329	b	b	b
As Percent of Persons in Each Age Group									
All ages	1.2	1.1	0.6	0.2	0.2	0.2	0.1	a	0.1
Under 45	1.2	0.1	0.4	0.1	0.1	b	b	b	a
45-64	1.1	1.1	0.9	0.4	0.2	0.1	0.1	b	b
65 and over	1.7	8.7	1.2	0.7	1.2	1.8	b	b	b

NOTE: Data from National Center for Health Statistics, 1972, Table 3.
a. Less than 0.1 percent.
b. Base too small to be reliable.

movie attendance (53 percent). The purposes for which walking was least frequently employed were attendance at schools other than elementary (7 percent), outdoor recreational activities (only 8 percent), employment (9 percent), and major shopping (12 percent). The median distance for all walking trips was one-third of a mile.

In a 1969 sample survey of household heads and spouses in ten American community settings, some evidence on walking was obtained (Lansing, Marans, E. Zehner). The emphasis of the survey was on suburban and relatively recent developments, half of which were judged to be "planned communities" (including Columbia, Reston, Radburn, Southwest Washington and Lafayette-Elmwood in Detroit). Walking to stores or to friends was distinguished from walking or hiking for recreation. Selected findings are presented in Table 4.33. In planned communities, whether in town or peripheral, between 15 and 45 percent of respondents (household heads or spouses) reported walking to a grocery or other store in the preceding week; in less planned or least planned peripheral communities, these percentages ranged from 0 to about 10. In the whole scatter

Table 4.33: Percentage Walking, Having Sidewalks, and Bicycling in 10 Planned American Communities, 1969[a]

| Activity/Characteristic | Highly Planned Communities | | Less Planned | Least Planned |
	Two In-Town	Three Peripheral	Two Peripheral	Three Peripheral
Walking to grocery store last week	40-44	15-47	0-12	4-8
Walking to other stores last week	26-32	13-39	0-3	2-10
Walking to friend's house last week	46-50	50-60	57-66	30-52
Walking to two or more places last week	37-38	19-45	0-11	4-9
Hiking or walking for recreation	53-60	68-86	58-66	52-60
Sidewalks in front of or near home	98-99	62-67	0-100	38-98
Sidewalks going by home judged to be "very important"	69-75	47-60	64-88	39-71
Bicycling to at least one place last week	8-12	21-25	16-25	8-25
Bicycling for recreation	21	31-44	38-39	20-51

NOTE: Data adapted from Lansing et al., 1970, Tables 63, 64, 67.
a. These include only replies for household heads or spouses who reside in single-family homes or townhouses. Communities include: highly planned, in-town—Southwest Redevelopment, Washington, D.C., and Lafayette Park-Elmwood Park, Detroit; highly planned, peripheral—Columbia, Md., Reston, Va., and Radburn, N.J.; less planned, peripheral—Crofton, Md., and Montpelier, Md.; least planned, peripheral—Norbeck area, Md., Southfield area, Mich., and Glenn Rock area, N.J.

of community types, about half of the respondents had walked to a friend's house in the preceding week. Most respondents reported hiking or walking for recreation, and this rose to about three-fourths for the planned peripheral communities. Most respondents also judged sidewalks to be important.

A study of retired persons living in San Antonio, Texas, in the mid-1960s showed that for this admittedly special-age segment (although some were under fifty), walking was the most commonly used mode of transportation for going to the library (67 percent), to the senior center (45 percent), to visit friends (42 percent), and to church (34 percent) (Carp, 1971a). It was least used to go to sports events (8 percent), or to visit the doctor or to visit relatives (16 percent, in each case). Nearly half the respondents walked as a means of transportation several times each week, and one person in five went somewhere on foot "every day." However, nearly as many habitually walked to some destination less often than once a month, and some who considered themselves walkers had not done so for several years (Carp, 1971b: 36). But Carp (pp. 36-37) noted that walking was not well regarded as a means of transportation: "Only three percent of the walkers said walking was 'satisfactory' as a means of getting places while over half said it met their needs 'very poorly' or 'not at all'. The outstanding problem was that the places they needed and wanted to go were beyond walking range."

A subsequent sample survey of older persons in San Francisco—again, a special but important group—showed that walking was even more common among San Francisco people aged sixty-five and over than it was among retired people in San Antonio. Nearly 66 percent used their feet to take them some place every day, and more than 80 percent made several walking trips each week (Carp, 1972: 19-20). As Table 4.34 shows, the most common destination, ranked by the percentage using walking as the mode, is "food" (75 percent). "Friends and acquaintances," "religious services," and "park" rank next as destinations, with over 40 percent walking to these places.

However, walking was not popular as a means of transportation among the older residents of San Francisco. As in Texas, the more one walked, the less he

Table 4.34: Percentage of the Elderly in San Francisco Walking to Common Destinations, Late 1960s

Destination	Percentage Walking
Food	75
Friends and acquaintances	46
Religious services	44
Park	42
Medicine	38
Out to eat	25
Other shopping	23
Other recreation	21
Doctor	15
Other relatives	14
Children	10

NOTE: Data from Carp, 1972, p. 22.

Table 4.35: Percentage of the Elderly in San Francisco Reporting Problems and Advantages of Walking, Late 1960s

	Percentage of Respondents
Problem[a]	
Destinations too far	83
Depends on weather	78
Hills	72
Fears	65
Tired, feet hurt	55
Takes too long	52
Health problem	37
Traffic confusing	36
Advantages[b]	
Good for health	92
Inexpensive	90
Independent	85
Convenient	82
Contact with people	81

a. Carp, 1972, p. 20.
b. Carp, 1972, p. 24.

liked it as a means of getting places (Carp, 1972: 20). Table 4.35 shows percentages of the elderly reporting on certain disadvantages and advantages of walking. The main problems of walking cited were that a destination was too far and that the decision to walk depended on the weather. Advantages cited included the fact that walking is good for health and is inexpensive. We must remember that San Francisco, with its high density and its developed transit system is an unusual setting; walking is undoubtedly more prevalent and more helpful in San Francisco than in most American cities.

Regarding the use and relative satisfaction in walking trips for poor persons, we are not able to provide helpful information. As Gurin (1969: 25) notes:

> Little is known about the walking trips of the poor. No procedures for summarizing the large number of possible walking trip destinations, even within a neighborhood, have been prepared. Desired information on walking trips might include guidelines for transportation plans that involved walking as one phase of a trip. In particular, this information would help transportation planners to be able to estimate good bus stop space and route coverage in an area, based on people's tolerance for walking—controlled by the walker's income, age, trip purpose, time of day and year, topography, the number and age of traveling companions, and weather.

Gurin (1969: 74-75) goes on to discuss the many other elements that relate to walking and to mobility in more general terms: "Mobility, somewhat like civil rights, is taken for granted by those who have it. Until mobility is reduced or denied, a person rarely begins to appreciate how much his attitudes, hopes, aspirations, and even his faith in his own self-determination depend upon his ability to move when and where he desires." Gurin (pp. 19-20) also discussed the special circumstances which blacks face in regard to walking:

The poor as a group and the black people as a subset of the poor have many handicaps in common that restrain travel mobility—fear, financial deprivations, etc. The blacks, however, bear not only these burdens, but additional ones that are unique to them because of a racist social environment. Almost like aliens in an enemy land, black people in the U.S. must consider movements in this country which the 'natives' need not consider. . . . People from whom whites normally get travel aid and directions, such as police and gas station attendants, are often the very people with whom the blacks are most reluctant to get involved. This is especially true in certain regions of the country and in exclusively white communities.

Several studies have shown the impacts of suburbanization and dispersal on pulling employment opportunities away from low-income areas in inner cities. Jobs are not only spreading well beyond possible walking range; they become increasingly difficult or impossible to reach by public transit. A recent study of West Oakland, for example, showed that a majority of the jobs for which West Oakland residents might be qualified were more than 45 minutes away by bus (Oakland City Planning Department, 1970). This suggested, according to the report, that distance and cost, as well as an actual lack of transportation, become very serious impediments. A study (McMurry, 1972: 20-21) concludes:

Ghettoized Puerto Ricans are limited in their job search to the communications network of the local area, and consequently miss out on the employment opportunities far-removed from their homes. The latter are usually opportunities in the fast-growing suburban employment centers, which appear to be better-paying, more promising positions in the long-run. If Puerto Ricans living in the central city do obtain such jobs, our data suggest that the difficulties of transportation involved in the 'reverse commuting' from their residence areas to the suburban employment centers may be too much of a burden. Thus for some Puerto Ricans tenure in a suburban job is short-lived.

CONCLUSIONS

There are clearly many meanings that may be attached to the concept, "community." We have been looking at the functional-spatial aspect of facility use and of daily activity. As Hawley (1950: 257) has suggested "From a spatial standpoint, the community may be defined as comprising that area the resident population of which is interrelated and integrated with reference to its daily requirements, whether contacts be direct or indirect." It would appear now that those traditional notions that tie community to specific and precise geographic settings, featuring clear centers and sharp outer limits, involve a misplaced concreteness and are increasingly inappropriate as ways of viewing American metropolitan structure.

We have stressed that the structures of metropolitan areas have been undergoing tremendous change, involving the active circularity between dispersion and ever lower densities on the one hand, and the extremely heavy reliance on the auto on the other. Rising income and the ready use of autos, in fact, have given most metropolitan residents access to an unprecedentedly wide range of opportunities and have provided great scope for reaching out spatially to points where these opportunities are to be found—but points which are well beyond the bounds that would earlier have demarcated communities. This reaching out is characteristically highly selective and permits each person to put together a relatively unique configuration of the opportunities he opts to reach or use.

Reflecting these powerful changes, we might reinterpret and supplement Hawley's approach to "community." First, we might somewhat downplay the concept of a single area and, particularly with respect to the complex structure of "subcommunities" within any given metropolitan area, stress the multiplicity of, and the irregular overlayering of, subcommunities. We might stress the lack of generally clearcut boundaries; it is important that many of these subcommunities verge on functional, rather than literally geographic, boundaries in any event. Second, we might emphasize the degree to which individual residents come to operate with their own personalized configurations of facilities and persons to which or to whom they have customary access. And, third, we might invite increased recognition of *"community" as a sharing of access to opportunities,* in possible contrast to "community" as a sharing of actual facility-use and personal-contact patterns. This difference is rather fundamental and suggests that with rising income, more education, greater knowledge about one's metropolitan environs, and better transportation and communication, most metropolitan residents are able to benefit from the potential array of opportunities open to them over and beyond the actual contacts to which they customarily travel. This amounts to a greater freedom of opportunity and recognizes the significance of latent opportunities.

But in the midst of this general trend of rising accessibility to many and diverse opportunities, certain categories of residents, by reason of their household or personal characteristics, find themselves seriously deprived with respect to accessibility. These persons may lack financial resources, they may have personal physical disabilities, they may lack the knowledge and the coping abilities to get along in the complex metropolis, and they may lack the most versatile and essential transportation—the auto. Even more likely, they may suffer from combinations of these disadvantages such that the various deprivations become negatively reinforcing.

The public policy implications of this situation particularly suggest the need for improving the accessibility on the part of those persons who have failed to share the full benefits of residence in the metropolitan environs. This leads to many challenges, but to no simple, ready solutions. Improved access to shifting job opportunities is of high priority; probably the creation of jobs near present residence will prove even more difficult. Income maintenance would appear to be needed to provide an improved resource base. Concern for physical health and personal mobility is involved.

Several policy implications follow. Concern for latent opportunities as an active ingredient of "community" is, of course, consistent with a philosophy of pluralism that recognizes the prospects for alternative life-styles within the metropolis. It respects the basic rights of urban residents to select between nearby (local) contacts and more distant (less local) contacts; to choose their friends and be able to maintain relations with these friends wherever they may reside in the metropolis; to have considerable choice as to type and location of job; to be able to pursue one's particular leisure-time interests; to seek out the kind of immediate residential environment one wants for one's household; and to pursue one's preferred religious and political beliefs. We have, if anything, been moving into an era in which choice of life-style is a prominent characteristic. To a remarkable degree we have been moving beyond the point where residents' life-styles can be stereotyped on the basis of ethnic background, income, or occupation. We may helpfully view a resident's home and immediate residential environment as a base from which the resident may operate, rather than as a tight imposition of patterns and expectations associated with that "place."

In simple areal terms, community building must seek to provide both access to an ever broadening range of metropolitan opportunities, and a pleasant and convenient immediate residential environment with opportunities close at hand for those who opt (or, because of physical condition or other reasons, may find it necessary) to rely on them.

If anything, we have probably placed undue emphasis in recent years on the promise of improved transportation. This has merely served to reinforce the already powerful impacts of the auto. It has suggested that it was as important to permit the resident to travel sixteen miles as a half mile. And, as we have stressed, it has gradually squeezed out many who have lacked ready access to autos. It has led to land use patterns presuming auto-mobility.

The alternate thrust would seem to deserve fresh attention: namely the thoughtful provision of selected local opportunities. This certainly includes some basic facilities for food shopping, other convenience shopping, and other services. This is not a simple matter, however, for the economics have been such that many strictly local commercial ventures have not been able to hold their own against the vastly larger stores and service centers that continue to flourish.

Perhaps, too, we might seriously explore the possibilities of innovative types of service centers in local residential districts that specialize in providing information about, and contacts to, the larger web of essentially nonlocal facilities. This would respect the inappropriateness of offering anything approaching a full range of services in each district, but would seek to link the local resident more effectively into the broader potentials. Service centers might have local personnel and seek to provide what local residents particularly expressed interest in, but might well be linked to a hierarchically organized service-center system in which various higher-level or specialized centers provide information and contacts beyond the expertise of the local center. There could be legal-advice centers or medical clinics that were fewer in number and more specialized in character.

Even here, the overriding philosophy might best be to encourage residents to get to the facilities they would prefer to use. Some may head immediately for the large law office or the major medical center; some may appreciate the availability of smaller, but more proximate facilities.

There is also much that we have made no attempt to cover. We have deliberately not dealt with the political and governmental-administrative aspects of community. We have not grappled with political participation and its ties to community identification or alienation. Nor have we dealt with the difficult fiscal situations confronted in all metropolitan areas. It stands to reason that a concern for accessibility must be melded with many other aspects of community.

REFERENCES

Automobile Manufacturers Association. *1971 Automobile facts and figures.* Detroit: 1972.

Baltimore Regional Planning Council and National Capital Regional Planning Council. *Land use and transportation.* Baltimore-Washington Interregional Study, Technical Report No. 7. Baltimore: 1960.

Bellomo, S., Dial, R. B., and Voorhees, A. M. *Factors, trends and guidelines related to trip lengths.* National Cooperative Highway Research Program Report 89. Washington, D.C.: Highway Research Board, 1970.

Blumenfeld, H. *The modern metropolis: Its origins, growth, characteristics and planning.* Cambridge: MIT Press, 1967.

Carp, F. M. "Walking as a means of transportation for retired people." The Gerontologist, Summer 1971a, 11, 104-111.

Carp, F. M. The mobility of retired people. In E. J. Cantilli and J. L. Shmelzer (Eds.), *Transportation and aging.* Washington, D.C.: U.S. Government Printing Office, 1971b, 23-41.

Carp, F. M. The older pedestrian in San Francisco. Highway Research Record, November 1972 (403), 18-22.

Clawson, M. *Suburban land conversion in the United States: An economic and governmental process.* Baltimore: Johns Hopkins Press, 1971, for Resources for the Future, Inc.

Foley, D. L. Urban neighborhood facilities: A study of a residential district in northwest St. Louis. Unpublished doctoral dissertation, Washington University, Department of Sociology and Anthropology, 1948.

Foley, D. L. Differentials in personal access to household motor vehicles: Five-county San Francisco Bay Area, 1971. Working Paper No. 197/BART 9. Berkeley: University of California, Institute of Urban and Regional Development, December 1972.

Foley, D. L., Drake, R. L., Lyon, D. W., and Ynzenga, B. A. *Characteristics of metropolitan growth in California. Vol. I: Report.* Berkeley: University of California, Center for Planning and Development Research, December 1965.

Foley, D. L., and Redwood, Jr., III. Auto nonavailability as a component of transportation disadvantage: A pre-BART review of the Bay Area situation and the national context. Working Paper No. 168/BART 5. Berkeley: University of California, Institute of Urban and Regional Development, March 1972.

Gans, H. J. *People and plans: Essays on urban problems and solutions.* New York: Basic Books, 1968.

Greer, S. *The urbane view: Life and politics in metropolitan America.* New York: Oxford University Press, 1972.

Gurin, D. *The physical mobility of the poor: An introductory overview.* (M.C.P. thesis, Harvard University, Department of City and Regional Planning) Springfield, Va.: National Technical Information Service, 1969.

Haines, H., Jr., Simon, L., and Alexis, M. "An analysis of central city neighborhood trading areas." Journal of Regional Science, April 1972, 12, 95-105.

Hawley, A. H. *Human ecology: A theory of community structure.* New York: Ronald Press, 1950.

Hawley, A. H. *Urban society.* New York: Ronald Press, 1971.

Hawley, A. H., and Zimmer, B. G. *The metropolitan community: Its people and government.* Beverly Hills: Sage Publications, 1970.

Hurst, M. E. "The structure of movement and household behavior." Urban Studies, February 1969, 6, 70-82.

Kain, J. F. "Postwar metropolitan development: Housing preferences and auto ownership." American Economic Review, 57, May 1967, 223-234.

Lansing, J. B., and Hendricks, G. *Automobile ownership and residential density.* Ann Arbor: University of Michigan, Institute for Social Research, Survey Research Center, 1967.

Lansing, J. B., Marans, R. W., and Zehner, R. B. *Planned residential environments.* Ann Arbor: University of Michigan, Institute for Social Research, Survey Research Center, 1970.

Lee, T. Urban Neighborhood as a socio-spatial schema. Human Relations, August 1968, 21, 241-268. Reprinted in H. M. Proshansky, W. H. Ittelson, and L. G. Rivlin (Eds.), *Environmental psychology: Man and his physical setting.* New York: Holt, Rinehart and Winston, 1970, 349-370.

McMilland, K., and Assael, H. *National survey of transportation attitudes and behavior, Phase II: Analysis report.* national Cooperative Highway Research Program Report 49. Washington, D.C.: Highway Research Board, 1969.

McMurry, T. Residence, employment and mobility of Puerto Ricans in New York City. Unpublished doctoral dissertation (Abstract), University of Chicago, Department of Sociology, 1972.

March, M. S. "The neighborhood center concept." Public Welfare, April 1968, 26, 97-111.

Myers, S. "Personal transportation for the poor." Traffic Quarterly, April 1970, 24, 191-206.

National Center for Health Statistics. Use of special aids: United States, 1969. *Monthly Vital Statistics Report,* May 11, 1972, 21, Supplement 2.

Owen, W. *The accessible city.* Washington, D.C.: The Brookings Institution, 1972.

Oakland City Planning Department. *Getting to work from West Oakland.* Oakland: January 1970.

Pickard, J. P. *Dimensions of metropolitanism.* Research Monograph 14. Washington, D.C.: Urban Land Institute, 1967.

Thompson, W. R. "The national system of cities as an object of public policy." Urban Studies, February 1972, 9, 99-116.

U.S. Bureau of the Census, U.S. Census of Population: 1960. *Number of Inhabitants.* Final Report PC(1)-1A. U.S. Summary. Washington, D.C.: U.S. Government Printing Office, November 1961.

U.S. Bureau of the Census. *Special report on household ownership of cars, homes, and selected household durables: 1970, 1969, and 1960.* Current Population Reports, Series P-65, No. 33. Washington, D.C.: U.S. Government Printing Office, October 16, 1970.

U.S. Bureau of the Census. U.S. Census of Population: 1970. *Number of Inhabitants.* Final Report PC(1)-A1. U.S. Summary. Washington, D.C.: U.S. Government Printing Office, 1971.

U.S. Public Health Service. *Chronic conditions and limitations of activity and mobility: United States—July 1965-June 1967.* Data from the National Health Survey, Series 10, No. 61. Rockville, Md.: U.S. Department of Health, Education, and Welfare, January 1971.

U.S. Public Health Service. *Disability components for an index of health.* Data Evaluation and Methods Research, Series 2, No. 42. Rockville, Md.: U.S. Department of Health, Education, and Welfare, July 1971.

Webber, M. M. On strategies for transport planning. In *Organization for Economic Cooperation and Development, The urban transportation planning process.* Paris: OECD, 1971, 129-149.

Wildavsky, A. "Black rebellion and white reaction." The Public Interest, Spring 1968 (No. 11), 3-16.

PART II

QUALITY OF LIFE

In this section, three authors approach the quality of metropolitan life in very different ways. Because of the differing emphases, methodologies, and levels of approach, they illuminate different dimensions of metropolitan life. Fischer looks at what is distinctive about metropolitan life (in an implicit critique of what Wirth thought was distinctive); Marans and Rodgers look at what is distinctly good (i.e., the major variables in community satisfaction); and Suttles looks at the physical and social arrangements that at various times have been thought of as the key to improving and preserving the neighborhood or sub-community experience.

Gerald Suttles, a sociologist, has done much previous work attempting to pin down the meaning of "community" in an urban setting. Here, he begins by critiquing several popular misconceptions of the term. He feels that "community" now has a much more limited meaning than it did in the past, but that it is still a useful term in the analysis of urban life if certain qualifications are taken into account. The significance of the contemporary community, he suggests, lies in the fact that it is instrumental, rather than based on common sentiments. The use to which it is put varies by class and ethnicity.

After treating various community design arrangements, Suttles presents his own proposal for a multi-tiered arrangement of metropolitan areas, which is based on participation of existing neighborhoods. Thus, for Suttles, the quality of urban life is very much related to the functioning of the neighborhood or subcommunity as a unit. and as a vehicle for individual participation.

Claude Fischer analyzes the effect of urban life on individual experience— i.e., does size of place have any intrinsic effects on behavior and attitudes? Keeping in mind the difficulty of isolating intrinsic effects, Fischer provides a lucid analysis of the literature on urban life. Taking Wirth's formulation of urban life as a referent, he looks at reputed individual pathologies and the social and physical surroundings of urban dwellers. In behavioral terms, little emerges that is distinctively different about living in a large place compared to living in a small place—what differences there are seem to be largely mediated by social class. Rather, it is in the less tangible attitudes, values, and potential experiences that the city is distinctive. Fischer also attempts to distinguish city and suburban behavior, but finds that this distinction may be largely attributed to socio-economic differences.

Marans and Rodgers, on the other hand, are very much involved in the development of social indicators, one thrust of which is the determination of subjective reactions to various objective conditions. In this case, they are looking at attitudes toward various physical and service aspects of the neighborhood. While there is much literature on objective neighborhood conditions—e.g., on service levels in different parts of a metropolitan area, Marans and Rodgers take this a step further and attempt to determine the impact of these conditions on people's evaluations of their local areas. They posit that such personal factors as demographic characteristics and standards of reference combine with objective conditions to affect the evaluation. With use of multivariate analysis of three Institute for Social Research national attitude surveys, they attempt to operationalize this model. Thus, they provide us with more explicit referents of the quality of urban life.

Marans and Rodgers feel that their data can be used as a benchmark with which to compare future assessments of community satisfaction. They suggest that observing such attitudes through time can be useful to policy-makers at all levels of government, who must set spending priorities for physical improvements and social legislation.

One factor that is common to these three papers is the importance of the social-class variable in determining the function of the neighborhood, in selecting a place of residence, and in evaluating the community. Thus, to infer that the quality of urban life, broadly considered, is a function of social class would not constitute an oversimplification.

CHAPTER 5

THE METROPOLITAN EXPERIENCE

Claude S. Fischer

University of California, Berkeley

*The central problem of the sociologist of the city is to discover the forms
of social action and organization that typically emerge in relatively
permanent, compact settlements of large numbers of heterogeneous
individuals [Louis Wirth, 1938].*

THE ISSUE OF CONCERN in this paper is the social psychology of urban life.
This means that it will deal with questions such as: How is the nature of individual experience affected by residence in a metropolis? How are the cognitions,
beliefs, and behaviors of people shaped by life in more versus less urban places?
Our goal is to estimate the social psychological impact of variations in population distribution.

DEFINITIONS

Before any discussion can proceed, certain definitions and clarifications are
critical, for the confusion surrounding this topic is great and persistent.

Operational Definitions of Metropolitan and Urban

We will be concerned here with population concentration as a continuum
ranging from the great metropolises to the archetypal farm house, a dimension
commonly referred to as the "rural-urban continuum." In this paper, "rural/
urban" and "nonmetropolitan/metropolitan" are used as convenient terms for
making comparisons along this size-of-place scale, but we do not mean to imply

AUTHOR'S NOTE: This paper is based largely on a more technical review (Fischer, 1972b),
which the reader should consult for fuller documentation. The author acknowledges the
helpful comments of the other contributors, of the panel, and of Herbert J. Gans. The quotations from pages 288-289 of *The Levittowners,* by Herbert J. Gans, are used by permission
of Pantheon Books, a division of Random House, Inc. ©1962.

real dichotomies.[1] The working definition which will be used here is a relatively simple demographic one: population aggregation. The greater the number of people at a place of settlement, the more "urban" is that place; the greater the number of people in an individual's place of settlement, the more "urban" his or her experience. There are difficulties with this definition, which will not be belabored here, but it is a far more sensible interpretation than many others which abound. (And there are almost as many interpretations, explicit or implicit, of "urban" as there are authors on the topic; see Dewey, 1960.) Take as warnings three serious confusions:

(1) "Urban" as a cultural variable. In this usage, where "urban" is often interchanged with "urbane," the term refers to unique social forms and psychological sets which presumably differentiate city from country people. The assumption—that there *are* such differences—is so strong that the term "urban" is used equally to mean the physical, demographic phenomena and the cultural, psychological phenomena.[2] While it may indeed be true that there is such a correlation between demographic features of settlements and sociocultural forms, we can hardly *define* "urban" by those forms, since whether such a correlation exists is the problematic question of this paper. In short, to treat "urban" or "metropolitan" as a psychological or cultural variable is to beg the question.

(2) "Urban" as an attribute of a society. A similar usage crops up in the phrase "urban society." A society may be urbanized—that is, have a large proportion of its population in concentrated settlements—but, usually, the implicit translation of the phrase is "modern society," "industrial society," "bureaucratic society," or some such *cultural* statement. Again, this presumes that the cultural nature of a society is isomorphic with its demographic nature—a presumption we mean to test.

(3) Another type of confusion arises from equating "urban" with some apparent coincidental or contemporary correlate of population distribution. An example is housing. While apartment buildings are more common in places with larger populations, multidwelling housing and urbanism are hardly the same thing. (Compare, for example, American Indian pueblos and metropolitan single-family-home tracts.) One of the stereotypes behind such a confusion is not even true: crowding, at least in terms of the number of people per room, is slightly greater in more *rural* places (Duncan, 1957a; Carpenter, 1960; U.S. Bureau of the Census, 1971b).

The Meaning of Experience. In assessing the impact of metropolitan life, we will take a behavioristic approach. Important experiential differences due to size of place will, it is assumed, manifest themselves in differential human responses—i.e., behaviors. In this category are included verbal reports of internal states, as in expressions of loneliness, distrust, or unhappiness.

Expected Size of Effects. In dealing with significant psychological experiences and responses, one should, as a rule, not expect major or dramatic effects of size of place. The metropolis is a very general social context for people. The forces that have the greatest impact are those much more proximate to the individual personality: genetic factors, childhood, social class, race, sex, etc. Therefore, the discussion will revolve largely about modest differences.

Searching for Intrinsic Effects. The discussion will not only cover contemporary American differences in urban/rural experiences, but will also be concerned with the "intrinsic" effects of urbanism. By this is meant the social psychological effects that are due to population aggregation alone, rather than to some other factor currently associated with urban residence.[3]

This is important for at least two reasons: The association of urban residence with many of these factors changes over time. If we are not careful to control for these variables in our analysis, the conclusions become extremely time-bound and dated. In terms of policies governing population distribution, we must of course know what effects are due to that specific variable alone and would thus be changed by its manipulation.

The means for establishing "intrinsic" effects are essentially two: (1) examining cases of urbanism in other times and places where factors associated with it here and now are not present and seeing what effects occur; and (2) statistical procedures for simulating such cases. The following discussion will be based on social-science literature utilizing both methods.

Another problem in discovering "intrinsic" effects—one which is harder to deal with—is "self-selection." People migrate from place to place; they "select" themselves into different settlement types. It is therefore difficult to know, when we discover that urban people are more "x" than rural people, whether that difference is due to living in metropolitan areas or whether it is due to "x"-type people moving to and staying in cities. In regard to subtle social psychological differences, it is often not possible to decide which is the case.

Yet another complication arises from intercity differences. Communities of the same size vary among each other in many respects: economic structure, government, social composition, etc. Consequently, there are differential experiences (Milgram, 1970; Schuman and Gruenberg, 1970). What these differences are and why they exist is important. For example working-class communities of varying sizes are probably more similar to each other than they are to middle-class communities of the same size. However, for present purposes, these differences complicate the effort to assess the general metropolitan experience, the effects of population aggregation abstracted out of specific communities. Therefore, we will generalize across such intermetropolitan differences. (This paper will deal with intrametropolitan comparisons, in terms of city versus suburb, after the urban/rural discussion.)

A final prefatory caution: The state of *knowledge* (as opposed to opinion) in this field is definitely inadequate (cf. Fischer, 1972b). Therefore, what follows is often based on fragmentary data and should be read with the appropriate skepticism.

PUBLIC OPINION

Popular conceptions of and attitudes toward urban life are important for several reasons. They may reflect more or less accurately the real experience of urban life. They may create expectations, which, if not met, can lead to disappointment. They may determine the choices people make about where they live, and thus be a force in the self-selection process. They may shape actual experience and behavior by leading people to act in what they feel to be appropriate "urban" or "rural" ways.

Historically, American intellectual opinion about urban life has been negative. The city has been seen as a corrupting influence on the human spirit, that spirit finding its highest ascendancy in contact with the soil (see, for example, White and White, 1962; Howe, 1971). European views have been somewhat more charitable, stressing, for example, urban "civilization" as opposed to rural "savagery" (cf. Schorske, 1963). Nevertheless, some of the same warnings about urban life have existed for ages: sin and secularism, anxiety and anguish, estrangement and alienation, as well as noise, dirt, and crowds.

These attitudes persist today in various ways. For instance, surveys reveal a tendency for people to prefer places smaller than the ones within which they currently reside. Table 5.1 presents a composite of two Gallup polls on the topic. While people express preferences for places of the same size as the ones within which they presently reside, deviations from that preference are in the direction of small communities. A Harris (1970) survey revealed that two-thirds of the city-dwellers interviewed expressed a desire not to be living in a city ten years hence.[4]

The irony of these findings is that, historically, when people have "voted with their feet," they have overwhelmingly chosen the cities. And that movement continues today in the United States and in the world at large. One reason for this pattern can be seen in the other side of the urban image—the city as a place

Table 5.1: Preferences for Place of Residence by Present Size of Community, 1970-1971

| | Present Place of Residence[a] | | | | |
| | Nonmetropolitan | | Metropolitan | | |
Preferred Residence	Under 2,500	2,500- 50,000	50,000- 500,000	500,000- 1,000,000	Over 1,000,000
Farm	54.0	19.5	12.5	12.5	9.5
Small towns	28.0	56.0	30.0	22.0	25.5
Suburb	15.5	15.0	29.5	39.5	35.0
City	2.0	9.5	26.0	26.5	28.5

NOTE: Adapted from Gallup Opinion Index, February 1970 and August 1971. Figures were derived from averaging the results of the two surveys. Sample size was approximately 3,000. "No opinions" are not shown. The text of the question was, "If you could live anywhere in the United States that you wanted to, would you prefer a city, suburban area, small town or farm?" See Harris (1970) for similar results.
a. Size of city or central city if respondent lived in a suburb. Percentages add down.

of opportunity, largely economic opportunity, but also of chances for entertainment and excitement.[5]

One of the outcomes of this approach-avoidance dilemma is compromise when possible—i.e., the suburb. The suburb grew as an attempt to meld the best of the city and country and continues to exercise such an attraction (Donaldson, 1971). A recent study indicated just such a popular desire for the best of both worlds. In a Wisconsin survey (Zuiches and Fuguitt, 1971), a large majority of the respondents expressed a preference for residing outside a city but within easy commuting distance of it (see Table 5.2).

Perhaps the most accurate summary statement is that there is a general American value preference for the rural or small-town ideal, even if it can only be realized in the suburban tract home. At the same time, the reality of economic life means that metropolitan residence is chosen. The implication, which may be serious, is that many if not most urban residents benefit materially from their place of residence, but feel that this is not where the "good life" is led.[6] (An indication of such a feeling is provided by the first item in Table 5.3: The larger the community, the less satisfied are the people with the quality of life there.)

SOCIAL SCIENCE OPINION

Probably the first collection of writings on the city that one could term "social science" rather than social "philosophy" or "history" was that of the "Chicago school" led by Robert Park (1952). The central work of the group was a series of classic demographic and ethnographic descriptions of Chicago in the

Table 5.2: Wisconsin Preferences for Place of Residence Relative to a Large City, 1971

Preferred Place of Residence	Present Place of Residence[a]							
	Nonmetropolitan			Metropolitan				
	Rural	1,000-10,000	10,000-50,000	Rural	1,000-10,000	10,000-50,000	Suburb	CC
More than 30 miles from a large city								
Rural	40	8	9	14	2	8	4	3
Small city	8	33	10	6	7	6	4	5
Medium city	3	5	22	2	0	4	6	5
Within 30 miles of a large city								
Rural	36	11	11	54	23	14	18	12
Small city	7	32	8	15	42	18	10	15
Medium city	4	5	24	3	14	36	9	13
Suburb	2	3	8	3	7	14	40	19
Center city	0	3	8	3	5	0	9	28
(Sample sizes)	(195)	(131)	(93)	(66)	(43)	(66)	(79)	(233)

NOTE: Data adapted from Zuiches and Fuguitt, 1971, T. 3.
a. Percentages add down.

Table 5.3: Satisfaction with Community versus More Global Feelings by Community Size, c. 1970

Item	Community Size[a]				
	Under 2,500	2,500- 50,000	50,000- 500,000	500,000- 1,000,000	1,000,000 or more
"Would you say that you are satisfied or dissatisfied with the quality of life?"					
Percent satisfied[b]	84	81	69	77	61
"On the whole would you say that you are satisfied with the future facing you and your family?"					
Percent satisfied[c]	60	60	59	52	57
"Do you think life is getting better or worse in terms of happiness?"					
Percent better[d]	23	24	25	30	27
"Taking everything into account, is the world getting better or is it getting worse?"					
Percent better[c]	19	25	25	33	17

a. Size of city or of central city if respondent lived in suburb.
b. Gallup Opinion Index, October 1971.
c. Gallup Opinion Index, March 1972.
d. Gallup Opinion Index, November 1968.

first third of the century. The theoretical ideas about urban lifeways drew on the German sociologist Georg Simmel (1903) and were best expressed by Louis Wirth (1938).

In Wirth's statement, the essential nature of the city—population size, density, and heterogeneity—was described as producing a series of psychological and social consequences, in two mutually reinforcing ways:

(1) On the individual experiential level, urban life surrounds the resident with a constant bombardment of stimuli: sights, sounds, people, and social demands for attention, concern, and action. In response to this overstimulation, coping mechanisms are brought into play to defend the organism. Basically, they are means of isolating him from his environment and from other people. The urbanite becomes aloof from others, superficial in his contacts with them, and blasé, sophisticated, and indifferent to the events which occur about him. His relationships to others are restricted to specific roles and tasks in a businesslike way (in contrast to the personal relationships of the small town). Thus, the urban individual, it is theorized, is estranged from his fellow man. (See Milgram, 1970, for a modern elaboration of this thesis.)

(2) On the aggregate level, the concentration of great numbers, in conjunction with economic principles of competition and comparative advantage, leads to a multifaceted differentiation, or diversification. The larger the community, the more divided and specialized is the labor, the greater the number and variety of social groups, and the greater the differences among neighborhoods. This fractionation, combined with a psychological fractionation of the individual's attention, prevents the existence of a "community" in which people are bound by common social ties and understandings (e.g., commonality of values, personal attention, social pressure, tradition). To hold such a splintered society together at all, different social mechanisms are needed and do arise—means of formal integration such as written laws, impersonal rules of etiquette, and special agencies of social control, education, communication, and welfare.[7]

Within the "noncommunity," the primary social groups that tie the individual and society together, particularly the family, are also weakened. The individual's diversified interests, associations, and locales draw him or her away from the family; the specialized institutions of the city usurp family functions; the contacts with different persons and different value systems shake the normative foundations of the primary group.

The formal institutions that partly supplant these primary groups are, however, inadequate to avoid a state of anomie. This is a condition of society in which social bonds between individuals and their groups are weak, and, consequently, the norms—rules of proper and permissible behavior—are also weak. Such a state of anomie results in social and personality disorganization, deviance, and, once again, individual isolation.

Thus Wirth predicted that the urban experience would generate a series of interrelated social-psychological phenomena, including relationships that are "impersonal, superficial, transitory and segmental," "anonymity," "sophistication," "rationality," "secularization," "competition," "aggrandizement," "mutual exploitation," and "depersonalization," among others.

This theoretical perspective had been the dominant one in sociology. In the 1950s, it increasingly came under attack by a group of urban ethnographers, who have been labeled the "non-materialists" (Sjoberg, 1965). Basing their arguments on the "re-discovery" of kinship, social ties, and effective norms in certain urban communities, they argued that the ecological factors of numbers and space were essentially unimportant in determining social-psychological consequences (cf. Lewis, 1965; Gans, 1962b). What matters is class, ethnicity and life-cycle.

There are several other sociological formulations about urban life (cf. Fischer, 1972b), but the debate over the Wirthian theory is the most central and important. It is also unresolved (Hauser, 1965). In the following discussion, it is essentially the Wirthian theory which will be used to orient the empirical review.

ELEMENTS OF THE URBAN EXPERIENCE

Characteristics of Urban Individuals

As a general rule, the more urban a person's place of residence, the higher his social class—education, occupation, income, and self-definition (cf. Blau and Duncan, 1965; Schnore, 1963; and from the author's research). The degree of association between community size and socioeconomic position is low,[8] but it is consistent cross-culturally and historically. (One aspect of this pattern is the traditional location of elites within urban centers; see Sjoberg, 1960.) Some variations to this pattern occur, in particular, the presence of deprived groups— many of rural origin—in the center cities of large American metropolises. It is difficult to foretell whether this variation indicates future trends of whether it is transitory. The most accurate statement is that social class, with its accompanying perquisites, increases mildly with urbanism. This point must be constantly kept in mind.

To the degree to which urban residence is responsible for the high social class of individuals (Alonso and Fajans, 1970) and that, in turn, affects their life experiences and behaviors, urbanism can be said to have an indirect social psychological impact. To the degree to which urbanism increases the rates of social mobility (Lipset and Bendix, 1964), and that mobility in turn disrupts social relationships (Janowitz, 1970), it may have a deleterious social effect. However, our concern here is with the consequences of urbanism, if any, above and beyond such indirect effects (cf. Fischer, 1972b, for further discussion).

The more urban a place of settlement, the more socially heterogeneous the population. That is, the greater is the presence of minority religious and ethnic groups (see Schnore, 1963). This may not be a necessary consequence of urbanism, for anthropologists have noted many large settlements in underdeveloped societies composed of single, homogeneous groups. However, it does appear to be a general correlate in Western societies, most likely due to the economic opportunities of cities and their position on transportation paths. With these opportunities and placement, population aggregation increases heterogeneity by *attracting* widely scattered groups to a central place.

Another form of heterogeneity is probably *internally* generated by population size. This is the variety of occupational, common-interest, and life-style subcultures (e.g., bohemia, the academic community, the small-business community, the criminal underworld, the "singles set"). Specialization and diversification increase with size and thereby spur the development of somewhat distinctive subgroups. At the same time, large numbers provide "critical masses" of people necessary for sustaining these communities of interest as distinctive and separate groups (see Fischer, 1973b).

Urban persons are more likely to be single, usually beginning their careers, than are less urban persons. There is a fairly substantial increase in the proportion of persons living outside a family as community size increases (Fischer, 1972a: 154, n. 3).

It should also be noted that urban persons are more likely to be non-Southern, and, given the historical migration pattern, more urban persons are raised in rural areas than the reverse.

The relevance of these individual differences is that (1) in comparing urban vs. rural people on social-psychological dimensions, it must be remembered that one is dealing with different populations in each case and, (2) the metropolitan experience includes living within an area inhabited by somewhat higher class, heterogeneous, and more frequently single people than does the rural experience.

The Physical Context of Urban Life

The physical nature of the city seems to be a persistent source of distress. A number of irritants increase in frequency with increases in community size, particularly noise and pollution. A recent National Research Council (1972) study found air pollution to be fifteen times greater in large cities than in more rural areas. The subsequent question is whether these irritants are inevitable concomitants of city life, or whether one can build quiet, clean, large cities. Most probably, some increase in both noise and dirt accompanies all population aggregation, though the degree to which it occurs can probably be reduced below today's level.

Taking the analysis another step, are there differential biological or psychological effects of these irritants on urban vs. rural persons? Regarding noise, a recent national examination of children ages six to eleven found no association between community size and hearing sensitivity (U.S. Department of Health, Education, and Welfare, 1972). And, experimental studies suggest that noise per se may not impair personality, but only unpredictable noise (Glass and Singer, 1972). Furthermore, there is little evidence of urban-rural differences in the psychosomatic symptoms that one might expect from noise. It seems that this disadvantage of urban life has been exaggerated.

Pollutions might be expected to influence health, and, historically, cities have been unhealthy places because of sewage problems and epidemics. In recent times, this difference has been reduced or erased by modern health methods and by the advantages of cities in health facilities. Yet, the difference is probably still to the rural advantage. For example, the National Research Council air-pollution study concluded that the cost of smog for urban communities was a lung-cancer mortality rate twice that of rural areas.[9]

On the whole, some amount of unpleasant irritants is probably an inevitable concomitant of urban life, imposing a degree of biological damage. The psychological consequences, however, are probably small, if at all existent.

Large numbers of people form part of the setting of city life, and crowds are often considered one of the irritants of the city. We do not know to what extent people actually spend time in crowds, but the real picture can be nowhere near the stereotypic image. The assumption behind much of the current pop-ethology literature on urban life—that city people spend a significant part of their lives crowded—is questionable. Similarly, the other premise—that population density has serious negative social consequences—is also questionable. Other than a few animal studies with dubious relevance, there is little data to support that view. Both experimental work and studies of natural variation in population density done to date fail to support the proposition.

A sense of "crowding" is, of course, a subjective feeling, dependent on the individual's needs and on cultural norms (see the Marans and Rodgers paper in this volume). To the degree to which available space does not meet the personal demand, people will feel "crowded," and psychological effects perhaps result. Research on these issues is just beginning, but so far, it indicates that density per se has little effect (see review and experimental studies in Freedman, Klevansky, and Ehrlich, 1971).[10]

Related to this issue is that of housing. As argued earlier, multiple-dwelling units are not an intrinsic feature of urban life, but they are more common in American cities than in the countryside. Apartments are not the American dream homes, but neither do they seem to have serious negative effects if social needs are met—that is, if the space arrangement permits tasks to be performed and the cultural standards of privacy to be attained. The general thrust of the research is that there are few social-psychological effects attributable to multiple-dwelling housing per se, other than some mechanical problems such as supervising children from apartments on the higher floors or inviting guests into the home (see reviews in Mitchell, 1971; Schorr, 1966).

One element of the physical environment that does vary to an important degree with community size is the presence of what might be termed "facilities": stores, amusements, public and private services, organizations, and the like. Around 1940, Fenton Keyes (1958) tabulated cities by size and by whether or not they possessed 94 different sorts of facilities and services. A partial set of the results are presented in Table 5.4. As size increases, the variety of services does also. One conclusion Keyes drew was that the 25,000 population level was an important "break" point for whether cities have facilities or not.

Similarly, the presence of specialists of various sorts seems to require minimum levels of population (Ogburn and Duncan, 1964). While these differences between rural and urban are being mitigated by efficiencies in transport (Webber, 1970), they persist and will probably continue to exist. The larger the community, the more likely is the individual to find the particular goods or services he is seeking.

The Social Context of Urban Life: The Individual's Groups

A simple truth too often forgotten in discussions at the level of towns and cities is that people actually lead their lives in much smaller milieus—their immediate families, friends, and co-workers. These are the groups which influence and, to a great extent, circumscribe the individual's experience, both in country and city. Relatively few persons, mostly only those at the upper rungs of the social ladder, have in any sense large parts of cities as their meaningful social environments. And only a tiny fraction can be considered "cosmopolitans" of

Table 5.4: Association of City Size and the Presence of Facilities: Threshhold Size Levels for Probability of Presence, c. 1930

	Minimum City Size at Which	
	50+%	95+%
Facility or Service	of Cities Have Facility	
Grocery store	2,000	2,000
Restaurant	2,000	5,000
Furniture store	2,000	25,000
Dry goods	2,000	50,000
Household supplies	2,500	50,000
Automotive supply	2,500	5,000
Paint store	5,000	50,000
Book store	25,000	100,000
Hospital	5,000	100,000
Home for the aged	50,000	250,000
Psychiatric clinic	100,000	500,000
School for the deaf	100,000	500,000
College	250,000	500,000
Art school	250,000	500,000
Nursery school	250,000	1,000,000
City planning board	25,000	500,000
Airport	25,000	250,000
Daily newspaper	10,000	250,000
Radio station	50,000	250,000
Lions club	25,000	250,000
Music organization	100,000	250,000
YMCA	25,000	250,000
Municipal tennis courts	25,000	250,000
Playground	25,000	250,000
Symphony orchestra	500,000	1,000,000

NOTE: Data selected and adapted from Keyes, 1958, Table 1.

the sort to whom "BosWash" and "SanSan" have any meaning. Thus, the metropolitan experience is largely an experience mediated by the individual's small number of significant others (his "networks"), usually within one portion of a city.

The most immediate personal context is the family. It was long part of sociological lore that urban life weakened, if not destroyed, the family institution. It is true that the traditional family structure appears less frequently in the more urban areas, where unmarried, childless, or divorced households are disproportionately present. As discussed earlier, the problem of self-selection makes it difficult to call this an *effect* of urban life. Cities apparently attract young singles and unmarrieds without children (Zuiches and Fuguitt, 1971).

A more general issue is whether the social force of kinship is affected by urbanism. The best conclusions that can be drawn from the fragmentary and largely qualitative data (and considering the differences in individual characteristics discussed above) are the following: Urban residence, ceteris paribus, probably affects kinship by encouraging the geographic dispersal of relatives and by reducing the degree to which the family is called upon to provide aid and other services (Greer, 1956; Smith, Form, and Stone, 1954; Wellman, Craven, Whitaker, Stevens, and DuToit, 1971). (The urban milieu provides alternative institutions to supply these needs; cf. Table 5.4.) However, contact with kin is probably no less frequent, and they are still the major source of aid (Wellman et al., 1971). Nor is there sufficient evidence that the social-psychological importance or the moral suasion of kin is any less in urban than in rural places. To some extent, though probably not a great one, the family is a more specialized, specifically socio-emotional, institution in cities. Whether this strengthens or weakens the family is debatable.

The same general statements can probably be made about nonkin primary ties. The proposition has been forwarded that friendships should be fewer or more shallow in the urban setting. There is little data to support either hypothesis and no empirical reason as yet to believe that urban life isolates people from important social relationships. As with the family, these ties are probably more dispersed, but still present. One study concluded: "Spatial mobility makes for city-wide ties; stability for local area ties; and most urban residents have both" (Smith et al., 1954).

Expanding the circle of the individual's associations, we can consider his more general membership groups—particularly ethnic or religious groups—but also including occupational or life-style subcultures. For descent-related ones such as ethnic communities, the expectation, based on standard sociological analysis and immigrant experience in America, is that the cohesiveness and importance of these subcultures should be reduced in the disruptive and distracting urban environment. However, anthropological studies from around the world (and America) suggest that this expectation is weakly met, if at all. In fact, there is some evidence that ethnocultural identification and unity is greater in the city, especially the larger city, than in the country. For example, Africanists have described the rise of tribal consciousness in the new African metropolises (cf. Epstein, 1967). This phenomenon is probably caused by (1) contrast and conflict with other groups which, as social psychologists have long known, strengthens the internal ties of the collectivity, and (2) the presence of sufficient numbers of members to support a vital subculture (cf. Fischer, 1973b).

The geographical locality, or neighborhood, is another membership group for the individual. The stereotypic picture of urbanites being anonymous to their neighbors is, as with many other urban images, quite exaggerated, given the accumulating research revealing the existence of meaningful neighborhood communities (e.g., Gans, 1962a; Suttles, 1968). However, it is probably the case that the degree to which a person knows his neighbors, the importance of those people to him and of him to them, and his attachment to the locality do decrease with increases in community size. (For one thing, friends, relatives and co-workers are less likely to be neighbors.) Thus, urbanites are somewhat more isolated from their neighbors than are ruralites. But, this does not mean that they are more isolated in toto (Fischer, 1973a).

The Social Context of Urban Life: Strangers

The stranger is the central character of the urban scene for many writers on this topic. While residence in a small town is depicted as a life among friends and acquaintances, residence in the large city is described as a life "in the presence of strangers" (Lofland, 1972).

This contrast has been much exaggerated, for the turnover of population in small communities is often high. (In 1969, it was equal to that of metropolitan communities [U.S. Bureau of the Census, 1971a].) The general disorder of small towns has also been ignored (Lane, 1971; Smith, 1968). Nevertheless, as a general rule, it is probably the case that, the larger the community, the greater the number of encounters with "strange" people—strange both in the sense that they are unknown and in that they are likely to look and act somewhat "strangely." The consequences of this situation have been the focus of theorists such as Simmel (1903), Wirth (1938), and Milgram (1970).

Two types of consequences can be specified: (1) psychological effects presumed to result from an environment of strangers, and (2) a set of adaptations that arise to protect the individual from these strangers. The first category includes anxiety due to the unpredictability of interaction with unknown others. Related to this anxiety is what James Q. Wilson (1968) has recently termed the "urban unease," which he sees as the crux of the "urban problem."[11] In the analyses of Simmel and Wirth, the frequent encounters with (relatively) exotic strangers result in a blasé outlook on life: world-weary and cosmopolitan, perhaps sophisticated, and certainly jaded. In Milgram's analysis, these masses of strangers are part of the overstimulation of city living; they must be watched and guarded against. Thus, they contribute to psychic overload, with consequent irritation and nervousness.

The second category, protective adaptations, includes mechanisms described earlier to handle overstimulation and overdemands: isolation from others and the maintenance of superficial, task-oriented contacts. Such role-specific relationships imply that the other persons are treated mainly as means or obstacles to certain ends (e.g., the bus driver is only a means for transport; someone in front in a bank queue is only an obstacle to reaching the teller). In that way, people are simply objects and not full personalities in their own right. In such goal-directed, dehumanized encounters, mutual economic exploitation is an unsurprising outcome. In general, the adaptations involve maintaining a barrier between one's self and others, a barrier of constant suspicion and distrust.[12]

In the midst of this negative-sounding description, it should be stressed that the rarely noted concomitant of all this isolation and estrangement is personal, individualistic freedom. (Indeed, the moral and philosophical tension between community and individualism is frequently a subliminal theme in the urban literature.)

Whether these attitudes and modes of interaction are indeed effects of large community size is in many cases an essentially untouched research topic and, therefore, completely open. Other cases will be treated later in the paper.

One of the important points about the list of adaptive mechanisms is that these modes and attitudes are not only means of dealing with strangers, but also come to permeate the entire lives of urbanites (so the theory goes). However, the discussion in the preceding section implies that there is little empirical indication of such predicted estrangement in urban people's own personal circles.[13]

That the proximity of strangers is a concomitant of urban life more so than of rural life seems undeniable. (It would be interesting, though, to see figures on the degree to which urban residents actually encounter strangers.) The experiential importance of this fact is, however, another matter. It may be neither the case that the stranger makes a major impact on city-dwellers (he may fade into the scenery, and the more strangers, the more fading) nor the case that adaptations, positive or negative, have relevance to anything beyond the stranger. All the above speculation remains just that.

In this discussion, the "stranger" has been treated as a blank figure. In point of fact, he is almost always embedded within his own social groups. Thus, a more accurate image of the urban resident is that he is more likely, relative to rural persons, to be in the midst of diverse social groups (whose members are, with rare exception, strangers to him). And, there is, as far as we know, an internal cohesion and vitality to these groups equal to rural ones. The implication this leads to is that urban life is not so much life in the presence of strangers as it is life among distinctly different others.

Thus, the metropolitan experience is more likely than the rural one to involve proximity to, and perhaps contact with, identifiably "foreign" groups. Based on our knowledge of small-group processes, one could expect this situation to be accompanied by contrasts of the "us" vs. "them" kind, highlighting clear boundaries between the groups. And, there are some bits of evidence that such intergroup lines are sharper and conflicts greater, the larger the size of community. For instance, social classes seem more distinctive (Lasswell, 1959) and more politically important (Ennis, 1962) in larger cities.

While population aggregation may lead to separate and conflicting subgroups, the presence of large, vital subcultures in close proximity probably also leads to positive contacts. Thus, the diffusion of beliefs and practices between culturally distinct groups is likely to be greater in cities than in less urban places (where the other groups are either absent or present in weak numbers). Again, there are fragments of data indicating that this may be the case, at least in terms of the diffusion of new ideas from the more to the less educated.

Put grossly, part of the urban experience is (we suggest) to be both offended and influenced by "odd" people.

In the last two sections, we have sought to stress the point that cities are not composed, as much popular literature suggests, of masses of atomistic individuals crowded together at pathogenic densities, but are composed, rather, of many complex and vital social networks within which individuals lead lives not much social-psychologically different from those led by rural persons.

The Social Context of Urban Life: Crime

A major contemporary concern about the metropolitan experience is crime. Though crime statistics are seriously questionable, there seems little doubt that the large-city individual is more likely than the person in the small town to encounter criminality of all sorts. Table 5.5 presents the 1970 FBI crime statistics by community size. A recent survey in which respondents reported known crimes showed that FBI statistics greatly underestimated the frequency of crime, but the relative urban-rural differences were substantiated (Ennis, 1967).

The higher urban crime rates are reflected in individual awareness of danger. A Gallup poll, displayed in Table 5.6, shows that fear of walking the streets increases with community size.

As a general rule, the larger the community, the greater the rates of property crimes, crimes against the person, and vice crimes. The degree to which this is true—i.e., that there is a cost in serious crime for each increment in population— is unknown, but if there is a cost, it is probably not high, all else being equal. The reasons for this pattern—that is, the relation of crime to urbanism—are partially known.

Property crime and vice seem to accompany population size in almost all cases. One probably will get the former with the latter, other factors held constant. This can be explained without recourse to ideas that the city generates social disorganization. It probably results from the fact that size creates the

Table 5.5: Crime Rates by City Size, 1970

City Size	Crime Rates[a]						
	Total	Violent	Property	Murder	Rape	Robbery	Burglary
Over 250,000 (N = 56)	7,152	980	4,355	18	40	589	1,948
100,000-500,000 (N = 98)	6,238	450	3,746	10	24	199	1,684
50,000-100,000 (N = 252)	4,693	274	2,686	5	15	110	1,114
25,000-50,000 (N = 504)	4,031	214	2,334	4	11	82	940
10,000-25,000 (N = 1,177)	3,354	159	1,822	3	9	42	785
Under 10,000 (N = 2,394)	2,682	141	1,450	3	7	24	631
Suburban[b] (N = 2,415)	3,150	177	1,960	4	13	58	872
Rural (N = 1,563)	1,271	102	883	6	10	13	477

NOTE: Data adapted from Federal Bureau of Investigation, 1971, pp. 104-105.
a. Offenses known to police per 100,000 population.
b. Suburban jurisdictions also included in other city-size categories.

Table 5.6: Fear of Walking the Streets, by Community Size, 1972

"Is there anywhere right around here—that is, within a mile—where you would be afraid to walk alone at night?"

	Community Size[a]				
	Under 2,500	2,500- 50,000	50,000- 500,000	500,000- 1,000,000	Over 1,000,000
% Yes	24	42	49	43	53

NOTE: Data from Gallup Opinion Index, April 1972.
a. Size of city or of central city if respondent lived in suburb.

"markets" for such crimes—centralized accumulations of property (especially given the greater wealth of urbanites) and of "consumers" of vice. Also, the aggregation of large numbers of criminals fosters the rise of underworld facilities (e.g., fences) and organization.

Violent crime is a different matter. (In this connection, one must always keep in mind that crimes against the person, for example, 90 percent of the cases of homicide, occur most of the time between relatives and acquaintances; Wolfgang, 1967.) To a great extent, the metropolitan nature of violent crime in America is due to the concentration in Northern ghettos of poor blacks (and Southern culture groups generally).[14] When factors such as class and ethnicity are taken into account, it is not clear that cities per se breed violence. Indeed, cross-culturally and historically, rural areas have predominated in violent lawlessness (see U.S. National Commission on the Causes and Prevention of Violence, 1969).[15]

Contemporary American city-dwellers pay a price for their place of residence in terms of property loss and potential violence (with some accompanying anxiety). The cost in property probably comes with the city itself; the violence probably need not.

The Social Context of Urban Life: Ambience

There are other elements of the metropolitan experience which are harder to specify but which involve the sights, sounds, and smells of a place, and the activities that one can or does engage in. To some, the buildings, people, facilities, and bustle of cities are attractions; others will gladly forsake them for fewer people and more trees. These are the "intangibles," hard to measure or even define, which fall within the category of personal taste. We can say little about this ambience, except (1) it is *not* a major concern in residential moves (cf., for example, Rossi, 1956; Gans, 1967)—housing needs are; and (2) to the degree to which affluence permits freedom of choice, town and country will come more and more to be inhabited by persons with the appropriate personal inclinations.

EFFECTS OF THE URBAN EXPERIENCE

On Personality

Many of the hypotheses about urban life predict certain effects, usually deleterious, on the individual personality. One set of such effects might be termed "stress, strain, or tension." The sensory stimulation, the demands for concern, the strangers to guard against in the city are so great as to seriously overtax the organism. In the discussion earlier, doubts were raised about the assumptions behind these arguments—that such overstimulation is indeed a significant part of the average urbanite's experience, or that it cannot be handled. And, as far as consequences of stress are concerned, there is little evidence to support the theory that they are more common in cities. For instance, one international survey (Inkeles, 1969) reported no real urban-rural differences in psychosomatic symptoms.

Such strain, it is theorized, together with the hypothesized disintegration of close, supportive social ties, should also lead to behavioral manifestations of the type called "psychiatric disorders." It is difficult to assess whether rates of such disorders increase with urbanism. One difficulty, for example, is that admissions to mental hospitals are partly a function of the availability of such institutions, and this availability is greater in urban areas. Also, forthrightness about psychological difficulties is affected by potential social stigmatization, which also varies by community size. One recent review of nine varied and international epidemiological studies concludes that there is a tendency for neuroses to be greater in urban areas and psychoses to be greater in rural ones (Dohrenwend and Dohrenwend, 1971). The most trustworthy conclusion is that there is little support for the prediction that city life impairs mental functioning in ways termed "psychiatric disorders." However, most of the available data are mixed and generally inconclusive, especially if one seeks to isolate the specific effects of urban life per se.

There is a whole assortment of social-psychological states labeled "alienation." That term has been nearly killed by overuse and misuse, but some statements can be made, if we employ the distinctions presented by Seeman (1959, 1972).

One type of alienation is powerlessness—a sense of low control over one's life. It would be consistent with the theoretical lines discussed earlier to find more powerlessness in urban areas, but that is not the case in any substantive way (Fischer, 1973a).

Meaninglessness is a sense of low predictability and comprehension about the events occurring to the individual. This has been little studied, but "doomsday" questions asked in various surveys (i.e., questions reflecting a general pessimism about the future) generally fail to indicate any meaningful differences.

Social isolation, a sense of rejection and loneliness, is one of the core predictions of the Simmel-Wirth theory. Isolation is one of the means of adapting to the omnipresence of strangers and is also a consequence of the social disorganization of the city (so goes the theory). As discussed earlier, there is little evidence that urban people are actually more isolated than nonurban ones. Nor is there any reason to believe that urban people sense an isolation, except perhaps in one regard. In American surveys, there is a tendency for urbanism to be associated with a general sense of distrust about "other people" (Fischer, 1972a: ch. 4; Robinson and Shaver, 1969). (An example of the tendency which elicits this response is, "Generally speaking, would you say that most people can be trusted or that you can't be too careful in dealing with people?") This effect is real but weak. It might be attributable to the greater crime rate in cities, or to the presence of those "strange" other people. At the same time, this finding should be placed in perspective. Ethnographers in many parts of the world report high levels of interpersonal suspicion and distrust within small, rural communities (see discussion in Foster, 1960-61).

Normlessness is a sense that normative, socially approved of, means of achieving ends are unlikely to be effective compared to illegal or immoral ones. Survey items designed to measure this dimension (especially the Srole Anomia Scale, [see Srole, 1956]) generally fail to show any urban-rural differences. However, given the greater crime rate and the greater frequency of deviant beliefs in cities (see below), this form of alienation is probably somewhat higher in urban areas.[16]

Value isolation refers to holding values discrepant with the general values of the society (e.g., the archetypal bohemian). Little research has been done specifically on this alienation, but the fact that urban populations are more heterogeneous and the data on values discussed below imply that this alienation probably increases mildly with urbanism.[17]

Another personality dimension sometimes considered to be positively affected by urbanism is intellectual ability, usually measured by I.Q. A study just published contends that the "multi-faceted" nature of city life—during childhood—promotes "psychological functioning" (Schooler, 1972). In this study, as in others, small differences are found to the advantage of the urban-bred. However, the differences are slight and explainable by correlated variables (e.g., class, ethnicity) and by self-selection.

In sum, there is little empirical reason to believe that the urban experience disturbs or changes the human personality in any significant way. Urban life may incline people to somewhat deviant perspectives and to suspect deviance by others (at least in the contemporary United States), but even such an effect is small.

We can also consider one global state of mind: general satisfaction with one's life situation. Worldwide, the persistent trend is for urban people to express *greater* satisfaction than do rural people, largely, though perhaps not only, because of a better economic situation. However, in the United States today, there are slight differences in the direction of urban dissatisfaction (controlling for associated factors).[18]

Modes of Interaction

Certain ways of interacting with others are presumed to be more frequent in urban settings, for reasons outlined earlier. One long-standing distinction in sociology is between "primary-group" and "secondary-group" relationships. In the former type, people relate as whole personalities involved with each other in a variety of ways (examples: family, close friends). In secondary relationships, people interact with, and know only a single facet of, each other (for example: store clerk and customer; teacher and pupil). In urban life, human interaction presumably becomes more secondary (one cannot personally know every clerk, customer, bus driver, etc., as one presumably does in a small town). Simultaneously, primary ties are weakened for reasons discussed earlier, and because formal distance becomes a way of life.

There is a commonsensical appeal to the prediction that the frequency of secondary contacts increases with population size, but we do not know the degree to which it is true. And it does not appear that such an increase has any important consequences, anyway. We know that there is little, if any, decline in the number or depth of primary relationships with increases in urbanism; nor are there any particular personality changes. Perhaps we should view urban life as offering a large number of potential secondary relationships in addition to, rather than in substitution for, personal ones.

Part of the urban style is described as an impersonality and superficiality in social interactions. (Recall that these are considered ways of protecting the individual against an overload of demands.) Again, there is little empirical reason to believe that this is true.

Living in a world of many strangers is hypothesized to develop an exploitative, materialistic orientation. There is some suggestion that American large-city-dwellers have slightly more distrust for "others," but little indication that they actually are more exploitative. One study of the "Machiavellian" personality (a type which has a cold, calculating approach to people) revealed no urban-rural differences in its frequency (Christie and Geis, 1970).

One of the most dramatic images of the urban mode of interaction is that of the city-dweller who refuses to "get involved" in aiding another person in need. The public slaying of Kitty Genovese spurred a series of studies on "pro-social behavior" (e.g., intervening to help others). Pilot studies reported by Milgram (1970) showed somewhat less willingness on the part of large-city (especially New York) people to extend themselves than on the part of small-town people. Other research (e.g., Forbes and Gromoll, 1971) has come up with mixed results. Since the research has but begun, it would be premature to conclude whether there are urban-rural differences in this regard, and certainly whether any differences would be due to urbanisn per se.[19]

A comment should be made about mob-psychology descriptions of urban life: What evidence exists suggests that city people are not any more likely than rural persons to fall sway to such collective behavior (see, for example, Tilly, 1969).

We conclude this section, as we did the previous one, by noting that differences, if they exist at all, are small. Changing population distribution alone is unlikely to have a significant social psychological impact on the way people interact.

Values and Beliefs

If there are substantial associations between size of place and social-psychological phenomena, this is where they exist. It is a repeated finding that, the larger the city, the less traditional and conservative are the expressed opinions and behaviors of people. And the differences are noticeable. This is true for several realms of life, including religion, life-style, law, race, drugs, sex, the family, and politics. Table 5.7 illustrates these differences with poll results on marijuana.

A major reason for this correlation is the association of community size with factors such as region of the country, social class, and the presence of minority groups. When these factors are taken into account, urban-rural differences become a good deal smaller, though still in an urban-liberal direction (Fischer, 1972a: ch. 6).

Table 5.7: Attitudes Toward and Reported Use of Marijuana by Community Size, 1972

	Community Size[a]				
	Under 2,500	2,500- 50,000	50,000- 500,000	500,000- 1,000,000	Over 1,000,000
"Do you think that the penalties for the use or possession of marijuana should be less strict than they currently are, or not?"					
Percent Yes (less)	23	20	29	42	43
Percent No	72	72	63	55	51
Percent No Opinion	5	8	8	3	6
"Do you think that marijuana should be made legal, or not?"					
Percent Yes (legalize)	7	9	19	24	23
Percent No	90	88	77	72	70
Percent No Opinion	3	3	4	4	7
"Have you, yourself, ever happened to try marijuana?"					
Percent Yes	3	10	13	15	20
Percent No	97	90	87	85	80

NOTE: Data from Gallup Opinion Index, April 1972.
a. Size of city or of central city if respondent lives in a suburb.

The "deviant" nature of cities is consistent historically and cross-culturally, suggesting that it may be an "intrinsic" feature of urban life. Though the modal urban citizen (say, a middle-class WASP) holds about the same beliefs as does his rural counterpart (middle-class WASP), the city, more so than the country, harbors groups holding differing values and beliefs. Though it varies greatly by the composition of specific cities, generally it is to the urban centers that deviants of all sorts have been able to come, find supportive comrades, and maintain distinctive subcultures. These subgroups have protected their members and also have affected the community around them by disseminating their values.

In this way, cities have historically been the scenes of scientific, economic, social, and political innovation. Combined with the earlier discussion of crime, we can generally say that population aggregation is associated with deviance— some "bad" and called crime, some "good" and called invention, depending on one's values.

It is frequently argued that urban-rural differences are decreasing. In this context, at least, such differences will persist and will probably continue to persist (Willins, Bealer, and Crider, 1973). As long as cities are the generators of new ideas and there is lag in their diffusion, there will continue to be urban-rural contrasts.

Attitudes Towards the Community

One of the diagnoses of contemporary urban ills is that there has been a "loss of sense of community." If by community we mean the local neighborhood, then there is some evidence that it is weaker in the metropolis. (That is, the community of associates and the physically proximate community overlap less.) And, if we mean the incorporated city, then there is evidence that this, too, has weaker attachments, the greater the size of population. As a real, though quite weak, trend, the larger the legal city, the less people are politically oriented to it and the more they are oriented to the national or international level (see, for example, Verba and Nie, 1972; Nie, Powell, and Prewitt, 1969; Fischer, 1972a: ch. 4). The reason for this trend is partly, though not totally, the higher class-level of urbanites. It is difficult to apportion the relative contributions of urbanism to this pattern between (1) the large size of metropolitan governments, which might cause a sense of political futility (a sense that might be reduced by decentralization), and (2) the general decline of the importance of locality that comes with city size.

(As an indication of how individuals' personal worlds may be independent of their orientation to the local community, consider again Table 5.3. The first entry in the table shows the association between community size and satisfaction with local "quality of life." The other entries show the association of community size with items reflecting either more personal or more existential concerns. The larger the community, the more the dissatisfaction with it. But there is essentially no relationship with the other feelings.)

To summarize, the best estimate at the moment is that the urban experience (that is, size of place) does not affect individual personality in any substantial way, nor does it seem to change the ways in which people relate to each other (or to whom they relate). The urban experience includes the presence of people with nontraditional beliefs, and, to some degree, these "deviant" values may be picked up by other city people. The criminal deviants can affect the urban citizen in less innocent ways. Finally, since the urban individual's groups are more dispersed from the local area than the rural person's groups, so may his attention and concern with the locality be less. The central thrust of the research is that personality effects of urbanism per se are essentially nonexistent; the effects on attitudes and values are present—in a nontraditional direction—but modest.

CITY AND SUBURB

An important aspect of the metropolitan experience involves location within the metropolis. Central city vs. suburb is the distinction that is usually made. However, there are critical conceptual difficulties in employing this distinction for social-psychological purposes. For one, the definition of "suburb" is usually a political one: a suburb is a district outside the city limits of the largest city of the metropolis. These lines—usually arbitrary, often historical accidents or gerrymanderings (e.g., Los Angeles)—do have serious consequences for society and are justifiably the concern of political scientists (and, by those consequences, of sociologists). However, it is doubtful that living on one or the other side of a town marker has important psychological repercussions. Yet the research that exists, small as it is, depends on this distinction.

The second conceptual problem with employing this distinction is that we may be simply mystifying a commonplace in urban sociology: neighborhood differences. Cities are divisible into sections with distinguishable populations— blacks, Jews, Italians, young singles, families with children, poor, nouveau riche, alcoholics, etc.—and with accompanying housing and physical appearance. The general tendency in America—and increasingly elsewhere—is for the socioeconomic and ethnic rank of neighborhoods to increase with distance from the central business district, though there are a great number of exceptions to this pattern. Accompanying the higher class-level and the better physical surroundings, one can expect less social and personal disorganization, more happiness, trust, and friendship, less crime (other than white-collar crime), and more liberal attitudes. This heterogeneity among neighborhoods applies to suburbia as well, for there are blue-collar suburbs, black suburbs, singles suburbs, etc. In short, there may be very little sociologically interesting about city-suburb contrasts that are not also present in neighborhood contrasts within cities.

To make the suburban question a more sociologically meaningful one would require redefining it, perhaps in the following way: How is the nature of the metropolitan experience affected by residence at greater or lesser distances from city centers, all else being equal? Even so, most of our data remain based on political lines. (One argument that city-suburb differences vary by size of metropolitan area is probably based on just such an artifact of boundary lines; see Schnore, 1972.)

The third problem is that people sort themselves out in terms of neighborhoods. They choose which places to live on the basis of the kind of people who are there, the life-style, the facilities—in sum, on whether the experience will suit them. This is particularly true about city and suburb (Bell, 1959; Fava, 1959; Zelan, 1968; Zuiches and Fuguitt, 1971).[20] It therefore becomes quite difficult to attribute interneighborhood differences to the nature of the areas rather than the nature of the people who choose those areas. (One rare study that could do that, because the subjects were moved en masse to suburbia by their company, concluded that there was no significant change due to suburban residence; see Berger, 1960.)

All this is to caution the reader about the following discussion.

ELEMENTS OF THE SUBURBAN EXPERIENCE

Characteristics of Suburban Individuals

The stereotypic pattern of suburbs being white and wealthy is generally true, though younger and smaller cities show this pattern less than do older, larger ones (Schnore, 1972; see Zimmer, this volume).[21] This class distinction is relatively large, and accounts for most city-suburb differences.

Suburbs are also more likely to have families, while cities contain a disproportionate number of younger and older singles and of the childless (see, e.g., Hawley and Zimmer, 1970).

Suburbs are probably also more homogeneous in the sense that, within a given physical distance of his home, the average suburbanite is less likely to encounter different types of people than is the average city-dweller.

The Physical Context. Distance from city center usually means lower population density and less noise, traffic, pollution, and crowds. It also usually implies more housing space. Whether these elements have important social-psychological consequences is doubtful or unknown, but the market prices for these commodities certainly imply that people are happier with them than without them.

"Facilities" are at a relative premium in suburbs (Hawley and Zimmer, 1970). However, as the center of gravity of the population and of the wealth moves out, it appears that facilities (stores, meeting halls, amusement complexes) are doing the same, perhaps eventually reversing the pattern. The same thing is happening with government services, as city centers starve and suburbs grow.

The Social Context: The Individual's Groups. The thrust of most research is that there really are not major differences in the social lives of urban and suburban people, once account is taken of the characteristics of the individuals, the recency of their move, and the age of the suburb. We have already noted the demographic differences in the populations. Recency of move is critical because suburbs are composed to a large degree of recent migrants. The act of moving itself may have effects. More importantly, people move for certain goals. In most cases, those goals, be they an extra bedroom or an all-white neighborhood, are achieved, and thus the move is social-psychologically positive. Finally, new suburbs may have an esprit that will fade over time.

City and suburban residents, who are otherwise similar, have probably the same total degree of personal involvement. For suburbanites, though, it includes more local contact—neighboring, community civic groups, the immediate family—and less contact with other relatives and former friends (Tallman and Morgner, 1970; Fava, 1959; Tomeh, 1964).

The Social Context: Strangers. The people immediately around the suburban-ite are less likely to be strange or to be strangers than is the case for the city-dweller, but the differences are not great. One can speculate, however, that political identification as a small separate entity may increase the "sense of com-munity" for suburbanites.

A critical variable is distance. Given the automobile, it can be of little signifi-cance for the adult who is able to drive to facilities and other neighborhoods (though it has been shown that church attendance has decreased; see Hawley and Zimmer, 1970). The major impact is probably on relatively immobile children and car-less housewives, such that those in the city can more easily encounter strangers and diversity than those in the suburbs (see Foley, this volume).[22]

Crime. The average crime rate is lower in the suburb than in the city (cf. Table 5.5), but increasing at a more rapid rate.

EFFECTS OF THE SUBURBAN EXPERIENCE

Two points must be understood regarding the following comments, in addition to the cautions advanced earlier: (1) little quantitative research has accumulated that would permit confident generalizations about city-suburb comparisons, and (2) the better qualitative work (e.g., Berger, 1960; Gans, 1967; Willmott, 1963) generally implies that the effects are negligible.

Personality. Popular imagery suggests both that a respite from the maddening crowd is available in suburbia and that a neuroticism is engendered by the sub-urban rat-race. Given the lack of research, the best conclusion is that there are probably no substantial effects on stress or tension. For example, British studies comparing residents of new towns with those of old city boroughs generally fail to find differences in psychosomatic or psychiatric symptoms attributable to the environment (Pahl, 1970: 125-127).

Neither can much be generalized about forms of alienation. Feelings of social isolation tend to be greater among those just separated by long distance from kin and friends, but this is compensated for among many by involvement in local circles. One recent survey of neighborhoods in Los Angeles found few social-psychological differences among them (Seeman, Bishop, and Grigsby, 1971).

Satisfaction and happiness, at least about their town, is likely to be greater among new suburbanites than among city-dwellers, both because of greater affluence and because their move permitted them in most cases to achieve certain desires—space, land, a life-style, quiet, etc. Whether second-generation suburbanites are more satisfied than their otherwise similar, city counterparts is uncertain.

Modes of Interaction. One element of suburban imagery is that of perhaps overly sociable kaffee-klatsching. To a certain extent, this may be true. With somewhat greater mutual compatibility than in most city areas and with the greater importance of the neighborhood, a larger proportion of the suburban-ite's local interactions may be close and personal than in the city. However, hard data are difficult to come by, and the Los Angeles study (Seeman et al., 1971) reports little evidence to support the proposition.

Values and Beliefs. It used to be thought that the suburban move "Repub-licanized" people, but that tends to be dismissed now. Perhaps the new affluence, which permitted the suburban move, conservatized, but there is little reason to conclude that suburban residence per se affects values. Suburbanites are likely to be liberal on social issues (though a recent study showed this was not so with regard to race; see Campbell, 1971), but that is largely attributable to class and ethnic differences.

Attitudes Toward the Community. In spite of the greater importance of the locality, suburban residents—once social class is accounted for—are probably less involved politically in their communities than are city-dwellers, though exceptions to this pattern no doubt exist in cases of community threat (e.g,, busing) and in new towns. This relatively lower interest in politics, we speculate, is due to the apparent triviality or invisibility of suburban government in metro-politan areas dominated by single, large cities (Verba and Nie, 1972: ch. 13; Fischer, 1972a: ch. 4).

To summarize, an apt conclusion about the suburban experience—as best we know of it—is provided by Herbert Gans (1967: 288-89) in his almost definitive study, *The Levittowners:*

> The findings on changes and their sources suggest that the distinction between urban and suburban ways of living postulated by the critics (and by some sociologists as well) is more imaginery than real. Few changes can be traced to the suburban qualities of Levittown, and the sources that did cause change, like the house, the population mix, and newness, are not distinctively sub-urban. Moreover, when one looks at similar populations in city and suburb, their ways of life are remarkably alike. For example, when suburbs are com-pared to the large urban residential areas beyond the downtown and inner districts, culture and social structure are virtually the same among people of similar age and class. Young lower middle class families in these areas live much like their peers in the suburbs, but quite unlike older, upper middle class ones, in either urban or suburban neighborhoods.

The crucial difference between cities and suburbs, then, is that they are often home for different kinds of people. If one is to understand their behavior, these differences are much more important than whether they reside inside or outside the city limits. Inner-city residential areas are home to the rich, the poor, and the nonwhite, as well as the unmarried and the childless middle class. Their ways of life differ from those of suburbanites and people in the outer city, but because they are *not* young working or lower or upper middle class families. If populations and residential areas were described by age and class characteristics, and by racial, ethnic, and religious ones, our understanding of human settlements would be much improved. Using such concepts as 'urban' and 'suburban' as causal variables adds little, on the other hand, except for ecological and demographic analyses of communities as a whole and for studies of political behavior.

COMMENTS

The bulk of this report has dealt with what the metropolitan experience was thought to be and is not. We should state what the metropolitan experience *is*. It is, first and foremost, plural. Depending on the social characteristics of the individual, it is the experience of affluence or poverty; of being black, Italian, or Jewish; of being young or old; of being a professional or a laborer. Beyond that, there is a crude sort of commonality of the following sort. The metropolitan experience (relative to the nonmetropolitan one) is noisy and somewhat dirty. It involves a wide range of alternative opportunities, in terms of people, places, and things. It means some isolation from the neighborhood, but involvement in translocal communities of interest. These communities are large and vital, and they touch other vibrant subcultures, both in conflict and in trade. In this milieu, new, exciting, and sometimes frightening events and ideas occur, for it is the vortex of change.

Before we take this description too seriously, we should reconsider Gans' statements about city-suburban differences, for they also express his nonecological position on urban-rural differences—that, by and large, the correlation of size of place with social behavior is due to the composition of the populations that inhabit those places rather than to their spatial features.

The truth is that we lack adequate research to confirm Gans', or Wirth's, or our position. What is needed are comprehensive studies that place individuals within their meaningful social circles and then systematically explore the impact of urbanism on the structure and functioning of those personal worlds.

To the extent to which we can rely on the existing empirical data, it does support Gans' view, with certain important qualifications. That is, in the spectrum of meaningful life experiences, dimensions of personality and styles of interpersonal relationships, there are very few urban-rural differences that can be attributed to place of residence, and even those few are of modest size. This is our major conclusion.

However, those few differences deserve some attention. Thus, one of the consequences of urbanism is spatial dispersion of personal networks. Perhaps due to the absence of alternatives, a rural person's neighbors are his friends and relatives (or vice versa). In the city, these important associates are dispersed and neighbors relatively ignored. In suburbia, neighbors are rediscovered, perhaps because (1) the distances are now too great for extended ties and/or (2) the neighbors are more compatible.

Another feature of population concentration is the popular preference for less-dense areas, combined with a desire to be near the social and economic opportunities of the metropolis. This implies a continuing push for suburbanization.

The facilities and opportunities of the metropolis are generated by size, and their ready availability is an intrinsic element of the urban experience.

Granting that population composition is the primary causal variable, there remains a critical question for Gans' analysis: Why do the populations of city and country differ in consistent ways, historically and cross-culturally? It is the intrinsic features of urbanism per se—of population aggregation—that attract and retain certain types, repel and lose others. Population size means major and diverse economies, with consequent effects on social class.[23] Aggregation leads to the services and opportunities of the city which, depending on the individual, do or do not compensate for the physical context. And, more importantly, urbanism provides the opportunity to be among similar people—an opportunity more precious and dependent on the city, the more unique the individual. For example, the "Middle American" of media fame can probably find a suitable community of interest across the entire range of physical community sizes. However, an ethnic Italian-American or Jewish-American would usually be an outlander away from his metropolitan home. Similarly, an artist, intellectual, or chess fiend would have great difficulty supporting his interests away from a sizable number of like-minded people—i.e., away from a major city. In short, it is population size that makes the composition of urban places disproportionately one of groups outside the American mainstream.

A number of these groups are deviants of a serious and harmful sort: heroin addicts, organized criminals, skid-row residents, etc. Others are deviants in approved ways: ethnic or religious minorities, artists, scholars, scientists, etc. Yet others have an ambiguous position: Life-style experimenters, ethnic-culture militants, etc. The existence of all these groups (and their contacts with each other) means that the city is the site of cultural innovation of various sorts: pop art and the methadone black market, new fashions and the systematic burglary of school buildings, and so on. These inventions start among small urban groups, spread to other urban people, and then to the nation. Donald Cook (1963: 87) stated it this way in an article entitled "Cultural Innovation and Disaster in the American City": "Today's city is seen at once as the source of the most important values of our culture, and, at the same time, as the source of its most characteristic and pressing problems. . . . The same basic structural conditions may in fact be responsible for both outcomes."

One of the "outs" from what Cook calls a "dilemma" has been the search for an optimum city size—one which would maximize facilities, services, and innovation with a minimum of congestion, dirt, and crime. The issue of optimal city size has rarely been tackled by sociologists (which is not surprising, given the rarity of any comparative studies). However, Otis Dudley Duncan (1957b) examined the distribution of various public goods across community sizes and concluded that no such simple optimum could be found, for it depended on the good to be maximized. Political scientist Robert Dahl (1967) used some of Duncan's data in his argument that the optimal city size, particularly for achieving a viable participatory democracy, was in the 50,000 to 200,000 range. Some data examined by this author (Fischer, 1973a, 1973c) imply that residence in the very largest metropolises may have a quite small, but real, disquieting or alienating effect.

The policy problems with seeking sociologically optimal city sizes include not only that mentioned by Duncan (deciding what value to optimize), but also what measure of good one uses (average returns, minimum standards, modal levels, etc.). Take an example used by Dahl: cultural institutions. Statistics show that the optimal size for achieving minimum standards and per capita use of cultural items (e.g., libraries and museums) peaks at a city-size level well below that of our largest cities. In that sense, the lower size is optimal for maintaining the highest average institutional use. This ignores, however, the fact that peaks in cultural attainments come disproportionately in (and may require) large metropolises. Perhaps this is one area where one might wish to optimize the chances for greatness (e.g., the Museum of Modern Art in New York) rather than the average rate.

A similar issue, put more broadly, is whether that which optimizes the average return to the average American may not minimize the return to the nonaverage American. For example, in the optimal community, there may be enough books, delicatessens, and youth facilities for the average citizen, but will there be enough for the scholars, Jews, and teen-agers?

The problems of optimizing social variables introduces the broader policy issues. We can speculate as to the sociological and psychological effects of redistributing the population in the direction of smaller cities. We will assume that the economic factors remain constant. This is a precarious presumption, for individual and national income may well depend on the present hierarchy of city sizes. It is also a critical assumption, in that most urban-rural and city-suburb differences are a function of class. But if smaller cities were the rule, with the present proportional distributions of class, occupational and life-cycle population characteristics, what might we expect to be different? Not very much.

What might change, modestly, is the following: If more people could, without economic cost, move to smaller cities and more suburban areas, more people would be pleased with their communities. In that sense, redistribution would be consonant with the popular will. It is unlikely that the national average of happiness with other aspects of life would change. For the average person, the networks of people important to him would be more constricted spatially, and he may take a little more interest in his neighborhood and local town. The crime rate is likely to be slightly lower, as is the rate of noncriminal deviance.

On the other hand, the number of special services and institutions would probably be reduced somewhat. So would the size and vitality of minority subcultures. Noncriminal forms of innovation—social, cultural, and political—would also be likely to become less frequent. In that way, social change, desirable and undesirable, would probably slow down.

More direct, fundamental, impacts on individual personality and personal relationships would be unlikely.

NOTES

1. For an extended discussion of these terms as meaningful categories, see the paper by Rex Campbell (this volume).

2. One result of this usage has been the devotion of many printed pages to higher-level semantic elaborations of the following sort: "While urban places are usually more urban and rural more rural, sometimes (and more and more these days) one finds urbanism among the rural and rurality among the urban."

3. Among the factors associated with urban residence in the United States are: ethnicity, religion, social class, region of the country, stage in the life-cycle, as well as the whole conglomeration of things currently labeled "urban problems."

4. The French tradition is somewhat different, with preferences inclined toward cities (Girard, Bastide, and Pourcher, 1970). However, Dutch tastes are more like Americans (The Netherlands, 1967: 66).

5. While economic reasons are by far the most often cited by urban migrants, this does not deny that there are other factors explaining urban migration. For instance, many peasant immigrants to the United States had planned to become farmers, but stayed in their ports of disembarkation because of lack of funds (Handlin, 1969).

6. The group which could be called "urbane," who view city life as the good life, are a small minority.

7. A current television announcement makes a similar point. The speaker states that, in the past, one could depend on one's neighbors for emergency help, but today one cannot, and must therefore instead turn to the Red Cross.

8. For example, in a survey analyzed by the author, the correlation coefficients between size of SMSA and class variables were: education, 0.2; occupational prestige, 0.18; and income, 0.17 (Fischer, 1972a: Appendix B).

9. A challenge to the conclusions of that report illustrates some of the difficulty in making these sorts of urban-rural comparisons. The challenger argued that the mortality statistics were biased for reasons including (1) rural persons go to cities for hospital care and die there, and (2) the unavailability of specialists results in lung-cancer deaths in rural areas being attributed to "senility" (Melnick, 1972).

10. A recent study suggests that high person-per-room density may have deleterious effects (Galle, Gove, and McPherson, 1971). However, that type of density does not increase with urbanism.

11. In Wilson's analysis, contemporary urbanites are surrounded and upset by what they sense to be public misbehavior, serious and otherwise. This is the sort of display strangers make.

12. Further adaptations include the use of impersonal media of interchange, such as newspapers, because of the impossibility of knowing all other urban persons; and the use of status symbolism (clothes, possessions, styles, etc.) because of the impossibility of all these strangers personally knowing each other's social position. A more ambivalent adaptation is

moral relativity—a suspension of judgment, or at least, action, against others' values and beliefs—which is necessary if one is to conduct business with, and pass peacefully among, strangers. This relativism has harmful repercussions, according to the theory, in the resultant weakening of attachments to one's own values.

13. Much of the influence of these ideas is due to the powerfully compelling logic with which the authors originally presented them. However, as Reiss (1955) has shown with some of these propositions, persuasive and equally plausible arguments can be made from the other side. For example, a line of analysis could begin with the proposition that life among strangers requires an etiquette of *politesse* as a social lubricant, one which culminates not in an atmosphere of ceremony but in one of mutual regard and friendliness (see, for example, the chapter on "The City" in Wood [1934]).

14. For a challenge to this viewpoint, see Loftin and Hill (1973).

15. One can dismiss most of the best-selling pop-ethological descriptions of urban life in terms of "behavioral sinks" populated by crowded "killer apes" as nonsense.

16. A clarification is necessary in regard to normlessness or "anomia." The complexity in this area involves whose norms are used as a reference. The conclusion that the crime rates indicate a higher urban normlessness means that such criminals are less likely to believe in the *general society's* rules. However, normlessness can also refer to the rules of the individual's *specific subculture,* rules which may differ from those of the wider society. In that case, there are probably no major urban-rural differences. That is, the urban ghetto-dweller is probably no less attached to his own group's rules of behavior than is the farmer attached to the traditional Protestant morality.

17. Self-estrangement—alienated labor—is another of Seeman's dimensions, but it is not directly relevant to this paper.

18. This slight trend appears, in one analysis, to be due to relatively greater despair in the very largest metropolises, rather than to monotonic increases with population size (Fischer, 1973c).

19. A caveat to this conclusion: Research by Darley and Latane (1968) indicates that, the more people at the scene of an emergency, the less likely any individual is to act (though this finding has recently been challenged by Darley, Tiger, and Lewis, 1973). This is due to the psychological processes involved in defining a situation as being indeed an emergency. To the degree to which crises in cities are more likely to occur in the presence of many people than are rural emergencies, one could find urban-rural differences in helping. However, this does not imply that city people are actually less caring. Presumably, the same dynamics would operate in a crowd of country people.

20. To clarify this statement with a previous one: Residence moves are made largely for housing reasons; social, life-style reasons are secondary, but exist. *Where* a person finds his new home can be more affected by the population or social climate than whether he moves.

21. Historically, and in many places around the world, this pattern was and is reversed—the wealthy gathered in the city center. Efficiencies in transport made it possible for the well-to-do to have their access to facilities and to spacious lands. In either case, the poor received the residue.

22. Second-generation suburbanites, who would be better subjects for comparative study, are rarely studied. One analysis of survey data (Zelan, 1968) found no major differences in intellectual attitudes between suburban and center-city-raised college students. (It did show that, in a sample of graduate students, those who were raised in a suburb, were married, and were relatively uninterested in intellectual cultural entertainment, preferred suburban life over those who differed in these characteristics.)

23. H. Gans, personal communication, October 23, 1972.

REFERENCES

Alford, R. R., and Lee, E. C. "Voting turnout in American cities." American Political Science Review, September 1968, 62, 796-813.

Alonso, W., and Fajans, M. Cost of living and income by urban size. Working Paper No. 128. Berkeley: University of California, Institute of Urban and Regional Development, 1970.

Ardrey, R. *The territorial imperative.* New York: Atheneum, 1966.

Bell, W. Social choice, life styles, and suburban residence. In W. M. Dobriner (Ed.), *The suburban community.* New York: Putnam, 1959. 225-247.

Berger, B. N. *Working-class suburb.* Berkeley: University of California Press, 1960.

Blau, P. M., and Duncan, O. D. *The American occupational structure.* New York: Wiley, 1967.

Campbell, A. *White attitudes toward black people.* Ann Arbor: University of Michigan, Institute for Social Research, 1971.

Carpenter, D. B. "Urbanization and social change in Japan." Sociological Quarterly, July 1960, 9, 155-166.

Christie, R., and Geis, F. L. *Studies in Machiavellianism.* New York: Academic Press, 1970.

Cook, D. A. Cultural innovation and disaster in the American city. In L. Duhl (Ed.), *The urban condition.* New York: Simon and Schuster (Clarion ed.), 1963. 87-96.

Dahl, R. A. "The city in the future of democracy." American Political Science Review, December 1967, 61, 953-970.

Darley, J. M., and Latane, B. "When will people help in a crisis?" Psychology Today, December 1968, 2, 54 ff.

Darley, J. M., Tiger, A., and Lewis, L. D. "Do groups always inhibit individuals' responses to potential emergencies?" Journal of Personality and Social Psychology, June 1973, 26(3), 395-399.

Dewey, R. "The rural-urban continuum: Real but relatively unimportant." American Journal of Sociology, July 1960, 66, 60-66.

Dohrenwend, B. P., and Dohrenwend, B. S. The prevalence of psychiatric disorders in urban versus rural settings. Paper presented at the Fifth World Congress of Psychiatry, Mexico City, November 28-December 4, 1971.

Donaldson, S. *The suburban myth.* New York: Columbia University Press, 1971.

Duncan, O. D. Community size and the rural-urban continuum. In P. K. Hatt and A. J. Reiss, Jr. (Eds.), *Cities and society.* New York: Free Press, 1957. 35-45. (a)

Duncan, O. D. Optimum size of cities. In P. K. Hatt and A. J. Reiss, Jr. (Eds.), *Cities and society.* New York: Free Press, 1957. 759-772. (b)

Ennis, P. H. The contextual dimension in voting. In W. M. McPhee and W. A. Glaser (Eds.), *Public opinion and congressional elections.* New York: Free Press, 1962. 180-211.

Ennis, P. H. *Criminal victimization in the United States: A report of a national survey.* Chicago: National Opinion Research Center, 1967.

Epstein, A. L. "Urbanization and social change in Africa." Current Anthropology, October 1967, 8, 275-296.

Fava, S. F. Contrasts in neighboring: New York City and a suburban county. In W. M. Dobriner (Ed.), *The suburban community.* New York: Putnam, 1959. 122-130.

Federal Bureau of Investigation. *Uniform crime reports—1970.* Washington, D.C.: U.S. Government Printing Office, 1971.

Fischer, C. S. Studies in the social psychology of urban life. Unpublished doctoral dissertation, Harvard University, 1972. (a)

Fischer, C. S. "Urbanism as a Way of Life: A review and an agenda." Sociological Methods and Research, November 1972, 1, 187-242. (b)

Fischer, C. S. "Urban alienation and anomie: Powerlessness and social isolation." American Sociological Review, June 1973, 38, 311-326. (a)

Fischer, C. S. Toward a subcultural theory of urbanism. Paper presented at the meeting of the American Sociological Society, New York, August 1973. (b)

Fischer, C. S. "Urban malaise." Social Forces, December 1973, 53, (c)

Forbes, G. B., and Gromoll, H. F. "The lost-letter technique as a measure of social variables: Some exploratory findings." Social Forces, September 1971, 50, 113-115.

Foster, G. M. "Interpersonal relations in peasant society." Human Organization, Winter 1960-61, 19, 174-185.

Freedman, J. L., Klevansky, S., and Ehrlich, P. R. "The effect of crowding on human task performance." Journal of Applied Social Psychology, March 1971, 1, 7-25.

Galle, O. R., Gove, W. R., and McPherson, J. M. Population density and pathology. Paper presented at the meeting of the American Sociological Association, Denver, 1971.

Gans, H. J. The urban villagers: Group and class in the life of Italian-Americans. New York: Free Press, 1962. (a)

Gans, H. J. Urbanism and suburbanism as ways of life: A re-evaluation of definitions. In A. M. Rose (Ed.), Human behavior and social processes. Boston: Houghton Mifflin, 1962. 625-648. (b)

Gans, H. J. The Levittowners: Way of life and politics in a new suburban community. New York: Vintage, 1967.

Girard, A., Bastide, H., and Pourcher, G. Geographic mobility and urban concentration in France: A study in the provinces. In C. J. Jansen (Ed.), Readings in the sociology of migration. Oxford: Pergamon, 1970. 203-253.

Glass, D. C., and Sincer, J. E. Urban stress. New York: Academic Press, 1972.

Greer, S. "Urbanism reconsidered: A comparative study of local areas in a metropolis." American Sociological Review, February 1956, 21, 18-25.

Handlin, O. Boston's immigrants. (Rev. ed.) New York: Atheneum, 1969.

Harris, L. "A Life poll." Life, January 9, 1970, 102-106.

Hauser, P. H. Urbanization: An overview. In P. H. Hauser and L. F. Schnore (Eds.), The study of urbanization. New York: Wiley, 1965. 1-48.

Hawley, A. H., and Zimmer, B. G. The metropolitan community. Beverly Hills: Sage, 1970.

Howe, I. "The city in literature." Commentary, May 1971, 51, 61-68.

Inkeles, A. "Making men modern: On the causes and consequences of individual change in six developing countries." American Journal of Sociology, September 1969, 75, 208-225.

Janowitz, M. Social and political consequences of social mobility. In M. Janowitz (Ed.), Political conflict. Beverly Hills: Sage, 1970. 71-87.

Keyes, F. "The correlation of social phenomena with community size." Social Forces, May 1958, 36, 311-315.

Lane, R. Address to the Eastern Sociological Society, New York, April 1971.

Lasswell, T. E. "Social class and size of community." American Journal of Sociology, March 1959, 64, 505-508.

Lewis, O. Further observations on the folk-urban continuum and urbanization with special reference to Mexico City. In P. H. Hauser and L. Schnore (Eds.), The study of urbanization. New York: Wiley, 1965. 491-503.

Lipset, S. M., and Bendix, R. Social mobility in industrial society. Berkeley: University of California Press, 1964.

Lofland, L. "Self-management in public settings: Part 1." Urban Life and Culture, April 1972, 1, 93-108.

Loflin, C., and Hill, R. H. Regional subcultures and homocide? An examination of the Gastil-Hackney theory. Paper presented at the meeting of the American Sociological Society, New York, August 1973.

Melnick, N. "Pollution cancer link disputed." San Francisco Examiner, September 14, 1972.

Milgram, S. "The experience of living in cities: A psychological analysis." Science, March 13, 1970, 167, 1461-1468. Reprinted in F. Korten (Ed.), Psychology and the problems of society. Washington, D.C.: American Psychological Association, 1970. 152-173.

Mitchell, R. E. "Some social implications of high density housing." American Sociological Review, February 1971, 36, 18-29.

National Research Council. Committee on Biologic Effects of Atmospheric Pollutants. Particulate polycyclic organic matter. Washington, D.C.: National Academy of Sciences, 1972.

The Netherlands. Polls, Summer 1967, 2(4), 66-70.

Nie, N. H., Powell, G. B., and Prewitt, K. "Social structure and political participation: Developmental relationships, Parts 1 and 2." American Political Science Review, June 1969, 63, 361-378; September 1969, 63, 800-832.

Ogburn, W. F., and Duncan, O. D. City size as a sociological variable. In E. W. Burgess and D. J. Bogue (Ed.), *Urban sociology.* Chicago: University of Chicago Press (Phoenix), 1964. 58-76.

Pahl, R. E. *Patterns of urban life.* London: Longmans, Green, 1970.

Park, R. E. The city as a social laboratory. In E. C. Hughes, C. S. Johnson, J. Masuoka, R. Redfield, and L. Wirth (Eds.), *Human communities: The city and human ecology.* Vol. 2. *Collected papers of Robert Ezra Park.* Glencoe: The Free Press, 1952. 73-87.

Reiss, A. J., Jr. An analysis of urban phenomena. In R. M. Fisher (Ed.), *The metropolis in modern life.* Garden City: Doubleday, 1955.

Robinson, J. P., and Shaver, P. R. *Measures of social psychological attitudes.* Ann Arbor: University of Michigan, Institute for Social Research, 1969.

Rossi, P. *Why families move.* Chicago: Free Press, 1956.

Schnore, L. "Some correlates of urban size: A replication." American Journal of Sociology, September 1963, 69, 185-193.

Schnore, L. *Class and race in cities and suburbs.* Chicago: Markham, 1972.

Schooler, C. "Social antecedents of adult psychological functioning." American Journal of Sociology, September 1972, 78, 299-322.

Schorr, A. *Slums and social insecurity.* U.S. Department of Health, Education, and Welfare. Washington, D.C.: U.S. Government Printing Office, 1966.

Schorske, C. E. The idea of the city in European thought: Voltaire to Spengler. In O. H. Handlin and J. Burchard (Eds.), *The historian and the city.* Cambridge: MIT Press, 1963, 95-115.

Schuman, A., and Gruenberg, B. "The impact of city on racial attitudes." American Journal of Sociology, September 1970, 76, 213-262.

Seeman, M. "On the meaning of alienation." American Sociological Review, December 1959, 24, 783-791.

Seeman, M. Alienation and engagement. In A. Campbell and P. E. Converse (Eds.), *The human meaning of social change.* New York: Russell Sage, 1972. 441-466.

Seeman, M., Bishop, J. M., and Grigsby, J. E., III. Community and control in a metropolitan setting. In P. Orleans and R. Ellis (Eds.), *Race, change and urban society.* Urban Affairs Annual Review, Vol. 5. Beverly Hills: Sage Publications, 1971. 423-450.

Simmel, G. The metropolis and mental life. Dresden: V. Zahn and Jaensch, 1903. As translated in K. Wolfe (Ed.), *The Sociology of Georg Simmel.* New York: Free Press, 1950. Pp. 409-424. Reprinted in P. K. Hatt and A. J. Reiss, Jr. (Eds.), *Cities and society.* New York: Free Press, 1957. 635-646.

Sjoberg, G. *The preindustrial city.* New York: Free Press, 1960.

Sjoberg, G. Theory and research in urban sociology. In P. H. Hauser and L. F. Schnore (Eds.), *The study of urbanization.* New York: Wiley, 1965. 157-190.

Smith, J., Form, W. H., and Stone, G. P. "Local intimacy in a middle-sized city." American Journal of Sociology, November 1954, 60, 276-284.

Smith, P. *As a city upon a hill: The town in American history.* New York: Knopf, 1968.

Srole, L. "Social integration and certain corollaries: An exploratory study." American Sociological Review, December 1956, 21, 709-716.

Suttles, G. D. *The social order of the slum.* Chicago: University of Chicago Press, 1968.

Tallman, I., and Morgner, R. "Life-style differences among urban and suburban blue-collar families." Social Forces, March 1970, 48, 334-348.

Tilly, C. Collective violence in European perspective. In H. D. Graham and T. R. Gurr (Eds.), *The history of violence in America.* New York: Bantam, 1969. 4-44.

Tomeh, A. K. "Informal group participation and residential patterns." American Journal of Sociology, July 1964, 70, 28-35.

U.S. Bureau of the Census. Mobility of the population of the United States: March 1969 to March 1970. *Current Population Reports,* Series P-20, No. 210. Washington, D.C.: U.S. Government Printing Office, 1971. (a)

U.S. Bureau of the Census. U.S. Census of Population and Housing: 1970. General demographic trends for metropolitan areas, 1960 to 1970. U.S. Summary, Final Report PHC (2)-1. Washington, D.C.: U.S. Government Printing Office, 1971. (b)

U.S. Department of Health, Education and Welfare. Hearing levels of children by demographic and socioeconomic characteristics. DHEW Publication No. (HSM) 72-1025. Washington, D.C.: U.S. Government Printing Office, 1972.

U.S. National Commission on the Causes and Prevention of Violence. *Crimes of violence: A staff report.* Vol. 12. Washington, D.C.: U.S. Government Printing Office, 1969.

Verba, S., and Nie, N. H. *Participation in American life: Political democracy and social equality.* New York: Harper and Row, 1972.

Webber, M. M. Order in diversity: Community without propinquity. In R. Gutman and D. Popenoe (Eds.), *Neighborhood, city and metropolis.* New York: Random House, 1970. 792-811.

Wellman, B., Craven, P., Whitaker, M., Stevens, H., and DuToit, S. *The uses of community: Community ties and support systems.* Research X10. 47. Toronto: University of Toronto, Center for Urban and Community Studies and Department of Sociology, August, 1971. Reprinted in L. S. Bourne, R. D. MacKinnon, and J. W. Simmons (Eds.), *The form of cities in Central Canada: Selected papers.* Toronto: University of Toronto, Centre for Urban and Community Studies, 1973.

White, M., and White, L. *The intellectual versus the city.* New York: Mentor, 1962.

Willins, F. K., Bealer, R. C., and Crider, D. M. "Leveling of attitudes in mass society: Rurality and traditional morality in America." Rural Sociology, Spring 1973, 38, 36-45.

Willmott, P. *The evolution of a community.* London: Routledge and Kegan Paul, 1963.

Wilson, J. Q. "The urban unease." The Public Interest, Summer 1968 (12), 25-39.

Wirth, L. "Urbanism as a way of life." American Journal of Sociology, July 1938, 44, 3-24.

Wolfgang, M. E. Urban crime. In J. Q. Wilson (Ed.), *The metropolitan enigma.* Garden City: Anchor, 1970. 270-311.

Wood, M. *Stranger: A study in social relationships.* New York: Columbia University Press, 1934.

Zelan, J. Does suburbia make a difference. In S. F. Fava (Ed.), *Urbanism in world perspective.* New York: Crowell, 1968. 401-408.

Zuiches, J. J., and Fuguitt, G. V. Residential preferences: Implications for population redistribution in nonmetropolitan areas. Paper presented at the meeting of the American Association for the Advancement of Science, Philadelphia, December 1971.

CHAPTER 6

COMMUNITY DESIGN: THE SEARCH FOR PARTICIPATION IN A METROPOLITAN SOCIETY

Gerald D. Suttles

State University of New York, Stony Brook

THE WORDS "COMMUNITY DESIGN" arouse numerous associations which run from the utopias discussed by Greek, Roman, Renaissance, and modern authorities to the new suburban developments and public housing projects which have taken shape in the U.S. The hope that one could find a particular kind of community in which man would always prosper and satisfy spiritual or collective values, or at least find happiness and contentment, has been a major preoccupation of Western thinkers. The local community, next to the family, has been thought of as the most universal form which could mold human thoughts, actions, and ambitions to produce a desirable citizen. To thoroughly cover the ideas on community design would require an encyclopedic knowledge running from the ancient Babylonians to current times. However, such an effort might result in a series of discrete articles by specialists tracing the descending ideas of their predecessors.

My aim is to respond more narrowly to the issues of the specific times. The issues of community control, decentralization, the quality of public services and the financial imbalance within metropolitan areas are the most apparent ones which need settling at this moment. It may be seen as the problem of how localities should relate to one another and to supracommunity groups. Such a focus on organizational patterns tends to place the discussion of physical location and architectural design in the background and to neglect the whole range of "Skinner boxes" and "city beautifuls" discussed heretofore by psychologists, engineers, and city planners. Indeed, the very concept of community design tends first to arouse thoughts of how and where to build physical structures rather than of how and why to build social structures.[1]

Our problem here is largely one of the normative, legal, and administrative arrangements among communities and supracommunity organizations. There seems to be an unwieldy agglomerate of community groups, supracommunity organizations, and governmental referees who produce unwanted outcomes or outcomes which benefit only a limited number of people. This is a major issue in modern societies, and it is not one that can be resolved by building a new type of building or by a particulâr placement of roads and public buildings. Brick and mortar solutions seem simply not to work and something more seems to be called for (Gans, 1968a: 57-77; Altshuler, 1965; Von Eckardt, 1965; Fagin, 1967). What does seem to be called for is a notion of community design that places emphasis on the normative, legal, and administrative relationships among local groups.

MASS SOCIETY AND "THE DECLINE OF COMMUNITY"

A trend which seems to have become prominent around the time of the First World War was the increasing scale of both public and private organizations (Nisbet, 1967; Schulze, 1961; Warner and Lowi, 1947; Hawley, 1971: 199-218). This trend was accompanied by the increasing centralization of organizational control, and a functional rather than a territorial division of labor. This trend, when joined with the widespread use of the automobile, served to reduce considerably the significance of the local community. The centers of power and decision making became distant and remote; public and private organizations were often narrowly specialized and unable to respond to communities as groups; and the mobility of the population was so increased that nonterritorial voluntary organizations seemed likely to replace locality groups.

This trend was sustained after World War II. Aside from a defense of the local community on sentimental and nostalgic ground, there was little immediate concern with the decline of community. Perhaps the prevailing sociological point of view was that expressed by Richard Dewey (1950: 504):

> It is often overlooked that there are two types of primary groups operating in the rural setting. In the first group, membership is voluntary and is made up of friends and associates of one's own choosing. The second group is made up of those whose attention is unsolicited and often unwelcome, but the small town resident cannot escape membership in this primary group. The former type of primary group is essential to man's welfare regardless of his residence, but the latter type is neither essential nor desirable, and it is frequently the reason for persons migrating from rural areas. The sociologist and social psychologist can aid planners by pointing out that a large primary group is not essential to the development of an adequate personality.

Thus, the small town was not a model for the urban local community and, by implication, voluntary associations were everywhere preferable to territorial ones.

This rather sanguine view seems to have persisted until the 1960s when there began to develop a series of social movements aimed at restoring the local community (for example, see Ellis, 1969; Mayer, 1969; Kotler, 1969; Altshuler, 1970; Lipset and Altback, 1968; Hallman, 1970: 3-11). Both black militants and white segregationists began a loud outcry for local determination. A significant number of young people expressed grievances over the "lack of community," and many of them have since formed fitful and short-lived communes. The riots of the mid and late 1960s disclosed the depths of the alienation of local residents from the large and impersonal agencies meant to serve them.

Sociologists, as well as others, were rather unprepared for these social movements and have made only limited efforts to diagnose them and rethink their ideas about the local community. Although more data would be useful in doing this, a large part of the problem seems to be conceptual. This conceptual confusion seems to exist among both proponents for the local community and analysts of local communities. Since each group tends to feed upon the misconceptions of the other, it may be best to start with a critical review of several widespread notions that form the background for most discussions of community.

Some assumptions underlying analyses of U.S. Communities. Members of the local community are bound together primarily by bonds of sentiment rather than the instrumental usefulness of residents for one another. In part, this point of view derives from Tönnis' concept of Gemeinschaft, which portrayed the local community as a sort of overgrown primary group. The same imagery is often voiced by those who wish to restore the local community and defend it by clothing their argument in nostalgic and altruistic garb. In the negotiations between defenders of the local community and those of supracommunity organizations, the former apparently think it useful to portray the local community as an especially precious human collectivity.

This conception is quite misleading, and even Tönnis' would have emphasized the way in which instrumental and expressive associations are undifferentiated in the Gemeinschaft. But a more serious problem with this point of view is that it may detract attention from some of the more important instrumental uses that members of local communities have for one another. With the recent panic over "safety in the streets," it is becoming apparent that co-residents depend very much upon one another for some sort of informal surveillance. Some level of community loyalty may be a prerequisite even for the person who has no personal contacts with his neighbors but must assume some minimum of mutual trust.

In this sense, sentiment may play only a small role in the development and character of modern local communities, and we should be especially attuned to the possibility that some communities are essentially secondary associations with instrumental goals. This applies particularly when we think of local communities as co-consumers of public services and as collectivities which must maintain some minimal level of safety and security.

The rural village and small town are the model for the local community, and they persist in urban areas only in a weakened form of the original. There are two counts on which this generalization is misleading and overly simple. While it is certainly true that some small towns and rural areas have developed into compact and solid communities, not all of them do so. As work in the South reveals, many small towns are sharply fragmented, with elitism rather than democratic consensus being their outstanding feature (Pope, 1942; Caudill, 1963; Moreland, 1965; Rubin, 1951). Research from some areas of the great plains tends to show no distinct "community" boundaries among farmers but only an unbroken network of personal relations which continue until intercepted by some physical obstruction.

But the above statement is also misleading because it suggests that the local urban community is a sort of heritage from rural and small town areas. The mass of descriptive and analytical material we possess on local communities in America, however, derives from thoroughly urban areas. Almost all of the early work of Park, Burgess, Zorbaugh, and their followers is based upon urban examples. Indeed, the word "neighborhood" itself seems to be restricted almost entirely to urban authors. Studies of local communities in London show that some of them have persisted over great lengths of time (Young and Wilmot, 1957). Also, studies of new areas undergoing urbanization show that these areas develop local subcommunities (Little, 1965; Plotnicov, 1967). These findings, along with others, would seem to suggest that the local urban subcommunity which does not coincide with a legal unit such as a town or county may have entirely urban roots—it may not be similar to the rural community to which it is so often compared. These urban subcommunities may be as cosmopolitan as Greenwich Village or as provincial as the Addams Area on the West Side of Chicago. In retrospect, however, it is hard to visualize either of these subcommunities as having originated in a rural or small town setting. Indeed, the development of subcommunities such as the neighborhood may depend upon population growth and heterogeneity to the point at which residents find it impossible to conceive of themselves as residing within a single territorial unit. In this respect, the city is more likely to produce subcommunities than is the countryside, and those subcommunities which develop in urban areas are to be accounted for by processes distinctly urban.[2] The processes of population differentiation and segregation are especially prominent here. But one must also include the possibility that co-residents can become interest groups and that the differentiation of subcommunities is a means of expanding the opportunities for diverse experience. Were the population of New York City randomly distributed, it would certainly materially reduce the opportunities one has to enjoy the city's ethnic and cultural centers.

The urban subcommunity is a detached and singular residential group which competes with supracommunity organizations for its members' loyalty. Ever since Park's phrase about "little worlds which touch but do not interpenetrate," we have thought of the city as a mosaic of provincial village-like units which stay to themselves and closely control their members. This view applied best to the ethnic colonies which developed around the "Loop" in Chicago and in several other large cities. Other areas, however, were never so provincial or detached from the wider community. Even the ethnic colonies were not so encapsulated as has been suggested. In Chicago only about half of the Italian migrants settled in Italian colonies; the other half were quite dispersed (Nelli, 1970). For this dispersed population, the Italian colonies functioned as cultural centers where they could visit, buy ethnic goods, and maintain certain cultural establishments. No doubt there are many areas of the metropolis which continue to function as places of first settlement for migrants and immigrants. Many of these are cultural centers which serve a much wider population, as in the case of Chicago's Chinatown.

Participation or residence in these communities is often voluntary and is to be distinguished from many of the black ghettos which are genuine places of confinement. Some of these black ghettos are cultural centers for blacks who do not live there (e.g., Harlem), but for their residents they are also very much places of confinement. This coercive aspect of the local community, however, seems to derive less from the nature of local communities than from the widespread racial prejudice present in the wider society.

In any case the "mosaic of little worlds which touch but do not interpenetrate" does not seem to adequately capture the way most urbanites conceive of their residential communities. Recent research seems to indicate that the smaller and more localized areas are conceived of as belonging to larger areas and, in some instances, different localities are seen as having a symbiotic or cooperative relationship (Hunter, 1972). Also, the subcommunity may be only one of the areas of voluntary participation that a person selects (Janowitz, 1952: 195-213). Community participation is not necessarily coerced, nor does it necessarily make a person less cosmopolitan. Indeed, there is some reason to think that a part of the reason for the growth and militancy of some community groups is the feeling of their members that they are unable to influence the nonterritorial professional and interest group associations in any other way. These associations were at one time seen as a source of relief from coercive and provincial community groups.

The principal virtues of the local subcommunity are its contributions to personality and social solidarity. This contradicts any attempt to conceive of it as a service area. This generalization is explicit in both Issacs' (1948a, 1948b) and Dewey's (1950) critiques of Clarence Perry's concept of the neighborhood unit as a plan for community design. It is possible, however, to agree with these authors' criticisms of Perry's followers without accepting the generalization. Much of the debate hinges on how one considers the relationship of personality development to the wider society. Clearly, the rural village or small town is not a good model for training people to live easily in a metropolitan community. On the other hand, a tier of progressively inclusive areas which continually widen the experience and opportunities of individuals may be quite appropriate to preparing people for urban life. This system also preserves some continuity for people, as they move from community to community or through the life cycle. Since many of these experiences and opportunities are provided by service agencies, the idea of community as a service area may not be contrary to the designation of a community for other purposes.

The Urban Subcommunity

It is not necessary to turn each of these misconceptions on its head to produce a more viable body of initial assumptions. Our starting point, however, ought to be made explicit. Members of local communities may develop bonds of shared sentiments, but there must be some instrumental basis for community definition and organization. Currently, instrumental activity is most likely to include the shared consumption of public and private goods and services, the provision of safety and security, and the development of an environment which increases the opportunities for social participation.

These are not the surviving functions of a rural or village form of life, but are genuine necessities brought more sharply into relief by urban living conditions. The urban resident belongs to public and private service areas which comprehensively encompass him and his neighbors as a homogeneous "unit." By contrast, the typical rural or small town resident might negotiate face to face with a variety of local suppliers, entrepreneurs or governmental representatives. While there is a wider variety of products and services distributed by large-scale public and private organizations in metropolitan areas than in rural or small town areas, the products and services are less responsive to the demands of any single individual.

More importantly, the urban resident finds himself more dependent on the public definition of his residential area and its reputation for decency, safety, and prestige. Rural and small town residents often know one another personally. Just exactly where they live may not concern them much since "everyone" knows that they are honorable, respectable, or law abiding citizens. It is in the anonymity of the urban environment that it is more important for people to be able to make assumptions about each other's reputability, trustworthiness and lack of predatory intent on the basis of territorial residence (LaFland, in press). Presumptions of this sort are most essential to "cosmopolitans," who know least about the personal character of their co-residents. Paradoxically, it is probably they who find it most essential to use territorial stereotypes as a basis for avoidance or association.

Finally, the urban dweller views the mosaic of areas in the metropolis not just as a series of barriers to movement and association, but as a differentiated set of cultural, social, and recreational areas in which he may partake. New York and Boston, for instance, are cities which provide a relatively rich range of experiences precisely because they are so spatially differentiated as compared, say, to Los Angeles or Detroit. Here again it is often the most urbane and cosmopolitan resident who makes the widest use of this *opportunity* provided by the city.

Taken from this perspective, the local community is a service area, a basis for defining the mutual prospects of trustworthiness, and one of the many units which help make for a varied and more cosmopolitan life. This is an entirely urban notion of the local community and one to which we will regularly return in attempting to develop principles of community design.

A HISTORICAL OVERVIEW OF
COMMUNITY DEVELOPMENT IN THE U.S.

No doubt there has been a dearth of planning in U.S. cities, but it is easy to overemphasize the mindless play of market forces. Throughout the colonial period, most of the towns and cities along the eastern seaboard were carefully planned and centrally directed (Glaab and Brown, 1967: 124). The narrow, winding streets of the older parts of Boston were intentionally and carefully laid out by the city fathers to conform to the contours of the landscape. Savannah, Norfolk, and Philadelphia were also planned towns, where proprietors and local enthusiasts made room for the development of great centers of commerce, culture, and industry. The models for these early towns were drawn from Europe and, like their predecessors, they tended to emphasize a single central and accessible location for most public and commercial activities. Little provision was made for the separate development of distinct subcommunities; the legal and social communities were thought to be one. Subcommunities did develop, however, as people settled within walking distance from their place of work or business, and as the price of land or lot size sorted out different groups.

Nonetheless, it was only after the Revolution that the play of market forces attained legitimacy and the role of planning was regarded as unnecessary governmental intervention. One should not overemphasize the decline in planning, however, because the main result was to shift the role of planning from public to private agents. The development of the trans-Appalachian region towns shortly after 1800 fell into the hands of private boosters and land speculators who operated with a rather common and definite model of what was to be done (Glaab and Brown, 1967). The theories of Von Humbolt being widely accepted, towns were generally located as close as possible to water or other lines of transportation.[3] Since the foundation and platting of these towns preceded settlement of them or the countryside around them, the grid pattern was almost universally employed. This pattern produced lots of uniform frontage which could be sold at uniform prices to a buyer, sight unseen.[4] As in the previous period, public and commercial facilities were centrally located on some main transportation line. Parks and open spaces were limited because they did not provide direct revenue to the developer. The grid pattern favored by most developers did not make any provision for the development of distinct subcommunities. The prevailing assumption seems to have been that people would orient themselves to a single center of community life. Of course, subcommunities did develop as people sorted themselves out, in order to be close to their work or according to their ability to purchase more or less expensive lots. While these subcommunities were unanticipated, no one seems to have marveled at their appearance.

As these new towns became settled, they often grew by a process of marginal accretion in which the urban booster, developer, and land speculator played a large part. The platting of fairly large units of land at the margin of the town and the sale of lots for individual development was a common pattern (Wade, 1959).

While no provision was usually made for community institutions, occasionally land was reserved for sale to a church or a school. Subcommunities developed unintentionally, with little provision for their corporate life. The general public took little notice of them.

This early pattern of subcommunity development seems to have been guided by two basic considerations: transportation and income. The early towns depended on transportation by foot, draft animals, and water craft. Residence and place of work could not be separated very far, and residential communities often looked like communities of co-workers. These transportation constraints tended to generate a kind of primitive residential democracy in which maids, businessmen, fine ladies, mechanics, slaves, and day laborers clustered within walking or buggy distance of the same place of occupation. There was at the same time, however, a powerful undertow which tended toward residential segregation.[5]

Even by 1820 the income differences in urban America were substantial and the advantages of residential segregation considerable. High land (which facilitated avoidance of the malarial swamps) was progressively a privilege of the well-to-do, who could afford the more costly home lots and had more time to go to work. The pleasure of living in a prestigious area, away from the noisome clamor of the central city, and the safety of areas away from the main line of transit were benefits realized early, and they were soon available to those who could pay for them. Already the rapid rate of growth of most of the eastern seaboard cities had made residence at the periphery a costly relief from deterioration and conversion. Almost from the start, then, there was a good deal of segregation in the larger cities of the country. It probably grew as the cities became larger—host to an unruly and frightening number of transients, "foreigners," and lower-status individuals.[6]

This tendency toward residential segregation and subcommunity formation was impelled forward most sharply by the development of systems of mass transportation, first horsedrawn and then steam driven. The streetcar system not only made possible a massive reassortment of the residents of the city; it also led to the prolific development of subcommunities whose most distinctive characteristic was their socioeconomic homogeneity. Once again, this pattern of peripheral growth was guided by private land developers who platted out tracts to be sold in lots. Community or public facilities were lacking, except in instances where a church or school might be expected to buy property. Subcommunities were being developed then, but they lacked much provision for a corporate life.

This tendency toward homogeneous residential subcommunities was catapulted along by massive immigration of Europeans into the country, and created an additional dimension to stratification which warranted a greater concern for personal safety, prestige, and living around people similar to oneself. Gentlemen's agreements, restrictive covenants, and the planned location of tenement housing reached out to create especially homogeneous subcommunities. The immigrant colony was in some ways the counterpart to the exclusive Gold Coast or suburb.

The interpersonal fear and conflict between these groups was so great that only the defended, segregated neighborhood seemed to keep them at arm's length.

The internal migration from rural to urban areas in the country had somewhat the same consequences, especially when southern hillbillies and southern blacks were the invaders. Both groups seem to have spread fear in the hearts of native urbanites, driving them further into protected and defended residential enclaves.

The deconcentration of industry, the widespread usage of the automobile, and extensive highway development extended and intensified these trends after the First World War. The automobile made it possible for people to locate in a wider range of residential areas. Electrical power and truck transport made it feasible for industries to disperse widely beyond their sources of power supply. At each stage of mobility, it became progressively more possible for Americans to locate their residence and business on the basis of noneconomic considerations. The general drift seems to have been to give additional weight to prestige, safety, and the public service potentials of residential choice.

Throughout this development, the general course was toward the segregation of ethnic, socioeconomic, and racial groups into different subcommunities. In those parts of the city already constructed, the pattern was one of expanding growth, a rapid change of usage, and successive waves of invasion in which residential groups were often crowded out by persons of somewhat lower status. At the periphery of the city, new housing was developed in blocks of single family dwelling units which were occupied by relatively high status people. While these people felt they belonged to a distinct residential unit, they often shared little provision for a corporate life.

This broad pattern of segregation and subcommunity formation continued after World War II. Most new housing construction occurred at the periphery of cities in the form of developments for middle and high income families. Low income residents were concentrated in the inner core of the city, where the processes of conversion and deterioration continued to press upon them. During the two decades following World War II, over seventeen million people left farms and small towns for metropolitan areas. The interstate highways promoted greater mobility and the further deconcentration of industry allowed cities to sprawl extensively beyond their original corporate limits. While there was great homogeneity in residential areas, there was also a great amount of mobility. Places of work, residence, and friendships became progressively disassociated.

The net result seems to have been perplexing to sociologists, and by 1960 two somewhat contradictory views began to develop. One view regarded the local residential subcommunity as a passing entity which might be maintained only so long as temporary patterns of racial and socioeconomic segregation persisted. Ultimately the local community would decline as people found more preferable, nonterritorial bases for association (Dewey, 1950; Nisbet, 1967; Webber, 1963). Territorial groups, it was thought, were coercive in character and far less attractive than voluntary forms of association. The latter would shortly replace local community ties and these "interest communities" would get a more sympathetic response from government and big business. The local community would decline as racial and socioeconomic segregation declined; interest communities would replace residential communities. Even the fragmented governmental structure of the sprawling metropolitan area was not a matter of great concern because it was assumed that the essential negotiations went on between interest communities and supracommunity bureaucracies.[7] The local community and even the corporate city government were simply considered irrelevant to the basic transactions between the individual and the wider society.

The alternative viewpoint was not nearly so well developed into a coherent position, but consisted mainly of a series of reservations, afterthoughts, and critical assessments. For some, the primary problem was the failure of the corporate city government to keep pace with the growth of metropolitan areas through the process of annexation (Hawley and Zimmer, 1961, 1970). In this view, the city is a single economic entity requiring a single political form to govern its inflow of taxes and outflow of services. Others noted that residential segregation in the United States did not seem to be declining but instead was increasing, especially between racial and socioeconomic groups. Ethnic groups might not be so territorially confined as previously, but the centers founded by these groups often seemed to be viable and to have broad social support for their continuity (Gans, 1962). The view that interest communities would be more democratic than territorial communities was doubted by some because interest communities seemed equally restrictive on membership, and even more coercive about how members were to express their interests, (Janowitz, 1961; Greer, 1962: 168-192). There were others who doubted the efficacy of interest organizations altogether and entered a plea for the sort of face-to-face relationships which could reestablish personal responsibility in the interaction between citizen and public servant (Alinsky, 1946).

Looking over both the development of local communities in the United States and what various interpreters have said about it, it seems that much of the controversy is traceable to a series of false dichotomies, an overly optimistic appraisal of the local community, and a tendency to see the local community as an isolated enclave rather than a building block in a variegated and changing society. First, the local community in the United States was never a coercive and entirely ascriptive institution, but one of a series of groups to which people might belong. Reducing its importance and position in people's lives meant only a reduction in the number of groups to which people could belong (and thus a change in the market position and bargaining power of the remaining groups). The predilection of some for voluntary groups was a sort of social-scientific argument for oligopoly: the dominance of voluntary groups excluded communal ones.

Second, there always seems to have been great variability in Americans' attachment to their local communities. It may have been this variability which led some to predict a "decline of community" from some mythical past when people were thought to be wholly absorbed in their local communities. American communities vary from the very provincial ethnic colony to such cosmopolitan centers as Haight-Ashbury. In turn, individual Americans vary from those whose lives are heavily centered in a very localized area to those who have a foot in a much more extended area to those who totally absent themselves from communal activities. This sort of individual variation may occur over the life cycle of a single individual. The nature of an American's attachment to his local community is also quite variable. Sometimes an individual may not participate in community life at all, yet want the community to "be there" as something to fall back on if needed.

Third, many of those looking at the local community seem to have thought of it primarily as a means of meeting the need for close, intimate association. Undoubtedly some American communities do provide this type of social contact, and a large proportion of the American population probably want to have such communities available even when they do not wish to live in them at any given time. But a more enduring function of the local community has been to serve as a basis of unity that is intermediate between the family and supracommunity institutions. Like the voluntary association, the local community is a basis for social mobilization and a counterbalance against vast, bureaucratic, supracommunity organizations. Since the need to counterbalance these supracommunity organizations is often episodic, participation in or attachment to the local community is often episodic as well. Also such participation may be entirely instrumental and lacking in the intimacy which is associated with our image of the local community. This does not make the local community less important, but it gives it a purpose that is apt to grow as supracommunity organizations and "interest communities" increase in scale and become more impersonal and more bureaucratic.

THE TRADITION OF PHYSICAL DESIGN

Most attempts to plan or design U.S. cities and communities have had as their objective some sort of physical arrangement. Behind this approach lay an implicit assumption of physical determinism which reasoned that if we could only create the right kind of physical plant, citizens and organizations would go about their business without friction or disappointment. No doubt some elements of physical structure, such as transportation, do have an overpowering effect on subsequent locational decisions. But, following Gans (1968b), one can probably say that the long-term attempt to create communities by physical planning has had these results: the plans were always far more grandiose than anything actually implemented; even when the plans became accepted in principle they were not followed in practice; the hoped for effects of physical design were seldom realized; no single plan seems to have gained widespread enough support to insure its spread and adoption elsewhere; and none of the plans seemed flexible enough to match the variability of the U.S. population and their communities (Banfield, 1967; Fagin, 1967).

One of the most ambitious of these plans and the one which may have come closest to complete implementation was the construction of Pullman in 1881 on Lake Calumet, south of Chicago. Essentially a company town for employees of the Pullman company, it nonetheless housed over 12,000 people, was carefully arranged to include a full complement of public facilities (shopping center, hotel, post office, library, theatre, etc.), and met high standards for sanitation and housing. Despite much admiration for the community's appearance and facilities, there were difficulties from the start. Many of the residents felt that the fact that their employer was also their landlord allowed him to invade and regulate their private lives (see Budes, 1967, for a general review). A series of strikes against the Pullman Company aroused accusations that the company was manipulating its rental policy to undermine the strikers. Regulation by a "Town Agent" appointed by the Pullman Company and the lack of citizen participation were said to lead to an absence of civic pride. In 1898 Pullman simply became another part of Chicago, and a decade later the homes ceased to belong to the company.

The failure of Pullman seems to have discouraged any further experimentation with industrial towns under different conditions of ownership and local government. Despite the much admired physical design of the community, it did not produce the sense of community originally expected, and no similar efforts were undertaken by other industrialists or developers. Ironically, the period architecture of the community has subsequently attracted a number of middle class admirers to settle in Pullman. They have been able to get the community declared a national monument to preserve it from recent threats of conversion to industrial usage.

Another early design for planned communities was Ebenezer Howard's Garden City, which was widely discussed and praised in the U.S. after the turn of the century. Suburban developers began dubbing their developments "garden villages," "garden suburbs," and so on. In 1911, the Russell Sage Foundation financed Forest Hills Gardens on Long Island, and the planner, Frederick Law Olmsted, Jr., attempted to incorporate some of Howard's ideas. The community lacked its own industry and other service units and became essentially a suburb for well-to-do commuters. Shaker Heights, built by the Van Sweringens brothers, turned out to be essentially the same thing—an upper-middle-class suburb left in a relatively natural setting with curved streets rather than a grid pattern. The idea of the garden city seems to have languished, then, (except for the labeling habits of realtors) until Rexford Tugwell, the head of the Resettlement Administration during the New Deal, attempted to develop Greenbelt Towns. These were to be relatively self-sufficient communities with varying functions, and a means of resettling people currently living in slums. Tugwell hoped to build 3,000 Greenbelt Towns; the Resettlement Administration selected 25 sites; Roosevelt approved 8; Congress reduced the number to 2. In the end, the 2 Greenbelt Towns completed housed 2,267 families. Neither of them came close to being a self-sufficient community with its own industry and a mixed-income population.

The City Beautiful Movement was another physical planning effort. Initially a grandiose body of ideas for making the city a healthy and attractive place to live, it ended by embellishing the downtown areas of many cities with parks and by developing a series of zoning principles which increased the segregation of income, ethnic, and racial groups (Lubove, 1967: 59-62). The City Beautiful Movement was based on the argument that if the city could be reconstructed so that it was attractive, clean, and uncrowded, then the behavior of slum dwellers would dramatically improve. In principle, the City Beautiful Movement meant to concentrate its efforts on slums or the more deteriorated sections of cities. Since it lacked any powers of its own, however, only portions of the movement's ideas were adopted. The ideas adopted tended to be those which fulfilled the desires of business interests to attract tourists and customers to downtown areas. These included the construction of nearby parks, tree-lined boulevards and other patches of natural scenery.

In general, other attempts at planning have started with the same emphasis on a holistic design for the entire city. The usual result has been that narrowly defined interest groups selectively applied elements of the design to continue the very patterns the designs were supposed to arrest or reverse. Proponents of the garden cities or the City Beautiful had little power to enforce their full vision of the city. Realtors turned the garden cities into middle class suburbs. Businessmen turned the City Beautiful Movement into a publicly financed program for maintaining the commercial importance of the central business district.

Somewhat the same consequences can be traced for planning commissions and zoning regulations. Both were originally meant to reduce the uncertainty of land usages, raise standards of sanitation and construction, and avoid conflicting uses of an area. Planning commissions flourished in U.S. cities between 1920 and 1930, when over 700 were formed. The planning commissions remained advisory, however, and various interest groups could easily select those proposals which suited their purposes. This was especially the case where an established group of commercial land users found the commission a way of "planning out" competing industries and businesses (Glaab and Brown, 1967: 291-298).

Zoning regulations became popular in the United States in the 1920s, and by 1930 there were 981 zoned cities and towns in the country. Although the intent of those who favored zoning was to make American cities more attractive and less congested, the result was often the reverse. Early zoning practices were openly used for segregating blacks, and, despite restrictions on building size and heights, traffic congestion continued to mount in U.S. cities. Zoning also proved to be a tool in the hands of some suburban land developers who were anxious to exclude low income and minority groups. Zoning has doubtless had some effect in limiting the potential harm from congestion and the reduction of light and air in some parts of some cities. However, the overriding conclusion of most students of land use is that zoning regulations tend to be extremely pliable and rather ineffective as a way of avoiding the deterioration and blight which come at the interface of land conversion (Hoover, 1969).

The master, comprehensive, or general plans that a number of cities developed after the 1920s went a considerable way beyond zoning regulations and planning commissions. The master plan was an attempt to project the demographic and economic possibilities for a particular community, establish goals for the community, and then schedule and locate the public and private facilities needed. Essentially a blueprint for long-term development, the master plan was supposed to insure that private and public facilities kept pace with growth and that locational choices were made so as to benefit the entire community. From the outset, most master plans were hampered by being confined to the corporate city, whereas most urban growth was occuring beyond the city limits. But master planners also became the captives of their larger clients. By depending upon the larger public and private agencies to estimate their own growth needs, they simply built into the master plan their maximum demands for budgeting and services (Gans, 1968a: 60-65; Banfield, 1967; Fagin, 1967). In addition, however, the master plan often simply "planned out" a number of public and private facilities which some people regarded as unattractive or morally debatable: cheap taverns, marginal housing, service stations, and night clubs. The master plan seemed to share with the City Beautiful Movement a certain Christian moralism which simply chose to ignore the needs or desires of a large segment of the population. The result was often disastrous for poor populations which found some of their vital facilities (neighborhood taverns, cheap housing, small shops, etc.) simply scheduled for destruction.

Like planning commissions and zoning regulations, master plans seldom went very far toward realizing their professed objectives (Churchill, 1945). The master planners also had relatively weak authority, and different interest groups could select from among their proposals those which suited them. The power of such interest groups as builders and large corporations is bound to be very great, since only the larger firms and public agencies are likely to be able to undertake a major project within the corporate city. Yet practically all attempts at planning in the United States have given the planners relatively little authority and made them dependent upon large scale organizations for their information (Gans, 1965a).

The record of urban renewal runs somewhat the same course. To pacify the owners and builders of private housing, they were given a large voice in the development of subsidized housing for moderate or low income people (Greer, 1965). A result was that far more housing was destroyed than constructed, and the housing which was constructed was reduced in quality so as to make it uncompetitive with private housing. These public housing projects also lacked any type of public facilities in which people might develop a social life outside their own apartments.

The generally poor record of physical planning in the United States has certainly not stopped people from dreaming, and a variety of even more grandiose schemes have been put on paper. Frank Lloyd Wright's Broadacre City represents an almost complete abandonment of present cities for a much lower density of settlement. Doxiadis has attempted to develop a comprehensive set of principles which he claims provide an equally comprehensive means of meeting people's needs through spatial and physical arrangements. Neither of these idealized cities has ever been constructed and, in some ways, it is unfortunate that the plans of other physical designers of the city have been so infrequently and incompletely executed. The general lack of implementation makes it hard to evaluate these plans. The evidence against such grandiose plans does not come from their own failures so much as from other studies which show that drastic alterations in people's physical environment does not have that dramatic an effect on their behavior. As Gans (1968a) points out, the movement of people from inner city communities to the suburbs really had rather little impact on their life-style. Providing relatively roomy, clean, and attractive living quarters did not reform the poor, nor has the construction of community centers suddenly promoted a great sense of community pride.

Perhaps the most promising direction in physical planning in the United States has been that taken by a few private builders who see themselves constructing total communities rather than only a subdivision of marketable homes. Columbia, Maryland, and Reston, Virginia, are the best known examples and seem to have been reasonably successful in meeting many of the public and private needs of their residents. Available research tends to indicate that these communities are somewhat more satisfactory to their residents than less planned communities (Lansing, Marans, Zehner, 1970; Eichler and Kaplan, 1967). Columbia, in particular, seems to be both a financial success for its developers and a popular success among its residents. This seems to have been achieved in part by its flexibility of design and by the continued willingness of its creators to negotiate the form and shape of separate subdevelopments with potential builders and residents. The result has been more heterogeneity of design than we expect from urban planners and a consequent ability to appeal to a range of tastes in styles of residential life (modern and Cape Cod, apartments, single-family dwelling units, town houses, etc.). Of equal importance may be the Columbia Association, which is financed by liens on each dwelling unit and is able to act as a sort of private government on behalf of local residents. In the United States, with its traditions of pluralism and individual choice, it may be especially important to emphasize "process" as against "product" planning and to include some form of private government alongside the existing public ones (Fagin, 1967).

None of the builders, including those of Columbia, seem to have intended to develop communities with a heightened sense of unity and widespread social participation, and there is little reason to believe that exceptional levels have occurred. Perhaps by aiming for less, these new builders are achieving more. In Sweden, where new communities have been built with an even fuller complement of non-residential facilities, it has been found that participation in local social activities is moderate—about the same as in older communities (Astrom, 1967: 49-126). Such moderate participation, however, may be what we should expect and aim toward.

Still, one wonders if urban planning in the United States has been ineffective only because it has been bad planning. Other countries seem to have made planning work better by carrying it out on a national level and by aiming for more modest goals. A large part of the difficulty in the United States seems to have been caused by the overly ambitious vision of remaking the behavior of urban dwellers by remaking the physical plants of the city. In fact, the two were never very closely related in the first place. Many of these physical designs and facilities may be desirable in their own right and ought to be pursued for that reason. But the physical plans, whether they are the direct construction of new communities or the indirect control of growth through zoning and advisory commissions, are not the basic issue. The development of communities which can serve their residents, give their residents a sense of mutual respect, and provide a range of social experiences requires an ordering of social life which goes well beyond considerations of the physical plant. It bears directly on the normative, legal, and administrative arrangements of the city.

MOVEMENTS TOWARD URBAN AND SOCIAL PLANNING

A number of social reformers and planners took the physical plant of the city as a vital starting point for community design, but their efforts also reached directly into the city's normative, legal, organizational, and administrative structure. Perhaps the clearest early example was Jane Addams and the Settlement House Movement which she helped found. From her view and that of her followers, the settlement houses were not there primarily to change the physical structures of local communities. Instead, they operated as a sort of indigenous focus around which working class residents and immigrants could gather to develop a consensus among themselves, partake in a self-defined form of social life, and mobilize either to serve their local community or to negotiate with public and private bureaucracies (Addams, 1961). The settlement house workers themselves were to be people who had cast their lot among the residents they aimed to serve, and their burden was to respond to communal needs rather than impose those needs.

The Settlement House Movement

Undoubtedly the Settlement House Movement had some limited success. Especially in the immigrant colonies, it became a focus for organization, for self-help ventures, and for mobilizing the poor to make demands of supracommunity organizations. There were a number of crucial elements that seem to have made the Settlement House Movement an early success and subsequently a declining fixture which was unable to inspire other people to parallel efforts (Davis, 1970; Lubove, 1965). First, the Settlement House Movement demanded a heavy commitment from its workers, requiring them to become part of the community they served by living there and giving up some of the opportunities for occupational advancement elsewhere. Second, while the Settlement House Movement may have had its own self-righteous notions about what its clients should do, in its early stages it was quite flexible and responsive to the residents it aimed to serve. Third, while those in the Settlement House Movement aimed to join in the communities of those they served, they also maintained a continuous association with leading thinkers, social innovators, and the public media. Jane Addams' autobiography documents her full intention of becoming absorbed into the provincial life of Taylor Street on the West Side of Chicago. But in the course of her attempt to do so, a constant round of public dignitaries, revolutionists, and inquiring social scientists came to see her. Finally, the Settlement House Movement did not consist of a group of professionals looking for a safe career line, but a group of people who were willing to challenge established powers by mobilizing local communities for political purposes.

The early stages of the Settlement House Movement had a remarkable amount of influence on the thinking of outsiders, although its net social impact was rather less. The movement confirmed John Dewey in his view of the local community as the microcosm of the wider society which would teach people the rudiments of wider social responsibilities. The settlement house workers provided the intellectual justification for the Small Park Movement and the attempt of recreational supervisors to provide for the needs of local communities. The Chicago School of Sociology was deeply influenced, and Park (1955: 72) felt that:

> these communities in which our immigrants live their smaller lives may be regarded as models for our own. We are seeking to do, through the medium of our local community organizations, such things as will get action and interest for the little world of locality. We are encouraging a new parochialism, seeking to initiate a movement that will run counter to the current romanticism with its eye always on the horizon, one which will recognize limits and work within them. Our problem is to encourage men to seek God in their own villages and to seek social problems in their own neighborhood.

The Chicago community areas were defined by Burgess and have remained relatively intact as a basis for identifying the city's communities, despite great change and movement. Clifford Shaw's work on delinquency received part of its inspiration from this social movement and has persisted in a program known as the Chicago Area Project (Kobrin, 1959). Both Zorbaugh and Burgess were active in trying to get the city of Chicago to adapt its administrative districts and political wards to coincide with community areas, although they achieved almost no success.

Nonetheless, the settlement house has become almost invisible among contemporary attempts to reorder community life. The common reason given for this is the shift in population from immigrant colonies to black ghettos which were not understood by settlement workers. But a deeper and more basic reason seems to have been the loss of an esprit de corps among settlement house workers. They became career social workers or were replaced by local residents; they failed to maintain their contacts with the intellectual circles of the wider community; and they settled upon early principles of operation which could not be adapted to new groups such as blacks, Puerto Ricans, and Appalachian whites. Above all, the Settlement House Movement seemed to have lost any sense of being an innovative, unpopular group mobilizing territorial groups to contest the decisions which supracommunity groups made for them.

Clarence Perry's Neighborhood Unit Concept

Clarence Perry's work on the Neighborhood Unit developed somewhat independently of the Settlement House Movement, although he often made use of their work. Perry was interested in providing neighborhoods for all Americans rather than just recent immigrants or problem populations. His work often took on a more general character than that pressed forward during the Progressive Era, with its exclusive concern with poor and problematic urban residential groups. Perry was interested in establishing sharply bounded, physically distinct territorial units. He also wished to establish unequivocal positive values of local unity. These were concepts which proved to be operational and were widely adopted by the engineers who were the main group recruited into urban planning.

A resident of Forest Hills Gardens, Perry seems to have been most influenced by his own early observations of this version of Ebenezer Howard's Garden City. On becoming a member of the Russell Sage Foundation, he developed a conception of the local subcommunity which was in many ways separate from and more influential than the conception of community design modeled on the immigrant colony of Chicago. Perry's idea was to generate social communities in the larger cities by building a variety of social service agencies around a single territorial focus. His starting point was the local school system and the basic unit was the high school district. All other social agencies were to use the same district boundaries and locate their distributional centers so as to provide a shared focus of community activity. Traffic patterns, shopping centers, and recreational facilities were to direct people to a common spatial focus for interaction, creating among residents a sense of common purpose (Perry, 1939; Dahir, 1947; Perry and Williams, 1931). This was a plan which not only gave a rationale for its selection of community boundaries but also suggested a clear pattern for the location stations. There was a firm hope that residents would mobilize to protect their interests and look after each other as well.

The model described by Perry seems to have had a profound and widespread effect on planning commissions, zoning boards, and those who sought to bring together the traditions of physical and social planning. It was a rather complete plan which included locational decisions and organizational outcomes. Perry's critics pay him the tribute of saying that his model became an accepted doctrine for city planners; it is doubtful that any subsequent thinker on the problem of community design has had such widespread social acceptance (Dewey, 1950: 504). The neighborhood unit was at least a definable goal and a describable entity, and it did figure into engineered versions of the city in a way that alternative conceptions found difficult to countermand.

Perry's notion of the "neighborhood unit," however, was never fully embodied in any particular locale, and partial versions were often discarded or unduly praised on the basis of insufficient evidence. Perry pled his own cause by favorable case studies (Perry and Williams, 1931). Isaacs argued against his plans because they tended to crystalize and worsen existing patterns of segregation (Isaacs, 1948b). In a widely read article, Richard Dewey (1950) critically discharged the neighborhood unit concept as a confused and incompatible combination of service areas and "natural communities" in a nation where residential propinquity was no longer a cause for social solidarity or preferential association. The service area designated by a high school district was not the same as a natural community; in any case, Americans preferred alternative and nonterritorial forms of association. This was essentially Dewey's judgment of community planners in the early 1950s.

Alinsky's Industrial Areas Foundation

Perhaps the main inheritor of the Settlement House Movement was Saul Alinsky, who continued to see residential groups as potential sources of social solidarity which could counterbalance the growth of big business, big labor, and big bureaucracies. Alinsky's Industrial Areas Foundation exists as a sort of loud echo of the Settlement House Movement, and like its progenitor, it has achieved a modest success (see Alinsky, 1946, for the general plan). The Back of the Yards Council in Chicago has been generally regarded as an effective community organization, although the Woodlawn Organization in the same city has had more limited success up to this time. Ironically, such militant community organizations seem to work best where there is a powerful political machine, as in Chicago, which possesses the power to coordinate and deliver more or different public services to a local community. The Woodlawn Organization has had great difficulty in negotiating with relatively autonomous public agencies (e.g., the Board of Education) or city employee unions (e.g., the police) (The Woodlawn Organization, 1970). These relatively autonomous city bureaus—what Lowi (1968) calls the new machines—are growing phenomena while city political machines are definitely a declining one. Perhaps neither Alinsky's Industrial Areas Foundation nor the Settlement House Movement is an appropriate model any more, simply because their adversaries have changed. They now consist of numerous and independent public and private bureaucracies which do not recognize in their boundaries or their clients any single community or any rational grounds for consulting with "nonspecialists."

Mobilization for Youth

Mobilization for Youth, a Ford Foundation Program started in the early 1960s, is a program which seems to have drawn from both the Settlement House

Movement and Alinsky's Industrial Areas Foundation. The scientific rationale for the program seems to have been drawn from an article by Solomon Kobrin (1951) which summarized Clifford Shaw's experience with the Settlement House Movement, and his own offspring, the Chicago Area Project (see Cloward and Ohlin, 1960: 156-186). Basically, the article pointed to two types of lower class communities, those mature enough to mobilize and seek their own legal benefits, and those which were still so new, ill-formed, and anonymous that their residents spent most of their time fighting among themselves. In the hands of Ohlin and Cloward, this idea was transformed into a formula in which outside advocates would play the role of indigenous leaders. These advocates would arouse the more disorganized subcommunities to settle upon their natural leaders, find a consensus among themselves, and use territorial unity as a basis for negotiating with city hall. Both the Ford Foundation and the federal government bought this idea and helped establish Mobilization for Youth in the Lower East Side of Manhattan (Moynihan, 1969: 45-59).

Mobilization for Youth was one of the largest private programs ever undertaken in this country. It included a number of projects aimed at community self-help and mobilization to make increasing demands from the wider community. No categoric evaluation of Mobilization for Youth is possible, but it is certain that the organization brought a number of unaffiliated persons into various forms of community organization and that it dramatized the plight of the Lower East Side of Manhattan relative to the remaining areas of the city.[8] This strategy may have increased the public services delivered in the area, but it is unclear whether this increase in organization and services has really reduced the Lower East Side's problems: a high delinquency rate, poor health care, garbage on the streets, drug addiction, and the mutual fear of its residents (see Weissman, 1969; Brager and Purcell, 1967).

The major impact of Mobilization for Youth may have been its influence on the War on Poverty (Moynihan, 1969: 38-73). Mobilization for Youth was a "demonstration program," meant to influence subsequent private and public policies in social welfare. At the same time the federal government was being heavily influenced by advisors who pressed forward a "culture of poverty" interpretation of the nation's urban ills.[9] The culture of poverty theory stressed the continuity of values between generations among the urban poor and explained their predicament as self-inflicted. In order to break up this "pathological cycle," outside help was seen as essential to bestir local residents to reject their apathy, arouse themselves for community improvement, and engage in self-help ventures. The best known program then engaged in *some* of these efforts was Mobilization for Youth. Thus, some of the program's leaders were eager to lend their advice to ensure that the program was effective (Moynihan, 1969).

The proponents of the culture of poverty expected that intervention was necessary to break the intergenerational passage of beliefs and values which made it impossible for the urban poor to organize to help themselves. The Mobilization for Youth model included an additional provision that outside intervention should promote agitation for greater public services and community control.

The model developed by Shaw and Kobrin (and the Settlement House workers) argued that communal organization and self-help were preliminary to any major onslaught on city hall. Indeed, their approach suggested that local subcommunities which became organized could "slip" into the wider political organization without any major confrontation. Mobilization for Youth attempted to carry both things on at the same time. The culture of poverty was an altogether different interpretation of urban lower-class behavior and, while it included adequate grounds for the introduction of outsiders into slum areas, it forewarned no one that they might become agitators against city hall or other established centers of authority. Politicians were rightfully offended when they found that the federal government was funding "outside agitators" in local communities. Many blacks and lower-class residents of slum areas were offended by the culture of poverty explanation of their behavior, with its view that they had to rub shoulders with middle-class persons or college students in order to become "normal" (Rainwater and Yancey, 1967). Even many of the workers for the War on Poverty became disillusioned and cynical because of the restriction in their mandate to encourage "maximum feasible participation."

There is no broad, general, empirical account of the War on Poverty. Debate on the program is still confined to those who helped guide the program, and their writings are more like apologies than genuine evaluations. Only two ideology-free conclusions seem to have emerged: (1) the War on Poverty lacked sound intellectual guidance and (2) many of the programs initiated by the War on Poverty will be retained because they have proved popular with some constituencies.

Head Start, Vista, and Model Cities are the main programs which seem to have enough political or popular support to insure their inclusion in the federal budget for the immediate future. What most clearly distinguishes these programs from others originally included in the War on Poverty is that they have few political enemies. They also have a definite constituency which depends upon them for funds and/or occupational support.

This aftermath of the War on Poverty raises serious questions about the practice of starting a large number of social programs and assuming that the winners among them are successes in terms of their original intent. This sort of political market place approach has been regarded by some political scientists as a *description of* pluralistic decision-making and by others as a *prescription for* pluralistic decision making. This supply and demand approach to social programs assumes that the attrition of programs is based on a fully informed public. It is also assumed that small numbers of activists who take part in opposing or supporting a program do not have their judgments clouded by self-interest of ideological persuasion (see Lowi, 1969, for a critique of this approach).

Model Cities

An idea which was present during the formulation of the War on Poverty was the general notion of decentralization of political decision-making. There was the hope that a more localized level of administration would make government more sensitive to public demands. This sort of thinking was most apparent in the federal government's provision for "maximum feasible participation" of citizens in programs which affected them. But the same idea has been incorporated into a number of municipal programs by federal guidelines governing funds transferred to municipalities and states. Among federal programs, Model Cities is the main one remaining from the War on Poverty and the most ambitious in its overall aims.

The Model Cities program is just now emerging from the planning stages and it is too early to judge its success in reaching two main objectives: (1) active involvement of local citizens in the future planning of their communities; and (2) the stimulation of coordination among city, county, and state agencies. Up to this point, it is clear that Model Cities has not lived up to the ambitious expectations spelled out by its initial sponsors. Some modest accomplishment of its goals, however, considering the funds alloted to it, might still warrant its continuation. In Chicago, Gary, and a number of other larger cities, genuine efforts on the part of local citizens were often ignored by city planners, or the citizens were simply replaced by city administrations. Other cities have had greater success in including local citizens (Hallman, 1970: 191-204).

Some coordination seems to have been promoted among the vast number of agencies which serve the areas designated as Model Cities areas. The hoped for "spillover effect," the creation of additional areas in which state, local, and federal agencies would coordinate their efforts, has not occurred. Nonetheless, the modest accomplishments of the Model Cities program in its own areas are sufficient to warrant a wait-and-see attitude. Any attempt to yoke various city, state, and federal agencies into a single team which addresses the problems of a single area is bound to run into difficulties.

Municipal Programs: Little City Halls, Community Corporations, and Neighborhood Service Centers

In the last decade, the efforts of the federal government have dominated our consideration of how to manage metropolitan areas. Yet this has also been a period when municipalities have tried to be inventive and to respond to the general call for decentralization. One of the best known innovations in this area is Mayor Lindsay's effort to institute "little City Halls" in New York City. The publicity following Mayor Lindsay's announcements has not been followed by much reportage on performance. Competing politicians quickly diagnosed the "little City Halls" as a disguised attempt by the Mayor to create a new "political machine" with a vast store of patronage afforded by his appointment rights (Bornfriend, 1969; Kaufman, 1969).

Preliminary and fragmentary reports indicate that the "little City Halls" operate as a "brokerage" between the administrators of public services in New York and some citizens in search of someone responsible for recognizing their desires. As a result, those few residential areas which have a little City Hall have been able to receive some favors. This has not influenced the rules which govern the contracts of public employees or the district boundaries of the public service agencies. This may be far too much to ask of such a minor innovation. The difficulties which are lodged in the interface between city administrators and the public they serve may be so "overdetermined" that small changes may have only minuscule effects. That is, the many variables and conditions may be so numerous that each contributes very little to change. Perhaps an alteration in any one of them will not produce so noticeable a change that citizens can determine whether it has been a success or failure. If their achievement is positive but small, the little City Halls may only move from the attention of sociologists into the archives of historians. Changes of this order will not produce a fulcrum or inchpin in approaching metropolitan change.

The commentary of Mayor Lindsay's political adversaries on efforts at decentralization is, however, a telling judgment. The little City Halls have been prejudged as a little city machine because their management is largely in the hands of the mayor. Americans have a long and enduring belief in the effectiveness of community organizations which are independent of political guidance. The "grass-roots" must be independent of political controls so that nothing considered unnatural or unspontaneous is imposed. Essentially this belief derives from a radical individualism which takes as its starting point the existence of individual desires apart from a general social interest, and attributes to these desires great authenticity, naturalness, and reality. It is probably useless or futile to wean Americans away from these beliefs; it would be rather like trying to convince them that what they want to do and what they ought to do are the same. In U.S. history, this choice has been assumed to be conflictive. There is little reason to believe that Americans will ever accept an organizational structure which both shapes and responds to public opinion. The little City Halls may prove to be a broker between city administrators and residents, but they are suspect organizations which are unlikely to spread to other communities because they do not emphasize enough the voluntarism that Americans associate with community organizations.

Somewhat the same judgment seems to hold for community corporations. These joint stock companies of local residents seem to develop mostly under the guidance of charismatic leadership or in communities which have already undergone severe crises. Robert Kennedy's sponsorship of Bedford-Stuyvesant Neighborhood Development Corporation is a well-known example (Gifford, 1970; Hallman, 1970). The organization has been relatively successful, but even its strongest supporters would concede that prominent leadership is essential. Other community corporations seem to have enlisted support only when the community was in such dire straits that all else had been tried. Charismatic leadership is scarce and desperation is too late a point to begin the business of community reconstruction.

The neighborhood service center is an interesting although relatively untried option for municipal decentralization. This was billed as a sort of supermarket, where private and public services could be located in the same walking area. The resident could bank, shop, and negotiate complaints with city service agencies in one location. Actually, little has been done to implement this idea. According to available reports, some private welfare organizations have agglomerated their operations in neighborhood centers, but it is unclear whether they have located themselves at nodes where people were already congregating (O'Donnell, 1969).

Since the agencies undertaking this form of human service shopping center are highly specialized, it has been the case up until now that the center they can form is equally specialized. For all practical purposes, we do not have a "single-stop" neighborhood service center to discuss or evaluate in North America. While such centers could make some contribution to the management of cities, they would have little effect because of the complexity and scale of U.S. society. The centers are a form of social organization merging voluntary and politically guided behavior in a manner which is contrary to widespread American beliefs about man's individualism.

One cannot say much for or against these efforts because the task they are pitted against is far larger than they. The revitalization of American cities by means of little City Halls, community corporations, and neighborhood centers raise two problems: (1) how to recognize the utility of efforts which may make only small changes, given the general scope and complexity of U.S. society; and (2) how to get public support for programs which attempt to merge voluntary community effort with public administrative sponsorship. What seems to be needed is a more sweeping structural framework, within which communities can mobilize and aggregate themselves without depending so much upon administrative, political, or individual leadership.

Decision-Making Models

During the period of these attempts at community design, community organizers, social planners, and sociologists have remained active, especially in the development of "decision-making models" for community planning. Such decision-making models tend to stress the procedures for community planning rather than a particular "package" in terms of a type of community organization or physical design. The aim is to make the decision-making process one in which knowledge, expertise, costs, goals, and clients are thoroughly considered so that the outcome is satisfactory to the community and uses the best technical information available. Decision-making models, then, tend to schedule in a series of decisions and decision-makers in the hope that a favorable outcome will be reached (see Fagin, 1967; Fagin and Tarr, 1967; Biddle and Biddle, 1965).

Gans (1968: 78-83), for example, has suggested a "goal-oriented" system of urban planning which would rely heavily on clients developing their own goals, while professional specialists assist in making them aware of options, alternative costs, and other people's experience with the same undertaking. While other decision-making models have less emphasis on residential clients, all of them seem to have some sort of representation formula.

There is no doubt that these decision-making models allow for a broader consultative process and help insure that social planning will be adaptive. The representation formula may help build in a sort of "demand schedule" similar to that of market mechanisms. For such decision-making schemes to work, however, they need a prior structure of "representatives" who can speak with some authority about either the wishes of the public or the concrete impact that alternative plans will have on specific organizations and activities. For example, the "community" needs some sort of definition of its boundaries and leadership structure in order to participate in the decision-making. Also, as Gans has noted, the inclusion of municipal agency leaders in the decision-making process has the danger of "planning in" the growth of their agencies unless the planning group has its own independent source of estimates and projection for demand.

A broader problem is the scale on which this representational formula should work. Not every decision needs to be reviewed by every person or agency within the metropolitan area, but it is often impossible to restrict this review to some very localized group of residents and organizations. Many decisions (e.g., those regarding traffic lights, zoning changes, and sporting events) do have spillover effects on adjacent areas, although they need not concern the entire city or metropolitan area. In the U.S. we have very little organizational structure between the local subcommunity and the entire corporate city. This tends to delimit client participation to the residents of a single neighborhood or to expand participation to the point that some of those present are not really clients.

There are other difficulties which have been noted in the literature. Such decision-making models tend to prolong the time of planning; it is difficult to get professional planners to accept so reduced a role in planning; and the decision-making process still leaves undone the vital process of creating the options among which it is to choose (Altshuler, 1965; Webber, 1967). Nonetheless, the decision-making model seems to be a defensible approach and is certainly likely to grow. There is a widespread demand for participation in decision making, and most decisions simply cannot be made without some information from a variety of cooperative groups and organizations.

The Committee for Economic Development's Proposal for Metropolitan Government

After looking over these various proposals for community design, it is surprising that the most radical and comprehensive plan for urban change has been developed by a most conventional source, the Committee for Economic Development, a group of social scientists supported by established businessmen. In three publications (1967a, 1967b, 1970), the CED has suggested a major overhaul of municipal governments. These changes would yield a two-tier metropolitan government which allocates functions between levels according to where they can best be performed. Administrative and governmental units would follow this functional pattern. The size and boundaries of each level would be determined by functional considerations which ignore or abolish present jurisdictional boundaries.

There is much to be said for the CED plan. It is an administrative, legal, and normative solution to metropolitan problems which does not hide behind the unsupported hopes of physical designers. The movement toward a metropolitan form of government and administration is a major step toward aggregating the problems of municipalities and the resources and organizations which must address those problems. Undoubtedly there are flaws in the CED plan. It is easy to point to functions which need a metropolitan administrative structure, but it is uncertain that there are any functions which are best suited to a lower level. There is also the problem of matching electoral districts with government units.

For our purposes, however, the main problem with the CED plan is that it does not indicate how some form of voluntary assortment of locality groups can relate themselves to this proposed governmental and administrative structure. Representative government is primarily a way of developing a leadership which can sort among goals and voice common ones; administration is the means by which these common goals get implemented. Voluntary citizen groups are a way in which these priorities and procedures may be legitimized between elections. Thus, alongside governmental and administrative structures, one needs some sort of recognized structure of voluntary citizen groups to review and judge the short-term efforts of elected or appointed officials. The CED proposal seems admirable, then, but incomplete.

This appears to be a crucial omission. There is the implicit hope in the CED plan that an improvement in metropolitan services will itself be enough to reduce criticism and social unrest. This is doubtful, however; the main result of changes in metropolitan government and administration would be a reduction of inequities and probably small, uneven increases in public services. Thus, a metropolitan form of government, alone, cannot effect legitimacy in public policies, even though it may be more productive or equitable because of the advantages of scale, or because of a general improvement in the quality of public services. The difficulty is not only what people get from their government by way of public services, which are totally contractual transactions. There is also the problem of assuring that people are full citizens of this society in the sense that Shils (1960) or T. H. Marshall (1964) use the term.

The code word for dramatizing this broad demand during the last few years has been "participation." It is not enough for government to give people a good buy for their tax dollar; it is also essential that government give them a sense that they are something more than well-served "clients." A democratic "government of the people" cannot simply treat its citizens as "customers" or "stockholders." The ghetto youth who may have to sacrifice his life in armed combat for his society requires not just a "good deal" from the Social Security Administration, but also some sense that the society he lives in is worth dying for.

Such an analysis suggests that representative government, administration, and citizen participation are equally essential ingredients for ensuring domestic tranquility. Each of these sectors must maintain some independence, but they also must have ready access to one another. The CED proposal is admirable in fitting together governmental and administrative functions embracing a single metropolitan area so that the goals of the first and the performance of the second can be articulated. An additional function, however—that of citizen participation—is also needed, to assure people that they are citizens rather than just clients.

Summary

Looking over these various attempts at community organization and participation, one can count some successes. None of them, however, seems to provide a compelling blueprint for the future, at least in its present shape. The role of the Settlement House Movement and its successors, that of working mainly in lower income immigrant colonies, has declined. The newly important social welfare profession, with its dependence on public funds, is not congruent with the great personal commitment and the frequent adversarial relationship to political and administrative units required of the participative function. The community groups fashioned by the Settlement House Movement and its successors seemed to work best in the old machine-governed cities. The new machines composed of municipal agencies and their employee unions appear to be relatively insensitive to client pressures.

Federally and municipally guided attempts at decentralization and community participation have frequently run aground because they have developed an adversarial relationship between community groups and public agencies. More recently, it appears that attempts to decentralize public service administration and to include community decision makers have aroused a great deal of competition for political control among local leaders, leaving them little time for or interest in developing programs. While this may be a temporary situation, there does seem to be confusion about the role of community groups in the administration of public agencies. Should they be grievance committees, political mobilizers, watchdogs, fellow decision makers, or veto groups? So long as this confusion persists, it is likely that some groups will take the opportunity to compete for political control. The issue has not been settled in an administrative fashion.

In the meantime, some of the new "community builders" seem to have achieved a modest success in building satisfactory new communities. None, however, seems to have intended to create social units with a high degree of self-consciousness and self-determination. A greater range of public facilities has been included in these communities than in the typical suburban development. The new community builders, however, have characteristically turned over their buildings and buyers to existing forms of government and administration. One exception is the development of Columbia, Maryland, where the residents have been provided with a community foundation, a type of private government supported by liens on their property which is able to supplement services provided by the county. Aside from this rather unique attempt at process planning, there seems to be a good deal of difficulty in defining who ought to be the actors in a community development situation. Ideas of who constitutes "the community" may vary among leaders even in areas which are already built up.

Many of the problems with these various approaches seem to derive from a notion of local subcommunities as exclusive territorial units separately engaged in a zero-sum struggle with supracommunity organizations. Perry's notions of the neighborhood unit was of such a discrete form, as was the portrait of Chicago developed by Burgess. Nisbet and others have seen the decline of community as an inevitable concomitant to the growth of supracommunity organizations. Theories of mass society have persistently aroused the fear that the encroachment of mass organizations would destroy the local community and democracy as well.

Another group of writers, represented in particular by Greer and Janowitz, have suggested that this view of the local subcommunity is wrong in its initial assumptions. They feel that communities are not invariably competitors with supracommunity organizations; that membership in mass organizations is not necessarily destructive of one's ties to the local community; that the character of residents' ties to their community is variable; and that some of the commercialized or contrived forms of community life have a real social function although they contrast sharply with a nostalgic version of Gemeinschaft. Instead of a continuing accumulation of power within supracommunity organizations, Janowitz (1961: 17) and Greer identify the problem of the local community (as well as that of the wider community) as that of lacking an articulated system for making decisions at all: "The issue is not the manipulation of the [facts] to create the conditions required for making decisions." Since we might hope for a society in which elites and administrators could serve communities while serving themselves, it may be useful to look at the emerging characteristics of American communities to see if they provide some guidelines in this direction.

AMERICANS AND THEIR LOCAL COMMUNITIES

Any analysis of Americans and their local communities must take into account an enormous amount of variability. Americans vary in their agreement on neighborhood boundaries; in their loyalty to their local community; in their extent of local participation; and in what they want out of the place they live. In turn, the communities in which Americans live vary as much or more in their racial, ethnic, and socioeconomic composition; in their available life-styles; in the physical features which can be used to create images and boundaries; and in their historic claims to a distinct reputation or identity. I will examine this variability among Americans and their subcommunities with an eye to maximizing choice and opportunity in any subsequent considerations of community design.

Community Awareness

Preliminary to any discussion of the local subcommunity is a consideration of its boundaries. If a residential population cannot point to territorial limits which separate it from other territorial groupings, then the subcommunity must be said not to exist or must become a contrived social entity (as are most others in our society). The corporate community has its legal boundaries to define it, but sub-communities have no similar boundaries and sometimes trespass on those of incorporated areas. The prevailing tendency has been to regard local subcommu-nities as "natural social units" which, rather like the family, defined themselves without external help, premeditation, or specific designs. As I will try to point out, this view has its limits, although its failings are no argument against using current community boundaries where they exist.

The vast majority of Americans seem to have a name for the area they live in and there is often a good deal of agreement among them on its boundaries (see Greer, 1962: 107-137; Janowitz, 1952; Hunter, 1972). While this is the major trend, it should not obscure other tendencies. Some people feel that the people they really know, or consider neighbors, make up a much smaller spatial con-figuration: the people whose property or apartments directly abut their own; people on the block; the people who walk to a particular establishment; or those who come out for sociability on the streets during the evening. For still others, the smallest named area is too small to really reflect their sense of territorial placement (Hunter, 1972). They have additional terms and areas which denote whole segments of the metropolitan community and various foci in it. Some see themselves as members of a tier of community areas which stretch from the smallest named area to progressively larger ones including one to which they "belong." And there will be a few, for example, the merchant mariner and the "jet setter" who think of themselves as altogether rootless or as belonging only to communities which have no territorial boundaries.

Most Americans, of course, are confined to their residential and occupational locations and spend most of their lives there. A majority of them have some choice in deciding whether they will cast their lives among those who are espe-cially near—within walking distance—or use the inexpensive reach of the auto-mobile and other cheap forms of transportation. The majority pattern, then, is one which trades off the selection of social affiliations with the costs of trans-portation.

Still, there is ample room and income for movement and Americans show that these opportunities will be taken. People vary considerably in their movement and in their choice of social affiliation. To make these choices, however, they seem to rely upon a rather common cognitive mapping of alternatives which, for most, range across a common set of territorial junctures: adjacent households; the block; the named community; a sector of the city; and the entire metro-politan area. This schematic outline, however, only hints at the actual terms used and the multiple choices available. Adjacent households may mean adjoining single family dwelling units, facing apartments, or a single floor, depending upon the type of structure one lives in. The "block" may mean a face block in the city's grid pattern, or anything within eyesight of a mother looking after her children. In the inner city, a named community is apt to be an old ethnic colony subsequently settled by different ethnic groups or a new housing project named after some New Deal public servant. In suburbia a named community is apt to be a development with a name chosen to lure buyers or celebrate some relative of the builder. Some sectors of the city tend to be faceless, often being indicated by a central focus (e.g., a park or statue), or by their cardinal relation to the remainder of the city (east, west, etc.). The corporate municipality, of course, often has a rich body of imagery associated with it ("the city of broad shoulders," or "Fun City"), but its city limits seldom leave much room for argument (Strauss, 1961). The entire SMSA is a more obscure and faceless entity and, while some people may feel it their bailiwick, they have a difficult time circumscribing it. We should not forget, of course, that there are significant portions of the metropolitan area which are nameless and anonymous, as well as significant numbers of people who know nothing of the metropolitan area or its various territorial components.

Nonetheless, the boundaries of most community areas can probably be roughly approximated in the following list:

(1) Neighbors—People who live on either side of one's single-family dwelling unit, in facing apartments, on the same floor of a single apartment building.

(2) Block—Houses, apartments, or buildings that face a single street, play area, or focus of interaction over which the residents have or claim some form of social control.

(3) Minimal Named Area—The smallest named area which may or may not be included in a larger named area. The use of the name and boundaries need only deviate from chance expectations and its boundaries need only be described by an isoline indicating where popular agreement and disagreement on boundaries converge. Sometimes this is an old ethnic colony, since resettled by one or several other ethnic groups but which keeps the same name and some elements of its previous reputation. The minimal named area could, however, be a new suburban housing development, a small incorporated community within the metropolitan area; a contrived social area established by a developer's promises, protected by outlawed restrictive covenants, and kept together by artificial social centers; or a new housing development constructed and named by total outsiders.

(4) Higher Order Named Areas—Areas which include two or more minimal named or unnamed areas which in turn may be encompassed in larger named areas (e.g., Near West Side and West Side of Chicago).

(5) Residual Areas—Areas which are bounded by minimal named areas but lack a name of their own. They are likely to be included in higher order named areas.

The order of this structure and public agreement on it should not be overemphasized. There are a large number of people who know relatively little about the boundaries of these subcommunity areas, and there are vast areas of any large city which can only be called "residual areas." In large part the reason for this is that subcommunity areas in the United States seldom have any official standing. They are not recognized by city governments; they are not data gathering units for reports on social problems; nor do they have any officials assigned specifically to them. *A central problem in the development of subcommunities, then, is the absence of any authorative way in which residents can appeal to a single set of boundaries.* What is remarkable is that any structure of subcommunities exists at all, given the lack of support for them by supracommunity organizations (see Hunter and Suttles, 1972).

The development of this structure is all the more remarkable considering the lack of conformity between named community areas and agency districts (Greer, 1962). Indeed, in some communities there seems to be an attempt to avoid using existing community boundaries for agency districts, lest agencies run into fairly strong and solid citizens' groups. Nonetheless, these community areas are frequently bases for civic associations, voluntary self-help groups, and community action groups.

Style of Life

The styles of life which seem to have developed in various subcommunities are quite variable and, judging from the literature, most understandable in terms of ethnicity, race, socioeconomic status, and family life cycle. The style of life attributable to these factors primarily characterizes what I have called the minimal named community. We may think of these communities in terms of the following ideal types: ethnic center, ghetto, working class community, cosmopolitan center, Gold Coast, suburban development, and exclusive suburb.

Since these community types have developed from a long pattern of segregation, the life-styles which characterize them tend to derive from a rather homogeneous population with similar opportunities and preferences. Table 6.1 summarizes what seem to be the main findings. From these findings it should not be inferred that an overwhelming majority of the residents are heavily involved in each life-style. These are the modal trends and certainly there are people who find the minimal named community too small for their style of life and either participate in the community life of a much larger area or simply avoid local associations altogether. There are, however, probably a large number of people who find that their own preferences do not fit well with the style of life in their local community and that not much else is available. Indeed, this seems to be one of the central deficiencies in American subcommunities—without a change in residence, which may be impossible because of low income or discrimination, it is difficult to "shop" for a community in which one can share in an appropriate life-style. The mutual exclusiveness of local communities tends to confine people to limited opportunities for seeking out new life-styles and thus limits overall participation in community life. This problem must be most acute for teenagers and young couples who are not already heavily enmeshed in

(Text continues on page 270)

Table 6.1: Styles of Life and Distinctive Features of Seven Types of Local Community

Participation in Organization	Ethnic Center[a]	Black Ghetto[b]	Working Class Neighborhood[c]	Cosmopolitan Center[d]	Gold Coast[e]	Exclusive Suburb[f]	Suburban Development[g]
Voluntary	Very low	Very low	Low	Cultural associations, reformist, militant, and utopian social movements.	High rates of membership in high-status conventional associations.	High rates of membership in high-status conventional associations.	High rates of membership.
Occupational	Low rates of union membership.	Nominal union membership.	Convergence of union and political party activities.	Low rate of membership in unions.	Professional or managerial associations.		Union and professional association membership.
Ethnic or Racial	Center for organizations drawing widespread membership.	Low but increasing membership in local organizations.	Participation in ethnic associations on ceremonial occasions.	Sporadic expressions of support for ethnic life.	Little public acknowledgement of ethnicity.	Little public acknowledgement of ethnicity.	Little development of local ethnic association but occasional participation on ceremonial occasions.

Table 6.1 (Continued)

Participation in Organization	Ethnic Center[a]	Black Ghetto[b]	Working Class Neighborhood[c]	Cosmopolitan Center[d]	Gold Coast[e]	Exclusive Suburb[f]	Suburban Development[g]
Political	Precinct level politics with emphasis on patronage.	Uneven development of precinct politics with emphasis on patronage.	Convergence of union and political party activities.	Minority party membership and participation in social movements.	Connections with local politicians through specialists in clubs and civic associations.	Connections with local politicians through specialists in clubs and civic associations.	Variable: older suburbs having the greatest participation.
Church	Ethnic congregation with heaviest involvement among females.	Autonomous congregations with heaviest participation among females.	Church is social center with widespread secular participation.	Center for church reform.	Church membership limited to liturgical celebrations and charitable efforts.	Church membership limited to liturgical celebrations and charitable efforts.	Church attendance as part of family life.
Informal Associations	Street corner tavern groups.	Street corner groups.	Athletic groups: tavern groups.	Groups centered around activities: art, music, politics, drugs, sex.	Entertaining, attendance at events receiving wide publicity.	Entertaining, attendance at events receiving wide publicity.	Sports teams, school groups, dances, casual contact in back yards.

Table 6.1 (Continued)

Participation in Organization	Ethnic Center[a]	Black Ghetto[b]	Working Class Neighborhood[c]	Cosmopolitan Center[d]	Gold Coast[e]	Exclusive Suburb[f]	Suburban Development[g]
Informal Associations (continued)							
Cross Sex	Segregation	Sex segregation endorsed but not enforced.	Segregation	Equalitarianism	Managed cross sex relations.	Managed cross sex relations.	Movement toward equalitarianism.
Cross Age	Segregation	Segregation	Segregation	Segregation	Stages of progressive involvement between age groups.	Stages of progressive involvement between age groups.	Efforts to create occasions for co-participation.
Family Relations	Honorific authority of father.	Heightened respect for expressive role of women.	Honorific authority of father.	Equalitarianism.	"Team" view of husband-wife relation.	"Team" view of husband-wife relation.	Companionate family.
Relations With Wider Community:							
Services Provided	Ethnic foods, entertainment.	Entertainment for those seeking action, music.	Little provided.	Center for nightlife and offbeat cultural offerings.	Center for some cultural events: high-status clubs.	Few local events.	Little provided.

Table 6.1 (Continued)

Participation in Organization	Ethnic Center[a]	Black Ghetto[b]	Working Class Neighborhood[c]	Cosmopolitan Center[d]	Gold Coast[e]	Exclusive Suburb[f]	Suburban Development[g]
Visitors	Tourist looking for "ethnic flavor".	Action seekers.	Relatives of residents.	Tourists, action.	Sightseers.	Sightseers.	Relatives of residents.
Organized Crime	Limited but routine connections with gambling and rackets.	Customer status in widespread availability of prostitution, drugs, stolen goods.	Limited but routine connections with gambling.	Limited but routine connections for drugs, porno, ordinance violations.	Limited but routine connections for gambling, call girls, city services.	Limited but routine connections: mostly for local services.	Variable: control of some local services: e.g., sanitation.
Drug Use	Small, invisible group of regular users.	Waves of drug usage with a sizeable group of regular, private users.	Low drug usage.	Small group of regular users: waves of usage in remaining population.	Small, invisible group of regular users.	Small, invisible group of regular users.	Waves of drug usage especially among the young.

a. Suttles, 1968, and Gans, 1962.
b. Abrahams, 1970.
c. Kornblum, in press.
d. Jacobs, 1961.
e. Zorbaugh, 1929.
f. Ringer, 1967.
g. Gans, 1967.

a particular life-style and find themselves casting about for "something better" or different than what they see among their parents or peers.

Local Community Participation

While residents of subcommunities often share a rather widespread life-style, social participation in community affairs is usually more limited. The long-term trend in the U.S. seems to be toward specialization in participation and an increasing use of professionals and formal organizations. In *working-class communities, ghettos, and ethnic centers,* the broad pattern has been one where informal meeting places (the tavern or carry-out place), street corner gangs, church groups, and precinct politics tend to dominate the collective forms of communal life. Conversely, it has been difficult to recruit many people into formal associations closely related to public agencies (e.g., PTA, YMCA, etc.). In recent years, however, there seems to have been an upsurge of protest groups in low-income areas although these may be episodic in their formation and their activity.

In *middle-income, familial areas,* informal relations seem to be heavily shaped by the management of children—babysitting pools, Little League teams, splash parties, etc. Formal organizations, however, are much more extensively developed than in lower income areas. The PTA, recreational centers, community centers, civic associations, and voluntary associations find an ample constituency in these communities. Frequently these groups are linked to national or regional structures which give residents some sense of being part of a social structure larger than their local community. Political groups manage to maintain small cadres of activists which swell during elections but maintain consistent issue orientations. Despite this rather rich organizational life, participation is always limited. People maintain an interest in the school, recreational centers, or charitable activities only so long as they have children, are physically active, or are socially ambitious for acceptance. This is the community of limited liability, a community in which people invest their efforts and resources for achievable gains within the short term, expecting that they can "pull out" on short notice without losing much. Still they are communities and, indeed, this type of community is probably the "working ideal" of most social planners and the mass media.

Recently there have occurred two trends in these familial, middle-income areas which seem somewhat new. One is the increasing use of professionals to look after community affairs, especially taking responsibility for recreation, counciling, and communication. Specialists in these areas have been hired by a number of community groups, and it is likely that this type of reliance on professionals will continue if the budgets of these groups and the availability of public funds hold up. Paradoxically, this trend may mean that the number of amateur resident participants will diminish, although this should not be interpreted as a "decline of community"; the professionalization and specialization of community leaders may signal only the passage of community responsibilities to a narrowing circle chosen because it is apt to be effective and versatile in negotiations with supracommunity organizations.

A second trend, similar to one developing in working class communities, ghettos, and ethnic centers, is the emergence of militant groups which oppose themselves to established public or private administrations and corporations. In these middle income communities, the emphasis is often upon zoning regulations, environmental quality, consumer protection, and the intrusion of public facilities (highways, electrical power plants, atomic energy installations, public housing, and the like). These protest groups are relatively rare and episodic in their occurrence, but they seem to denote a broad undercurrent of dissatisfaction which is so pervasive that it infects what most people would consider the ideal type of American community.

The cosmopolitan centers which have long existed in some of our major cities seem to be sprouting up in other cities which, as they grow, are able to provide a critical mass of locally grown talent and misfits, creating their own symbiotic milieus of tolerance. Typically, these are communities composed of people who are more tolerant of one another than others are tolerant of them, including intellectuals, artists, homosexuals, radicals, eccentrics, and the footloose. University communities, Greenwich Village, Haight-Ashbury, the North Beach of San Francisco, the North Side of Chicago, and Fire Island are older and recognized examples of this type of refuge, and mutual tolerance (and tourism). In the past, such areas have organized themselves mainly around intellectual and appetitive circles. They have been the centers of intellectual cliques and private forms of recreation. More recently, however, these communities have also spawned militant and adversarial groups, mainly those which have objected to close policing and the attempts of sanitation and housing inspectors to turn their residences into examples of puritan cleanliness and safety. They also function as the starting point for unpopular social movements, such as abortion and gay liberation.

The Gold Coast and the exclusive suburb generally have a private mode of interaction and organization, which includes social clubs, private schools, country clubs, businessmen's associations, and a host of invitational groups such as the Junior League. Because of their high income and reputed power, these communities find it hard simply to withdraw into private pleasure; there is a broad although ill-defined expectation that their members will be socially active on behalf of the wider community (Baltzell, 1958). This expectation is not very strong or clearly stated, for the U.S. has little aristocratic tradition. Still, the stereotype of the "idle rich" is one to be avoided, and money and power unbalanced by social responsibility leave the members of these elite communities with some difficulty in presenting themselves as more than mercenary self-seekers. Before the development of political machines, these elites do seem to have been the major source of leadership and social welfare programs for the metropolitan community. More recently, however, local elites seem to have had a declining role in service to the central city. In some places the leadership role played by elites has dwindled down to organizing the support of established charities through, for example, debutante charity balls. Like so many other groups, the elites have metropolitanized their investments and interests but lack an organizational form within which to serve either their interests or responsibilities. In a few cities (Philadelphia, Pittsburgh, Chicago) elites have been able to help in the revitalization of the central business district, but in numerous cities they have not even been able to take this kind of step, which appears to be so clearly within their own interests.

A number of conditions help account for this: the displacement of elites by political and professional leaders; the migration of elites into national service to the neglect of their local community; and the growth of corporate holdings so that great personal wealth is no longer closely linked to local enterprises. But there is also a broader problem in the relationship between elite communities and the remaining subcommunities of the metropolitan area. Some elite communities are legally and physically separated from the metropolitan community by their incorporation as separate suburbs. But even where elite communities retain a central location, the vaguely defined character of other communities, their lack of well-recognized leadership, and the relatively low status of most community leaders have made it difficult for the elites and representatives of other communities to approach one another. The number of community groups is so considerable that members of the elite cannot hope to meet with all of them; local leadership is not pyramided so as to materially reduce the task. Some members of the elite occasionally volunteer to meet with community groups only to find themselves "mau-maued" and accused of ulterior motives. The tendency of most business leaders must be to draw back from such local confrontations by turning over their local obligations to a public relations expert and shifting their personal involvement to national circles where the pyramid leadership of supracommunity organizations include relatively polite leaders of labor, the NAACP, and so on.

While this abandonment of responsibility by elites is apparent in some central cities, it should not be concluded that elites have no reason to be interested in (i.e., no stake in) their local community or other subnational units of organization. To a large extent, elites seem to have metropolitanized their investments (their residential, business, recreational, charitable, and political undertakings) so that any single city government is inadequate as an instrument for realizing their aims or responsibilities. The tendency to reach out and rely on state or federal agencies, then, must be partially due to the absence of any regulatory mechanism which encompasses the metropolitan area. In this respect, it should not be too surprising that the CED proposal for metropolitanization is being supported by some business elites, while the major objection to metropolitanization comes from minority constituencies currently concentrated in the inner city.

There also seem to be *emerging* elites who have a genuine interest in the local community, although they lack full recognition or a clear structure within which they can negotiate with *established* elites. For example, the new elites representing blacks and other minority groups (Mexicans, Puerto Ricans, Indians, Italians, and so on) are likely to become very powerful if they replace the Irish and WASPS as managers of the central city. However, they are not well recognized as elites, and there seems to be no well-elaborated government, administrative, or organizational structure within which they can begin negotiations with established elites to normalize their disagreements and take them out of the range of public confrontation.

Alongside these emerging elites, there seem to be a number of established elites who have more to gain from a metropolitan forum than from one which forces elites to seek out the smaller systems of city government or the overly large ones of state and federal government. Among these established elites are a number who have a substantial interest in the metropolitan community and every reason for continuing this interest: the downtown merchants, the descendants of the "founding fathers," whose reputations still depend somewhat on how well they demonstrate their loyalties to local clients and admirers; the new "professional community representatives"; the administrative elites who are the caretakers of sessile universities and hospitals entrapped in the central city; the new unionists organizing city employees, especially the police and school teachers; and the real estate operators whose holdings are concentrated in a central metropolitan area.

Some of these elites, especially the downtown merchants, administrative elites, and founding fathers, have an enduring and long-term interest in the central city and its adjacent communities. The other elites (professional community organizers, new unionists, and real estate operators) seem to be close to the point where they may kill the goose with the golden egg unless they are able to incorporate themselves in a larger metropolitan system in the near future. The new city unions, for example, have before them the prospect of dealing with a pauperized employer in most central cities. If the most militant community organizers and emerging minority mayors manage to frighten out the rich, they will be left presiding over an equalitarian but impoverished mass. And the local real estate operator will become a kind of pawn whose activities are governed by national and subnational policies in the hands of other elites.

To the extent that these elites wish to maintain their long-term interests ("pay-offs" or objectives) and their own autonomy, they seem to have some stake in the metropolitan community as a unit which lies between incorporated municipalities and the higher levels of the state and nation. By retreating to the suburbs, the established elites are restricted to dealing with either suburban toy governments or federal influence. The emerging elites are left in the central city arguing for home rule and federal subsidies (and court action, agency enforcement, and so on) at the same time. Neither group of elites seems able to match its interests to a currently recognized governmental unit. The city government seems too small and the federal government too remote. Yet in many respects these established and emergent elites have in common the problems of managing urban life: safety on the streets, service delivery, social equity, and their own political survival. At present there seems very little way of getting these groups together except at the federal level, through what Lowi calls "interest group liberalism."

Continuities in the Forms of Community Participation

These different forms of community participation are quite variable but there are certain continuities which ought to be highlighted. Those who participate in any type of community are probably a minority of the residents, but only in low-income subcommunities is the character of community participation such that many formal associations are not able to sustain themselves or claim much right to represent the community (Greer, 1962). Most of the formal associations are linked to the wider society, but in general there is extremely low attendance at public hearings to review or participate in agency decisions (planning boards, school boards, police "workshops," and so on). This may be partly caused by the limited participation provided by these meetings but it is also true that there is a great deal of indefiniteness about how participation at these meetings can represent the feelings of the community. Typically, these meetings are open to the general public and the few people who come have no special responsibility to speak for anyone other than themselves. Some may be able to ask embarrassing questions, but there is no designation of responsibility which would encourage those who attend either to survey public opinion or do their homework on upcoming issues.[10] As a result there is little incentive to attend unless a particular agency decision has become a widespread issue.

These occasional and sometimes violatile reactions to issues tend to make participation in these public meetings very episodic. But episodic activism is a common characteristic of many community organizations which swell in membership and attendance during a crisis and then slack off to a small and more permanent cadre thereafter. This is understandable so long as the absence of a crisis or issue means that things are going well. However, it does leave community residents in a weak position to monitor agency decisions and to have a more constant effect on their policies. A contributing condition is the specialization of city agencies and the lack of conformity among their district boundaries. The fragmentation of local communities by numerous non-overlapping agency districts allows agencies to define their own "community" and to fragment the efforts of indigenous community groups. The "town meeting" model is simply impossible to implement because there is no way of gathering the issues and clients into a single setting. Public agencies, then, tend to become unaccountable to any one other than their own employees.

This specialization of city agencies, the fragmentation of their district boundaries, and their lack of accountability seem also to contribute to the widespread outcry for community control and militant tactics to dramatize the insensitivity of city agencies. This type of demand cuts across community types and suggests that there is a profound alienation from professional and administrative service groups. It is not one-sided, with all groups demanding somewhat the same kind of service (e.g., less police harrassment or more emphasis on reading in the school). Rather, the local control movement seems to indicate a great deal of dissatisfaction with the standardization of public services so that they cannot be tailored at all to the preferences of local communities. Undoubtedly there are limits—even constitutional limits—to how public services can differentiate to suit a particular clientele. But still there are a host of decisions in which services could be modified to suit local communities without violating anyone's civil rights or thwarting good professional judgement. The placement of school crossing guards, the regulation of advertising signs, the mix of recreational programs, and many other issues of this kind can depend heavily upon community preferences. The decisions are often rather minor ones, but the unwillingness of some public agencies to consult communities on these minor issues seems to dramatize their inflexibility and their overgrown claims to authority.

This is not to say that Americans are very eager to engage in collective decision making on an extremely wide range of public services. Probably the preferred form of "influence" on public services is a highly individuated approach where a single person can air his grievances and suggestions with some assurance that they will be heard out. Perhaps this is one reason some community groups have expressed a desire for small-scale establishments for the delivery of services, although it may involve some lowering of the "quality" of services. Such small centers provide the opportunity for personalized interchanges and one form of feedback from the clients.

Barriers to Community Participation

The main problem of metropolitan subcommunities does not seem to be a lack of participation or a scarcity of elites, but the lack of any articulate structure through which participants can be effective. Those who have spent some time "working for the community" are apt to know that it is a hard and relatively unrewarding task for a number of reasons: there is no authorative definition of community areas; the specialization of agencies and the fragmentation of their boundaries forces community groups to deal with a large number of administrative units; small subcommunities have no regularized relationship to the larger community areas which frequently enclose them; the standardization of public services and the appeal of professionals to "objective" decision rules makes them inflexible in the face of community desires; the scale of public agency delivery points reduces the likelihood of individuated treatment and client feedback; public meetings on agency policies do not allow for any designation of responsibility among residents, leaving each resident to speak for himself only; and the necessity to use militant tactics to gain even the attention of agency administrations is distasteful to most residents and seldom increases the service orientation of public administrators.

With all of these obstacles it is surprising that community organization has survived at all in most American cities. Yet except for very low income communities, most subcommunities manage to maintain a small cadre of active participants in community organizations. Even low-income subcommunities have recently developed militant and formal community organizations, although much of this may be due to temporary external aid. None of these groups, including those manned by more affluent persons, seems to have achieved remarkable or persistent success. Community organizations seem most successful at self-help ventures and in the support of existing institutions. Some community groups have achieved moderate success by teaming up with large private institutions when their interests happen to coincide, and these groups are probably more successful in influencing elected representatives than public agency administrators. It is with the agency administrations that the community groups have been least successful, but it is also the agencies which most seriously influence the quality of life in subcommunities.

Despite the limited success of community groups, the problems they have helped dramatize are not likely to go away even if community groups themselves do decline and become less vocal. Instead, the further decline of subcommunity groups (if, in fact, there has been a long-term decline) may leave only a vacuum which allows discontent to grow without any articulate leadership to propose changes. I doubt that mass society theorists are correct in prognosticating a rootless and easily swayed electorate, subject to extremism if the local community is defeated. On the other hand, I also doubt that we have come to the millenium where each individual is so closely and prominently tied into "interest communities" that he can always effectively channel his grievances.

PROPOSALS FOR COMMUNITY DESIGN

In approaching community design, it is probably best to think in terms of "minimal" and "maximal" subcommunities with some intervening levels. In part this is because such tiers represent the preference structure of residents— some of them confine their attention and loyalty to very small areas while others seek a much enlarged area for participation. There are other reasons as well: small areas tend to be very homogeneous, perpetuating segregation, and most small neighborhoods have an insufficient population base around which to organize many activities. This tier of subcommunities would preserve the small scale units within which the most solidarity seems to exist. At the same time, there would be an expanded opportunity structure for wider participation, negotiation, association, and cooperation.

One way of reaching this goal is to use the minimal named subcommunity as a modular unit in a much larger subcummunity that emphasizes the very heterogeneity which is usually absent in the minimal named area. The general principle, then, would be to combine contiguous minimal named areas so as to achieve a balanced population, or one which is roughly representative of the racial, ethnic, and socioeconomic composition of the corporate city (or where possible, the metropolitan area). The maximal subcommunity should have a large enough population base to support several public service agencies (schools, welfare offices, auto registration, etc.), since a multiplicity of agencies would provide choice and differentiation of services for clients.

The maximal subcommunity should also have a large enough population base to produce prominent leadership—i.e., leadership with a sizable constituency and sufficient prestige to open the doors of mayors and administrative leaders. The maximal subcommunity, then, should include one elite community. If it does not contain the business elite, then the next best thing would be the elite settled around a university. Indeed, a useful decision rule may be to create as many maximal communities as there are elite communities.

This plan would require very large maximal subcommunities since the number of elite communities is always small, especially where the corporate city is surrounded by a growing expanse of suburban sprawl containing the departed elites. For this reason it may be useful to think of an intermediate subcommunity which balances the costs of transportation, the goal of heterogeneity, and the opportunity for small-scale, face-to-face meetings among community leaders. The costs of transportation suggest a contiguous aggregation of modular, minimal, named communities. The goal of heterogeneity suggests that these modular areas be as different as possible on the criteria of race, socioeconomic status, and ethnicity. Since the representatives of these intermediate subcommunities should be able to caucus in face-to-face interaction, the number of modular units should not be great—perhaps no more than five or so. Five may be enough to achieve heterogeneity without having to resort to parliamentary procedure. Essentially the number of such units reflects the number of lifestyles present: ghetto, ethnic center, working class community, cosmopolitan community, elite community, and middle class dormitory. Since these communities occur in unequal ratios, the best plan might be one which considers the number of modular types and aims for the maximum of heterogeneity while preserving territorial contiguity.

This procedure would produce a three-layered form of social order among most large SMSAs. The first would be a series of minimal named homogeneous communities which can appeal to historic claims of loyalty and solidarity as their basis for consideration by the wider society. The second level, with a heterogeneous membership broadly representative of communities, could claim that its decisions have matured in face-to-face encounter. The third level would be a broad sector of the city including a substantial portion of the city's population and some of its most prominent citizens. This tier would move toward a representational structure resting ultimately on social solidarity, with the opportunity to negotiate among different populations which would be pyramiding their preferences upward to where they might be heard with an accommodating ear.

The Definition of Community Levels

For these tiers of residential communities to take shape, a number of decision rules need to be made about how boundaries are to be designated and brought into conformity with other types of territorial boundaries now existing in the city. Since the modular units are used to compose the larger ones, their boundary definition is preliminary to any other. As suggested, the *smallest named residential unit* is a reasonable selection for this purpose since it already indicates some level of social solidarity. There are existing interview techniques for determining such boundaries and their refinement is fairly easy to manage (Hunter, 1972). The most significant problem is that of areas which have no name and in which there is no agreement on boundaries. These areas would have to be designated as distinct subcommunity areas by outsiders who need some rules to go by. A plausible rule would be to attempt to find the "walking community," with a focus on a number of public facilities: parks, schools, shopping facilities. While these "walking communities" will probably shade into one another, they will probably disclose gradients around centers of public facilities, which will show reasonable cutting lines. These contrived subcommunities can then be treated in the same way as minimal defined communities.

The construction of the next two tiers of more inclusive subcommunities is more troublesome and must be approached in a more flexible manner. The second tier should be a combination of contiguous minimal communities which maximizes heterogeneity. This heterogeneity can be achieved by numerous options, although an overall balance in the "maximal" community will determine the rough proportions. But since the minimal communities which are adjacent to one another are often similar, the combinatorial possibilities may be limited and some priorities should be established. One procedure would be to place priority on racial heterogeneity (rather than ethnicity or SES) because face-to-face negotiations seem most needed among racial groups in the United States, and because there already exists more ethnic and socioeconomic heterogeneity than racial heterogeneity within minimal named areas. Priorities might next be placed on socioeconomic heterogeneity and then ethnic homogeneity.[11]

This set of priorities would probably determine most combinations of subcommunities for the second tier. A flip of a coin might determine the remaining cases. The number of minimal named communities combined in this fashion should not be so numerous that community leaders representing them cannot easily gather in face-to-face negotiations, nor so few that it rules out the possibility of much heterogeneity. An upper limit of five minimal named areas is probably reasonable (between five and twenty leaders of community organizations). But obviously this is a decision which needs to be informed by research findings.

The maximal subcommunity does not depend upon the number of second-tier communities composing it, but on the number of elite communities lying within the city or metropolitan boundaries. It is not difficult to identify elite communities made up of wealthy businessmen and administrators; the problem is their scarcity, especially within the city limits. Many cities have only one "Gold Coast" and perhaps another university community. With such a shortage of elite communities, it may be necessary to make some compromises. The object in the maximal community is to create a leadership which has access to top political and administrative leadership in the city and also has a large constituency. In practical terms this means that the constituency must be so large that its leaders can threaten to go to state and federal leaders and receive a hearing. This argues for quite large maximal communities. Within any city, however, such maximal communities should not be so small in number that the leadership of only two of them can go into an easy coalition to overpower the remainder— i.e., there need to be more than three. Five is a nice minimun since it avoids the easy coalition among three and the deadlock which may occur among four maximal communities. On the other hand, it is desirable that there not be so many maximal communities that there is not much opportunity for their leaders to engage in informal face-to-face interaction. Perhaps a dozen maximal communities is the limit even for our largest city. For each of these maximal communities the "best" elite community available must be selected, although the choice in some instances may go far down into the middle classes.

Ideally, these maximal communities should be of roughly equal size and equal heterogeneity. This can only be approximated, but the difficult problem is continuity over time. Even a good choice of equally populous and heterogeneous maximal communities will alter as population shifts occur. Some procedure of review and a rule for "annexing" community areas from one maximal community to another must be instituted. In the main this rule should follow the intent of the entire structure: to maintain heterogeneity and the established boundaries of acknowledged communities. Minimal named subcommunities should definitely be regarded as indivisible modules, to be annexed as units or left where they are.

Official Recognition of Community Levels

Public recognition of the lowest tier of subcommunities is essential if the present vagueness of community boundaries is to be avoided and community leaders are to have stable constituencies which they can claim to represent. There are a number of ways this can be done and each of them can be argued for on grounds other than the above.

First, the minimal named units can become data gathering and reporting units; by aggregating them, the larger units can also be reported on. It would seem particularly helpful to use these units as a basis for reporting on the delivery of public services. There is a great deal of complaint about inequities in the distribution of public services, but we have no standard accounting system which would allow communities to argue their case on the basis of reliable information. It is also likely that the availability of such information would heighten "community awareness," since the residents could make genuine comparisons between themselves and other residential areas and each community would become the object of newspaper accounts and other public reports.

Second, leaders or groups from these subcommunities might be recognized by city governments as the appropriate informal negotiating bodies for residential groupings. That is, they could receive regular information on public hearings, be invited to such hearings and, in general, receive recognition as the appropriate constituencies for which higher level community leadership should speak. This would not only give leaders a known constituency to which they could appeal; it would reduce the likelihood of city governments arranging ad hoc communities which are gerrymandered so as to fragment existing communities and which reduce the solidarity or continuity of citizen representation. Such a system of recognition need not exclude other representative bodies not based on residential unity or drawn from residential units other than the lowest tier. What does seem to be necessary is some assurance that city government will not suddenly "redefine" subcommunities so as to undermine the constituencies which community leaders have developed.

Third, some degree of conformity between the community boundaries of this tier and the district boundaries of public agencies would probably be the single most important way of reducing the present barriers to community awareness and participation. Obviously the boundaries of this lowest tier of subcommunities could not be the appropriate district boundary for every public agency. However, the general direction might be to bring agency districts into as close conformity with subcommunity boundaries as is possible. This puts little limit on the size of district boundaries—they may coincide with the minimal named community, with the second tier of these communities, with the maximal community or be "nested" within one of these units. The general guideline would be to minimize the number of agency districts to which any one subcommunity belongs, given the number of districts which agency administrators feel is appropriate to their operation. The optimal situation would be achieved if all agency boundaries were brought into conformity with one another, and the smaller districts of some agencies were nested within the larger ones. Undoubtedly there must be some flexibility here, but the burden of proof might best lie on the agencies to demonstrate that their services are imperiled by such a districting.

These three steps would seem to be sufficient to give subcommunities a clear identity as well as a clear notion of who are the public servants with whom they must negotiate. In turn, public officials and administrators have a well-defined community with which they can consult and to whom they can go for support. The most important advantages, however, may lie in the new opportunities for: (1) decentralizing some public services; (2) introducing some choice among public services; (3) encouraging competition among public agencies; and (4) increasing the opportunity for voluntarism.

Increasing Choice in the Selection of Public Services

Ordinarily a resident is a captive client of a particular public agency distribution center. He can send his children to a particular school but no other; he can complain to a single police district, register to vote at a single place, obtain his auto license at only one distributional point. etc. This tends, however, to limit competition among agency distributors and is one reason given for the absence of quality public services. Clients often feel they have no choice and sometimes resent their inability to "shop" for a better school, better place for voting registration, and so on. Undoubtedly this sort of situation frequently cannot be avoided, especially where expensive community services must be brought to the client (police, sanitation, postal delivery), rather than the other way about (school attendance, registration for various reasons, applications for social benefits). Consider two examples: the public schools and controlled desegregation.

A tier of subcommunities makes it possible to create "super districts" in which there are alternatives among some public services. At the same time, the responsibility of agencies to serve a subcommunity which may be already organized to some extent is preserved. The most obvious example is the public school system. School personnel continue to claim that schools are operated best when they are neighborhood-based, and they frequently have widespread support in this claim. Nonetheless, there are a number of people who would prefer to shop for a better school. A super district which would include, say, four or five high schools could allow for this type of choice without requiring much alteration in a parent's representational capacity within his subcommunity. That is, a parent could still send his children to a school within a subcommunity where he is an active (or potentially active) member.

Districting school attendance areas in this manner may be especially helpful in allowing schools in close proximity to specialize somewhat and serve minority demands more than they do at present. Some schools, for example, might develop racially integrated programs to appeal to the small number of parents and students who would support this type of social contact. This type of voluntary racial integration is badly needed at the present time since more coercive measures that apply to an entire residential population (e.g., busing) are running into strong opposition.

This type of differentiation among public schools might also be the basis for incentive programs that increase competition among schools and reward them for meeting social demands or helping to fulfill constitutional goals (e.g., racial integration). A set of local school districts combined in a single super school district makes it possible to detect shifts in consumer preferences and reward schools and their faculties for this "popularity." The *net increase* in the number of students who cross local school district boundaries to attend another school in the super district is a fair measure of popularity, so long as we can assume that popularity indicates some difference in quality.

Similarly, it is possible to include incentives for voluntary racial and socioeconomic integration within the public school system. The subcommunity areas within the second-level district boundaries form a racial and socioeconomic mix which can be known, although it may not be stable over time. By this base population, it would be possible to approximate full racial and socioeconomic integration. A formula which rewards schools for serving more minority group members than those living immediately in its local district might make "self-busing" among poor whites and blacks a more popular pattern than it is at present.

One can probably build the strongest case for this type of super district for the public school system. It is an important service, one that has been widely criticized for overstandardization and it is a service where the client must do most of the traveling. No doubt there are other services for which similar forms of competition and incentive structures can be developed. The advantage of the tier of subcommunities suggested here is that they pyramid together to form large enough areas to accommodate super districts while preserving some form of local community organization as a continuing source of influence on public agencies.[12]

Residential desegregation remains a challenge which few American cities or governmental units are able to face head on or materially affect. This is also an area in which mass supracommunity organizations seem to be neutralized by the heterogeneity of their own membership. Such groups must base their objectives on a broad base of support from a majority of their membership. These mass associations have not been able to find among their membership much support for placing a high priority on residential racial desegregation (except in rare instances involving groups like the NAACP and ACLU which have formed specifically to reduce discrimination). Nonetheless, a large proportion of Americans indicate that they are tolerant of racial desegretion in their communities, and a small but probably growing proportion have definite preferences for residential desegregation (Hyman and Sheatsley, 1956).

So far, efforts at residential desegregation seem to have taken only one direction—mass desegregation of the entire society. This approach may be commendable but it tends to arouse mass resistance which frequently undermines the initial effort. Certainly it would be useful to have as well an approach which allows for incremental, voluntary local efforts at residential desegregation.

A few local communities in large cities have shown a popular willingness to establish a racial balance, but so far they have faced almost insurmountable problems (Bradburn, Sudman, and Glockel, 1971). First, they have a very limited organizational structure within which they may pursue this goal or which they can use to obtain help from city, state, and federal authorities. Second, the present discriminatory restrictions on black home seekers are such that areas which are open to them tend to be inundated in a short time—i.e., the prophecy that once an area received a few black residents it tends to become entirely black is largely self-fulfilling. Third, while many white Americans are willing to live in a "mixed" community, few seem willing to live in a community which seems to be shifting from all white to all black.

Surely it would be advantageous if a few local communities could work toward self-desegregation with the aid of governmental authorities and some assurance that a temporary "open residential policy" would not end in another segregated black community. Official recognition of community boundaries and community groups would at least open the channels of communication between community groups and governmental authorities on this topic.

It is more important, however, that subcommunities have some defensible quotas for defining "integration" and maintaining acceptable levels of black and white residents. A maximal subcommunity which is a cross-section of the entire city (or metropolitan area, where possible) might contain in its racial makeup a racial balance which would be defensible as a measure of integration. Those minimal communities who were willing to work toward this racial balance might then be given both monetary and organizational support to reach their goal. One tactic would be to compensate minimal communities with less than their share of minority group members for any net increase in minorities, on the theory that such residential changes increase the costs of certain local services such as police protection and schooling. Thus, any net annual gain in minority group residents up to their percentage in the maximal community might be compensated by additional funds to the police and the local schools. (Incidentally, this tends to penalize minority communities for remaining segregated and to make the return of the white middle class more likely. This is an important step where "race power" has no offsetting disadvantages.)

A second and perhaps more likely tactic would be to support minimal community organizations in their efforts to regulate residential changes among existing communities in order to maintain a balance rather than to simply facilitate an exodus. Occasionally such groups have attempted to form associations which could maintain a balance of incoming residents and disperse those who are different in race. It is easy to mistake these groups for gatekeepers who attempt to maintain outlawed restrictive covenants or to take in a token number of minority group members. Often this is the case, but frequently it is only a relatively liberal white community which is willing to take its share of invasion in order to maintain some vestiges of its previous character. Such groups have solid and self-interested reasons for racial integration and should not be overlooked in our search for ways to meet constitutional requirements. It would not be too difficult to give them an incentive to meet acceptable levels of desegregation in the form of additional support to police protection and schooling on the basis of net annual gains in the proportion of minority group residents in the minimal subcommunity. This formula requires a lot of counting but is not unmanageable.

Obviously such a system requires a maximal community which reflects the residential mix of racial, ethnic, and socioeconomic groups in a single city so nearly that it can become a defensible basis for defining residential quotas. In such a system there is sufficient local and supracommunity organization to effect the task without undue coercion and uncertainty. This would seem to argue for a maximal community which could establish the limits which define integration and a minimal community which could employ those limits.

The popular argument for decentralization seems to be that it would restore a more personalized treatment of clients. Decentralization may have as much benefit for the public servant as for the private citizen. The clinic physician who can recall nothing about his patients, the school teacher who never seems to recognize the parents of her students, and the policeman who does not even remember those most inclined to recidivism on his beat are ill-equipped to make the most rudimentary judgments required by typical on-the-spot predicaments. Residents may long to be recognized by their public servants but the public servants have a harder task; there are more clients than there are servants.

We are in a period of extraordinary geographic and social mobility which makes personal recognition difficult for everyone, but especially for the distributors of public goods and services in regard to their clients. This lack of prior acquaintanceship has been aggravated by a swollen number of younger people (mostly clients) born since World War II and a peculiarly diminished number of older people (some public servants) born during the Great Depression. The exodus of people from the city to the suburbs has not helped this situation because it has included both an abandonment of prior service areas and the taking up of residence in different ones. The disenchantment between the distributors of public services and their clients takes four forms: the dislike of old public servants for their new clients; the dislike of new residents for their old public servants; the dislike of old suburban residents for those invading them; and the resentment of new suburban residents for the scorn shown them by older residents. Each group has been thrust upon the other without much chance to settle in and get acquainted.

One can hope with the recent lowered birth rate and a more rectangular population pyramid that some of these problems will diminish. But in any case, they are chronic problems in a society which constantly chooses impersonal (or "universalistic") modes for the delivery of public services, and which has a high level of residential and occupational mobility. Within such a society some special efforts seem to be needed to moderate the difficulty of getting acquainted.

One version of this attempt to decentralize public services has been the one-stop public service center, which promises not only to reduce the scale of public service agencies but also to bring client and public agent into a kind of multidimensional contact by reducing the latter's specialization. The comprehensive service distribution center would seem to require the prior recognition of subcommunity areas and the support of local community residents.

Either a minimal community area or the second-tier community area might be considered for such an all-purpose one-stop center, so long as residents and their representative organizations were willing to support it. Obviously it is important that most or all local groups give it support because such a center needs to be "invited" if it is to mollify the present alienation toward some public agencies.

The designation of official community areas would make the one-stop center more feasible for subcommunities than before. For the most part, municipal and federal governments seem to have sponsored more localized service units where it was thought trouble was brewing. Such distribution centers have had to develop without any prior basis for cooperation, and the result has often been a controversy over community control.

A tier of community areas which shares its district boundaries with public agencies might be the basis for moving toward a genuinely comprehensive one-stop service center including a wide range of public services. The original conception of the one-stop center included a wide range of services now being taken care of by several public agencies with their separate delivery stations. Coordination and cooperation among these agencies would have been difficult in any case, but the lack of common districts and a common clientele made it more difficult. The tier of subcommunities and coincident agency districts avoids this drawback.

The extent to which such one-stop centers can develop, of course, depends upon many other things as well, especially the ability of government and private groups to engender broad cooperative efforts among municipal agencies. The major sources of resistance lie within the agencies themselves: the administrators' unwillingness to share budgets, responsibilities, and authority; and the employees' unwillingness to give up highly specialized roles, change their working conditions, or work extensively with subprofessionals. These sources of resistance are a sort of constant force that helps fragment the city.

One concept which should be explored is the idea of the one-stop center as a *subcontractor* for some public services. This would mean that in some subcommunities the one-stop center would be directly contracted to provide some limited forms of city services. Presently, city governments do this with private contractors and, indeed, some suburban governments "farm out" practically all their functions. The one-stop center might be similarly regarded. No doubt the number of services which can be farmed out in this fashion is limited. Also, it seems most likely to work best in affluent subcommunities where residents might help capitalize such ventures. Even without these limitations, however, such a plan might give city administrations some leverage in what is now a very stubborn situation. It would also allow for some of the experimentation necessary in order to develop a more complete model of the one-stop center.

Coordination Among Public Agencies

We have found numerous occasions like those above to point to the absence of cooperation and coordination among municipal service agencies. While the self-interest of public administrators and employees is largely the reason for this situation, there are also few requirements for coordination and cooperation among administrators. Agency administrators, of course, do get together occasionally, but this is sporadic and sometimes only for purposes of supporting each other's budgets or wage increases for their employees. Indeed, cooperation among municipal agencies has often been regarded as a license for conspiracy. Because of this "incestuous" relationship among some administrators, it has been suggested that their opportunity to associate ought to be even further limited. What actually seems to be required, however, is an explicit administrative and legal requirement that agency heads at every level consult with one another regularly in order to develop joint goals which can incorporate their various functions and be justified before a broader public than presently available (i.e., their own superiors and employees).

No amount of community design is going to fully rectify this problem. It is basically a legislative problem and must be settled there despite recent and rather grim evaluations of the legislative process (Lowi, 1969). A tier of subcommunity areas with conforming agency district boundaries will move in a direction which *permits* such explicit and above-board cooperation among municipal agencies.

Several features of this community design are relevant to administrative coordination. First, it helps to bring the districts of various agencies into conformity with one another so that several public bureaucracies administer to the same set of residential clients. It is possible to imagine, for example, a public meeting at which the clients of some local municipal bureaucracies are able to get their police commander, fire chief, school superintendent, and welfare official on the same auditorium floor. While not offering the bureaucrats an actual cooperative procedure, this situation might make cooperation among them more likely.

Second, a tier of subcommunity areas coinciding with agency districts makes clear which levels of various functional bureaucracies need most to cooperate. Those administrators with the same clients are the obvious parties who need to get together for consultation. As things presently stand, it is not clear among the mosaic of public agency districts which levels of authority should or can have access to one another. Does a school principal, for example, approach a local police commander whose district includes most of his school district, or does he ask that his school superintendent (whose district lies largely outside of any particular police district) do this? At present, any attempt to coordinate the efforts of district administrators is likely to run into the problem of status mismatches or the probability that senior district administrators of various functions have little overlap in district boundaries or clientele.

Third, an authoritative definition of subcommunities might prevent public bureaucracies from defining their own clients as a "natural community"; they frequently claim that they are beholden only to their own clients and cannot consider cooperation with agencies which have "another community"; the contriving of distinct clienteles by district administrators has reached the point where no one else can assert any more what is a community. By this means, district administrators hope to avoid agency cooperation and confrontation with clients who have some prior solidarity and the convenience of a cheap means of consulting with one another.

This tier of subcommunity areas will not lead directly to the necessary legislative procedures which allow district administrators to establish joint goals and to serve a single, territorial clientele. But it may make it more likely that they will voluntarily do this because of their own self-interest.

Assurances of Participation under Metropolitan Government

One of the central problems of metropolitan areas is their fragmentation along jurisdictional lines. The metropolitan area is not a single city, but a mosaic of cities, towns, villages and unincorporated areas. Thus, an attempt to tier and merge local community areas within one or even several jurisdictions will probably still leave the metropolitan area poorly coordinated, with continuing disparities in public services and public responsibilities. The Committee for Economic Development (1967a), fully recognizing these difficulties, has proposed a two-tiered metropolitan government in recent publications. However, metropolitanization has inched forward very slowly in the U.S. and its prospects are rather dim at the present time.

The main barriers to metropolitan government seem to be the fear of significant losses of local control and the fear that the central city will "export" some of its problems to surrounding communities in an inequitable manner. These fears are not unwarranted. The recent controversy surrounding the Forest Hills housing project on Long Island is a good case in point. The project consists of 20,000 units of moderate- and low-income housing proposed by New York City for a middle class community. Since similar housing projects are not under consideration for other local communities, it would appear that the present residents of Forest Hills have some grounds for saying that they are having to take "more than their share" of a certain population (some of it low income and black) and housing stock (apartments). If the metropolitanization of political and administrative authority implies similar fates for other communities, their resistance is well grounded.

The CED proposal attempts to reduce this fear with a first tier of local government which would retain some powers. It may be necessary, however, to build in some further structure for local participation through something like the community design being discussed here. Such a community design develops comparable areas in which one can say what is a community's "fair share" of low-income housing, polluting industry, freeways, school funds, and so on. Without some system of comparable areas around which to develop such an accounting system, it seems extremely unlikely that public planning can proceed in what will be seen as a fair and equitable manner. In this respect, the community design outlined here may help "sell" people on metropolitanization if it can build in some assurances of participation and the equitable treatment of all community areas.

The concurrent development of metropolitanization and a community design for local participation may be essential to the public acceptance of either. There is a deeper reason, however, for giving Americans every assurance of local participation and an accounting system to monitor the distribution of public benefits and costs. Americans deeply suspect a strong government, not only because many of them are strongly committed to a free enterprise ideology, but also because they fear that strong government might fall into the hands of a small minority or, worse, an oppressive majority. The religious, ethnic, racial, regional, and socioeconomic diversity of the country's population is so great that there is an understandable hesitancy to risk the concentration of strong governmental powers in the hands of any single group. In the past these fears have been assuaged by the weakness of governmental units and a system of counterbalancing powers. In all likelihood, the move toward metropolitanization will have to include some of these counterbalancing powers in the form of a community design which provides for participation from roughly equivalent territorial units. As I will point out below, however, this does not mean merging voluntary, political, and administrative groups in this tier of community areas.

Representative Structure

The present representative structure of subcommunity areas depends on voluntarism and on some commonly recognized need for people, especially those who cannot afford to travel widely, to establish their own solidaristic unions for negotiating with the wider society. The subcommunity group remains a highly voluntary all-purpose association which attempts to aggregate its wishes rather than to present a united front behind one predominant issue or goal. Since most nonterritorial forms of associational life in the U.S. are either somewhat coercive in their membership (e.g., labor unions, professional associations), or have a single objective (e.g., NAACP), or have local units which are heavily dependent on national support (e.g., political parties), it seems worthwhile to keep intact some form of associational life which makes virtues of voluntarism and a wide range of social goals.

Paradoxically, then, the subcommunity emerges as perhaps the most voluntaristic form of association available to select among a multiplicity of goals. Common Cause and numerous other experimental associations have tried to develop some representational structure to do the same thing—appeal to voluntary effort and at the same time set priorities among a multiplicity of goals. As Simmel put it, however, mass associations can be best brought together by a single cause. And as Weber and countless others have reiterated, organizations find their own survival a central concern, one that frequently makes them dependent on broader organizational efforts. These are the two central problems which community organizations must manage to avoid. Community groups must remain voluntary and multipurpose if they are to help the wider society plumb the depths of its mixed attitudes and select among its goals. For that reason it may be best to provide community groups with some framework within which they can organize but with no direct regulatory or administrative powers. The incentives for community organization, then, are its intrinsic benefits.

To stress this limited incentive seems essential because the tier of subcommunities described so far might be construed as mirroring existing forms of political representation or merely repeating what has already been tried in existing representative bodies, such as city councils. These elective forms of government may be as useful as the Federalist Papers insist, but they seem to lack a set of further ingredients which are essential to citizen influence in government. Local, state, and national legislatures are heavily indebted to organizational sponsors who seem to paralyze them when it comes to taking any course which would endanger opportunities for reelection. Because of gerrymandering, legislatures have only safe constituencies to which they can appeal; they are heavily dependent on national or supracommunity groups to support them; and, like TV stations, they seem sensitive only to the masses rather than to significant minorities (see U.S. National Commissions on Urban Problems, 1969: 346-359).

For these reasons, it is best to leave the representational structure of subcommunities to develop as a voluntary effort. The structure lays emphasis on voluntarism and on the ability to develop a "balanced ticket" of leaders and issues able to arouse or develop widespread support. Perhaps that is the reason why community organizations have dwindled—they depend on esprit de corps and issues which can mobilize people with concerns beyond narrow professional or class interests. This diagnosis of voluntary community groups is not overly optimistic but it does suggest that they are in a crucial position. They are not dependent on single purpose supracommunity organizations for their continuity and they are able to establish priorities among multiple goals.

This does not mean that subcommunity groups should not apply for foundation or federal grants to support them and allow them to carry out experiments. Community organizations, however, must mobilize themselves without publicly decreed methods of election, appointive procedures, or special social guidance. It may be enough to give subcommunity groups an organizational and territorial framework within which they can mobilize to face their advocates and adversaries. Undue public sponsorship will do little more than compromise the voluntarism and broad spectrum of goals. Left to their own, some community groups may appeal to and become dependent on outside sponsors, some may align themselves with special interest groups, and others may struggle with the problem, in a pluralistic society, of establishing goal priorities. External help can be available to subcommunities if they solicit it, but no effort beyond this seems necessary or advisable.

Matching service delivery districts with community areas and aggregating both according to some common territorial framework is not a drastic move toward community control. What it does essentially is to match up community, political, and administrative representatives so that each has a corresponding adversary or advocate among the others. The powers of the local community, however, are limited and advisory, as will be evident to any strong proponent of "community control," "separatism," or "home rule."

This absence of formal political or administrative control at the subcommunity level seems to be warranted for two basic reasons. First, there is the danger of "balkanizing" metropolitan areas by dividing them further into small, semi-autonomous units. This is already one of the main problems of metropolitan areas and to further it would only institutionalize and appear to justify the inequitable distribution of public services and the narrow interests of public leadership. Low income, inner city minority communities might be able to control their public service agencies, but their limited resources would not seem to be a result of local popular preference.

Second, the merging of voluntary community representation with formal political or administrative powers would narrow rather than broaden the representative base of community organization. Both political and administrative organizations seem to develop narrow constituencies, and they have understandable reasons for doing so. By developing small and reliable constituencies with a narrow range of interests, political and administrative leaders can return themselves to office by satisfying only a small and dependent number of people. This is especially likely to happen where political and administrative leaders can manipulate sizable amounts of patronage or make decisions which heavily benefit some groups while the costs are diffused throughout the remaining population. The advantage of voluntary community groups is that they can develop a broad constituency. To give local community groups sizable amounts of patronage and considerable decision-making power would seem only to encourage them to develop small, reliable, homogeneous, and dependent constituencies.

Implications for Other Forms of Participation: Political Representation and Interest Groups

Since the aims of this community design are to increase the opportunity for widespread participation, there is an emphasis on the role of voluntarism and localism. This argues for the independence of community groups from the more direct representative political process. However, this design does not argue against reforms which would also broaden our selection of political representation. Under current arrangements, the tendency is toward single-member districts in municipal, state, and national legislative bodies. The argument for this form of political representation is that it makes political power available to minority groups (or narrowly defined groups) which are heavily localized in a particular local, state, or national legislative district. The result of this type of selection is frequently a state legislator, congressman, or ward councilman with a dependable constituency and little interest in national goals outside of his particular constituency. Thus, political negotiation tends to boil down to log rolling and trade-offs among opponents. The result is the "interest group liberalism" portrayed by Theodore Lowi (1969).

One might hope that state and national legislators, as well as city councilmen, could have a broader conception of the public interest, and seek to define a hierarchy of collective goals. Representative political authorities, however, seem likely to develop such a broad hierarchy of shared goals only when they are dependent on equally broad constituencies. As I read the evidence, it points toward a "mix" of electoral districts: some single member districts to insure the representation of rather small minority groups and a majority of at-large districts heterogeneous enough to insure that legislative leaders will try to respond to a range of interest groups and social goals. On somewhat similar grounds, one might argue that nonterritorial interest groups should be deflected from their present tendency to pursue single issues. They should be reshaped into all-purpose groups which have to defend a balance of national, regional, and more localized goals in terms of their relative primacy.

It seems to me that one cannot argue with measures which would so clearly operate to broaden constituencies and encourage an assortment of social goals among political representatives and interest groups. But neither of these avenues of social reform excludes the ideas of reform which have been elaborated in this approach to community design. They are basically complementary in that they both seek to create broader and more heterogeneous constituencies and to force representational groups to select among competing alternatives rather than defending isolated goals.

CONCLUSION

One of the central problems of modern industrial nations seems to be their difficulty in finding a workable interface between voluntary, political, and administrative institutions. The overwhelming trend in the short run seems to be one in which citizens are regarded (especially by administrators and politicians but also by themselves) as mercenary customers of governmental services, happy if they are well taken care of, unruly if they are not. But in the long run, the great Western democracies have been able to claim the loyalty of their members by the extension of citizenship, and this seems the only moral justification which places them above a benign and efficient dictatorship. The voluntary community is defensible primarily because it extends citizenship, and that must be its moral raison d'etre.

The present community design attempts to observe this moral dictate by pairing a tier of community areas with administrative areas. The community areas are then able to voluntarily confront political representatives because of their common interests and members. This pattern of subcommunity formation may not be the only one that could be proposed at this point in time, but it does embody two principles which are worthy of fuller consideration. On the one hand, there is the attempt to align citizens or "customers" with the units which do the serving. On the other hand, there is the attempt to maintain the autonomy of citizen groups so that they do not become the captive constituency of political organizers. Our aim then, has been to give administrators, politicians, and citizens a chance to confront each other while maintaining their independence of one another. Other community designs aim toward these same two principles; I doubt whether any community design can succeed in the U.S. without embodying them. Our conclusion grows then, not only from the examination of past experience, but from an attempt to project the structural principles of future experiences.

(1) The tier of subcommunities laid out here has its basis in a cognitive mapping of named areas which range from the most local, homogeneous, and unified areas to large sectors which encompass the cosmopolitanism and heterogeneity of large metropolitan centers.

(2) This tier of community areas is compatible with suggested reforms in metropolitan administration. The tier of administrative and representative units can be brought into conformity with, for example, the recent proposals of the Committee for Economic Development. This community design, however, also preserves the voluntary character and independence of community organization rather than fully encompassing it within the official representative structures of proposed changes.

(3) This community design attempts to yoke together unified local residential groups with more heterogeneous residential groups by promoting negotiations and contacts among heterogeneous representatives of the minimal communities. The tier arrangement aims to give an orderly structure to negotiations among heterogeneous residential groups rather than leave them to contest all their differences at the national level.

(4) This community design can increase the opportunities for choice in selecting among public services especially for small minorities. They can patronize certain public service distributors without forcing others to do so.

(5) The lowest tier of this design gives an authoritative definition to community areas, avoiding both the controversy about what is the "real" subcommunity and the self-interested attempts of public agencies to create communities out of their local service areas. While the communities may be contrived in many instances, once defined, subcommunities will at least have the opportunity to become "real" and will not be constantly subject to the fragmentation enforced by administrative and political agencies.

(6) This community design allows for comparison of service delivery among community areas and a genuine judgment on the equity of public services. The lowest tier of community areas can also be given "bonuses" for helping to meet national goals, for example, desegregation, or high quality in the delivery of public services.

(7) This community design permits coordination among public agencies and makes them jointly accountable to a unified clientele. While this may not force public agencies to coordinate their efforts, it makes it more profitable for them to do so.

(8) This community design increases the opportunities for participation within a potentially more effective structure of voluntary community organization. It provides both a very localized and much more cosmopolitan range of participation than currently recognized. While it does not force participation in the local community, it makes such participation a viable alternative to supracommunity organizations which currently monopolize many of the avenues for citizen influence.

(9) This community design attempts to reenlist elites into the service of their local communities and allows them to play a role consistent with their status and their desire for orderly social relations. It aims to make elites responsible leaders or helpers rather than a disliked or privileged class pursuing only its own interests.

(10) This community design depends on the active interests of a minority of community residents and assumes that it is primarily their instrumental goals which will mobilize residents to take an active course. It does not depend upon sentimental attachments to "the old neighborhood," although it does not preclude people from becoming active for this reason.

(11) This community design allows residents to experiment with more comprehensive and decentralized modes of service delivery for public goods without forcing them to do so. The idea of the "one-stop service center" as a subcontractor for public service delivery is worth consideration, although its viability may be limited in the number and kinds of services which can be distributed most effectively and humanely in this manner. The design permits residential groups to experiment with this type of public service delivery without fully challenging the continued existence of public service agencies.

(12) This community design provides a structure of community groups that can make inputs into public decision making, especially in areas like "city planning," which require some orderly consideration of residential groups and their interests. Authoritatively defined community groups make it difficult for city planners to enlist their friends and ignore their enemies when attempting to ascertain "public opinion."

(13) This community design takes account of the high mobility of the American population, of its variable attachment to place of residence, and of the general preference for an individualized mode of relating to public bureaucracies. The tier of community areas allows for voluntarism among those who care to act on behalf of collective goals. The element of choice leaves some room for a "demand schedule" in community participation.

(14) This community design allows for a continuation in the variety of community areas which have attracted Americans in the past, ranging from cosmopolitan centers to homogeneous dormitory suburbs. While the design asks a variety of areas to engage in some joint decision making, it leaves their bigots, racists, artists, and intellectuals free to withdraw into homogeneous local communities.

(15) The community design developed here does not exclude other ways of transforming narrowly based interest groups or political party organizations into multipurpose institutions. The development of multipurpose community groupings by any means creates a "competitor" to current interest and political groups and is a possible stimulus to transform these groups.

(16) The aim of this community design has been to provide a framework within which citizens, administrators, and political representatives can negotiate toward adaptive courses of action rather than common brick and mortar solutions. The results of such a design are apt to be quite variable. Such a situation would be a great improvement over the present bureaucratically detailed programs that are carried out with such uniformity that there can be no subsequent selection among the more or less successful of them.

It should be emphasized that while this analysis is based largely on the American experience with community, this is not the only reason for considering it. Since the Enlightenment, the long-term fate of national states has depended on the extension of citizenship. The relationship between citizens, administrators, and political representatives is problematic almost everywhere in the world, even in Soviet Russia. Streamlining and simplifying the relationship between citizen, administrator, and politician is an issue which is worldwide. Riots and revolutions, cynicism and corruption, terrorism and tyranny: each type of disorder seems to be infectious and seems to arise from our inability to reach the ideals of the Enlightenment, where the citizen, the administrator, and the politician could arrive at common goals. In my own view, there are no other ultimate values which have such universal importance at this time.

NOTES

1. For example, Skinner (1968) makes the only attempt at community design included in the International *Encyclopedia of the Social Sciences.*

2. Oddly enough, this point was made in an early landmark study by Roderick McKinzie (1968). Despite its availability, McKinzie's work has gone neglected by social scientists, and planners have continued to regard the local urban community as a legacy of rural life.

3. This often had the unfortunate consequence of placing residences, in areas subject to malarial epidemics, which subsequently resulted in extensive drainage or the change of residential locations.

4. This resulted in uncommonly precipitous streets in some cities, such as Cincinnati.

5. For a finely detailed account of this pattern of subcommunity development, see Goheen (1970).

6. This fear of an urban rabble is well documented in Johnson (1972).

7. Lowi (1969) has traced in some detail how this interest group liberalism has become transformed into a process which attempts to reduce all negotiations with government and big business to negotiations between interest communities and nonterritorial bureaucracies.

8. The Chicago Youth Development Project, a similar but more modest Ford Foundation program in Chicago, seems to have concluded that it was rather successful in mobilizing people into various forms of community organization but relatively unable to affect the incidence of most indicators of social disorganization.

9. These included Daniel Moynihan, whose ideas appeared in President Johnson's address at Howard University, June 4, 1965.

10. There seems to be a fatal flaw in this modern adaptation of the town meeting. It must be remembered that the original town meeting considered a wide range of issues which might mobilize a number of people, and those who presided at the town meeting could be replaced by those attending.

11. This ordering follows the argument made above; there is probably less socioeconomic heterogeneity within adjacent minimal areas than there is ethnic heterogeneity. Another rule might be to construct an index based on the overall racial, ethnic, and socioeconomic status of the maximal subcommunity and adopt that combination of minimal subcommunity areas which most nearly approximates it.

12. A variety of public services would seem to require no districting, either because most of their business could be handled by mail (e.g., auto registration) or because computer technology makes it possible for any particular distribution center to retrieve all the necessary records (e.g., applications for welfare benefits).

REFERENCES

Abrahams, R. D. (Ed.) *Deep down in the jungle.* Chicago: Aldine-Atherton, 1970.

Addams, J. *Twenty years at Hull House.* New York: New American Library, 1961.

Alinsky, S. *Reveille for radicals.* Chicago: University of Chicago Press, 1946.

Altshuler, A. "The goals of comprehensive planning." Journal of the American Institute of Planners, August 1965, 31 (3), 186-194.

Altshuler, A. *Community control: The black demand for participation in large American cities.* New York: Pegasus, 1970.

Astrom, K. *City planning in Sweden.* Stockholm: The Swedish Institute, 1967.

Baltzell, E. D. *Philadelphia gentlemen.* Glencoe: The Free Press, 1958.

Banfield, E. C. The uses and limitations of metropolitan planning in Massachusetts. In H. W. Eldredge (Ed.), *Taming megalopolis: How to manage an urbanized world.* Vol. 2. New York: Anchor Books, 1967. 710-719.

Biddle, W. W., and Biddle, L. J. *The community development process: The rediscovery of local initiative.* New York: Holt, Rinehart and Winston, 1965.

Bornfriend, A. J. Political parties and pressure groups. In R. H. Connery and D. Caraley (Eds.), *Governing the city.* New York: Praeger, 1969. 55-67.

Bradburn, N., Sudman, S., and Glockel, G. *Side by side.* Chicago: Quadrangle, 1971.

Brager, G. A., and Purcell, F. P. *Community action against poverty.* New Haven: College and University Press, 1967.

Buder, S. *Pullman.* New York: Oxford University Press, 1967.

Caudill, H. M. *Night comes to the Cumberlands.* Boston: Little, Brown and Co., 1963.

Churchill, H. S. *The city is the people.* New York: Reynald and Hitchcock, 1945.

Cloward, R. A., and Ohlin, L. *Delinquency and opportunity.* Glencoe: The Free Press, 1960.

Committee for Economic Development. *Modernizing local government.* New York: CED, 1967a.

Committee for Economic Development. *Modernizing state governments.* New York: CED, 1967b.

Committee for Economic Development. *Reshaping government in metropolitan areas.* New York: CED, 1970.

Dahir, J. *The neighborhood unit plan.* New York: Russell Sage Foundation, 1947.

Davis, A. F. *Spearheads of reform: The social settlements and the Progressive movement.* New York: Oxford University Press, 1970.

Dewey, R. "The neighborhood, urban ecology, and city planners." American Sociological Review, August 1950, 15(4), 502-507.

Eichler, E. P., and Kaplan, M. *The community builders.* Berkeley: University of California Press, 1967.

Ellis, W. W. *White ethics and black power.* Chicago: Aldine Press, 1969.

Fagin, H. The evolving philosophy of urban planning. In L. Schnore and H. Fagin (Eds.), *Urban research and policy planning.* Beverly Hills: Sage Publications, 1967. 309-328.

Fagin, H., and Tarr, C. H. Urban design and urban development. In L. F. Schnore and H. Fagin (Eds.), *Urban Research and policy planning.* Beverly Hills: Sage Publications, 1967. 413-459.

Gans, H. *The urban villagers: Group and class in the life of Italian-Americans.* New York: The Free Press, 1962.

Gans, H. *The Levittowners: Way of life and politics in a new suburban community.* New York: Vintage, 1967.

Gans, H. *People and plans.* New York: Basic Books, 1968a.

Gans, H. Planning, social: II Regional and urban. In D. Sills (Ed.), *International Encyclopedia of the social sciences.* Vol. 1 New York: Macmillan and Free Press, 1968b, 129-137.

Gifford, K. D. Neighborhood development corporations: The Bedford-Stuyvesant experiment. In L. C. Fitch and A. H. Walsh (Eds.), *Agenda for a city.* Beverly Hills: Sage Publications, 1970. 421-450.

Glaab, C. N., and Brown, A. T. *A history of urban America.* New York: Macmillan, 1967.

Goheen, P. G. *Victorian Toronto: 1850 to 1900.* Research Paper No. 127. Chicago: University of Chicago, Department of Geography, 1970.

Greer, S. *The emerging city.* New York: The Free Press, 1962.

Greer, S. *Urban renewal and American cities.* Indianapolis: Bobbs-Merrill, 1965.

Hallman, H. *Neighborhood control of public programs.* New York: Praeger, 1970.

Hawley, A. H. *Urban society: An ecological approach.* New York: Ronald Press, 1971.

Hawley, A. H., and Zimmer, B. G. Resistance to unification in a metropolitan community. In M. Janowitz (Ed.), *Community political systems.* Glencoe: The Free Press, 1961. 184-184.

Hawley, A. H., and Zimmer, B. G. *The metropolitan community.* Beverly Hills: Sage Publications, 1970.

Hoover, E. Introduction: Suburban growth and regional analysis. In D. K. Zschock (Ed.), *Economic aspects of suburban growth.* Stony Brook: State University of New York, Economic Research Bureau, 1969. v-vii.

Hunter, A. D. Symbolic community. Paper delivered at the American Sociological Association Meetings, New Orleans, August 1972.

Hunter, A. D., and Suttles, G. D. The expanding community of limited liability. In G. D. Suttles, *The social construction of communities.* Chicago: University of Chicago Press, 1972. 44-81.

Hyman, H. H., and Sheatsley, P. B. "Attitudes toward desegregation." Scientific American, December 1956, 195, 35-39.

Isaacs, R. "Are urban neighborhoods possible?" Journal of Housing, July 1948, 5, 177-180.

Isaacs, R. "The 'neighborhood unit' is an instrument for segregation." Journal of Housing, August 1948, 5, 215-219.

Jacobs, J. *The death and life of great American cities.* New York: Vintage Books, 1961.

Janowitz, M. *The community press in an urban setting.* Chicago: University of Chicago Press, 1952.

Janowitz, M. Converging perspectives in community political analysis. In M. Janowitz (Ed.), *Community political systems.* Glencoe: The Free Press, 1961, 13-17.

Johnson, D. The search for an urban discipline: Police reform as a response to crime in American cities: 1800-1875. Unpublished doctoral dissertation, University of Chicago, Department of History, 1972.

Kaufman, H. Bureaucrats and organized civil servants. In R. H. Connery and D. Caraley (Eds.), *Governing the city.* New York: Praeger, 1969. 41-54.

Kobrin, S. "The conflict of values in delinquency areas." American Sociological Review, October 1951, 16, 653-661.

Kobrin, S. "The Chicago Area Project: A 25 year assessment." The Annals of the American Academy of Political and Social Science, March 1959, 322, 20-29.

Kornblum, W. *Steel and community.* Chicago: University of Chicago Press, in press.

Kotler, M. *Neighborhood government: The local foundations of political life.* Indianapolis: Bobbs-Merrill, 1969.

Lansing, J. B., Marans, R. W., and Zehner, R. B. *Planned residential environments.* Ann Arbor: University of Michigan, Institute for Social Research, 1970.

Lipset, S. M., and Altback, P. G. The quest for community on the campus. In E. D. Baltzell (Ed.), *The search for community in modern America.* New York: Harper and Row, 1968. 123-147.

Little, K. *West African urbanization.* Cambridge: Cambridge University Press, 1965.

Lofland, L. *A world of strangers.* New York: Basic Books, in press.

Lowi, T. Gosnell's Chicago revisited via Lindsay's New York. In H. F. Gosnell (Ed.), *Machine politics.* (2nd ed.) Chicago: University of Chicago Press, 1968. v-xxiv.

Lowi, T. *The end of liberalism.* New York: W. W. Norton and Co., 1969.

Lubove, R. *The professional altruist.* Cambridge: Harvard University Press, 1965.

Lubove, R. *The urban community.* Englewood Cliffs: Prentice-Hall, 1967.

Marshall, T. H. *Class, citizenship and social development.* Garden City: Doubleday and Co., 1964.

Mayer, M. *The teachers strike: New York, 1968.* New York: Harper and Row, 1969.

McKinzie, R. "The neighborhood: A study of local life in the city of Columbus, Ohio." American Journal of Sociology, September 1921. 27, 145-168. November 1921, 344-363. Reprinted in A. Hawley (Ed.), *On human ecology.* Chicago: University of Chicago Press, 1968. 51-93.

Moreland, J. K. *The millways of Kent.* New Haven: College and University Press, 1965.

Moynihan, D. P. *Maximum feasible misunderstanding.* New York: The Free Press, 1969.

Nelli, H. S. *The Italians in Chicago.* New York: Oxford University Press, 1970.

Nisbet, R. A. History as the decline of community. In R. A. Nisbet (Ed.), *Community and power.* London: Oxford University Press, 1962. 75-97.

O'Donnell, E. J. "The neighborhood service center." Welfare in Review, November-December 1969, 6, 1-11.

Park, R. R. *Society.* Glencoe: The Free Press, 1955.

Perry, C. A., and Williams, M. P. *New York school centers and their community policy.* New York: Russell Sage Foundation, 1931.

Perry, C. A. *Housing for the Machine Age.* New York: Russell Sage Foundation, 1939.

Plotnicov, L. *Strangers to the city.* Pittsburgh: University of Pittsburgh Press, 1967.

Pope, L. *Millhands and preachers.* New Haven: Yale University Press, 1942.

Rainwater, L., and Yancey, W. *The Moynihan Report and the politics of controversy.* Cambridge: MIT Press, 1967.

Ringer, B. *The edge of friendliness.* New York: Basic Books, 1967.

Rubin, M. *Plantation county.* Chapel Hill: University of North Carolina Press, 1951.

Schulze, R. O. The bifurcation of power in a satellite city. In M. Janowitz (Ed.), *Community political systems.* Glencoe: The Free Press, 1961. 19-80.

Shils, E. "Mass society and its culture." Daedalus, Spring 1960, 89(2), 288-314.

Skinner, B. F. The design of experimental communities. In D. Sills (Ed.), *International encyclopedia of the social sciences.* Vol. 16. New York: Macmillan Co. and the Free Press, 1968. 271-275.

Strauss, A. *Images of the American city.* Glencoe: The Free Press, 1961.

Suttles, G. D. *The social order of the slum.* Chicago: University of Chicago Press, 1968.

(U.S.) National Commission on Urban Problems. *Building the American city.* New York: Praeger, 1969.

VonEckardt, W. *The challenge of megalopolis.* New York: Macmillan, 1965.

Wade, R. C. *The urban frontier.* Chicago: University of Chicago Press, 1959.

Warner, W. L., and Low, J. O. *The social system of the modern factory—The strike: A social analysis.* New Haven: Yale University Press, 1947.

Webber, M. M. Order in diversity: Community without propinquity. In L. Wingo, Jr. (Ed.), *Cities and space: The future use of urban land.* Baltimore: Johns Hopkins University Press for Resources for the Future, Inc., 1963. 23-54.

Webber, M. M. The role of intelligence systems in urban-systems planning. In W. W. Eldredge (Ed.), *Taming megalopolis: How to manage an urbanized world.* Vol. 2. New York: Anchor Books, 1967. 644-666.

Weissman, H. H. *Community development in the Mobilization for Youth experience.* New York: Association Press, 1969.

Woodlawn Organization. *The Woodlawn Model Cities Plan.* Northbrook, Ill.: Whitehall Co., 1970.

Young, M., and Wilmot, P. *Family and kinship in East London.* Baltimore: Penguin Books, 1957.

Zorbaugh, H. W. *The Gold Coast and the slum.* Chicago: University of Chicago Press, 1929.

CHAPTER 7

TOWARD AN UNDERSTANDING OF
COMMUNITY SATISFACTION

Robert W. Marans and Willard Rodgers

University of Michigan

THIS PAPER REPORTS on a continuing research effort dealing with one aspect of the quality of American life—people's levels of satisfaction with their residential communities. The research is being conducted at the Survey Research Center of the Institute for Social Research at the University of Michigan and uses data collected as part of several independent studies. It attempts to build on the work of others who have investigated people's responses to residential environments and at the same time outlines a conceptual model within which these and subsequent data can be investigated.

During the past decade, there have been a number of empirical studies dealing with people's responses to their residential environments. Two phenomena have played a catalytic role in fostering much of this research. First, the postwar housing boom of the fifties and early sixties and the concomitant growth of suburban developments have created new residential environments and living patterns for many Americans—environments and living patterns which heretofore have not been experienced. During the same period, an active program of slum clearance and central city rebuilding has focused attention on the plight of the central city resident, with particular emphasis on his housing and established way of life. How people respond to these environments and the patterns of living associated with them have been the subject of inquiry of social scientists interested in factors affecting the quality of people's lives and more specifically, environmental conditions under which this quality is viewed favorably or unfavorably. Before presenting a model within which such studies can be organized, we will briefly review some of the past work related to community satisfaction.

COMMUNITY SATISFACTION RESEARCH

During the fifties and sixties, it was fashionable among writers, architects, urban planners, and others from higher socioeconomic backgrounds to characterize the housing patterns emerging around metropolitan areas as drab, ugly, and monotonous. Such physical development, it was asserted, could not help but foster a way of life which was equally dull and inhuman. In an attempt to understand and describe the ways of life of people in one such community, Gans (1967) conducted a study which focused on social patterns, political organization, and community satisfaction. Among his findings was the fact that most people in the new suburb reported being extremely happy and well-adjusted after their move there. Many had chosen the community because of a desire to change their life-styles and found that they succeeded. Similarly, the systematic assessments of residential environments by planners and other nonresidents have been shown by others to be at variance with the evaluations of the people living in them (Lansing and Marans, 1969; Kaiser, Weiss, Burby, and Donnelly, 1970; Troy, 1971). Researchers in the U.S. have found that the vast majority of residents in a variety of community settings report being moderately to very satisfied with both their communities and their residential neighborhoods (Wilson, 1962; Gulick, Bowerman, and Back, 1962; Lansing and Hendricks, 1967).

Research on community satisfaction and its relation to specific features of the community and dwelling environment has also been in process for several years in Great Britain and Australia. In one study, Metcalf (1967) reported that general satisfaction in three English towns was more strongly related to attitudes toward the individual dwelling than to characteristics of the town itself. When considering the quality of the residential environment in four Sydney suburbs, Troy (1971) found that satisfaction with the individual dwelling and the social setting were more important aspects of people's assessments of the quality of their environment than their assessments of convenience or environmental factors, such as noise or air pollution. With respect to convenience and physical environment characteristics, the assessment of the former was more important in explaining overall satisfaction than assessments of specific attributes of the physical environment. Similarly, Lamanna (1964) reported that a sample of urban residents in a North Carolina community valued their physical environment to a lesser degree than their social relations when assessing the livability of their town.

Strong attachments to the social setting as a principal source of community satisfaction were also expressed by residents of a well-known central city development area in Boston (Fried and Gleicher, 1961; Gans, 1962). Although it was considered a slum by many outsiders, three out of four residents in the area reported it to be a highly satisfactory place to live. Other researchers investigating residents of lower income households have found them to be reasonably content with their place of residence, despite poor housing conditions (Hollingshead and Rogler, 1963; Andrews and Philips, 1970; Young and Wilmott, 1957; Suttles, 1968). In most instances, satisfaction was associated with strong attachments to family and friends living in the community.

Finally, the type of housing and proximity to neighboring dwellings are aspects of the individual dwelling most strongly associated with community satisfaction. Lansing and Hendricks (1967) and Michelson (1969) showed that people living in single family houses on large lots evaluated their neighborhood environments highly, compared to people living in other types of residential structures, including single family houses on small lots.

In sum, most people, including many of those living in "substandard" environments tend to be fairly content with the community in which they live. The social setting, including interpersonal relations and living in single family housing, are salient factors influencing an individual's level of satisfaction with his residential community. Other important factors which are related to general community satisfaction are the physical conditions in the environment and the convenience of having nearby public and private facilities and services.

While numerous researchers have considered the way in which people evaluate their residential communities, it is not always clear just why these efforts have been made. Beyond a general desire to determine the relative importance of various attributes of the environment which are subject to alteration, few researchers have presented a clear statement of why efforts to measure community satisfaction levels are useful. To avoid repeating this omission, it seems appropriate to preface our discussion with a rationale for the importance of measuring community and neighborhood satisfaction.

Community Satisfaction as a Social Indicator

One aspect of the interest in satisfaction measures is related to the growing movement toward more and better social reporting. Community satisfaction can be considered an important social indicator, justified on the basis that knowledge about its distribution and change is important in the formulation of social policy. For example, it may facilitate the assessment of new and emerging housing and community designs and transportation systems and, at the same time, document trends in patterns of living that may be occurring within residential communities and within our society as a whole.

However, proposals to try to measure community satisfaction, and indeed to measure any so-called subjective indicators, have been strongly challenged by those who doubt either the ability of surveys to provide valid measures of community satisfaction, or the usefulness of the concept regardless of how well it can be measured. Such criticisms need careful consideration before a major commitment to the measurement of subjective indicators is undertaken by the nation.

The title of a recent volume, *The Human Meaning of Social Change* (Campbell and Converse, 1972), which reviews much of the work on subjective indicators, is perhaps the most succinct statement of the justification for such indicators. Objective indicators such as the gross national product, the unemployment rate, the price index, number of housing starts, high school graduations, and birth and death rates are well known and useful in understanding the diversity of national life and changes that are taking place within it. However, taken by themselves, such indicators are colorless—only when human meanings are attached to them do they become important. Although it is often assumed that the human meaning of an objective indicator is self-evident and that a consensus exists within society as to what constitutes a desirable level of change, there are many instances in which the human meaning attached to objective indicators is not obvious. Only recently has the axiom that "a constantly rising gross national product is good" been seriously challenged. Perhaps most poignant is the quoted statement of the late Robert Kennedy (Ross, 1968: 351):

> We cannot measure national spirit by the Dow Jones average or national achievement by the gross national product. For the gross national product includes our pollution and advertising for cigarettes, and ambulances to clear our highways of carnage. It counts special locks for our doors and jails for the people who break them. The gross national product includes the destruction of the redwoods, and the death of Lake Superior. It grows with the production of napalm and nuclear warheads.

This theme has now become a political cliche, but it raises the question of how many objective indicators in which we place stock should be challenged in a similar manner. What is accepted as good or bad by those who do the measuring or by those who use the indicators to make policies may appear different to those segments of the population whose lives are affected by such policy decisions. Moreover, even if there is consensus as to what is desirable or undesirable, this consensus may at times be based on universal ignorance of the actual impact of social changes on the quality of life of people. Only when subjective indicators of the human meaning of social change are instituted and collected over time can we as a society begin to have confidence in the usefulness of objective indicators.

Subjective indicators are needed to supplement objective indicators for the obvious, but often overlooked, reason that an individual's satisfaction with any set of circumstances is dependent, not only on those circumstances as viewed objectively, but on a whole set of values, attitudes, and expectations that he brings into the situation. As an example, satisfaction with a meal depends not only on such objective characteristics of the food as its nutritive value and its temperature, but also on how hungry the individual is, his attitudes toward the particular foods, and his expectations, given the prices of the items on the menu.

At least two stages can be conceptualized as intervening between any aspect of a person's environment and his evaluation of that aspect, and at both stages the characteristics of the person must be considered. The first intervening stage is the perception by the individual of his environment. Discrepancies between reality and perception often occur, and such discrepancies can be investigated in relation to traits of the perceiver.

The second intervening stage between an objective situation and its evaluation by an individual can be labelled as the fit between the situation, as perceived by the individual, and the standard against which the individual measures that perception. The concept of a standard is undoubtedly a complex one, and is probably multiply determined and perhaps situation specific. Determinants might include such concepts as needs and values, expectation levels and aspirations.

To move from the abstract to a specific example, an individual's evaluation of his standard of living depends on a complex process, one that almost certainly depends on some implicit or explicit comparison. Objective measures of income and need are insufficient to explain satisfaction with income. In a paper by Easterlin (in press), data from cross-national studies are summarized, and the conclusion is drawn that life satisfaction as expressed by respondents within any particular nation is related to income, but that differences in average satisfaction levels across nations are unrelated to differences in mean incomes within those nations. This can be interpreted as evidence that evaluation of one's standard of living depends on a comparison of the standard of living of a reference group which is primarily national in scope. As Cantril (1965) illustrated by quotations from respondents to a cross-national study of life satisfaction, the best possible life as imagined by residents of different nations can be strikingly diverse.

Another example of the influence of characteristics of an individual on how he evaluates a particular situation comes from Campbell's (1971) study of satisfaction with various city services, housing, job, and other life aspects. He compared satisfaction levels of black and white respondents in 15 cities in the United States, and found that the blacks generally expressed considerably less satisfaction with their situations than did the whites. This is hardly surprising, given the objective situation of black people in the United States. However, Campbell found that the discrepancies persisted even when he equated black and white respondents on income and education. Such discrepancies can be interpreted as reflecting different attitudes and expectations, as well as real differences in the objective situation. Campbell (1971: 105) expresses this thought as follows:

> Our evidence is not conclusive but it raises the question of whether the major source of discontent and protest among urban Negroes is primarily their below-average income, occupation, and housing, or is instead the pattern of exclusion, subordination, and denigration which white society has traditionally assigned them.

In sum, we can see that the objective characteristics of a person's situation cannot necessarily be equated with how he feels about that situation. It would appear, therefore, that subjective indicators of life quality are quite distinct from the more traditional objective indicators. *The implication, however, is not that either objective or subjective indicators are better or more useful than the other. Rather, there is urgent need for both kinds of indicators; each type takes on depth of meaning as it can be related to the other.* By themselves, objective indicators are often misleading and will remain so until indicators of the human meaning attached to them are obtained. Likewise, by themselves, subjective indicators are insufficient as guides to policy. In some circumstances, they might be used to justify preservation of the status quo, because the population being questioned is unaware of alternatives to what may be considered intolerable conditions by outside observers. When it is possible to bring to bear objective indicators on the interpretation of subjective indicators, the policy implication may be the need for an educational effort to raise the aspirations of a population (e.g., about its physical fitness, or the purity of its water, or the quality of city services).

The actual usefulness of the concept of satisfaction with community as a subjective social indicator will necessarily remain an open question until considerably more methodological work on its measurement, and experience with its relevance to policy decisions, have been accumulated. Until more is known about its reliability (i.e., the degree to which it corresponds to the concept it was intended to measure), little confidence can be placed in an indicator of community satisfaction. Confidence in the relevance of such indicators to policy decisions will probably increase gradually as the utility of using such indicators is discerned in various situations.

Community Satisfaction and the Quality of Life

Apart from its conceptualization as an important social indicator, community satisfaction can be seen as a component of the broader concept of the quality of life. One way in which quality of life has been conceptualized is as a composite of the quality of various aspects of life experiences. Assuming that adequate measures of gratification and dissatisfaction derived from life domains such as work, marriage, health, financial situations, and friendships can be developed, it may be meaningful to go one step further, that is, to combine these components into an overall measure of the quality of life. The relationships of these components to one another, and how they can be meaningfully combined, remain topics of speculative but increasingly empirical study.

If the concept of life satisfaction is a meaningful and useful one, the relation of satisfaction with community to measures of life satisfaction would be of considerable interest and would constitute another important reason to study community satisfaction. In comparison with many other aspects of life experience, the community and its component parts are subject to potential influence by policy makers. To the extent that a person's satisfaction with his community can influence his satisfaction with more private spheres of his life, or his satisfaction with his life in general, the importance of measures of community satisfaction as social indicators is multiplied.

CONCEPTUAL MODEL

In the first part of this paper we have discussed some of the past research on community satisfaction and have presented a rationale for continued investigation of people's responses to their community and its component parts. We now present a conceptual model within which future investigations of people's satisfaction with their residential environments can take place. The model is not a highly theoretical one that introduces a plethora of unmeasurable concepts, and it goes considerably beyond much of the work on community satisfaction

that has heretofore been presented. Furthermore, it provides a conceptual framework within which our own data can be discussed.

The basic purpose of the model is to suggest the manner in which objective
attributes of the environment are linked to subjective experiences of people in
that environment. Various levels of subjective experience are included in the
model; these levels differ in the directness of their assumed association with the
objective environment. One level of experience is presented as being directly
linked to the environment, although it is influenced by other factors as well, so
that even at this level a perfect relationship between objective and subjective
measures is not expected. Other levels of the subjective experience, in particular
the satisfaction measures, are indicated in the model as being indirectly linked to
environmental attributes. Furthermore, additional factors such as personal
characteristics are shown to influence the subjective experiences. Therefore, the
relationship of the indirect levels of experience to objective attributes are
expected to be weak. To ignore the indirectness of the relationship between
objective attributes and satisfaction would be to risk the misinterpretation that
objective attributes of people's environments are almost irrelevant to their
experience of those environments. It is the intention of the model to make
explicit the linkages between objective attributes and satisfaction measures, and
in this manner to minimize the risk of misinterpretation.

Elements of the Model

Figure 7.1 shows the basic elements of the conceptual model. Satisfaction
with an environment as expressed by an individual is seen as dependent on his
evaluations or assessments of several attributes of that environment. Which
attributes are most relevant to satisfaction is an empirical question. For the community environment, it might include city services (such as fire and police
protection), population composition and population density, the amount of
open space, the responsiveness of local government officials to citizen complaints, or the kinds and amounts of citizen involvement in governance.

How a person assesses a particular attribute of his environment is considered
to be dependent on two things: how he perceives that attribute and the standard
against which he judges that attribute. The concept of a standard or reference
level is left rather vague at this time since little data are available to clarify it.
Alternative concepts that may be equivalent to or components of such a
standard include: expectation levels (i.e., what a person expected to be true
about the environment before he moved there, or before he had any experience
with which to evaluate it on a particular dimension); aspiration levels (i.e., what
a person thinks could, or should, be true of the place in which he now lives, or
of the type of community in which he hopes eventually to live); equity levels
(i.e., what a person thinks should be true of his community, given how much he
pays in local taxes; or how he should be treated in the community relative to
others, given their relative contributions); reference group levels (i.e., what the
person believes to be true of the communities in which others with whom he

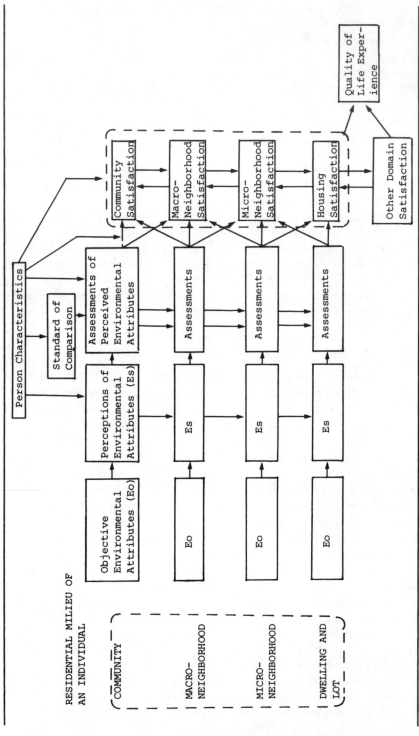

Figure 7.1: Elaborated model of environmental satisfaction

identifies live—his friends, his family, others of his income, race, occupation, etc.); needs (i.e., how much of a particular commodity does a person need—how much police protection to be reasonably safe, the frequency of garbage collection in order to avoid unsightly or unsafe conditions); and values (i.e., how does a condition or status on a dimension conform to a person's basic values, such as his values for freedom, equality, and so on). This list, which could be lengthened, emphasizes the fact that the notion of a reference level or standard is a complex one.

To reiterate, the model presents the notion that a person's evaluation of a particular environmental characteristic or attribute depends upon his perception of that attribute in relation to internal standards against which he measures that perception. Moving back one step in the model, a person's perception of any environmental attribute is shown as dependent on, but distinct from, the objective environment. We believe that the way in which a person perceives the environment is not necessarily equivalent to the environment as it actually is; the possibility of bias or inaccuracy in perception is recognized explicitly. This link may be of considerable interest not only to psychologists concerned with the dynamics of such distortions, but also to environmentalists and social planners concerned with the extent to which characteristics of the environment are inaccurately perceived.

The objective environment that is referred to in the model could be defined in physical, social, organizational, economic, or fiscal terms. One problem that is not included explicitly in the model, but which nonetheless must be recognized as we move from theorizing to data collection and analysis, is that any measure of the objective environment is inevitably fallible and to a degree unreliable.[1] In particular, when we attempt to match objective indicators with subjective experiences, we are often forced into the development of new techniques for measuring the objective environment in such a way that these measures can be directly linked to individual respondents in a sample survey study.

A final element in the model is a set of variables known as "Person Characteristics." This is a general term that is meant to include all characteristics and experiences of the individual that influence his perceptions and evaluations. With respect to perceptions, the model suggests that biases and inaccuracies in perception may be systematically related to person characteristics. For instance, persons of different ages, races, or incomes may have diverse perceptions of the police protection or the recreational facilities provided by the same community. Person characteristics can also influence an assessment of the physical or social environment or of a component of those environments. For example, people might be characterized by a general pessimism or optimism, or by a particular response style (e.g., a tendency to report what is thought to be a socially acceptable evaluation).

Finally, person characteristics can have an effect on an individual's standards of comparison. In addition to socioeconomic characteristics such as age, race, and income, background characteristics, including the kinds of environments a person has experienced and his perceptions of presently available alternative environments, may determine the standards against which perceptions are evaluated.[2]

Multiple Environmental Satisfaction

The model presented in Figure 7.1 includes the basic elements by which we suggest that subjective experiences are linked to environmental characteristics. Implicit in the model is the notion that satisfaction with one's environment is related to the assessments and perceptions of *many* attributes of that environment. At the present time, we do not know whether these assessments and perceptions are additive or interactive; we hope our investigations will provide us with answers. Nor do we know how the different levels of the environment interact with one another. While the principal environment under consideration is the community, it is difficult to discuss it without reference to attributes of the neighborhood and dwelling. This was shown in the research reviewed earlier in the paper. Figure 7.1 also presents a more complete model of environmental satisfaction which includes not only the community but also the neighborhood and the individual dwelling. The neighborhood is presented under two headings: macro-neighborhood, by which is meant an area often defined by grade-school districts or by major thoroughfares; and the micro-neighborhood, by which is meant the immediate cluster of perhaps six or so adjacent houses. These environments constitute a set of concepts which comprise the residential milieu of an individual.

The model suggests that community satisfaction has multiple determinants, some of which are associated with other levels of the environment. In other words, there is the expectation that the attributes that determine satisfaction with any level of the residential environment may overlap those that determine satisfaction with another level. In particular, many of the attributes relevant to satisfaction with community are also expected to be relevant to satisfaction with the macro-neighborhood. For example, evaluation of city services may be one factor that influences satisfaction with the macro-neighborhood as well as satisfaction with the city.

Finally, the model shows that the different residential environments represent only one of a set of interacting domains which together comprise the total life space. Other domains include those of family life and marriage, occupation, physical health, financial status, and education. We hope to clarify the extent to which adjustment in each of these aspects of the individual's life influences his adjustment in the remaining aspects. For example, we are interested in the question of the extent to which satisfaction with one's community is reflected in satisfaction with his family life. Furthermore, as the model suggests, we are interested in exploring the concept of the quality of life experience. To the extent such a concept seems to warrant further attention, we will be interested in determining the relative importance of different domains to this overall satisfaction. In particular, we will be very interested in the extent to which satisfaction with one's residential environment contributes to his satisfaction with his life as a whole.

SOME EMPIRICAL DATA

In an attempt to amplify the conceptual model dealing with environmental satisfaction, this part of the paper presents an analysis of data from three independent studies recently conducted at the Survey Research Center. While varying extensively in their objectives, the studies are bound together by their mutual efforts to understand how people respond to the environments in which they live. Prior to discussing the data on satisfaction with each type of environment, an overview will be presented of the three studies from which the data derive.

Sources of Data

The earliest of the studies focused on people's attitudes and behavioral responses to residential environments subject to varying degrees of planning (Lansing, Marans, and Zehner, 1970). In this study of planned communities, data were collected in 1969 by personal interviews with over 1,200 residents in ten residential environments. These environments included completely self-contained new towns, redeveloped central city neighborhoods, and sections of incorporated suburban communities. Since a fundamental objective of the study was to see if people who live in highly planned residential communities respond differently to their place of residence than residents of less planned environments, efforts were made to control the sample population along several socio-economic dimensions. These controls to a large extent determined the selection of sample communities whose residents were atypical of the national population. For the most part, they had very high family incomes, were relatively young, and had high levels of educational attainment.

In addition to identifying behavioral patterns with respect to transportation, recreation and social interaction, the Planned Communities study investigated people's attitudes toward their communities and the micro-neighborhoods within which they lived. The study identified respondents' levels of satisfaction with each environment and salient components of these satisfactions. The specific findings will be discussed below within the context of the model.

The second study for which data are available is currently under way at the Survey Research Center and is scheduled for completion in the fall of 1973. This study of the quality of American life by Campbell, Converse, and Rodgers is concerned with satisfaction with several domains of life satisfaction, and is based on a 1971 survey of a national sample of the population of the United States. More than 2,100 respondents were asked a series of questions dealing with their housing, their macro-neighborhood, and community, as well as with their work, health, income, friendships, family life, and other domains of life. In the domains of the community and neighborhood, respondents were asked to evaluate certain services normally provided by the local government (including schools, parks, streets, and police protection) and other characteristics such as convenience of location, how well kept up the neighboring houses are, and safety in walking outside at night. Preliminary findings from this study will be discussed below.

Finally, data on people's responses to their micro-neighborhoods are available as part of a study of participation in outdoor recreation and factors influencing it (Mandell and Marans, 1972). Data were collected in 1971 from approximately 1,300 respondents in a national sample of households. Besides reporting the extent of their involvement in outdoor activities, people were asked to describe their micro-neighborhoods along dimensions similar to those used in the planned-communities study. Assessments of additional micro-neighborhood attributes considered to be potentially stressful were also made by respondents. The relations between these assessments and overall neighborhood satisfaction are presented below.

Findings on Community Satisfaction

The focal point of our data is the concept of community satisfaction, as expressed by the respondents in two of the studies just described. In the conceptual model (see Figure 7.1), satisfaction with community is viewed as an integrative function of component assessments, which in turn are functions of objective characteristics of the community and of the individual's frame of reference. Community satisfaction also is related to satisfaction with other aspects of the individual's life, particularly with his neighborhood and housing environment, but also with other life domains such as his family life and his job. Finally, community satisfaction and satisfaction with other aspects of life are viewed as components of a global concept labelled the "quality of life experience."

Given the central position of satisfaction with the residential environment indicated by our model, it seems appropriate to begin our consideration of data by examining the levels of satisfaction and dissatisfaction with community which were expressed by people in a national sample. In the Quality of Life Study, respondents were asked to report how satisfied they were with the town or city (or county, if in a rural area) in which they lived.[3] As shown in Table 7.1, over a third (38 percent) of the respondents reported that they were

Table 7.1: Level of Community Satisfaction: Percentage Distribution of Respondents in the Quality of Life Study

Respondents were:	Percent
(1) Completely satisfied	38
(2)	22
(3)	15
(4) Neutral	16
(5)	5
(6)	2
(7) Completely dissatisfied	2
Total	100
Number of Respondents	2,153

"completely satisfied" with the community in which they lived, while fewer than one out of ten (9 percent) reported that they were dissatisfied to some degree. As in the studies reported earlier, we found that most people (three out of four) were satisfied with their community as a place to live. However, not all subgroups of the population gave such favorable ratings. Before discussing levels of satisfaction for different subgroups, the question of how people assess various community attributes will be considered.

In the Quality of Life Study, respondents were asked to evaluate nine attributes of their local communities, including services provided by the local government, local taxes, and the climate. Our primary interest in these assessments at this point is how they relate to overall community satisfaction. However, the distributions of responses for these items are also of interest. Table 7.2 shows, for example, that the public service which people were most likely to rate highly was "garbage collection," while the service they were most likely to evaluate negatively was "parks and playgrounds" for children.

Taken one at a time, these assessments are related positively to the overall satisfaction with community although in some instances the relationships are weak. The first column of Table 7.3 shows that among the attributes rated by people, evaluation of public schools was most strongly related to community satisfaction.

Table 7.3 also presents results of considering the entire set of nine assessments in predicting community satisfaction.[4] Together, the nine assessments explain 19 percent of the variation in responses to the community satisfaction question; that is, if we know how a respondent evaluated each of the nine aspects of his community, we reduce the uncertainty about how he evaluated his community by 19 percent.[5] Finally, Table 7.3 presents, for each assessment, beta coefficients reflecting the relative importance of each item in predicting community satisfaction. The ranking by importance is similar to the ranking by decreasing correlation.

The considerable degree of uncertainty in predicting community satisfaction from a set of specific assessments can partially be explained by the fact that we are using measures of satisfaction and assessments that are quite imperfect; that is, the measures are unreliable. Unreliability arises from several sources. For example, questions may be interpreted to mean slightly different things to different respondents—some may interpret their community as encompassing the entire metropolitan area of a large city while others may think only of the central city. Assessments of a service, such as police protection, may depend on some particular events that occurred recently; or the respondent's neighbor may answer with another set of events in mind. Such sources of unreliability limit the ability to measure the concepts which the researcher is trying to investigate and thus the precision with which he can assess the relationship among such concepts. This is especially true in studies of the type reported here in which the breadth of concern limits the number of questions that can be used to measure any particular concept.

Table 7.2: Assessments of Specific Community Attributes: Percentage Distribution of Respondents in the Quality of Life Study

Attributes[a]	Evaluated as:						
	Very Good	Fairly Good	Neither Good Nor Bad	Not Very Good	Not Good At All	Total	Number of Respondents
Garbage collection[b]	56	28	5	6	5	100	1,703
Public schools	38	42	6	8	6	100	1,678
Police-community relations	36	43	9	9	3	100	1,904
Climate[c]	36	42	11	8	3	100	2,152
Police protection	33	40	11	10	6	100	2,007
Parks and play-grounds[b]	30	43	7	14	6	100	1,476
Public transpor-tation[d]	30	38	10	15	7	100	884
Streets and roads	22	51	7	15	5	100	2,152
	Very Low	Low	Moderate	High	Very High		
Local taxes[e]	1	4	36	39	20	100	1,921

a. Respondents were asked to evaluate the way streets and roads were kept up, the quality of public schools, garbage collection, parks and playgrounds, police protection, police-community relations and public transportation in their neighborhood or in the area "around here."
b. Residents in rural areas were not asked questions about neighborhood garbage collection and parks and playgrounds.
c. The question was: "Another way people judge a place to live is what the weather throughout the year is like — as far as you are concerned, how good is the climate here?"
d. If no local public transportation was available respondents were not asked to make this evaluation.
e. The question was: "Would you say that the local taxes in (NAME CITY OR COUNTY) are very low, low, moderate, high or very high?"

Table 7.3: Multiple Classification Analysis of 2,153 Respondents in the Quality of Life Study: Multivariate Analysis of Community Satisfaction Using Ratings of Specific Community Attributes

Attributes	Correlation Ratio	Beta Coefficient
Public schools	0.27	0.17
Climate	0.23	0.17
Streets and roads	0.22	0.13
Parks and playgrounds	0.19	0.13
Police-community relations	0.25	0.12
Local taxes	0.17	0.10
Garbage collection	0.18	0.08
Public transportation	0.15	0.08
Police protection	0.21	0.07
Adjusted Multiple R^2 (explained variance)		19%

Besides the unreliability of the measures, other factors contribute to the uncertainty in predicting community satisfaction from assessments of specific community attributes. There are many attributes which the respondents were not asked to assess, such as fire protection, quality of stores, fairness of public officials, and the amount of air and water pollution. While an attempt was made to ask about attributes that seemed to concern people in preliminary investigations, many respondents might have felt that the most important community attributes, as far as their own satisfaction was concerned, had been overlooked. Furthermore, within the set of attributes that were included, considerable variation undoubtedly exists among respondents as to the importance of each. Perceived low quality of public schools might make a community completely unsatisfactory as a place to live for parents of school age children, but for unmarried respondents, a low quality of public schools may be of little or no concern.

The distribution of responses to the question discussed earlier on community satisfaction takes on more meaning as we consider differential responses of various population subgroups. Our model suggests that characteristics of the population can influence levels of satisfaction with community and with attributes of that community. As a means of amplifying our understanding of community satisfaction and as a prelude to testing relationships implied by the model, the distribution of community satisfaction responses for different population subgroups is shown in Table 7.4.

The first panel presents the data for different racial groups, and shows that white respondents were more satisfied with their communities than black respondents. In fact, blacks were nearly twice as likely to report being neutral about or dissatisfied with their communities as are whites. This is not a surprising finding given the conditions of our society at the time these data were collected in the summer of 1971.

The second panel of Table 7.4 shows the distribution of community satisfaction at different levels of reported family income for the year. There is not a strong relationship, but it is clear that those with the lowest income levels (below $5,000) were, if anything, more likely than those with higher incomes to express complete satisfaction with their communities (44 percent vs. 36 percent).[6] A similar pattern is seen in the third item, where community satisfaction was associated with low educational attainment. Indeed, among those with only a grammar school education, over half (54 percent) said that they were completely satisfied.

The inverse relationship between education and satisfaction in part reflects differences in age cohorts, since older respondents tend to have less education than younger respondents. The clear relationship between respondent age and community satisfaction is shown in the fourth item of Table 7.4. Only one in five (20 percent) of the respondents aged 18 to 24 said that they are completely satisfied, as compared to over half (56 percent) of those aged 65 or older.

A variable that is related to age is that of the life cycle. The fifth item of Table 7.4 shows that respondents who were most likely to express as much or

Table 7.4: Percentage Distribution of Respondents in the Quality of Life Study: Satisfaction with Community Expressed by Different Subgroups

| | Respondents were: | | | | |
Characteristics	Completely Satisfied (percent)	Satisfied (percent)	Neutral or Dissatisfied (percent)	Total	Number of Respondents
Race					
White	39	38	23	100	1,874
Black	29	28	43	100	219
Other	18	45	37	100	53
Family Income					
Less than $3,000	44	32	24	100	291
$3,000-4,999	44	29	27	100	287
$5,000-6,999	32	36	32	100	266
$7,000-9,999	37	38	25	100	364
$10,000-11,999	35	42	23	100	271
$12,000-16,999	37	42	21	100	320
$17,000- or more	38	45	17	100	264
Educational attainment					
Eighth grade or less	54	26	20	100	468
Some High School, no diploma	41	29	30	100	395
High School diploma	37	38	25	100	708
Some college, no degree	23	49	28	100	333
College degree(s)	24	60	16	100	238
Age					
18-24	20	48	32	100	331
25-44	30	42	28	100	810
45-64	47	31	22	100	649
65 or older	56	29	15	100	360
Family Life Cycle					
Single, age 18-29	16	46	38	100	167
Single, age 30 or older	33	34	33	100	93
Married, no children; age 18-29	14	61	25	100	95
Married, no children; age 30 or older	46	31	23	100	105
Married, youngest child age 5 or younger	30	43	27	100	434
Married, youngest child aged 6-17	39	38	23	100	410
Married, youngest child aged 18 or older	48	33	19	100	402
Separated or divorced	34	34	32	100	178
Widowed	62	23	15	100	255
Job Status					
Work for pay	34	42	24	100	1,230
Housewife	46	29	25	100	607
Retired	53	30	17	100	187

Table 7.4 (Continued)

	Respondents were:				
Characteristics	Completely Satisfied (percent)	Satisfied (percent)	Neutral or Dissatisfied (percent)	Total	Number of Respondents
Job Status (continued)					
Student	12	52	36	100	54
Unemployed, other	25	33	42	100	75
Length of Residence in Area					
Less than 2 years	29	47	24	100	293
2-7.9 years	28	46	26	100	422
8-19.9 years	35	38	27	100	526
20-39.9 years	40	35	25	100	540
40 years or more	53	27	20	100	407

more dissatisfaction than satisfaction were young single people. Equally unlikely to express complete satisfaction, but less likely to express dissatisfaction, were young married respondents with no children. Satisfaction was expressed more frequently by people at later stages in the life cycle. Those who were married and had older children and those who had never had children though over thirty years old expressed high levels of community satisfaction. The group most likely to express complete satisfaction was that of the widowed respondents. These people tend to be older, and their distribution can be viewed as the continuation of the trend seen through the earlier stages of married people.[7]

Workers, housewives, and retired people also tended to be more satisfied with their communities than students and the unemployed. Finally, the level of satisfaction was greater among those who had lived longer in an area.

In sum, white respondents with little education and a family income under $5,000, who had lived in one area for a long time were most likely to express complete satisfaction with the communities in which they resided. Moreover, levels of satisfaction tended to increase with increasing age or, more appropriately, with the later stages of the life cycle. In contrast, a typical dissatisfied respondent would be a young single person who is black and who is a high school dropout earning about $6,000 a year.

In our conceptual model we suggested that "Person Characteristics" influence community satisfaction both directly and indirectly, the latter through assessments of particular community attributes. At the same time, the model implies that person characteristics may modify the relationship between these assessments and overall community satisfaction.

In our preceding discussion of person characteristics, the respondents' stage in the life cycle, race, educational attainment, and job status appeared to be most strongly related to community satisfaction responses. The measure of the strength of these relationships, as represented by the correlation ratio, is shown in the first column of Table 7.5.[8] As seen by the relatively high ratio (0.22), the life-cycle variable is most strongly related to community satisfaction. When

Table 7.5: Multiple Classification Analysis on 2,153 Respondents in the Quality of Life Study: Multivariate Analysis of Community Satisfaction Using Six Person Characteristics

Person Characteristics	Correlation Ratio	Beta Coefficient
Family life cycle	.22	.16
Race	.15	.13
Educational attainment	.15	.12
Family income	.09	.09
Job status	.15	.06
Length of residence	.12	.05
Adjusted Multiple R^2 (explained variance)		7%

the six person characteristics are considered simultaneously with respect to community satisfaction, life cycle retains its role as the most important predictor. Together, these six characteristics explain only 7 percent of the variation in community satisfaction responses. It may be recalled that the set of assessments of community attributes accounted for 19 percent of the variance. Later, we shall see how much variance can be accounted for when both sets of are used to predict community satisfaction.

The model also indicates that relationships exist between person characteristics and assessments of specific attributes of the community. Space does not permit us to report these relationships, which tend to be similar in magnitude to the relationships between person characteristics and overall community satisfaction. It is possible that the relationship between person characteristics and community satisfaction can be explained by treating attribute assessments as intervening variables. For example, life cycle groups differ in their assessments of city services and since these assessments are related to satisfaction Age is also related to satisfaction. Another possibility is that life cycle and other person characteristics are directly related to community satisfaction.

To distinguish between these possibilities, a multivariate analysis predicting community satisfaction from both sets of variables (assessments and person characteristics) was considered. The critical test is the comparison between the total variance explained by both sets of variables and that previously explained by just the set of assessments. As seen in Table 7.6, the two sets together explain 21 percent of the variance in community satisfaction, as compared to 18 percent of the variance explained by only the assessments of community attributes.

The results of these analyses can be interpreted in different ways. On one hand, it suggests that person characteristics explain an additional 3 percent of the variance above that which can be explained by the assessment variables alone. Person characteristics, therefore, do have some effect on community satisfaction which is independent of the assessments, or at least the set of assessments measured in the quality of life study. On the other hand, the result indicates a considerable overlap in the explanatory power of the two sets of variables. If they were completely independent, the explanatory power of each set taken separately (18 percent and 7 percent) would yield a total explanatory power of 25 percent—considerably more than the actual combined explanatory power. Thus, it is apparent that the relationship between person characteristics and community satisfaction is mediated, to a large extent, by the influence of the person characteristics on assessments of community services and attributes. We therefore can regard the arrow directly linking person characteristics and community satisfaction as a weak one at best.[9]

Finally, the model shows another arrow which suggests the possibility of person characteristics influencing the relationship between attribute assessments and overall community satisfaction. A careful search for such interactions in our data failed to reveal any such relations.[10]

To summarize, the quality of life data indicate that satisfaction with community is partially based on assessments of various attributes of the community, in particular the public schools, police-community relations, the local taxes, and the climate. It also appears that population subgroup differences in community satisfaction responses are mediated to a large extent by differences in how these subgroups assess these community attributes.

As suggested by the model and confirmed by the above data, a primary set of predictors of community satisfaction are assessments of various characteristics or attributes of the community. Such assessments, in turn, are partially a function of a set of variables labeled "Person Characteristics." The model also indicates that such evaluations depend on attributes of the community as perceived by the respondent, or, more precisely, the discrepancy between such perceptions and the individual's standard of comparison. The individual's perceptions of community attributes, in turn, are shown as being influenced by the attributes themselves. These attributes or characteristics of the community are referred to in the model as objective environmental attributes and are measured by techniques independent of the respondent.

Data relevant to this portion of the model are sketchy at the present time although greater efforts to devise objective measures are envisioned in the near future. However, some data are available that are at least suggestive and can be reported. In the Quality of Life Study, the only presently available objective datum about the community in which respondents reside is the population size of that community.[11] Table 7.7 shows that substantial differences in satisfaction levels were expressed by residents living in communities of different sizes. Whereas only one out of every five residents in the central cities of the twelve largest SMSAs said they were completely satisfied with their community as a place to live, nearly half of all respondents in rural areas expressed complete satisfaction. Indeed, the proportion of respondents who were neutral about their communities or dissatisfied with them increased for communities as their size classification increased.

Furthermore, size of community of residence has been shown to be related to a number of community characteristics, including dwelling unit density (Marans and Mandell, 1972). While we are missing explicit links, it is reasonable to assume that in the Quality of Life Study, the size of the community in which

Table 7.6: Multiple Classification Analysis on 2,153 Respondents in the Quality of Life Study: Variance Explained Using Assessments of Community Attributes and Personal Characteristics as Sets of Variables

Assessments/Characteristics	Correlation Ratio	Beta Coefficient (Ranking of Importance)		
		Assessments Only	Characteristics Only	Assessments and Personal Characteristics
Assessments of Community Attributes				
Streets and roads	0.22	0.13 (4)		0.11 (4)
Public schools	0.27	0.18 (1)		0.18 (1)
Parks and playgrounds	0.19	0.11 (5)		0.09 (8)
Police-community relations	0.25	0.14 (3)		0.13 (3)
Climate	0.23	0.18 (1)		0.16 (2)
Local taxes	0.17	0.11 (5)		0.11 (4)
Personal Characteristics				
Length of residence in area	0.12		0.05 (6)	0.04 (12)
Educational level	0.15		0.12 (9)	0.11 (4)
Job status	0.15		0.06 (5)	0.05 (11)
Family income	0.09		0.09 (4)	0.08 (9)
Race	0.15		0.13 (2)	0.06 (10)
Life cycle	0.22		0.16 (1)	0.11 (4)
Adjusted Multiple R^2 (explained variance)		18%	7%	21%

the respondents reside is also related to some of the attributes of those communities that the respondents were asked to assess. We also expected that the size of community would be related to the assessments of some or all of these attributes.

As seen in Table 7.8, this expectation was confirmed. In particular, residents of the largest cities were less likely to evaluate characteristics of their communities in a favorable manner compared to residents of communities of smaller size. For all attributes except public transportation, a smaller proportion of central city residents than of residents of other sized communities evaluated them as "very good." [12] Large city residents also were more likely than others to think that they were paying too much for what they get. Table 7.8 shows that only one in six (17 percent) large city residents considered their local taxes to be moderate or low, compared to four in ten (41 percent) of the sample as a whole.

Despite the substantial differences in assessments of community attributes given by residents of communities of different size, it is not obvious that these differences should be attributed to objective differences in the characteristics of such places. Earlier investigations have indicated that residents in different sized communities differ in background characteristics, including race, life cycle stages, and educational attainment. It is possible to argue that differences in these background characteristics, which were shown above to be related to community satisfaction, explain the association between size of place and the assessments.[13] We can examine the data to see how much variation in assessments can be explained by size of place over and above what can be explained by person characteristics. For brevity, an assessment of a single attribute, that of the public schools, is considered. As shown at the bottom of the second column of Table 7.9, size of place by itself explains 7 percent of the variation in respondents' assessments of public schools. When a set of size-selected person characteristics is considered, only 2 percent of the variation is accounted for. Combined, the seven variables explain 8 percent of the variation in people's assessments of their public schools. Thus it is clear, at least for this assessment, that the predictive power of size of place cannot be explained by knowing differences in respondent family life cycle, race, and other person characteristics.

In our model, we suggest that attributes of the community environment are related to perceptions of those attributes which in turn are related through the attribute assessments to community satisfaction. No direct linkage between objective attributes of the community environment and community satisfaction is suggested. Taking size of place as a surrogate for measures of more specific attributes such as population density, we can examine the quality of life data for evidence concerning these indirect links.

As we indicated earlier, size of place of residence is related to community satisfaction. The correlation ratio is 0.24, shown in the first column of Table 7.10. A fundamental question is whether this relationship is dependent upon assessments of community attributes or if size of place has an effect on satisfaction which is independent of these assessments. In the third column of

Table 7.7: Percentage Distributions of Respondents in the Quality of Life Study: Level of Community Satisfaction for People in Communities of Different Sizes

Size of Community[a]	Respondents were:				
	Completely Satisfied (percent)	Satisfied (percent)	Neutral or Dissatisfied (percent)	Total	Number of Respondents
Central cities	20	38	42	100	226
Large cities	29	32	39	100	239
Suburbs	36	41	23	100	455
Small cities and towns	40	40	20	100	683
Rural areas	48	34	18	100	550

a. Communities were categorized by the degree to which they were urbanized, based on 1960 census data. The central cities are those of the 12 largest SMSAs. Large cities are other cities over 100,000 population. Suburbs are places with a population of less than 100,000 in the 12 largest SMSAs and rural places of less than 2,500 in all SMSAs. Small towns and cities are places with a population between 2,500 and 100,000 which are not in the 12 largest SMSAs while rural areas contain populations of less than 2,500 and are not situated in an SMSA.

Table 7.8: Proportion of Respondents in the Quality of Life Study Who Gave Very Good Evaluations: Residents' Evaluation of Specific Community Attributes in Communities of Different Sizes

Attributes	Size of Community[a]					All Commu-nities	Number of Respond-ents[b]
	Central Cities	Large Cities	Suburbs	Small Cities and Towns	Rural Areas		
Garbage collection	38	50	58	62	56	56	1,703
Local taxes[c]	17	29	46	44	49	41	1,921
Public schools	17	25	41	47	36	38	1,678
Police-community relations	27	30	43	38	33	36	1,904
Climate	24	40	29	39	41	36	2,152
Police protection	26	30	40	39	25	33	2,007
Parks and playgrounds	21	28	31	33	33	30	1,476
Public transpor-tation	42	38	19	27	12	30	884
Streets and roads	10	17	27	24	21	22	2,152

a. Communities were categorized by the degree to which they were urbanized based on 1960 census data. The central cities are those of the 12 largest SMSAs. Large cities are other cities over 100,000 population. Suburbs are places with a population of less than 100,000 in the 12 largest SMSAs and rural places of less than 2,500 in all SMSAs. Small towns and cities are places with a population between 2,500 and 100,000 which are not in the 12 largest SMSAs while rural areas contain populations of less than 2,500 and are not situated in an SMSA.
b. Respondents for whom a service was not available are not included in the base upon which the indicated proportions are calculated.
c. Proportions refer to those respondents who say local taxes are low or moderate.

Table 7.9: Multiple Classification Analysis on 1,678 Respondents in the Quality of Life Study: Multivariate Analysis of Assessments of Public Schools Using Size of Place and Selected Person Characteristics

	Corre-lation Ratio	Beta Coefficients (Ranking of Importance)		
		Size of Place Only	Person Char-acteristics Only	Size of Place Person Char-acteristics
Size of Place	0.27	a		0.26 (1)
Person Characteristics				
Family life cycle	0.14		0.12 (1)	0.11 (2)
Race	0.12		0.11 (2)	0.02 (7)
Educational attainment	0.06		0.04 (6)	0.03 (6)
Family income	0.08		0.07 (4)	0.06 (4)
Job status	0.10		0.08 (3)	0.08 (3)
Length of resident	0.06		0.05 (5)	0.05 (5)
Adjusted Multiple R^2		7%	2%	8%

a. Since the beta coefficient indicates the ranking of importance of predictors, no value is provided when only size of place is considered.

Table 7.10, the combined effects are shown when both size of place and six assessments are used in predicting to community satisfaction. The 19 percent of the variance accounted for is almost identical to that explained when only the six assessments were used in the analysis as seen in the second column. Thus, an independent effect of size of place has not been demonstrated. This is not to say that the size of the place where a person lives is not an important determinant of his level of satisfaction with his community. On the contrary, the size of place is related to the way in which residents assess various community attributes which, in turn, is related to overall community satisfaction.

Earlier, we suggested that size of place is also related to a number of person characteristics such as race and life cycle which have been shown to be related to community satisfaction. In the last column of Table 7.10, the combined effects of assessments, size of place and person characteristics are presented. Together, these three sets account for 21 percent of the variance, the same proportion accounted for when only the assessments and person characteristics were considered (see Table 7.6). This further confirms the lack of any direct (i.e., unmediated by other variables) effect of size of place of residence.

Although objective data from the Quality of Life Study are limited to a single measure which is considerably less specific than what is implied by the model, the above analysis does offer evidence in support of the model. That is, objective environmental measures influence community satisfaction only indirectly, with assessments of specific community attributes serving as mediating factors. The respondents' perceptions, another set of mediating factors between the objective environmental attributes and the respondents' evaluations of these attributes, are missing from the data and therefore cannot be appraised at this time.

Table 7.10: Multiple Classification Analysis on 2,153 Respondents in the Quality of Life Study: Multivariate Analyses of Community Satisfaction Using Assessment of Community Attributes, Size of Place, and Person Characteristics

Assessment of Community	Correlation Ratio	Beta Coefficient (Ranking of Importance)		
		Assessments Only	Assessments and Size of Place	Assessments, Size of Place and Person Characteristics
Attributes				
Public schools	0.27	0.18 (1)	0.16 (2)	0.16 (1)
Climate	0.23	0.18 (1)	0.17 (1)	0.16 (1)
Police-community relations	0.25	0.14 (3)	0.14 (3)	0.12 (3)
Streets and roads	0.22	0.13 (4)	0.12 (5)	0.11 (4)
Local taxes	0.17	0.11 (5)	0.10 (6)	0.10 (9)
Parks and playgrounds	0.19	0.11 (5)	0.09 (7)	0.08 (9)
Size of Place (Objective Attribute)	0.24		0.14 (3)	0.11 (4)
Person Characteristics				
Family life cycle	0.22			0.11 (4)
Race	0.15			0.04 (13)
Educational attainment	0.15			0.10 (7)
Family income	0.90			0.08 (9)
Job status	0.15			0.05 (11)
Length of residence	0.12			0.05 (1)
Adjusted Multiple R^2 (explained variance)		18%	19%	21%

It will be recalled that in the study of residential environments, ten communities were selected which differed in the extent to which their physical environments were planned. The extent of planning is a function of the manipulation of specific attributes of the physical environment according to accepted planning principles. For instance, the amount of open space, the density of residential development, the presence of trees and water, and the time-space distance between housing and shops, schools, swimming pools, parks, and other facilities are attributes of the environment which can be measured, observed, and assessed. They can also be varied by planners for economic, aesthetic, or other reasons.

While the Planned Communities Study did not systematically identify specific attributes in each community and sort out resident responses to them, it was possible to identify a general set of characteristics representative of planned environments and use it as a guide in selecting and classifying the communities to be studied.[14]

As part of the study, respondents were asked to indicate their current satisfaction with the area in which they lived. To give them an idea of what we had in mind, they were asked to consider an area outlined on a map which corresponded approximately to the main political or natural boundaries of the community involved.[15]

Table 7.11 shows the ten communities selected for the study, their classification according to the extent to which they were planned and respondents' ratings of them as places to live. In general, these ratings were high. More than two-thirds of the people rated their communities as "excellent" or "good." However, the proportion of residents who rated their communities "excellent" varied across the sample. For the most part, there was a tendency for high levels of planning to be associated with high overall ratings. There were

Table 7.11: Percentage Distributions of Respondents in the Planned Communities Study: Overall Ratings of Select Communities as a Place to Live

| Communities | Degree of Planning | Ratings (in percentages) | | | | | |
		Excellent	Good	Average	Below Average; Poor	Total	Number of Respondents
Reston	High	61	33	4	2	100	198
Radburn	High	54	37	7	2	100	102
Lafayette-Elmwood	High	53	39	6	2	100	102
Columbia	High	52	40	6	2	100	208
Glen Rock	Low	49	38	9	4	100	105
Crofton	Moderate	42	39	13	6	100	98
Norbeck	Low	41	44	13	2	100	97
Southfield	Low	36	49	12	3	100	108
Southwest Washington	High	26	59	10	5	100	106
Montpelier	Moderate	18	51	22	9	100	104

exceptions, however. Moderately planned Montpelier and highly planned South-west Washington received particularly low ratings from their residents.[16]

When exploring reasons underlying these relatively low ratings, respondents in Montpelier most often mentioned inadequate or poorly planned facilities, poor access to jobs and shopping, and a lack of open space or a feeling of crowd-ing. Southwest Washington residents most often mentioned the problem of crime or lack of traffic safety when asked to elaborate on their evaluations. On the other hand, residents in highly planned Reston gave the most favorable over-all ratings and attributed them to good planning, good access, the existence of trees, hills, lakes, and plenty of open space.

In reviewing these and other reasons offered freely by respondents, no clear patterns of attributes liked or disliked are associated with communities of different degrees of planning.[17] Had we been able to determine systematically residents' assessments of specific attributes, it would have been possible to analyze relations between the assessments and overall community satisfaction. Moreover, the availability of objective measures of these community attributes would have enabled us to determine how these attributes were related to people's assessments of them and, in turn, to overall satisfaction.

What is clear from the analysis conducted is that people who respond freely to their community think of numerous environmental attributes ranging from those existing in their immediate neighborhood to those beyond the confines of the communities as we defined them. The quality of schools, the safety of streets, the availability of public transportation and other public services as well as access to freeways and downtown were often mentioned by respondents. This range of responses supports the notion that people's perceptions of their residential environments vary in both scale and attribute content.

Findings on Macro-Neighborhood Satisfaction

In the Quality of Life Study, the data on satisfaction with the neighborhood appear similar to the data on satisfaction with community. Since no attempt was made to define a concept of macro-neighborhood for the respondents, they may have had quite diverse areas in mind when answering questions concerning their neighborhood. Preliminary investigations indicate that respondents generally considered a larger area than the micro-neighborhood defined by the planned communities and outdoor recreation studies. At the same time, this frame of reference was smaller than the political jurisdiction which defined the commu-nity. Therefore, we will refer to this middle level of the residential environment as the macro-neighborhood.

It was suggested above that in the Quality of Life Study, the relationship between community satisfaction and macro-neighborhood satisfaction was fairly strong.[18] Table 7.12 shows that nearly half of the respondents were "completely satisfied" with their macro-neighborhoods while less than one out of ten said they were more dissatisfied than they were satisfied. As we will see below, these high levels of satisfaction are not uniform across all segments of

Table 7.12: Percentage Distribution of Respondents in the Quality of Life Study: Level of Macro-Neighborhood Satisfactions[a]

Respondents Were:	Percent
(1) Completely satisfied	46
(2)	21
(3)	13
(4) Neutral	11
(5)	4
(6)	2
(7) Completely dissatisfied	3
Total	100
Number of Respondents	2,159

a. Respondents were handed a card with a 7-point scale and asked the following: "And what about this particular neighborhood in (NAME CITY OR COUNTY)? All things considered, how satisfied or dissatisfied are you with this neighborhood as a place to live? Which number comes closest to how satisfied or dissatisfied you feel?

the population. First, however, neighborhood attributes will be considered which are assessed by people in different ways and which are viewed as major determinants of overall satisfaction.

In the Quality of Life Study, respondents were also asked to assess five attributes of their neighborhoods—its convenience, how well neighboring houses are kept up, their neighbors, personal safety for walking outside at night, and the importance of locking their houses when out for brief periods. Each of these correspond to the box in our model labelled "Assessments of Perceived Environmental Attributes."

Before discussing how the data support the model, we can divert our attention briefly to the distributions of answers to these questions, as shown in Table 7.13. Neighborhood characteristics were evaluated rather positively by most of the respondents. There were few complaints about convenience. Only one in six (16 percent) felt that the place where they live is not "convenient enough." With respect to the condition of housing, two in five (41 percent) said that houses in the neighborhood were kept up "very well." Over half (54 percent) of the respondents said they had "very good" neighbors. More than one-fourth of all respondents (28 percent) expressed some reservations about the safety of walking outside at night, or, to interpret the same data in a more positive way, almost three-fourths of the respondents did not express any such fear, despite the widely expressed concern about rising crime statistics. At the same time, over half (56 percent) of the respondents said they felt it was "very important" to lock up their houses even when leaving them for only a brief period.

As shown in Table 7.14, the five assessments considered together predict almost one-third of the variance in macro-neighborhood satisfaction. The most important predictor is the respondents' assessment of their neighbors, although the assessment of the upkeep of neighboring houses is also important. As we shall see, these assessments remain strong when several other predictors are included in the analysis.

Table 7.13: Percentage Distribution of Respondents in the Quality of Life Study: Assessments of Specific Macro-Neighborhood Attributes

Attributes	Percent	Number of Respondents
Convenience of location[a]		
Very convenient	42	
Convenient enough	42	
Not very convenient	13	
Not convenient at all	3	
Total	100	2,157
Condition of housing — upkeep[b]		
Very well	41	
Fairly well	48	
Not very well	8	
Not well at all	3	
Total	100	2,149
Neighbors[c]		
Very good	54	
Fairly good	33	
Neither good nor bad	9	
Not very good	3	
Not good at all	1	
Total	100	2,138
Safe to walk at night[d]		
Yes	74	
No	26	
Total	100	2,058
Importance of locking doors[e]		
Very important	56	
Somewhat important	17	
Not very important	15	
Not at all important	12	
Total	100	2,161

a. The question was: "Now I have some questions about this neighborhood. First, thinking about the kinds of things you would like to have near where you live—places you go fairly often—how convenient would you say this location is: is it very convenient, convenient enough, not very convenient, or not convenient at all?
b. The question was: "What about the condition of the houses in this neighborhood? Overall, would you say they are very well kept up, fairly well, not very well, or not kept up well at all?
c. The question was: "What about the people who live around here? As neighbors, would you say they are very good, fairly good, neither good nor bad, not very good, or not good at all?
d. The question was: "Would you say that it is safe to go out walking around here at night?
e. The question was: "How important do you feel it is to lock your doors when you are going out of the house for just an hour or two? Would you say it is very important, somewhat important, not very important, or not at all important?

Table 7.14: Multiple Classification Analysis of 2,159 Respondents in the Quality of Life Study: Multivariate Analysis of Macro-Neighborhood Satisfaction Based on Ratings of Specific Neighborhood Attributes

Attributes	Correlation Ratio	Beta Coefficient
Neighbors	0.48	0.37
Condition of housing: upkeep	0.41	0.25
Safe to walk at night	0.27	0.11
Convenience	0.18	0.10
Importance of locking doors	0.15	0.07
Adjusted Multiple R^2 (explained variance)		32%

As in the case of community satisfaction, there are numerous dimensions along which respondents who differ are related to their evaluation of overall macro-neighborhood satisfaction. Table 7.15 shows that satisfaction is higher among whites than among black respondents. While there is virtually no relation between family income and satisfaction, another correlate of socioeconomic status—educational attainment—appears to be inversely related to expressions of complete satisfaction. Whereas 56 percent of the respondents with no more than an eighth grade education said they were completely satisfied with their neighborhood, only 35 percent of those with at least some college training responded in this manner.

Similarly, young single people tended to be the least satisfied with their neighborhoods, while older respondents without children living at home were the most satisfied. With respect to work status, the pattern of satisfaction to a large extent is a reflection of age, that is, the most satisfied were retired while students and the unemployed were the least satisfied. Length of residence in community is also related to age. The last item in Table 7.15 shows that the proportion of respondents who report complete satisfaction increases as the number of years in the area increases.

When these six person characteristics are considered simultaneously, in Table 7.16, they account for only 8 percent of the variance in responses to macro-neighborhood satisfaction. As in the case of community satisfaction, the most important predictors in the set are the family life cycle and race variables. After considering other elements of the model, the effects of person characteristics together with assessments of specific attributes and objective environmental measure will be analyzed with respect to macro-neighborhood satisfaction.

In the Quality of Life Study, data were gathered for what could be considered the respondents' perceptions of a true or objective environmental attribute of their neighborhoods. Perceptions of the racial composition were identified by asking respondents whether their neighborhood was "all white, mostly white, about half and half, mostly black, all black or what?" This perception can be compared to an objective indicator of the racial composition of the neighborhood.[19] It was found that there is a high correlation (the product moment

Table 7.15: Percentage Distribution of Respondents in the Quality of Life Study: Satisfaction with Macro-Neighborhood Expressed by Different Subgroups

Characteristics	Completely Satisfied (percent)	Satisfied (percent)	Neutral or Dissatisfied (percent)	Total	Number of Respondents
Race					
White	49	33	18	100	1,877
Black	28	36	36	100	222
Other	28	42	30	100	53
Family Income					
Less than $3,000	49	29	22	100	291
$3,000-4,999	48	30	22	100	287
$5,000-6,999	42	32	26	100	268
$7,000-9,999	44	33	23	100	366
$10,000-11,999	46	38	16	100	272
$12,000-16,999	46	38	16	100	320
$17,000 or more	49	35	16	100	265
Educational Attainment					
Eighth grade or less	56	27	17	100	467
Some High School, no diploma	50	27	23	100	398
High School diploma	47	31	22	100	710
Some college, no degree	34	43	23	100	334
College degree(s)	35	51	14	100	239
Family Life Cycle					
Single, age 18-29	22	41	37	100	167
Single, age 30 or older	37	40	23	100	93
Married, no children; age 18-29	31	47	22	100	95
Married, no children; age 30 or older	56	29	15	100	105
Married, youngest child aged 5 or younger	36	38	26	100	436
Married, youngest child aged 6-17	50	35	15	100	412
Married, youngest child aged 18 or older	60	27	13	100	402
Separated or divorced	40	31	29	100	179
Widowed	61	26	13	100	256
Job Status					
Work for pay	42	37	21	100	1,234
Housewife	54	28	18	100	608
Retired	62	24	14	100	187
Student	11	55	34	100	54
Unemployed, other	40	25	35	100	76

Table 7.15 (Continued)

| | Respondents Were: | | | | |
Characteristics	Completely Satisfied (percent)	Satisfied (percent)	Neutral or Dissatisfied (percent)	Total	Number of Respondents
Length of Residence in Area					
Less than 2 years	39	36	25	100	254
2-7.9 years	40	37	23	100	423
8.19.9 years	43	35	22	100	530
20-39.9 years	47	32	21	100	541
40 years or more	61	28	11	100	406

correlation is 0.84) between the objective and subjective indicators. There is reason to interpret this finding as more a reflection of the segregated character of most neighborhoods than of the perspicacity of the respondents. Nevertheless, whatever the explanation, the high correlation provides some justification for treating the respondents' perceptions of the racial composition of their neighborhoods as an objective measure. For purposes of this paper, this equivalence will be assumed in several of the multivariate analyses described in the following sections.

In the Quality of Life Study, one direct measure of an objective environmental attribute and one indirect measure were considered in relation to macroneighborhood satisfaction. The direct measure was an interviewer rating of the upkeep of structures in the neighborhood, on a four-point scale from "very well kept up" to "very poorly kept up or dilapidated."[20] The indirect objective measure is again the size of the community in which the respondent lives.

A relationship between the interviewers' ratings of the upkeep of structures in the neighborhood (objective environmental attribute) and the respondents' assessment of neighboring structures (subjective evaluation) can be posited. Since the conceptual model is concerned with this relationship as mediated by the respondents' perceptions of the reality of structural upkeep, the data are incomplete. However, the data indicate a strong relationship between the two

Table 7.16: Multiple Classification Analysis on 2,159 Respondents in the Quality of Life Study: Multivariate Analysis of Macro-Neighborhood Satisfaction Using Six Person Characteristics

Person Characteristic	Correlation Ratio	Beta Coefficient
Family life cycle	0.24	0.17
Race	0.15	0.12
Length of residence	0.16	0.09
Family income	0.06	0.07
Educational attainment	0.10	0.06
Job status	0.15	0.06
Adjusted Multiple R^2		8%

measures (gamma = 0.71). In cases in which the interviewer considered the neighboring structures to be kept up "very well," almost two-thirds (64 percent) of the respondents evaluated the condition of their neighbor's houses as "very well kept up," compared to only 7 percent of the respondents giving this reply when the interviewer rated the nearby structures as kept up pporly.

Since size of place is not a direct measure of any neighborhood attribute, its relationships to assessments of neighborhood attributes do not constitute direct evidence on the adequacy of the model. However, the data that are available do offer indirect support of the model. For instance, if we accept the statistics showing crime rates to be higher in central cities than in other places, it is not surprising to find relationships between the size of place and two crime-related assessments—fear of walking outside at night and the importance people attach to leaving house doors unlocked.

Prior to considering objective environmental attributes along with attribute assessments and person characteristics in the analysis of the macro-neighborhood satisfaction, it is worth discussing the relative importance of each of the three objective measures with respect to neighborhood satisfaction. As shown by the correlation ratios of Table 7.17, housing upkeep, followed closely by the size of place of the community, is most strongly related to macro-neighborhood satisfaction. When the three variables are considered simultaneously, upkeep of neighboring structures, size of place, and racial composition explain 14 percent of the variance in macro-neighborhood satisfaction. This is considerably less than that explained by the set of attribute assessments (32 percent), but more than the variance explained by person characteristics (8 percent). The effects of the three sets taken together are shown in the next paragraph.

In the previous pages, we have considered three sets of measures that, according to the model, directly or indirectly predict macro-neighborhood satisfaction. These sets are the respondents' assessments of specific environmental attributes, the characteristics of the individuals making the assessments (person characteristics), and objective environmental attributes. Earlier, we showed that the five available respondents' assessments, taken together, accounted for 32 percent of the variance in neighborhood satisfaction. Furthermore, the set of person characteristics explained 8 percent of the variance in the same satisfaction measure.

Table 7.17: Multiple Classification Analysis of 2,159 Respondents in the Quality of Life Study: Multivariate Analysis of Macro-Neighborhood Satisfaction Using Objective Environmental Attributes

	Correlation Ratio	Beta Coefficient
Upkeep of neighboring structures	0.28	0.22
Size of place	0.27	0.22
Racial composition of neighborhood	0.24	0.15
Adjusted Multiple R^2 (explained variance)		14%

As seen in Table 7.18, when these two sets are considered together, a total of 35 percent of the variance is explained. When the objective environmental attributes (including respondents' perceptions of racial composition) are included in the analysis, the proportion of variance explained increases slightly, to 36 percent, an increase of only 4 percentage points over and above the variance explained by just the assessments. Thus, it appears that the objective environmental attributes and the person characteristics are affecting macro-neighborhood satisfaction indirectly through their effects on assessments of specific attributes. This is consistent with the model in the case of the objective measures of environmental attributes. In the case of person characteristics, the results of the analyses imply that the direct link shown in the model from these characteristics to macro-neighborhood satisfaction is a weak one at best.

Findings on Micro-Neighborhood Satisfaction

As we have suggested throughout the paper, people have difficulty in clearly differentiating between attributes of their community and attributes more clearly associated with the particular district or section of the community in which they live—i.e., their neighborhood. Indeed, a subsequent multivariate analysis of the data from the Planned Communities Study revealed that one's level of satisfaction with his immediate environment (micro-neighborhood) is the strongest single predictor of community satisfaction (Maklan, unpublished paper, University of Michigan). Similarly, data from the Quality of Life Study showed that satisfaction with the macro-neighborhood and satisfaction with community are highly correlated. These findings tend to support the belief that neighborhood is a rather fuzzy concept having various connotations for different people.

In the studies of planned communities and outdoor recreation, attempts were made to give respondents a clear definition of a neighborhood environment to which responses were elicited. In the questionnaires, neighborhood was defined as: "Just what you can see from (your front door/the front door of this building), that is, the five or six other buildings nearest to you around here." There were several reasons for focusing on this micro-neighborhood rather than more traditional neighborhoods such as those defined by major thoroughfares and natural boundaries or those centered around elementary schools. First, the micro-neighborhood is an area with which most residents—even commutors— have day-to-day experiences. Second, it is the area where children are raised, where interactions with close neighbors occur, and where leisure interests may be pursued. Finally it is an area where homeowners often have a sizeable investment. It is for these reasons that the micro-neighborhood has been considered in our model as another important dimension of the residential environment.[21]

The two studies cited above provide data on the micro-neighborhood which enable us to amplify the model. During the administration of questionnaires, respondents were asked to evaluate their immediate environment (according to the micro-neighborhood definition) along several dimensions. Three of these

Table 7.18: Multiple Classification Analysis of 2,159 Respondents in the Quality of Life Study: Multivariate Analysis of Macro-Neighborhood Satisfaction Using Assessments, Person Characteristics and Objective Environmental Attributes

Attributes/Characteristics	Correlation Ratio	Beta Coefficient (Ranking of Importance)		
		Assessments Only	Assessments and Personal Characteristics	Assessments, Personal Characteristics and Objective Environmental Attributes
Assessment of Attributes				
Condition of housing: upkeep	0.41	0.25 (2)	0.25 (2)	0.24 (2)
Neighbors	0.48	0.37 (1)	0.34 (1)	0.31 (1)
Safe to walk at night	0.27	0.11 (3)	0.14 (3)	0.10 (5)
Convenience	0.18	0.10 (4)	0.10 (4)	0.11 (4)
Importance of locking doors	0.15	0.07 (5)	0.07 (6)	0.05 (11)
Person Characteristics				
Family life cycle	0.24		0.10 (4)	0.09 (7)
Race	0.15		0.02 (11)	0.08 (8)
Length of residence	0.16		0.06 (8)	0.05 (11)
Family income	0.06		0.04 (10)	0.05 (11)
Educational attainment	0.10		0.07 (6)	0.06 (9)
Job status	0.15		0.06 (8)	0.06 (9)
Objective Environmental Attributes				
Upkeep of neighboring structures	0.28			0.05 (11)
Size of place	0.27			0.12 (3)
Racial composition of neighborhood	0.24			0.10 (5)
Adjusted Multiple R^2 (explained variance)		32%	35%	36%

were general measures and were used to construct a satisfaction measure. The items enabled the respondent to rate his micro-neighborhood on three semantic differential-type dimensions ("attractive-unattractive," "pleasant-unpleasant," and "very good place to live-very poor place to live"). The zero order correlations of the items with the scale and with each other suggest that the items did, in fact, measure a single dimension.[22]

In the Planned Communities Study, a high degree of neighborhood satisfaction was found across the sample communities. This concurred with findings from studies reported in the first part of this paper, suggesting that these expressions of satisfaction were not atypical. It was therefore decided that data for all communities would be combined and that the satisfaction measure would be considered in relation to people's responses to other neighborhood attributes.

In the Planned Communities Study, respondents were asked to assess several characteristics of the micro-neighborhoods in which they lived. They were also asked to describe these neighborhoods on a different set of dimensions. While these concepts (assessments and perceptions) are treated separately in the model as parts of a causal chain, differences between them were not considered in the study. The assumption was made that descriptions (perceptions) carried implicit evaluative meanings (assessments). This may not have been a good assumption in every instance. Nevertheless, the distinction between descriptions and assessments, with one exception, is not possible in the present discussion since measures of each for the same attribute were not obtained.

Table 7.19 presents a partial set of these descriptive and evaluative items and their relationships to satisfaction with the micro-neighborhood.[23] Not surprisingly, residents who reported hearing their neighbors often and those who reported living in a "noisy" neighborhood evaluated their neighborhoods less favorably than those who "almost never" heard their neighbors and those who said their neighborhood was "quiet." Similarly, people who had no privacy in their yard from neighbors and those who had too little outdoor space for family activities were less inclined to assess their neighborhood favorably than people who had privacy and adequate outdoor space near their home. Among other items evaluated, how well the neighborhood was maintained was strongly related to satisfaction, as was the perception of neighbors as friendly people and as being similar to themselves.

In the Outdoor Recreation Study, respondents were asked to describe an additional set of attributes of their micro-neighborhoods. Table 7.20 shows that people who said they lived in neighborhoods which were crowded, which had dangerous streets with too much traffic, and which were lacking trees and clean air were much less likely to evaluate their micro-neighborhoods as favorable than people who perceived the opposite conditions to exist.

Table 7.21 displays the findings from a multivariate analysis in which five of the neighborhood descriptive items used in the Outdoor Recreation Study were used to predict satisfaction with micro-neighborhoods. Over half of the variance is explained (58 percent), with perceived maintenance level of neighborhood structures being the most important predictor.[24]

Table 7.19: Micro-Neighborhood Satisfaction for Responses Related to Select Environmental Attributes (Planned Communities Study)

	Percent Giving Area Highest Rating on Neighborhood Satisfaction Scale	Number of Respondents
Frequency of Hearing Neighbors		
Very often	36	44
Occasionally	41	191
Almost never	54	1,013
Noise Level		
Noisy	23	31
	20	54
	34	198
	37	337
Quiet	67	615
Privacy in Yard from Neighbors		
Yes	57	646
No	44	602
Adequacy of Outdoor Space for Family Activities		
More than needed	54	158
Right amount	54	861
Too little	35	224
Neighborhood Maintenance Level		
Well kept up	71	705
	28	398
	12	97
	4	24
Poorly kept up	18	11
Neighbors		
Friendly people	70	640
	37	343
	21	266
	29	38
Unfriendly people	9	11
People similar to me	81	298
	43	306
	46	433
	24	119
People Dissimilar to me	29	68

We noted earlier that in the Planned Communities Study, efforts were made to select communities whose populations did not vary extensively along several socioeconomic and demographic dimensions. Perhaps because of the relatively homogeneous population, the analysis of person characteristics with respect to micro-neighborhood satisfaction revealed no relationships.

In the study of outdoor recreation, the use of a national sample resulted in respondents with more diverse characteristics than those in the planned commu-

Table 7.20: Micro-Neighborhood Satisfaction for Responses Related to Select Environmental Attributes (Outdoor Recreation Study)

	Percent Giving Area Highest Rating on Neighborhood Satisfaction Scale	Number of Respondents
Level of Neighborhood Crowding		
Crowding	11	108
	15	125
	23	272
	34	215
Uncrowded	63	575
Safety of Neighborhood Streets		
Safe streets	68	425
	35	250
	30	266
	19	150
Dangerous streets	21	194
Traffic Level in Neighborhood		
Not much traffic	66	366
	42	209
	33	305
	23	172
Too much traffic	22	224
Availability of Trees in Neighborhood		
Many trees	59	589
	31	258
	26	273
	17	102
No trees	19	74
Quality of Air		
Clean air	63	478
	36	250
	29	261
	21	141
Polluted air	21	166

nities study. Several of those characteristics were shown to be related to community and neighborhood satisfaction and were therefore considered in relation to micro-neighborhood satisfaction. These relationships are presented in Table 7.22.

As in the case of community and neighborhood satisfaction, white respondents gave higher ratings to their micro-neighborhood than black and other respondents. Similarly, people over forty-five and married people with the youngest child age six or older tended to be more satisfied with their immediate environment than young single people or young married people without children. On the other hand, while little relationship was shown between family income and community and macro-neighborhood satisfaction in the Quality of Life Study, data from the Outdoor Recreation Study revealed that people whose family income was over $15,000 were nearly twice as likely to give a high rating

Table 7.21: Multiple Classification Analysis of 1,300 Respondents in the Outdoor Recreation Study: Multivariate Analysis of Micro-Neighborhood Satisfaction Based on Ratings of Specific Neighborhood Attributes

Attributes	Correlation Ratio	Beta Coefficient
Maintenance: well kept up — poorly kept up	0.63	0.40
Noise level: noisy — quiet	0.56	0.22
Crowding: crowded — uncrowded	0.51	0.14
Trees: no trees — many trees	0.43	0.15
Neighbors: similar people — dissimilar people	0.42	0.19
Adjusted Multiple R^2 (explained variance)		58%

Table 7.22: Micro-Neighborhood Satisfaction Expressed by Respondents with Select Person Characteristics (Outdoor Recreation Study)

	Percent Giving Area Highest Rating on Neighborhood Satisfaction Scale	Number of Respondents
Race		
White	43	1,136
Black	29	131
Other	11	36
Family Life Cycle		
Single; age 18; no children	18	84
Single; age 45 or older; no children	48	218
Married; age 18-44; no children	30	90
Married; age 18-44; child aged 5 or younger	40	230
Married; age 18-44; child aged 6 or older	47	148
Married; age 45 or older; with children	52	159
Married; age 45 or older; no children	48	296
Separated, widowed, divorced; with children	19	78
Family Income		
Less than $3,000	30	193
$3,000-4,999	20	172
$5,000-7,499	41	186
$7,500-9,999	43	167
$10,000-14,999	42	327
$15,000 or more	55	222
Education of Head		
Eighth grade or less	37	323
Some high school, no diploma	35	227
High school graduate	46	186
High school graduate, some college or technical school training	44	364
College graduate	43	195

to their micro-neighborhood as people whose annual family income was less than $5,000. A discrepancy between the Outdoor Recreation Study for the micro-neighborhood and the Quality of Life data for the community and macro-neighborhood is seen for educational levels. The relationship for the micro-neighborhood data is slightly positive, while data from the Quality of Life Study showed that people with limited education were more likely to say that they were "completely satisfied" with their community and macro-neighborhood than those with higher levels of education.

The extent to which each of these person characteristics is related to micro-neighborhood satisfaction is shown in the first column of Table 7.23. The table also shows that when the four characteristics are considered together, only 9 percent of the variance is explained, with family life cycle being the most important explanatory variable. As we will see shortly, the importance of these person characteristics in explaining overall micro-neighborhood satisfaction is diminished considerably when the assessment of specific micro-neighborhood attributes are entered into the analysis.

Although the logical causal chain begins with the objective environment, only one aspect of that environment was considered, measured, and used in our analysis of the data from the Outdoor Recreation Study.[25] This was the dwelling unit density at which people lived. Most available data from the study represent the next set of variables in the model—the environment as perceived by the respondents. With the one exception of crowding and density, we are unable to compare people's perceptions with objective measures of reality.

Dwelling unit density was considered in our analyses because it is an attribute of the physical objective environment which can be manipulated, and concomitantly, can have relevance to transportation and land use patterns in metropolitan areas. Furthermore, a body of social science literature has dealt with the impact of living at different densities on a range of individual and social behaviors. Because much of the research reported in the literature is inconclusive, attempts to understand better the effects of various densities on responses pertaining to the micro-neighborhood have been made within the context of several studies at the Survey Research Center.

Given our definition of micro-neighborhood, the precise number of dwelling units within a given area of land could be objectively determined and the density

Table 7.23: Multiple Classification Analysis of 2,159 Respondents in the Outdoor Recreation Study: Multivariate Analysis of Micro-Neighborhood Satisfaction Using Person Characteristics

	Correlation Ratio	Beta Coefficient
Family life cycle	0.23	0.21
Family income	0.20	0.12
Race	0.18	0.13
Education of head	0.12	0.11
Adjusted Multiple R^2 (explained variance)		9%

Table 7.24: Percentage Distribution of Respondents in Outdoor Recreation Study: Micro-Neighborhood Response Related to Density, by Dwelling Unit Density

	Dwelling Units per Acre						
	Less than 1.0	1.00-3.49	3.50-6.49	6.50-11.49	11.50-19.49	19.50-39.49	39.50 or more
Frequency of Hearing Neighbors							
Very often	2	6	8	38	19	35	22
Occasionally	10	20	26	28	44	36	43
Almost never	88	74	66	34	37	29	35
Total	100	100	100	100	100	100	100
Noise Level in Neighborhood							
Noisy	4	7	9	21	11	22	25
	2	5	8	8	17	19	11
	6	19	20	32	22	24	33
	15	23	23	21	24	16	9
Quiet	73	46	40	18	26	19	22
Total	100	100	100	100	100	100	100
Available Outdoor Space							
No	1	1	6	14	29	35	62
Yes — without privacy	8	30	34	52	40	47	27
Yes — with privacy	91	69	60	34	31	18	11
Total	100	100	100	100	100	100	100
Traffic Level in Neighborhood							
Too much traffic	12	14	19	26	18	28	39
	8	13	14	11	20	20	22
	22	23	22	25	21	32	17
	16	17	22	18	16	15	3
Not much traffic	42	33	23	20	15	5	19
Total	100	100	100	100	100	100	100
Dangerous streets	13	12	12	20	14	34	28
	7	12	11	15	16	16	19
	17	19	20	25	32	25	20
	17	20	22	18	23	19	11
Safe streets	46	37	35	22	15	6	22
Total	100	100	100	100	100	100	100
Level of Crowding							
Crowded	1	5	6	9	12	28	31
	2	7	9	18	21	21	30
	7	21	25	31	40	32	3
	8	23	22	11	10	11	8
Uncrowded	82	44	38	21	17	8	28
Total	100	100	100	100	100	100	100
Number of Respondents	285	415	258	132	85	80	36

in terms of housing units per acre calculated. This procedure was used in the work reported here.[26]

From the data in the Planned Communities Study, dwelling unit density was found to have variable effects on residents' responses.[27] Reporting a "noisy" neighborhood and "hearing neighbors" increased fairly regularly with greater densities. On the other hand, variation in density under 12.5 dwellings per acre had little systematic effect on private yard space for outdoor activities or adequacy of children's play areas near home.

In the Outdoor Recreation Study, a national sample of households was selected providing a greater range of density. A significant portion of the sample (21 percent) was found in low density areas of less than one dwelling per acre. At the other extreme, about 9 percent of the households were located in neighborhoods with densities of 20 dwelling units per acre or more.

The effects of density on a number of perceptions of attributes is shown in Table 7.24. At densities of 6.50 dwelling units per acre or greater, for instance, about two-thirds of the people are likely to report hearing their neighbors. Furthermore, about one-third of them are likely to describe their neighborhoods as "noisy."

With increasing density, the feeling that one has private outdoor space decreases regularly as does the probability of having any outdoor space associated with one's dwelling increases. Perceptions of too much traffic and dangerous streets also increase regularly with rising density up to 11.49 dwelling units per acre, at which point they remain constant until densities above 20 dwellings per acre are reached.

One of the strongest relationships is shown in the last item of Table 7.24 where people's perceptions of the level of crowding in the micro-neighborhood increase precipitously with rising dwelling unit densities. This is not surprising since the level of crowding is the best subjective measure of the objective density attribute we have available.

Having examined the relationships of the objective density measure to people's perceptions of conditions in the physical environment, we can now explore its relationship to neighborhood satisfaction. In the Planned Communities Study for low to moderate density levels (2.50 to 8.49 dwellings per acre), there was little relationship to satisfaction. However, in the least dense category (under 2.50 dwellings per acre), satisfaction was found to be noticeably higher, and in the most dense level (12.5 to 25 dwellings per acre), satisfaction was relatively low. Table 7.25 presents the relation between micro-neighborhood density and satisfaction using data from the Outdoor Recreation Study. Because of the wider range of density categories, we are able to amplify findings from the Planned Communities Study. Once again for low to middle range densities there was found to be little relationship to satisfaction, but this range now has as its upper limit a density of approximately six or seven dwelling units per acre, rather than the eight or nine dwelling units per acre as suggested by the data from the Planned Communities Study. Once again, people living in areas of very low densities (less than one dwelling per acre) are the most satisfied with their micro-neighborhoods while those living in areas of high densities (19.50 dwellings per acre) are least satisfied.

Table 7.25: Neighborhood Satisfaction Related to Density (Outdoor Recreation Study)

Dwelling Unit Density (in dwelling units per acre)	Percent Giving Area Highest Rating on Neighborhood Satisfaction Scales	Number of Respondents
Less than 1.0	58	286
1.0 – 3.49	48	417
3.50 – 6.49	40	254
6.50 – 11.49	18	133
12.50 – 19.49	22	87
1950 – 39.49	14	80
39.50 and over	14	37

When density is used to predict satisfaction with micro-neighborhood in a one-way analysis of variance, the correlation ratio is 0.39. That is, it explains about 15 percent of the variance in satisfaction. However, according to our model, density as an objective attribute of the environment is expected to affect satisfaction indirectly through the individual's perception and assessment of it. To examine the data for support of this aspect of the model, we turn to a series of multivariate analyses of the type presented earlier in our discussion of macro-neighborhood and community satisfaction.

Using data from the Planned Communities Study and the Outdoor Recreation Study, we have shown that a number of perceptions of the attributes of the physical and social environment are related to micro-neighborhood satisfaction. When five of the most important perceptions are considered simultaneously, they account for 58 percent of the variance in micro-neighborhood satisfaction. How well the environment is maintained is by far the most important predictor of satisfaction.

When the set of person characteristics is added to the perceptions, the amount of variance explained increases slightly to 59 percent. This is not surprising after the comparable analyses of community and macro-neighborhood satisfaction. To determine whether the objective environment attribute has any effect apart from that mediated by the perception, the dwelling unit density measure was included in a further analysis; the proportion of explained variance remained unchanged at 59 percent. This implies that the relationship of density to micro-neighborhood satisfaction is entirely mediated by the perceptions.

Community Satisfaction and Macro-Neighborhood Assessments

The fact that respondents in the Qualityof Life Study did not clearly differentiate between their neighborhoods and their communities has been mentioned several times. In part, this was suggested in the model which indicated that respondent assessments of some neighborhood attributes would be related to community satisfaction and, similarly, that their assessments of some community attributes would be related to neighborhood satisfaction. What was not implied by the model, but was revealed by the data, is that assessments of some community attributes are related as strongly to neighborhood satisfaction as to community satisfaction, and vice versa. This indicated considerable overlap in the residential concepts as manifested by the way in which the questions were asked or by the way in which these questions were interpreted by the respondents.

According to the presently available data, then, the distinction made in the model between community and macro-neighborhood attributes is not a very useful one. In order to better understand the determinants of community satisfaction, it might be useful to treat these attributes as conceptually equivalent. This idea was tested by a regression analysis predicting community satisfaction from a set of assessments that included not only community attributes, but also five attributes originally conceptualized as being associated with the macro-neighborhood.

The model also suggests a relationship between community and macro-neighborhood satisfaction, apart from that implied by their common determinants. That is, the macro-neighborhood per se is a significant characteristic of the community, and therefore satisfaction with neighborhood might well be a significant determinant of community satisfaction. While 22 percent of the variance in community satisfaction was accounted for by just the assessments, with the addition, the proportion of variance explained increases by more than half, to 35 percent. This may reflect, in part, a methods artifact since the ratings of neighborhood and community satisfaction used the identical scale. It is also possible that there are important attributes of the neighborhood which respondents were not asked to assess but which contribute to community satisfaction as well as to neighborhood satisfaction. Nonetheless, the data support the plausibility of direct linkages between macro-neighborhood and community satisfaction, as are suggested by the model.

Community Satisfaction, Other Life Domains, and the Quality of Life

In the Quality of Life Study, relationships of satisfaction with community and macro-neighborhood to satisfaction with other life domains were examined. The results are summarized in Figure 7.2, which shows a two-dimensional representation of proximities between satisfaction measures as measured by product-moment correlations.[28] The diagram reveals a clustering of the three residential domain satisfactions and to a lesser extent, a link between community satisfaction and satisfaction with life in the United States.[29] When correlations with other domain satisfactions are examined in relation to the broader concept of "quality of life experience," it is found that each domain contributes to this quality of life experience as suggested by the model. Community satisfaction, macro-neighborhood satisfaction, and housing satisfaction are correlated with a life quality index as are most of the other domain satisfactions.

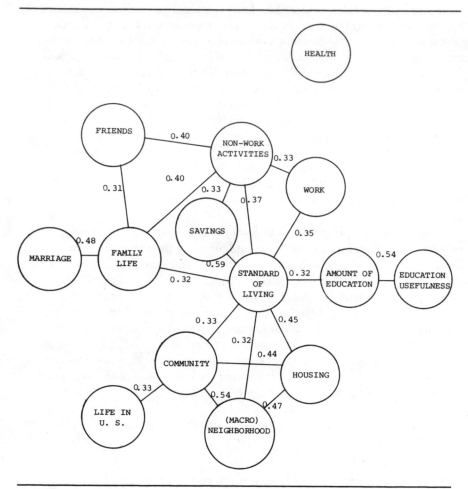

Figure 7.2: Cluster analysis of domain satisfaction variables (correlogram where distances between domains are proportional to product moment correlations).

In a multivariate analysis, it was found that a set of ten domain satisfaction measures, including those dealing with financial situation, friendships, work, and marriage, accounted for over half (56 percent) of the variance in the life quality index. However, among the ten measures, community satisfaction and housing satisfaction were relatively unimportant, ranking eighth and seventh respectively. Their beta coefficients were 0.06 and 0.04 compared to the beta coefficients (0.22) of the two most important predictors, non-working activities and family life satisfactions.

In other words, the data indicate that in order to increase overall satisfaction by a given amount, a considerably larger change would be required in community or housing satisfaction than in, say, satisfaction with family life. It should be emphasized, however, that such a statement is at best tentative, based as it is on cross-sectional survey data. Data from a longitudinal study in which changes over time could be observed would be more definitive, especially if significant changes in place of residence of some of the respondents took place during the period of investigation.

SUMMARY, IMPLICATIONS,
AND PROGRAM FOR FUTURE RESEARCH

In this paper we have presented a model within which studies of people's responses to different environments and attributes of those environments can be undertaken. We have also suggested several reasons for undertaking such empirically based studies. Finally, using data from three independent studies conducted at the Institute for Social Research, we have presented findings which suggest that the postulated relationships between elements of our model, for the most part, are correct.

In this part of the paper we will first review the theoretical model which links the concepts of environmental attributes and levels of satisfaction with community and neighborhood. Then, based on the discussion of the data from the three studies, implications of our findings for people in policy making and community development roles will be discussed. Finally, suggestions for a program of continued research dealing with community and other environmental satisfaction will be outlined.

The Theoretical Model—An Overview

The data presented in the preceding section have been organized within a theoretical framework for understanding community and other environmental satisfaction. The model suggests that satisfaction with a particular life domain, such as one's community, is primarily dependent on assessments of various attributes of that domain. These assessments, in turn, depend on the fit between how each of the attributes is perceived, and the standard of comparison against which an individual judges it. The individual's perception of an attribute, for the most part, corresponds to the attribute itself although the possibility of distortion between perception and reality is clearly recognized.

Thus, the model as outlined above makes a critical distinction between objective indicators (the reality) and subjective indicators (perceptions, assessments, and satisfactions) of the quality of the residential environment. This distinction is based on the assumption that characteristics of the individual intervene so as to influence the subjective indicators. Specifically, the manner in which an objective environmental attribute is perceived and assessed by individuals is modified by their present situation, their attitudes, and their past experiences. These considerations underlie the basic contention of our paper, namely, that objective measures of environmental attributes are inadequate in themselves as indicators of life quality. Only as their relationships to subjective indicators are understood do they begin to take on human meaning and provide reliable guidance for policy decisions.

Using data from the three studies, the theoretical model has been tested and illuminated although it is clear that considerable work remains to be done. The link from the assessments of particular attributes of an environment to overall satisfaction with the environment was found to be more or less strong in each of the three environments considered: the community, and the macro- and micro-neighborhoods. Person characteristics such as age, race, and educational level and objective characteristics, such as size of population of the community and dwelling unit density, also were related to environmental satisfaction measures. These latter relationships seem to be almost entirely mediated by the assessments of particular attributes of the environment.

Satisfaction with community is so strongly related to satisfaction with the macro-neighborhood that the usefulness of the distinction between these two concepts is called into question. Satisfaction measures with these as parts of the environment are also related to satisfaction with other domains of life experience. Finally, satisfaction with these residential environments, as well as satisfaction with other domains of life experiences, are related to expressed satisfaction with life as a whole.

Implications of the Data

As we indicated earlier, an important use of empirical data on people's responses to their environments is related to the concept of social reporting. Data from the studies presented in this paper can be considered initial measures in developing social reports on how different people feel about their residential environments, namely their communities, their macro-neighborhoods, and their micro-neighborhoods. At the same time, these data describe those attributes of the various environments which are most influential in determining overall levels of satisfaction.

While our measurements of satisfaction with different environments may be questionable and undoubtedly can be improved in subsequent research, our data nevertheless can be useful in several respects. These data, based on samples of the national population, can provide benchmarks against which subsequent assessments of people's responses to their environments can be compared. That is, subsequent national studies and studies of specific localities or of subgroups of the population can be compared to findings from the studies reported in this paper.

The importance of observing the changes that may occur in people's responses to their environments over time cannot be overemphasized. A constant monitoring of people's perceptions of the environment and the objective attributes of the environment can be valuable to policy makers at the local and state as well as national levels. For any given locality, such information can indicate to public officials and policy planners what attributes of the environment are deemed important by various segments of the population. This knowledge can be useful in setting priorities for governmental services, physical improvements, and social legislation. At the same time, the information can be of value to community builders, whether public or private, in that it can point out what things are important to overall levels of satisfaction and what attributes of the environment can be made marketable.

Specifically, in the Quality of Life Study we found that attitudes toward a number of public services and facilities were strongly related to overall satisfaction with the community. These findings concur with a basic premise of the model which states that one's overall level of satisfaction is a function of specific assessments of the component parts of the environment acting together. At the macro-neighborhood level, our data showed that people's assessments of their neighbors and of housing conditions were the most important factors in determining their overall satisfaction. Indeed, without neighbors who at least warrant neutral responses, an individual's feelings of satisfaction with his neighborhood would be relatively low, even in environments which offered good housing and other environmental amenities. These findings concur with studies reported earlier which show the social setting to be most critical to people's overall levels of satisfaction with their residence.

While perceived similarity of neighbors is related to overall satisfaction with one's immediate environment—his micro-neighborhood—the single most important determinant is one's perception of how well the neighborhood is maintained. To the extent that developers can design neighborhoods to favor ease of maintenance and general upkeep of buildings and grounds, they can influence, if not fully determine, residents' subsequent levels of satisfaction.

Our analysis found other salient attributes of the micro-neighborhood that can be designed in such a way as to influence satisfaction levels. In the Planned Communities Study, residents indicated that having adequate outdoor space for family activities and children's play were important to them. In addition, the evaluation of the micro-neighborhood on the noisy-quiet dimension contributed appreciably to the explanation of variation in overall satisfaction.

Further investigation of other attributes of the micro-neighborhood in the Outdoor Recreation Study showed that the presence of trees and perceived low levels of traffic and air pollution were also important. Finally, perceptions of crowding, reflecting the effects of density, were related to levels of micro-neighborhood satisfaction. It is clear then that community builders are able to make substantive contributions to people's satisfaction with the immediate environment within which they live.

Another possible implication of the data arises from the failure to find any effect of personal characteristics on overall satisfaction that is independent of the assessments of particular attributes of the environment. Personal characteristics such as race and age are related to satisfaction measures, but these relationships seem to be mediated by how these characteristics affect assessments of environmental attributes. Neither was any evidence obtained for strong interactions; that is, it was not found that the strength or direction of relationships between assessments of particular attributes and overall satisfaction were markedly different for different parts of the sample. These findings suggest that policy makers may not face different problems in different types of communities or with respect to different constituencies, nor are they forced into a position of having to play off the interests of one group against those of other groups. The same attributes seem to matter to people of all sorts; the sources of dissatisfaction for one type of person are likely to be sources of discontent for everyone.

Finally, it is plausible that within the framework of the model, a group of people living in a residential environment considered to be favorable by outsiders may express less satisfaction than another group living in a less favorable environment. One explanation is that the first group may have higher expectations than the second group and therefore view its situation less favorably. Similarly, as subjective and objective indicators are monitored over time, it is possible that levels of satisfaction may decline even as objective conditions are being improved—a manifestation, perhaps, of the "revolution of rising expectations." Under these two conditions, the need for both objective and subjective indicators is clearly revealed, since either type alone would be misleading. Having both types of indicators may present the policy maker with an embarrassment of riches. He may prefer the less ambiguous, albeit misleading, situation of having only a single type of indicator. However, with objective and subjective indicators, the policy maker would be made aware that he has at his disposal a wider set of variables that may be subject to manipulation. In some instances, for example, serious consideration might be given to the alternative of raising or lowering the expectations of people rather than modifying their objective situation.

Program for Future Research

As a continuing program of research dealing with people's responses to their environment, there are several areas of study that could be pursued simultaneously. One would focus on refining and modifying the conceptual model we have presented. These refinements and modifications can take place as data from empirical studies become available and either confirm or disprove relationships hypothesized between model elements. As we indicated earlier, a considerable literature has appeared in recent years which has focused on people's responses to their residential environments. Inevitably, additional research in this area will take place in the future. Hopefully, the model we have presented can provide one point of departure for these efforts.

While new data on attributes of environments need to be collected and linkages between them analyzed, an important part of any research dealing with people's responses to their residential environments must concern itself with the development of adequate measures of objective environmental attributes. Although we are able to develop a procedure for measuring dwelling unit density on the basis of dwelling units per given unit of land, other attributes of the environment whether physical, social, or economic, require definition and quantification. For instance, we are unclear as to how school quality, to which people attach great importance, can be measured objectively. Traditional measures such as pupils per teacher or dollars spent per pupil are incomplete in themselves and may require new qualitative dimensions to supplement them.

At the same time, measures relating to traffic, noise, crime, and pollution, as well as elements or features of the natural environment, need to be operationalized for analytic purposes. A third type of measurement problem deals with the objective measurement of public services. When people attach great importance to garbage collection, we are uncertain as to whether they are talking about the frequency of garbage pickups or other qualitative aspects of the service. Furthermore, good police-community relations, while having different meanings for different people, require objective quantification.

At the other end of our model, better methods are needed for measuring the complex concept of satisfaction. When we ask people about their level of satisfaction with their community we do not know whether a single question is sufficient to encompass all the dimensions of satisfaction that the respondent has. Nor do we know the meanings that various groups of people attach to the concept of community. Earlier in this paper we pointed out that several researchers have shown that people do not clearly differentiate between the various levels of environment within which they live. Indeed, our data support the notion that the residential environment of an individual encompasses everything from his dwelling through his community.

The definition of the micro-neighborhood is one attempt to define a uniform environment to which people can respond. Furthermore, our attempt to use a graphic representation of a geographic entity to elicit responses may offer another useful device. Undoubtedly, there are other techniques and definitions of environments available.

Earlier we pointed out that problems existed in obtaining data which clearly differentiate between people's perceptions of an environmental attribute and their assessment or evaluation of it. When we asked people to indicate whether their neighborhood had many trees or few trees, we assumed that they gave a perceptual response to an objective environmental attribute rather than an attitude toward or an evaluation of the number of trees. On the other hand, to ask people about whether their neighborhood is crowded or uncrowded implies a subjective evaluation as well as a perception of what actually exists. In this instance, the distinction between perception and assessment is less clear.

One aspect of the environment to which we have given little attention in this paper is that of the individual dwelling and the land associated with it. While this level of concern may be of little interest to policy makers at the community or national levels, research related to it can have significant implications for residential developers, architects, and site planners as well as lending institutions. Indeed, much more information is needed about the relative importance people attach to attributes of their dwellings ranging from the number and size of rooms and their relationship to one another to outdoor privacy and landscape features.

Another area of investigation would involve monitoring changes in people's responses over time. Although data presented in this paper are cross-sectional and therefore descriptive of conditions, attitudes and relationships at a single point in time, it would be of considerable interest and value to obtain repeated sets of data interviewing a panel of respondents over a period of years. This would permit the establishment of forecasting models based on time series data and, at the same time, enable us to estimate the probability of change in any of the elements in the model. More important, it would open the door to causal analysis of relationships among these elements. For instance, while people's assessments of an environmental attribute may change over time, this may be accounted for more in terms of changes in the standards against which people judge their perception of the attributes than in terms of objective changes.

Finally, a basic question to be addressed is whether the model and data base should be expanded to include other dependent variables besides environmental satisfaction—a concept that has been central to this paper. Aside from the faith that more data is better, other types of indicators may prove to be more relevant to policy decisions. For example, considerable interest has been expressed in the plans and behaviors of individuals and groups with respect to moving, participation in community, organizations, home improvements, and so on. The relationship between such measures and levels of satisfaction would be of considerable theoretical and practical interest.

NOTES

1. The literature, both theoretical and data-based, on objective social indicators is large and will not be reviewed here. (See Sheldon and Moore, 1968; Wilcox, Brooks, Beal, and Klonglan, 1972.)

2. The discussion of the conceptual model outlined in Figure 7.1 is sufficient for the purpose at hand, though necessarily rather sketchy. A more complete discussion of the concepts will be presented in a forthcoming paper (French, Rodgers, and Cobb, in press). ·

3. Overall proportions answering in the different categories provided for survey questions are to some extent a function of the wording of the question and so should be interpreted with caution.

4. The principle multivariate technique used in the analysis throughout the paper is the multiple classification analysis or MCA technique. For a complete discussion of the MCA, see Andrews, Morgan, and Sonquist (1969).

5. Although this is not a very impressive reduction in uncertainty, it is considerably better than what is possible by knowing any one of the set of nine assessments. For example, by knowing how an individual assesses public schools in his neighborhood, the uncertainty about how he evaluates his community would be reduced by only 9 percent.

6. This relationship is especially noteworthy because family income is a measure that is often used as an objective indicator of life quality, in contradistinction to the subject indicator, community satisfaction, presented here.

7. In order to reduce the number of variables used in the multivariate analysis of community satisfaction, age of respondent will not be used. It is believed that the life cycle variable not only accounts for marital status and the presence of children but it implicitly reflects the age of the respondent in broad but sufficient classes.

8. The correlation ratio is similar to a product-moment correlation except that it does not assume the relationship to be linear. This is an appropriate measure since characteristics such as race and life cycle are categorically defined.

9. It should be noted, however, that the person characteristics included in the present study are restricted to demographic variables. If measures of personality traits (such as "optimism-pessimism," "repression-sensitization," and "active-passive") were available, a quite different conclusion about the mediation of their effects on satisfaction might be reached.

10. In the process of searching for interaction effects, a number of hypotheses were investigated. One suggested that evaluations of public schools would be more strongly related to community satisfaction for parents of school-age children. This relationship was considered separately for respondents at each of the nine levels of the life cycle variable. No consistent pattern emerged. Similarly, no consistent patterns were found when the respondents were stratified by race and income, and where the relationships between each of the attribute evaluations and community satisfaction were compared across strata.

11. It is anticipated that additional objective data will be obtained and incorporated in subsequent analyses.

12. Over four out of ten (42 percent) of the large city residents said that the available public transportation was "very good," compared to three in ten (30 percent) of the sample as a whole. The difference would appear even larger if we included in the base for the percentages the respondents who reported that there is no available public transportation, and so were not asked to evaluate it; only 1 percent of the residents of large cities said no public transportation was available, compared to over half (53 percent) of the sample as a whole. Including those who said no transportation was available, 41 percent of the large city residents said it is "very good," compared to only 13 percent in the sample as a whole.

13. The causal direction of this association is not at all clear since it could be argued that one reason for the differences between racial groups, educational groups, etc., is the differential distribution of such groups in places of different sizes, rather than the other way around.

14. For a more complete review of characteristics of planned environments, see Lansing, Marans, and Zehner (1970: 7).

15. The question used was: 'I'd like to ask you how you feel about this area as a place to live—I mean the area outlined on the map (SHOW MAP). From your own personal point of view, would you rate this area as a place to live as excellent, good, average, below average, or poor?" A complete discussion of the method used in ascertaining people's levels of satisfaction is covered in Lansing et al. (1970: ch. 3).

16. The relatively low satisfaction expressed by residents of the Southwest Washington community may be partially explained by factors that produce lower community satisfaction among residents of large cities in general. Person characteristics that differ between communities also may account for further differences. For example, a high proportion of the residents of Southwest Washington are single and young, a group seen in Table 7.4 to be less satisfied than those in most other life cycle stages.

17. For a more complete discussion of the reasons underlying evaluations of different communities, see Lansing et al. (1970: ch. 3) and Zehner (1971).

18. The product moment correlation coefficient is .54 while the ordinal measure, gamma, is .61.

19. The only objective indicator available at the present time is a crude one based on the race of the respondents themselves. Samples used in national studies at the Survey Research Center, including the present studies, are drawn by a multistage procedure in which the next-to-last level consists of clusters of households, typically on a single block within cities. The racial proportions of the respondents in each such cluster can be treated as a reflection of the racial composition of the entire neighborhood within which each respondent lives, and it is this measure that is utilized in the present analysis in the absence of more reliable indicators. The analysis is restricted to residents of cities living in clusters from which at least three interviews were obtained.

20. It is true, of course, that the interviewer ratings of housing conditions could be treated as a subjective measure in another context. However, in the present context we con-

sider these ratings to be "objective" in the sense that they are not made by the respondents whose assessments and satisfactions we are trying to predict. Furthermore, while no special effort was made to train the interviewers to make this observation, there is evidence that they were respectably reliable in their judgments. To assess the reliability of measures used in the study, a subsample of the respondents was selected and reinterviewed approximately eight months after the original interviews were taken. For the interviewer observation of the condition of structure, the test-retest correlation was high (gamma = 0.83).

21. An additional justification for considering the small residential unit relates to sampling. In many of the Survey Research Center studies, including the three mentioned here, cluster sampling techniques were used, enabling us to collect information from four to six contiguous dwellings.

22. In the Planned Communities Study an additional item was used in the satisfaction measure. See Lansing et al. (1970: 103) and Zehner (1970: ch. 2) for further discussion of the items and the scale's validity.

23. A complete set of items used in the Planned Communities Study and their relationships to neighborhood satisfaction are shown in Tables 32, 33, 37 and 38 of Lansing et al. (1970).

24. The proportion of explained variance is considerably higher in the case of micro-neighborhoods than was found in the case of the community (19 percent) or the macro-neighborhood (32 percent). This may reflect the more defined, delineated character of the micro-neighborhood concept. However, there may also be a methods artifact, in that the assessments of micro-neighborhood attributes were made on the same semantic-differential type scales as the components of the micro-neighborhood satisfaction index. In the analyses of community and macro-neighborhood satisfaction, on the other hand, different formats were used for the attribute assessment items.

25. In the Planned Communities Study, several items were analyzed which may be considered objective environmental attributes. These items were based on the respondent's housing costs (and income) relative to the housing cost (and income level) of others in his micro-neighborhood and his community. While some of these measures were found to be related to neighborhood satisfaction, their importance in a multivariate analysis was relatively low, contributing less than 1 percent to the total explained variance. Consequently, they are excluded from the discussion in this paper. For a more detailed consideration of these measures, see Lansing et al. (1970: ch. 5) and Zehner (1970).

26. For a more thorough discussion of the rationale and procedure used in measuring residential density, see Marans and Mandell (1972); Marans, Wineman, and Fox (1972), and Lansing et al. (1970). Undoubtedly there are other ways to define and measure density including the number of people per room, people per acre, and people per square mile.

27. Since apartment dwellers were excluded from the sample, mean densities in the communities were relatively low. Residents did not live at densities exceeding 25 dwellings per acre and only 4 percent of the sample lived in the highest density category of 12.50 to 25 dwellings per acre.

28. Factor analysis resulted in a similar grouping of life domains.

29. It should be remembered that data on the micro-neighborhood satisfaction were not collected as part of the Quality of Life work.

REFERENCES

Andrews, F. M., Morgan, J., and Sonquist, J. *Multiple classification analysis.* Ann Arbor: University of Michigan, Institute for Social Research, 1969.

Andrews, F. M., and Philips, G. W. "The squatters of Lima: Who they are and what they want." Journal of Developing Areas, January 1970, 4, 211-229.

Campbell, A. *White attitudes toward black people.* Ann Arbor: University of Michigan, Institute for Social Research, 1971.

Campbell, A., and Converse, P. E. (Eds.), *The human meaning of social change.* New York: Russell Sage Foundation, 1972.

Cantril, H. *The pattern of human concerns.* New Brunswick: Rutgers University Press, 1965.

Easterlin, R. A. Does economic growth improve the human lot? Some empirical evidence. In P. A. David and M. W. Reder (Eds.), *Nations and households in economic growth: Essays in honor of Moses Abramovitz.* Palo Alto: Stanford University Press, in press.

French, J.R.P., Jr., Rodgers, W., and Cobb, S. Adjustment as person-environment fit. In G. V. Coelho, D. Hamburg, and J. Adams (Eds.), *Coping and adaptation.* New York: Basic Books, in press.

Fried, M., and Gleicher, P. "Some sources of residential satisfaction in an urban slum." Journal of the American Institute of Planners, 1961, 27, 305-315.

Gans, H. J. *The urban villagers.* New York: The Free Press of Glencoe, 1962.

Gans, H. J. *The Levittowners.* New York: Random House, 1967.

Gulick, J., Bowerman, C. and Back, K. Newcomer enculturation in the city: Attitudes and participation. In F. S. Chapin and S. Weiss (Eds.), *Urban growth dynamics.* New York: John Wiley and Sons, 1962.

Hollingshead, A. B., and Rogler, L. Attitudes towards public housing in Puerto Rico. In L. Duhl (Ed.), *The urban condition.* New York: Basic Books, 1963.

Kaiser, E., Weiss, S., Burby, R., and Donnelly, J. Neighborhood environments and residential satisfaction: A survey of occupants and neighborhoods in 166 single family homes in Greensboro, N.C. Chapel Hill: University of North Carolina, Center for Urban and Regional Studies, 1970.

Lamanna, R. A. "Value consensus among urban residents." Journal of the American Institute of Planners, 1964, 30, 317-323.

Lansing, J. B., and Hendricks, G. *Automobile ownership and residential density.* Ann Arbor: University of Michigan, Institute for Social Research, 1967.

Lansing, J. B., and Marans, R. W. "Evaluation of neighborhood quality." Journal of the American Institute of Planners, 1969, 75, 195-199.

Lansing, J. B., Marans, R. W. and Zehner, R. B. *Planned residential environments.* Ann Arbor: University of Michigan, Institute for Social Research, 1970.

Maklan, M. Unpublished paper, University of Michigan.

Mandell, L., and Marans, R. W. *Participation in outdoor recreation: A national perspective.* A report prepared for the Bureau of Outdoor Recreation. Ann Arbor- University of Michigan, Institute for Social Research, 1972.

Marans, R. W., and Mandell, L. "The relative effectiveness of density related measures for predicting attitudes and behavior variables." Proceedings of the American Statistical Association Meetings, Social Statistics Section, 1972, 360-363.

Marans, R. W., Wineman, J., and Fox, B. *A methodology for measuring residential density in national samples.* Ann Arbor: University of Michigan, Institute for Social Research, 1972.

Metcalf, J. *Satisfaction and housing standards.* An Internal Note of the Building Research Situation, Urban Planning Division, Garston, Watford, Herts; England. 1967.

Michelson, W. Analytic sampling for design information: A survey of housing experiences. In H. Sanoff, and S. Cohn (Eds.), *EDRA I.* Proceedings of the 1st Annual Environmental Design Research Association Conference, 1969.

Ross, D. *Robert F. Kennedy: Apostle of change.* New York: Pocket Books, Inc., 1968.

Sheldon, E. B., and Moore, W. E. *Indicators of social change.* New York: Russell Sage Foundation, 1968.

Suttles, G. *The social order of the slums.* Chicago: University of Chicago Press, 1968.

Troy, P. N. *Environmental quality in four suburban areas.* Canberra: Australian National University, Urban Research Unit, 1971.

Wilcox, L. D., Brooks, R. M., Beal, G. M. and Klonglan, G. E. *Social indicators and societal monitoring.* San Francisco: Jossey-Bass, 1972.

Wilson, R. L. Liveability of the city: Attitudes and urban development. In F. S. Chapin, Jr. and S. Weiss (Eds.), *Urban growth dynamics.* New York: John Wiley and Sons, 1962.

Young, M., and Wilmott, P. *Family and kinship in East London.* London: Routledge and Kegan Paul, 1957.

Zehner, R. B. Satisfaction with neighborhoods: The effects of social compatability, residential density and site planning. Unpublished doctoral dissertation, University of Michigan, 1970.

Zehner, R. B. "Neighborhood and community satisfaction in new towns and less planned suburbs." Journal of the American Institute of Planners, 1971, 37, 379-385.

PART III
GOVERNANCE OF METROPOLITAN COMMUNITIES

Most aspects of the metropolitan system, including its social organization and functional distribution of economic activities and land use, have undergone a substantial increase in scale during the present century. Of the key elements, only the structure of general government has avoided major alteration. The effectiveness and equity of government have become increasingly important questions to which the three papers in this section are addressed. Taken together, they present a comprehensive discussion of many of the proposals to change the form of local government and the problems inherent in each.

Campbell and Dollenmayer and Fitch discuss the array of restructuring devices, but from different perspectives, while Zimmerman concentrates more intensively on the analysis of a more limited number of devices.

Campbell and Dollenmayer are particularly interested in the redistribution of social and economic activity between country and city and between central city and suburb, and the pressures that this process has put on governmental institutions. The inability of fragmented jurisdictions to deal with mismatches of needs and resources is a central focus of their paper. Thus, they present their evaluations of several suggested changes in governmental form in the context of the effect these changes will have on the racial, social, and economic disparities that have been associated with population movements.

While the federal government and the states have the constitutional and fiscal resources to deal with urban problems, the means they have chosen so far either have been ineffectual in obtaining social equity or have aggravated existing conditions. Recent state court decisions, however, particularly in the area of education, may have the effect of encouraging a much-needed redistribution of resources.

Fitch is largely concerned with evaluating various government reforms in terms of fiscal efficiency. He discusses various models of social choice, and uses the Tiebout market model (of which he is critical) as a reference point in much of his essay. Fitch is also pessimistic about many of the governmental adaptations that have been proposed.

Campbell and Dollenmayer and Fitch feel that some form of metropolitan government could effectively deal with both the efficiency and the equity problems of urban areas, but are well aware of the political infeasibility of relying solely on local initiative. These authors are also skeptical about the ability of decentralization to solve problems either in the production and delivery of services or in equity and redistribution.

Zimmerman focuses particularly on those structural adaptive methods that fall short of general reorganization, such as intergovernmental service agreements, transfer of functions, and special districts. He presents data on the growth and frequency of these arrangements derived from a major national survey that correlates the use of these adaptive methods with such variables as city size and region of the country. He concludes that most of these adaptive methods are merely short-term solutions that really perpetuate the problem of fragmentation.

All the authors, while recognizing the desirability of some federal initiative in this area, find fault with federal revenue-sharing as a response to urban problems, feeling that it aggravates the fragmentation of jurisdictions. This fragmentation, in turn, contributes to both the social (Campbell and Dollenmayer) and the fiscal (Fitch) difficulties of metropolitan areas. The authors also agree that some form of revenue-sharing within metropolitan areas, perhaps adapting the Minneapolis-St. Paul, Minnesota, model, may be a more beneficial device.

CHAPTER 8

GOVERNANCE IN A METROPOLITAN SOCIETY

Alan K. Campbell and Judith A. Dollenmayer

Maxwell School of Citizenship and Public Affairs
Syracuse University

METROPOLITANISM, a phenomenon created by the redistribution of population and economic activity, has already greatly affected the policies and institutions of American government. However, since any clear response of government inevitably lags behind economic and social change, it can always be demonstrated that public institutions and policies are inadequate, when measured against the pace and magnitude of change. The demonstration of inadequacy, however, is not a sufficient prerequisite for institutional and policy changes. An understanding of one's assumptions about what is desirable, and about the causes of social and economic change, is also necessary. Finally, the kind of impact institutional and policy changes can exert on social and economic phenomena must be determined. The implicit values that underlie suggested changes should be explicitly identified.

This essay assumes that an effective metropolitan system of government must meet several tests. An obvious problem of metropolitan analysis is that these tests can be stated only in general. The empirical evidence on which to base fair, specific tests of the productivity and satisfactions created by existing or proposed systems of local government does not exist. Nonetheless, if the structure of local government is at all determining, it can be said with authority that the present system fails to answer the needs of an increasingly metropolitan society.

A revised structure should more closely reflect the actual geographic area of economic interaction, while easing the application of environmental control technologies across boundary lines. One important aim should be to minimize the fiscal and other externalities that now flow across boundaries. Second, an equitable distribution of the public goods of an affluent society—notably education, health, and social services—should be encouraged, not retarded, by the local system. Ideally, local government should be flexible enough to allow changes in conceptions of what society should guarantee to its citizens, for, in Richard Sennett's (1970: 8) phrase, "the idea of history is that a society will come to be different than it expected to be in the past." Finally, the system should be so arranged that functions best performed across large areas can be placed in area-wide jurisdictions, while those that can fall to smaller units should remain there, allowing both economies of scale and the continued viability of communities that identify themselves as such.

Metropolitanism, the redistribution of people and economic activity between countryside and urban area and between city and suburb, is the phenomenon that currently presses hardest upon existing governments. Metropolitanism has grown visibly more influential in formulating prescriptions for change in institutions and policies alike.

For analytical purposes, it is useful to separate substantive policy responses from responses that urge the restructuring of government, though the two are often reciprocally related. For example, new policies to alleviate poverty, to improve education for the poor, to cleanse polluted air and water, to reduce crime, and to move people and goods expeditiously can be undertaken through the established institutional system. Like changes in the substance of policy, however, changes in the structure of government can also respond to the perceived inadequacy of present institutions to address metropolitan-born ills. Classically, political scientists would recommend restructuring governments to reflect the wider metropolitan area of interaction, even if metropolitanization drew *no* social problems in its wake (see Studentski, 1930; Jones, 1942: esp. 334; Maass, 1959; Gulick, 1962).

Suggested structural changes include a redistribution of functions among levels of government; the restructuring of governmental administration or jurisdiction at local or intermediate levels of the system (county, regional, or state); and the reallocation of policy-making, administrative, and financial responsibilities among levels of government and among jurisdictions on the same level. This paper focuses upon structural responses but stresses their hoped-for substantive results.

To understand the relation of structural change to metropolitan-generated problems, it is necessary first to describe the metropolitanizing process in broad strokes. The consequent redistribution of people and economic activity is noted, as well as the relation of this shifting pattern to the prevailing system of jurisdictions, particularly local ones. Next, a number of restructuring responses are explored: Do they address the problems they were designed to solve? The political ambience of restructuring is discussed; it suggests that only a complex political calculus can create reasonable prospects for effective metropolitan governance.

THE SORTING OUT OF PEOPLE AND ECONOMIC ACTIVITY

The metropolitanization process and its demographic consequences are relatively well understood. If anything, generalizations about metropolitanization have grown too gross, overlooking many deviations from the average. Before commenting on any of these exceptions, however, it may be well to state the generalizations briefly.

Since before the turn of the century, Americans have been "sorting themselves out" between rural and urban areas, and, within urban areas, between central cities and the areas outside central cities normally called suburbs (see Goist, 1971, for a reassessment of Park's importance to the theory of metropolitanization). This process gathered momentum during the 1920s, braked during the Depression, changed in character during the war (little suburbanization, but rural workers were drawn to cities), and took off with a vengeance following World War II. Since then, the population of metropolitan areas has grown continuously; concurrently, people have been redistributing themselves within these areas.

Moving to metropolitan areas from farms and small towns, Americans sought greater economic opportunity and fled the decline of such opportunity in their home areas. Of the two motivations, whether the "pull" of new jobs or the "push" of no jobs was greater has not been determined. Movement to urban areas, however, still brings higher incomes to some migrants in their new place of residence. In particular, there are substantial initial increases in income for black males who migrate north (Wertheimer, 1970: 57 ff.). As Table 8.1 shows, between one to five years after moving, black males with some college education had gains in annual income of $3,000 or more, approximately the same gains as were made by white males.

As the migration from rural to urban places progressed, a simultaneous movement gathered speed within metropolitan areas—a dispersal from central cities to suburban areas. This process was not random. People of higher incomes, mostly white, moved outward, relegating the central city to people of lower socioeconomic status. For example, within SMSAs in 1970, 13.4 percent of central-city residents were living below the poverty level, which was $3,968 for a nonfarm

Table 8.1: 1967 Annual Earnings Gains of Migrants from Rural South to Urban North Compared with Rural South Nonmigrants of Same Education, Race and Sex

Years after Moving	To Small Northern Cities[a]		To Very Large Northern Cities[b]	
	Elementary Education	College Education	Elementary Education	College Education
White males				
0-5	—	$3,075	$ 600	$3,075
6-35	$1,550	2,175	2,700	3,700
Black males				
0-5	800	3,875	1,400	3,875
6-35	1,550	2,175	2,000	3,000

NOTE: Data from It can pay to move: An estimate of income gains of rural-to-urban and south-to-north migrants, 1971, p. 7. Adapted from Wertheimer, 1970.
a. Under 50,000 people.
b. Over 750,000 people.

Table 8.2: Family Characteristics in Metropolitan Areas, 1970

Item	Central City	Outside Central City
Percentage of persons below poverty level[a]	13.4	6.3
Percentage aged 25-29 with less than high school education	25.3	19.2
Percentage of population over 65	11.1	7.4
Female-headed families as a percentage of all families[b]	17.0	8.8
AFDC[c] families as a percentage of all families[b]	9.8	2.4

NOTE: Data adapted from Schultze, Fried, Rivlin, and Teeters, 1972, p. 295.
a. 1969 data.
b. 1971 data.
c. AFDC-Aid to families with dependent children.

family of four (U.S. Bureau of the Census, 1971: 19).[1] The comparable figure for outside central cities was 6.3 percent. Tied to the greater poverty in central cities were higher proportions of the aged, female-headed families, and welfare recipients (shown in Table 8.2).

The economic disparities created between city and suburb by these population shifts are large and significant. They are greatest in the largest metropolitan areas. The largest metropolitan areas attain the highest income levels, but these areas also show the widest gap between city and suburb (Campbell and Sacks, 1967: 23). In the smallest areas, the exact reverse is true. Small central cities, in fact, have higher income levels than their suburbs.

Although exactly comparable data are unavailable for 1970, it is possible to compare the ratio of those who live in poverty (as federally defined) to the relatively affluent (incomes over $15,000) in central cities; then this ratio is held against the same ratio for the suburbs (see Table 8.3). A comparison of the two ratios demonstrates that the relative position of the central cities has deteriorated since 1960. If the ratios of poverty to affluence in both areas were alike, their

Table 8.3: Relationship of Ratio of Poverty to Affluence in Central Cities to the Same Ratio for Areas Outside the Central City, 1959 and 1969

Population of SMSA	1959	1969
All SMSAs	0.55	0.44
Over 3,000,000	0.41	0.20
1,000,000 to 3,000,000	0.41	0.33
500,000 to 1,000,000	0.58	0.55
250,000 to 500,000	0.90	0.78
100,000 to 250,000	1.10	0.93
Less than 100,000	1.78	1.74

NOTE: Source—unpublished census data analyzed by Professor Seymour Sacks, Maxwell School, Syracuse University.

relationship would appear as unity (1.0). A figure less than 1.0 in Table 8.3 shows that the central-city's ratio is less favorable than the suburban one. In 1959, this relationship of widely varied ranges of low incomes to high for all metropolitan areas was 0.55; by 1969, it had declined to 0.44. The deterioration occurred in metropolitan areas of every size.

These differences in suburban-central city income levels are partially explained by the higher proportion of blacks who live in central cities. Since incomes of blacks fall considerably below those of whites, the growing proportion of black population in central cities depresses central-city income levels. As Table 8.4 shows, the black proportion of central-city population grew from 17.8 percent to 21.9 percent between 1960 and 1970. Insufficient incomes and suburban discriminatory practices (through zoning and the unavailability of mortgages, among other devices) continue to block access to the suburbs for blacks and other minorities.

Some analysts predicted, or at least hoped, that the movement to suburbia would gradually decelerate or even be reversed. These hopes were raised, in part, by a belief that urban renewal and related development programs would draw middle-income families back to the cities from the suburbs. This hasn't happened. In recent years, a few writers, encouraged by the "youth revolt" of suburban-bred and -bored people in their twenties, began to hope that more than a few of these young people would choose to raise their families in the denser culture of the cities. Again, this hasn't happened. Neither data from the 1960 and 1970 censuses nor public-opinion polls give any clue that this reversal has occurred or will occur.

People's attitudes about where they prefer to live are especially revealing. As Table 8.5 shows, about half the interviewees who live in large cities and about half who live in suburbia are dissatisfied. But those in cities, especially the largest cities, would prefer to live in small towns, or, increasingly, on farms, while less than a quarter of the suburbanites would choose city life. What appears to be a

Table 8.4: Nonwhite Proportion of Population in the United States and Within Metropolitan Areas, 1900-70

Date	Nonwhite Population as a Percentage of:			
	Total U.S. Population	Total SMSA Population	Total CC Population	Total OCC Population
1900[a]	12.1	7.8	6.8	9.4
1910	11.1	7.3	6.9	8.1
1920	10.3	7.2	7.3	7.0
1930	10.2	8.1	9.0	6.4
1940	10.2	8.6	10.1	6.0
1950	10.7	10.0	13.1	5.7
1960	11.4	11.7	17.8	5.2
1970	12.3	13.7	21.9	5.5

NOTE: Data from U.S. Bureau of the Census, 1963.
a. Data for 1900-1960 refer to the coterminous United States, whereas data for 1970 include Hawaii and Alaska.

Table 8.5: Where Americans Would Like to Live and Where They now Live, by Occupation, 1966 and 1971

Group	City	Suburb	Small Town	Farm	No Opinion
March 1966					
All adults over 21	22	28	31	18	1
City size where living now					
500,000+	36	37	21	5	1
50,000-499,999	34	31	24	9	2
2,500-49,999	6	24	60	9	1
Under 2,500, rural	1	7	23	69	—
Occupation					
Prof. and bus.	20	42	28	9	1
White collar	24	31	32	13	—
Manual	22	26	33	17	2
Farmers	4	6	19	71	—
June 1971					
All adults over 18	17	26	31	25	1
City size where living now					
1 million+	28	31	29	11	1
500,000-999,999	27	44	17	12	—
50,000-499,999	23	35	29	12	1
2,500-49,999	10	13	51	26	—
Under 2,500, rural	2	15	31	52	—
Occupation					
Prof. and bus.	18	31	31	20	—
White collar	18	32	32	18	—
Manual	14	27	33	26	—
Farmers	2	—	12	86	—

NOTE: Data adapted from Gallup International, Inc., **Gallup Opinion Index,** March 1966, p. 23, and August 1971, p. 28.

growing distaste for cities among professional and white-collar groups, as well as among manual workers, the constituency traditionally considered most "upwardly mobile," is ominous. If preference plays a significant role in place of residence, it can be predicted that most central cities will continue to lose population.

As population has shifted, so has economic activity. Some of this relocation is directly related to population movements; other changes are not. The substantial shift in manufacturing employment from central city to suburbs, for example, has been relatively independent of outward migration. As technology has made the single-level production line most efficient, the need for land—and for highways to serve new sites—has greatly increased (Birch, 1970; Hoover and Vernon, 1959). Such land is usually most available on the fringe of metropolitan areas. Since, however, labor and market determinants dictate location near large population concentrations, this movement is not so much to the countryside as to the fringe of urban concentrations. The result is a large growth of employment in suburban manufacturing, while central-city manufacturing is declining or, at best, holding its own.

There are, however, significant regional differences. Manufacturing employment continues to increase in southern cities and in some western cities, while declining in nearly all eastern cities (see Sacks, Ranney, and Andrew, 1972: 68-69). A mixed pattern appears in the Middle West. City age, the stage of metropolitanization, and the size of the area are all important determinants of these differences (Birch, 1970). Whether the pattern of eastern cities will be duplicated in other regions as they mature is unknown, but seems likely.

Retail activities have tended to follow their customers to the suburbs, ramifying into branch stores (see Table 8.6). The central-city parent stores sometimes close or, if they remain open, often provide a decreasing percentage of the company's total business. Again, regional differences exist.

Wholesaling, which by its nature must locate at the point of least cost of distribution, has historically settled near the geographic center of the urban area it served. Now wholesaling, too, is on the move, for congestion and traffic patterns do not inevitably place the least-cost point at the geographic center. Like their retail counterparts, many service activities that contact the general consumer directly—from hairdressers to medical practitioners—have pursued their clients to the suburbs. In some places, finance, communications, and government offices have mitigated the severest effects of this exodus by remaining at the center.

Economic analysts (e.g., Wilbur Thompson, 1965) are not prepared to decide the direction of causation in this metropolitan diffusion. Whether services follow their clients, or vice versa, is presently a chicken-and-egg problem. It is significant that the outward movement of economic activities has caused suburban employment to grow very much more rapidly than central-city employment.[2]

For many suburbanites, dispersal means living and working in suburbia. The number of suburbanites who also work there rose 40 percent (to 8.7 million) between 1960 and 1970 (Salpukas, 1972). Many higher-income, white-collar office jobs remain in the central city, preserving commuting as a way of life for many others. Numerous job-seekers who live in the central city could fill the new jobs in suburbia, but because of their low income, lack of transportation, discrimination, or a combination of these, they find following jobs to the suburbs extremely difficult. Despite the obstacles, preliminary 1970 census data show significantly more "reverse commuting" to the suburbs than in 1960—up from 845,000 workers to 1.46 million, an increase of 72.7 percent that is especially marked in the blighted urban areas—Cleveland, Baltimore, Detroit (Salpukas, 1972). The reverse commuting grows increasingly necessary, for more and more central-city jobs do not fit the skills of the population who continue moving into cities from the countryside and small towns.

These demographic and economic changes have created pervasive social problems which, in large part, can be solved only by government action. The

Table 8.6: 1958-67 Percent Increase in Retail Sales[a] in Selected Large Standard Metropolitan Statistical Areas, by SMSA Region

SMSA	Percent Increase	
	Central City	Outside Central City
Northeast	− 0.3	75.2
Washington, D.C.	−10.5	134.8
Boston, Ma.	− 1.4	79.2
Paterson-Clifton-Passaic, N.J.	0.9	74.5
New York, N.Y.	9.7	60.2
Rochester, N.Y.	18.1	91.3
Philadelphia, Pa.-N.J.	6.2	65.4
Pittsburgh, Pa.	7.8	28.7
Midwest	9.5	127.1
Chicago, Ill.	5.3	86.6
Detroit, Mi.	0.7	86.4
Minneapolis-St. Paul, Mn.	7.9	149.7
St. Louis, Mo.-Ill.	− 7.6	76.2
Cleveland, Oh.	−15.2	269.1
Dayton, Oh.	− 3.6	125.5
Milwaukee, Wi.	7.5	108.3
South	28.7	108.3
Miami, Fl.	− 2.5	98.2
Atlanta, Ga.	−37.7	153.9
Louisville, Ky., In.	14.0	101.8
New Orleans, La.	21.0	141.9
Dallas, Tx.	36.6	119.2
San Antonio, Tx.	36.4	79.9
West	20.2	119.0
Los Angeles-Long Beach, Ca.	22.2	75.4
San Francisco-Oakland, Ca.	16.3	81.6
Denver, Col.	11.1	132.4
Portland, Ore.-Wa.	28.1	180.3
Seattle, Wa.	18.0	152.5
Unweighted average, 37 SMSAs	12.6	105.8

NOTE: Data from U.S. Bureau of the Census, 1961a, 1970a. Adapted from Sacks, Ranney, and Andrew, 1972, pp. 66-67.
a. Deflated by general price increase.

poor, the disadvantaged, and the elderly are disproportionately present in the central city. Concentration aggravates the demand for social services directed to the needs of this population. Adequate housing, decent schools, livable incomes, and effective health care are all required if central cities are not to become the backwaters of American society.

Beyond these familiar, egregious, social problems, a variety of other problems emerge from the new spread pattern of settlement. Some of these can be characterized by the economists' concept of "externalities"—that is, the benefits and costs of activities flow across jurisdictional lines. All aspects of pollution—land, water, and air—fall into this category, as do the transportation system, water supply, and other public services that cannot (due to technological consider-ations) be adequately handled by the present fragmented jurisdictional system.

CROSSING GOVERNMENT BOUNDARIES

The movement of higher-income people outward from the center, as the technology of transportation makes that possible, is a long-standing phenomenon of American urbanization.[3] After World War II, two distinguishing character-istics of outward migration were the great numbers of people involved and the crossing of political jurisdictions. The latter phenomenon multiplies the difficulty of making an effective governmental response to shifting demographic patterns (Bollens, 1956). Instead of incorporating the new areas within city boundaries through annexation, as in the past, independent suburban governments—including special districts, counties, towns, villages, and school districts—sprang up, or old ones were remodeled to provide municipal services that formerly came only from city governments.[4] Tables 8.7 and 8.8 show the fragmentation of government caused by this proliferation of jurisdictions and the outward movement of popu-lation into existing jurisdictions. School-district consolidation, as Table 8.8. suggests, is an exception to the general dynamic, while special-district creation has recently been the most popular form of meeting service demands because it does not painfully alter the political system by changing or erasing general local-government boundaries. It thereby protects local office holders and others with a stake in those boundaries.

Table 8.7: SMSAs with Greatest Fragmentation of Local Government, 1967[a]

SMSA	1967 Local Governments			1970 Population (000)		
	Total	CC	OCC	Total	CC	OCC
Chicago, Il.	1,113	12	1,101	6,979	3,367	3,612
Philadelphia, Pa.-N.J.	876	5	871	4,818	1,949	2,869
Pittsburgh, Pa.	704	11	693	2,401	520	1,881
New York, N.Y.	551	3	548	11,572	7,895	3,677
St. Louis, Mo.-Il.	474	6	468	2,363	622	1,741
Portland, Or.-Wa.	385	17	368	1,009	382	627
San Francisco-Oakland, Ca.[b]	312	18	294	2,988	956	2,032
Indianapolis, In.[c]	282	7	275	1,110	500	610
Kansas City, Mo.-Ks.	272	22	250	1,254	502	752
Denver, Co.	269	6	263	1,228	515	713
Seattle-Everett, Wa.[d]	268	12	256	1,238	401	837
Cincinnati, Oh.-Ky.-In.	266	6	260	1,385	453	932
Peoria, Il.	261	12	249	342	127	215

NOTE: Data from Census data worksheets, U.S. Bureau of the Census, 1969, 1970b.
a. Including school and special districts.
b. Of 18 CC governments, Oakland has 11 and San Francisco has 7.
c. These 1967 figures have been radically changed by 1969 state legislation, which instituted "Unigov" for Indianapolis, drawing a far larger proportion of the OCC population under an umbrella metro government.
d. Of 12 CC governments, Seattle has 7 and Everett has 5.

Table 8.8: 1962-67 Changes in Governmental Units Within SMSAs, by Number and Percentage

Type of Local Government	Local Governments in the 227 SMSAs		Increase or Decrease 1962-67	
	1967	1962	Number	Percent
Total	20.703	21,817	−1,114	−5.1
School districts	5,018	7,072	−2,054	−29.0
Other Local Governments	15,685	14,745	940	6.4
Counties	404	407	−3	−0.7
Municipalities	4,977	4,903	74	1.5
Townships	3,255	3,282	−27	−0.8
Special Districts	7,049	6,153	896	14.6

NOTE: Data from U.S. Bureau of the Census, 1969, p. 1.

Aggravating the administrative disabilities caused by overlapping, fragmented governments is the mismatch between resource base and social need that is also a consequence of the present system. The shift in population and economic activities makes it more and more difficult for the central city and its lower-income residential suburbs to find locally the revenues that remain the sine qua non of responsiveness to genuine problems. The piecemeal system of governments hampers attempts to assemble the resources needed to build area-wide metropolitan infrastructural systems for transportation, waste disposal, water, etc. The present differences in tax base make responses to social problems unequal and inequitable.

This fragmented governmental system lays widely disparate tax burdens upon the jurisdictions and generates greatly varied expenditure levels and patterns (Advisory Commission on Intergovernmental Relations, 1967). Of particular importance are differential tax burdens (taxes as a percentage of personal income) between central cities and suburbs; on the average, central-city burdens run 40 to 50 percent higher (see Table 8.9).

There are, however, important differences among the suburbs. As Table 8.10 shows, the burden that New York City taxpayers bear is substantially heavier than the tax burden of people who live in Westchester County, but the gap is not

Table 8.9: Local Government Taxes as a Percentage of Personal Income, 1970 (Regional Averages Based on Data from 72 Largest SMSAs)

Region	Central City (Percent)	Outside Central (Percent)	CC/OCC Ratio (Percent)
Northeast	7.7	5.5	1.41
Midwest	7.2	4.8	1.48
South	5.3	3.4	1.56
West	7.3	6.3	1.14
Total (unweighted avg.)	6.9	5.0	1.39

NOTE: Data from unpublished computations of the Advisory Commission on Intergovernmental Relations, 1972.

Table 8.10: New York Area Local Government Taxes as a Percentage of Personal Income, 1966-67

	Type of Tax		
Area	State	Local	Total
% SMSA	7.18	9.25	16.43
% City	7.96	10.47	18.43
% Westchester County	4.82	5.76	10.58
% Nassau County	5.71	6.98	12.59
% Suffolk County	6.20	8.03	14.22
% Rockland County	6.39	8.12	14.51

NOTE: Data from Advisory Commission on Intergovernmental Relations, 1971, Tables G-8 and G-11; New York State Department of Commerce, 1970.

so great when compared to Rockland and Suffolk Counties. Within these counties, some subcounty jurisdictions doubtless carry tax burdens as high as New York City's.

Another significant fiscal aspect of metropolitan life finds suburban areas spending a much higher proportion of their total public expenditures on education than do central cities, while just the opposite is true for noneducational municipal expenditures. Despite higher expenditures for education in the suburbs, total per capita expenditures in each central city generally surpass average per capita expenditures in the suburbs (see Table 8.11).

Fiscal disparities are only one product of the current local government system. Not only are resources and needs mismatched, but little ability to plan for the future of the area exists, because each jurisdiction seeks its own advantage through zoning practices and other public policies. Over ten years ago, Robert Wood (1959: 41) noted:

A single-minded fixation on the service concept of government, an insistence on the preservation of political autonomy and multiplicity, mean, first of all, that it is impossible to have a vision of what the metropolitan regions might become. When each jurisdiction goes on its separate way, urban sprawl continues, with its companions of spreading blight, cheap commercial developments along major highways, inadequate parks, congested schools, mediocre administration, smog, traffic jams, recurrent crises in mass transportation, and the hundred and one irritations of undirected growth. The 'gray belt' which Raymond Vernon has so graphically described continues to expand, and the municipalities caught directly in its path are left to grapple with its consequences, one by one. In place of a coordinated attack on the less attractive by-products of urbanization, each jurisdiction tries to avoid the conditions it regards as unpalatable, to protect its own, and to let its neighbors fend for themselves. When local government disclaims responsibility for the regional environment, the capacity to realize the potential of that environment is irrevocably lost.

Table 8.11: Per Capita Total Public Expenditures, 1957 and 1970
(Regional Averages Based on 37 Largest SMSAs)

Region	1957			1970		
	Central City	Outside Central City	CC/OCC Ratio	CC	OCC	CC/OCC Ratio
Northeast	$207	$165	1.25	$613	$419	1.48
Midwest	190	152	1.23	498	360	1.38
South	165	124	1.33	395	308	1.28
West	224	176	1.27	577	459	1.26
Total						
(unweighted average)	196	154	1.27	524	385	1.36
(weighted average)	213	170	1.25	600	419	1.43

NOTE: Data from unpublished computations of the Advisory Commission on Intergovernmental Relations, 1972.

THE GOVERNMENTAL RESPONSE

Although no coordinated national policy has responded to these by-products
of metropolitanization, all levels of government have undertaken certain specific
programs or actions.

The federal government has attempted various programmatic, structural, and
fiscal responses in combination. In general, the amount of federal resources
available to state and local governments has risen, while the federal government
has sometimes laid down corollary requirements that affect the structure of local
government. Through aid, the federal government has promoted a variety of
state and local actions to address the social and hardware difficulties of metropolitan areas. Through housing, urban renewal, grants for sewage and water
systems, aid to education and manpower training, and aid for mass transit and
other purposes, the federal government has tried to provide some fiscal resources
to enable the state-local system to be at least partially responsive. New programs
with a strong city orientation were developed in the 1960s; by 1973, expenditures
for them exceeded four billion dollars (see Table 8.12).

In some state-local grant programs, the federal government has required
regional coordination and planning of the aided function. First used in airport-
aid legislation, this provision was later added to other programs (transportation,
water, waste disposal, etc.). Often it led to the creation of multi-jurisdictional
cooperation for specific aided functions, but sometimes the effects of aid provisions battled their intent.[5]

A more general structural impact on local government occurred when the
federal government began to encourage the formation of local councils of
governments (COGs) by making councils eligible for federal planning grants.
Although COGs now exist in most metropolitan areas, they are voluntary organizations of local officials which, at best, can encourage rather than mandate
cooperative activities.

Table 8.12: Levels of City-Oriented Federal Grant-in-Aid Programs Fiscal Years 1971-73 (Millions of Dollars)

Program	1971	1972	1973
Model Cities	521	620	620
Urban renewal	1,029	1,450	1,000
Community action	410	353	384
Urban mass transit	334	606	1,000
Public housing	626	886	1,105
Open-space land	75	100	100
Neighboring Facilities	40	40	40
Total	3,035	4,055	4,249

NOTE: Data from Schultz et al., 1972, p. 311. In turn, from U.S. Office of Management and Budget, 1972a, 1972b.

In 1966, federal legislation in the Demonstration Cities and Metropolitan Development Act granted to a metropolitan-wide agency in each urban area the power to comment on numerous kinds of grant applications. Under a directive of the Office of Management and Budget, the metropolitan agency is empowered to return an application to the local jurisdiction that submitted it, together with suggested alterations. The metropolitan agency may even urge abandonment of the proposal. The local jurisdiction can amend its application or submit it to the federal agency together with the remarks of the metropolitan review agency. In most areas, this review authority (known as the "A-95 power," after the OMB circular that instituted it) belongs to the COG.

How well do COGs meet the need for effective area-wide action? One study of COGs (Mogulof, 1971: 110-111) concludes:

> We are convinced . . . that there are tasks requiring a capacity for metropolitan governance, and we are equally convinced that the COG does not and cannot have this capacity. Given previous failures in developing regional governing structures, the COG has been a major achievement . . . *provided the COG is seen developmentally,* and not as a final form. Over the short pull the COG will continue to be worth the effort, provided that HUD and OMB have this developmental sense, and . . . are not prepared to 'rescue' the COG from the strain it is experiencing and should continue to experience as a result of federal requirements.

The author's conditional optimism may be soured by the possibility that COGs, far from seeing themselves (or being seen) as transitional organizations en route to metropolitan governance, are likely to become defensive mechanisms for existing jurisdictions and the prerogatives of their elected officials, who in fact are the COG.[6]

The most recent federal response is revenue-sharing, which passes federal revenues to state and local governments according to a formula that supposedly recognizes need and state-local tax effort alike. If revenue-sharing did overcome existing fiscal disparities, its contribution to overcoming a major fault of the present system would be substantial. But even if revenue-sharing corrected disparities, it would reinforce another major fault of the system, the patchwork of jurisdictions. As it is, revenue-sharing does not respond to the deep causes of the present system's impotence to solve the substantive problems of metropolitan areas.

The program fails to correct disparities, because its formula for distributing funds inadequately recognized the enormous fiscal disadvantage of most central cities and low-income residential suburbs. The present formula's character is illustrated by the fact that many central cities are receiving less money than originally expected—the use of 1970 census data and current tax burdens reduce the projected benefits even further for many cities. If revenue-sharing were to recognize need, their population losses (mostly middle-income residents), far from reducing the amounts received by cities, would increase the urban share, for the exodus of middle-income wage-earners intensifies urban need. By the same token, under the current formula the suburbs receive much more than they anticipated, as noted below.

Another factor increases the inability of the local portion of revenue-sharing to overcome local disparities: the states' use of their share of the money. State funds are now deployed in a manner that reflects the distribution of political power. Cities, because of centrifugal population movement and provincial political characteristics, wield considerably lighter political weapons in state legislatures than do their suburbs. Since state resources now flow in channels of political power, not social need, one can fairly predict that revenue-sharing money will buttress disparities between cities and suburbs as well as between high-, middle-, and low-income suburbs. Even though disparities may be preserved at higher levels of expenditure because of the golden touch of revenue-sharing (although even that is uncertain), the program will not offset them.

Nevertheless, the new revenue flowing to all jurisdictions will provide a fiscal breathing space for most of them. Revenue-sharing must therefore be seen as a step away from regionalization, because fiscal stringency, more than any other single pressure, has encouraged political leaders to think in regional terms. In the short term, at least, that pressure is partly relieved, especially for central-city mayors and (to a lesser degree) governors.

The inability of revenue-sharing to overcome disparities, and its tendency to preserve existing jurisdictions, have drawn criticism. Donald Canty (1972a: 36) judges that:

The federal government's role should be that of equalizer, undoing past damage to the victims of poverty and racism and making up for jurisdictional disparities.

The backward step in terms of metropolitan change would be enactment of stringless revenue sharing as the primary, if not exclusive, form of federal aid to states and localities.

It would be a backward step because, first, revenue sharing of the 'general' variety proposed by the Administration would distribute its benefits with disturbing evenness among needful and well-to-do jurisdictions alike, perpetuating the disparities between them.

Second, these benefits would go to jurisdictions rather than individuals, which could only harden the metropolitan pattern. Since the money would not be tied to need or targeted on the needy, it would not follow them across jurisdictional boundaries, so that these boundaries would remain class and racial barriers.

Finally, in the long term it is doubtful that revenue-sharing can overcome the fiscal crisis of state and local governments, despite the ardor of states and localities to embrace this money now. In New York State and New York City, the anticipated revenues from the new program were incorporated into 1973 budgets months before the checks began to arrive. Further, for jurisdictions that perform the welfare function, the cut in social services (most dramatically in day care, services to the aged, and drug-addiction programs) that was tied to the revenue-sharing bill will severely reduce its potential contribution to local budgets.[7] Finally, the emphasis of revenue-sharing formula on more aid for areas of population growth, baldly considered in terms of these numbers alone, gives some suburban towns and counties as much money in the first half of 1973 as they anticipated for the entire year (Madden, 1972).

Overall, the federal government's transfusions of money and exhortations to reorganize have made no major contribution to solving the social problems that press upon central cities. Education remains inadequate, housing is being abandoned apace, and the manpower training program (after skimming off the people, like high-school graduates, who are most likely to succeed) has not equipped ghetto residents for the available jobs within their commuting range.[8]

If the federal response has been inadequate or misconceived, the same generalization can be leveled with double force at the role of states.[9] Long criticized for their inattention to city problems, state governments were thought to be waking to their urban responsibilities after the 1962-63 Supreme Court decisions (Baker v. Carr and Sanders v. Gray) required application of the "one-man, one-vote" principle. Unfortunately from the cities' viewpoint, the judicial requirement of fair representation in state legislatures came too late. By the mid-1960s, cities had already lost to the suburbs their preeminent position in state populations. The chief beneficiaries of reapportionment are suburban jurisdictions, and suburbs will gain even more as population continues to move outward. As the 1970 census is used to redraw legislative districts, this impact will become fully visible because the areas of greatest population growth are the outer suburbs.

State governments might respond to the difficulties of their large-city jurisdictions along three general lines. They could assume full responsibility for selected functions of government, thereby enlarging state-wide the tax base to support these activities. Welfare and education are usually discussed as best suited to state assumption. States could also increase the amount of state aid and, more important, concentrate that aid in areas of greatest need. Finally, states could promote local government reorganization through redrafting their mostly antiquated local-government statutes or amending their constitutions.[10]

Some states have moved on all fronts, but no state has shown dramatic innovation in any of these directions. Recently, a few more states have assumed full financial responsibility for welfare, while other states have paid for public assistance ever since it was instituted in the 1930s.

Another kind of state assumption is under way in New York, where an Urban Development Corporation has been charged with providing greater housing opportunities across the state. UDC is empowered to do this not only by promoting housing developments, but also by building entire new communities. The legislature gave the corporation the financial powers to bond and borrow in order to generate housing, as well as the power to override local zoning and building codes. UDC's supercession power stirred bitter controversy and has been used sparingly; in a 1972 pullback from Westchester County, UDC found that the power of local political outrage could thwart its statutory powers. Governor Rockefeller in 1973 acquiesced to legislative curbs on UDC. Nonetheless, other states have been attracted to this device, and legislation creating similar public corporations is now being actively considered by many legislatures.[11]

States have increased their aid to local governments, but, on the whole, such state aid has not gone to the areas of greatest need (Advisory Commission on Intergovernmental Relations, 1967). For example, the steepest increase in aid to education has benefited suburban jurisdictions, not central-city ones (Berke, Sacks, Bailey, and Campbell, 1972: 18-20). Only where the welfare function looms large in the city budget has state aid for welfare risen sharply. Further, such aid increases mirror increases in the number of welfare recipients and are therefore automatic responses rather than deliberate policies.

In 1967, the Committee for Economic Development (1970: 35) assessed the flow of aid this way:

> The anti-central-city, and to a lesser extent, the anti-metropolitan biases of existing state and federal aid programs demonstrate the need not only for more resources, but for a reallocation of those already being used. Today direct state and federal aid supports 27 percent of all expenditures within central cities but 29 percent of those in suburban areas and 37 percent of all local expenditures in the remainder of the nation. If examined relative to local tax effort, direct federal and state aid is equivalent to only 44 percent of central city taxes, while the comparable figures for suburbia and the rest of the nation are, respectively, 53 and 74 percent.

Today, though state and federal aid support a higher proportion of both central-city and suburban expenditures, the suburbs have pulled even farther ahead of central cities in the race for aid, except in the Northeast (see Table 8.13). There is an obvious political dimension to this development, which will be reinforced by the pro-suburban reapportionment that will emerge from the 1970 census.

Perhaps the states have faltered most seriously in failing to encourage local government reorganization. Except for state action in Indiana, which consolidated the city of Indianapolis and the county of Marion, the creation of the Metropolitan Regional Council in Minneapolis-St. Paul, and permissive legis-

Table 8.13: State and Federal Aid as a Percentage of Total Expenditures in the 72 Largest SMSAs, 1970

	Central City	Outside Central City	CC/OCC Ratio
Northeast	35	32	1.09
Midwest	27	35	0.77
South	26	40	0.65
West	35	38	0.92
Total (unweighted average)	30	36	0.83

NOTE: Data from an unpublished tabulation of the Advisory Commission on Intergovernmental Relations, 1972.

lation in a number of states, no major impetus to local government reorganizations is visible today.

In most states, the permissive legislation now on the books allows general interlocal cooperation. This cooperation must, of course, serve the interests of every jurisdiction involved; consequently, the most pressing problems of many jurisdictions are not eagerly alleviated by their neighbors. It would be very difficult, for example, to convince a suburb that it should help to support its central-city's schools.

In regard to some functions, cooperation exists because every jurisdiction gains by it—or at least none loses. Such interlocal cooperation takes many forms, from informal agreements to formal contracts.[12] A recent tally (Zimmerman, 1973) shows that of the 2,248 towns and cities surveyed, 61 percent participate in some form of interlocal agreement for services. Central cities are apparently less able to make intermunicipal arrangements (37 percent of the central cities surveyed have them, and 56 percent of the suburbs do), but agreements with public authorities are more common among central cities (32 percent of central cities have them, while 18 percent of suburbs do).

Besides such interlocal agreements, area-wide, one-function special districts may be created. To handle water supply, sewage disposal, and transportation, local governments often turn to a regional authority, which is delegated partial responsibility for one of these functions. Occasionally regional authorities are given taxing power, but more often they are financed by user charges. One of the best known region-wide bodies is the Port of New York Authority.

There also have been created a few multifunctional, area-wide authorities. The oldest and best known is Boston's Metropolitan District Commission, which provides some transportation services and water supply and is partly responsible for sewage disposal.[13] Multifunction districts have also been created in Portland, Oregon, and Seattle. The most recent large-city establishment of a multifunction special district is the Metropolitan Council of Minneapolis-St. Paul.

The Council, created in 1967, is a relatively autonomous regional unit that covers a seven-county area, two major cities, about 130 lesser municipalities, and 1,800,000 people. The Minnesota legislature created the Council partly in order to curtail a proliferation of special districts. It holds important fiscal and substantive powers that can be exercised without state or local approval.

All fifteen members of the Minneapolis-St. Paul Council are appointed by the Governor—fourteen are selected from combinations of legislative districts, while the chairman is appointed at large. Thus constituted, the Council appears to have an independent base of power. It is financed by a limited tax it levies on all property in the seven counties. By law, the Council (among other activities) may:

(1) Review comprehensive plans of special districts and suspend them;

(2) review comprehensive plans of municipalities and any zoning changes of metropolitan significance, and suspend those plans and changes for sixty days, after which the municipality may continue the action;

(3) exercise A-95 review; and

(4) appoint one of its members to any metropolitan commission.[14]

The first of these powers is potentially the greatest.

An important underlying idea is that the Council will become the "holding company" for single-function special districts that provide area-wide services. The 1967 law that created the Council stipulated this relationship with sewer services. The Council appoints the seven-member board of the new Metropolitan Sewer Service and generally controls the Service, now the sole sewer authority for the metropolitan area. General obligation bonds may be issued by the Council on behalf of the board, which finances sewer services by charges to the municipalities and districts. A 1969 law gave the council similar supervision of a Metropolitan Park Board, though the courts rescinded this action on the basis of a technicality about adjournment of the legislature. Solid-waste disposal is a county responsibility—subject, however, to plans developed by the Council. Under point one of the statute cited above, the Council holds planning authority over a Metropolitan Airports Commission and has recently twice vetoed a new airport site. The fate of the Minneapolis-St. Paul Council hinges partly on the assumption that several other special districts will be tied to it as the Metropolitan Sewer Service is.

Local and area-wide sentiment for change prompted the state legislature to create the Council, whose early support in the region has continued. The Council seems to consider itself an extension of state government and has become politically more controversial as it has begun to act. For example, there has been an argument recently that seats on the Council should be elective. Governor Wendell Anderson, who now appoints Council members, recommended to the 1972 session of the legislature that the Council be made elective, ostensibly to make it more accessible and open to the public. Opponents, particularly state legislators, fear that an elected Council would compete for public attention and loyalty with both local government officials and the state legislative delegation from the area covered by the Council (O'Keefe, 1973).

Only one genuine metropolitan federation exists in the United States—Miami/Dade County. In this Florida case, a number of formerly local functions were assigned to the county, and the county also agreed to deliver local services to its unincorporated areas. Dade County now serves both as a coordinator of the activities of municipalities within it, and as a prime deliverer of services to unincorporated areas.

The best-known governmental federations exist outside the United States, in Toronto and London. In London, the first-tier governments are the 32 boroughs, which have powers independent of the regional Greater London Council, and the Council holds powers independent of the boroughs. The Council and the boroughs share functions, but each holds independent powers over aspects of those functions.[15]

Representatives to the legislative body of the Greater London Council are elected from legislative districts drawn without regard to borough lines. Thus they represent people, not jurisdictions. In Toronto, the system is genuinely federal, for the jurisdcitions are represented on the legislative body of the Municipality of Toronto, the de facto regional government.[16]

As another measure, not always explicitly designed to cope with the problems of metropolitanism, some states have created substate regions. The types of substate districts they have formed range from simple administrative decentralizations of state activities to regional authorities which operate a service that once belonged wholly or partly to local governments. Substate regions have become an attractive device, in view of the frequent immobility of local governments in planning (Council of State Governments, 1971). The U.S. Office of Management and Budget (1971; see also USOMB, 1967) also promotes the creation of substate regions "to encourage the state to exercise leadership in delineating and establishing a system of planning and development districts in each state which can provide a consistent geographic base for the coordination of federal, state, and local development programs."[17]

The federal initiative has produced substate regions that are in some places state-founded, in some places local creations. The most widespread response has been to assemble Councils of Governments, discussed earlier. Leaving aside COGs, however, many administrative devices that are clearly state-originated and state-oriented have emerged with federal encouragement. Many are simply planning, rather than operating, agencies (in Tennessee, Maine, California, and New York, for example).

Some states are moving to establish common geographic areas as the basis of all departmental decentralization, similar to the common regions drawn by the federal government for a variety of its domestic departments and agencies. Under strong leadership from the state, these regions might become a new layer of government between states and localities, though for political reasons this may be difficult. In time, some local functions may be absorbed by the regions, and some state activities may be decentralized to them. Such an evolution in the system seems unlikely to arouse the bitter political opposition that sudden, dramatic structural changes elicit.

DECENTRALIZATION—AN ALTERNATIVE RESPONSE

Recent demands of some central-city people for decentralization or community control urge a quite different restructuring response. In some sense, this neighborhood-born desire in cities echoes the defensive affection of suburbanites for their village jurisdictions. Whether urban decentralization would likewise produce the unhappy consequences of suburbanization is an open question.

Whatever the social-psychological or ideological issues raised by decentralization—and in our present state of knowledge, these are often obscure or tendentious—this essay presumes that some irreducible community interests exist beneath the clamor for decentralization. People do care whether the neighborhood's garbage is collected, whether their streets are safe for walking, whether local schools offer their children an equal chance to make good. These identifiable interests can be the subject of governmental responses in the form of planned or actual decentralization programs.[18]

At first, decentralization proposals may respond as much to the presumed psychological needs of people in low- and middle-income neighborhoods as to the need for better services in those neighborhoods. But if decentralization provides a more independent base of political power for these communities, it may reduce disparities in service levels among different districts within a metropolitan area, offering a larger slice of the service pie to the lower-income districts. On the other hand, greater fiscal autonomy for poor neighborhoods that would require them to lean more heavily upon their already overburdened tax bases would merely increase disparities. The small number of large-city decentralization schemes now operating have been in existence too briefly for a clear empirical determination of which outcome is the more likely.

In fact, most large-city decentralization schemes in the United States today are "plans." Schools have been decentralized in New York City and Detroit, while Dayton has adopted a small-scale decentralization of its general government, clearly controlled by City Hall. The Indiana legislature has initiated a system of "mini-governments" for Indianapolis's new Unigov system. In the recently consolidated government of Jacksonville-Duval County, Florida, there is talk of adopting a variant of decentralization, while the Citizens League of Minneapolis (1970) began in 1970 to press for "suburbs in the city" to ensure minority representation in Minneapolis-St. Paul's government.

In addition to these actual or preoperative decentralizations, numerous plans exist for decentralizing the government of New York City. Mayor Lindsay's scheme, called "command decentralization," is in experimental operation already (Office of the Mayor, 1971). As designed, the plan is more a management device than a devolution of political power.

Most New York City services (police, fire, sanitation, health, housing, etc.) have long been geographically decentralized into subcity areas that are not coterminous. The purpose of command decentralization is to coordinate services effectively. Using the already established community planning districts as the geographic base of the new system, the plan will appoint a manager for each district. Reporting to the mayor, the manager will preside over a "service cabinet" of the field supervisors from each participating city agency. The service cabinet is supposed to develop a new information system that will help link agency services to local conditions and priorities, maintain the delivery of services to the district's residents, and, eventually, redraw the boundaries of each functional subregion of the city to make them coterminous.

Five experimental districts (of the eight which are planned) have been established so far: one in Manhattan, two in Brooklyn, one in the Bronx, and one in Queens. Districts vary in population size from 118,808 to 212,957. Though command decentralization is too new to be assigned blame or praise, it appears that the original design for management decentralization alone may evolve into a system with significant political characteristics. The community advisory councils in the districts have increasingly strong voices in establishing priorities for their areas and in stipulating how city services will operate there.

Beyond command decentralization, six more-far-reaching decentralization schemes are currently proposed for New York City. Four have been designed by borough presidents (Robert Abrams of the Bronx, Sebastian Leone of Brooklyn, Donald Manes of Queens, and Percy Sutton of Manhattan), one by the Association of the Bar of New York City, and the last by a task force of the state-established Study Commission for New York City (Scott Commission). Each plan divides the city into neighborhood units, but the borough presidents, as might be expected, want to enhance the role of their units. The suggested optimum population size of the subdistricts varies from a 100,000 maximum (Manes proposal) to 200,000-300,000 (Scott Commission). Every plan but one substantially agrees about which functions or aspects of functions should be decentralized: sanitation, code enforcement, street maintenance, selected health services, park and playground operation. The exceptional plan would grant neighborhood units only the power to hold public hearings. Each of the plans goes considerably further than Lindsay's command decentralization in the area of delegating decision making and establishing formal neighborhood political institutions. The plans would all feature elected neighborhood councils, with elected or appointed chief executives. Only the Bar Association plan would grant any revenue-raising power to the neighborhoods.[19]

All of these schemes, and more, were to be considered by a City Charter Commission appointed by Governor Rockefeller. Politically, the proffer of these plans has moved the decentralization issue to center stage in New York City. The decentralizers base their case on the need for participation and redistribution of power (Costikyan, 1972; Costikyan and Lehman, 1972). Their opponents argue that participation will be slight, if past experience is any guide, and that decentralization will only exacerbate disparities among neighborhoods (Sayre, 1972a, 1972b).

Speculation about decentralization's effects demands careful consideration of how fiscal responsibility will be divided between the decentralized tier (neighborhoods or districts) and the city- or metropolitan-wide tier. The resource bases of decentralized units are bound to vary greatly, just as they do now among the suburbs. If these decentralized units were assigned any inde-pendent revenue-raising responsibility—and many argue that the units must be given such power if they are to have any sense of fiscal accountability—the differences in their abilities to raise money would be enormous.[20]

The potential degree of their variation as fundraisers can be illustrated by the disparities that exist among suburbs today. The raising of equal amounts of revenue in different suburban jurisdictions requires widely varied tax rates and therefore inposes heavier tax burdens upon less affluent jurisdictions. For example, identical property tax rates in Levittown and Great Neck, two New York City suburban school districts, raise vastly different sums of money per pupil: $1,684 in Great Neck, but only $410 in Levittown. As Table 8.14 implies, the Levittown rate would have to be four times as high as the rate exacted from Great Neck to produce equal local resources per student. Since family income is considerably lower in Levittown, a similar rate substantially understates their actual tax burden. Further, Table 8.14 shows that differences in the amount of state aid do not nearly compensate for the disparity in local resources.

Because equally great differences in resource base exist among urban neigh-borhoods, it follows that burdens would vary within a decentralized city system just as they do in suburbia. Of course, aid formulas could correct these disparities, but it is difficult to believe that they would be devised to do so,

Table 8.14: A Comparison of the Revenue Sources of Two New York State School Districts, 1968-69

Revenue Sources	Per Pupil Enrolled
Great Neck: (Student enrollment: 9,869)	
Revenue from local property tax	$1,684.07
Revenue from tuition and other local sources	29.29
Revenue from state sources	364.16
Revenue from federal sources	—0—
Total	$2,077.52
True value assessed property: $64,400 per pupil	
Tax rate: $2.72 per $100	
Levittown: (Student enrollment: 17,280)	
Revenue from local property tax	$ 410,31
Revenue from tuition and other local sources	13.87
Revenue from state sources	764.48
Revenue from federal sources	.71
Total	$1,189.37
True value assessed property: $16,200 per pupil	
Tax rate: $2.72 per $100	

NOTE: Data from New York State Commission on the Quality, Cost and Financing of Elementary and Secondary Education, 1972, p. 58.

given the inequity of current formulas. Perhaps for these reasons, most decen-tralization plans do not call for independent taxing powers for the decentralized units. Instead, they propose that all revenue flow from the city- or region-wide government. The impact of such a structure on the character and quality of decision making within the neighborhood units is unclear.

From a third perspective, other analysts argue that unless decentralization is combined with simultaneous regionalization of some sort, the basic problems of central cities will be untouched (Campbell, 1973). The need to combine region-alization and decentralization is at the heart of a recent plan for general metro-politan reorganization. Crucial to the plan is a genuine sharing of power over functions. The Committee for Economic Development's policy statement, *Reshaping Government in Metropolitan Areas* (1970: 17) argues that:

> It is clear . . . that what is needed is a system of government that adequately recognizes both forces, centralization and decentralization. Such a system must permit a genuine sharing of power over functions between a larger unit and a smaller unit. It must recognize a larger unit to permit economies of scale, area-wide planning, and equities in finance. It must recognize a smaller unit to permit the exercise of local power over matters which affect the lives of local citizens.

OTHER GOVERNMENTAL ADAPTATIONS

Except as the suburbs themselves can be considered historically the proto-typical "decentralized units" of modern American government, the movement favoring decentralization has thus far affected the governmental institutions of metropolitan areas less than have other kinds of adaptation to metropoli-tanism.[21]

Despite its handicaps, the weblike system of local government in American metropolitan areas has performed almost miraculously in providing services. Delivering services has required adaptations ranging from the interlocal agree-ments discussed earlier, through contractual arrangements like the Lakewood Plan, to the more fundamental change that comes with a metropolitan-wide special district that performs a single function.

These adaptations have not necessarily reduced fragmentation, but they have sometimes softened its unhappy consequences. In short, the governmental system has grown used to a policy of accommodation, not reform. The result is that local governments have been able to keep house. Water continues to flow, sewage is disposed of (though it may pour downstream to pollute other juris-dictions), highways are built, fires are extinguished, public health is protected, children educated (after a fashion), and welfare checks are mailed (though delivery is another matter).

The relevance of governmental fragmentation to services is thus at bottom a question of equity. Do the public services that people need reach them in the right places at the right times, and are they of high quality; The arguments based in economics of scholars like Charles Tiebout or political scientists like

Edward C. Banfield and Vincent Ostrom tend to see the fragmentation of local governments another way. To them, it represents different marketbaskets of services being offered to consumer taxpayers with different tastes and needs. Hence, metropolitan chaos is seen less as chaos than as the embodiment of market principles, with choice being exercised by choosing a community with the "right combination" of services and costs. This paper, by contrast, views fragmentation from the standpoint of resources available to meet those consumer taxpayers' needs, and finds them woefully maldistributed, rendering a consumer-choice view of community-of-residence inequitable from the start.

The phenomenon noted earlier of inequities in educational expenditures between city and suburbs, for example, indicates that equitable distribution does not always—or even often—happen. Further, the housekeeping orientation of the present system of local government makes effective area-wide planning impossible. Consequently, basic decisions about metropolitan-wide issues are simply not made, because no institution has the authority to make them. The metropolitan-wide planning agencies that now exist are basically advisory, possessing few of the tools needed for effective planning. It seems fated that responses to the current dispersal of metropolitan population and economic activities will continue in the present haphazard fashion. Another result, and perhaps not even the most important one, is the tremendous and growing fiscal pressure exerted by the expense of providing government services, particularly capital plant, for the present residential pattern.[22]

RECOMMENDED APPROACHES

Thus far, the failure of most governmental adaptations to help significantly in overcoming fiscal disparities or in enabling long-range, coordinated attacks on social and physical problems raises the question of what changes might help to accomplish these ends. Three approaches seem promising.

To overcome fiscal disparities, boosting the flow of funds from outside the metropolitan area—state and/or federal aid—is one possibility. Another is to develop a system whereby all local governments in a region share that region's entire tax base without disturbing the present jurisdictional system. Finally, major metropolitan reorganization would make possible both fiscal equity and long-range planning.

Recent court decisions seem likely to influence the selection of instruments to be used in attacking these problems. The equitable distribution of public services within a jurisdiction was the issue in Hawkins v. Town of Shaw. The U.S. Court of Appeals, Fifth Circuit, in ruling on this Mississippi case in 1971, found that the town violated the Constitution by providing inferior sewers, paving, fire hydrants, street lighting, and other services to black neighborhoods. The decision requires municipalities (and, in all likelihood, other types of local government jurisdictions) to provide an equal level of services to all parts of the jurisdiction if service inequality reveals a pattern of racial discrimination. While the Shaw decision does not address the issue of differences in service levels among jurisdictions, an extension of the logic of the case could support more general applications of it. Commenting on the Shaw case and a series of decisions about the financing of education, one scholar, Joseph Ohren (1972), speculates that further interpretations of the Fourteenth Amendment could address the delivery of general governmental services:

> Of primary concern to the authors of the 14th Amendment was the prevention of state discriminatory actions against any group. It has been interpreted to mean that all persons in the same situation must be treated alike by the state and hence has served to protect any person or group from being singled out for hostile legislation or action by state government. Certain recent court decisions on Shaw and education finance raise the question as to whether in fact all municipal services are included in the equal protection clause. Such a finding would make it unconstitutional for one city to provide public services substantially inferior to other cities within the same state.

> In essence, this is to say, equal protection may mean equal public services. With distinctions based on race or income already held suspect, radically different levels of service occurring between different income and/or racial groups could be declared unacceptable by the courts. Accepting the view that local governments have no constitutional standing—that, in fact, they are instruments created by the state—would result in the interpretation that the states are designated to secure equal protection for citizens. If the maintenance of the present system of local government results in discrimination in a provision of public services among different local units, the states may have a constitutional obligation to equalize spending for local public services.

Recent federal and state court decisions about the financing of public education, emerging from over fifty cases in thirty-one states, have produced a number of plans (none adopted yet) that try to end the present dependence of the level of public education spending upon the taxable value of the property base of individual school districts.

At least four courts have found the present system, in which differences in wealth produce differences in educational expenditures, objectionable. Mr. Justice Sullivan's opinion for the six-to-one majority of the California Supreme Court in Serrano v. Priest argues that California's school-finance system "invidiously discriminates against the poor by making the quality of a child's education a function of the wealth of his parents and neighbors." [23]

A federal district court makes the same argument against Minnesota's system of school finance:

> The issue posed by the children . . . is whether pupils in publicly financed elementary and secondary schools enjoy a right under the equal protection guarantee of the 14th Amendment to have the level of spending for their education unaffected by the variations in the taxable wealth of their school district or their parents. This court concludes that such a right indeed exists and that the principle announced in Serrano vs. Priest is correct. Plainly put, the rule is that the level of spending for a child's education may not be a function of wealth other than the wealth of the state as a whole.[24]

The Rodriguez decision was unfavorably reviewed by the Supreme Court in the 1972-73 term. The judicial criteria could be met by states in various ways, from totally assuming the financing of education to refining the education-aid formula so that more resources flow to districts with weaker tax bases. It is probable, however, that the issues raised by the case will remain litigious, because the phraseology of many state constitutions is vulnerable (Benson, 1972). Five states are at present under state mandate to reform their financing systems (Campbell and Gilbert, 1973).

Possibly, plans adopted under either category will not correct the fiscal disparities that now exist between central cities and suburbs. If the state adopts full state financing, its fiscal impact will depend upon the tax system chosen to finance this new responsibility. If (as has been suggested in a number of states, including New York) a state-wide property tax is established to replace the loss of local revenue and its proceeds are distributed to all school districts on an equal dollars-per-student basis, the outcome will not necessarily benefit cities.

Since cities tax themselves less heavily for education because of the burden of noneducation services, an average state-wide tax rate may well tax city people more heavily to support education than they are now taxed locally. Further, if the money is distributed equally, the gain for most cities will be small—and some will actually suffer losses.

Let us briefly summarize the impact on the major cities of a projected shift to a statewide property tax for education. Assume equal dollar expenditure per pupil throughout the state, and a state-wide property tax rate that would raise the same amount of revenue that local property taxes now raise for education. For nine of the thirteen cities, tax burdens (taxes as a percentage of personal income) would be heavier after state assumption, while expenditures per pupil would be cut in six of the cities. If changes in taxes are compared to changes in expenditure under state assumption, only four cities would show a net gain (i.e., taxes increase less than educational spending).

These outcomes are caused, first, by the higher burden cities carry for non-education purposes. Second, although cities spend less for education per pupil than do their suburbs, cities spend much more than rural areas. When the system is averaged, the result thus will not automatically remedy the plight of central cities (Berke and Callahan, 1972; see also Benson, 1972; Campbell and Gilbert, 1973).

A similar result is likely if the state aid system is used to overcome current unequal expenditures per pupil among districts. Again, since only the existing tax base used for education (rather than total local tax burden) seems likely to be taken into account in computing aid, the cities will emerge at a disadvantage.

This is not to suggest that court action will not improve the fiscal situation of cities relative to their suburbs. It does indicate that the simple requirement of fiscal equality that appears to be the courts' demand will not suffice to produce such improvement.

As suggested above, the influx of funds from outside the area has made, at best, a negligible contribution to overcoming fiscal disparities within a metropolitan area. The overall impact of the revenue-sharing program is not clear, but it seems unlikely to overcome intrametropolitan disparities. Nor does it seem that future state and federal programs will correct disparities, given the changing political composition of state legislatures and Congress.

Beyond the potential of external funds to overcome intrametropolitan disparities, existing local jurisdictions might share the entire regional tax base. The only metropolitan area to try such general sharing is Minneapolis-St. Paul.

In 1971 the Minnesota State Legislature established a system under which all local governments in the region must share all of the new and improved nonresidential property tax base. The local jurisdiction where the new or improved facilities are located is allotted 60 percent of the tax base they create. The other 40 percent must be shared among all the jurisdictions within the metropolitan area, according to a formula based primarily on the proportion of the region's total population in each jurisdiction, and to a lesser extent on the jurisdiction's fiscal need. Each jurisdiction applies its own tax rate to its share of the tax base (Birkhead et al., 1972).

Major metropolitan reorganization offers a third possibility to overcome fiscal disparities and also to permit long-range planning as well as coordinated physical and social programs. The evidence is not yet in on whether reorganized metropolitan governments will, in fact, redistribute resources. Melvin Mogulof (1972b: 82-83) summarizes the current state of knowledge this way:

> Metro agencies, because they have all of the governments of a metropolis as their purview, can be redistributive, provided that the resources to be redistributed come from outside the metropolitan system. However, metro governments may be even more handicapped than first-tier governments in making redistributive decisions *within* local resources. Unlike first-tier governments (or Jacksonville's consolidated system) metros have as their major constituency, units of government, rather than individual citizens. As evidenced by . . . the Toronto area, metros tend to redistribute resources to their constituent governments in some relationship to the tax contributions of these governments to metro . . . (By contrast, the more unitary system of) Jacksonville may be freer to rearrange the distribution of resources within its consolidated area . . . there is some evidence that Jacksonville's government is more responsive to the needs of poor black areas of residence than previous governments have been. But this responsiveness may be enabled by new resources coming into the community rather than by any rearrangement of existing resources . . . Jacksonville's willingness to upgrade public services through institution of new user charges must fall particularly hard on the lowest income beneficiaries of these services. As a result, despite its potentially greater freedom to redistribute, Jacksonville's experience is mixed.
>
> The core of the evidence seems to be that metros are only useful vehicles for redistribution of public resources which are newly arrived from outside the metropolitan system.

However mixed the actual experience of metros, metropolitan-wide government would make possible resource redistribution and effective planning. Despite these possibilities (or perhaps because of them), efforts to adopt thoroughgoing reorganization have met fierce political resistance.[25]

Table 8.15: Rate of Voter Support for Local Government Reorganization in 33 Referenda, 1945-72

Year	Reorganization Referendum	% of Reorganization Support (Numbers in columns equal the "pro" vote.)	
		Success	Defeat
1949	Baton Rouge-E. Baton Rouge Par., La.	51.1	
1952	Hampton-Elizabeth Cty., Va.	88.7	
1953	Miami-Dade Cty., Fla.		49.2
1957	Miami-Dade Cty., Fla.	51.0	
	Newport News-Warwick, Va.[a]	66.9	
1958	Nashville-Davidson Cty., Tenn.		47.3
1959	Alburquerque-Bernalillo Cty., N.M.		30.0
	Knoxville-Knox Cty., Tenn.		16.7
	Cleveland-Cuyahoga Cty., Oh.		44.8
	St. Louis-St. Louis Cty., Mo.		27.5
1960	Macon-Bibb Cty., Ga.		35.8
1961	Durham-Durham Cty., N.C.		22.3
	Richmond-Henrico Cty., Va.		54.0[b]
1962	Columbus-Muscogee Cty., Ga.		42.1
	Memphis-Shelby Cty., Tenn.		36.8
	Nashville-Davidson Cty., Tenn.	56.8	
	South Norfolk-Norfolk Cty., Va.	66.0	
	Va. Beach-Princess Anne Cty., Va.	81.9	
	St. Louis-St. Louis Cty., Mo.		40.1[c]
1964	Chattanooga-Hamilton Cty., Tenn.		19.2
1967	Jacksonville-Duval Cty., Fla.	64.7	
	Tampa-Hillsborough Cty., Fla.		28.4
1969	Athens-Clarke Cty., Ga.		48.0
	Brunswick-Glynn Cty., Ga.		29.6
	Carson City-Ormsby Cty., Nev.	65.1	
	Roanoke-Roanoke Cty., Va.		66.4[b]
	Winchester City-Frederick Cty., Va.		31.9
1970	Charlottesville-Albemarle Cty., Va.		28.1
	Columbus-Muscogee Cty., Ga.	80.7	
	Chattanooga-Hamilton Cty., Tenn.		48.0
	Tampa-Hillsborough Cty., Fla.		30.7
1971	Augusta-Richmond Cty., Ga.		41.5
	Charlotte-Mecklenburg Cty., N.C.		30.5
1972	Athens-Clarke Cty., Ga.		48.3
	Macon-Bibb Cty., Ga.		39.6
	Fort Pierce-St. Lucie, Fla.		36.5
Total Outcome (Number)		10	26
Local Reorganizations attempted		36	

THE POLITICS OF REORGANIZATION

Since the end of World War II, thirty-six major metropolitan reorganizations, including city-county consolidations, have been tried; ten have been adopted. The historical pattern in Table 8.15 clearly shows that voter approval is extremely difficult to obtain. Nor are the political prerequisites of success easy to determine.

Significantly, all successful attempts to reorganize by referendum took place in the South, while major efforts in other regions failed. The stronger role played by county government in the South may partly explain the region's willingness to consolidate cities with counties. Further, of the ten successes, four occurred in Virginia, whose unique annexation laws provide especially strong motivation for reorganization. In Virginia, the power to separate cities from their counties by judicial process may make county residents more willing to accept city-county consolidation than is true where such encouragement is absent (Bollens and Schmandt, 1965: 422-423, 425; Gulick, 1962).

Larger areas find reorganization more difficult to attain than smaller ones. In fact, if "large" means over one million population, no major reorganization has occurred since the New York City area adopted metropolitan government in 1898.

Nor does there appear to be any historical trend that favors reorganization. Recent rejections have been as frequent and substantial as past defeats; in some cases, even second or third reorganization attempts in the same community have failed by greater margins than the first proposals. Cleveland is a case in point.

Lack of success, however, does not cause reorganizers to stop trying. Vincent Marando (1973) reports that today more than 60 major reorganizations are being considered in the United States. Most of these are city-county consolidations, and a substantial number of these are in the South. Not surprisingly, study commissions are much more easily approved—even by referendum—than are the study commissions' recommendations. The average vote in favor of the study commissions that created the reorganization plans proposed since the end of World War II was 72.8 percent, but the average vote in favor of adopting their plans was 46.8 percent.

Marando (1973) has also tried to pinpoint the political factors that affect the adoption of reorganization. He concludes, in effect, that primary importance must be attached to unique situations in each community, though metropolitan

---

NOTES TO TABLE 8.15:
NOTE: Data from Marando, 1973.
a. Warwick, Virginia, was a city at the time of the referendum. It had incorporated in 1952, but it was included in this analysis because of its suburban and rural character (in 1958) and because it was Warwick County just six years prior to the referendum.
b. The type of majority requirement is vital in consolidation referenda. In these two instances, city-county consolidation was not possible despite the majority voting percentage in its support. In both of these attempts, the "double majority requirement," which stipulates separate approval by city voters and county voters, resulted in defeat, since a majority of county voter support was not achieved.
c. St. Louis-St. Louis Cty. portions of the 1962 statewide referendum are reported in this table.

areas of more than one million people seem less likely to approve reorganization. For example, success in Jacksonville-Duval County was doubtless linked to the fact that numerous local officials were under indictment for corruption at the time of the campaign, while county schools had been disaccredited. In the case of Nashville-Davidson County, success seemed to hinge upon the major annexation of surrounding territory by the central city between the first vote, which defeated reorganization, and the second, which approved it. Similar events surrounded the Columbus-Muscogee County, Georgia, reorganization, which passed because central-city residents formed 95 percent of the total city-county population at the time of the vote. As these examples suggest, Marando has verified the political science commonplace that reorganization is most likely to occur in Southern states, whose traditions and statutes reflect more assertive roles for counties and states than exist elsewhere.

Generally, the Marando study finds that, the higher the city vote turnout relative to turnout in the county outside the city, the more likely reorganization is to succeed (and vice versa). It is helpful, too, if municipalities within the county are not included in the reorganization plan. The nature of the political campaign for reorganization matters in that grassroots efforts are much more likely than mass-media campaigns to produce favorable results.

A high degree of fragmentation is a negative factor. As fragmentation grows, and larger numbers of local governments are drawn into reorganization plans, success becomes less likely. The double majority requirement that asks majorities in both central cities and outlying jurisdictions is generally fatal to reorganizations, Marando found. If a single majority is stipulated, however, reorganization has a fighting chance.

If economic factors are stressed in a campaign, it is unlikely that the reorganization proposal will be successful. The possibility of new services does not appear to outweigh citizens' anxiety over higher taxation for either city or county voters.

Marando's study found what statements of black politicians also suggest: that the reduction of black majority control entailed in reorganizations in certain cities negatively affects the likelihood of reorganization. The overall size of the voter turnout, the quality of the research standing behind the proposal, and "get-out-the-vote" campaigns appear to have no effect on the acceptance or rejection of reorganization proposals.

The ideological issues that emerge during reorganization campaigns are helpful in understanding the political process. Very often, such issues play a larger role in reorganization campaigns than they do in campaigns where political parties are deeply involved. Political parties, given their internal divisions and emphasis on immediate rewards, tend to mute ideological issues. Normally they do not participate in reorganization campaigns; consequently, these campaigns lack their moderating influence (Advisory Commission on Intergovernmental Relations, 1962).

The greatest opposition to metropolitan reform originally came from the suburbs and the right wing of American politics. The political right long ago decided that the "metro" concept is part of a broad Communist plot to weaken American democracy. One publication of the right (The Dan Bell Report, 1958: 3) ludicrously suggested that "Perhaps the choice of the word Metro is not coincidental as a name for this type of regional government, since the underground railway which connects Moscow with its suburbs is also called 'Metro.' "

Recently, blacks have severely criticized metro government. Many black community leaders see this new governmental form as another ruse to dilute black political power, just when blacks are attaining significant political influence in a number of cities. Of interest on this point is the change in the black vote in Cleveland between early and later reorganization referenda. As their proportion of central-city population grew and the possibility of capturing City Hall became a reality, a majority of blacks in favor of reorganization became a majority against it.

The black community is somewhat divided over the issue of metropolitan reform, but at the moment most black leaders are in the opposition camp. Gary's Mayor Richard Hatcher (League of Women Voters Education Fund, 1972: 30) represents their view when he notes that:

> Enlightened leaders make a persuasive case for metro government. They talk sensibly of the proliferation of tax districts without contiguous boundaries, from mosquito abatement districts to school districts, they deplore with some justification and good reason the confusion that these many overlapping authorities cause, but they also speak of political and social problems which do not end at traditional political lines and for a need for coordination and overall planning. They are right. . . . But to people in the ghetto it still looks as if they are trying to mute new black voices by diluting the vote of those new huddled masses. And the ghetto too is right. Whatever the motive for metro government at the theory's end, the practical effect is to undermine growing black political power. Indeed if the choice is between deferring the black dream already deferred beyond all human consideration or of deferring the eminent logic of metropolitan government, to me the choice is clear. Metro government has to wait.[26]

A somewhat different position is taken by a black political scientist, Dale Rogers Marshall (1972: 26-27), who argues that the most promising strategy for blacks today is

> to continue criticizing metropolitan government but to stop ignoring it. Minorities should become active in the efforts to shape metropolitan reorganization at local, state, and national levels, opposing proposals detrimental to minorities and devising alternative proposals in order to be included in the bargaining process . . . the content of the alternative plans . . . will vary according to the situation in each metropolis. . . . Since whites have become more interested in regional solutions to environmental problems, one promising approach might be for minorities to withhold support for such solutions until they are assured that multipurpose units will handle certain aspects of the social problems that are not amenable to mere local control, yet permit community control over the other aspects. For example, minorities could demand a multipurpose district which equalizes the tax base for education—yet places the control of schools at the community or city level.

The actual metro reorganization that touches a large black constituency is Jacksonville. The recency of Jacksonville's consolidation, the large size of the old city's black population, and the fact that the consolidation was voted on locally, all contribute to speculation among black leaders as to whether the consolidation has advantaged them. A summary of some of the black leaders' comments demonstrates their ambiguity (Mogulof, 1972b: 115-116):

> (1) by not opposing consolidation the black community has forever given up the likelihood of political control of the city; (2) the corollary argument to the first point is that if the blacks controlled the old city they would have had a major pawn in the bargaining with white leadership who have economic stakes in the central city; (3) the converse of course, is that the old city was no longer a viable community,—therefore the blacks would have been left with a 'hollow' prize; (4) the consolidated government is the lesser of two evils for blacks; (5) the five at-large seats on the Jacksonville City Council are viewed as an antiblack maneuver in that they undercut district representation by which blacks are assured a certain number of seats. Conversely, one analyst of the consolidation says that whites favored district elections because blacks exercise the balance of power in at-large elections; (6) a consolidated government would enable new housing opportunities, and of course the converse: that an attempt to disperse the black population would be aimed at diluting the strength of the black vote . . .; (7) one final comment (reflects) the depth of black cynicism about any restructuring . . . a black interviewee noted that a corrupt city government is not necessarily bad for the black community.

The last remark indicates an attitude that is not unique to blacks, but that is widespread in the current literature. Just as the intricate interdependence of metropolitan areas becomes clearly demonstrable, especially its negative effects due to small, independent jurisdictions, many look fondly back to the personalized aspects of the old urban machines. Indisputably, these machines are felt to have been more effective in the life of "the little guy" excluded by income or ethnicity from the benefits of middle-class reform.[27]

Scott Greer (1972; see also Minar and Greer, 1969) concludes from his lengthy research into St. Louis reorganization attempts that metropolitan reformers have seriously mistaken the kind of dissatisfaction voters feel toward local government. The value they give to local autonomy far surpasses their concern with the cost or efficiency or equity of government services. It must be concluded that any reorganization proposal with a hope of political success must offer a way of preserving localism of sorts, while adjusting the system to the realities of economic and environmental interaction.

CONCLUSIONS

The system of local government in American metropolitan areas today causes far-reaching externalities and underscores fiscal disparities. Further, it forbids public decisions based on the socioeconomic interdependence of the metropolitan region, though the seamlessness of that area has been recognized for at least half a century.[28] Metropolitan social problems—crime, inadequate housing, poor education, unemployment—are caused only in small part by the system, but it makes solving them many times more difficult.

Federal and state governments hold the constitutional and fiscal resources to erase the system's structural and fiscal deficiencies. But neither the "carrot" of categorical grants nor the "stick" of conditions tied to them has remedied these weaknesses to any great degree. Federal aid has grown by leaps and bounds. Often, though, it reinforces rather than reduces fragmentation and overlooks disparities. Revenue-sharing injects more money into the sluggish metropolitan bloodstream, but it, too, strengthens the pernicious aspects of the system.

Councils of governments, regional planning agencies, and citizen participation have all been promoted by federal action. The COGs, however, are generally forums wherein local officials protect the autonomy of their jurisdictions. Too often they justify law professor Lawrence Sager's (Trillin, 1972) rueful remark that municipalities act more like property owners' associations than arms of the state concerned with the general welfare. Under COGs, regional planning is advisory and carefully monitored by spokesmen for governmental units that make up the governing board. Groups of citizens, frustrated by their lack of funds, also lack competent expert analysis on which to base their positions.

The somnolent states were used to protecting their rural and small-town areas, except for occasional forays into cities to capture resources or to investigate official mal- or non-feasance in order to remind their rural constituencies of the corrupt ways of city folk. Events of the 1960s forcibly made the states aware of the cities. Many states, dominated by suburban legislators, flinched and demanded that the federal government do something, anything, because the states themselves were not willing to embroil themselves in urban problems. A few, however, are trying.

Most states have enabled local units of government to work together voluntarily. This permissive legislation has been helpful concerning problems that affect more than one jurisdiction. Many states contribute to federal aid programs that require a local share, while single-function authorities have been created for a few activities that clearly cross local boundaries. At least two states have established a form of region-wide (i.e., metropolitan) government for their major city or cities. Others are considering the possibility.

In few metropolitan areas has local initiative won major reform. The political resistance encountered in most places suggests that this avenue of change will hardly be thronged. Negotiation of interlocal agreements doubtless will continue, but it contributes little to fiscal equity or coordinated, region-wide planning.

Standing alone, decentralization offers little hope of resolving problems that are created by regional and national economic or social forces. More localized participation can be effective only if these smaller units of government receive adequate resources and sufficient authority to use them.

Metropolitan government, if it were encouraged by appropriate state and federal support, could provide a promising alternative. At least, it is economically and socially rational, if not politically easy. Such a government probably should have two tiers: one neighborhood-oriented; the other embracing the metropolis. A base of participation and genuine influence could be built upon the neighborhood unit; meanwhile, the area-wide government's capacity to plan comprehensively and to meet infrastructural needs such as waste disposal, pollution control, and transportation might redeem the local governments' defeat in these matters. Further, a two-tier system offers the possibility, if not the guarantee, of overcoming fiscal disparities.

Beyond promoting metropolitan government, states could act in other significant ways. Assumption of welfare and education financing by the state could cut fiscal disparities. State opposition to discriminatory zoning might reduce social inequities, as might the focusing of state resources upon areas of densely concentrated social ills. The federal government need not restrict its help to ladling out more resources. If, for example, the Administration had followed the Humphrey-Reuss suggestion that tied revenue-sharing to state and local government reform, the program could now be reducing, rather than reinforcing, the immutability of the system.

While the social and economic logic that recommends these changes is persuasive, the political logic to back their adoption is weaker. Currently, the federal government holds out no hope of vigorous action. The localities that need change most urgently lack the political muscle to achieve it by themselves. One must conclude that state governments are the best immediate hope.[29] Legislators from low-income suburbs may find that their interests are better served by coalition with large cities than by alliance with high-income suburbs. But before realignments like this can occur, a distressing history of deep ethnic and social antagonisms must be overcome.

By and large, American metropolitan areas have no spokesmen. Jurisdictions and functional interests are gifted with the politically resonant voices, which they seldom raise in behalf of metropolitan reorganization, because it rarely serves their immediate interests. The occasional champion of metropolitan government lifts a weaker voice; no established, organized constituency firmly backs the concept. A single-function, area-wide jurisdiction, however limited its powers, can attract a certain following and may form the base for a general area-wide government. When George Romney was Secretary of Housing and Urban Development, he often talked of "the Real City," by which he meant the metropolitan area, exhorting all groups within it to recognize their interdependence and work together for their mutual well-being. Not wholly by coincidence, George Romney has left the Administration.

Whatever the political obstacles that confront reorganization, effective government in metropolitan areas must eliminate externalities and correct the disparities that hinder fiscal—and ultimately social—equity. Fiscal justice is no romantic ideal; indeed, in social services like education it is not known whether money can guarantee achievement. Even so, though equity in the distribution of American resources may not be a sufficient condition of an open society, it is surely a necessary one.

NOTES

1. This definition of poverty was drawn up in 1964 by the Social Security Administration and revised by a federal interagency committee in 1969. It represents an average annual income threshold of poverty for a family of four. In 1970, the annually revised "poverty line" was about $3,968 per family—several hundred dollars lower for farm families of four, very slightly higher for male-headed households, and slightly lower for families headed by women.

2. Rosenthal (1972) has a striking table on the swift drain of the central-city share of metropolitan employment between 1960 and 1970.

3. Warner (1962) is representative of American studies of this outward movement. Comparative studies, as well as data on railway development, suggest that the "long-standing" nature of suburban dispersal by upper-income residents began in the last third of the nineteenth century in America and just before mid-century in Britain. Earlier, railway development often helped to depopulate rural areas (see Kellett, 1969), while early Victorian suburbs in England were as likely to be *faubourgs* of industrial workers as superior residence property (see Briggs, 1970). Useful general discussions of urban history today are Oscar Handlin's introduction to Handlin and Burchard (1963) and Gordon Craig (1970).

4. Gulick (1962) discusses why annexation will do little to remedy metropolitan fragmentation. Sengstock (1960) reviews annexation procedures. Although annexation was alive and well in the 1960s in a few sections of the country, especially in the Southwest, it created a rash of new incorporations intended to prevent annexation by central cities.

5. For a critique of such unanticipated effects, see Haefele and Kneese (1972). Beyond the fact that local jurisdictions hurt each other in regard to handling their physical interdependence, local governments are often kept from doing helpful things by higher-level governmental restrictions or program provisions. For example, federal subsidies to municipalities for their own sewage treatment plants will probably foreclose the hope of realizing economies of scale in building and operating plants for more than one jurisdiction.

6. See also Mogulof (1972a). Harris (1970) reviews 74 COGs largely in terms of black reaction to them, and Hanson (1966) reviews COGs in terms of their hopeful future. Marando (1971) is also more optimistic about the growing political effectiveness of COGs.

7. Miller (1972), in an analysis of the effect of revenue-sharing on New York City, shows that program cuts will offset the new money. This is because New York was one of the few states to take full advantage of a 1969 measure attached to the Social Security law which allowed states 75 percent reimbursement on practically any project to help "past, present, or potential" welfare recipients. In New York City, $395 million in federal tax money will be pumped directly into the general fund. But thirteen major social services will be cut as much as 75 percent, including (in order) day care, special services in schools, drug-addiction programs, foster care, services to the mentally retarded, social services staff, programs for the aged, probation and youth services, among others. These cuts reduce precisely those services most needed by a population that is disproportionately composed of the aged, the poor, and working mothers as heads of households. A skeptical view of revenue-sharing's impact upon programs aimed at black poverty is detailed in Joint Center for Political Studies (1973).

8. For a qualified pessimistic assessment and bibliography of manpower training programs, see Goldstein (1972: 16, 39, 55-56). Schultze et al., (1972: 449-468) analyze the general ineffectiveness of the social programs of the 1960s.

9. Campbell (1970) details the constitutional, political, and fiscal failures of the states in urban affairs. Herzberg and Rosenthal (1972: 26) find fault with state legislatures. They feel that the current reform movements in state government are a reaction to the 1960s "love affairs" between cities and the federal government, cities and foundation grants, and cities and corporate public affairs programs which say, in effect, " 'Forget the states.' They are not going to make it. The crisis is in the cities and we have to get at it there."

10. See Shalala (1972: ch. 1) for a fuller discussion of these alternatives as they affect state constitutional provisions regarding city powers.

11. For example, the New Jersey legislature has approved a development corporation for the Hackensack Meadows area. The political tribulations of UDC through 1972 can be followed in the New York *Times*. UDC finally shelved its plan, which was supported by the League of Women Voters, the Regional Plan Association, and local builders, to build 100 units of low- and middle-income apartments in each of nine Westchester towns. Pressure came from United Towns for Home Rule, an organization formed by several dozen residents when the plan was announced in June. Soon the group claimed hundreds of members, who marshalled the entire Westchester state legislative delegation to oppose the plan. This was done despite the embarrassment it caused the Governor, who in May 1972 had vetoed a bill that would have forced UDC to comply with local zoning laws. The incident illustrates the commonplace that local government action excites little interest and less participation, except when something disagreeable to local voters occurs. (See Greenhouse, 1972a, 1972b, 1972c; Housing opposed in Westchester, 1972; Narvaez, 1972a, 1972b; Regional Plan Association backs state housing plan, 1972; Shipler, 1972a, 1972b; Sponsor suspends housing protest, 1972; State gets order on housing unit, 1972; metropolitan briefs: Harrison drops building ban suit, 1972; Metropolitan briefs: Town upheld on UDC suit, 1972.)

12. For case studies of different interlocal methods in operation, see Martin (1963) and Advisory Commission on Intergovernmental Relations (1969).

13. Birkhead, Campbell, and Weissman (1972) analyze the Metropolitan District Commission and compare it to the Minneapolis-St. Paul Council.

14. Minnesota, *Statutes,* Chaps. 473 B-E.

15. The term "federation," as used to describe the London system is unacceptable to some because responsibility is sharply divided between the two tiers.

16. The best academic assessments of the politics of London reorganization are Rhodes (1970); Ruck and Rhodes (1970); and Smallwood (1965). The fiscal, as well as the political, outcomes of the transition are discussed by a London School of Economics research unit, the Greater London Group (1968). For reorganization proposals of the 1960s and their influence outside London, see Foley (1972). On Toronto, see Kaplan (1967).

17. Proximate legal authority is in Sec. 204 of P.L. 89-754, Nov. 3, 1966.

18. The following are a sample of decentralization literature: Kotler (1969) presents the localist view of the desirable degree of autonomy; Sennett (1970) marshals arguments for decentralization from social and ego psychology; Shalala (1971) reviews recent decentralization literature; Washnis (1972) analyzes case studies of 12 cities.

19. For a comparative summary of the six proposals, see Shalala and Merget (1973). See also Frarr, Lieberman, and Wood (1972).

20. New York City began in 1972 to assemble studies of how much the city actually spent per capita to provide services in each of 62 community planning districts, in order to gain preliminary empirical knowledge of what decentralization may cost (how much the city expended to provide services in each of 62 neighborhoods, 1972).

21. Smith (1966) and Zuckerman (1970) are sophisticated recent examples of the tendency in American cultural and social history for small units of government to be regarded as the communal context of the American character. This has been true whether the units were the sterile suburbs of 1950s' sociology or the towns of provincial Massachusetts. It is an ironic comment on our preoccupation with community that Zuckerman finds homogeneity far more important to Massachusetts towns than their vaunted town-meeting democracy. He (p. 258) writes that a townsman who differed in his politics, religion, or lifestyle "had the option of his forebears: he could reform or he could leave."

22. For capital costs, see Regional Plan Association of New York (1962). Factors in rising public employment are discussed in Bahl, Greytak, Campbell, and Wasylenko (1972) and Horton (1971).

23. 5 Cal. 3d 584, 487P. 2d. 1241, 96 Cal. Rptr. 601 (Aug. 1971).

24. The Minnesota opinion, following Serrano by six weeks, was handed down by the Federal District Court in U.S.L.W. 2228 (D. Minn. Oct. 12, 1971).

25. Greer (1963) studies the defeat of the St. Louis District Plan and looks briefly at reorganization campaigns in Cuyahoga (Cleveland) and Dade (Miami) Counties.

26. Two academic leaders of the welfare reform movement have reacted similarly. See Piven and Cloward (1967a, 1967b).

27. Sociologists are especially drawn to this argument, for they believe the decline of personalized politics is partly responsible for the alienation that survey data of recent years abundantly reflects. In the 1950s, Maurice Stein (1960) and David Riesman (1950, 1952) suggested that the loss of a sense of community might be partly a consequence of the growth of bureaucratized governmental organizations. A recent example from a huge literature is Richard Sennett (1970). Politicians have also joined the chorus, as Governor Nelson Rockefeller's 1972 State of the State address attests: "Serious students of big city government say the ordinary citizen actually had a better chance of being heard and getting help in the old days . . . because there was a direct relationship between the people and the clubhouse right down to the block level. . . . Today New York City has neither an effective, city-wide old-line political organization, eager to respond to the individual's needs, nor does it have true community or neighborhood elective government."

28. The first studies to recommend metropolitan government appeared in the 1920s. Even earlier, in 1879, Frederick Law Olmsted was persuaded of metropolitan interdependence in an even wider sphere, perhaps from his perspective as a physical planner: "When we speculate on the future of New York as a metropolis we must not think of it as confined by arbitrary political boundaries. As a metropolis, Newark, Newport and Bridgeport, as well as Brooklyn, Yonkers and Jersey City are essential parts of it" (Whitney Museum of American Art, 1972).

29. On the changing role of states in urban areas, see Sharkansky (1972) and LeMay (1972). Of forty-six states responding to LeMay's 1970 survey, twenty-six states had passed legislation covering metropolitan functional authorities. State action ranged from simple enabling legislation to actually setting up such authorities with only advisory powers or multipurpose functional powers. Mogulof (1973) is convinced that states will play the critical role in establishing metro government, acting as final arbiters among conflicting special authorities, COGs, and traditional local governments. In effect, this argument takes the notion that "cities are creatures of the state" (which has been viewed in the recent literature as a constricting reality) and turns it around, by asking the state to produce a new creature, metro-government. But, given the suburbanizing of state legislatures anticipated by this paper, one must question whether a state-sponsored metropolitan government will improve the situation of large central cities.

REFERENCES

Advisory Commission on Intergovernmental Relations. *Factors affecting voter reaction in governmental reorganization in metropolitan areas.* Washington, D.C.: U.S. Government Printing Office, 1962.

Advisory Commission on Intergovernmental Relations. *Fiscal balance in the American federal system.* Vol. 2: Metropolitan fiscal disparities. Washington, D.C.: U.S. Government Printing Office, 1967.

Advisory Commission on Intergovernmental Relations. *Urban America and the federal system.* Washington, D.C.: U.S. Government Printing Office, 1969.

Advisory Commission on Intergovernmental Relations. *Measuring the fiscal capacity and effort of states and local areas.* Washington, D.C.: U.S. Government Printing Office, March 1971.

Bahl, R., Greytak, D., Campbell, A. K., and Wasylenko, M. J. "Intergovernmental and functional aspects of public employment trends in the United States." Public Administration Review, No. Dec. 1972, 32, 815-832.

Benson, C. S. "The Serrano decision: Where will the money go?" Public Affairs Report (Institute of Governmental Studies, University of California at Berkeley), December 1972, 13(6), 1-5.

Berke, J. S., and Callahan, J. J. "Serrano v. Priest: Milestone or millstone for school finance?" Journal of Public Law, 1972, 21(1), 23-71.

Berke, D. S., Sacks, S., Bailey, S. K., and Campbell, A. K. Federal aid to public education: Who benefits? In J. S. Berke and M. W. Kirst, *Federal aid to education: Who benefits? Who governs?* Lexington: D. C. Heath, 1972. 1-59.

Birch, D. L. *The economic future of city and suburb.* New York: Committee for Economic Development, 1970.

Birkhead, G. S., Campbell, A. K., and Weissman, M. Massachusetts substate government. Occasional Paper No. 7, Metropolitan Studies Program. Syracuse: Syracuse University, 1972. (Mimeo.)

Bollens, J. C. *The states and the metropolitan problem.* Chicago: Council of State Governments, 1956.

Bollens, J. C., and Schmandt, H. J. *The metropolis: Its people, politics, and economic life.* (2nd ed.) New York: Harper and Row, 1965.

Briggs, A. *Victorian cities.* (Rev. ed.) New York: Harper and Row, 1970.

Campbell, A. K. (Ed.) *The states and the urban crisis.* Englewood Cliffs: Prentice-Hall, 1970.

Campbell, A. K. The fiscal setting for reforming government structure in New York City. In State Study Commission for New York City, *The neighborhoods, the city, and the region: Working papers on jurisdiction and structure.* New York: State Study Commission for New York City, January 1973.

Campbell, A. K., and Gilbert, D. A. The governance and political implications of educational finance. Santa Monica: Rand Corporation, 1973. (Mimeo.)

Campbell, A. K., and Sacks, S. *Metropolitan America: Fiscal patterns and governmental systems.* New York: Free Press, 1967.

Canty, D. "Metropolity." City, March-April 1972, 6(2), 29-44.(a)

Canty, D. "Nixon's urban record, Part 2." City, Fall 1972, 6(4) 59-60.(b)

Citizens' League of Minneapolis. Sub-urbs in the city. Minneapolis: CLM, May 1970. (Mimeo.).

Committee for Economic Development. *Reshaping government in metropolitan areas.* New York: CED, 1970.

Costikyan, E. A proposed new structure of city government. State Study Commission for New York City Working Paper. New York: State Study Commission for New York City, 1972. (Mimeo.).

Costikyan, E., and Lehman, M. *Restructuring the government of New York City: Report of the Scott Commission Task Force on Jurisdiction and Structure.* New York: Praeger, 1972.

Council of State Governments. *Sub-state district systems.* RM-468. Lexington, CSG, September 1971.

Craig, G. A. "The city and the historian." Canadian Journal of History, March 1970, 5(1), 47-55.

Foley, D. L. *Governing the London region.* Berkeley: University of California Press, 1972.

Frarr, W. G., Jr., Lieberman, L., and Wood, J. S. *Decentralizing city government: A practical study of a radical proposal for New York City.* New York: Praeger, 1972.

Goist, P. D. "City and 'community': The urban theory of Robert Park." American Quarterly, Spring 1971, 23(1), 46-59.

Goldstein, J. H. The effectiveness of manpower training programs: A review of research on the impact on the poor. Staff study for the Subcommittee on Fiscal Policy of the Joint

Economic Committee of the Congress. Washington, D.C.: U.S. Government Printing Office, 1972.

Greater London Group. *The lessons of the London government reforms.* London: HMSO, 1968.

Greenhouse, L. "Low-income state housing due in rural Westchester." New York Times, June 21, 1972. (a)

Greenhouse, L. "Suburbs fighting state agency's plan to override local zoning." New York Times, July 17, 1972. (b)

Greenhouse, L. "Westchester towns win a moratorium on UDC housing." New York Times, August 2, 1972. (c)

Greer, S. *Metropolitics: A study of political culture.* New York: John Wiley, 1963.

Greer, S. *The urbane view: Life and politics in metropolitan America.* New York: Oxford University Press, 1972.

Gulick, L. H. *The metropolitan problem and American ideas.* New York: A. E. Knopf, 1962.

Haefele, E. T., and Kneese, A. V. Residuals management and metropolitan government. In L. Wingo (Ed.) *The governance of metropolitan regions: Metropolitanization and public services.* Washington, D.C.: Resources for the Future, Inc., 1972. 57-69.

Handlin, O., and Burchard, J. (Eds.) *The historian and the city.* Cambridge: MIT Press, 1963.

Hanson, R. *Metropolitan COG's.* Washington, D.C.: Advisory Commission on Intergovernmental Relations, August 1966.

Harris, W. *Regional COG's and the central city.* Detroit: The Metropolitan Fund, 1970.

Herzberg, D., and Rosenthal, A. (Eds.) *Strengthening the states: Essays on legislative reform.* New York: Doubleday, 1972.

Hoover, E. M., and Vernon, R. *The anatomy of a metropolis.* Cambridge: Harvard University Press, 1959.

Horton, R. D. "Municipal labor relations: The New York City experience." Social Science Quarterly, Winter 1971, 52(3), 680-696.

"Housing opposed in Westchester: 2,000 attend rally against state's plan for building." New York Times, November 13, 1972.

"How much the city expended to provide services in each of 62 neighborhoods." New York Times, November 13, 1972.

"It can pay to move: An estimate of income gains of rural-to-urban and south-to-north migrants." Search (A Report from the Urban Institute), January-February 1971, 1(1), 2, 7.

Joint Center for Political Studies. Public Policy Series. *The black community and revenue sharing.* Washington, D.C.: January 1973.

Jones, V. *Metropolitan government.* Chicago: University of Chicago Press, 1942.

Kaplan, H. *Urban political systems: A functional analysis of Metro Toronto.* New York: Columbia University Press, 1967.

Kellett, J. P. *The impact of railways on Victorian cities.* London: Routledge and Kegan Paul, 1969.

Kotler, M. *Neighborhood government: The local foundations of political life.* New York: Bobbs-Merrill, 1969.

League of Women Voters Education Fund. *Shaping the metropolis.* Washington, D.C.: 1972.

LeMay, M. C. "The state and urban areas: A comparative assessment." National Civic Review, December 1972, 61(11), 542-548.

Maass, A. (Ed.) *Area and power.* New York: The Free Press, 1959.

Madden, R. L. "Revenue sharing bonuses for Long Island," New York Times, December 10, 1972.

Marando, V. L. "Metropolitan research and councils of government." Midwest Review of Public Administration, February 1971, 5(1), 3-15.

Marando, V. L. *Local government reorganization: An overview.* Washington, D.C.: National Academy of Public Administration, 1973.

Marshall, D. R. Metropolitan government: Views of minorities. In L. Wingo (Ed.), *The governance of metropolitan regions: Minority perspectives.* Washington, D.C.: Resources for the Future, Inc., 1972, 9-30.

Martin, R. C. *Metropolis in transition.* Washington, D.C.: Housing and Home Finance Agency, 1963.

"Metropolitan briefs: Harrison drops building ban suit." New York Times, August 8, 1972.

"Metropolitan briefs: Town upheld on UDC suit." New York Times, August 11, 1972.

Miller, L. "Dollar sharing seen costly to the city." New York Post, October 16, 1972.

Minar, D. W., and Greer, S. (Eds.) *The concept of community.* Chicago: Aldine, 1969.

Mogulof, M. B. *Governing metropolitan areas.* Washington, D.C.: The Urban Institute, 1971.

Mogulof, M. B. "Metropolitan councils of government and the federal government." Urban Affairs Quarterly, June 1972, 7, 489-507. (a)

Mogulof, M. B. *Five metropolitan governments: An exploratory comparison.* Paper No. 713-27. Washington, D.C.: The Urban Institute, 1972. (b)

Mogulof, M. B. *A modest proposal for the governance of America's metropolitan areas.* Washington, D.C.: The Urban Institute, 1973.

Narvaez, A. A. "Urban development curbs are voted." New York Times, April 13, 1972. (a)

Narvaez, A. A. "Rockefeller signs bill for panel to site power plants." New York Times, May 25, 1972. (b)

New York State Commission on the Quality, Cost and Financing of Elementary and Secondary Education. *The Fleischman report on the quality, cost, and financing of elementary and secondary education in New York State.* Vol. 1. New York: Viking, 1973.

New York State Department of Commerce. *Personal income in counties of New York State, 1968.* Research Bulletin 28. Albany: March 1970.

"1971 Survey of buying power." Sales Management. June 10, 1971.

Office of the Mayor, New York City. Program for command decentralization and integration of services in selected New York City neighborhoods. New York: Office of the Mayor, December 1971. (Mimeo.)

Ohren, J. Memorandum to K. Mathewson. Cited in K. Mathewson, Regionalism: An idea whose time has come. President's Annual Message, Metropolitan Fund, Detroit, 1972. (Mimeo.)

O'Keefe, R. "Elected metro council argument ahead." St. Paul Pioneer Press, January 14, 1973.

Piven, F. F., and Cloward, R. "Black control of cities: Heading it off by metropolitan government." New Republic, September 30, 1967, 157(14), 19-21. (a)

Piven, F. F., and Cloward, R. "Black control of cities: How the Negroes will lose." New Republic, October 7, 1967, 157915), 15-19. (b)

Regional Plan Association of New York. *Spread city.* Bulletin 100. New York: RPANY, 1962.

"Regional Plan Association backs state housing plan." New York Times, June 22, 1972.

Rhodes, G. *The government of London: The struggle for reform.* London: London School of Economics, 1970.

Riesman, D., with Glazer, N. *Faces in the crowd: Individual studies in character and politics.* New Haven: Yale University Press, 1952.

Riesman, D., with Glazer, N., and Denney, R. *The lonely crowd.* (2nd ed.) New Haven: Yale University Press, 1961.

Rockefeller, N. A. 1972 State of the State address. Albany: 1972.

Rosenthal, J. "Large suburbs equal cities as providers of employment." New York Times, October 15, 1972.

Ruck, S. K., and Rhodes, G. *The government of Greater London.* London: Allen and Unwin, 1970.

Sacks, S., Ranney, D., and Andrew, R. *City schools/Suburban schools.* Syracuse: Syracuse University Press, 1972.

Salpukas, A. "Reverse commuters increasing." New York Times, December 2, 1972.

Sayre, W. S. Political decentralization: A mare's nest for New York City. Internal memorandum to State Study Commission for New York City. New York: State Study Commission for New York City, 1972. (Xerox) (a)

Sayre, W. S. "Smaller does not mean better, necessarily." New York Times, April 8, 1972. (b)

Schultze, C. L., Fried, E., Rivlin, A., and Teeters, N. *Setting national priorities: The 1973 Budget.* Washington, D.C.: The Brookings Institution, 1972.

Sengstock, F. S. *Annexation: A solution to the metropolitan area problem.* Ann Arbor: University of Michigan Law School, 1960.

Sennett, R. *The uses of disorder: Personal identity and city life.* New York: A. E. Knopf, 1970.

Shalala, D. E. *Neighborhood governance: Issues and Proposals.* New York: American Jewish Committee, 1971.

Shalala, D. E. *The city and the constitution.* New York: National Municipal League, 1972.

Shalala, D. E., and Merget, A. E. *Decentralization: Implications for service delivery.* Washington, D.C.: National Academy of Public Administration, 1973.

Sharkansky, I. *The maligned states.* New York: McGraw-Hill, 1972.

Shipler, D. K. "Levitt criticizes bidding policy of unit for urban development." New York Times, April 3, 1972. (a)

Shipler, D. K. "UDC housing agency: Paper tiger." New York Times, August 5, 1972. (b)

Smallwood, F. *Greater London.* Indianapolis: Bobbs-Merrill, 1965.

Smith, P. *As a city upon a hill.* New York: A. E. Knopf, 1966.

"Sponsor suspends housing protest: Westchester group acts after UDC delays plans." New York Times, August 9, 1972.

"State gets order on housing unit: Must show cause for project in Westchester town." New York Times, August 3, 1972.

Stein, M. *The eclipse of community.* Princeton: Princeton University Press, 1960.

Studentski, P. *The government of metropolitan areas in the United States.* New York: National Municipal League, 1930.

Thompson, W. R. *A preface to urban economics.* Baltimore: Johns Hopkins Press, 1965.

Trillin, C. "U.S. Journal: The coastline: Some reflections on land as real estate." The New Yorker, November 18, 1972, 215-224.

U.S. Bureau of the Census. U.S. Census of Business: 1958. Vol. 2: *Retail trade—area statistics, Parts 1 and 2.* Washington, D.C.: U.S. Government Printing Office, 1961. (a)

U.S. Bureau of the Census. U.S. Census of Population: 1960. *Number of inhabitants.* Final Report PC(1)-1A. U.S. Summary. Washington, D.C.: U.S. Government Printing Office, November 1961. (b)

U.S. Bureau of the Census. U.S. Census of Population: 1960. *Standard metropolitan statistical areas.* PC(3)-1D. Washington, D.C.: U.S. Government Printing Office, 1963.

U.S. Bureau of the Census. U.S. Census of Governments: 1957. Vol. 5: *Local governments in metropolitan areas.* Washington, D.C.: U.S. Government Printing Office, November 1969.

U.S. Bureau of the Census. U.S. Census of Business: 1967. Vol. 2: *Retail trade, Parts 1-3.* Washington, D.C.: U.S. Government Printing Office, 1970. (a)

U.S. Bureau of the Census. U.S. Census of Population: 1970. *General population characteristics.* U.S. Summary. PC(1)-B1. Washington, D.C.: U.S. Government Printing Office, 1970. (b)

U.S. Bureau of the Census. Current Population Reports. *Characteristics of the low-income population, 1970.* Series P-60, No. 81. Washington, D.C.: U.S. Government Printing Office, 1971.

U.S. Department of Health, Education, and Welfare. *Statistics of local public school systems: Finances 1968-69.* Washington, D.C.: U.S. Government Printing Office, 1971.

U.S. Office of Management and Budget. Circular A-80. Washington, D.C.: January 1967.

U.S. Office of Management and Budget. Circular A-95. (rev. ed.) Washington, D.C.: February 1971.

U.S. Office of Management and Budget. *The budget of the United States Government: Fiscal year 1973.* Washington, D.C.: U.S. Government Printing Office, 1972. (a)

U.S. Office of Management and Budget. *The budget of the United States Government: Fiscal year 1973—Appendix.* Washington, D.C.: U.S. Government Printing Office, 1972. (b)

Warner, S. B., Jr. *Streetcar suburbs.* Cambridge: Harvard University Press, 1962.

Washnis, G. J. *Municipal decentralization and neighborhood resources.* New York: Praeger, 1972.

Wertheimer, R. F., II. *The monetary rewards of migration within the U.S.* Washington, D.C.: The Urban Institute, 1970.

Whitney Museum of American Art. Gallery notes to "Frederick Law Olmsted's New York." Exhibition October 19-December 3, 1972. New York City.

Wood, R. C. *Metropolis against itself.* New York: Committee for Economic Development, 1959.

Zimmerman, J. F. Meeting service needs through intergovernmental agreements. In International City Management Association, *Municipal yearbook, 1973.* Vol. 40. Washington, D.C.: ICMA, 1973, 79-88.

Zuckerman, M. *Peaceable kingdoms: New England towns in the eighteenth century.* New York: A. E. Knopf, 1970.

CHAPTER 9

FISCAL AND PRODUCTIVE EFFICIENCY
IN URBAN GOVERNMENT SYSTEMS

Lyle C. Fitch

Institute of Public Administration

THIS PAPER looks at the organization of urban government primarily from the viewpoints of economics and public administration, somewhat tempered by viewpoints usually associated with political science and sociology.

In this context, the main business of government has to do with providing certain services and benefits not furnished, for whatever reason, by the private sector. These services and benefits, here called "public goods," are the "outputs" of government, analogous to the products that a business firm creates and offers for sale.

The discussion assumes three main "values" or objectives, again reflecting the concerns of economics and public administration. The first of these is efficiency, both in determining what kinds and amounts of public goods urbanites want and in producing and delivering them at least cost. The second objective is equality of income distribution. Other things being equal or not too unequal, the more evenly the economy's income is divided, the better. A third objective is conflict resolution and the preservation of domestic tranquility, an objective which requires both the efficiency and equality principles, and in addition a participation principle: the opportunity for all persons affected by government to participate therein and have access to those who wield power and make decisions.

Accepting efficiency as a desideratum in choice making does not require that we go overboard, as some economists continue to do, by assuming that collective choice making ultimately rests on the decisions of individuals, concerned only with achieving their respective Pareto optimum conditions (see Wagner, 1971, for an uncompromising statement of this viewpoint). The Pareto optimum, it should be remembered, is not a state of nature; it is a state of mind derived from social conditioning and is subject to whim and circumstance. Neither must we assume that the state has life and purpose of its own, transcending that of the individuals making it up. We assume, rather, an intense interaction between individual and society, whereby public decisions are continually being influenced by individual preferences, and individual preferences, in turn, are continually

[397]

molded by social interaction. This requires also that we accept the legitimacy of that somewhat vague concept "the public welfare" as incorporated in broadly accepted social goals and aspirations (Colm, 1955: 33-34).[1]

While economists have largely abandoned attempts to construct social-welfare functions from individual preference functions, some are still endeavoring to rescue as much as possible of individual preference by tailoring political jurisdictions in ways discussed below. Other economists have thrown broad questions of social choice, which is what politics is mostly about, back to the political scientists to wrestle with, catch-as-catch-can.

Normative convictions of efficiency and economy have not greatly impressed many political scientists in recent years, however. Though closer to the real world than economists, they have been interested more in describing how it works, according to their own methodological preconceptions, than in how it should work under economic restraints. This leads to other subtle sets of norms. Theodore Lowi has said that "In the mid-twentieth century polity, the conceptual equivalent to the nineteenth century concept of nature's market system is the pluralist political process." The pluralist political process, of course, is what the unreconstructed economics, still attached to the "sovereignty" of individual consumers as the ultimate value, would like to ignore.

MAIN ECONOMIC FUNCTIONS OF URBAN GOVERNMENT

With the above as a backdrop, I shall discuss the implications of the organization of government in urban areas for three main government functions and one ancillary function. (Functions are here described from the viewpoint of economics.) The three main functions are: social choice making, production and delivery of public goods, and income redistribution.

Social choice making is concerned with (1) allocating community purchasing-power between public and private goods and services—deciding what proportion of public goods to buy out of a limited total income, and (2) deciding upon the kinds, quality, and quantity of public goods to be purchased. Choice making, as the term is used here, implies the whole range of activities associated with planning and budgeting.

Urban governments customarily produce most of the goods and services they deliver to taxpayers/consumers, although some types of production, such as road building and heavy construction, are generally contracted out. Some general government jurisdictions contract out most of the goods they provide and perform only the most elementary production services. This implies that choice making, rather than production, is the essential element of the governmental economic process.

Most tax-financed governmental activities involve some degree of income distribution, in the sense that the incidence of benefits is usually different from the incidence of taxation.[2] This is one of the income redistribution problems to be solved by the governmental process, though urban jurisdictions, subject to tax constraints laid down by the sovereign state governments, seldom have much flexibility in determining how the community's tax burden will be distributed. The other main redistribution problem is that of outright income transfers, the most conspicuous and troublesome at the present time being public assistance in its various forms.

The ancillary function referred to above is that of financing the choice making and production delivery functions, or finding the wherewithal to pay for public goods. In some instances, efficiency is achieved by relating the amounts paid by individual beneficiaries as closely as possible to the costs of the benefits they receive through public prices or benefit taxes.[3]

PROPOSALS FOR REBUILDING URBAN GOVERNMENT

Another premise of this paper is that urban governments in the United States are performing inadequately, at best, in meeting the demands laid upon them, and that, at worst, they are failing miserably as measured by general discontent with public services, taxpayer revolts, the mounting desperation of urban government financial conditions, the transformation of large central cities into reservations for the poor, and the downward trend of many social indicators. This paper focuses particularly on proposals for curing the troubles of American cities by restructuring their governments. There are several families of such proposals around, reflecting the long-standing American penchant for seeking to improve governmental performance by changing the structure of governmental institutions. Three types of proposal are of particular interest here: (1) to make urban governments smaller, and their constituencies more homogeneous, (2) to make them larger and their constituencies more heterogeneous, and (3) both.

The notion of large, or metropolitan-scale, government has been around for decades, but had its main run in the 1950s. Many people became much exercised then over the phenomenon of urban areas spilling out over city boundaries. The clutch of problems thereby created was blamed on the "fragmentation" of local governments in urban areas—the well-publicized 1,400 governments in the New York metropolitan region, for example.

The notion that fragmentation may be beneficial came along a bit later; it is more a child of the 1960s. It has had two main roots: (1) the concept of giving a larger piece of the political action to the urban poor, who until recently have lacked a political voice, and (2) the concept, widely associated with Charles Tiebout (1956, 1961), that the existence of many jurisdictions in a metropolitan area, each able to control its own levels and patterns of spending, will enable each individual family and firm to find a jurisdiction most congenial to its tastes, thereby more nearly approximating a market situation.

After several decades, advocates of metropolitan government consolidation have only a few successes. The most pressing needs for metropolitan-wide jurisdiction have been met, if at all, by the establishment of limited-function agencies—a process in which the federal government has taken a prominent part. Pressures for decentralization have been met both by the continuation of existing fragmentation and, in the larger cities, by various organizational innovations such as Model Cities and Concentrated Employment programs, and moves to put service centers in neighborhoods close to the people. But after the first flush of enthusiasm for maximum feasible participation, decentralization also has lagged. Many cities, however, are attempting to cope with the rising indignation about service deficiencies by going part way toward decentralization, with neighborhood service centers and other devices.

Decentralization by radical surgery is now being pushed harder in New York City than anywhere else in the United States. The state governor is apparently convinced that the existing monolithic city government is beyond salvation, and that the city can be rescued only by breaking it up. The State Study Commission on New York City (1972) turned in a report calling for a plan whereunder various functions now exercised by the highly centralized city government would devolve downwards to 30-35 newly created "service delivery districts." These would be legally designated as operating governmental units, with a central service-delivery sector being retained for those services requiring city-wide administration. The local service-delivery districts would be governed by local councils, and each would have local executive officers—professional-manager types.

TWO MODELS OF THE URBAN GOVERNMENTAL PROCESS: THE MARKET MODEL AND THE GAMES MODEL

This section is concerned with two of the numerous views of the governmental process advanced by different social science disciplines. These are employed primarily as points of reference, rather than as systematic frameworks for analysis.

The *market model* regards government as the analogue of the producer-firm in the private sector: It arranges for the production and delivery of public goods to voter/taxpayers, who are the analogue of sovereign consumers in the private market. The market analogy suggests that governmental institutional arrangements should approximate market conditions as closely as possible. The market model is usually associated with the values of efficiency, in both choice making and production, and equity.

Efficiency in choice making involves equating the marginal benefit of each public good with its marginal cost. Marginal cost is measured in terms of other goods and services that must be sacrificed to enjoy an additional unit of the particular good. Richard Wagner (1971: 2) states the condition as follows:

> For any given supply of police service (or other public good), there will be some value that each citizen will place upon a slight increase in the level of protection. This is the citizen's marginal valuation for police service, which would normally fall as the level of protection increased. There will also be some sacrifice of private consumption required to generate a slight increase in the level of protection; this is the marginal cost of police protection, which would normally rise with increases in the level of protection. . . .

Budgetary efficiency will be attained only when the supply of police service has been expanded to the point where the marginal valuation of police service equals the marginal cost.

With respect to any public good, a taxpayer theoretically has three variables to consider: the value to him of the service, at least at the margin; the cost of the service; and the amount of tax he pays because the service is provided. In a perfectly functioning market model, the values of the three variables are equal; in practice, they may differ widely. The first variable—service value—is largely subjective; it is molded by community political and social processes. It may, and frequently does, change over time. The other two variables in the market model are largely independent of the taxpayer in the short run.

The difficulty in attaining efficiency lies in reconciling differences in individual preference for various public and private goods. Some people may prefer more police, some may prefer more parks, some may prefer greater expenditures on education, while still others may prefer less public goods and lower taxes. Attempts to construct public welfare functions, which would yield optimal allocations, have proved futile. Majority rule is no answer: It is not difficult to show that, for instance, fiscal inefficiency will result if a majority chooses a level of police or other public service which it prefers only *mildly* over alternatives, while the minority *greatly* prefers other alternatives. Majority rule will be efficient only by accident (Wagner, 1971: ch. 1).

One organizational solution for this dilemma, discussed in a following section, is to make choice-making jurisdictions as small as possible and their constituencies as homogeneous in preferences as possible.

In the market model, government agencies are assumed to produce and deliver public goods with reasonable efficiency, meaning that production functions and output-input ratios cannot be greatly improved in the short run.[4] In this context, the main policy problems concern economies of scale—the size of jurisdiction required for most effective planning, decision making, and actual production or delivery of goods. The problems may be simplified by the fact that these three elements of the administrative process—planning, decision making, and decision implementation—may be performed by different organizational entities.

Fiscal equity, which aims at a "fair" distribution of income after taxes, requires that equal taxes be imposed on individuals of equal economic capacity (as measured by income and wealth), and that tax rates be progressive-higher for individuals of higher economic capacity. The first requirement is fairly unambiguous, though there may be practical difficulties in measuring economic capacity, and though there may be other efficiency arguments for taxing some forms of income and wealth (e.g., land rents) more heavily than other forms (e.g., earned income). The second requirement is more difficult, because of the lack of knowledge respecting the degree of progressivity required for maximum efficiency, though it is generally thought that progressivity must stop well short of 100 percent to avoid unduly impairing incentives.[5]

Here the economist can only appeal to the community's sense of justice or, on more practical grounds, to political feasibility. But political feasibility, at the state-local government level at least, does not require equity through progressive taxation—most state and local tax structures are notoriously regressive.

The *games model* views the governmental (and, more broadly, the communal) process as a system or systems of games in which various players strive for various prizes. In the games model, many different individuals and groups want different, often conflicting, things from government (of which public goods, as ordinarily defined, are only one) and employ different kinds of tactics (only one of which is appeal to voters) to get what they want. Some of the prizes, for example, include positions of power and influence, jobs and contracts, wages and working conditions (of interest to employee unions), zoning and other regulations favorable to specific interests, and favorable enforcement of statutes and regulations (Long, 1958).[6]

Thus, in the games model, allocation issues are much more complicated than the two-way bargaining process between taxpayer-consumers and producer-governments. By way of illustration, I identify four sets of players whose conflicting interests have to be resolved by the governmental process. They are input suppliers, elected officials, taxpayers, and beneficiaries—consumers of public goods or outputs.

Input suppliers are interested in such matters as more pay, less work, and organizational status. They have long protected themselves by civil service and the so-called merit system, as well as by attempts to manipulate the political system to their advantage through the use of money and votes. In recent years, this protection has been fortified by the growth of unions, frequently militant, whose purpose it is to provide their members with more muscle in playing the community game. Even those inveterate pussycats, the teachers, have turned into snarling wildcats in seeking to raise their pay and protect their professional status against intrusion by outsiders (particularly outsiders colored black and brown).[7] Government unions do not have many of the constraints that affect industrial unions, such as the market and profit situation, and the body of law defining unfair practices is safely ignored. Nor do government unions have the fairly standard set of moves and countermoves, understood and followed by both parties, that keep the game within bounds.

Government agencies, in the games model, lack the incentives for economic efficiency that are imposed on private firms by competition. The service bureaucracies are in the position of monopolies who need not worry overmuch about consumer reaction to inefficient performance and high prices. Even private monopolies, however, are goaded to some extent by the profit motive, whereas, in the public sector, the prerogatives of supplying inputs tend to be more important and to bear more heavily on the production process than do either the profit motive or the objective of satisfying customers.

Elected officials perform their political function of reconciling interests, making decisions, and, in direct or indirect fashion, supervising the bureaucracy (which tries to ignore them, and generally succeeds). Their interests are varied: power, prestige, financial reward, party success, and, for many, the desire to render public service.

Taxpayers can be divided into two groups: those who are aware of the taxes they are paying, and those who are not. The *aware* group may make a tenuous connection between the taxes they pay and the benefits they receive, and, typically, they would prefer to pay less and get more. As a group they object particularly to paying taxes for income-redistribution purposes and tend to avoid jurisdictions that offer relatively large welfare and other benefits to the poor. The *unaware* taxpayers are usually unaware because their taxes are hidden or indirect, a common example being property taxes on rental housing. Such taxes are highly popular with elected officials because they elicit less squawking. In one way or another, the poor get caught with a heavy burden of taxes—e.g., state and local tax systems are grossly regressive.

Beneficiaries of government can also be divided into two groups. The first includes the upper and middle classes who do not, or think they do not, depend on government for most of their consumption. They look rather to the market, a habit which has been bolstered by rising incomes and purchasing power. They depend on government only for basic housekeeping and protective services, and education, which last is the largest expenditure item in most urban areas. Of this group Raymond Vernon (1962: 31) said a decade ago:

> To most Americans the personal experience of urban living seems not one of personal retrogression but of continuous improvement. Let the central city weep; let the sociologists fume; for most people things are getting slightly better all the time.

The betterment mentioned by Vernon was facilitated by the fact that the middle- and upper-income groups (particularly the whites, but more recently the blacks as well) could escape from the stresses and strains of large-city life by moving out.

One must doubt whether Vernon's optimistic note fits the situation today. Many of the lower-middle class, overtaken by rising taxes and inflation, made little or no progress during the last half of the 1960s. Proud of their self-reliance, yet unable to share in the general progress, and convinced that their hard-earned tax payments are going to support the idle and dissolute, these people have been frustrated, and even spurred to more-or-less open revolt. They are joined in this resentment by some of their better-off blue-collar colleagues who have mobilized union power to extract disproportionate wage increases from the economy while resisting tax increases and tax reform.[8]

Moreover, one senses a rising disenchantment with urban conditions among even the upper-middle- and upper-class groups troubled by such unpleasantness as congestion, pollution, crime and delinquency, restrictions on choice, and the ugliness of the "urbanscape." In self-defense, they must turn to collective action, but in doing so their instincts are less creative than conservative; they lean toward preserving amenities and eliminating abominations. Most have not made the connection between their growing discomfort and the need for better planning and design.

The second category of beneficiaries is the lower class, who must look to government for gratification of their most elementary wants, such as basic subsistence, housing, education, and a viable social environment (e.g., neighborhoods free of violence, dope pushers, and vagrants).

The two models differ in the objectives that they implicitly stress. The market model is value-oriented. Its most important feature is its stress on efficiency (in the economic sense) in both choice of public goods (by aiming for maximum satisfaction of taxpayer-consumers) and production and delivery of public goods (by aiming for maximization of output-input ratios).

The games model, by contrast, is essentially value-free in that it does not entail ends, such as efficiency, though the games model does depend on the existence of, and adherence to, rules under which the community's games will be played. Various players continually seek to change the rules in order to give themselves an advantage, and many succeed; this is also part of the game. The games break up when any considerable number of players decide that the rules are too heavily biased in favor of other players and decline to play any longer under the allegedly unfair rules.

SOCIAL CHOICE MAKING

There are two central issues of collective choice making. The first has to do with achieving maximum gratification of urban residents' demands for public goods—demands as expressed in various forms of communication and, ultimately, in the voting booth. The second, closely related, issue is to provide a sense of participation in, or identification with, processes whereby choices are made and services are provided.

Approaches Based on the Market Model

Market-based approaches conceive of a situation similar to that of the individual consumer shopping in the market, able to buy within the limits of his purchasing power the items that he wants. Of course, the market in fact does not work as well as some enthusiasts would have us believe. Purchases may be ill-informed, regretted later, harmful, or beyond the means of the people making them. It is not always possible to buy exactly what is needed, because some items are "lumpy" in the sense that people have to buy more than they need—for example, household capital items such as automobiles, lawn mowers, and other implements. In some cases, however, it may be possible to attain economies of scale through informal arrangements, such as by carpools or the sharing of implements with friends and neighbors. The preference scales of individuals and households are to some degree changeable, capable of being modified by various influences such as advertising and the play of fad and fashion. While some of these influences have their counterparts in the public sector, the imperfections of the private market to some degree narrow the advantage of precision that it is supposed to enjoy over the public sector.

In applying the market model to the public sector, it is not difficult to show that a majority of voters desiring a certain level of service can coerce a minority (which would prefer a less expensive service, or no service) into paying for the level desired by the majority. While exploitation of the minority may be prevented by rules requiring uniform taxation, an incremental expenditure may be wasteful if the aggregate amount of benefit to the majority desiring it (as measured by what they would be willing to pay over what they actually do pay) exceeds the aggregate amount of excessive payments by the minority (Wagner, 1971: ch. 1).

The market model leads to two principles of government organization, homogeneity and smallness. The first principle, homogeneity, says that voters of choice-making government jurisdictions should be as homogeneous as possible, with similar preferences as to the amounts and kinds of public services they desire. The second principle, smallness, states that the number of voters should be small, so as to reduce the costs of interpersonal bargaining and negotiation necessary to arrive at mutually satisfactory public budgets. Hence Wagner (1971: 64) states that, "Efficiency conditions suggest that if a group of citizens within one state want to form a new state, they should be permitted to do so."

The validity of the smallness principle depends also on the assumption that small groups will be more homogeneous than large as to tastes and preferences. This homogeneity is achieved in the Tiebout theory; each firm and household gravitates to the community that most nearly fits its own preferences. "Voting by foot" is thus the adjustment mechanism in the social-political process that is analogous to the "invisible hand" in the private market.

There is some evidence that this "birds-of-a-feather" principle tends to operate in the real world, but mainly with respect to the wealthier classes. Variances between residential incomes tend to be higher among suburban towns than within individual towns, indicating a tendency of income classes to flock together. Thus, suburban towns tend to be rich, poor, or middle income. Public services tend to be better and expenditures higher in higher-income communities. In fact, expenditures on public goods and services are more closely correlated with income than with any other variable, which suggests that differences in preferences among persons of similar incomes are less important than the market analogy implies.[9]

There are some differences, to be sure. For example, older people and working-class families may oppose high expenditures on public education, or new residents in a suburban town may want improvements opposed by older settlers. Whether these differences are ordinarily sufficient to cause migration to other communities is another question. Considering the host of other considerations which tie people to a community, many individuals would rather "fight than switch." The flight of the middle class from central cities affords little support to the Tiebout principle, because the difference between central-city and suburban living far transcends differences in public services.[10]

The Tiebout argument, moreover, logically applies mainly to households with high enough incomes to afford some choice as to how their incomes should be allocated between private and public (tax-financed) goods. Low-income groups, largely dependent on government services, have no such latitude of choice. Also, the latitude they might otherwise have is frustrated by the tendency of higher-income groups already in place to resist incursions of lower-income residents, because the presence of the latter would raise taxes and otherwise spoil the community for the former. Foot-voting, in short, is largely the prerogative of the higher-income groups who play exclusionary politics to deny the foot vote to lower-income groups.

Problems of the Market Model

Three kinds of problems—economies of scale, externalities, and income redistribution—are recognized by the advocates of smallness and homogeneity. The first problem has to do with economies of scale in production; this is discussed in the section on production.

The second problem is externalities, having to do with the benefits conferred, or costs imposed, by the production activities of one jurisdiction upon residents of other jurisdictions. In the case of external costs, the producing jurisdiction, not having to bear the full cost, may produce more of the public good involved than is socially justified. The test is whether the resident-consumers of the public good involved would be willing to compensate fully nonresidents who are damaged; to the extent that they are not, production is presumptively not justified.[11]

The same reasoning applies to external benefits, but with a reverse twist. Where part of the benefits from the activity of one jurisdiction accrue to the residents of other jurisdictions, the acting jurisdiction, if it has to pay all the costs, is likely to produce less than the optimal amount. That is, other jurisdictions would be willing to pay it to produce more, and the social loss, however calculated, is greater than the cost of an increment to production.

A damaging instance of such underproduction may occur where the residents of a particular jurisdiction, preferring private goods to social goods, desire to economize on education (a conspicuous target, because it is the largest component of local government expenditures in most areas). Though the amount spent on education is not necessarily a reliable indicator of the quality thereof, if is usually true that, where education is less valued, it is less good. Poor education, however, is likely to spread "ignorance pollution," which adversely affects not only the community but also the society and economy at large. The same can be said of neglect of recreational and other cultural opportunities for young people and of law enforcement and health services.

In some cases, external benefits might be handled by voluntary intergovernmental cooperation, whereby other jurisdictions agree to pay the acting jurisdiction for increasing production of the externally beneficial good. But such arrangements are difficult, at best, to negotiate. External costs probably cannot be handled by intergovernmental arrangements—it is difficult to conceive of jurisdiction B paying jurisdiction A not to pollute the river or to upgrade jurisdiction A's educational program.

Income redistribution is the third problem. The notions of efficiency and choice making presuppose a socially acceptable distribution of income. If taxes have to be imposed to finance income transfers to the poor, the total amount of taxes imposed will exceed the total cost of public services produced and delivered, and this greatly complicates the mechanisms of collective choice. To overcome this problem, it is frequently proposed that the income-redistribution function be "moved upstairs," preferably to the federal government. A national jurisdiction can better effect equitable redistribution than can metropolitan areas or states, which in any case vary greatly among themselves in regard to per capita income and taxable resources.

In many respects, the market model fails to conform to the conditions of modern urban government and is simply irrelevant to the real world. Its prescriptions of homogeneity and smallness cannot be fulfilled. One weakness is that outputs in many functions are difficult to define, so that it is impossible for the citizen to discern any relationship between an increment (or decrement) in taxes and the quality of any particular benefit he receives. Demands for improved service are usually translated into more inputs, which may, or may not, increase or improve outputs. Moreover, once we abandon the two-dimensional world of the market model for the games model, the community negotiation process goes beyond taxpayers and producer-governments, and other claimants appear. Legislators and elected public officials, as previously mentioned, tend to be more interested in inputs and the resultant patronage than in outputs, which are difficult, at best, to measure.

Second, governmental bureaucracies are notoriously unresponsive to public demand; they tend to go their own way and to pressure officials and legislators to find the wherewithal to continue their support. The experience of the last few years has confirmed that pouring more money into education, or police, or highways does not necessarily provide better education, improved protection, or speedier transportation.

Few citizens have the requisite time or knowledge to evaluate services, or to take any action except that of complaining about gross deficiencies. Making decisions about preferred expenditures and quantities of services and putting together an optimal package of desired services is beyond the interest and competence of most citizens of the real world. Increasing the number of jurisdictions that provide services does not improve matters; it complicates the task of discovering and understanding what is going on. The budgeting process, in which attempts are made to weight community needs and priorities and to balance them against each other, is weakened.

Thus, one of the advantages of a general multifunctional government is that it relieves constituents of the necessity of making many decisions (some of a highly technical nature) that they would have to make if public services were supplied through the market. Voters in a multipurpose government, however, do have to accept whole packages of services in whose priorities most of them, typically, have had little part in shaping, except possibly as members of community interest groups. In the process, voters become far removed from their economic function as rational sovereign consumers and settle for other "rationalities."[12] As Shapiro (1969: 1118) notes:

> Some voters derive gratification from knowing that a given type of individual is in office, some are more concerned with the policy choices that an officeholder is likely to make, while others find fulfillment in making choices which they feel are congruent with the choices of others whom they admire or respect.

The mere fact that public-goods consumers may get more or less than they would have been willing to bid for is not an infallible indication of waste in public choice making, however. As previously noted, individuals' preferences are themselves conditioned by the community decision-making process, the debate over public issues, and the striking of compromises. It is common to find cases of people satisfied with the outcome of community decisions which they may have originally opposed. Ex post judgments are likely to be more informed, hence better, than ex ante judgments.

The small-jurisdiction prescription, based on the notion that the costs of negotiation and cooperation rise with the number of individuals concerned, fails, most political scientists would agree, because its basic assumption is mistaken. According to Wallace S. Sayre (1972: 29):

> The smaller the constituency, the *lower* [my italics] the level of electoral participation. . . . Small constituencies also display unstable, highly factionalized, personalized politics or tight oligarchical control supported by consensual politics, both representing low levels of citizen participation.
>
> One main explanation is the absence of an information system for small constituencies. The communication media provide information only about the issues, the leaders and the performance of large constituencies. Nor do any other information channels serve as useful substitutes. Thus the politics of small constituencies is word of mouth, rumor and gossip, misinformation or half-baked information.

Numerous case studies and other materials amply support the above points. To take one case, a study of "micro-city" in California found tight oligarchical control, which was resistant to innovation and reluctant to rock the boat. Individuals who get out of line are punished for their temerity, and in the goldfish bowl of a small community, endeavors to organize opposition are difficult or impossible.

Another disadvantage is the inability of small governments to bring countervailing power against muscular interest groups—business and labor groups, bureaucracies, and other groups seeking special consideration from government. Roscoe Martin (1965: 190) has observed:

> 'Bring government back home' and 'Return government to the people' are battle cries equally familiar in the cause of local economy and in that of states' rights. . . . In point of fact it is quite clear that the goal sought is often not local autonomy or states' rights as such but rather less government, and moreover government more immediately and more directly subject to control.

The case for homogeneity is no stronger. Homogeneity already exists to a large extent in suburbia, where groupings tend to be by income class rather than by finely differentiated preferences regarding the amount and composition of government expenditure. The impact of these existing homogeneous patterns is well known—in a word, the "haves" continue to freeze out the "have-nots," denying them access to housing and thus to jobs, better schools, recreation, and other advantages. It is unrealistic to imagine that these disadvantages will be overcome by anything the federal government does about income redistribution.

Differences over most of the basic urban issues of the times, such as the quality of education, environmental improvement, urban transportation, economic development, manpower development, health programs, and waste disposal, will not be resolved by small jurisdictions, homogeneous or not. And to the extent that they cannot be resolved within the confines of metropolitan areas, they will be moved to higher arenas of state or federal government.

Advantages of Larger Scale in Choice Making

In today's complicated urban society, informed decisions about expenditure and investment priorities require sophisticated planning and budgeting processes which lend themselves to the economies of scale which are impossible in small jurisdictions. Some economists have seen other advantages of scale in choice-making jurisdictions. As Julius Margolis (1961: 241-242) points out:

> The normal pattern of public choice is one of choosing a package rather than a single product. It is reasonable to hypothesize that the greater the number of products offered in the package to the voter the greater the likelihood of adoption. . . . The success of the multipurpose package is based upon the existence of consumers' surpluses of enough voters for specific projects so that they are willing to endorse the entire package rather than lose the specific project.

James M. Buchanan and Gordon Tullock (1962), accepting the possibility of such logrolling, think that it results in raising expenditures on public services above optimal levels. Anthony Downs (1957), on the other hand, suggests that the dynamics of the political-electoral process works to reduce public services below optimal levels.

The Margolis proposition argues for governments that are more comprehensive not only in regard to function but also in regard to geography and population. A multiplicity of governments, whatever their respective degrees of homogeneity, tends to reduce the possibility of agreement on broad public programs in a metropolitan area. Political scientists generally have tended to favor larger governmental jurisdictions, at least until recently, though some minds have been changing, as large city governments have come into fashion.

Meltsner and Wildavsky (1970: 311-312), however, contend that the concern with resource allocation by urban governments is mostly academic flapdoodle:

> There is loose talk to the effect that budgeting involves resource allocation. So far as the few American cities we know about are concerned, we believe

this rumor to be unfounded. . . . Since cities are in a financial strait jacket and officials can make only small changes in their budgets, the rationale for resource allocation is not entirely evident. Our detailed analysis of the budgetary process in Oakland shows that choices among alternative allocations of resources are not at the center of anyone's concern.

It should be pointed out, however, that Oakland, a main inspiration for this generalization, is a poor city. In the urban area of San Francisco Bay, there are numerous urban issues involving large public expenditures—e.g., urban transportation.

Voice and Control

Aside from the efficiency argument, which turns out to lack substance, the main argument for multiple jurisdictions, and particularly for decentralization of large city governments to create these, is that, as the Committee for Economic Development (1970) puts it: "Units of government should be small enough to enable the recipients of government services to have some voice and control over their quality and quantity."[13]

This version of "maximum feasible participation" might go so far as to include the power to allocate part or all of the funds available for public services in the community, the power to implement such decisions by hiring personnel, purchasing materials, and making contracts, and the power to sign checks—in other words, the budgetary-expenditure powers ordinarily exercised by municipal general government. No corresponding decentralization of revenue-raising powers is advocated, however. On the contrary, the poor communities who are the principal intended beneficiaries of decentralization presumptively lack adequate revenue bases, so their revenues must come mainly from higher jurisdictions.[14]

Urban political historians record that, in the past, political and government assistance operated to speed acculturation and to ease things for the poor in several ways. The large city political machines delivered a modicum of welfare assistance in exchange for votes, turning a tidy profit in the process. The worst misfortunes of the poor were alleviated by various kinds of subventions—food, fuel, and shelter when necessary, and intervention—with city agencies, the police, the courts. But while it may be true that the poor have never been so well represented since, descriptions of actual living conditions in large cities around 1900 dispel any notion that this was the "golden age" of poverty.

In the last few decades, political control, including control of large cities, has been exercised predominantly by the middle class, because they are the most numerous, although less dependent on government for services. Moreover, with the institutionalizing of welfare services, the poor, who once had political clout because of sheer numbers, have been forced to depend on the large welfare bureaucracies, which have been more or less impervious to political intervention, for satisfaction of their wants and needs. But with the increasing concentration of the poor in central cities, and the large amount of political patronage from Washington, which bypassed both state and city administrative and political machinery, the situation in the central cities changed somewhat in the 1960s.[15]

As previously noted, the social-choice argument for decentralization rests upon the familiar notion that community residents, knowing their needs and desires better than anyone else, can make more efficient decisions respecting the allocation of funds.[16] The exercise of such powers is justified also by the "maximum feasible participation" principle, which holds that participation in civic decisions is of value in itself, partly because it reduces the sense of alienation associated with nonparticipation (Boone, 1972: 451-452).

Another argument, to be considered later, has to do with the production function. It is thought that giving a community greater control over suppliers, through the power to hire and fire and make contracts, will compel the bureaucracies to pay more attention to clients' needs and to serve them more effectively.

"Voice and control" over budget decisions, however, raises some difficult questions:

(1) Is it in fact possible to create efficient decision-making and administrative machinery in poor communities? Experience to date shows a notable lack of participation through voting, political activity, or community organization. The disabilities of small political jurisdictions, summarized in the preceding quotation by Wallace S. Sayre, tend to be even more pronounced in poor neighborhoods, partly because of the lack of participation.[17]

(2) Will the necessity of making hard choices between more sanitation service or more police services, or between more housing or more health service, enhance the sense of responsibility and political maturity of neighborhood residents and their leadership?

(3) Will poor communities become more politically sophisticated and howl less loudly about deprivation if they have to get down to hard choices in the allocation of scarce resources? Will budget-making exercises, largely with funds granted under arbitrary allocation formulas by other governments, lead to a better understanding of the difficulties of imposing taxes, or of the political and economic constraints imposed by the necessity of keeping taxes and expenditures in some sort of balance?

(4) Where so many needs—such as housing, public protection, sanitation, education, and recreation—are inadequately met, should communities spend large amounts of time and energy deciding on marginal allocation of resources?

To ask these questions is to suggest that the answer to all of them is no. As Meltsner and Wildavsky (1970) point out, there is little latitude, where funds are chronically scarce, for significant allocation decisions. In most cities, budgeting is mainly concerned with keeping existing machinery in operation, and budgets are instruments of expenditure control rather than instruments for economizing by making the "best" use of public funds. Only the richer suburbs have the financial latitude for significant decisions about resource allocation. Observation of urban government today confirms that adequate resources—not only fiscal, but also administrative, political, and organizational—are a first requisite of effective government. The only way for a community to have access to adequate resources is to be a member of a larger and richer community (city, state, or federal).

It does not follow that the urban poor generally, and the large-city poor minority groups in particular, should not be more involved with the public decisions that affect them. But there are ways short of radical surgery on exist-ing city governments to improve both citizen involvement and identification with government (Jones, 1970; Altshuler, 1970). There is a spectrum of degrees of participation—the right to be advised, the right to be consulted, the right to veto measures and policies affecting an area or group concerned, and the right to participate actively in neighborhood planning processes. All these fall short of creating new jurisdictions with powers to allocate resources and administer service-delivery programs. These less drastic mechanisms include community councils which are consulted on development plans, service priorities, and similar matters; neighborhood service centers to make health, welfare, and other services more readily accessible to clients, both in regard to hours and locations; and devices for improving communication between neighborhoods and central-agency administrators. Even such relatively simple measures have not been exploited by most cities, though an increasing number are moving to improve communication and access, including access to services. Otherwise, the main thrust for community involvement has come from the poverty programs of the 1960s.

Geographic vs. Political Decentralization

Most decentralization schemes concentrate on geographic decentralization, because physical boundaries enclosing territory, artifacts, and people are so integral a part of the concept of organized local government that it is difficult to imagine getting along without them (Maas, 1959).[18] Geographic central-ization, or decentralization, which refers to the number of jurisdictions govern-ing an urban area, however, must be distinguished from political centralization or decentralization, which refers to political power, or, in games-model terms, the number and strength of the players in the game.

The difference in the two concepts is illustrated by New York City, where a monolithic city government presides over a large geographic area containing eight million people, but where political power is widely dispersed among many political, civic, and other organizations. Annmarie Hauck Walsh (1972: 8-9) has observed that:

> Every serious student and avid practitioner of politics in New York City
> knows that real power is highly fragmented; that despite his impressive formal
> authority, there is very little that the mayor can do without complex, lengthy
> and uncertain bargaining. What we have is a high degree of decentralization,
> not along geographic lines, but along functional lines. Power is fragmented

among specialized pockets of single purpose interest groups, entrenched bureaus, public corporations, public employee associations, local, state, and federal officials.

The high degree of political decentralization has suggested to some observers that geographic decentralization would only compound the existing pluralism which makes it so difficult to formulate, adopt, and implement coherent public policies in the city today. Some have concluded that New York City's main need for governmental improvement is not geographic decentralization, but rather a greater degree of political centralization. For example, Wallace Sayre (1970) has suggested that the mayor's office be restructured to promote this objective.

Much of the rationale behind geographic decentralization, on the other hand, is that this is the only effective means of putting more power in the hands of blacks and other minority groups who have no other means of exercising real power over the governmental process by majority rule. In this view, attempts to increase participation of the poor ("poor" is generally a euphemism for the blacks and the browns) in large heterogeneous jurisdictions has for the most part failed.[19]

A generic difficulty with geographic decentralization has to do with carving out, from already existing jurisdictions, the geographic areas to be endowed with general governmental powers. There has been little experience in drawing boundaries in already established jurisdictions (except for special purposes, such as electoral districts); most reorganization has aimed at consolidation and the obliteration of boundaries, rather than the establishment of new ones.

The objective (implicit, at least) of most decentralization proponents is greater homogeneity of the decentralized jurisdiction. There are a number of possible bases of homogeneity. Thus, communities might be historically defined areas, ethnic or racial concentrations, income-class concentrations, or the like. Even to mention such distinctions is to emphasize the inconsistency of drawing lines to focus group homogeneities in an age that stresses the values of heterogeneity, particularly in urban government jurisdictions. One possible expedient is to base jurisdictions on already existing political units; thus, it has been suggested that decentralized New York City units be based on existing councilmanic districts (Hertz and Walinsky, 1970). This expedient, however, would seem to have little to commend it except convenience, since the mere fact of being represented by an individual whose name typically is known by only a few constituents is not much of a basis for "community."

Communities suitable to be decentralized governmental jurisdictions sometimes already exist, but more often they do not. Annmarie Hauck Walsh (1972: 8) has observed that

> power never did reside in general population groups within the neighborhoods of our big cities, and it remains to be seen if there is any sense of community in most of them. The image of neighborhood power has cultural roots in our ideology—namely our yearning for a town-meeting society, but it has little place in urban political history.

There has been little attention to the criteria for establishing new decentralized units. "Power to the poor" implies a principle of homogeneity, as previously observed, but some decentralists prefer heterogeneity, and would opt for jurisdictions that are microcosms of the whole metropolitan area, a concept which would require ingenious gerrymandering in most urban areas. Then there is the question of size: Is there an optimal population size range for urban jurisdictions? Conceivably, the answers may vary according to the function involved. The optimal size may differ for the functions of (1) intracommunity bargaining and choice making, (2) production and delivery of services (and within this category the scale economies associated with particular services), and (3) redistribution of income.

Most speculations respecting the optimal size range of urban governments have included both production-delivery functions and social choice making functions. One does not often see reference to actual numbers. Presumably, the jurisdiction for functions that, because of their production characteristics, need to be metropolitan in scale should be coterminus with the metropolitan area. As for submetropolitan units, there seems to be general agreement that at least 40,000 people are required for an effective jurisdiction providing a full range of urban services.

Still another difficulty with smallness and pluralism as principles of urban government organization is that pluralistic local-government fiscal structures, and the budget-making process, are disjointed by what has been termed the "peripatetic propensities of metropolitan man." According to Fitch (1957), a metropolitan family

> may reside in one jurisdiction, earn its living in one or more others, send the children to school in another, and shop and seek recreation in still others. Such dispersal of activities among jurisdictions can, and in practice frequently does, confuse the voting process which to a considerable extent still reflects the presumption that the voter's various activities are concentrated in the jurisdiction of his residence, where he casts his vote.

THE PRODUCTION-DELIVERY SYSTEM

The Politics of Production: The Games Model

Where, as in the market model, jurisdictions can buy services economically from other public or from private agencies, the scale and efficiency of production need not be a primary consideration in determining the size of the purchasing jurisdiction. But, as the games model indicates, things are seldom so simple.

First, the production and delivery of services in most jurisdictions is the heart of the political-governmental process. It produces many "outputs" such as jobs and contracts, high offices, and ego satisfaction, which tend to be regarded more highly than public goods delivered to beneficiaries.

Second, government bureaucracies typically do not stand or fall, as do most private firms, on customer satisfaction with the product. In the games model, only the beneficiary-consumers have a direct interest in delivery of services; the other players have different interests. An observation made by Robert Wood (1963: 107) a decade ago is still substantially valid:

> The urban political process is not directly concerned with the provision of goods and services except when these 'problem-solving' activities can be translated into useful resources for the resolution of political conflict or its avoidance, or when, at infrequent intervals, in times of breakdown and emergency, an outright failure of law and order seems imminent.

The urban governments ordinarily rated highest in efficiency and service delivery tend to be medium-sized or smaller and to have constituencies that are predominantly middle-class and interested mainly in adequate service. They are run by professional city managers, who can concentrate on the technical aspects of administration instead of being obliged, as are so many large-city mayors, to devote much of their time to conflict resolution.

Such smaller middle-class-dominated cities more nearly fit the market model, while the larger cities are better described by the games model. Charles Adrian (1969: 512) has observed that:

> The efficiency and economy movement contributed much to the modern management of America's small and moderate-sized cities. But it was little help to our larger cities, perhaps chiefly because the reformers' two basic assumptions—that politics and politicians are evil and untrustworthy, and that city government is almost entirely a matter of applying the principles of efficient business management—could not be reconciled with the political realities of a large city.

The fact that large city governments take after the blind-to-efficiency games model does not mean that the larger cities are rapidly becoming unglued and in danger of collapse, or that things are worse than in grandfather's day—they are certainly much better in New York, for example, than the conditions described by Jacob Riis and Lincoln Steffens at the turn of the century. Nor does it mean that the city government is doing worse than some of the private industries that serve urban populations—for instance, the Penn Central Railroad. Nor is there reason to suppose that the "megacentropolis" is governed worse than many other jurisdictions—one has only to compare New York City with other governments in the New York region for confirmation.

It would not be correct to conclude, either, that middle-sized and smaller units as a class are generally well governed, for good government depends on possessing both human and financial resources, and many smaller cities are insufficiently endowed with either. There already exist many examples of the dubious benefits that self-determination may bestow on poor jurisdictions. Out in suburban land one finds many low-income enclaves even more economically bereft, and worse-governed, on the whole, than are the central cities. Where funds are scarce, the level of political sophistication low, the supply of professional, managerial, and technical manpower limited, and communications poor, community leadership is more likely to focus on jobs and handouts—the traditional concern of patronage—than on improving services (Stanley, 1963; Eisinger, 1970; Reiss, 1970).

Aside from political and economic factors such as those mentioned in the preceding paragraphs, the size of agency required for efficient production and delivery of public goods depends on a number of other considerations, of which few lend themselves to quantitative analysis. One is the type of goods. It has long been established that some goods can be efficiently planned and administered only by agencies of at least metropolitan-wide jurisdiction.

The Case for Metropolitan Planning and Administration

Metropolitan-scale planning and administration may be essential, or at least more efficient, for a number of reasons, including the following:

(1) Economies of scale in production: for example, maintenance, certain aspects of the police function, and museums and other cultural centers;

(2) Externalities that cannot be adequately handled by interjurisdictional agreement: for example, air- and water-pollution control;

(3) Interdependence of elements of a public service: for example, intraurban transportation;

(4) Necessity of resolving conflicts of interest among various sub-metropolitan areas, as in the planning and zoning functions.

The list of functions that are candidates for metropolitan-scale administration appears to be expanding rather than contracting. Fifteen years ago, the principal candidates were water supply, air- and water-pollution control, and intraurban transportation. Now the list may be expanded to include health services, economic development (emphasizing jobs for the unemployment-prone), manpower-development programs, housing, and general environmental control.

In some cases, where economies of scale or administrative efficiency clearly require metropolitan-scale governmental institutions, these have been created or are in the process of evolving. Mainly, they take the form of limited-purpose jurisdictions designed specifically for only one or two services. For other types of service, economies of scale should in principle be a consideration in establishing the size of administrative jurisdictions.[20] But for other than metropolitan-scale functions (where scale is dictated more by the need for comprehensive coverage and coordination than by production technology), the literature on the subject demonstrates little evidence of economies or diseconomies of scale in a broad population bracket which might range between forty thousand and four million.

Even where scale economies do exist, it is not necessary to tailor the size of jurisdictions to take advantage of them. Several jurisdictions can cooperate in functions requiring large productive units, such as police academies or incinerators. Or services can be obtained under contract with larger jurisdictions, the most notable example of which is Los Angeles County, which sells service packages to local municipal jurisdictions. The size and content of packages is determined by the individual jurisdictions. Under such an arrangement, only the function of choice making is left to the individual jurisdictions.

Suburban areas around many large cities need a rationalization of their own governmental structure. With the rapid growth and aging of the suburbs have come many of the problems of the central cities—congestion, pollution, deficient water, sewage, and sanitary services, and an increasing number of poverty-prone residents. These have been superimposed upon the existing suburban problems of providing for rapid growth and development while maintaining open space and environmental quality.

Most suburban-area governments are not organized to cope with either the development or service needs of rapid growth. Structurally, there are two difficulties. One is the existence of many general government jurisdictions that are too small to achieve economies of scale, not only in the production-delivery functions, but also in the administrative functions—planning, management, and finance. The other is the existence of numerous entangled and overlapping special districts, which have been created absentmindedly over the years to serve special needs as they arose. In many cases, these districts have no adequate supervision or control, no compulsion to cooperate with other governmental units, and even no excuse for continued existence.[21] Most of the attention devoted to metropolitan government organization in recent years has focused on metropolitan-scale planning and jurisdiction and upon decentralization-participation issues. The problems of suburban governments per se have received little attention, and the situation needs changing.

The Case for Decentralization

It is hoped that, by putting control over service bureaucracies closer to the people, in smaller jurisdictional units, the community can put more heat on the bureaucrats to do a better job. Thus Lance Liebman (1972: 49) sees the following objectives (among others) in decentralization:

To produce contact between employee and consumer, so that the . . . needs of the consumer come to influence the employee.

To increase the extent to which jobs go to the people, or at least the kinds of people, who live in an area so that the workers care about the level of service.

To place responsibility for policy questions, especially over service allocations, on political leaders whose careers can depend on public satisfaction with their decisions.

To shake up all processes—labor, budget, planning, politics—enough so that the newly responsible persons get some of the flexibility necessary to their success, and some of the bottlenecks can be identified and public indignation mobilized against them.

This last point is supported by observation of the "arteriosclerotic" tendencies of bureaucracy and the governmental production process. As Smith and Hague (1970: 72) have noted:

All bureaucratic systems seem to suffer from a built-in entropy, a tendency to run down in efficiency. Goal displacement, or the deflection of initial objectives into such other aims as organizational maintenance, is a familiar phenomenon noted by observers of bureaucratic behavior.

So much for logic. The hard fact is that any move toward decentralization of an already existing large city government will encounter the problem of what to do about the existing production organization. Bureaucracies do not readily disappear or wither away.

If New York City were decentralized according to the broad prescriptions now being advocated (State Study Commission, 1972), certain large city agencies would be broken up and reconstituted as smaller, decentralized units. We may be sure, however, that unscrambling the government omelet will not produce fresh eggs again. Existing bureaucracies, fortified by strong unions, will not go along, or will exact tolls—in the form of organizational prerogatives, job security, and wage and pension increases—for going along.

There is no reason to think that administrators of decentralized bureaucracies will find employee groups any easier to deal with by virtue of decentralization. On the contrary, the personnel function probably will remain highly centralized, for personnel management is increasingly a matter of negotiation and collective bargaining, which require both a high degree of skill and a measure of counter-vailing power. Decentralized jurisdictional units would be at a disadvantage in both these respects, and there is no reason to think that big employee groups will obligingly decentralize when the government does.

The potential advantages of decentralization listed by Liebman, therefore, more nearly resemble the gold at the foot of the rainbow than money in the bank, as he readily admits. Unfortunately, there has been little experience with decentralization with which to test judgments. The New York City school decentralization experience, however, does not follow the optimistic script. By any hard-nosed test of performance, it has neither brought the schools closer to the people, in any constructive sense, nor improved the quality of education. Reports in the fall of 1972, for example, showed that reading achievement scores had continued falling during the new era of decentralization. Also, it has the effect of considerably raising the cost of education in New York City, another probable effect of decentralization which is commonly disregarded.

Other community-run enterprises in large cities have scored notable successes only in a few cases where there has been strong leadership. More generally, experience has followed that of such ventures as the community-run Concentrated Employment Programs, which were much more effective in dispensing patronage than in training people and putting them into jobs. [22]

Decentralization which puts control in the hands of minority groups previously underrepresented in urban government would doubtless increase the jobs, contracts, and other fallouts from the production-delivery system available to such groups. In so doing, it offers a way up the political and economic ladder not afforded by any other means. While this process might be retarded by the above-mentioned bureaucratic intractability, it would not be stopped entirely.

There is little hope that decentralization will improve the allocation process, however. Nor is there much hope that it will raise productivity or otherwise improve the production and delivery functions. It seems likely to promote further racial segregation, at least in the short run. But possibly it can accelerate absorption of minority groups into the governmental process and enable them to command a larger share of the prizes for which players contend in the games analogy model.

It is possible, however, that decentralization might not cause deterioration of services in the ghettos. Karl Hess (1972) states this view:

> In every large city the problems of crime, of welfare, of health care, of education have outpaced the ability of metropolitan planners and bureaucrats. There is no successful big city in this nation. And no amount of enlargement of the bureaucracies and spending in the cities has changed this. The alternative seems, clearly, to be toward decentralization.

> [The neighborhoods] have been gobbled up by the urban imperialism of downtown. They have been insulted as ethnic or racial while the downtown WASPS milked them dry for renewal or zoning. And yet they persist—occupied by strange police, harassed by criminals who have more connections downtown than any of the victims, impoverished by absentee landlords and tax collectors, abandoned by metropolitan hospitals, and treated like skinnerian mice by visiting school teachers.

> To survive, the people in neighborhoods are going to have to secede. 'Let us have the funds which the city has been spending in this area [health, education or whatever],' goes the demand. 'We can't do worse and we might do better, and at least we will have the satisfaction of trying.' But it seems likely that the satisfaction of trying will be the chief positive result. I conclude that this is the chief benefit which decentralization might confer on minorities.

INCOME REDISTRIBUTION AND
THE METROPOLITAN FINANCIAL PERSPECTIVE

Inter- and Intrametropolitan Disparities

The most intractible single problem of metropolitan finances is the prevalence of great disparities in taxable capacity—among states, among metropolitan areas, and among suburbs. The impossibility of treating metropolitan areas (here defined as SMSAs) as economic equals is indicated by the fact that, in 1970, per capita income of the highest income areas was 137 percent of the national average, while that of the lowest income area was only 50 percent of the national average (U.S. Department of Commerce, 1972: Table 2). Poverty tends to be concentrated primarily in central cities. The median family income of suburbanites, black and white, is higher than that of central-city dwellers. The disparities between per capita taxable resources in many suburbs, however, are greater than those between central cities and the suburbs as a whole. At one extreme is the bedroom town inhabited by low- and middle-income workers, having little industry to tax; at the other extreme are the wealthy tax colonies, carefully zoned and otherwise fortified against low-income intruders.

Like metropolitan areas, central cities themselves vary greatly as to taxable capacity and trends therein, and, indeed, metropolitan area disparities reflect in part the economies of central cities. The simplest generalization is that the national and regional business, financial, and political capitals are growing, with white-collar and service industries replacing older manufacturing industries. In many other central cities, however, outmoving industries and other economic activities have not been replaced (except by parking lots), and taxable capacity has declined, relative to continuing needs and in some cases absolutely. But such is the measure of need stemming from higher concentrations of the poor that even the cities, in which taxable capacity continues to grow, have difficulty making ends meet. The suburbs, including the better-off ones, which have been building and maintaining dikes to keep out central-city ghetto refugees, manifest elaborate unconcern with and disinclination to share the central-city burdens of health, welfare, and other problems of poor populations.

Suburban populations around most large central cities increasingly outnumber central-city populations. The effect of the "one-man, one-vote" rule (once thought to be of advantage to central cities) has been to shift power to the suburbs. The suburbs, to fortify their advantage, line up with rural areas against central cities to oppose state financing of special services to the poor, urban mass transportation, low-income housing, and so on. In New York State, for example, per capita education and other grants (except welfare) to suburbs around central cities substantially exceed grants to central cities.[23] In this situation, the best that can be said for equal per capita grants such as those proposed by various general revenue-sharing plans is that such grants would not accentuate present inequality, though perhaps we should not underestimate the ability of state governments to manipulate federal funds, including broad grant funds, with pass-through requirements which favor the politically potent suburbs and rural areas.

The size of the economic disparities between outside-central-city areas and central cities, and among their respective states, is the most compelling reason why urban areas cannot be expected to move toward greater fiscal self-sufficiency. These disparities are an argument for continuing and increasing federal grants. There are several reasons for thinking that the greatest contribution the federal government can make toward relieving urban government financial burdens in the immediate future is assumption of larger shares of the cost of services required by the urban poor, such as welfare, education, and manpower development—i.e., income redistribution functions.

Reasons for Federal Intervention

First, the main political-financial issues in most urban areas today concern income redistribution and programs specifically formulated to raise the economic and cultural status of those at the bottom end of the scale. Such issues cannot be resolved in poor suburban jurisdictions or central cities with high concentrations of poor people. They cannot be resolved fiscally below the metropolitan level, and even at the metropolitan level, only in the wealthier metropolitan areas. Politically, metropolitan-level resolution is blocked because of conflicts between central cities and suburbs, and between rich and poor suburbs.

Second, welfare assistance is a dead weight on communities with a disproportionate number of poor residents, since taxpayers (at least those who are conscious of paying taxes) will shun the high-welfare-cost communities and go elsewhere. Such communities thus are caught between the millstones of neglecting their poor or losing their tax bases, though the tax bases may dwindle in any event if the neglect of the poor leads to civil disorder and other manifestations of revolt.

Third, the welfare issue is likely to becloud other community issues. For example, taxpayers whose taxes rise to meet increased labor costs are prone to blame not public-employee organizations but the stereotype welfare deadbeat. The policeman whose wages are not as high as he thinks they should be also blames high welfare payments.[24]

Fourth, gross disparities among states and among metropolitan areas in levels of public assistance tend to encourage migration, which may be uneconomic and otherwise undesirable. At best, this is a purposeless way of offering incentives for location.

Fifth, as Musgrave and Polinsky (1970) have pointed out, the rich should contribute to the relief of the poor, no matter where they live.

Even at the national level, however, the growing political power of the suburbs outweighs the growing needs of central cities, and this fact inevitably will influence general-revenue-sharing formulas.

Assuming that the main burdens of income redistribution are taken over by the federal government, at least part of the argument for metropolitan-scale government—that having to do with fiscal equalization—would disappear. Conversely, as income redistribution and other measures reduce the economic differences among urban communities, and as lower-income individuals and communities achieve more nearly equal levels of public services, shares of public jobs, and political recognition, a large part of the argument for decentralization will also disappear.

The Case for Metro

The disparity in resources among jurisdictions in most metropolitan areas is so great, however, that it will not be overcome by anything the federal government conceivably may do by way of income redistribution. It is more important to solve this problem than to work for a multiplicity of jurisdictions, either for the purpose of offering variety in the types and quantities of public services or for affording "voice and control" to the nighttime residents of decentralized jurisdictions.

Such disparity of resources can be alleviated by metropolitan consolidation, although this has not usually been a main objective of consolidation in the United States. (Metropolitan Toronto, on the other hand, was established in part because of the necessity of mobilizing resources to assist poor suburban governments to finance crucial services, particularly education.) In principle, costs of central-city services might be "equalized" over a metropolitan area by area-wide financing and administration, or grants to local jurisdictions financed by area-wide taxes.

It does not necessarily follow that metropolitan organization would eliminate serious service discrepancies, considering the fact that they have not been eliminated within the confines of existing large-city, or for that matter small-city, jurisdictions. One of the main complaints against many city governments is the low level of services afforded poor communities (witness the riots in New York City over the low state of garbage collection).

It appears probable, however, that as a result of recent court decisions such as Hawkins vs. Town of Shaw (in 1969) and the Serrano case (in 1971), which respectively urge municipal corporations to provide equal services to all sectors of a single jurisdiction and state governments to equalize per-pupil public-school expenditures, states and metropolitan areas will have to undertake substantial reductions in service disparities between rich and poor districts. Such developments may be explained in terms of the games model by observing that the courts are reinterpreting the rules of the game to decrease the disadvantages hitherto suffered by less affluent peoples and governments.

The case for metropolitan consolidation as a means of achieving redistribution may be strengthened by court decisions requiring intraurban equality. However, urban blacks as a class do not see any solution to their problems in metropolitan consolidation. For instance, they resisted consolidation in the Cleveland area and are resisting it in the Atlanta area today.

Equalization Grants

Equalization grants by a metropolitan-wide revenue-collecting jurisdiction have as yet been little explored in the United States, though grants are the principal means of financing proposed by advocates of urban government decentralization, at least for poorer areas. Experience with state equalization grants indicates that they can be subverted to comply with the old maxim "to him that hath shall be given," and there is no reason to expect that the situation would be different in metropolitan jurisdictions. In fact, redistribution goals can probably be better attained in higher (state or federal) arenas than at the urban level. Large-city mayors, the most vociferous poverty pleaders, have been directing their pleas to federal and state governments, not to the cause of metropolitan consolidation.

However tax proceeds are distributed, there is no doubt that local tax administration can be greatly improved by metropolitan-wide organization, which can better afford trained personnel, costly equipment, and professional direction and research. Metropolitan-wide tax areas would also be large enough to minimize the avoidance of taxes that occurs when residents and business establishments move over boundary lines or go outside high-tax jurisdictions to shop.

SOME TENTATIVE CONCLUSIONS

Although the propositions advanced in this paper are tentative and incomplete, they weigh heavily against some of the proposals being advanced for reorganizing urban government, particularly those which would fragment decision-making units either through decentralizing large-city government or maintaining numerous small jurisdictions in metropolitan areas.

The notion that small jurisdictions make for better public choice rests on a market-model concept of government and assumes that the constituencies of smaller jurisdictions are relatively more homogeneous than those of larger jurisdictions, and that taxpayer-consumers will locate in the jurisdictions whose tax and expenditure patterns most nearly meet their respective preferences. But informed choice making in small jurisdictions tends to be impeded by poor political machinery—communication typically is deficient, participation is low, and self-interested manipulation by cliques and individuals is relatively easy. Many smaller jurisdictions, particularly poor ones, do not meet a basic market-model condition—i.e., that constituents be well-informed about the public services they want and the costs and conditions under which public services are produced. Insofar as it has any validity, the smaller-jurisdiction concept applies mainly to middle- and upper-income taxpayers and to services without large externalities.

"Centralization" and "decentralization" are usually construed in geographic terms. In fact, there are many other bases of representation, including the interest groups that abound in large urban areas. Local political structures and patterns of control may not follow geographic boundaries. Thus, political power may be highly diffused in a single large urban jurisdiction (e.g., New York City) or highly concentrated in an area containing numerous jurisdictions (the Chicago area, for example). Geographic decentralization for the purpose of increasing the power of particular groups therefore may miss the main issues of representation and the exercise of political power.

In any discussion of this issue, we should draw a sharp line between *decentralization,* here defined to mean breaking up existing jurisdictions into smaller geographic ones, and *participation,* which suggests a fuller integration of hitherto neglected areas or groups into the social, economic, and political framework of the larger community. The two concepts have quite different implications. Decentralization implies further isolation of the constituency of each new jurisdiction—the creation of a new "game," as it were—while participation implies a larger measure of intercourse with, and absorption into, the larger community, with hitherto weaker players wielding more power and influence.

Advocates of decentralization will inevitably encounter great difficulties in carving out territories that can become "communities" that are meaningful for government or other social purposes. However communities come about, they are seldom created by drawing boundary lines. The notion of "community" is, of course, fundamental to concepts of government jurisdiction in a democratic society, where government is presumed to derive its authority from the consent of the governed. While such governments may be said to derive from communities, it is also true that communities derive from governments which serve them, and many communities may have as their main unifying force a local government of long standing. "Instant governments" and "instant communities," however, are a contradiction in terms.

Decentralization for the psychological purpose of giving poor communities greater voice and control over public services may have little to commend it. In particular, the power to allocate public funds lacks significance when funds for all purposes are desperately short. If control over production and delivery of public goods could be decentralized, leaders in poor communities *might* gain by acquiring a larger stake in the inputs, but at the expense of a deterioration in outputs (goods produced and delivered). The possibility of such deterioration, however, does not worry many advocates of decentralization who claim, not always without reason, that public services in poor neighborhoods could not possibly be worse.

Aside from better communication and information, there are certain economies of scale in social choice making that argue for larger, rather than smaller, jurisdictions, particularly where heterogeneous constituencies with different and conflicting preferences are involved. There is a class of public goods and services, exemplified by intraurban transportation and air- and water-pollution control, which can be effectively provided only by metropolitan-scale jurisdictions. The case for geographic centralization of governmental powers to provide such services is more persuasive than the case for decentralization of existing large-city governments.

Both the established suburbs and developing areas in large urban concentrations are confronted with many governmental problems, which to date have tended to be neglected because of the concentration on metropolitan areas as a whole. Suburban governments particularly are handicapped by too-small jurisdictions, a proliferation of overlapping jurisdictions, and wide disparities in taxable capacity relative to need. Reorganization and rationalization of suburban governments deserves a priority at least equal to that accorded to establishing metropolitan-scale jurisdictions and improving central city government.

Income redistribution presents a greater problem than either social choice making or production and delivery of public goods, because the greatest tensions arise from disparities of wealth and income among families, and disparities in public services provided to rich and poor neighborhoods, even in the same governmental jurisdiction. No amount of urban government reorganization (whether in the direction of metropolitan consolidation or decentralization of existing large-city governments) will do much to ease such tensions as things now stand, although recent court decisions may compel both large and smaller jurisdictions to move toward greater equality of public services.

While metropolitan areas, being the chief repositories of the nation's wealth, should, in principle, be able to pay for their own public services and income redistribution measures, the configuration of urban politics (particularly conflicts between central cities and suburbs) militates against their doing so. The greatest conflicts concern income-redistribution measures and special services required by the poor, particularly the blacks and browns, the majority of whom congregate in central cities. Also, there is great variation among metropolitan areas in financial capacity.

These considerations argue that responsibility for financing income redistribution and special services should be assumed by the federal government, even though redistribution conflicts rage at higher as well as lower levels. Since the main sources of urban tension concern the poor, federal funding for income maintenance, education, and special services should take precedence over unconditional grants. It appears unlikely, however, that in the foreseeable future the federal government will go much further than it has already gone in the direction of equalization. A major impediment lies in the fact that the substantial efforts made thus far, as in the antipoverty and related programs, have had such small visible effect. A large share of the equalization problem will therefore remain with the states and metropolitan areas for the foreseeable future. Further progress with equalization appears most likely in public services provided to rich and poor areas, and this largely as a result of recent court decisions.

Another main goal of federal policy should be to raise the level of competence of state and local governments. It is necessary to continue encouraging the establishment of metropolitan-scale organizations to handle the increasing number of functions that require metropolitan-scale administration. It is also necessary that the federal government look more specifically at the growing problems of suburban government, and at means of structuring and equipping suburban governments to cope more adequately with these problems. In addition, the federal government must continue to encourage participation and to draw upon, but not necessarily follow, the experience accumulated thus far in poverty and related programs. Unconditional grants (general revenue sharing) are not well suited for meeting any of these needs.

NOTES

1. For an excellent review of the whole economic discussion of public versus private preferences, see Burkhead and Miner (1972: ch. 1-4).

2. In other words, for most taxpayers (households or firms) the ratio B/I varies from the ratio C/I, where "B" is the dollar value of benefits of public goods and services to the ith taxpayer, and "C" is the dollar amount of taxes paid by the ith taxpayer, and "I" is the dollar amount of ith taxpayer income.

3. See Mushkin (1972) for a discussion of this subject.

4. There are two kinds of tests: (a) comparisons of unit costs of similar products produced by private and other public agencies, and (b) observations of the degree to which organization and operating procedures accord with accepted standards of good management and use of available technology.

5. Some political scientists place small stock in equity as an objective. Meltsner (1970: 105), for example, comments that "equity, tax justice, and similar notions are not realistic guides to action, but just sources of bureaucratic anxiety."

6. Sayre and Kaufman (1960), among others, have systematically classified the players and prizes in New York City.

7. The hullabaloo about decentralized education in New York City represents mainly an attempt by blacks and Puerto Ricans to gain teaching and supervisory positions in a bureaucracy hitherto dominated by the Jews. Unions of the Police Department, which is Irish turf, and the Sanitation Department, where the Italians have held sway, still concentrate on pay and status rather than the black-brown incursion, but their time is coming.

8. Thus the New Jersey State AFL-CIO in the spring of 1972 lent a hand in defeating Republican Governor William Cahill's badly needed state-tax-reform program, which among other things would have partially substituted a personal income tax for the grossly inequitable property tax.

9. Robert Wood (1961: app. 3) and others have had little success in discovering relationships between local-government expenditure patterns and various sociocultural characteristics.

10. For a discussion of the behavior of different socioeconomic classes, see Banfield (1970: ch. 3) and Dobriner (1963).

11. External costs, of course, may be imposed upon a jurisdiction's own residents—those without the political clout to stop the offending activity or to obtain full restitution—as well as upon the residents of other jurisdictions.

12. See Downs (1957: ch. 1).

13. For further support of the community-control thesis, especially as it applies to blacks and other minorities, see Sundquist and Davis (1969) and Altshuler (1970). On the other side, see Moynihan (1969) and Banfield (1970). For a relevant case study, see Derthick (1970).

14. The preliminary plan for decentralizing New York City government, prepared by the State Study Commission on New York City (1972), proposed that the city-wide government retain control over revenue-raising and exercise broad budgeting powers under which allotments of funds for operating purposes would be made to the 30-odd newly created borough governments.

15. In New York City, it is alleged that the rate of acceptance of applications for public assistance has been manipulated for political purposes. Moreover, the Department of Community Services, which administers the public-assistance program, has come to be heavily staffed by blacks and Puerto Ricans, who (it is alleged) take a much more lenient attitude toward welfare applicants than did preceding generations of welfare workers.

16. This notion is advocated in a proposal to give elected councils in New York's 62 Community Planning Boards the powers, subject to specific constraints, to reallocate budget funds that have been allocated to various public functions in each district (Danzig and Heineman, 1971). The authors of the proposal took no account of the fact that, with few exceptions, the 62 existing community councils are inert, nor did they examine why the proposed community councils should behave differently.

17. Kenneth Clark (1972), the black educator, has expressed his disappointment with the lack of interest shown by the boards of New York City's decentralized school districts in improving educational programs and with their preoccupation with politics and patronage.

18. There are, of course, many other bases of social organization—familial, occupational, economic interest, racial-ethnic, and the like (Webber and Webber, 1967).

19. For a discussion of the family of participation issues, see *Public Administration Review* (1972).

20. Under the plan of the State Study Commission on New York City (1972) for decentralizing New York City government, local districts would have the responsibility for delivering the following services: garbage collection, street cleaning, social services (other than welfare administration), housing management and maintenance, code enforcement, local parking, street maintenance and lighting, community hospitals, health services and outpatient clients, police precincts, local libraries, local sewers and sewer maintenance, local parks and markets, air pollution code enforcement, local cultural affairs, personnel administration for local agencies, local budgets, and local planning.

The city's central government would have responsibility for waste disposal, delivery of welfare funds, housing construction and financing, relocation standards and building codes, traffic, tax regulation, main highways, police operations, medical centers, central library, fire department, major parks, public utilities, air pollution control standards, cultural affairs, civil service, collective bargaining, city-wide budget, central management services, human rights, strategic city-wide planning, and zoning.

Obviously there would be much argument about economies of scale implicit in these recommendations.

21. For an excellent summary discussion of this problem, see Committee for Economic Development (1966).

22. This opinion is based on several unpublished evaluations for the U.S. Department of Labor.

23. A study of New York State aid distribution patterns found that state aid per capita to suburbs of the six largest cities in 1966-67 was 18 percent higher than to the cities themselves. Excluding New York City, per capita grants to suburbs of the other five cities were 16 percent higher than to the cities (Pettingill, Chen, and Uppal, 1970).

24. Few city governments (New York City is an exception) finance and administer welfare programs. This does not mean, however, that local governments escape all welfare obligations. Some 27 percent of total government welfare expenditures were financed by county governments in 1966-67, and the poor impose many costs on local governments outside of direct public assistance.

REFERENCES

Adrian, C. Recent concepts in large city administration. In E. C. Banfield (Ed.), *Urban government.* (Rev. ed.) New York: The Free Press, 1969. 512-524.

Altshuler, A. *Community control.* New York: Pegasus, 1970.

Banfield, E. C. *The unheavenly city.* Boston: Little, Brown, 1970.

Boone, R. W. "Reflections on citizen participation and the Economic Opportunity Act." Public Administration Review, Sept. 1972, 32, 444-456.

Buchanan, J. J., and Tullock, G. *The calculus of consent: Logical foundations of constitutional democracy.* Ann Arbor: University of Michigan Press, 1962.

Burkhead, J., and Miner, J. *Public expenditure.* Chicago: Aldine-Atherton, 1972.

Colm, G. *Essays in public finance and fiscal policy.* New York: Oxford University Press, 1955.

Committee for Economic Development. *Modernizing local government.* New York: CED, 1966.

Committee for Economic Development. *Reshaping government in metropolitan areas.* New York: CED, 1970.

Danzig, R., and Heineman, B., Jr. "Decentralization in New York City: A proposal." Harvard Journal on Legislation, March 1971, 8, 407-453.

Derthick, M. "Defeat at Fort Lincoln." The Public Interest, Summer 1970, No. 20, 3-39.

Dobriner, W. *Class in suburbia.* Englewood Cliffs: Prentice-Hall, 1963.

Downs, A. J. *An economic theory of democracy.* New York: Harper & Row, 1957.

Eisinger, P. J. The impact of anti-poverty expenditures in New York: Determination of basic strategies at the neighborhood level. In J. P. Crecine (Ed.), *Financing the metropolis.* Beverly Hills: Sage Publications, 1970. 539-559.

Fitch, L. C. "Metropolitan financial problems." The Annals of the American Academy of Political and Social Science, November 1957, 314, 66-73.

Hertz, D., and Walinsky, A. Organizing the city: What cities do is what cities think. In L. C. Fitch and A. H. Walsh (Eds.), *Agenda for a city: Issues confronting New York.* Beverly Hills: Sage Publications, 1970. 451-501.

Hess, K. "Why neighborhoods must secede." New York Times, January 31, 1972.

Jones, V. "New local strategies." National Civic Review, March 1970, 59, 127-134.

Liebman, L. Metropolitanism and decentralization. In L. Wingo (Ed.), *Reform of metropolitan governments.* Washington, D.C.: Resources for the Future, 1972. 43-56.

Long, N. E. "The local community as an ecology of games." American Journal of Sociology, November 1958.

Maass, A. (Ed.) *Area and power.* New York: The Free Press, 1959.

Margolis, J. Metropolitan finance problems.: Territories, functions and growth. In National Bureau of Economic Research, *Public finances: Needs, sources, and utilization.* Princeton: Princeton University Press, 1961. 229-293.

Martin, R. *The cities and the federal system.* Chicago: Atherton Press, 1965.

Meltsner, A. J. Local revenue: A political problem. In J. P. Crecine (Ed.), *Financing the metropolis.* Beverly Hills: Sage Publications, 1970. 103-135.

Meltsner, A. J., and Wildavsky, A. Leave city budgeting alone!: A survey, case study, and recommendations for reform. In J. P. Crecine (Ed.), *Financing the metropolis.* Beverly Hills: Sage Publications, 1970. 311-358.

Moynihan, D. P. *Maximum feasible misunderstanding.* New York: The Free Press, 1969.

Musgrave, R. A., and Polinsky, A. M. Revenue-sharing—a critical view. In *Financing state and local government.* Proceedings of the Monetary Conference, June 14-16, 1970. Nantucket, Rhode Island. Boston: Federal Reserve Bank of Boston, 1970. 17-45.

Mushkin, S. (Ed.) *Public prices for public products.* Washington, D.C.: The Urban Institute, 1972.

Perlmutter, Emanuel. "Decentralization of schools fails, Kenneth Clark says." The New York Times, May 8, 1972.

Pettingill, R. B., Chen, K., and Uppal, J. S. Cities and suburbs: The case for equity. Part 1. *State aid to big cities in New York State and to their suburbs.* Albany: New York Conference of Mayors and Municipal Officials, 1970.

Public Administration Review. "Special Issue on Citizen Action in Model Cities and CAP Programs: Case Studies and Evaluation." September 1972, 32.

Reiss, A. J., Jr. Servers and served in service. In J. P. Crecine (Ed.), *Financing the metropolis.* Beverly Hills: Sage Publications, 1970. 561-576.

Sayre, W. S. The mayor. In L. C. Fitch and A. H. Walsh (Eds.), *Agenda for a city: Issues confronting New York.* Beverly Hills: Sage Publications, 1970, 563-601.

Sayre, W. S. "Smaller does not mean better, necessarily." New York Times, April 8, 1972.

Sayre, W. S., and Kaufman, H. *Governing New York City.* New York: Russell Sage Foundation, 1960.

Shapiro, M. J. "Rational political man: A synthesis of economic and socio-psychological perspectives." American Political Science Review, December 1969, 63, 1106-1119.

Smith, L. R., and Hague, D. C. *The dilemma of accountability in modern government.* New York: St. Martin's Press, 1970.

Stanley, D. T. *Professional personnel for the city of New York.* Report of the Study of Professional, Technical and Managerial Manpower Needs of the City of New York. Washington, D.C.: The Brookings Institution, 1963.

State Study Commission on New York City. *Restructuring the government of New York City.* Report of the Task Force on Jurisdiction and Structure. New York: State Study Commission, March 15, 1972.

Sundquist, J. P., and Davis, D. *Making federalism work.* Washington, D.C.: The Brookings Institution, 1969.

Tiebout, C. M. "A pure theory of local expenditures." Journal of Political Economy, October 1956, 64, 417-424.

Tiebout, C. M. An economic theory of fiscal decentralization. In National Bureau of Economic Research, *Public finances: Needs, resources, and utilization.* Princeton: Princeton University Press, 1961. 79-96.

U.S. Department of Commerce, Bureau of Economic Analysis. Metropolitan area income in 1970. *Survey of Current Business,* May 1972, 52, Part 1.

Vernon, R. *The myth and reality of our urban problems.* Cambridge: Massachusetts Institute of Technology—Harvard Joint Center for Urban Studies, 1962.

Wagner, R. E. *The fiscal organization of American federalism.* Chicago: Markham, 1971.

Walsh, A. H. "What price decentralization in New York." City Almanac, June 1972, 7, 1-11.

Webber, M. M., and Webber, C. C. Culture, territoriality and the elastic mile. In H. W. Eldridge (Ed.), *Taming megalopolis.* Vol. 1. New York: Praeger, 1967. 35-53.

Wood, R. C. *1400 governments: The political economy of the New York metropolitan region.* Cambridge: Harvard University Press, 1961.

Wood, R. C. Contributions of political science to urban life and form. In W. Z. Hirsch (Ed.), *Urban life and form.* New York: Holt, Rinehart and Winston, 1963. 99-127.

CHAPTER 10

THE PATCHWORK APPROACH:
ADAPTIVE RESPONSES TO
INCREASING URBANIZATION

Joseph F. Zimmerman

Graduate School of Public Affairs
State University of New York at Albany

TO THE SURPRISE OF MANY REFORMERS, the fragmented metropolitan governmental system in no metropolitan area in the United States has collapsed as the result of rampant urbanization since 1945. Collapse of the system has been averted by what can be labelled an adaptive or patchwork response to problems associated with increasing metropolitanization.

Our primary concern in this paper is with actions short of general reorganization being undertaken by governments in metropolitan areas to cope with area-wide problems—regional planning, establishment of Councils of Governments (COGs), intergovernmental service agreements, upward transfer of functional responsibility, creation of special district governments, tax sharing, and direct state government action. We will also consider briefly significant court decisions in the areas of reapportionment of local government bodies, school consolidation, and school finance.

REGIONAL PLANNING
AND COUNCILS OF GOVERNMENTS

Urbanization has made regional planning imperative if costly mistakes are to be avoided and problems transcending local political boundaries are to be solved. The objective of regional planning is to end haphazard growth by drafting and implementing a comprehensive and coordinated plan to guide the development of the area and rectify the unplanned heritage of the past.

Possessing only advisory powers, a metropolitan planning commission must work closely with cities and towns, state agencies, federal agencies, and private organizations whose activities and programs affect the development of the area.

To be successful, the commission must persuade the other organizations to plan and execute their programs within the framework of the commission's comprehensive plan.

The first type of official metropolitan planning was conducted by single-purpose special districts organized to solve a particular area-wide problem. Comprehensive metropolitan planning is principally a post-World War II development, although a few earlier isolated instances may be cited. The most famous early plan is the Regional Plan for New York and Its Environs, which was a private undertaking sponsored by the Russell Sage Foundation and completed in 1929. The plan was prepared by a committee of the Foundation which in 1929 was converted into the Regional Plan Association, a citizens organization, whose original purpose was the promotion of the plan's recommendations. According to Association President John P. Keith (1972: 1):

> The legacy of the 1929 Plan is seen throughout the Tri-State Region: the system of radial and circumferential highways and bridges and tunnels that tie the Region together; the parkways that lead to the Plan's major recreational areas like Bear Mountain; the air and marine ports operated by the Port Authority; zoning concepts and building standards; design innovations like the superblock carried out at Rockefeller Center; all these and much more attest to the vision of the Association's founders.

Although metropolitan planning commissions are established under provisions of a state enabling act, the federal government has been primarily responsible for the growth in the number of commissions by using conditional grants-in-aid to persuade local governments to organize commissions.

In 1961, the Advisory Commission on Intergovernmental Relations (1961: 34) issued a report opposing the creation of metropolitan planning commissions "comprised solely of part-time commissioners, and dominated by professional planning staff. Rather, a body including as ex officio members a small number of mayors, councilmen, and county commissioners in the metropolitan area, as well as private citizens, with adequate authority and funds to employ the requisite planning staff, is believed to be a preferable pattern." The Commission (1961: 49) stressed the need for integrating planning with decision making, and recommended that Congress enact legislation requiring that local governments' applications for federal grants for public facilities be reviewed by a metropolitan planning agency.

The year 1965 witnessed a significant change in federal strategy relative to metropolitan planning. Federal officials concluded that such planning had not been fully effective because of the schism existing between the planners and the decision makers. The conclusion was reached that the implementation of co-ordinated areawide plans is dependent upon the involvement of the local decision makers in the planning process. In consequence, a provision was inserted in the Housing and Urban Development Act of 1965 [1] amending the Housing Act of 1954 [2] which declared organizations of public officials in metropolitan areas eligible to receive federal grants for the preparation of comprehensive metropolitan plans.

To be eligible for a grant, a COG must consist primarily of elected representatives of municipalities and counties rather than officials of special agencies and authorities.[3] A grant, in an amount not exceeding two-thirds of the cost of the work, may be made to a council to undertake studies, collect data, develop regional plans and programs, and engage in other activities designed to provide solutions for metropolitan problems. The remaining one-third of the cost of the work must be met by the council in the form of cash or professional and technical services contributed by the jurisdictions comprising the council's membership.

The following year Congress provided an additional stimulus for the formation of COGs by enacting a requirement—popularly known as Section 204 review—that all local government applications for federal grants and loans for thirty specified projects must be submitted for review to a metropolitan organization responsible for areawide planning "which is, to the greatest practicable extent, composed of or responsible to the elected officials of a unit of areawide government or of the units of general local government."[4]

Each application for a federal loan or grant must be accompanied by the comments of the reviewing agency "concerning the extent to which the project is consistent with the comprehensive planning developed or in the process of development for the metropolitan area . . . and the extent to which such project contributes to the fulfillment of such planning."[5]

A further stimulus to metropolitan planning is contained in the act's authorization of supplementary grants up to 20 percent of project costs to units of general local government, provided they demonstrate to the Secretary of Housing and Urban Development that they will carry out their projects "in accord with metropolitan planning."[6] The supplementary grants are limited by the stipulation that the total federal contribution may not exceed 80 percent of the project cost. In making his determination, the Secretary must consider the comments of the metropolitan planning commission.

The importance of metropolitan planning has been further enhanced by passage of the Intergovernmental Cooperation Act of 1968[7] and the National Environmental Policy Act of 1969.[8] Parts of these two acts and Section 204 of the Demonstration Cities and Metropolitan Development Act of 1966 are implemented by the United States Office of Management and Budget Circular A-95 (1971) which broadens the coverage of the Section 204 review to 106 programs and extends the review to nonmetropolitan areas and the state level.

Part I of circular A-95 established the Project Notification and Review System (PNRS), an "early warning system" designed to facilitate the coordination of local, regional, and state planning and development programs assisted with federal funds. Currently, there is a state clearinghouse in each state and over 400 substate clearinghouses. The latter are designated metropolitan and regional (i.e., nonmetropolitan) clearinghouses. Any potential applicant for federal assistance under a program covered by Circular A-95 is required to notify both the state and substate (metropolitan or regional) clearinghouses of his intent to file an application and submit a brief summary description of the proposed project. Each clearinghouse has thirty days in which to indicate interest in the project and to arrange for consultation on the project.

If a conference identified conflicts over the proposed project, the clearing-house(s) may assist in the resolution of such conflicts. The intent of the Circular is to ensure that conflicts, with the assistance of the clearinghouse(s), will be either resolved or clearly identified. Upon request, a clearinghouse may have an additional thirty days in which to file comments to accompany the application. Part IV of Circular A-95 is designed to counteract the tendency of federal agencies administering grant-in-aid programs to promote functional planning independent of comprehensive regional planning. Part IV also encourages states to establish substate systems of comprehensive regional planning, and directs federal agencies to conform their planning regions to the regions established by the state. Applicants for a particular federal grant must coordinate their planning with planning for related programs in the region.

The formation of COGs, voluntary associations of local governments, was actively promoted in the mid-1960s. The COG in a metropolitan area is a device to facilitate the solution of areawide problems without changing the structure of the local government system (Zimmerman, 1968a). Most COGs are composed only of general purpose local governments, but a few COGs include representatives of school and other special districts as members. A small number of COGs have appointed public officials and representatives of civic organizations as members. One COG—the East-West Gateway Coordinating Council in the St. Louis area—has four state officials as nonvoting members.

The Demonstration Cities and Metropolitan Development Act of 1966 induced a number of metropolitan planning commissions to convert themselves totally or partially into COGs while retaining their original names, and others to change their membership and names. Furthermore, a number of COGs have assumed responsibility for planning (Zimmerman, 1968b; Zimmerman and Snyder, 1967). Consequently, it is difficult in many areas to make a sharp distinction between a COG and a regional planning commission.

Metroplan, the COG in the Little Rock area, is unusual in that it operates the regional public transportation system. The COGs in only one state are authorized to perform a traditional governmental function other than planning and training. In 1972, the state of Rhode Island and Providence Plantations enacted a law authorizing cities and towns to form a COG, which, in addition to the usual COG functions, can "exercise such other powers as are exercised or capable of exercise by the member governments and necessary or desirable for dealing with problems of mutual concern." [9] Three COGs have been formed in Rhode Island, but none exercises a traditional governmental function.

It is possible that other states will authorize COGs to perform functions in addition to planning and training. The Texas Urban Development Commission (1971: 63) recommended "the enactment of permissive legislation giving COGs authority to provide selected region-wide public services when specifically authorized to undertake these services by vote of their member governments."

Advantages

COGs have several obvious advantages. One of the greatest advantages is ease of organization. In contrast to proposals for a restructuring of the local governmental system, a proposal to create a COG usually encounters little opposition. Very few individuals believe the creation of a council is a threat to "home rule," and the by-laws of many councils explicitly state the council has no power to force its will on individual members.

According to the agreement establishing the Association of Central Oklahoma Governments (1966), "It is not the intention of the parties to form a super-government, but to organize a voluntary association of local governments . . . and to thereby seek by mutual agreement solutions to mutual problems for the benefit of all citizens." And Mayor Robert F. Wagner (1959) of New York has stated "the Metropolitan Regional Council is one way to avoid super-government. It is one way to preserve the values of local self-rule, while giving to the local community a voice in regional matters, a voice it has never had before."

The most common legal basis for the formation and operation of a COG is a joint exercise of power act which authorizes two or more units of local government to exercise jointly any power each government is authorized to exercise individually. A few states, including Rhode Island [10] and Connecticut [11] have enacted laws specifically authorizing local governments to form COGs.

A second advantage of a COG is that it establishes a representative form for the discussion, on a regular basis, of areawide problems. The forum should facilitate the identification and understanding of area-wide problems, and hopefully may lead to a program of cooperative action to solve the problems.

Third, a COG is an organized body which can lobby at the State House and in Washington for passage of favorable legislation and defeat of unfavorable legislation. In particular, a COG can defend the interests of its members against further federal and state encroachment.

Fourth, a COG may serve as a coordinating mechanism for local governments and/or a central secretariat which provides assistance to member governments upon request. Joint training programs, joint purchasing programs, and a procedure for the sharing of expensive equipment have been developed by COGs. A COG can also promote the signing of inter-local agreements providing for the joint operation of facilities, joint provision of services, and the provision of services by one government to other units.

Fifth, a COG has territorial boundaries capable of being expanded in most instances by a vote of the members. COGs may play an important role in facilitating the resolution of interstate metropolitan problems since a COG can be formed in such areas with considerably less difficulty than an interstate compact or federal-state compact agency.

Finally, a COG is a flexible instrument in that any and all units of government, including school districts, may be members.

Disadvantages

The magnitude of problems in the typical region compels one to question whether the most desirable type of areawide development can be achieved by reliance upon voluntary cooperation, strengthened by the "carrots" of federal grants-in-aid. The council of governments approach to metropolitan problems suffers all the disadvantages of the United Nations approach to the resolution of world problems (Zimmerman, 1967a). Although a large number of COGs were organized in the latter half of the 1960s, they have failed to solve a major problem in any area and many have become inactive.

Melvin B. Mogulof (1971, p. 112) of the Urban Institute has concluded that "the COG is not now capable, and must be severely strained and restructured if it is to become capable, of performing the necessary tasks of regional governance." He feels that COGs have carved out a place for themselves because they have been useful, without being painful to member governments.

The reasons why COGs have not scored major successes are not hard to find. Conflicts between the central city and suburban communities have been of long standing in many areas, and COGs have been unable to resolve these conflicts. Second, political leaders generally have been interested only in area-wide problems which affect their individual communities and have not adopted an area-wide viewpoint. In most cases, the number of elected officials active in a COG has been small, and the average delegate to the annual COG meeting does not identify himself closely with the COG.

Third, many COGs have proved to be little more than debating societies and their accomplishments have been limited to the preparation of area-wide plans which cannot be implemented. Assuming a council is able to agree upon a common course of action for its member governments, the council lacks the power to enforce its decision because decision-making authority remains fractionated. The difficulties of persuading the member and nonmember governments in the area to initiate action the council favors should not be underestimated. Should a municipality with a key location refuse to cooperate with contiguous municipalities, effective area-wide action may be frustrated. Central cities, for example, have refused to extend their sewer and water lines to suburban communities for fear such action will promote suburban development and accelerate central city decline.

The fact that the representative from a given city or town to the COG endorses a course of action agreed upon by the COG is no guarantee the city or town will implement the course of action. Representatives from cities and towns to a COG tend to be oriented toward an area-wide viewpoint, whereas other officials in their communities may lack such an orientation. If a representative to a COG is a political rival to the other political leaders in his city or town, he probably will be unable to persuade them to follow the COG's recommendations.

Fourth, it is axiomatic that a council, in order to achieve major results, must be composed of representatives of all cities and towns in the area. If several major units of government, for whatever reason, refuse to join the council, its future as an effective coordinating mechanism is limited.

Fifth, a COG is a voluntary association and every member city and town reserves the right, which frequently is stipulated in a COG's by-laws, to withdraw from membership.

Finally, a COG may decide that the most effective way to solve a particular functional problem is the creation of a special district, thereby further fragmenting the area's governmental system. To cite only one example, the Denver Regional Council of Governments currently is promoting the formation of a regional service authority (National Association of Regional Councils, 1972).

Conclusions

Several studies in the mid-1960s were relatively optimistic regarding the future effectiveness of councils of governments. Professor Royce Hanson (1966) of American University studied eight COGs and concluded that "the future of this form of metropolitan cooperation and action seems bright. The councils of government offer one of the most productive means of translating plans into action for many of America's metropolitan areas."

The San Francisco Bureau of Governmental Research (1965: 1) concluded that "the Association of Bay Area Governments is transforming itself from one of the myriad discussion forums into a vigorous and potent governmental force." This conclusion was supported by the Institute for Local Self Government (1965: 5), which maintained that the Association "has conclusively demonstrated that it can stimulate and guide factual analyses which are essential first steps to reasonable regional action. It has proven its worth as a desirable public forum for debate and consideration of vital issues, and it has developed organizational machinery for successfully considering and adopting meaningful alternatives for policy considerations."

A metropolitan council of governments representing all units of local government within a given area may act as a catalytic agent in developing and assisting the implementation of areawide programs. However, doubts must be raised about the adequacy of a COG as a mechanism for solving complex areawide problems. Its potential is limited, in view of the fact that decision-making authority remains fractionated. The only agreement the council may be able to reach is likely to be a negative one: opposition to a major action proposal.

The success of a COG depends heavily upon local conditions. If areawide problems are not of serious magnitude and complexity, the prospects of solving them satisfactorily by the COG approach are good. If each local government has a dominant and persuasive political leader who is willing to devote the necessary time and energy to the work of the COG, the prospects of implementing agreements reached by the COG are increased immeasurably. On the other hand, if local governments are motivated by narrow self-interest, attempts to secure cooperative action will prove to be of no avail.

Evidence to date warrants the conclusion that COGs will continue to concentrate on the solution of relatively noncontroversial functional problems and avoid highly controversial issues such as the housing problems of the metropolis. If COGs are unwilling or unable to solve certain difficult problems, public pressure may grow for a major restructuring of the government of the metropolis, including the transfer of responsibility for solving difficult area-wide problems to the state and federal government.

INTERGOVERNMENTAL SERVICE AGREEMENTS

Formal and informal intergovernmental service agreements have been used for at least a century and a quarter by local governments for the provision of services to their citizens by other local governments.[12] Such agreements facilitate the solution of local and areawide problems without necessitating the structural reorganization of the governmental system of a metropolis. Hence, service agreements may be viewed as an adaptive procedural response to problems associated with metropolitanization.

The popularity of intergovernmental service agreements is easily explained. A local government may be able to obtain, by means of an agreement, a service or a product which the government itself cannot produce or could produce only at an excessively high cost. The provider of the service can benefit from an agreement if it enables the provider to take advantage of economies of scale.

Intergovernmental agreements are popular also because they do not restrict significantly the freedom of action of the governments receiving services and can be terminated in most cases on short notice. Hence, service agreements are viewed by local officials as a flexible method of obtaining services when needed.

With very few exceptions, service agreements are entered into voluntarily by local governments. On rare occasions, a state government has ordered a local government to provide a service or a product to a contiguous government. Counties in a few states (e.g., Texas) are required by law to provide specified services if requested to do so by a city.

The number of service agreements has increased sharply in the period since 1945 as functional problems have become more acute, as the pace of urbanization has quickened and as states have removed constitutional and statutory barriers restricting the ability of municipalities to enter into service agreements.

In 1957, the Committee of State Officials on Suggested State Legislation of the Council of State Governments drafted a model interlocal contracting act. Forty-two states currently have enacted all or part of the act. Of these states, twenty-nine authorize local units to cooperate with their counterparts in neighboring states. Michigan has empowered its local units to cooperate with their Canadian counterparts.

The ability of local governments to enter into service agreements is unfortunately impeded by two provisions found in many general interlocal cooperation acts. In thirty-two states, a power may not be exercised jointly unless each government possesses the power. This means that a city and a town, for example, could not jointly exercise a power if only the city possessed authority to exercise the power. Furthermore, the general interlocal cooperation statute found in thirteen states explicitly stipulates that individual statutes authorizing cooperation in a specific functional area are not superceded. In New Jersey, there are approximately two hundred specific statutes (New Jersey County and Municipal Government Study Commission, 1970: 38).

Services Received

In 1972, the Advisory Commission on Intergovernmental Relations and the International City Management Association, jointly sponsored the sending of a 20-page questionnaire to 5,900 incorporated municipalities of over 2,500 population seeking data on intergovernmental agreements involving 76 services. Returns from 40 percent of the municipalities were classified by population categories, geographic region, form of government, and metro/city type. Contracting municipalities were also classified by the type of jurisdiction in which they contracted.

Sixty-three percent of the 2,375 responding municipalities have entered into formal and informal agreements for the provision of services to their citizens by other governmental units or private firms. Table 10.1 reveals that the tendency to enter into agreements is related to population size. Larger units of local government generally have a greater propensity to enter into service agreements than smaller ones. Units in the 50,000 to 100,000 population category, however, enter into agreements with a slightly greater degree of frequency than larger units. Units in the 25,000 to 50,000 population category enter into agreements more frequently than units in the 100,000 to 250,000 category.

Nonmetropolitan municipalities (53 percent) enter into service agreements with less frequency than central cities (75 percent) and suburban governments (71 percent). This finding can be explained by the facts that governmental problems usually are more acute and there are a larger number of service suppliers in metropolitan areas than in nonmetropolitan areas.

Service agreements are most common in the West (79 percent) and least common in the South (54 percent). Agreements with a local government in a neighboring state were reported by only 14 respondents. We know, however, that 16 Rhode Island cities and towns have joined with Attleboro and Seekonk, Massachusetts, in a police communication network (Zimmerman, 1972a: 2).

Relative to forms of governmental administration, council-manager governments (69 percent) enter into service agreements with the greatest degree of frequency. This finding agrees with Vincent L. Marando's (1968: 193) finding in the Detroit area that "council-manager municipalities participate in joint

Table 10.1: U.S. Municipalities with Agreements for Receipt of Services, 1972

	Number of Reporting Cities	Having Agreement for Services		Number of Contracting Municipalities Contracting With:													
		n	%	Munici-pality		County		School District		Other Special Districts		Public Authority		State		Other	
				n	%	n	%	n	%	n	%	n	%	n	%	n	%
Total, all cities	2,375	1,491	63	600	40	919	62	380	25	412	28	249	17	429	29	217	15
		(Total: 1,491) (of 1,491)															
Population Group																	
Over 500,000	10	8	80	1	13	3	38	1	13	2	25	0	0	1	13	3	38
250,000-500,000	10	8	80	3	38	7	88	6	75	7	88	5	63	7	88	6	75
100,000-250,000	50	36	72	18	50	27	75	15	42	18	50	14	39	22	61	12	33
50,000-100,000	110	89	81	42	47	67	73	36	41	35	39	31	35	39	44	21	24
25,000-50,000	236	180	76	81	45	118	66	60	33	60	33	46	46	64	36	31	17
10,000-25,000	532	357	67	156	44	225	63	114	32	106	30	51	14	93	26	41	11
5,000-10,000	618	360	58	141	39	217	60	77	21	86	24	52	14	98	27	41	11
2,500-5,000	812	446	55	154	35	251	56	69	15	96	22	49	11	104	23	62	14
Under 2,500	17	7	41	1	8	4	37	2	29	2	29	1	14	2	29	0	0
Geographic Region																	
Northeast	502	275	55	149	54	83	30	72	26	55	20	67	24	79	29	37	13
North Central	791	513	65	224	44	317	62	126	25	142	28	58	11	122	24	73	14
South	706	380	54	118	31	253	67	66	17	81	21	81	21	123	32	66	17
West	398	313	79	109	35	266	86	116	37	134	43	43	14	105	34	41	13

Table 10.1: (Continued)

	Number of Reporting Cities	Having Agreement for Services		Number of Contracting Municipalities Contracting With:												
				Munici-pality		County		School District		Other Special Districts		Public Authority		State		Other	
	n	n	%	n	%	n	%	n	%	n	%	n	%	n	%	n	%
				(Total: 1,491) (of 1,491)													
Form of Government																	
Mayor-council	1,148	645	56	257	40	357	55	136	21	152	24	91	14	167	26	88	14
Council-manager	1,098	762	69	315	41	519	68	249	33	238	31	157	21	233	31	118	15
Commission	78	46	59	11	24	34	74	8	17	9	20	5	11	16	35	4	9
Town meeting	57	30	53	12	40	6	20	15	50	9	30	6	20	11	37	4	13
Representive town meeting	14	8	59	5	63	3	38	2	25	2	25	1	13	2	25	2	25
Metro City Type																	
Central	155	117	75	43	37	81	69	41	35	46	39	37	32	53	45	39	33
Suburban	1,076	762	71	426	56	458	60	201	26	241	29	142	19	201	26	112	13
Non-Metropolitan	1,164	612	53	131	21	380	62	128	21	27	21	70	11	176	29	76	12

NOTE: Data from Zimmerman, 1973.

cooperative agreements to a markedly greater degree than do mayor-council municipalities."

Municipalities most commonly enter into service agreements with counties (62 percent of contracting municipalities) and other municipalities (40 percent). Nevertheless, the state government (29 percent of contracting municipalities) and public authorities (17 percent) are major suppliers of services to local governments. State governments chiefly provide police training, criminal identification, police patrol, fireman training, traffic control, and water pollution abatement services.

Few service agreements involve a package of services. The bulk of the agreements relate to only one service and only two governments—the provider and the recipient of the service. In addition, most binary agreements relate to relatively noncontroversial functions—civil defense, fire and police mutual aid, jails, and water supply. This finding is not surprising in view of the fact that few local governments have the ability and desire to provide a package of services. In addition, most recipients of services are interested only in a service which they cannot provide economically themselves or a product which they cannot produce themselves.

The concept of a single contract providing for a package of services did not originate until 1954 when the newly incorporated City of Lakewood contracted to have all municipal-type services provided by Los Angeles County.[13] Although few local governments had received more than one service from another local government on a contract basis prior to 1954, the 32 cities incorporated in the county since 1954 have followed Lakewood's lead by contracting with the county for a package of services. Most agreements are for a term of five years.

Typically, a service package includes animal regulation, election services, emergency ambulance services, enforcement of city health ordinances, engineering services, fire and police protection, library services, planning and zoning, street construction and maintenance, and street lighting. Certain services, e.g., animal regulation, are financed by fees. Other services—fire protection, library, sewer maintenance, street lighting—are financed by means of special districts administered by the county. The remaining services provided by the county are financed by direct reimbursement of costs by the recipient cities.

Several Lakewood Plan cities have terminated their service contracts with the county. Contracts have been terminated primarily because of public pressure reflecting a belief that the municipality would be more sensitive and responsive to local needs if it provided the services itself.

Local governments are generally satisfied with agreements, however. Only 6 percent of the 2,367 respondents have discontinued agreements. Not surprisingly, council-manager municipalities (9 percent) have terminated agreements with a greater degree of frequency than mayor-council municipalities (3 percent). It would appear that professional managers are more critical in their evaluation of the performance of the providers of services and terminate agreements if the providers fail to meet the terms of the agreements. The fact that nonmetropolitan municipalities (3 percent) have terminated agreements only one-fourth as often as central cities (12 percent) no doubt is a reflection of the fact that the former municipalities have few if any alternative methods of providing or obtaining the services.

Joint Agreements

Thirty-five percent of the 2,061 municipalities reporting on this item are parties to agreements for the joint provision of services; larger municipalities enter into these agreements most often. Such agreements are most common in the West (49 percent of contracting cities) and least common in the South (28 percent). In regard to forms of administration, council-manager governments (43 percent of contracting cities) have the greatest proclivity for entering into joint agreements. Central cities (62 percent) enter into these agreements with a greater degree of frequency than other metro/city types, apparently because they have more opportunities to enter into conjoint agreements, particularly with the county.

Twenty-one percent of the 2,120 responding municipalities are parties to agreements for the joint construction or joint leasing of a facility. As with joint service agreements, larger units and council-manager governments participate most often in joint construction and leasing agreements.

We find in a number of metropolitan areas that the central city and the county have incrementally consolidated functions over the years. The City of Charlotte and Mecklenburg County in North Carolina currently have consolidated school, public health, and public welfare systems and jointly finance a single agency responsible for elections, a second agency responsible for planning, and a third agency responsible for property tax administration.

In Georgia, the City of Albany and Dougherty County jointly provide 21 services. In Oregon, over a five-year period, Portland and Multnomah County entered into joint agreements for a city-county annex, combined duplication and reproduction facilities, combined mail and distribution service, central data processing, a Metropolitan Human Relations Commission, a Metropolitan Youth Commission, a Council on Aging, a city-county civil service study, an Office of Economic Opportunity Metropolitan Steering Committee, and a city-county Detoxification Center. It appears that these joint city-county activities are a prelude to complete city-county consolidation, as the 1971 Oregon legislature created a City-County Charter Commission charged with the task of drafting an amalgamation charter for submission to the electorate in 1974.

The most difficult problem associated with the joint provision of a service and joint construction and operation of a facility is the equitable allocation of the costs incurred. Disputes over the apportionment of costs have led to the termination of a significant number of joint agreements.

Joint leasing of equipment is uncommon; only 55 units are parties to such agreements. More common are agreements for the loan of personnel or equip-

Table 10.2: Counties Supplying Services on a Contract Basis, 1971

Population	Number of Counties	Number of Responding Counties	Provide Services		Do Not Provide Services	
			Number	% of All Counties	Number	% of All Counties
Over 500,000	58	22	16	5.7	6	1.1
250,000-500,000	70	39	16	5.7	13	2.3
100,000-250,000	185	62	32	11.4	30	5.5
50,000-100,000	326	94	40	14.2	54	9.0
25,000-50,000	566	153	48	17.1	105	18.8
10,000-25,000	998	258	73	26.0	185	32.6
Under 10,000	844	230	56	19.9	174	30.7
Total	3,047	858	281	100.0	567	100.0

NOTE: Data from a 1971 survey of county governments by the Advisory Commission on Intergovernmental Relations, International City Management Association, and National Association of Counties. Zimmerman, 1973.

ment—15 percent of the 2,109 reporting units are parties to agreements of this nature. As with other types of agreements, the larger units and council-manager units have the greatest tendency to enter into agreements.

Providers of Services

Although the bulk of the service agreements involve only local governments, a significant number of agreements for the provision of services are entered into by local governments with state governments or private firms. Fifty percent of the incorporated municipalities obtaining personnel services by means of agreements receive the services from state governments. The corresponding percentage is 48 for police training, 44 for water pollution abatement services, 41 for crime laboratory services, 40 for training of firemen, and 40 for criminal identification services.

As is well known, private firms are major suppliers of certain services. Eighty-eight percent of the 385 incorporated municipalities obtaining refuse collection service under agreements receive the service from private firms. The corresponding percentage is 86 for engineering services, 84 for legal service, 79 for street lighting, 67 for public relations services, and 64 for microfilm services.

Few services are provided by school districts, other special districts, councils of governments, and other regional units under agreements with incorporated municipalities. School districts provide a significant number of school crossing guards, and other special districts are parties to a small number of agreements for the provision of fire services, sewage disposal, irrigation, and parks.

Services Provided by Counties

In 1971, the Advisory Commission on Intergovernmental Relations, International City Management Association, and National Association of Counties cooperatively surveyed 3,047 counties in regard to the services they provided for individual local governments within each county on a contract basis, provided on a joint basis with local governments in each county, and provided jointly or under contract with another county.

Table 10.2 reveals that one-third of the responding counties provide contract services to local governments located within the county. Although 73 percent of the reporting counties with a population in excess of 500,000 provide contract services, these counties account for less than 6 percent of the total number of service agreements. Slightly more than one-quarter of the responding counties furnishing services are in the 10,000 to 25,000 population class, a reflection of the greater number (998) of counties in this population class.

Jails and detention centers are the subject of the largest number of agreements (82), followed by police protection (72), roads and highways (65), planning (44), libraries (39), public welfare (38), fire protection (30), education (29), hospitals (25), parks and recreation (22), and refuse collection (22). The largest number of agreements are in Texas (68), followed by Georgia (36),

Table 10.3: Factors Inhibiting Intergovernmental Service Agreements

	Number of Cities Reporting	Limitations on Independence of Action		Inequitable Apportionment of Cost		Adverse Public Reaction		Restriction on Terminating Agreements		Other	
		Number	Percent	Number	Percent	Number	Percent	Number	Percent	Number	Percent
Total, All Cities	463	718	49	339	23	137	9	29	2	247	17
Population Group											
Over 500,000	3	1	33	2	67	0	0	0	0	0	0
250,000-500,000	10	4	40	3	30	1	10	0	0	0	30
100,000-250,000	35	14	40	8	23	3	9	2	6	8	23
50,000-100,000	77	37	48	17	22	6	8	1	1	16	21
25,000-50,000	162	80	49	43	27	13	8	4	2	22	14
10,000-25,000	349	174	50	83	24	30	9	7	2	55	16
5,000-10,000	368	190	52	69	19	39	11	10	3	64	17
2,500-5,000	452	215	48	110	24	44	10	5	1	79	17
Under 2,500	7	3	43	4	57	1	14	0	0	0	0
Geographic Region											
Northeast	309	168	54	58	19	24	8	6	2	56	18
North Central	478	225	47	110	23	54	11	10	2	81	17
South	409	180	44	115	28	40	10	5	1	69	17
West	267	145	54	56	21	19	7	8	3	41	15
Form of Government											
Mayor-council	624	318	51	132	21	64	10	11	2	105	17
Council-manager	758	355	47	194	26	66	9	15	2	129	17
Commission	44	20	45	9	20	5	11	2	5	8	18
Town Meeting	26	16	62	3	12	2	8	1	4	4	15
Representative Town Meeting	11	9	82	2	18	0	0	0	0	1	9

Iowa (36), Nebraska (36), Minnesota (35), Virginia (34), Kansas (33), and North Carolina (31).

Two hundred and fourteen, or 76.2 percent, of the reporting counties which supply services are in nonmetropolitan areas and 67, or 23.8 percent, are in metropolitan areas. This finding was to be anticipated since about 85 percent of all counties (2,589) are located in nonmetropolitan areas.

Nearly 38 percent of the reporting counties jointly provide services with other local governments located within the county. As in the case of contract services, joint service agreements are most common among nonmetropolitan counties in the 10,000 to 25,000 population category. The most popular joint county-local agreements are police protection (58), libraries (56), jails and detention homes (52), fire protection (38), planning (37), roads and highways (37), refuse collection (29), public welfare (23), and education (22). The largest number of joint agreements with another unit in the county was reported by Texas (65), followed by Georgia (35), Nebraska (34), Virginia (34), Iowa (33), and Kansas (32).

Two hundred and twenty-six out of 744 reporting counties are parties to joint agreements with another county for the provision of services. Such agreements are most common among nonmetropolitan counties in the 10,000 to 25,000 population class. The most popular joint functions are planning (37), jails and detention homes (29), libraries (27), education (16), roads and highways (14), and fire protection (11). Texas counties report 58 joint service agreements with other counties. There are 37 such agreements in Minnesota, 34 in Nebraska, and 32 in each of three states—Georgia, Kansas, and Virginia.

Adverse Factors

The principal factors which have the most adverse effect on the willingness of local governments to enter into an agreement with another governmental unit to obtain services are summarized in Table 10.3. Nearly one-half of the 1,463 reporting incorporated municipalities checked a political reason—"limitations placed on independence of action by the agreement"—as the principal adverse factor.

The written comments of many municipal officials reflected the intensity of the opposition to entering into service agreements with another governmental unit. A New Jersey local official wrote that "many municipalities are hesitant to cooperate because of the fear of loss of home rule." A Mississippi mayor wrote: "I think until we start doing things for ourselves and quit leaning on the federal government and others we will continue to get deeper and deeper into trouble." A California city manager believes that greater intergovernmental cooperation in the provision of services is inhibited by local pride and vanity under the guise of more "local control." And in Ohio, a mayor is of the opinion that use of agreements is limited because "people are afraid of the big city."

Nearly one-quarter of the incorporated municipalities cited "inequitable apportion of the cost of the service" as a reason for refusing to enter into agreements. A village manager in Michigan, for example, wrote that "our biggest problem is that township and rural areas want city services but don't want to pay what the services cost."

"Adverse public reaction to services presently being provided by another unit" was the only other factor checked by a significant number of officials (9 percent). Responses did not vary much by form of government, region, and central city, suburban, or nonmetropolitan type.

The ability of the county government to provide additional services was questioned by several respondents. One city manager indicated he was convinced that many services should be provided by the county, yet wrote: "I assume the county government setup will be changed by statutes before they take over and perform all these services. Presently they could not function effectively in Michigan." A second city manager wrote: "Until we get the nineteenth century representatives out of the county courthouse, cooperation between cities and counties will remain limited." And a third city manager reported that "the county fights any move to join forces."

The New Jersey County and Municipal Government Study Commission (1970: iv) found "great hope in the fact that the overwhelming majority of officials in over 400 municipalities polled and interviewed are willing and anxious to enter into joint service agreements on a wide variety of areas." Our national survey did not yield as optimistic a finding—478, or 20 percent, of the 2,383 reporting incorporated municipalities are contemplating entering into initial or additional agreements with other units for the provision of services. In general, a greater percentage of the larger units are contemplating such agreements. More than one-third of the cities over 250,000 population are contemplating entering into agreements, but only 17 percent of the units in the 2,500 to 5,000 population category are considering taking this action. Forty-one percent of the units in the 25,000 to 50,000 population category, however, are weighing new agreement possibilities. This finding appears to be a reflection of the prevalence of council-manager governments in this population class.

Geographically, there is little difference in the distribution of units of local governments contemplating entering into new agreements. In regard to forms of government, one-quarter of the council-manager units are pondering such agreements compared to only 16 percent of the mayor-council cities. Twenty-eight percent of the central cities are considering new agreements, as compared to only 20 percent of the suburban units and 19 percent of the nonmetropolitan units. The relative lack of interest in entering into new agreements by nonmetropolitican municipalities undoubtedly is related to their smaller size and the lack of opportunity to enter into agreements.

State and Federal Encouragement

State and federal governments clearly can take a number of actions, principally providing incentive grants-in-aid, to encourage local governments to enter into cooperative service agreements.

Only 44 (2 percent) of the 1,765 reporting municipalities indicate that the state constitution prohibits them from entering into agreements for the receipt of services or inhibits their ability to enter into such agreements. Six percent, or 109 out of 1,808 units, report that state statutes inhibit their ability to enter into service agreements.

On the other hand, 1,440 (76 percent) of the 1,904 responding units indicate that their state governments actively encourage the intergovernmental provision of services. Forty-eight percent of the municipalities report state incentives via grants-in-aid, 42 percent mentioned financial assistance for studies, and 56 percent report that the state provides technical assistance.

Only 28 out of 1,859 local governments felt that federal statutes and regulations restricted their ability to enter into agreements for services with another governmental unit. In contrast, 701 (49 percent) of the 1,445 units replied affirmatively to the question, "Do federal statutes and regulations encourage intergovernmental contracting and cooperation?" most comments mentioned incentive federal grants-in-aid for cooperative and regional water and sewer projects.

Summary

Our national survey of nearly 6,000 incorporated municipalities reveals that they receive a significant number and a large variety of services from other governmental units by means of informal and formal agreements. Although more than three-fifths of the reporting units receive services from other units, most agreements are limited in scope and involve only a single service.

One of our principal findings is that the tendency of a local government to enter into service agreements is positively correlated with population size. The larger the unit, the more agreements it enters into. That council-manager governments have the greatest proclivity for entering into agreements, and that the dominant motive for entering into agreements is to take advantage of economies of scale, are two other major findings. The factor most inhibiting the willingness of local governments to enter into service agreements is the fear that their independence of action will be curtailed by the agreements. In addition, some central cities have been hesitant to extend water supply and sewer lines to suburban municipalities for fear that the exodus of citizens and business firms to the suburbs will be accelerated as they acquire additional municipal-type services. In some instances, intensive bargaining occurs between a central city and a suburban town, resulting in a trade-off, i.e., the central city agrees to supply water to the town in exchange for a solid waste disposal site.

We may view the use of service agreements as a limited and temporary form of functional consolidation based upon a partnership approach in which administration is centralized and policy making is decentralized. We must point out that the use of a large number of agreements is a desultory approach to the solution of service problems which complicates the local governmental system and may make it less responsible to the needs and wishes of citizens.

The cooperative, or ecumenical, approach to the solution of service problems will continue to be popular with local government officials in the future because this approach allows units to take advantage of economies of scale and has a minimal disruptive impact on local governments. It is not unreasonable to forecast that most state governments will expand their efforts to encourage local governments to enter into service provision agreements and will in special cases order one unit to provide a service to one or more contiguous units.

We conclude this section by pointing out that not all governmental service problems lend themselves to solution by means of service agreements. The potential of intergovernmental cooperation is limited chiefly to the solution of relatively minor and non-controversial problems involving a small number of local governments.

TRANSFER OF FUNCTIONAL RESPONSIBILITY

Interest in solving governmental problems by transferring responsibility for certain functions from cities, towns, villages, and other local units to the county and state levels appears to be mounting. The California Council on Intergovernmental Relations (1970) has conducted a study of the reallocation of the responsibility for governmental functions, and the New York State Temporary Commission on the Powers of Local Government, chaired by former Mayor Robert F. Wagner of New York City, is conducting a similar study.

To collect data on the transfer of functions for this paper, a letter requesting such information was sent to the forty-nine state municipal leagues, the forty-seven state associations of counties, and the twenty-six state agencies for local affairs.

Transfers to the County

Increasing recognition of the fact that certain services can best be provided on an areawide basis has led to the resurgence of efforts to modernize county government, especially in urban areas, and authorize it to perform additional functions—such as airport regulation, air pollution control, civil defense, fire and police protection, industrial development, sewage disposal, and water supply. Municipal officials traditionally have been hostile to proposals for the transfer of functions to the county, but they are now found among the initiators of such proposals.

A second reason for the resurgence of interest in modernizing county government stems from the widely held belief that serious political obstacles lie in the path of any proposal to reform the government of the metropolis by consolidating existing local governments or creating a new unit of areawide government. Since organized county government exists in all but three states,[14] and 130 Standard Metropolitan Statistical Areas fall within the confines of a single county, a number of reformers have concluded that the most feasible method of creating an areawide government is to restructure the existing county and incrementally increase its powers (Advisory Commission on Intergovernmental Relations, 1972).

Counties originated as quasi-municipal corporations and were viewed as administrative subdivisions of the state for the convenient performance of limited functions. In addition to lacking home rule, most counties suffer from a long ballot, the filling of offices on a patronage basis, and the lack of a chief executive. The vast majority of the 3,047 counties have a plural executive—the county board or commission—which typically shares governmental power with a relatively large number of independent officers and special purpose boards.

Counties historically have been highly resistant to reform, but the application of the United States Supreme Court's "one-man, one-vote" principle to county governing boards has facilitated general reform of county government in several states.[15]

Alaska, California, Florida, Illinois, Michigan, New York State, Ohio, Pennsylvania, and Tennessee have specific constitutional provisions authorizing municipalities to transfer functions to the county (borough in Alaska). The requirement that a proposed charter must be approved by the voters of cities considered as a unit and the voters of the remainder of the county considered as a second unit is a hindrance to the adoption of county charters transferring city and town functions to counties in New York State.[16] If a proposed charter provides for the transfer of a village function to the county, a one-third majority affirmative vote—villages affected as a unit—is required.

To encourage state legislatures to authorize the shift of functions to the county level, the Advisory Commission on Intergovernmental Relations (1971: 10-11) has prepared "Suggested Legislation" for the voluntary transfer of functions between municipalities and counties.

None of the organizations responding to our letter of inquiry reported that a survey had been conducted of the transfer of functions from municipalities to counties in their states. Respondents indicated that no transfers of municipal functions to the county level have occurred in Arkansas, Arizona, Illinois (under its 1970 constitution), Massachusetts, New Hampshire, New Mexico, Vermont, or Washington.

The Advisory Commission on Intergovernmental Relations in 1971 surveyed counties in regard to the transfer of functions. Forty-six of the 133 responding metropolitan counties reported that functions had been transferred to the county government by cities, towns, villages, and other local units. Limited available evidence suggests that the incremental strengthening of county government by means of functional transfers in a number of states during the past decade is a significant governmental trend. The following are several examples of recent constitutional and statutory changes and transfers to illustrate the nature of the trend.

In Mississippi, municipal health departments are automatically abolished when the county creates a health department.[17]

An amendment to the Pennsylvania Constitution, approved by the voters in 1968, classifies the county as a municipality and extends home rule to it. In other words, by adopting a home rule charter, a county becomes a municipal corporation and may perform the same functions as any city, township, or borough, provided the charter authorized the performance of the functions. In 1972, the Pennsylvania legislature for the first time enacted a law allowing the transfer of functions between units of government.[18]

The Illinois Constitution, which became effective July 1, 1971, authorizes a county treasurer to act as the treasurer of any unit of local government or school district within the county; no transfers have occurred to date.

In 1958, home rule was extended to counties in New York State. Fifteen of the 57 counties outside of New York City have adopted charters. Two counties—Monroe and Schenectady—have a county manager appointed by the county legislature and eleven other counties have an elected county executive. These charters also make the county responsible for several new functions. In addition, cities, towns, and villages are authorized by general law to voluntarily turn functions over to the county and many have done so.

A survey of fifty-two New York counties during the fall of 1972 revealed that the average charter county provides thirty-five services compared with twenty-one services provided by the average noncharter county (Jorgensen, 1972). The number of services provided by the charter counties ranges from twenty-two to fifty-one.

The following functions have been transferred to Monroe County (New York) since 1947: airport (1947), civil defense (1954), public health (1958), major parks (1961), and public safety laboratory (1961). In addition, the City of Rochester and Monroe County are jointly responsible for planning (1953), civic center (1957), port authority (1958), youth board (1960), human relations (1961), probation (1968), vital statistics (1969), consumer protection (1968), library services (1968), museum services (1968), and public defender (1968).

The Genesee/Finger Lakes Regional Planning Board and the Rochester Chamber of Commerce have engaged the International Association of Chiefs of Police to develop an implementation plan for unified police services in the county. At the request of the Rochester City Council and the County Legislature, the Rochester Center for Governmental and Community Research studied the police systems within the county and issued a report in 1970 which concluded that a unified police system was necessary. Support for the consolidation of police services also is growing in Broome, Erie, Westchester, and Yates Counties. On August 21, 1972, Commissioner Sal J. Prezioso of the New York State Office for Local Government recommended the consolidation of local police services at the county level, particularly in metropolitan areas.

A final New York State example is Onondaga County, which assumed responsibility for welfare and civil service during the depression, civil defense during World War II, and water pollution abatement, public health, and solid waste disposal in the post-war period.

In Florida, Dade County voters in 1968 defeated a proposed charter amendment which would have transferred all municipal firefighting and police functions to the County Public Safety and Fire Departments. Defeat of the amendment is attributable to the well-financed opposition of the Dade County League of Municipalities. Nevertheless, Florida City and North Miami turned their fire departments over to the county in 1968 and 1969, respectively, under a charter provision authorizing a city council by a two-thirds vote to turn functions over to the county.[19]

Also in Florida, Volusia County voters on June 30, 1970 approved a proposed home rule charter which grants the county the power of preemption with respect to protection of the environment: "County ordinances shall prevail over municipal ordinances whenever the County shall set minimum standards protecting the environment by prohibiting or regulating air or water pollution or the destruction of the resources of the County belonging to the general public."[20]

Although Winston-Salem, North Carolina, reports that it is not a party to any intergovernmental service agreements, the city has transferred the following functions to Forsyth County since 1955: assessing, tax collections, election administration, registration of voters, public health, jail, ambulance service, animal control services, hospitals, library services, and schools.

Similarly, Wilmington and New Hanover County (North Carolina) over the years have consolidated nine important functions: airport, civil defense, public health facilities, hospitals, jail, property tax assessment, mental health, schools, and welfare.

In Minnesota, Minneapolis has turned over its jail, municipal court, and hospital to Hennepin County. The City of Alexandria transferred public welfare to Douglas County in 1972.

As a final example, there have been efforts to revise county lines in eastern Massachusetts to create a metropolitan Boston County. In 1970, Representative Paul W. Cronin filed a bill in the Massachusetts General Court providing for the redrawing of county boundaries throughout the Commonwealth to create a metropolitan county in the Boston area, eight urban counties, and four rural counties.[21] The Metropolitan Area Planning Council, a COG, is currently considering the use of county government as the basis for a new regional government for the Boston area (Zimmerman, 1972c).

Transfers to the State

A recent trend promising to accelerate in the future is the upward shift of responsibility for certain traditional local functions to the state level. In abolishing county governments in 1968, Connecticut transferred their functions to the state level.

In Massachusetts, responsibility for public welfare was transferred from cities and towns to the Commonwealth in 1968. In 1972 the General Court eliminated funds for forest fire patrols from all county budgets, making the function entirely a Commonwealth responsibility.

In Delaware, responsibility for welfare payments has been shifted to the State Department of Health and Social Services.

Pressure is increasing in New York State for the transfer of responsibility for public welfare and the Medicaid program to the state level, and for shifting responsibility for financing public education completely to the state level.

In concentrating upon the upward shift of functional responsibilities we must not lose sight of the fact that functions can be devolved from the state level to the local level. Such a reverse transfer is taking place in California, as control of mental health programs is being shifted to the county level to make the programs more responsive to community needs.

Who Should Provide the Services?

Our questionnaire to municipal officials seeking information on intergovernmental service agreements also requested the officials to indicate the services which they believe should be provided by county governments, regional special districts, councils of governments, or the federal or state government. An examination of Table 10.4 leads to the conclusion that many mayors, managers, and other municipal executives believe that the county should play a more important role in providing services. A number of respondents, however, qualified their answers by stipulating that responsibility for additional functions should not be transferred to county governments until they are modernized.

Municipal officials displayed the greatest willingness to assign the following services to counties: all public health services (692), jails and detention homes (680), assessments (608), tax collection (557), probation and parole (554), juvenile delinquency programs (507), election administration (505), welfare (503), and all civil defense services (481).

The same officials were most unwilling to assign to counties responsibility for the following services: utility billing (22), treasury functions (45), records storage and maintenance (60), water distribution (67), snow removal (70), legal services (72), water supply (79), recreational facilities (83), sewer lines (87), and irrigation (93). Four of these services—utility billing, public relations, street lighting, and legal services—often are performed by private firms, and a fifth service—snow removal—is partially provided by private firms in many communities.

Regional special districts, according to these municipal respondents, should be responsible primarily for environmental and public protection services—air pollution abatement (392), flood control (359), water pollution abatement (356), crime laboratory (322), police training (311), sewage disposal (291), solid waste disposal (282), civil defense communications (272), criminal identification (264), noise pollution abatement (261), and training of firemen (255).

As a general rule, respondents were reluctant to assign responsibility to regional special districts for the functions they were reluctant to assign to counties—treasury functions (21), election administration (22), licensing (23),

Table 10.4: Preferences of Municipal Officials for Jurisdictional Placement of Services

Service	County Government	Regional Special District	Council of Governments	Federal or State Government
Assessing	608	59	21	31
Payroll	31	23	53	38
Tax Collection	557	44	26	38
Treasury Functions	48	21	39	24
Utility Billing	22	49	49	42
Election Administration	505	22	29	19
Legal Services	72	30	47	31
Licensing	104	23	31	28
Microfilm Services	125	70	32	27
Personnel Services	33	42	40	28
Public Relations	31	31	45	29
Record Maintenance and Storage	60	37	36	26
Registration of Voters	549	29	24	12
All Public Health Services	692	192	22	52
Air Pollution Abatement	327	392	33	86
Alcoholic Rehabilitation	337	243	17	76
Ambulance Service	342	144	33	51
Animal Control Services	423	90	23	21
Cemetries	169	64	27	43
Hospitals	352	180	19	37
Mental Health	397	237	14	73
Mosquito Control	394	206	18	26
Noise Pollution Abatement	212	261	24	64
Nursing Services	314	133	13	29
Water Pollution Abatement	231	356	19	123
Welfare	503	149	7	166

Table 10.4: (Continued)

Service	County Government	Regional Special District	Council of Governments	Federal or State Government
Flood Control	238	359	29	114
General Development Services	85	163	55	27
Housing	124	152	52	61
Industrial Development	130	180	65	43
Irrigation	93	171	19	29
Mapping	312	184	47	28
Planning	186	239	109	43
Soil Conservation	221	234	30	64
Urban Renewal	108	106	47	64
Zoning and Subdivision Control	145	105	65	48
Parks	245	186	53	53
Recreation Facilities	83	58	19	26
All Police Services	150	117	56	53
Crime Laboratory	308	322	29	74
Criminal Identification	316	264	26	103
Patrol Services	127	93	41	69
Police Communications	248	219	44	45
Police Training	186	311	52	112
School Crossing Guards	115	52	44	71
Traffic Control	101	82	48	53
Jails and Detention Homes	680	189	20	34
Juvenile Delinquency Programs	507	207	27	46
Probation and Parole	554	206	19	68
Work Release Programs	401	148	21	55

Table 10.4: (Continued)

Service	County Government	Regional Special District	Council of Governments	Federal or State Government
All Fire Services	148	139	63	46
Fire Communications	178	151	58	35
Fire Prevention	131	130	49	38
Training of Firemen	170	255	55	77
All Civil Defense Services	481	203	35	72
Civil Defense Communications	268	272	28	51
Civil Defense Training	257	184	27	59
Bridge Construction and Maintenance	269	73	31	66
Building and Mechanical Inspection	136	58	42	48
Electrical and Plumbing Inspection	120	64	45	52
Electricity Supply	57	99	25	72
Engineering Services	106	55	52	48
Refuse Collection	179	111	56	49
Sewage Disposal	143	291	49	33
Sewer Lines	87	140	49	47
Snow Removal	70	62	49	40
Solid Waste Disposal	325	282	48	37
Street Construction and Maintenance	89	47	52	56
Street Lighting	45	50	47	64
Water Supply	79	224	52	51
Water Distribution	67	167	46	49
Special Transportation Services	140	265	40	28
Management Service for Publicly owned Transit System	74	195	36	21
Library Services	379	161	35	34
Museums	268	160	20	28
Schools	218	192	25	58

NOTE: From Zimmerman, 1973.

voter registration (29), public relations (31), records maintenance and storage (37), personnel services (42), street lighting (50), and recreational facilities (58). These officials displayed a greater willingness to assign responsibility for sewer lines (140) and water supply (224) to regional special districts than to counties.

Data in Table 10.4 support the conclusion that a sizable number of municipal officials are willing to assign responsibility for many important functions to regional units. The comments of two local officials highlight some of the reasons why they are willing to shift functional responsibility upwards. The Chairman of the Board of Selectmen in a Massachusetts town wrote that "a change from town services to regional services, while an explosive emotional issue, is necessary if we are to serve greater numbers of people at less cost." An Ohio mayor wrote that "township and small political subdivisions are inefficient and today should be abolished in favor of a regional approach."

SPECIAL DISTRICT GOVERNMENTS

Unifunctional, special district governments within towns were developed because of the need for a mechanism which would provide a municipal-type service to the urban core of the town without imposing an additional tax burden upon all residents of the town. As such, local special district governments may be viewed as service and tax districts. Although the vast bulk of the special district governments are unifunctional, incorporated villages within towns, as in New York State, may be viewed as multifunctional special district governments because they originated as mechanisms for providing several municipal-type services to the residents of the urban core of towns.

Despite a sharp reduction in the number of school districts, the total number of special districts in the United States has increased substantially. The largest absolute increase in the number of special districts between 1962 and 1972 occurred in nonmetropolitan areas, yet the largest relative increase occurred in metropolitan areas—45 percent compared to 24 percent. Regionally, the sharpest increase in the number of special districts within metropolitan areas occurred in the South (105 percent).

The bulk of the increase is attributable to Texas, where the number of special districts rose from 214 to 512. Consideration should be given to the abolition of many special districts and the transfer of their functions to local governments or to a new upper tier unit of local government.

Forty-one states report that they have special districts responsible for housing. Thirty-nine states have soil conservation districts, thirty-four states have sewer and water districts, and twenty-eight have fire protection districts. Only two states have school building districts.

Nearly 35 percent of the special districts are located within SMSAs. The most common districts, according to Table 10.5, are fire protection (1,491), water supply (877), sewer (822), housing (691), and drainage (436). Special

Table 10.5: Distribution of Special Districts Within Standard Metropolitan Statistical Areas (SMSAs) by Type, 1972

Type of Special District	Number	Percentage Within SMSA	Percentage of SMSA Total
Total, SMSA Special Districts	7,842	32.8	100.0
Cemetery	157	10.5	2.0
School building	619	57.1	7.9
Fire protection	1,491	38.5	19.0
Health	101	39.3	11.3
Hospitals	150	22.9	1.9
Highways	139	19.9	1.8
Housing	691	30.4	8.8
Drainage	436	19.9	5.6
Library	148	29.7	1.9
Other natural resources	92	39.8	1.2
Parks and recreation	377	50.3	4.8
Flood control	131	19.4	1.7
Irrigation and water conservation	271	28.1	3.5
Sewers	822	58.5	10.5
Soil conservation	416	16.2	5.3
Other general functions	329	37.0	4.2
Water supply	877	37.8	11.2
Electric power	13	17.6	0.2
Gas supply	7	14.6	0.1
Transit	31	93.9	0.4
Natural resources and water supply	44	65.7	0.6
Sewer and water	379	60.3	4.8
Other multiple functions	121	58.5	1.5

NOTE: Data from U.S. Bureau of the Census, **Special Runs, 1972 Census of Governments.**

districts today are created for a variety of reasons, including a desire to tax only those who benefit from a service and to avoid civil service requirements and constitutional debt and tax limits.

Metropolitan Special Districts

Currently, there are nine hundred metropolitan special districts, but only eighty-seven are located within the seventy-two largest SMSAs. The boundaries of 25 percent of these districts are coterminous with the boundaries of general purpose local governments.

The failure of comprehensive metropolitan reorganization plans to win voter approval has promoted the organization of metropolitan special districts, which are more politically acceptable, to solve critical areawide service problems. Creation of such districts is facilitated by state laws which usually do not require a popular referendum on the question of the creation of the districts. Existing local governments continue to perform all the regular functions with the exception of the one(s) assigned to the special districts.

Metropolitan special districts are assigned responsibility for area-wide facilities and services such as airports, bridges, housing, tunnels, terminals, sewage disposal, public transportation, water supply, and parks and recreational facilities. The vast majority of these districts are unifunctional, but a few have been assigned responsibility for the performance of more than one governmental function. The Metropolitan District Commission in the Boston area is responsible for water supply, sewage disposal, and certain parks and recreational facilities. Voters in the Portland, Oregon, area in 1970 approved the formation of a metropolitan special district responsible for sewage treatment and disposal, public transportation, solid waste disposal, and flood control. Other functions can be assigned to the district with voter approval. In the State of Washington, the Municipality of Metropolitan Seattle is responsible only for sewage disposal and public transportation, but may be assigned other functions by the area's municipalities. As a final example, a 1972 Colorado law authorizes the City and County of Denver and Adams, Arapahoe, and Jefferson Counties to form a regional service authority responsible for as many as sixteen functions. [22] Formation of an authority is being actively promoted by the Denver Regional Council of Governments.

A metropolitan special district has several advantages. It is not restricted by traditional local government boundaries—its jurisdictional area may include an entire metropolitan area or the greater part of it. A district may be the only feasible mechanism for the resolution of critical areawide problems which extend beyond the boundaries of a single county or state. Since most areawide special districts rely upon user charges, they are not restricted by constitutional and statutory tax limits. And revenue bonds exempt from debt limits can be issued without a popular referendum. Furthermore, concentration upon the provision of a single service in a relatively large geographical area often allows a metropolitan special district to achieve economies of scale and specialization.

That a metropolitan special district has certain advantages is not denied by reformers who favor a comprehensive approach to the resolution of metropolitan problems. The reformers, however, raise several objections to the creation of such districts.

A new special district further fragments an already fractionated political system and makes the government of the metropolis more complex. Within a given metropolitan area, it is not unusual to have more than one special district and each one may have different geographical boundaries. In addition, the relations between metropolitan special districts and other local governments have not always been good, and coordination of district and local government activities has been less than satisfactory. Furthermore, a special district may make the achievement of a comprehensive approach to metropolitan development more difficult since the activities of a special district may adversely affect other governmental programs. A special district, for example, may facilitate the movement of automobiles by constructing and operating bridges and tunnels and thereby injure the public transportation program.

Critics often charge that metropolitan special districts exceed their authority and are responsible to no one. Only a small minority of the governing bodies of these districts are popularly elected. The members of most governing bodies are appointed or hold office by virtue of other offices they hold.

Finally, it is charged that the creation of a metropolitan special district may deprive a central city of the bargaining power it gains from having dependent suburbs. As an illustration, a suburban community dependent upon the central city for sewage disposal may be more willing to cooperate in programs designed to solve the central city's water supply and solid waste disposal problems.

State-Controlled Metropolitan Districts

The creation of state authorities has been a major organizational response to metropolitan exigencies. Massachusetts created the Metropolitan Sewage Commission in 1889, the Metropolitan Parks Commission in 1893, and the Metropolitan Water Commission in 1895. The present day Metropolitan District Commission was created in 1919 by the merger of the Metropolitan Parks Commission and the Metropolitan Water and Sewage Board; the latter was formed in 1901 by the consolidation of the Metropolitan Sewage Commission and the Metropolitan Water Commission. Other state authorities in the Boston area include the Massachusetts Bay Transportation Authority, Massachusetts Port Authority, Massachusetts Turnpike Authority, and Metropolitan Boston Air Pollution Control District.

New York State, under Governor Nelson A. Rockefeller, decided to use its plenary authority to directly solve areawide problems, and has adopted the authority approach. Both statewide and regional authorities have been created for special purposes. The Urban Development Corporation (UDC), Environmental Facilities Corporation, Job Development Authority, Metropolitan Transportation Authority, Niagara Frontier Transportation Authority, Rochester-Genesee Transportation Authority, Central New York Transportation Authority, and Capital District Transportation Authority are among the more prominent authorities. UDC has received the most publicity outside New York State because the Corporation has the power to override local codes and laws by a two-thirds vote of its nine-member board of directors.

The rationale for the creation of state authorities is a simple one: only the state has the authority and resources to solve critical metropolitan problems. Other reasons for the use of authorities in New York State include a desire to avoid the constitutional debt limit and civil service, and to remove items from the state budget and annual appropriation processes.

THE TWIN CITIES METROPOLITAN COUNCIL

Responding to acute problems in the seven-county Twin Cities area, the Minnesota Legislature in 1967 created a fifteen-member Metropolitan Council for the area.[23] This action may be deemed an adaptive response to problems stemming from urbanization.

Fourteen council members are elected for overlapping, six-year terms from equal population districts by the Governor, with the advice and consent of the senate. The Governor also appoints the chairman, subject to senate confirmation. No local units of government were consolidated by the legislature when the Metropolitan Council was established, and no provision was made for a popular referendum on the question of the council's creation.

The Twin Cities model is basically a federated one with powers divided between the upper tier unit—the Metropolitan Council—and the lower tier units— counties and municipalities. The Council assumed the functions of the Metropolitan Planning Commission, which was abolished, and was granted authority to review and indefinitely suspend plans of each "independent commission, board, or agency," in conflict with the Council's development guide. An agency may appeal the suspension of its plans to the legislature. The Council also was authorized to appoint one of its members as a non-voting member of the boards of metropolitan special districts, conduct research, operate a data center, and intervene before the Minnesota Municipal Commision in annexation and incorporation proceedings.

Shortly after the Council's formation, it signed contracts with the State Highway Department and Metropolitan Transit Commission, thereby assuming responsibility for transportation planning in the area. The Council also has been designated the criminal justice planning agency by the Governor's Crime Commission. Furthermore, the Council has appointed and provides guidance to a health board responsible for coordination of planning for health facilities, manpower, and services. To finance its activities, the Council is authorized to levy a tax not exceeding "seven-tenths of one mill on each dollar of assessed valuation of all taxable property."

The Metropolitan Council was designed by the state legislature to be a policy forming rather than an operating agency. However, it assumed responsibility in 1969 for overseeing the performance of two governmental functions. Acting upon the Council's request, the legislature created two seven-member functional service boards and provided for their appointment by the Council. The Metropolitan Sewer Board[24] and the Metropolitan Park Reserve Board[25] were designed to be operating agencies which would execute policies developed by the Council in their respective areas. The Park Reserve Board's role as an operating service body was terminated in 1970 by a Minnesota Supreme Court ruling invalidating laws passed on the one hundred twenty-first day (one day past the constitutional limit) of the 1969 legislative session.[26] The Board, however, was retained by the Council as an advisory body. Opposition from the Inter-County Council, which wants the counties to operate the parks, and the

Hennepin County Park Reserve District, which has acquired large areas for parks, was sufficient to block reenactment of the original Park Reserve Board bill by the legislature.

The Twin Cities model is an interesting one in that policy making is divorced from policy execution. The model provides for the Metropolitan Council to determine regional policies which are to be carried into execution by service boards appointed by the Council. In theory, the Council can devote its full attention to broad policy making for the region. Routine administrative problems in many governmental units preempt the attention and energy of the governing body, leaving little time for the study of major problems and the development of a long-range program to solve the problems.

The Model in Action

Glowing accounts of the Twin Cities Metropolitan Council have been published. After studying the origin and development of the Metropolitan Council, Stanley Baldinger (1971: 215) concluded that "the Twin Cities area has developed the most promising and innovative means yet to plan and govern major metropolises." He adds (p. 3) that "the Council . . . plans, coordinates, and controls the comprehensive development of an urban region containing 1.9 million people, seven counties, two large central cities, and some 300 units of local government." Writing in the New York *Times,* John Herbers (1971) concluded that the Metropolitan Council "is unique in that it has taxing authority and the power to coordinate the overall social, physical, and economic development in the 3,000-square mile area."

Are these assessments accurate? Has the Metropolitan Council been an effective coordinating body during its first five years? Is overall development occurring in a less haphazard manner than in the pre-1967 period? Definitive conclusions cannot be drawn regarding the Council's effectiveness, in view of the fact that the system is relatively new and is still in the process of evolution. However, we can raise several questions about the operation of the model.

One fact is indisputable. The Twin Cities regional governmental system is still a fragmented one in which many units of government—the Metropolitan Council, regular state departments, Metropolitan Airport Commission, Metropolitan Transit Commission, Mosquito Control Commission, counties, and municipalities—share governmental powers and responsibilities.

The umbrella concept underlying the Metropolitan Council appears to have considerable merit, yet the legislature has demonstrated a marked reluctance to grant strong powers to the Council. In fact, the legislature specifically rejected the Council's proposals that a seven-member zoo board be established and placed under the Council's control, and that the Metropolitan Airport Commission be reorganized as a service board under the Council. The legislature also created the Metropolitan Transit Commission in the same year as the Metropolitan Council, and in 1969 specifically rejected a proposal to authorize the Council to appoint the members of the Commission (Kolderie, 1969: 321).

Furthermore, the legislature has refused to reestablish the Park Reserve Board as an operating board under the Council, following the 1970 State Supreme Court ruling invalidating the act creating the Board.

Is the legislature opposed to the establishment in the Twin Cities area of a strong, popularly elected regional governing body because it might play a dominant role in Minnesota politics? Stanley Baldinger (1971: 222) maintains that "the rural and conservative legislators felt they had a substantial stake and role to play in the future of the Twin Cities area. The Legislature, therefore, sought to maximize the State's role in the operation of the Council by making it an appointed rather than an elected body. A more local (elected) Council might not be as responsive to the needs of the rest of the State or to the wishes of the Legislature." It has also been argued that the caliber of the Council's members will be higher if they are appointed rather than elected, because many highly qualified individuals will not seek an elective post but would accept an appointive one.

Although the consensus in the Twin Cities area is that the Metropolitan Council should be popularly elected, there appears to be strong legislative opposition to the election of Council members. A proposal for the popular election of some members and the appointment of others, including the chairman, may stand a better chance of enactment.

Operationally, the Twin Cities model suffers from three major weaknesses. First, it appears that major problems, as in the past, will be attacked on a piecemeal basis and the legislature will play a major referee role between competing regional bodies and interests. This situation is not the most desirable one since a coordinated attack on regional problems will be difficult to launch, and representatives and senators elected outside the Twin Cities area will continue to play an important role in the governance of the region.

A second operational weakness of the model—deadlocks between the various regional entities failing to operate on the basis of comity—also stems from political fragmentation on the regional level in the Twin Cities area. An example of this problem involves the selection of a site for a new jetport. The Metropolitan Council twice exercised its power to indefinitely veto a site for a new jetport proposed by the Metropolitan Airport Commission. The Council can prohibit the development of the jetport at the site favored by the Commission, yet the Council must rely upon its persuasive powers since it cannot order the Commission to construct the jetport at a site selected by the Council. Consequently, a continuing deadlock between these two regional entities may block the development of a facility that both bodies agree is needed. The dispute may have to be settled by the legislature. The Commission is authorized to bring the dispute to the legislature for resolution, but has not yet chosen to do so.

The Twin Cities model may have an inherent defect—the possibility of disputes between the Council and its service boards. Such a dispute involving the Council and the Sewer Board did occur in regard to the Board's 1971 construction program. According to Ted Kolderie (1972: 4), the Citizens League believes that the present organizational arrangement "is useful . . . indeed, indispensable

. . . for the public. It represents, to use an old-fashioned term, the 'check and balance' in the system . . . which exists between President and Congress . . . or between Governor and Legislature . . . or between Mayor and Council." We may question the aptness of the analogy in that an executive veto can be overriden by the legislative body.

To reduce friction between the Council and the service boards, Mr. Kolderie (1972: 4) suggests that "perhaps this would be a good time to revive the Citizens League's 1968 proposal—not implemented—that the subordinate boards be served, in their planning, by staff from the council."

To avoid entirely disputes between the Council and any of the service boards, the device of the interlocking directorate can be utilized, as it was by New York state in 1967. The board of directors of the newly created Metropolitan Transportation Authority (MTA) was made the ex officio board of directors of the Long Island Railroad, New York City Transit Authority, Manhattan and Bronx Surface Transit Operating Authority, and Triborough Bridge and Tunnel Authority.[27] What we are suggesting as a possibility is the establishment of an umbrella agency whose board would be the ex officio board of each of the existing regional operating agencies. This approach is somewhat similar to the current Twin Cities model, but differs in that the Metropolitan Council has no direct operating responsibilities.

Concluding Comments

The basic question that remains unanswered in the Twin Cities area is whether one body—the Metropolitan Council—or several bodies will exercise regional power. It is reasonable to conclude that there will be a continuing struggle to centralize responsibility for additional functions in the Metropolitan Council. The evidence of the past five years suggests that the Council's potential for acquiring additional formal powers is limited. If additional legal powers are not granted by the legislature to the Council, its effectiveness as the regional coordinating body will be determined primarily by its ability to persuade other governmental units to follow its development guide.

REVENUE-SHARING

One of the most recent and interesting adaptive responses to problems associated with urbanization was the passage by the Minnesota Legislature in 1971 of the Metropolitan Fiscal Disparities Law,[28] which enables all local governments in the seven county Twin Cities region to share in the tax revenue produced by new commercial-industrial development, regardless of where it occurs in the region.

Since January 1, 1972, the property tax revenue produced by 40 percent of the net growth in commercial-industrial valuation in each municipality has been shared on a regional basis. Each community receives a share of the total revenue thus produced, based upon a formula which stresses population, but also adjusts the share according to the percentage by which a community's valuation exceeds or falls below the metropolitan average on a per capita basis. It is anticipated that the shared property will be 2 percent of the region's total property tax base in 1972, and increase to approximately 25 percent by 1985. A major purpose of the Act is to encourage municipalities to make land-use decisions on a basis other than that of the need for additional tax resources.

Pressures have been building for many years for the establishment of a program of federal revenue-sharing which would allow state and local governments more programmatic flexibility than existing grants-in-aid, promote the use of the income tax by states, help to equalize resources between wealthier and poorer states and local governments, and assist state and local governments in meeting their obligations.

The report of the (U.S.) National Commission on Urban Problems (1968) urged that federal revenue-sharing be utilized as a catalyst to encourage small local units—those under 50,000 population—to consolidate. According to the Commission, one of the major barriers to the solution of housing and other problems in metropolitan areas is the multiplicity of local governments with complex building and zoning codes often designed to keep low-income persons out of the communities.

Under the Commission's plan, a local government with a population under 50,000 would not share in the revenue, and one between 50,000 and 100,000 would receive funds based on the percentage by which its population exceeds 50,000. The shared revenue would be in addition to grants-in-aid and unrestricted as to its use.

The Commission conceded that its proposal did not "provide an overwhelming incentive" for consolidation, and it appears that most suburban municipalities would have reacted negatively if the plan had been enacted into law. Many citizens, for a variety of reasons, choose to live in a high-tax suburban community and probably would not be enticed to consolidate by the prospect of receiving shared revenue. One of the Commission's major reasons for advocating consolidation is the belief that consolidation is necessary to guarantee the proper guidance of land development. Few suburban municipalities, however, would give up control of land use in exchange for shared revenue. Furthermore, two or more contiguous suburban municipalities with restrictive codes could consolidate to qualify for federal shared revenue under the Commission's proposal. The consolidated government would be in control of a larger area, which the Commission favored, but fiscal zoning undoubtedly would be continued.

Congress has displayed no interest in the Douglas Commission's revenue-sharing proposal, but it did enact the State and Local Fiscal Assistance Act of 1972 which the President signed into law on October 6, 1972. The Act appropriates $30,236,400,000 for the period January 1, 1972 through December 31, 1976. Funds are being distributed to state and local governments by a complex formula which assigns various weights to population, local tax efforts, and per capita income.

The Act has been criticized on a number of grounds. Opponents charge that the Act favors the fast-growing affluent suburbs, when in fact the greatest need for financial assistance is in the older central cities, the home of high-cost citizens. Typical of the criticism of the Act is the following statement by Professor Jay G. Sykes (1972: 2) of the University of Wisconsin-Milwaukee:

> The fragmentation of local government need not be documented here. But we ought never to forget that the disintegrated, almost anarchical, state of local government in the United States has frustrated the solution of most problems of the late 20th century. Federal revenue sharing will further imbed the disorder and postpone the solutions.

One implication of federal revenue-sharing is clear. It will help to perpetuate the atomistic government of the metropolis because the shared revenue will enable many small units to survive, perhaps delaying the formation of a metropolitan government. Congress would have chosen a wiser course of action had the enabling act contained a clause providing incentives for the formation of a two-tier system of local government in metropolitan areas. The upper tier could be either a modernized county government or a new areawide government.

THE ROLE OF THE COURTS

Of the external forces influencing the governmental system of metropolitan areas since 1962, none has had a greater impact than the federal courts. In this section we will briefly examine the implications for metropolitan governance of court decisions in three areas—reapportionment, school finance, and school consolidation.

Until 1962, the United States Supreme Court refused to hear malapportionment cases involving state legislatures. In that year, however, the Court ruled that federal courts had jurisdiction in such cases, but did not mandate population as the basis for apportionment.[29] The following year the Court for the first time used the term "one-man, one-vote" and ruled unconstitutional Georgia's county-unit system for electing state officials.[30] In a 1964 case, the Court rejected the federal analogy of one house apportioned on the basis of area as violating the equal protection of the law clause of the Fourteenth Amendment to the United States Constitution, and ruled that both houses of the state legislature must be apportioned on the basis of one-man, one-vote.[31]

In a case involving a Michigan school board, the Supreme Court refused to extend its one-man, one-vote principle to all local governments. The Court held that the board's membership was "basically appointive rather than elective," and that the board's functions were "essentially administrative."[32] This case was unusual in that local district school boards, elected at large, each sent one delegate to a biennial meeting of the county school board.

Since the Fourteenth Amendment to the United States Constitution applies to local governments as well as to state governments, it was inevitable that the

Court would extend its one-man, one-vote principle to local governments. In April 1968, the Court, in a five-to-three decision, held that the apportionment of the board of commissioners of Midland County, Texas, violated the federal Constitution.[33] The Court ruled that population equality must be the basis for precinct equality, in view of the fact that the commissioners perform legislative functions, including setting a tax rate, equalizing assessment, issuing bonds, adopting budgets, and levying taxes.

The Court's one-man, one-vote principle has had no effect on metropolitan governance in states where county commissioners are elected at large, e.g., in Massachusetts and New Hampshire, or in states where county governments lack legislative powers. But the principle has promoted the modernization of some counties, including the assumption of additional powers, in states such as New York where town supervisors were ex officio members of the county board of supervisors. The necessity of reapportioning the county board induced a number of counties to establish charter commissions charged with drafting a charter which would modernize county government as well as reapportion its governing body.

Court cases in the area of public school finance and school district consolidation also have implications for the governance of metropolitan areas. The California Supreme Court, on August 30, 1971, ruled that the State's system of financing public schools violated the equal protection of the law clause of the Fourteenth Amendment to the United States Constitution because the system "makes the quality of a child's education a function of the wealth of his parents and neighbors."[34] The Court added:

> Although private residential and commercial patterns may be partially responsible for the distribution of assessed valuation throughout the State, such patterns are shaped and hardened by zoning ordinances and other governmental land use controls which promote economic exclusivity. . . . Governmental action drew the school boundary lines, thus determining how much wealth each district would contain.

Because of misinterpretations of the Serrano opinion, the California Supreme Court modified its original opinion by stating that the Court had not forbidden the use of the property tax to finance public education, nor had the Court ruled that school property tax rates must be uniform statewide.

The Serrano decision has been followed by somewhat similar decisions in several other states. The United States Supreme Court has accepted the State of Texas' petition for a review of a federal court of appeals ruling in the case of Rodriguez v. San Antonio Independent School District.[35]

If the United States Supreme Court declares the present system of financing public schools unconstitutional, each state government except Hawaii (which has only one school district) may have to assume complete responsibility for financing public schools. The impact of state assumption of public school costs obviously depends upon the tax or taxes used to finance the system and whether local districts will be allowed to levy a supplemental tax.

A second possible state response would involve the reformulation of state aid formulas to ensure that equal educational resources are available in all school districts (see Coons, Clune, and Sugarman, 1970).

A third possibility is the consolidation of all local school districts in each metropolitan area into a metropolitan school district, thereby making possible the elimination of fiscal disparities formerly existing between the local districts in the area.

A fourth possibility would be the establishment of a two-tier school system in each metropolitan area. Existing school districts would be continued but deprived of their revenue raising function. A newly created metropolitan school district would be assigned responsibility for raising funds for all local school districts and the elimination of fiscal disparities existing between the districts. Such districts could be organized on the model of the Metropolitan Toronto School Board.[36]

In Virginia, a United States District Court on January 11, 1972 ordered the establishment by September 1st of a metropolitan school system in the Richmond area by the merger of the school districts of Richmond, Chesterfield County, and Henrico County.[37] The Richmond system presently has a student population that is approximately 70 percent black and each of the county systems has a student population that is over 90 percent white. The Court ruled "that meaningful integration in a biracial community, as in the instant case, is essential to equality of education and the failure to provide it is violative of the Constitution of the United States."

The Fourth Circuit Court of Appeals on June 6, 1972, by a vote of five to one, reversed the opinion of the District Court.[38] Referring to Spencer v. Kugler[39] the Circuit Court stated:

> Because we think that the last vestiges of state-imposed segregation have been wiped out in the public schools of the City of Richmond and Henrico and Chesterfield and unitary systems achieved, and because it is not established that the racial composition of the schools in the City of Richmond and the Counties is the result of invidious state action, we conclude that there is no constitutional violation and that therefore the district judge exceeded his power of intervention.[40]

Should the United States Supreme Court reverse the Circuit Court decision, many suits will be entered in courts to force the consolidation of central city and suburban school districts.

CONCLUDING COMMENTS

Bollens and Schmandt (1970: 444) to the contrary, it does make an important difference whether certain service delivery systems in metropolitan areas are fractionated or unified. A fragmented local government system has endured because it is advantageous to segments of our pluralistic society. While certain individuals and groups gain, however, the system has failed to solve numerous major problems and provide quality services to all segments of our society.

The key question is whether we wish to perpetuate the fragmented local governmental system in the typical metropolitan area. If the answer to this question is yes, we should support the patchwork approach and urge greater federal and state support for metropolitan planning, COGs, intergovernmental service agreements, special districts, and the current type of federal revenue sharing.

Tinkering of this nature, however, will not enable the system to solve many major metropolitan problems, nor is tinkering apt to lead to the formation of metropolitan governments in most areas. While it is true that the establishment of metropolitan Dade County and the amalgamation of Jacksonville-Duval County were preceeded by functional consolidation, special circumstances account for the formation of these two metropolitan governments and the metropolitan government of Nashville and Davidson County (see Zimmerman, 1970, 1972b). If the effort to solve pressing service problems by tinkering is successful, the fragmented government of the metropolis probably will be perpetuated since reformers will be deprived of some of their most compelling arguments.

We can state with reasonable confidence that major problems which local governments cannot cope with will be solved in time on the state or federal levels unless a new areawide mechanism is developed on the local level. As we pointed out above, Massachusetts and New York State have established state-controlled public authorities charged with solving areawide functional problems. Furthermore, in the 1960s the federal government commenced to preempt what had been considered to be traditional state and local government responsibilities. Congress has partially preempted the regulation of air, water, and noise pollution abatement [41] and is continually establishing higher standards. One regulatory area—automotive emissions—has been completely preempted by Congress. Unless state and local governments take forceful action to solve areawide problems, it is reasonable to predict that the federal governmen will preempt additional governmental functions.

We conclude by suggesting that a strong case can be made for the establishment in most metropolitan areas of a popularly controlled regional government with sufficient powers, including financial and implementation ones, to solve areawide exigencies and promote the orderly and rational development of the region. The metropolitan government might be either a new unit of areawide government or a modernized county government. It might be called an Environmental Council because most of its powers would be concerned with enhancement of the environment—air and water pollution abatement, refuse disposal, public transportation, major parks and recreational facilities, and certain land-use controls. Establishment of Environmental Councils would reduce the need for a further upward shift of responsibility for solving areawide problems to the state and federal levels.

NOTES

1. Housing and Urban Development Act of 1965, 79 Stat. 502 (1965), 40 U.S.C. 461 (g) (1965).

2. Housing Act of 1954, 68 Stat. 590 (1954), 40 U.S.C. 461 (1965).

3. Housing and Urban Development Act of 1965, 79 Stat. 502 (1965), 40 U.S.C. 461 (2).

4. Demonstration Cities and Metropolitan Development Act of 1966, 80 Stat. 1255, 42 U.S.C. 3301-314 (1966).

5. Ibid.

6. Ibid.

7. Intergovernmental Cooperation Act of 1968. 82 Stat. 1103, 42 U.S.C. 4201-243 (1970).

8. National Environmental Policy Act of 1969. 83 Stat. 852, 42 U.S.C. 4321 and 4331-332 (1972).

9. State of Rhode Island and Providence Plantations Public Laws of 1972, Ch. 248.

10. Ibid.

11. Connecticut General Statutes Annotated, Ch. 578, Sec. 32-7 (1965).

12. This section is based on data collected for a larger study of substate regionalism being conducted by the Advisory Commission on Intergovernmental Relations under the direction of Dr. Carl W. Stenberg (see Zimmerman, 1973).

13. See the California Government Code, Sec. 51301, and Los Angeles County Charter, Sec. 56 1/2.

14. Rhode Island and Connecticut abolished county government in 1842 and 1960 respectively, and Alaska entered the Union without county government in 1959.

15. Avery v. Midland County, Texas et al., 390 U.S. 474 (1968). See below for a discussion of reapportionment cases.

16. Constitution of the State of New York, Art. IX, Sec. 1 (h).

17. Mississippi Code, Secs. 7082 and 7129-150.

18. Pennsylvania Acts of 1972, Act 180.

19. The Charter of Metropolitan Dade County Florida, Art. 1, Sec. 1.01.

20. Volusia County (Florida) Charter, Sec. 1305.

21. Massachusetts General Court, House 4013 (1970).

22. Colorado Revised Statutes, Ch. 89, Art. 25.

23. Minnesota Statutes, Ch. 473B.

24. Ibid., Ch. 473C.

25. Ibid., Ch. 473E.

26. Knapp v. O'Brien, 179 N.W. 2d 88 (1970).

27. New York Laws of 1967, Ch. 717.

28. Minnesota Statutes, 1971 Special Session, Ch. 24.

29. Baker v. Carr, 369 U.S. 186 (1962).

30. Sanders v. Gray, 372 U.S. 368 (1963).

31. Reynolds v. Sims, 377 U.S. 533 (1964).

32. Sailors v. Kent Board of Education, 387 U.S. 105 (1967).

33. Avery v. Midland County, Texas et al., 390 U.S. 474 (1968).

34. Serrano v. Priest, 5 Cal. 3d 584 (1971).

35. Rodriguez v. San Antonio Independent School District, 299 F. Supp. 476.

36. The Municipality of Metropolitan Toronto Act, 1953, Part VII, Sec's. 129-49a.

37. Carolyn Bradley et al. v. The School Board of the City of Richmond, 338 F. Supp. 67 (1972).

38. Bradley v. School Board of Richmond, Virginia, 562 F. 2d 1058 (1972).

39. Spencer v. Kugler, 404 U.S. 1027 (1972).

40. Bradley v. School Board of Richmond, Virginia, 462 F. 2d 1070 (1972).

41. Water Quality Act of 1965, 33 U.S.C. Sec. 466; Air Quality Act of 1967, 42 U.S.C. Secs. 1857-1971; Noise Control and Abatement Act of 1972, Public Law 92-574.

REFERENCES

Advisory Commission on Intergovernmental Relations. *Governmental structure, organization and planning in metropolitan areas.* Washington, D.C.: U.S. Government Printing Office, 1961.

Advisory Commission on Intergovernmental Relations. *For a more perfect union—County reform.* Washington, D.C.: U.S. Government Printing Office, April, 1971.

Advisory Commission on Intergovernmental Relations. *Profile of county government.* Washington, D.C.: U.S. Government Printing Office, January, 1972.

Association of Central Oklahoma Governments. Agreement for the organization of the Association of Central Oklahoma Governments. Oklahoma City: ACOG, March, 1966 (Mimeo.).

Baldinger, S. *Planning and governing the metropolis: The Twin Cities experience.* New York: Praeger, 1971.

Bollens, J. C., and Schmandt, H. J. *The metropolis: Its people, politics, and economic life.* (2nd ed.). New York: Harper and Row, 1970.

California Council on Intergovernmental Relations. *Allocations of public service responsibilities in California.* Sacramento: CCIR, June, 1970.

Chamber of Commerce of the U.S. Twin Cities Metropolitan Council anticipates and supplies orderly growth. *Urban Action Clearinghouse,* Case Study No. 20. Washington, D.C.: CCUS, 1971.

Coons, J. E., Clune, W. H., and Sugarman, S. D. *Private wealth and public education.* Cambridge: Harvard University Press, 1970.

Fischer, J. "The Minnesota experiment: How to make a big city fit to live in." Harper's Magazine, April, 1969, 238, 12-32.

Hanson, R. *Metropolitan councils of government.* Washington, D.C.: Advisory Commission on Intergovernmental Relations, August, 1966.

Herbers, J. "Minneapolis area council is emerging as a pioneer in strong regional government." New York Times, February 2, 1971.

Institute for Local Self Government. *ABAG Appraised.* Berkeley: ILSG, December, 1965.

Jorgensen, C. W. *Survey of functions at county level: Fall 1972.* Albany: County Officers Association of the State of New York, 1972.

Keith, J. P. Regional civic organizations. Address presented at the National Conference on Government, Minneapolis, November 28, 1972.

Kolderie, T. "Minnesota legislature aids metropolitan setup." National Civic Review, July 1969, 58, 321, 326.

Kolderie, T. "Keeping 'checks and balances' in metropolitan structure." (Minneapolis) Citizens League News, October 31, 1972.

Marando, V. L. "Inter-local cooperation in a metropolitan area: Detroit." Urban Affairs Quarterly, December 1968, 4, 185-200.

Mogulof, M. B. *Governing metropolitan areas: A critical review of councils of government and the federal role.* Washington, D.C.: The Urban Institute, 1971.

National Association of Regional Councils. "Denver COG seeks to establish regional service authority." National Association of Regional Councils Newsletter, November 7, 1972, (4), 6.

New Jersey County and Municipal Government Study Commission. *Joint services—A local response to areawide problems.* Trenton: CMGSC, 1970.

San Francisco Bureau of Governmental Research. *The Association of Bay Area Governments: A gathering force.* San Francisco: BGR, April 1, 1965.

Sykes, J. G. Revenue sharing: The new boondoggle? Address presented at the National Conference on Government, Minneapolis, November 28, 1972 (Mimeo).

Texas Urban Development Commission. *Urban Texas: Policies for the future.* Arlington, Texas: UDC, November, 1971.

(U.S.) National Commission on Urban Problems. *Building the American city.* Washington, D.C.: U.S. Government Printing Office, 1968.

U.S. Office of Management and Budget. Circular A-95. (rev. ed.), Washington, D.C.: February, 1971.

Wagner, R. F. Address to the Metropolitan Regional Council, Plainfield, New Jersey, June 16, 1959 (Mimeo).

Zimmerman, J. F. "Metropolitan ecumenism: The road to the promised land?" Journal of Urban Law, Spring, 1967a, 44, 433-457.

Zimmerman, J. F. (Ed.) *Metropolitan charters.* Albany: State University of New York, Graduate School of Public Affairs, 1967b.

Zimmerman, J. F. "The planning riddle." National Civic Review, April, 1968a, 57, 189-194.

Zimmerman, J. F. *1968 Survey of metropolitan planning.* Albany: State University of New York, Graduate School of Public Affairs, 1968b.

Zimmerman, J. F. "Metropolitan reform in the U.S.: An overview." Public Administration Review, September/October 1970, 30, 531-543.

Zimmerman, J. F. Solving areawide problems in Rhode Island. Newsletter. Kingston: University of Rhode Island, Bureau of Governmental Research, September, 1972a.

Zimmerman, J. F. "Mergers reviewed for local units." National Civic Review, September, 1972b, 61, 417-419.

Zimmerman, J. F. *Governing metropolitan Boston.* Boston: Metropolitan Area Planning Council, November, 1972c.

Zimmerman, J. F. Procedural adaptation: Intergovernmental service agreements. In Advisory Commission on Intergovernmental Relations, *Substate regionalism and the federal system.* Vol. 1. Washington, D.C.: U.S. Government Printing Office, 1973.

Zimmerman, J. F., and Snyder, M. E. "New trends seen in area planning." National Civic Review, September, 1967, 56, 470-474.

BIBLIOGRAPHY

Abrahams, R. D. (Ed.) *Deep down in the jungle.* Chicago: Aldine-Atherton, 1970.

Adams, R. F. "On the variation in the consumption of public services." Review of Economics and Statistics, November 1965, 47, 400-405.

Addams, J. *Twenty years at Hull House.* New York: New American Library, 1961.

Advisory Commission on Intergovernmental Relations. *Governmental structure, organization and planning in metropolitan areas.* Washington, D.C.: U.S. Government Printing Office, 1961.

Advisory Commission on Intergovernmental Relations. *Factors affecting voter reaction in governmental reorganization in metropolitan areas.* Washington, D.C.: U.S. Government Printing Office, 1962.

Advisory Commission on Intergovernmental Relations. *Fiscal balance in the American federal system.* Vol. 2: *Metropolitan fiscal disparities.* Washington, D.C.: U.S. Government Printing Office, 1967.

Advisory Commission on Intergovernmental Relations. *Urban America and the federal system.* Washington, D.C.: U.S. Government Printing Office, 1969.

Advisory Commission on Intergovernmental Relations. *Metropolitan disparities: A second reading.* Information Bulletin No. 70-1. Washington, D.C.: ACIR, January 1970.

Advisory Commission on Intergovernmental Relations. *Measuring the fiscal capacity and effort of states and local areas.* Washington, D.C.: U.S. Government Printing Office, March 1971.

Advisory Commission on Intergovernmental Relations. *Profile of county government.* Washington, D.C.: U.S. Government Printing Office, January 1972.

Advisory Commission on Intergovernmental Relations. *For a more perfect union—County reform.* Washington, D.C.: U.S. Government Printing Office, April 1971.

Advisory Commission on Intergovernmental Relations. *Substate regionalism and the federal system.* Vol. 1. Washington, D.C.: U.S. Government Printing Office, 1973.

Alford, R. R., and Lee, E. C. "Voting turnout in American cities." American Political Science Review, September 1968, 62, 796-813.

Alinsky, S. *Reveille for radicals.* Chicago: University of Chicago Press, 1946.

Alonso, W. "A theory of the urban land market." Papers and Proceedings of the Regional Science Association, 1960, 6, 149-157.

Alonso, W. *Location and land use.* Cambridge: Harvard University Press, 1965.

Alonso, W. "The economics of urban size." Papers and Proceedings of the Regional Science Association, 1971, 26, 67-83.

Alonso, W., and Medrich, E. Spontaneous growth centers in twentieth century American urbanization. Working Paper No. 113. Berkeley: University of California, Institute of Urban and Regional Development, January 1970.

Altshuler, A. "The goals of comprehensive planning." Journal of the American Institute of Planners, August 1965, 31 (3), 186-194.

Altshuler, A. *Community Control: The black demand for participation in large American cities.* New York: Pegasus, 1970.

Anderson, T. R., and Collier, J. "Metropolitan dominance and the rural hinterland." Rural Sociology, June 1956, 21, 152-157.

Andrews, F. M., Morgan, J. and Sonquist, J. *Multiple classification analysis.* Ann Arbor: University of Michigan, Institute for Social Research, 1969.

Andrews, F. M., and Philips, G. W. "The squatters of Lima: Who they are and what they want." Journal of Developing Areas, January 1970, 4, 211-229.

Ardrey, R. *The territorial imperative.* New York: Atheneum, 1966.

Astrom, K. *City planning in Sweden.* Stockholm: Swedish Institute, 1967.

Bahl, R., Greytak, D., Campbell, A. K., and Wasylenko, M. J. "Intergovernmental and functional aspects of public employment trends in the United States." Public Administration Review, November-December 1972, 32, 815-832.

Bailey, M. J. "Effects of race and other demographic factors on the value of single family homes." Land Economics, May 1966, 42, 215-220.

Baldinger, S. *Planning and governing the metropolis: The Twin Cities experience.* New York: Praeger, 1971.

Baltzell, E. D. *Philadelphia gentlemen.* Glencoe: Free Press, 1958.

Baltzell, E. D. (Ed.) *The search for community in modern America.* New York: Harper and Row, 1968.

Banfield, E. C. (Ed.) *Urban government.* (Rev. ed.) New York: Free Press, 1969.

Banfield, E. C. *The unheavenly city.* Boston: Little, Brown, 1970.

Baumol, W. J. "Macroeconomics of unbalanced growth: The anatomy of urban crisis." American Economic Review, June 1967, 57 (3), 415-426.

Bellomo, S., Dial, R. B., and Voorhees, A. M. *Factors, trends and guidelines related to trip lengths.* National Cooperative Highway Research Program Report 89. Washington, D.C.: Highway Research Board, 1970.

Benson, C. S. "The Serrano decision: Where will the money go?" Public Affairs Report (Institute of Governmental Studies, University of California at Berkeley), December 1972, 13(6), 1-5.

Berger, B. N. *Working-class suburb.* Berkeley: University of California Press, 1960.

Berke, D. S., Sacks, S., Bailey, S. K., and Campbell, A. K. Federal aid to public education: Who benefits? In J. S. Berke and M. W. Kirst, *Federal aid to education: Who benefits? Who governs?* Lexington: D. C. Heath, 1972. 1-59.

Berke, J. S., and Callahan, J. J. "Serrano v. Priest: Milestone or millstone for school finance?" Journal of Public Law, 1972, 21(1), 23-71.

Berry, B.J.L. "Cities as systems within systems of cities." Papers and Proceedings of the Regional Science Association, 1964, 13, 147-163.

Bhagwati, J. (Ed.) Economics and world order. New York: Macmillan, 1972.

Biddle, W. W., and Biddle, L. J. The community development process: The rediscovery of local initiative. New York: Holt, Rinehart and Winston, 1965.

Birch, D. L. The economic future of city and suburb. New York: Committee for Economic Development, 1970.

Bishop, C. E. "The organization of rural America: Implications for agricultural economics." Journal of Farm Economics, December 1967, 49, 999-1008.

Blau, P. M., and Duncan, O. D. The American occupational structure. New York: John Wiley, 1967.

Blumenfeld, H. The modern metropolis: Its origins, growth, characteristics and planning. Cambridge: MIT Press, 1967.

Bogue, D. J. The structure of the metropolitan community: A study of dominance and subdominance. Ann Arbor: University of Michigan, School of Graduate Studies, 1950.

Bollens, J. C. The states and the metropolitan problem. Chicago: Council of State Governments, 1956.

Bollens, J. C. (Ed.) Exploring the metropolitan community. Berkeley: University of California Press, 1961.

Bollens, J. C., and Schmandt, H. J. The metropolis: Its people, politics, and economic life. (2nd ed.) New York: Harper and Row, 1970.

Boone, R. W. "Reflections on citizen participation and the Economic Opportunity Act." Public Administration Review, September 1972, 32, 444-456.

Bourne, L. S., MacKinnon, R. D., and Simmons, J. W. (Eds.) The form of cities in Central Canada: Selected papers. Toronto: University of Toronto, Centre for Urban and Community Studies, 1973.

Bowles, G. Net migration from the farm population. Presented at the 1961 Annual Meeting of the Population Association of America.

Bradburn, N., Sudman, S., and Glockel, G. Side by side. Chicago: Quadrangle, 1971.

Brager, G. A., and Purcell, F. P. Community action against poverty. New Haven: College and University Press, 1967.

Brazier, H. E. City expenditures in the U.S. Occasional Paper No. 66. Washington, D.C.: National Bureau of Economic Research, 1959.

Briggs, A. Victorian cities. (Rev. ed.) New York: Harper and Row, 1970.

Buchanan, J. J., and Tullock, G. The calculus of consent: Logical foundations of constitutional democracy. Ann Arbor: University of Michigan Press, 1962.

Buder, S. Pullman. New York: Oxford University Press, 1967.

Burgess, E. W. "The growth of the city: An introduction to a research project." Proceedings of the American Sociological Society, 1923, 18, 85-97.

Burgess, E. W., and Bogue, D. J. (Eds.) Contributions to urban sociology. Chicago: University of Chicago Press, 1964.

Burkhardt, J. E., and Rothenberg, J. Changes in neighborhood social interaction. RMC Report UR-128. Washington, D.C.: U.S. Department of Transportation, Federal Highway Administration, 1971.

Burkhead, J., and Miner, J. *Public Expenditure*. Chicago: Aldine-Atherton,
1972.

Campbell, A. *White attitudes toward black people*. Ann Arbor: University of
Michigan, Institute for Social Research, 1971.

Campbell, A. K. (Ed.) *The states and the urban crisis*. Englewood Cliffs:
Prentice-Hall, 1970.

Campbell, A., and Converse, P. E. (Eds.) *The human meaning of social change*.
New York: Russell Sage, 1972.

Campbell, A. K., and Meranto, P. "The metropolitan education dilemma:
Matching resources to needs." Urban Affairs Quarterly, September 1966, 2,
42-63.

Campbell, A. K., and Sacks, S. *Metropolitan America: Fiscal patterns and governmental systems*. New York: Free Press, 1967.

Cantilli, E. J., and Schmelzer, J. L. (Eds.) *Transportation and aging*. Washington,
D.C.: U.S. Government Printing Office, 1971.

Cantril, H. *The pattern of human concerns*. New Brunswick: Rutgers University
Press, 1965.

Canty, D. "Metropolity." City, March-April 1972, 6(2), 29-44.

Canty, D. "Nixon's urban record, Part 2." City, Fall 1972, 6(4), 59-60.

Caplovitz, D. *The poor pay more: Consumer practices of low income families*.
New York: Free Press, 1963.

Carp, F. M. "Walking as a means of transportation for retired people."
Gerontologist, Summer 1971, 11, 104-111.

Carp, F. M. "The older pedestrian in San Francisco." Highway Research Record,
November 1972, 403, 18-22.

Carpenter, D. B. "Urbanization and social change in Japan." Sociological
Quarterly, July 1960, 9, 155-166.

Carlos, S. "Religious participation and the urban-suburban continuum." American Journal of Sociology, March 1970, 75, 742-759.

Casparis, J. "Metropolitan retail structure and its relation to population." Land
Economics, 1967, 43, 212-218.

Caudill, H. M. *Night comes to the Cumberlands*. Boston: Little, Brown, 1963.

Chapin, F. S., and Weiss, S. (Eds.) *Urban growth dynamics*. New York: John
Wiley, 1962.

Chinitz, B. "Contrasts in agglomeration: New York and Pittsburgh." American
Economic Review, Papers and Proceedings, May 1961, 51(2), 279-289.

Chinitz, B. (Ed.) *City and suburbs: The economics of metropolitan growth*.
Englewood Cliffs: Prentice-Hall, 1964.

Christaller, W. *Die zentralen orte in Suddeutschland*. Jena; Gustave Fischer
Verlag, 1933.

Christie, R., and Geis, F. L. *Studies in Machiavellianism.* New York: Academic Press, 1970.

Churchill, H. S. *The city is the people.* New York: Reynald and Hitchcock, 1945.

Clawson, M. *Suburban land conversion in the United States: An economic and governmental process.* Baltimore: Johns Hopkins Press, 1971.

Clawson, M. *Suburban land use conversion.* Baltimore: Johns Hopkins University Press for Resources for the Future, Inc., 1971.

Cloward, R. A., and Ohlin, L. *Delinquency and opportunity.* Glencoe: Free Press, 1960.

Coelho, G. V., Hamburg, D., and Adams J. (Eds.) *Coping and adaptation.* New York: Basic Books, in press.

Colm, G. *Essays in public finance and fiscal policy.* New York: Oxford University Press, 1955.

Committee for Economic Development, Research and Policy Committee. *Guiding economic growth.* New York: CED, 1960.

Committee for Economic Development. *Modernizing local government.* New York: CED, 1967.

Committee for Economic Development. *Reshaping government in metropolitan areas.* New York: CED, 1970.

Connery, R. H., and Caraley, D. (Eds.) *Governing the city.* New York: Praeger, 1969.

Coons, J. E., Clune, W. H., and Sugarman, S. D. *Private wealth and public education.* Cambridge: Harvard University Press, 1970.

Copp, J. H. Rural sociology and rural development. Presidential address, annual meeting of the Rural Sociological Society, Baton Rouge, Louisiana, August 26, 1972.

Costikyan, E., and Lehman, M. *Restructuring the government of New York City: Report of the Scott Commission Task Force on Jurisdiction and Structure.* New York: Praeger, 1972.

Council of State Governments. *Sub-state district systems.* RM-468. Lexington: CSG, September 1971.

Craig, G. A. "The city and the historian." Canadian Journal of History, March 1970, 5(1), 47-55.

Crecine, J. P. (Ed.) *Financing the metropolis.* Beverly Hills: Sage Publications, 1970.

Cressey, P. F. "Population succession in Chicago: 1898-1930." American Journal of Sociology, 1938, 44, 59-69.

Dahir, J. *The neighborhood unit plan.* New York: Russell Sage Foundation, 1947.

Dahl, R. A. "The city in the future of democracy." American Political Science Review, December 1967, 61, 953-970.

Danielson, M. N. Differentiation, segregation, and political fragmentation in the American metropolis. Presented at the U.S. Commission on Population Growth and the American Future, 1971.

Danzig, R., and Heineman, B., Jr. "Decentralization in New York City: A proposal." Harvard Journal on Legislation, March 1971, 8, 407-453.

Darley, J. M., and Latane, B. "When will people help in a crisis?" Psychology Today, December 1968, 2, 54ff.

Darley, J. M., Tiger, A., and Lewis, L. D. "Do groups always inhibit individuals' responses to potential emergencies?" Journal of Personality and Social Psychology, June 1973, 26(3), 395-399.

David, P. A., and Reder, M. W. (Eds.) *Nations and households in economic growth: Essays in honor of Moses Abramovitz.* Palo Alto: Stanford University Press, in press.

Davis, A. F. *Spearheads of reform: The social settlements and the Progressive movement.* New York: Oxford University Press, 1970.

Derthick, M. "Defeat at Fort Lincoln." The Public Interest, Summer 1970, No. 20, 3-39.

Dessel, M. D. Central Business districts and their metropolitan areas: A summary of geographic shifts in retail sales growth, 1948-1954. *Area Trend Series,* No. 1. Office of Area Development, U.S. Department of Commerce. Washington, D.C.: U.S. Government Printing Office, 1957.

Dewey, R. "The neighborhood, urban ecology, and city planners." American Sociological Review, August 1950, 15(4), 502-507.

Dewey, R. "The rural-urban continuum: Real but relatively unimportant." American Journal of Sociology, July 1960, 66, 60-66.

Dobriner, W. M. (Ed.) *The suburban community.* New York: Putnam, 1959.

Dobriner, W. M. *Class in suburbia.* Englewood Cliffs: Prentice-Hall, 1963.

Dohrenwend, B. P., and Dohrenwend, B. S. The prevalence of psychiatric disorders in urban versus rural settings. Presented at the Fifth World Congress of Psychiatry, Mexico City, November 28-December 4, 1971.

Donaldson, S. *The suburban myth.* New York: Columbia University Press, 1971.

Dorfman, R. (Ed.) *Measuring benefits of government investments.* Washington, D.C.: Brookings Institution, 1965.

Downs, A. J. *An economic theory of democracy.* New York: Harper and Row, 1957.

Duhl, L. (Ed.) *The urban condition.* New York: Simon and Schuster, 1963.

Duncan, O. D., and Duncan, B. "Residential distribution and occupational stratification." American Journal of Sociology, March 1955, 60, 493-503.

Duncan, O. D. "Gradients of urban influence on the rural population." Midwest Sociologist, Winter 1956, 18, 27-30.

Duncan, O. D., Scott, W. R., Lieberman, S., Duncan, B., and Winsborough, H. H. *Metropolis and region.* Baltimore: Johns Hopkins Press, 1960.

Edel, M. "Land values and the costs of urban congestion." Social Science Information, December 1971, 10(6), 7-36.

Edel, M., and Sclar, E. Differential taxation, land values and transportation. Presented at the Econometric Society, December 1971.

Edel, M., and Rothenberg, J. (Eds.) *Readings in urban economics.* New York: Macmillan, 1972.

Eichler, E. P., and Kaplan, M. *The community builders.* Berkeley: University of California Press, 1967.

Eldredge, H. W. (Ed.) *Taming megalopolis: How to manage an urbanized world.* New York: Doubleday Anchor, 1967.

Ellis, W. W. *White ethics and black power.* Chicago: Aldine Press, 1969.

Engle, R., Fisher, F., Harris, J., and Rothenberg, J. "An econometric simulation model of intra-metropolitan housing location." American Economic Review, Papers and Proceedings, May 1972, 62, 87-97.

Ennis, P. H. *Criminal victimization in the United States: A report of a national survey.* Chicago: National Opinion Research Center, 1967.

Epstein, A. L. "Urbanization and social change in Africa." Current Anthropology, October 1967, 8, 275-296.

Evans, A. W. "The pure theory of city size in an industrial economy." Urban Studies, February 1972, 9, 49-77.

Fava, S. F. (Ed.) *Urbanism in world perspective.* New York: Crowell, 1968.

Fischer, C. S. "Urbanism as a way of life: A review and an agenda." Sociological Methods and Research, November 1972, 1, 187-242.

Fischer, C. S. "Urban alienation and anomie: Powerlessness and social isolation." American Sociological Review, June 1973, 38, 311-326.

Fischer, C. S. Toward a subcultural theory of urbanism. Presented at the meeting of the American Sociological Society, New York, August, 1973.

Fischer, C. S. "Urban malaise." Social Forces, December 1973, 52.

Fischer, R. M. (Ed.) *The metropolis in modern life.* Garden City: Doubleday, 1955.

Fitch, L. C., and Walsh, A. H. (Eds.) *Agenda for a city: Issues confronting New York.* Beverly Hills: Sage Publications, 1970.

Floyd, F., and Robertson, T. D. "Some urban policy considerations of rural journey-to-work commuting." Review of Regional Studies, Spring 1972, 1, 29-36.

Foley, D. L., Drake, R. L., Lyon, D. W., and Ynzenga, B. A. *Characteristics of metropolitan growth in California.* Vol. I: *Report.* Berkeley: University of California, Center for Planning and Development Research, December 1965.

Foley, D. L. *Governing the London region.* Berkeley: University of California Press, 1972.

Foley, D. L. Differentials in personal access to household motor vehicles: Five-county San Francisco Bay Area, 1971. Working Paper No. 197/BART 9. Berkeley: University of California, Institute of Urban and Regional Development, December 1972.

Forbes, G. B., and Gromoll, H. F. "The lost-letter technique as a measure of social variables: Some exploratory findings." Social Forces, September 1971, 50, 113-115.

Foster, G. M. "Interpersonal relations in peasant society." Human Organization, Winter 1960-61, 19, 174-185.

Frarr, W. G., Jr., Lieberman, L., and Wood, J. S. *Decentralizing city government: A practical study of a radical proposal for New York City.* New York: Praeger, 1972.

Freedman, J. L., Klevansky, S., and Ehrlich, P. R. "The effect of crowding on human task performance." Journal of Applied Social Psychology, March 1971, 1, 7-25.

Fried, M., and Gleicher, P. "Some sources of residential satisfaction in an urban slum." Journal of the American Institute of Planners, 1961, 27, 305-315.

Fuchs, V. L. Differentials in hourly earnings by region and city size. Occasional Paper No. 101, National Bureau of Economic Research. New York: Columbia University Press, 1967.

Fuguitt, G. V. "The city and the countryside." Rural Sociology, September 1963, 28, 246-261.

Fuguitt, G. "The places left behind: Population trends and policies for rural America." Rural Sociology, December 1971, 36, 449-470.

Galle, O. R., Gove, W. R., and McPherson, J. M. Population density and pathology. Presented at the meeting of the American Sociological Association, Denver, 1971.

Gans, H. J. *The urban villagers: Group and class in the life of Italian-Americans.* New York: Free Press, 1962.

Gans, H. *The Levittowners: Way of life and politics in a new suburban community.* New York: Vintage, 1967.

Gans, H. *People and plans.* New York: Basic Books, 1968.

Ganz, A. *Our large cities: New light on their recent transformation; elements of a development strategy; a prototype program for Boston.* Cambridge: MIT, Laboratory for Environmental Studies, February 1972.

Gillette, J. M. *Rural Sociology.* New York: Macmillan, 1922.

Gist, H. P., and Fava, S. F. *Urban society.* (5th ed.) New York: Thomas Y. Crowell, 1964.

Gittell, M. (Ed.) *Educating an urban population.* Beverly Hills: Sage Publications, 1966.

Glaab, C. N., and Brown, A. T. *A history of urban America.* New York: Macmillan, 1967.

Glass, D. C., and Singer, J. E. *Urban stress.* New York: Academic Press, 1972.

Goheen, P. G. Victorian Toronto: 1850 to 1900. Research Paper No. 127. Chicago: University of Chicago, Department of Geography, 1970.

Goist, P. D. "City and 'community': The urban theory of Robert Park." American Quarterly, Spring 1971, 23(1), 46-59.

Gosnell, H. F. *Machine politics.* Chicago: University of Chicago Press, 1968.

Gottmann, J., and Harper, R. A. (Eds.) *Metropolis on the move: Geographers look at urban sprawl.* New York: John Wiley, 1967.

Graham, H. D., and Gurr, T. R. (Eds.) *The history of violence in America.* New York: Bantam, 1969.

Greater London Group. *The lessons of the London government reforms.* London: HMSO, 1968.

Grebler, L. "Measuring the suburbanization of manufacture." Land Economics, November 1956, 32, 380-381.

Greer, S. "Urbanism reconsidered: A comparative study of local areas in a metropolis." American Sociological Review, February 1956, 21, 18-25.

Greer, S. *The emerging city.* New York: Free Press, 1962.

Greer, S. *Metropolitics: A study of political culture.* New York: John Wiley, 1963.

Greer, S. *Urban renewal and American cities.* Indianapolis: Bobbs-Merrill, 1965.

Greer, S. *The urbane view: Life and politics in metropolitan America.* New Oxford University Press, 1972.

Grieson, R. E. The economics of property taxes and land values. Working Paper No. 72. Cambridge: MIT, Department of Economics, June 1971.

Grigsby, W. *Housing markets and public policy.* Philadelphia: University of Pennsylvania, Institute of Urban Studies, 1962.

Guest, A. "Urban growth and population densities." Demography, February 1973, 10, 53-69.

Gulick, L. H. *The metropolitan problem and American ideas.* New York: A. E. Knopf, 1962.

Gutman, R., and Popenoe, D. (Eds.) *Neighborhood, city and metropolis.* New York: Random House, 1970.

Haig, R. "Toward an understanding of the metropolis. Parts 1 and 2." Quarterly Journal of Economics, February 1926, 40, 179-208; May 1926, 402-434.

Haines, H., Jr., Simon, L., and Alexis, M. "An analysis of central city neighborhood trading areas." Journal of Regional Science, April 1972, 12, 95-105.

Hallman, H. *Neighborhood control of public programs.* New York: Praeger, 1970.

Hamovitch, W., and Levenson, A. "Projecting suburban employment." Urban Affairs Quarterly, June 1969, 4, 459-476.

Handlin, O., and Burchard, J. (Eds.) *The historian and the city.* Cambridge: MIT Press, 1963.

Handlin, O. *Boston's immigrants.* (Rev. ed.) New York: Atheneum, 1969.

Hanson, R. *Metropolitan councils of government.* Washington, D.C.: Advisory Commission on Intergovernmental Relations, August 1966.

Harris, L. "A *Life* poll." Life, January 9, 1970, 102-106.

Harris, W. *Regional COG's and the central city.* Detroit: Metropolitan Fund, 1970.

Hathaway, D. E., Beegle, J. A., and Bryant, W. K. *People of rural America.* 1960 Census Monograph Series. U.S. Department of Commerce. Washington, D.C.: U.S. Government Printing Office, 1968.

Hatt, P. K., and Reiss, A. J., Jr. (Eds.) *Cities and society.* New York: Free Press, 1957.

Hauser, P. H., and Schnore, L. F. (Eds.) *The study of urbanization.* New York: John Wiley, 1965.

Hawley, A. H. "An ecological study of urban service institutions." American Sociological Review, 1941, 6, 629-639.

Hawley, A. H. *Human ecology: A theory of community structure.* New York: Ronald Press, 1950.

Hawley, A. H. "Metropolitan population and municipal government expenditures in central cities." Journal of Social Issues, 1951, 7(1-2), 100-108.

Hawley, A. H. *The changing shape of metropolitan America: Deconcentration since 1920.* Glencoe: Free Press, 1956.

Hawley, A. H., and Zimmer, B. G. *The metropolitan community: Its people and government.* Beverly Hills: Sage Publications, 1970.

Hawley, A. H. *Urban society: An ecological approach.* New York: Ronald Press, 1971.

Hawley, A. H. "Population density and the city." Demography, November 1972, 9, 521-529.

Heinberg, J. H., and Oates, W. D. "The incidence of differential property taxes on urbanization: Comment." National Tax Journal, March 1970, 23, 92-98.

Herzberg, D., and Rosenthal, A. (Eds.) *Strengthening the states: Essays on legislative reform.* New York: Doubleday, 1972.

Hightower, J. *Hard tomatoes, hard times: The failure of the land grant college complex.* Washington, D.C.: Agribusiness Accountability Project, 1972.

Hillery, G. A. "Definition of community: Areas of agreement." Rural Sociology, 1955, 20, 111-123.

Hirsch, W. Z. (Ed.) *Urban life and form.* New York: Holt, Rinehart and Winston, 1963.

Hoover, E. M., and Vernon, R. *Anatomy of a metropolis.* Cambridge: Harvard University Press, 1959.

Horton, R. D. "Municipal labor relations: The New York City experience." Social Science Quarterly, Winter 1971, 52(3), 680-696.

Howe, I. "The city in literature." Commentary, May 1971, 51, 61-68.

Hoyt, H. *One hundred years of land values in Chicago.* Chicago: University of Chicago Press, 1933.

Hoyt, H. *Structure and growth of residential neighborhoods.* Washington, D.C.: U.S. Government Printing Office, 1939.

Hughes, E. C., Johnson, C. S., Masuoka, J., Redfield, and Wirth, L. (Eds.) *Human communities: The city and human ecology. Collected papers of Robert Ezra Park.* Glencoe: Free Press, 1952.

Hunter, A. D. *Symbolic community.* Chicago: University of Chicago Press, 1974.

Hurd, R. M. *Principles of city land values.* New York: The Record and Guide, 1903.

Hurst, M. E. "The structure of movement and household behavior." Urban Studies, February 1969, 6, 70-82.

Hyman, H. H., and Sheatsley, P. B. "Attitudes toward desegregation." Scientific American, December 1956, 195, 35-39.

Inkeles, A. "Making men modern: On the causes and consequences of individual change in six developing countries." American Journal of Sociology, September 1969, 75, 208-225.

Institute for Local Self Government. *ABAG Appraised.* Berkeley: ILSG, December 1965.

International City Management Association. Municipal yearbook, 1972. Vol. 39. Chicago: ICMA, 1972.

Isaacs, R. "Are urban neighborhoods possible?" Journal of Housing, July 1948, 5, 177-180.

Isaacs, R. "The 'neighborhood unit' is an instrument for segregation." Journal of Housing, August 1948, 5, 215-219.

Isard, W., and Whitney, V. "Metropolitan site selection." Social Forces, 1949, 27, 253-269.

Jacobs, J. *The death and life of great American cities.* New York: Vintage Books, 1961.

Janowitz, M. *The community press in an urban setting.* Chicago: University of Chicago Press, 1952.

Janowitz, M. (Ed.) *Community political systems.* Glencoe: Free Press, 1961.

Janowitz, M. (Ed.) *Political conflict.* Chicago: Quadrangle, 1970.

Jansen, C. J. (Ed.) *Readings in the sociology of migration.* Oxford: Pergamon, 1970.

Joint Center for Political Studies. Public Policy Series. The black community and revenue sharing. Washington, D.C.: January 1973.

Jonassen, C. T. *Downtown versus suburban shopping.* Columbus: Ohio State University, Bureau of Business Research, 1955.

Jones, V. *Metropolitan government.* Chicago: University of Chicago Press, 1942.

Jones, V. "New local strategies." National Civic Review, March 1970, 59, 127-134.

Kain, J. F. *Metropolitan form and the costs of urban services.* Cambridge: Harvard University Preprint, 1967 (6).

Kain, J. F. "Postwar metropolitan development: Housing preferences and auto ownership." American Economic Association, Papers and Proceedings, May 1967, 57, 223-234.

Kain, J. F., and Persky, J. J. The North's stake in Southern rural poverty. Discussion Paper No. 18. Cambridge: Harvard University, Program on Regional and Urban Economics, May 1967.

Kain, J. F. "Housing segregation, Negro employment and metropolitan decentralization." Quarterly Journal of Economics, May 1968, 82(2), 175-197.

Kain, J. F., and Quigley, J. M. Measuring the quality and cost of housing services. Discussion Paper No. 54. Cambridge: Harvard University, Program on Regional and Urban Economics, July 1969.

Kaiser, E., Weiss, S., Burby, R., and Donnelly, J. *Neighborhood environments and residential satisfaction: A survey of occupants and neighborhoods in 166 single family homes in Greensboro, N.C.* Chapel Hill: University of North Carolina, Center for Urban and Regional Studies, 1970.

Kaplan, H. *Urban political systems: A functional analysis of Metro Toronto.* New York: Columbia University Press, 1967.

Kasarda, J. D. "The impact of suburban population growth on central city service functions." American Journal of Sociology, May 1972, 77, 1111-1124.

Kellett, J. P. *The impact of railways on Victorian cities.* London: Routledge and Kegan Paul, 1969.

Keyes, F. "The correlation of social phenomena with community size." Social Forces, May 1958, 36, 311-315.

Kirschenbaum, A. "City-suburban destination choices among migrants to metropolitan areas." Demography, May 1972, 9, 321-335.

Kobrin, S. "The conflict of values in delinquency areas." American Sociological Review, October 1951, 16, 653-661.

Kobrin, S. "The Chicago Area Project: A 25 year assessment." Annals of the American Academy of Political and Social Science, March 1959, 322, 20-29.

Kolderie, T. "Minnesota legislature aids metropolitan setup." National Civic Review, July 1969, 58, 321-326.

Kornblum, W. *Blue collar community.* Chicago: University of Chicago Press, 1974.

Kotler, M. *Neighborhood government: The local foundations of political life.* New York: Bobbs-Merrill, 1969.

Krugel, D. L. "Metropolitan dominance and diffusion of human fertility patterns in Kentucky, 1935-1965." Rural Sociology, June 1971, 36, 141-156.

Lamanna, R. A. "Value consensus among urban residents." Journal of the American Institute of Planners, 1964, 30, 317-323.

Landis, P. H., and Hatt, P. K. *Population problems: A cultural interpretation.* (2nd ed., prepared by P. K. Hatt) New York: American Book Co., 1954.

Lansing, J. B., and Hendricks, G. *Automobile ownership and residential density.* Ann Arbor: University of Michigan, Institute for Social Research, Survey Research Center, 1967.

Lansing, J. B., and Marans, R. W. "Evaluation of neighborhood quality." Journal of the American Institute of Planners, 1969, 75, 195-199.

Lansing, J. B., Marans, R. W., and Zehner, R. B. *Planned residential environments.* Ann Arbor: University of Michigan, Institute for Social Research, Survey Research Center, 1970.

Lasswell, T. E. "Social class and size of community." American Journal of Sociology, March 1959, 64, 505-508.

Laurenti, L. *Property values and race.* Berkeley: University of California Press, 1960.

League of Women Voters Education Fund. *Shaping the metropolis.* Washington, D.C.: League, 1972.

LeMay, M. C. "The states and urban areas: A comparative assessment." National Civic Review, December 1972, 61(11), 542-548.

Lipset, S. M., and Bendix, R. *Social mobility in industrial society.* Berkeley: University of California Press, 1964.

Little, K. *West African urbanization.* Cambridge: Cambridge University Press, 1965.

Lofland, L. "Self-management in public settings: Part 1." Urban Life and Culture, April 1972, 1, 93-108.

Lofland, L. *A world of strangers.* New York: Basic Books, 1973.

Long, N. E. "The local community as an ecology of games." American Journal of Sociology, November 1958, 64, 251-261.

Losch, A. *The economics of location.* Trans. by W. H. Woglom. New Haven: Yale University Press, 1954.

Lowi, T. *The end of liberalism.* New York: W. W. Norton, 1969.

Lowry, I. S. Seven models of urban development: A structural comparison. In National Academy of Engineering, Highway Research Board, *Urban Development Models.* Special Report 97. Washington, D.C.: NAE, 1968.

Lowry, I. S. *Housing assistance for low-income families: A fresh approach.* New York City: Rand Institute, 1971.

Lubove, R. *The professional altruist.* Cambridge: Harvard University Press, 1965.

Lubove, R. *The urban community.* Englewood Cliffs: Prentice-Hall, 1967.

Lynch, K. *The image of the city.* Cambridge: Harvard University Press, 1960.

Maass, A. (Ed.) *Area and power.* New York: Free Press, 1959.

Marando, V. L. "Inter-local cooperation in a metropolitan area: Detroit." Urban Affairs Quarterly, December 1968, 4, 185-200.

Marando, V. L. "Metropolitan research and councils of government." Midwest Review of Public Administration, February 1971, 5(1), 3-15.

Marando, V. L. *Local government reorganization: An overview.* Washington, D.C.: National Academy of Public Administration, 1973.

Marans, R. W., and Mandell, L. "The relative effectiveness of density related measures for predicting attitudes and behavior variables." Proceedings of the American Statistical Association Meetings, Social Statistics Section, 1972, 360-363.

Marans, R. W., Wineman, J., and Fox, B. *A methodology for measuring residential density in national samples.* Ann Arbor: University of Michigan, Institute for Social Research, 1972.

March, M. S. "The neighborhood center concept." Public Welfare; April 1968, 26, 97-111.

Margolis, J. "Municipal fiscal structure in a metropolitan region." Journal of Political Economy, June 1957, 65, 225-236.

Margolis, J. (Ed.) *The analysis of public output.* New York: Columbia University Press, 1970.

Marshall, T. H. *Class, citizenship and social development.* Garden City: Double-day, 1964.

Martin, R. *The cities and the federal system.* Chicago: Atherton Press, 1965.

Martin, R. C. *Government and the suburban school.* Syracuse: Syracuse University Press, 1962.

Martin, R. C. *Metropolis in transition.* Washington, D.C.: Housing and Home Finance Agency, 1963.

Mayer, K. B., and Goldstein, S. "Population decline and the social and demographic structure of an American city." American Sociological Review, February 1964, 29, 48-54.

Mayer, M. *The teachers' strike: New York, 1968.* New York: Harper and Row, 1969.

McKenzie, R. "The neighborhood: A study of local life in the city of Columbus, Ohio." American Journal of Sociology, September 1921, 27, 145-168. November 1921, 344-363.

McKenzie, R. D. *The metropolitan community.* New York: McGraw-Hill, 1933.

McMilland, K., and Assael, H. *National survey of transportation attitudes and behavior,* Phase II: *Analysis report.* National Cooperative Highway Research Program Report 49. Washington, D.C.: Highway Research Board, 1969.

McNamara, R. L. Population change and net migration in the North Central States, 1960-70. Report of the North Central Regional Project. Population Changes in the North Central States. NC-97. Missouri Agricultural Experiment Station, 1972.

McPhee, W. M., and Glaser, W. A. (Eds.) *Public opinion and congressional elections.* New York: Free Press, 1962.

Meranto, P. *School politics in the metropolis.* Columbus: Charles E. Merrill, 1970.

Metcalf, J. *Satisfaction and housing standards.* An Internal Note of the Building Research Situation, Urban Planning Division, Garston, Watford, Herts; England, 1967.

Meyer, J. R., Kain, J., and Wohl, M. *The urban transportation problem.* Cambridge: Harvard University Press, 1965.

Milgram, S. "The experience of living in cities: A psychological analysis." Science, March 13, 1970, 167, 1461-1468.

Mills, E. S. "An aggregative model of resource allocation in a metropolitan area." American Economic Review, May 1967, 57, 197-210.

Minar, D. W., and Greer, S. (Eds.) *The concept of community.* Chicago: Aldine, 1969.

Mitchell, R. E. "Some social implications of high density housing," American Sociological Review, February 1971, 36, 18-29.

Mogulof, M. B. *Governing metropolitan areas: A critical review of councils of government and the federal role.* Washington, D.C.: Urban Institute, 1971.

Mogulof, M. B. "Metropolitan councils of government and the federal government." Urban Affairs Quarterly, June 1972, 7, 489-507.

Mogulof, M. B. Five metropolitan governments: An exploratory comparison. Paper No. 713-27. Washington, D.C.: Urban Institute, 1972.

Mogulof, M. B. *A modest proposal for the governance of America's metropolitan areas.* Washington, D.C.: Urban Institute, 1973.

Moreland, J. K. *The millways of Kent.* New Haven: College and University Press, 1965.

Moses, L., and Williamson, H. F., Jr. "The location of economic activity in cities." American Economic Review, Papers and Proceedings, May 1967, 57(2), 211-222.

Moynihan, D. P. *Maximum feasible misunderstanding.* New York: Free Press, 1969.

Moynihan, D. P. *Toward a national urban policy.* New York: Basic Books, 1970.

Mushkin, S. (Ed.) *Public prices for public products.* Washington, D.C.: Urban Institute, 1972.

Muth, R. "Economic change and rural-urban land conversions." Econometrica, January 1961, 29, 1-23.

Muth, R. *Cities and housing.* Chicago: University of Chicago Press, 1969.

Myers, S. "Personal transportation for the poor." Traffic Quarterly, April 1970, 24, 191-206.

National Academy of Sciences, Agricultural Board, Division of Biology and Agriculture. *The quality of rural living: Proceedings of a workshop.* Washington, D.C.: NAS, 1971.

National Bureau of Economic Research, *Public finances: Needs, resources, and utilization.* Princeton: Princeton University Press, 1961.

National Center for Health Statistics. "Use of special aids: United States, 1969." Monthly Vital Statistics Report, May 11, 1972, 21, Supplement 2.

National Commission on Urban Problems. *Building the American city.* New York: Praeger, 1969.

National Committee Against Discrimination in Housing. *The impact of housing on job opportunities.* New York: NCDH, 1968.

National Research Council. Committee on Biologic Effects of Atmospheric Pollutants. *Particulate polycyclic organic matter.* Washington, D.C.: National Academy of Sciences, 1972.

National Urban League and Center for Community Change. *National survey of housing abandonment.* New York: NUL and CCC, 1971.

Nelli, H. S. *The Italians in Chicago.* New York: Oxford University Press, 1970.

Neutze, G. M. *Economic policy and the size of cities.* New York: Augustus M. Kelley, 1968.

New Jersey County and Municipal Government Study Commission. *Joint services—A local response to areawide problems.* Trenton: CMGSC, 1970.

Newman, D. K. "The decentralization of jobs." Monthly Labor Review, May 1967, 90, 7-13.

New York State Commission on the Quality, Cost and Financing of Elementary and Secondary Education. *The Fleischman report on the quality, cost, and financing of elementary and secondary education in New York State.* Vol. 1. New York: Viking, 1973.

Nie, N. H., Powell, G. B., and Prewitt, K. "Social structure and political participation: Developmental relationships, Parts 1 and 2." American Political Science Review, June 1969, 63, 361-378; September 1969, 63, 800-832.

Niedercorn, J. H., and Hearle, E.F.R. *Recent land-use trends in forty-eight large American cities.* MEM, RM-3664-FF. Santa Monica: RAND Corp., 1963.

Niedercorn, J. H., and Kain, J. F. *Suburbanization of employment and population, 1948-1975.* Santa Monica: RAND Corp., 1963.

Nisbet, R. A. History as the decline of community. In R. A. Nisbet (Ed.), *Community and power.* London: Oxford University Press, 1962. 75-97.

North Central Public Policy Education Committee. Who will control U.S. agriculture? Policies affecting the organizational structure of U.S. agriculture. Special Publication 27. Urbana-Champaign: University of Illinois, College of Agriculture Cooperative Extension Service, 1972.

Oakland City Planning Department. *Getting to work from West Oakland.* Oakland: CPD, January 1970.

Oates, W. E. "The effects of property taxes and local public spending on property values: An empirical study of tax capitalization and the Tiebout hypothesis." Journal of Political Economy, December 1969, 77(6), 957-971.

O'Donnell, E. J. "The neighborhood service center." Welfare in Review, November-December 1969, 6, 1-11.

Office of the Mayor, New York City. Program for command decentralization and integration of services in selected New York City neighborhoods. New York: Office of the Mayor, December 1971. (Mimeo.)

Orleans, P. and Ellis, R. (Eds.) *Race, change and urban society.* Urban Affairs Annual Review, Vol. 5. Beverly Hills: Sage Publications, 1971.

Orr, L. L. "The incidence of differential property taxes on urbanization." National Tax Journal, September 1968, 21, 253-262.

Orshansky, M. "The poor in city and suburb, 1964." Social Security Bulletin, December 1966, 29, 22-37.

Ottoson, H. W., Birch, E. M., Henderson, P. A., and Anderson, A. H. *Land and people in the Northern Plain transition area.* Lincoln: University of Nebraska Press, 1966.

Owen, W. *The accessible city.* Washington, D.C.: Brookings Institution, 1972.

Pahl, R. E. *Patterns of urban life.* London: Longmans, Green, 1970.

Park, R. E., and Burgess, E. W. (Eds.) *The city.* Chicago: University of Chicago Press, 1925.

Park, R. R. *Society.* Glencoe: Free Press, 1955.

Parr, J. B. "Models of city size in an urban system." Papers and Proceedings of the Regional Science Association, 1970, 25, 221-253.

Perloff, H. S. (Ed.) *The quality of the urban environment.* Baltimore: Johns Hopkins University Press for Resources for the Future, Inc., 1969.

Perloff, H. S. and Wingo, L. (Eds.) *Issues in urban economics.* Baltimore: Johns Hopkins University Press for Resources for the Future, Inc., 1969.

Perry, C. A., and Williams, M. P. *New York school centers and their community policy.* New York: Russell Sage Foundation, 1931.

Perry, C. A. *Housing for the Machine Age.* New York: Russell Sage Foundation, 1939.

Pettingill, R. B., Chen, K., and Uppal, J. S. Cities and suburbs: The case for equity. Part 1. *State aid to big cities in New York State and to their suburbs.* Albany: New York Conference of Mayors and Municipal Officials, 1970.

Pfautz, H. W. (Ed.) *Charles Booth on the city: Physical pattern and social structure.* Chicago: University of Chicago Press, 1967.

Pickard, J. P. Dimensions of metropolitanism. Research Monograph 14. Washington, D.C.: Urban Land Institute, 1967.

Pinkerton, J. R. "City-suburban residential patterns by social class: A review of the literature." Urban Affairs Quarterly, June 1969, 4, 499-519.

Piven, F. F., and Cloward, R. "Black control of cities: Heading it off by metropolitan government." New Republic, September 30, 1967, 157(14), 19-21.

Piven, F. F., and Cloward, R. "Black control of cities: How the Negroes will lose." New Republic, October 7, 1967, 157(15), 15-19.

Plotnicov, L. *Strangers to the city.* Pittsburgh: University of Pittsburgh Press, 1967.

Pope, L. *Millhands and preachers.* New Haven: Yale University Press, 1942.

Pratt, S. A. "Metropolitan community developments and economic change." American Sociological Review, 1957, 22, 434-440.

President's Committee on Urban Housing. *A decent home.* Washington, D.C.: U.S. Government Printing Office, 1968.

Proshansky, H. M., Ittelson, W. H., and Rivlin, L. G. (Eds.) *Environmental psychology: Man and his physical setting.* New York: Holt, Rinehart and Winston, 1970.

Public Administration Review, Special Issue on Citizen Action in Model Cities and CAP Programs: Case Studies and Evaluation. September 1972.

Rainwater, L., and Yancey, W. *The Moynihan Report and the politics of controversy.* Cambridge: MIT Press, 1967.

Research Council of the Great Cities Program for School Improvement. *The challenge of financing public schools in great cities.* Chicago: Research Council of the Great Cities Program for School Improvement, 1964.

Rhodes, G. *The government of London: The struggle for reform.* London: London School of Economics, 1970.

Ridker, R. A., and Henning, J. A. "Determinants of residential property values with special reference to air pollution." Review of Economics and Statistics, May 1967, 49, 246-257.

Riesman, D., with Glazer, N. *Faces in the crowd: Individual studies in character and politics.* New Haven: Yale University Press, 1952.

Riesman, D., with Glazer, N., and Denney, R. *The lonely crowd.* (2nd ed.) New Haven: Yale University Press, 1961.

Ringer, B. *The edge of friendliness.* New York: Basic Books, 1967.

Robinson, E.A.G. (Ed.) *Backward areas in advanced countries.* New York: St. Martin's Press, 1969.

Robinson, J. P., and Shaver, P. R. *Measures of social psychological attitudes.* Ann Arbor: University of Michigan, Institute for Social Research, 1969.

Rodwin, L. *Nations and cities: A comparison of strategies for urban growth.* Boston: Houghton-Mifflin, 1970.

Rogers, A. *Matrix methods in urban and regional analysis.* San Francisco: Holden-Day, 1971.

Rose, A. M. (Ed.) *Human behavior and social processes.* Boston: Houghton Mifflin, 1962.

Rosenberg, T. J. *Residence, employment and mobility of Puerto Ricans in New York City.* Chicago: University of Chicago, Department of History, 1974.

Ross, D. *Robert F. Kennedy: Apostle of change.* New York: Pocket Books, 1968.

Rossi, P. *Why families move.* Chicago: Free Press, 1956.

Rothenberg, J. *Economic evaluation of urban renewal.* Washington, D.C.: Brookings Institution, 1967.

Rothenberg, J. An econometric simulation model of the metropolitan housing market for public policy evaluation. Report to the National Urban Coalition. Washington, D.C.: NUC, 1971.

Rubin, M. *Plantation county.* Chapel Hill: University of North Carolina Press, 1951.

Ruck, S. K., and Rhodes, G. *The government of Greater London.* London: Allen and Unwin, 1970.

Sacks, S., Ranney, D., and Andrew, R. *City schools suburban schools.* Syracuse: Syracuse University Press, 1972.

San Francisco Bureau of Governmental Research. *The Association of Bay Area Governments: A gathering force.* San Francisco: BGR, April 1, 1965.

Sayre, W. S., and Kaufman, H. *Governing New York City.* New York: Russell Sage Foundation, 1960.

Schaeffer, K. N., and Sclar, E. *Access.* Harmondsworth (Middlesex): Penguin Press, 1973.

Schnore, L. F., and Varley, D. W. "Some concomitants of metropolitan size." American Sociological Review, August 1955, 20, 408-414.

Schnore, L. F. "Some correlates of urban size: A replication." American Journal of Sociology, September 1963, 69, 185-193.

Schnore, L. F. "Urban structure and suburban selectivity." Demography, 1964,

Schnore, L. F. "The rural-urban variable: An urbanite's perspective." Rural Sociology, June 1966, 31, 131-143.

Schnore, L. F., and Fagin, H. (Eds.) *Urban research and policy planning.* Beverly Hills: Sage Publications, 1967.

Schnore, L. F. *Class and race in cities and suburbs.* Chicago: Markham, 1972.

Schooler, C. "Social antecedents of adult psychological functioning." American Journal of Sociology, September 1972, 78, 299-322.

Schorr, A. *Slums and social insecurity.* U.S. Department of Health, Education, and Welfare. Washington, D.C.: U.S. Government Printing Office, 1966.

Schultze, C. L., Fried, E., Rivlin, A., Teeters, N. *Setting national priorities: The 1973 budget.* Washington, D.C.: Brookings Institution, 1972.

Schuman, A., and Gruenberg, B. "The impact of city on racial attitudes." American Journal of Sociology, September 1970, 76, 213-262.

Seeley, J. R., Sims, R. A., and Loosley, E. W. *Crestwood Heights: A study of the culture of suburban life.* New York: John Wiley, 1964.

Seeman, M. "On the meaning of alienation." American Sociological Review. December 1959, 24, 783-791.

Semple, R. B., Jr. "Panel bids Nixon promote housing." New York Times, July 23, 1970.

Sengstock, F. S. *Annexation: A solution to the metropolitan area problem.* Ann Arbor: University of Michigan Law School, 1960.

Sennett, R. *The uses of disorder: Personal identity and city life.* New York: A. E. Knopf, 1970.

Shalala, D. E. *Neighborhood governance: Issues and proposals.* New York: American Jewish Committee, 1971.

Shalala, D. E. *The city and the constitution.* New York: National Municipal League, 1972.

Shalala, D. E., and Merget, A. E. *Decentralization: Implications for service delivery.* Washington, D.C.: National Academy of Public Administration, 1973.

Shaper, D. "Comparable living costs and urban size: A statistical analysis." Journal of the American Institute of Planners, November 1970, 36 (4), 417-421.

Shapiro, M. J. "Rational political man: A synthesis of economic and socio-psychological perspectives." American Political Science Review, December 1969, 63, 1106-1119.

Sharkansky, I. *The maligned states.* New York: McGraw-Hill, 1972.

Sheldon, E. B., and Moore, W. E. *Indicators of social change.* New York: Russell Sage Foundation, 1968.

Shils, E. "Mass society and its culture." Daedalus, Spring 1960, 89(2), 288-314.

Sills, D. (Ed.) *International encyclopedia of the social sciences.* New York: Macmillan and Free Press, 1968.

Sjaastad, L. "The costs and returns of human migration." Journal of Political Economy, October 1962, 70(5), Part 2 (supplement), 80-93.

Sjoberg, G. *The preindustrial city.* New York: Free Press, 1960.

Smallwood, F. *Greater London.* Indianapolis: Bobbs-Merrill, 1965.

Smith, J., Form, W. H., and Stone, G. P. "Local intimacy in a middle-sized city." American Journal of Sociology, November 1954, 60, 276-284.

Smith, L. R., and Hague, D. C. *The dilemma of accountability in modern government.* New York: St. Martin's Press, 1970.

Smith, P. *As a city upon a hill: The town in American history.* New York: A. E. Knopf, 1968.

Strole, L. "Social integration and certain corollaries: An exploratory study." American Sociological Review, December 1956, 21, 709-716.

Stanback, T. M., and Knight, R. V. *The metropolitan economy.* New York: Columbia University Press, 1970.

Stanley, D. T. Professional personnel for the city of New York. Report of the Study of Professional, Technical and Managerial Manpower Needs of the City of New York. Washington, D.C.: Brookings Institute, 1963.

State Study Commission on New York City. Restructuring the government of New York City. Report of the Task Force on Jurisdiction and Structure. New York: State Study Commission, March 15, 1972.

Stein, M. *The eclipse of community.* Princeton: Princeton University Press, 1960.

Sternlieb, G. "Abandonment: Urban housing phenomenon." Challenge, U.S. Department of Housing and Urban Development, May 1972, 3(5), 12-14.

Sternlieb, G. "The future of retailing in the downtown core." Journal of the American Institute of Planners, 1963, 29, 102-112.

Stoeckel, J., and Beegle, J. A. "The relationship between the rural farm age structure and the distance from metropolitan area." Rural Sociology, September 1966, 31, 346-354.

Strauss, A. *Images of the American city.* Glencoe: Free Press, 1961.

Studentski, P. *The government of metropolitan areas in the United States.* New York: National Municipal League, 1930.

Sundquist, J. P., and Davis, D. *Making federalism work.* Washington, D.C.: Brookings Institution, 1969.

Suttles, G. *The social order of the slum.* Chicago: University of Chicago Press, 1968.

Suttles, G. D. *The social construction of communities.* Chicago: University of Chicago Press, 1972.

Taeuber, K., and Taeuber, A. F. "White migration and socioeconomic differenced between cities and suburbs." American Sociological Review, October 1964, 29, 718-729.

Tallman, I., and Morgner, R. "Life-style differences among urban and suburban blue-collar families." Social Forces, March 1970, 48, 334-348.

Tarver, J. D. "Patterns of population change among Southern nonmetropolitan towns, 1950-1970." Rural Sociology, March 1972, 37, 53-72.

Tarver, J. J. "Suburbanization of retail trade in the Standard Metropolitan Areas of the United States, 1948-54." American Sociological Review, August 1957, 22, 427-433.

Taysby, F. A., Jr., Davidson, L. S., and Clark, D. D. "Flight to the fringes: An empirical study of office decentralization in Atlanta, Georgia." Review of Regional Studies, Fall 1970, 1, 117-140.

Texas Urban Development Commission. Urban Texas: Policies for the future. Arlington, Texas: UDC, November 1971.

Thompson, W. R. A preface to urban economics. Baltimore: Johns Hopkins University Press, 1965.

Thompson, W. R. "The national system of cities as an object of public policy." Urban Studies, February 1972, 9, 99-116.

Thompson, W. S. The growth of metropolitan districts in the United States: 1900-1940. Washington, D.C.: U.S. Government Printing Office, 1947.

Tiebout, C. M. "A pure theory of local expenditures." Journal of Political Economy, October 1956, 64, 410-424.

Tomeh, A. K. "Informal group participation and residential patterns." American Journal of Sociology, July 1964, 70, 28-35.

Troy, P. N. Environmental quality in four suburban areas. Canberra: Australian National University, Urban Research Unit, 1971.

U.S. Commission on Population Growth and the American Future. Population and the American Future. New York: New American Library (Signet), 1972.

U.S. National Commission on Urban Problems. Building the American city. New York: Praeger, 1969.

U.S. National Commission on the Causes and Prevention of Violence. Crimes of violence: A staff report. Washington, D.C.: U.S. Government Printing Office, 1969.

Vance, R. B., and Demerath, H. J. (Eds.) The Urban South. Chapel Hill: University of North Carolina Press, 1954.

Verba, S., and Nie, N. H. Participation in American life: Political democracy and social equality. New York: Harper and Row, 1972.

Vernon, R. "Production and Distribution in the Large Metropolis." Annals of the American Academy of Political and Social Science, November 1957, 314, 15-29.

Vernon, R. Metropolis 1985. Cambridge: Harvard University Press, 1960.

Vernon, R. The myth and reality of our urban problems. Cambridge: Massachusetts Institute of Technology—Harvard Joint Center for Urban Studies, 1962.

Vickrey, W. S. "Pricing in urban and suburban transport." American Economic Review, Papers and Proceedings, May 1963, 53(2), 452-465.

Vincent, P. E. Fiscal impacts of commuters on core cities with varying revenue structures. Report MR-130. Los Angeles: University of California, Institute of Government and Public Affairs, 1969.

Von Eckardt, W. *The challenge of megalopolis.* New York: Macmillan, 1965.

Von Thunen, J. H. *The isolated state.* New York: Pergamon, 1964.

Wade, R. C. *The urban frontier.* Chicago: University of Chicago Press, 1959.

Wagner, R. E. *The fiscal organization of American federalism.* Chicago: Markham, 1971.

Walsh, A. H. "What price decentralization in New York." City Almanac, June 1972, 7, 1-11.

Walters, A. A. "The theory and measurement of private and social costs of highway congestion." Econmetrica, October 1961, 29, 676-699.

Warner, S. B. *Streetcar suburbs: The process of growth in Boston, 1870-1900.* New York: Atheneum, 1969.

Warner, W. L., and Low, J. O. *The social system of the modern factory—The strike: A social analysis.* New Haven: Yale University Press, 1947.

Washnis, G. J. *Municipal decentralization and neighborhood resources.* New York: Praeger, 1972.

Webber, M. M. On strategies for transport planning. In Organization for Economic Cooperation and Development, *The urban transportation planning process.* Paris: OECD, 1971, 129-149.

Weissman, H. H. *Community development in the Mobilization for Youth experience.* New York: Association Press, 1969.

Wertheimer, R. F., II. *The monetary rewards of migration within the U.S.* Washington, D.C.: Urban Institute, 1971.

Wetzel, J. R., and Holland, S. S. "Poverty areas of our major cities." Monthly Labor Review, October 1966, 89, 1105-1110.

Wheaton, W. C., and Schussheim, M. J. *The cost of municipal services in residential areas.* Washington, D.C.: U.S. Government Printing Office, 1955.

White, M., and White, L. *The intellectual versus the city.* New York: Mentor, 1962.

Wilcox, L. D., Brooks, R. M., Beal, G. M., and Klonglan, G. E. *Social indicators and societal monitoring.* San Francisco: Jossey-Bass, 1972.

Wildavsky, A. "Black rebellion and white reaction." The Public Interest, Spring 1968, 11, 3-16.

Willins, F. K., Bealer, R. C., and Crider, D. M. "Leveling of attitudes in mass society: Rurality and traditional morality in America." Rural Sociology, Spring 1973, 38, 36-45.

Willmott, P. *The evolution of a community.* London: Routledge and Kegan Paul, 1963.

Wilson, J. Q. (Ed.) *Urban renewal: The record and the controversy.* Cambridge: MIT Press, 1967.

Wilson, J. Q. "The urban unease." The Public Interest, Summer 1968, (12), 25-39.

Wingo, L., Jr. *Transportation and urban land.* Baltimore: Johns Hopkins University Press for Resources for the Future, Inc., 1961.

Wingo, L., Jr. *Cities and space: The future use of urban land.* Baltimore: Johns Hopkins University Press for Resources for the Future, Inc., 1963.

Wingo, L., Jr. (Ed.) *The governance of metropolitan regions: Minority perspectives.* Washington, D.C.: Resources for the Future, Inc., 1972.

Wingo, L., Jr. (Ed.) *The governance of metropolitan regions: Metropolitanization and public services.* Washington, D.C.: Resources for the Future, Inc., 1972.

Wingo, L., Jr. (Ed.) *Reform of metropolitan governments.* Washington, D.C.: Resources for the Future, Inc., 1972.

Wirth, L., "Urbanisn as a way of life." American Journal of Sociology, July 1938, 44, 3-24.

Wolfe, K. (Ed.) *The Sociology of Georg Simmel.* New York: Free Press, 1950.

Wolfgang, M. E. "Urban crime." In J. Q. Wilson (Ed.) *The metropolitan enigma.* New York: Doubleday Anchor, 1970, 270-311.

Wood, M. *Stranger: A study in social relationships.* New York: Columbia University Press, 1934.

Wood, R. C. *Suburbia: Its people and their politics.* Boston: Houghton Mifflin, 1958.

Wood, R. C. *Metropolis against itself.* New York: Committee for Economic Development, 1959.

Wood, R. C., and Almendinger, V. V. *1400 governments: The political economy of the New York metropolitan region.* Cambridge; Harvard University Press, 1961.

Woodlawn Organization. *Woodlawn Model Cities Plan.* Northbrook, Ill.: Whitehall, 1970.

Young, M., and Wilmott, P. *Family and kinship in East London.* London: Routledge and Kegan Paul, 1957.

Zehner, R. B. *Satisfaction with neighborhoods: The effects of social compatibility, residential density and site planning.* Unpublished doctoral dissertation, University of Michigan, 1970.

Zehner, R. B. "Neighborhood and community satisfaction in new towns and less planned suburbs." Journal of the American Institute of Planners, 1971, 37, 379-385.

Zimmer, B. G., and Hawley, A. H. "Suburbanization and church participation." Social Forces, May 1959, 37, 348-354.

Zimmer, B. G., and Hawley, A. H. "Suburbanization and some of its consequences." Land Economics, February 1961, 37, 588-593.

Zimmer, B. G. *Rebuilding cities: The effects of displacement and relocation on small business.* Chicago: Quadrangle Books, 1964.

Zimmer, B. G., and Hawley, A. H. *Metropolitan area schools: Resistance to district reorganization.* Beverly Hills: Sage Publications, 1968.

Zimmerman, J. F. (Ed.) *Metropolitan charters.* Albany: State University of New York, Graduate School of Public Affairs, 1967.

Zimmerman, J. F. "Metropolitan ecumenism: The road to the promised land?" Journal of Urban Law, Spring 1967, 44, 433-457.

Zimmerman, J. F., and Snyder, M. E. "New trends seen in area planning." National Civic Review, September 1967, 56, 470-474.

Zimmerman, J. F. "The planning riddle." National Civic Review, April 1968, 57, 189-194.

Zimmerman, J. F. *1968 Survey of metropolitan planning.* Albany: State University of New York, Graduate School of Public Affairs, 1968.

Zimmerman, J. F. "Metropolitan reform in the U.S.: An overview." Public Administration Review, September/October 1970, 30, 531-543.

Zimmerman, J. F. "Mergers reviewed for local units." National Civic Review, September 1972, 61, 417-419.

Zimmerman, J. F. *Governing metropolitan Boston.* Boston: Metropolitan Area Planning Council, November 1972.

Zimmerman, J. F. Meeting service needs through intergovernmental agreements. In International City Management Association, *Municipal yearbook, 1973.* Vol. 40. Washington, D.C.: ICMA, 1973, 79-88.

Zorbaugh, H. W. *The Gold Coast and the slum.* Chicago: University of Chicago Press, 1929.

Zschock, D. K. (Ed.) *Economic aspects of suburban growth.* Stony Brook: State University of New York, Economic Research Bureau, 1969.

Zuckerman, M. *Peaceable kingdoms: New England towns in the eighteenth century.* New York: A. E. Knopf, 1970.

INDEX